Public International Law

Public International Law

Conventions, Cases and Commentary

John M. B. Balouziyeh

Wolters Kluwer

Published by:
Kluwer Law International B.V.
PO Box 316
2400 AH Alphen aan den Rijn
The Netherlands
E-mail: lrs-sales@wolterskluwer.com
Website: www.wolterskluwer.com/en/solutions/kluwerlawinternational

Sold and distributed by:
Wolters Kluwer Legal & Regulatory U.S.
920 Links Avenue
Landisville, PA 17538
United States of America
E-mail: customer.service@wolterskluwer.com

ISBN 978-94-035-2448-1

e-Book: ISBN 978-94-035-2458-0
web-PDF: ISBN 978-94-035-2468-9

A ti, Alexa, por tu maravilloso amor

Table of Contents

List of Abbreviations

Where appropriate, acronyms correspond to the names of treaties as they are commonly known (e.g., "MT" for Moon Treaty) rather than by the full treaty title.

A

ACHPR	African Commission on Human and Peoples' Rights
ACHR	American Convention on Human Rights (adopted in 1969, entry into force in 1978)
ACUNS	Academic Council on the United Nations System
ADRDM	American Declaration of the Rights and Duties of Man (1948)
AHRD	ASEAN Human Rights Declaration
AIC	Arab Investment Court
ALECSO	Arab League Educational, Cultural and Scientific Organization
AP I	Additional Protocol to the Geneva Conventions of 12 August 1949 and Relating to the Protection of Victims of International Armed Conflicts, 8 June 1977
AP II	Additional Protocol to the Geneva Conventions of 12 August 1949 and Relating to the Protection of Victims of Non-International Armed Conflicts, 8 June 1977
AP III	Additional Protocol to the Geneva Conventions of 12 August 1949 and Relating to the Adoption of an Additional Distinctive Emblem, 8 December 2005
APL	Anti-personnel landmine
Arab Charter	Arab Charter on Human Rights (2004)
ASEAN	Association of Southeast Asian Nations
ATCA	Alien Tort Claims Act (28 USC 1350) (also known as the Alien Tort Statute)

ATS	Antarctic Treaty System (Antarctic Treaty and related agreements) (1961)
AU	African Union
	B
BC	Berne Convention for the Protection of Literary and Artistic Works of 9 September 1886
BHRRC	Business & Human Rights Resource Centre
BIS	U.S. Bureau of Industry and Security
	C
CAEU	Council of Arab Economic Unity
Cairo Declaration	Cairo Declaration on Human Rights in Islam (1990)
CAT	Committee Against Torture
CBU	Cluster Bomb Unit
CC	Chicago Convention on International Civil Aviation (1944) (Chicago Convention)
CCW	U.N. Convention on Prohibitions or Restrictions on the Use of Certain Conventional Weapons Which May be Deemed to be Excessively Injurious or to Have Indiscriminate Effects (Geneva, 1980)
CDR	Cartagena Declaration on Refugees
CEDAW	Convention on the Elimination of All Forms of Discrimination against Women (1979)
CEDAW Committee	Committee on the Elimination of Discrimination Against Women
CERD	Committee on the Elimination of Racial Discrimination
CFC	Chlorofluorocarbon
CFREU	Charter of Fundamental Rights of the European Union (2000)
CGIAR	Consultative Group on International Agricultural Research
Charter	Charter of the United Nations (1945)
CISG	Convention on Contracts for the International Sale of Goods
CJCSI	Chairman of the Joint Chiefs of Staff Instruction (U.S.)
COAS	Charter of the Organization of American States (1967)
CoE	Council of Europe
Court of BiH	Court of Bosnia and Herzegovina
CPISA	Convention on Privileges and Immunities of the Specialized Agencies (1947)
CPIUN	Convention on the Privileges and Immunities of the United Nations (1946)
CPPG	Convention on the Prevention and Punishment of the Crime of Genocide (Genocide Convention) (1948)

CPT	"Carriage Paid To" (Incoterm)
CRC	United Nations Convention on the Rights of the Child (1989)
CRC Committee	Committee on the Rights of the Child
CRSR	Convention Relating to the Status of Refugees (1951)
CRSV	Conflict-Related Sexual Violence
CSDP Mission	Common Security and Defence Policy Mission (of the EU)
CSID	Convention on the Settlement of Investment Disputes Between States and Nationals of Other States
CTBTO	Preparatory Commission for the Comprehensive Nuclear-Test-Ban Treaty Organization (U.N.)
CTED	Counter-Terrorism Committee Executive Directorate
CWC	Convention on the Prohibition of the Development, Production, Stockpiling and Use of Chemical Weapons and on Their Destruction (entry into force on 29 April 1997)

D

DAP	"Delivered at Place" (Incoterm)
DARS	Draft Articles on the Responsibility of States for Internationally Wrongful Acts (2001) (Draft Articles on State Responsibility) (ILC document)
DAT	"Delivered at Terminal" (Incoterm)
DDA	Department of Disarmament Affairs (U.N.)
DESA	Department of Economic and Social Affairs (U.N.)
DGAACS	Department of General Assembly Affairs and Conference Services (U.N.)
DG ECHO	Directorate-General for European Civil Protection and Humanitarian Aid Operations
DHS	United States Department of Homeland Security
DM	Department of Management (U.N.)
DoD	Department of Defense (U.S.)
DPA	Department of Political Affairs (U.N.)
DPI	Department of Public Information (U.N.)
DPKO	Department of Peacekeeping Operations (U.N.)

E

EAC	Extraordinary African Chambers
ECA	Economic Commission for Africa (U.N.)
ECCC	Extraordinary Chambers in the Courts of Cambodia
ECE	Economic Commission for Europe (U.N.)
ECHO	European Civil Protection and Humanitarian Aid Operations

ECHR	European Convention for the Protection of Human Rights and Fundamental Freedoms (European Convention on Human Rights) (1953)
ECJ	European Court of Justice
ECLAC	Economic Commission for Latin America and the Caribbean (U.N.)
ECOSOC	Economic and Social Council
ECtHR	European Court of Human Rights
EEA	European Economic Area
ENMOD	United Nations Convention on the Prohibition of Military or Any Hostile Use of Environmental Modification Techniques (1976)
ESCAP	Economic Commission for Asia and the Pacific
ESCWA	Economic Commission for Western Asia
E.U.	European Union

F

FAO	Food and Agriculture Organization of the United Nations
FGM	Female Genital Mutilation
FM 27-10	Department of the Army, Field Manual 27-10, The Law of Land Warfare (July 1956) (U.S.)
FRY	Federal Republic of Yugoslavia

G

GATT	General Agreement on Tariffs and Trade (1949)
GC I	Geneva Convention I for the Amelioration of the Condition of the Wounded and Sick in Armed Forces in the Field (1949)
GC II	Geneva Convention II for the Amelioration of the Condition of Wounded, Sick and Shipwrecked Members of Armed Forces at Sea (1949)
GC III	Geneva Convention III relative to the Treatment of Prisoners of War (1949)
GC IV	Geneva Convention IV relative to the Protection of Civilian Persons in Time of War (1949)
GCTS	Geneva Convention on the Territorial Sea and Contiguous Zone

H

HC III	Hague Convention (III) relative to the Opening of Hostilities (1907)
HC IV	Hague Convention (IV) respecting the Laws and Customs of War on Land and its Annex: Regulations concerning the Laws and Customs of War on Land (1907)

HC V	Hague Convention (V) respecting the Rights and Duties of Neutral Powers and Persons in Case of War on Land (1907)
HC VIII	Hague Convention (VIII) relative to the Laying of Automatic Submarine Contact Mines (1907)
HC IX	Hague Convention (IX) concerning Bombardment by Naval Forces in Time of War
HCPIL	Hague Conference on Private International Law
HR IV	Regulations Concerning the Laws and Customs of War on Land, annexed to Hague Convention (IV) of 1907 respecting the Laws and Customs of War on Land
HRC	U.N. Human Rights Committee (of the ICCPR)

I

IAC	International armed conflict
IACHR	Inter-American Commission on Human Rights
IACtHR	Inter-American Court of Human Rights
IADC	Inter-American Democratic Charter
IAEA	International Atomic Energy Agency
IASC	Inter-Agency Standing Committee
ICAO	International Civil Aviation Organization
ICC	International Criminal Court
ICCPR	International Covenant on Civil and Political Rights (1966)
ICERD	International Convention on the Elimination of All Forms of Racial Discrimination
ICESCR	International Covenant on Economic, Social and Cultural Rights
ICISS	International Commission on Intervention and State Sovereignty
ICJ	International Court of Justice
ICRC	International Committee of the Red Cross
ICRPD	International Convention on the Rights of Persons with Disabilities
ICSID	International Centre for Settlement of Investment Disputes
ICSID Convention	Convention on the Settlement of Investment Disputes Between States and Nationals of Other States
ICTR	International Criminal Tribunal for Rwanda
ICTY	International Criminal Tribunal for the former Yugoslavia
IDA	International Development Association
IDLO	International Development Law Organization
IDP	Internally displaced person
IFAD	International Fund for Agricultural Development
IFC	International Finance Corporation

IFRC	International Federation of Red Cross and Red Crescent Societies
IHL	International humanitarian law
IHRL	International human rights law
IIIM	International, Impartial and Independent Mechanism to Assist in the Investigation and Prosecution of Persons Responsible for the Most Serious Crimes under International Law Committed in the Syrian Arab Republic since March 2011
IIMM	Independent Investigative Mechanism for Myanmar
ILC	International Law Commission
ILI	International Law Institute
ILO	International Labor Organization
IMO	International Maritime Organization
IMT	International Military Tribunal (at Nuremberg)
IMTFE	International Military Tribunal for the Far East
INSTRAW	International Research and Training Institute for the Advancement of Women
IOM	International Organization for Migration
ISA	International Seabed Authority
ITC	International Trade Centre
ITLS	International Tribunal for the Law of the Sea
ITO	International Trade Organization
ITPC	Indigenous and Tribal Peoples Convention
ITSR	Iranian Transactions and Sanctions Regulations
ITU	International Telecommunication Union
	J
JP 3-60	Joint Publication 3-60, Joint Targeting (U.S.)
	L
LAS	League of Arab States
LC	Charter of the International Military Tribunal (London Charter) (1945)
LoWM	Law of War Manual (U.S.)
	M
Maputo Protocol	Protocol to the African Charter on Human and Peoples' Rights on the Rights of Women in Africa (also referred to as the "African Women's Protocol") (2005)
MBT	Ottawa Convention on the Prohibition of the Use, Stockpiling, Production and Transfer of Anti-Personnel Mines and on their Destruction ("Mine Ban Treaty")
MICT	Mechanism for International Criminal Tribunals
MIGA	Multilateral Investment Guarantee Agency

MINUSCA	United Nations Multidimensional Integrated Stabilization Mission in the Central African Republic
MINUSMA	United Nations Multidimensional Integrated Stabilization Mission in Mali
MNF	Multinational force
MONUSCO	United Nations Organization Stabilization Mission in the Democratic Republic of the Congo
MSB	Swedish Civil Contingencies Agency
MT	Agreement Governing the Activities of States on the Moon and Other Celestial Bodies (1979) (Moon Treaty)
	N
NAT	North Atlantic Treaty
NATO	North Atlantic Treaty Organization
NGO	Non-governmental organization
NHRI	National human rights institution
NIAC	Non-international Armed Conflict
NRC	Norwegian Refugee Council
	O
OAS	Organization of American States
OAU	Organization of African Unity
OCHA	Office for the Coordination of Humanitarian Affairs (U.N.)
ODC	Office on Drugs and Crime (U.N.)
OHCHR	Office of the United Nations High Commissioner for Human Rights
OIC	Organisation of Islamic Cooperation (formerly the Organisation of the Islamic Conference)
OILPOL	International Convention for the Prevention of Pollution of the Sea by Oil (1954)
OIOS	Office of Internal Oversight Services (U.N.)
OIP	Office of the Iraq Program (U.N.)
OLA	Office of Legal Affairs (U.N.)
OPCW	Organization for the Prohibition of Chemical Weapons (U.N.)
OPEC	Organization of the Petroleum Exporting Countries
OSG	Office of the Secretary-General (U.N.)
OST	Treaty on principles governing the activities of States in the exploration and use of outer space, including the moon and other celestial bodies (1967) ("Outer Space Treaty")
	P
PCA	Permanent Court of Arbitration
PCIJ	Permanent Court of International Justice
PCT	Patent Cooperation Treaty (1970)

PoW	Prisoner of War
PRC	People's Republic of China
	R
R2P	Responsibility to Protect Doctrine
RC	Republic of China
RCA	Riot control agent
REACH	Registration, Evaluation, Authorization and Restriction of Chemicals (E.U. Regulation of 18 December 2006)
Refugee Protocol	1967 Protocol Relating to the Status of Refugees
RFR	Restatement 3d of the Foreign Relations Law of the U.S.
Rome Statute	Rome Statute of the International Criminal Court
RPF	Rwandan Patriotic Front
RUF	Revolutionary United Front (of Sierra Leone)
	S
SAR	Special administrative region of the People's Republic of China
SCSL	Special Court for Sierra Leone
SDN	Specially designated national
SDN List	Specially Designated Nationals and Blocked Persons List
SDR	Special Drawing Rights
SGBV	Sexual and Gender-Based Violence
SICC	Rome Statute of the International Criminal Court
SICJ	Statute of the International Court of Justice
SIDA	Swedish International Development Agency
SRoE	Standing Rules of Engagement (U.S.)
STL	Special Tribunal for Lebanon
	T
TBT Agreement	Agreement on Technical Barriers to Trade
TC	Trusteeship Council
	U
UDHR	Universal Declaration of Human Rights (1948)
U.K.	United Kingdom of Great Britain and Northern Ireland
U.N.	United Nations
U.N. Charter	Charter of the United Nations (1945)
U.N. Women	United Nations Entity for Gender Equality and the Empowerment of Women
UN-Habitat	United Nations Human Settlements Program
UN-INSTRAW	United Nations International Research and Training Institute for the Advancement of Women
UNAIDS	Joint United Nations Program on HIV/AIDS
UNAMI	United Nations Assistance Mission for Iraq

UNAT	United Nations Appeals Tribunal
UNAVEM	United Nations Angola Verification Mission
UNCCP	U.N. Conciliation Commission for Palestine
UNCED	United Nations Conference on Environment and Development (Earth Summit)
UNCHR	United Nations Commission on Human Rights (predecessor to the UNHRC)
UNCHS	United Nations Centre for Human Settlements
UNCITRAL	United Nations Commission on International Trade Law
UNCLOS	United Nations Convention on the Law of the Sea (1982)
UNCLOS I	First United Nations Conference on the Law of the Sea (1958)
UNCLOS II	Second United Nations Conference on the Law of the Sea (1960)
UNCLOS III	Third United Nations Conference on the Law of the Sea (1982)
UNCSW	United Nations Commission on the Status of Women
UNCTAD	United Nations Conference on Trade and Development
UNDCP	United Nations International Drug Control Program
UNDOF	United Nations Disengagement Observer Force
UNDPPA	United Nations Department of Political and Peacebuilding Affairs
UNDRIP	United Nations Declaration on the Rights of Indigenous Peoples (2007)
UNDT	United Nations Dispute Tribunal
UNEP	United Nations Environment Programme
UNESCO	United Nations Educational, Scientific and Cultural Organization
UNFCCC	United Nations Framework Convention on Climate Change (1992)
UNFF	United Nations Forum on Forestry
UNFICYP	United Nations Peacekeeping Force in Cyprus
UNFPA	United Nations Population Fund (formerly the United Nations Fund for Population Activities)
UNGA	General Assembly (of the U.N.)
UNHCR	Office of the United Nations High Commissioner for Refugees
UNHRC	United Nations Human Rights Council (successor to the UNCHR)
UNHSP	United Nations Human Settlements Program
UNICEF	United Nations Children's Fund
UNICRI	United Nations Interregional Crime and Justice Research Institute

UNIDIR	United Nations Institute for Disarmament Research
UNIDO	United Nations Industrial Development Organization
UNIDROIT	International Institute for the Unification of Private Law
UNIFEM	United Nations Development Fund for Women
UNIFIL	United Nations Interim Force in Lebanon
UNIIIC	U.N. International Independent Investigation Commission
UNITAD	United Nations Investigative Team for Accountability of Da'esh/ISIL
UNITAR	United Nations Institute for Training and Research
UNMAS	United Nations Mine Action Service
UNMIK	United Nations Interim Administration Mission in Kosovo
UNMISS	United Nations Mission in the Republic of South Sudan
UNMIT	United Nations Integrated Mission in Timor-Leste
UNODC	United Nations Office on Drugs and Crime
UNOG	United Nations Office at Geneva
UNON	United Nations Office at Nairobi
UNOPS	United Nations Office for Project Services
UNOV	United Nations Office at Vienna
UNRISD	United Nations Research Institute for Social Development
UNRWA	United Nations Relief and Works Agency for Palestine Refugees in the Near East
UNS	United Nations Secretariat
UNSC	United Nations Security Council
UNSCOP	United Nations Special Committee on Palestine
UNSECOORD	Office of the United Nations Security Coordinator
UNSMIL	United Nations Support Mission in Libya
UNSMIS	United Nations Supervision Mission in Syria
UNSSC	United Nations System Staff College
UNTAET	United Nations Transitional Administration in East Timor
UNU	United Nations University
UNV	United Nations Volunteers
UNWTO	World Tourism Organization
UPR	Universal Periodic Review
UPU	Universal Postal Union
U.S.	United States of America
USAID	United States Agency International Development
USC	United States Code
USCIS	United States Citizenship and Immigration Services
USPTO	U.S. Patent and Trademark Office
USSR	Union of Soviet Socialist Republics
UXO	Unexploded ordinance

V

VCCR	Vienna Convention on Consular Relations (1963)
VCDR	Vienna Convention on Diplomatic Relations (1961)
VCLT	Vienna Convention on the Law of Treaties (1969)
VCLTSIO	Vienna Convention on the Law of Treaties between States and International Organizations or between International Organizations
VRS	Army of Republika Srpska

W

WCED	World Commission on Environment and Development
WFP	World Food Programme
WHO	World Health Organization
WIPO	World Intellectual Property Organization
WMO	World Meteorological Organization
WSSD	World Summit on Sustainable Development (2002)
WTO	World Trade Organization
WWII	World War II
WWF	World Wide Fund for Nature

List of International Legal Instruments

These treaties and other international instruments are listed according to the year in which they were concluded and opened for signature—not necessarily the year in which they entered into force. They are listed according to the name or acronym by which they are commonly known.

1863	Lieber Code (also known as General Order № 100 of 1863 and Instructions for the Government of Armies of the United States in the Field)
1864	Geneva Convention for the Amelioration of the Condition of the Wounded in Armies in the Field
1868	Declaration of St. Petersburg Renouncing the Use, in Time of War, of Explosive Projectiles under 400 Grammes Weight
1891	Madrid Agreement Concerning the International Registration of Marks
1899	Hague Conventions on the Laws and Customs of War
1899	Hague Convention (II) of 1899 with Respect to the Laws and Customs of War on Land
1904	Hague Convention for the Exemption of Hospital Ships, in Time of War, from The Payment of all Dues and Taxes Imposed for the Benefit of the State of 21 December 1904
1906	Geneva Convention for the Amelioration of the Condition of the Wounded and Sick in Armies in the Field
1907	Hague Convention (IV) respecting the Laws and Customs of War on Land and its Annex: Regulations concerning the Laws and Customs of War on Land
1919	Convention Relating to the Regulation of Aerial Navigation ("Paris Convention")
1922	United Nations Declaration on the Rights of Minorities

1925	Protocol for the Prohibition of the Use in War of Asphyxiating, Poisonous or other Gases, and of Bacteriological Methods of Warfare (entry into force 8 February 1928) ("Geneva Protocol" or "Geneva Gas Protocol")
1929	Geneva Convention Relative to the Treatment of Prisoners of War
1929	Lateran Treaty
1929	Warsaw Convention for the Unification of Certain Rules Relating to International Carriage by Air ("Warsaw Convention")
1930	Convention providing a Uniform Law for Bills of Exchange and Promissory Notes (enacted 7 June 1930)
1933	Montevideo Convention on the Rights and Duties of States (signed on 26 December 1933)
1936	Tripartite Agreement between the United States, France and Great Britain
1940	Tripartite Pact signed between the Axis Powers of World War II (signed at Berlin on 27 September 1940)
1944	Chicago Convention on International Civil Aviation ("Chicago Convention")
1945	Charter of the United Nations and Statute of the International Court of Justice (signed 26 June 1945)
1945	London Charter of the Nuremberg International Military Tribunal ("London Charter") (issued 8 August 1945)
1946	Convention on the Privileges and Immunities of the United Nations (passed on 13 February 1946)
1947	General Agreement on Tariffs and Trade
1948	American Declaration of the Rights and Duties of Man (signed April 1948 and effective on 2 May 1948)
1948	Convention on the Prevention and Punishment of the Crime of Genocide (signed 9 December 1948)
1948	Universal Declaration of Human Rights (adopted 10 December 1948)
1949	Geneva Convention I for the Amelioration of the Condition of the Wounded and Sick in Armed Forces in the Field
1949	Geneva Convention II for the Amelioration of the Condition of Wounded, Sick and Shipwrecked Members of Armed Forces at Sea
1949	Geneva Convention III relative to the Treatment of Prisoners of War
1949	Geneva Convention IV relative to the Protection of Civilian Persons in Time of War
1949	North Atlantic Treaty
1950	Convention for the Protection of Human Rights and Fundamental Freedoms (colloquially known as the European Convention on Human Rights, "ECHR")
1951	Convention Relating to the Status of Refugees

1953 European Convention for the Protection of Human Rights and Fundamental Freedoms ("European Convention on Human Rights" or "ECHR") (entry into force 3 September 1953)

1954 Convention for the Protection of Cultural Property in the Event of Armed Conflict with Regulations for the Execution of the Convention (The Hague, 14 May 1954, entry into force 7 August 1956)

1954 International Convention for the Prevention of Pollution of the Sea by Oil ("OILPOL") (1954)

1958 Convention on the Recognition and Enforcement of Foreign Arbitral Awards ("New York Convention") (entry into force 7 June 1959)

1958 Geneva Convention on the Territorial Sea and Contiguous Zone

1958 Geneva Convention on the High Seas

1958 Geneva Convention on the Continental Shelf

1958 Geneva Convention on Fishing and Conservation of Living Resources of the High Seas

1961 Hague Convention Abolishing the Requirement of Legalization for Foreign Public Documents ("Apostille Convention") (concluded 5 October 1961)

1961 Vienna Convention on Diplomatic Relations

1961 Rome Convention for the Protection of Performers, Producers of Phonograms and Broadcasting Organizations

1963 Treaty Banning Nuclear Weapon Tests in the Atmosphere, in Outer Space and Under Water (also known as the "Nuclear Test Ban Treaty")

1963 Vienna Convention on Consular Relations

1965 International Convention on the Elimination of All Forms of Racial Discrimination ("ICERD") (entry into force 4 January 1969)

1966 International Covenant on Economic, Social and Cultural Rights, 16 December 1966 (entry into force 3 January 1976)

1966 International Covenant on Civil and Political Rights, 16 December 1966 (entry into force 23 March 1976)

1967 Charter of the Organization of American States

1967 Treaty on principles governing the activities of States in the exploration and use of outer space, including the moon and other celestial bodies ("Outer Space Treaty")

1967 Protocol Relating to the Status of Refugees

1969 American Convention on Human Rights ("Pact of San José")

1969 International Convention on Civil Liability for Oil Pollution Damage

1969 Vienna Convention on the Law of Treaties

1970 Patent Cooperation Treaty, done at Washington on 19 June 1970

1972 The Convention on the Prohibition of the Development, Production and Stockpiling of Bacteriological (Biological) and Toxin Weapons and on their Destruction ("Biological Weapons Convention") (entry into force 26 March 1975)

1976	United Nations Convention on the Prohibition of Military or Any Hostile Use of Environmental Modification Techniques (10 December 1976; entry into force 5 October 1978)
1977	Additional Protocol to the Geneva Conventions of 12 August 1949 and Relating to the Protection of Victims of International Armed Conflicts ("AP I"), 8 June 1977 (entry into force 7 December 1979)
1977	Additional Protocol to the Geneva Conventions of 12 August 1949 and Relating to the Protection of Victims of Non-International Armed Conflicts ("AP II"), 8 June 1977 (entry into force 7 December 1979)
1979	Agreement Governing the Activities of States on the Moon and Other Celestial Bodies ("Moon Treaty")
1979	Convention on the Elimination of All Forms of Discrimination against Women
1979	Statute of the Inter-American Commission on Human Rights
1980	United Nations Convention on Prohibitions or Restrictions on the Use of Certain Conventional Weapons Which May be Deemed to be Excessively Injurious or to Have Indiscriminate Effects
1981	African Charter on Human and Peoples' Rights (27 June 1981; entry into force 21 October 1986)
1981	Declaration on the Elimination of All Forms of Intolerance and of Discrimination Based on Religion or Belief (25 November 1981)
1982	United Nations Convention on the Law of the Sea
1984	Convention against Torture and Other Cruel, Inhuman or Degrading Treatment or Punishment (1984) (the "Convention against Torture") (entry into force 1987)
1986	Vienna Convention on the Law of Treaties between States and International Organizations or between International Organizations
1989	Indigenous and Tribal Peoples Convention
1989	United Nations Convention on the Rights of the Child
1990	Cairo Declaration on Human Rights in Islam
1992	United Nations Framework Convention on Climate Change
1993	Declaration on the Elimination of Violence Against Women
1994	Declaration on Measures to Eliminate International Terrorism (UNGA)
1994	General Agreement on Tariffs and Trade
1996	Comprehensive Nuclear Test Ban Treaty
1997	Convention on the Prohibition of the Development, Production, Stockpiling and Use of Chemical Weapons and on their Destruction (adopted in 1993, entry into force on 29 April 1997)
1997	Ottawa Convention on the Prohibition of the Use, Stockpiling, Production and Transfer of Anti-Personnel Mines and on their Destruction ("Mine Ban Treaty")
1998	Statute of the International Criminal Court ("Rome Statute") (entry into force 2002)

1999	Convention for the Unification of Certain Rules for International Carriage ("Montreal Convention")
2000	The Charter of Fundamental Rights of the European Union
2001	Inter-American Democratic Charter
2004	Protocol to the African Charter on Human and Peoples' Rights on the Establishment of the African Court on Human and Peoples' Rights (adopted 10 June 1998, entry into force 25 January 2004)
2005	Additional Protocol to the Geneva Conventions of 12 August 1949 and Relating to the Adoption of an Additional Distinctive Emblem ("AP III"), 8 December 2005 (entry into force 14 January 2006)
2007	U.N. Declaration on the Rights of Indigenous Peoples (adopted 13 September 2007)
2007	Statute of the Special Tribunal for Lebanon ("STL")
2008	Charter of the Organisation of Islamic Cooperation (concluded 14 March 2008)
2008	Convention on Cluster Munitions (signed 3 December 2008; entry into force 1 August 2010)
2017	Treaty on the Prohibition of Nuclear Weapons (adopted in New York 7 July 2017; opened for signature 20 September 2017; not in force as of 2019)

Acknowledgments

For more than two decades, I have been blessed with opportunities to study or work with some of the world's most innovative, thoughtful and tireless international law practitioners, pioneers and scholars. This book is the product of a journey that took me to universities in England, France, Spain, Turkey and the United States, where I studied international and comparative law with the world's leading minds, and to international courts, tribunals, NGOs and intergovernmental agencies in Abu Dhabi, Baghdad, Beijing, Caracas, Damascus, Guatemala City, Khartoum, Moscow, New York, Quito, Riyadh and Washington, DC, where I experienced firsthand how the law shapes international relations, trade and human rights. Throughout this trajectory, I came across lawyers, academics, judges and scholars who took me under their wing, patiently mentored me and helped me develop an understanding of international law that would become the foundation of this book. These individuals left an indelible mark on me. They selflessly invested their time in me, expecting nothing in return. In so doing, they exemplified the best of humanity. I would like to express my gratitude to each of them by way of these acknowledgments.

I wish to first thank the following individuals who provided their time in discussing the practical application and interpretation of international law by international organizations, courts and tribunals: Marko Milanovic of the University of Nottingham; Ardi Imseis of Queen's University; Amer Abu Khalaf of UNRWA; Kevin Jon Heller of the University of Copenhagen and the International Criminal Court; Kilian Kleinschmidt of UNHCR; and Craig Hollingsworth of the Norwegian Refugee Council. Many of my discussions with these distinguished lawyers found expression in this book.

My journey in international law began with a course I had taken with Dr. Hakan Baykal as an undergraduate exchange student in Turkey. In addition to presenting his weekly lectures, Dr. Baykal met with me one-on-one to discuss the practical application of the law of the sea and other branches of international law as they impacted Turkey's relations with other states. Dr. Baykal's passion for both international law and teaching marked me profoundly. Those one-on-one sessions set into motion what would ultimately become my career in international law. Dr. Baykal passed away in 2016. I will always remember him well.

After graduating from college, I returned to Turkey as a Fulbright Fellow to study Turkish legal reform through the prism of international law. During that time, Dr. Nilüfer Oral served as an extraordinary research mentor. I am deeply indebted to her. I am also grateful to the professors who shaped my legal thinking during my studies in France and Spain: Pablo Nuevo of Universidad Abat Oliba in Barcelona and Anne-Marie Lizin, Bernard Stirn and Onelia Cardettini of l'Institut d'Études Poliques de Paris (Sciences Po-Paris).

Over the following years, a number of educators made a mark on my understanding of international human rights and humanitarian law. They include Ahmed Shaheed, Naz Ghanea and Patti Sellers Viseur of Oxford University's master's program in international human rights law. I am also indebted to Dino Kritsiotos, who served as my dissertation advisor at Oxford University. Professor Kritsiotis helped me to read the Geneva Conventions of 1949 with a fresh pair of eyes and to consider the prisoner of war protections of Geneva Convention III in a manner that I had never before envisaged. His mentorship and guidance were key to a strategy I would later develop as a defense counsel at the Guantánamo Bay war crimes tribunals.

I am grateful to Professor Jeff Brauch of Regent Law School's Center for Global Justice. Professor Brauch encouraged my interest in international law and helped me to view it as a tool to seek justice and defend the oppressed. His life exemplifies the biblical mandate to "do justice, love mercy and walk humbly with your God" (Micah 6:8).

My first job as a licensed attorney was at the U.S. Department of State's Office of the Legal Advisor, where I learned from Mark Feldman, a leader in the State-investor arbitration team, how bilateral and multilateral treaties protected businesses in their foreign investments. I am grateful to Mark for his enduring support in the ensuing years. I later joined the law firm Dentons, where my managing partner, Amgad Husein, instilled in me his trust and let me build a refugee law practice while I simultaneously assisted foreign investors in their Middle East operations. At the time, I had built partnerships with international organizations and NGOs in the Middle East that had assisted hundreds of Syrian refugees just as the Syrian civil conflict had reached its peak. Amgad put logistical and financial support behind these initiatives that made them a reality. The ensuing understanding of international refugee law that I developed serves as the foundation of the refugee law chapter of this book.

I later went on to join the attorney corps of the U.S. military where, as a Judge Advocate, I met Major Jason Wright, who became a friend, mentor and ultimately a colleague. I know of no other lawyer who has invested as much in developing the next generation of lawyers as Jason. Leadership comes naturally to him. Selfless service and integrity are embedded in his DNA. To him, I am grateful.

I later joined the United Nations, where I experienced firsthand the application of international law in the assistance and protection of victims of human rights abuses and in the prosecution of international crimes. I am grateful to a number of colleagues and friends who guided me along the way and shaped my understanding of international human rights and international criminal law. They include Yousuf Khan, Daniel

Bell, Paula Silfverstolpe, Caroline Buisman and Douglass Hansen. I will forever cherish our meandering conversations on international law.

Finally, this book benefitted enormously from discussions I have had over the years with a range of scholars and practitioners on the intersection of public international law and Islamic law and how the latter complements or diverges from the former. These discussions added a layer of depth and comparative legal understanding that enriched this book. For this, I am grateful to Bernard Haykel of Princeton University; Ahmed Al-Dawoody and Omar Mekky of the ICRC; Melinda Taylor, Alka Pradhan, Felicity Gerry and Mohamed E. Badar of the International Criminal Court's *Al Hassan* defense team; Christopher Kidner and Saad Rustem of Geneva Call; Iyad Nasr of the London House of Consultants; Mohammad Fadel of the University of Toronto; and Dr. Mohamed A. Ibrahim of the United Nations Department of Peace Operations. I am also grateful to Sarah Gouia of Curtis, Mallet-Prevost, Colt & Mosle LLP for her research on the jurisprudence of the International Court of Justice.

Ten years ago, I reached out to Eleanor Taylor and the editors of Kluwer Law International to pitch an article on international law for the Kluwer Law blog. After that initial piece was accepted, I contributed several more. More recently, I reached out again to Eleanor Taylor, who now serves as acquisition manager and commissioning editor at Wolters Kluwer. This time, I pitched a full-fledged book on international law. I was pleased when Eleanor informed me that the publication committee wanted to proceed with my book. Over the past year, I have worked with Eleanor and the editors of Kluwer Law International in preparing my manuscript for publication. It has been a pleasure working with them, and it should go without saying that this publication would not have been possible without Eleanor, who believed in my proposal, recognized the need for my book and put her support behind it.

Finally, I am indebted beyond expression to my wife, Alexandra, for her unconditional support and wondrous love.

Foreword by Diego García-Sayán

Public international law applies—or should apply—every day in events all around us. One needs to look no further than the front page of any international news journal to find a plethora of international law issues: state disputes before the International Court of Justice; the right to peaceful assembly and protest-related violence; maritime claims and economic exploitation in disputed waters; climate change and the right to a healthy environment; armed conflict in Palestine, Sudan, Ukraine, Myanmar and beyond; legal reform and its impact on judicial independence; forced labor, child exploitation and modern slavery; the impact of AI on data privacy and access to information; intellectual property, genetic resources and associated traditional knowledge; the environmental impact of foreign investment on local communities ... the list goes on and on.

One sees perhaps most clearly the full prism of international law and the manifestation of its numerous facets during its most acute crisis—in acts of aggression. When one state invades another, a panoply of international law issues is triggered: the legality of the use of force (*jus ad bellum*); the rules governing military operations in armed conflict (*jus in bello*); status determinations of prisoners of war and other detainees; the law applicable in occupied and disputed territories; accountability for war crimes under international criminal law; the intersection of international human rights law and humanitarian law during armed conflict; state responsibility for internationally wrongful acts; reparations; the suspension of human rights during martial law; and the status of displaced persons under international refugee law, to name just a few.

International disputes are further complicated whenever states cannot agree on the status of a disputed territory, or, even more fundamentally, on what criteria should be used when determining whether an entity qualifies as a state. Does the objective test under the Montevideo Convention apply? Or does the subjective test under the constitutive theory of statehood apply? What are the rights and duties of entities such as Kosovo, Palestine and Taiwan, which some, but not all, states recognize as fulfilling the criteria for statehood? And what laws apply when the whole of the international community recognizes an entity as a state, but a single state does not? Is the latter bound by the determinations of the former?

For instance, in the event of an armed conflict between the Democratic People's Republic of Korea (North Korea) and the Republic of Korea (South Korea), would South Korea's non-recognition of North Korea as a separate state negate South Korea's obligations to accord Geneva Convention protections to captured prisoners of war and protected persons in South Korean territory? Could South Korea refuse to apply laws applicable to international armed conflict, and treat the North Korean government as a rebel group? Could South Korea refuse to grant refugee status to North Koreans who flee to South Korea, and argue that the Armistice Line does not represent an international border dividing sovereign states?

These are but a few of the countless legal questions that arise when states resort to the use of force. But international law comprises much more than the rules applicable to armed conflict. It applies every day in the ordinary course of business between states. It addresses interstate complaints brought before international courts and arbitral tribunals; it is used to adjudicate disputes involving international trade, sovereign rights, exclusive economic zones, diplomatic and sovereign immunity, the use of outer space and disputed territorial and maritime boundaries.

International law does much more than govern state conduct. It applies, increasingly so, to private actors. Today, individuals have standing as subjects under international law and may file claims against states under a variety of treaties, including, *inter alia*, the American Convention on Human Rights and the European Convention on Human Rights. Moreover, individuals may be prosecuted for international crimes by international criminal tribunals, as we have seen in the International Military Tribunals in Nuremberg and the Far East and, more recently, in the U.N.-created ad hoc tribunals for the former Yugoslavia and Rwanda, as well as in the permanent International Criminal Court.

Even businesses and corporate directors, officers and other corporate actors increasingly hold duties and obligations under international law. A range of international organizations have issued guiding principles and legal instruments governing business and human rights. A few worth mentioning include the U.N. Guiding Principles on Business and Human Rights, the OECD Guidelines for Multinational Enterprises and the ILO Tripartite Declaration of Principles Concerning Multinational Enterprises and Social Policy. There are many others.

It is no longer possible for multinational corporations following international best practice to invest in foreign jurisdictions without undertaking a human rights due diligence of their proposed operations abroad and assessing the impact that these operations will have on the environment, labor rights and human rights. To fail to do so exposes corporations to a litany of risks, including claims filed by victims, NGOs or human rights groups, and the possibility of universal jurisdiction claims if the alleged violations constitute international crimes.

These are not remote risks. Rather, they are very real, considering the proliferation of claims brought in national jurisdictions against individuals, corporations, corporate executives and government officials alleging violations of international humanitarian law, international criminal law, international human rights law and other branches of public international law. Some of the most high-profile cases, for instance, are being brought against multinational corporations alleging complicity in international crimes committed in conflict zones or in violations of international human rights law committed in mines, forced labor camps and occupied territories. Attorneys for these corporations are increasingly having to grapple not only with the national laws of domestic jurisdictions, but also with principles of public international law. Losing such a case can be crippling for corporations. The filing of a claim itself can be a public relations disaster for a multinational company that seeks to safeguard an unblemished reputation. Consequently, international law has become a topic of the corporate boardroom. Virtually every multinational corporation has by now adopted a human rights policy or environmental stewardship charter to direct its international operations and mitigate such risks.

This application of international law to corporations and other private actors, which has rapidly evolved in the past 20 years, is but one manifestation of the constant evolution of international law. As technology has advanced, with humankind closer than ever to activities in outer space, so too has international law been reinvented. Whether it is the *Woomera Manual on the International Law of Military Space Activities and Operations* or the *Tallinn Manual on the International Law Applicable to Cyber Warfare*, expert working groups and academic institutions have drafted a range of manuals and guidelines to address rising tensions in outer space, to clarify how international law applies to cyber conflicts, to ensure the protection of legal equities and to avoid unnecessary disputes. As computer technology takes leaps forward, so too does international law.

Around the world, on any given day, there are countless interstate legal disputes, transnational conflicts, tensions at sea and in space, international trade negotiations and boundary disputes that all carry with them unique questions of international law. In the current global economy, international law can no longer be the exclusive domain of lawyers. Diplomats, international civil servants, soldiers, human rights advocates and executives of multinational corporations all require knowledge of international law. This is especially true for the "hot button" topics of international law that impact not only states, but also multinational corporations, civil society groups, international organizations, NGOs and individuals. These topics include trade and investment, corporate accountability for international crimes, environmental law, banking and finance, human rights, the laws of war, international criminal law, labor rights, climate change, refugee and asylum issues and arms control.

Here is where this book comes in. It is an extensively researched and intensely readable handbook that covers all the aforementioned topics—and many more—with painstaking detail and sharp insight, but without technical jargon. It is written by an expert who brings wildly diverse experience to the subject of international law. John began his international law career at the Inter-American Court of Human Rights, where I was serving as a judge when we first met, and then went on to work for governments, international organizations and NGOs, advising on pressing topics of international law that shape the world around us. What is perhaps most impressive about this trajectory is the breadth of international law experience that John brings to this project—from serving as a legal advisor to his Department of State, to working as an international law officer for his military, to serving with the U.N. Office of the High Commissioner for Human Rights and later as a United Nations legal officer, all while teaching international law and running a range of clinics for refugees and other displaced persons. And finally, advising a diverse client base while serving at leading international law firms. This book, drawing on John's breadth of experience, expounds upon international law not only as it is written, but also as it is applied, from the perspective of a practitioner who has been at the ship's helm, reading both the currents of international law and its undercurrents.

I am proud to see this book—the culmination of John's work in international law since I worked with him years ago at the Inter-American Court—go to press. This solidly researched, clearly written and balanced exposition of international law is one that I commend to lawyers, diplomats, foreign investors, international arbitrators and any other person who seeks to understand international relations through the lens of international law.

- Diego García-Sayán
Special Rapporteur on the independence of judges and lawyers
of the United Nations
(2016-2022)
President and Judge, Inter-American Court of Human Rights
San José, Costa Rica (2007-2014)
Minister of Justice and Human Rights, Minister of Foreign Affairs
Lima, Peru (2000-2002)

Foreword by Charles L. O. Buderi

In this exhaustive and meticulously-researched book, John Balouziyeh sets out in *reference-book* style a virtual encyclopedia of the world of international law, its origins, sources, institutions, rules, developing trends and current challenges. The author's perspective, and his ability to cover the many topics addressed with clarity and deep familiarity throughout, has obviously been enriched by his diverse background and experiences. On a professional level, these have included roles in academia, the military, governmental and non-governmental organizations, multilateral institutions, and private law practice. Together these varied roles have brought him into close contact with both the theoretical basis and practical application of many of the rules of international law he covers in this work. On a more personal level, his immersion in and exposure to legal systems, cultures and currents of thought in multiple areas of the world, a hint of which is given by the author in his extended Acknowledgements, have given him a truly international vision of the importance of international law in today's world and the real-life consequences which flow from its application and respect or, in certain cases, its neglect or outright violation. The years-long development and writing of this book is a testament to the author's genuine dedication to the rules-based system of international law and his desire for it to be understood and respected.

It goes without saying that this lengthy and comprehensive book would be an important addition to the collection of any law library or law student having an interest in public international law as it addresses the very foundations of the law, as well as the role and impact public international law and institutions may have in contextualizing or resolving many of the world's conflict areas and crises which would likely be the focus of study in international law courses today. These might include such critical topics as climate change, the plight and status of the growing numbers of refugees in the world, or the responsibilities, obligations and consequences arising out of armed conflict, which has consumed so much global attention in areas such as Ukraine, Gaza, Myanmar and many other parts of the world during recent years. The book provides a review, commentary and relevant authorities which deal with each of these, and many other topics of international law, and which also guide the reader wishing to delve further into any of these topics through useful and relevant additional sources. The comprehensive manner in which the author deals with these and other discrete areas of international law can thus serve either as an introductory primer or, given the depth of the sources relied upon and referred to, as a basis for further academic study and refinement of research projects and analysis.

From the perspective of practicing lawyers, whether those whose work may only occasionally bring them into contact with one or more of the topics addressed in the book or those whose work revolves around public international law, this book will also prove to be of invaluable assistance. Its contents are readily accessible and present to the reader both the features of the area of international law under consideration, as well as a comprehensive review of the history, development and current status of that area of law, complemented by references to recent judicial and academic authorities. To mention a few examples, Chapter 2, which deals with international organizations, including the United Nations and its associated organs such as the International Court of Justice (ICJ), the Organization of American States, the Organisation of the Islamic Conference, the Arab League, the Andean Community, the African Union and the European Union, provides a comprehensive overview into the functioning of the international system and the rules which govern those organizations' activities which is so critical to understanding the framework in which the international rules-based system operates. Other chapters discussing international human rights law (Chapter 5), international humanitarian law and the law of armed conflict (Chapter 6), and international criminal law (Chapter 7) would be of particular interest to those following or involved in some of the most serious armed conflicts currently taking place in the world and whose work requires evaluating the legal position and responsibility of States for such conflicts. And Chapter 12, which deals with international economic and trade law, an already important topic of international concern, may become increasingly relevant if trade disputes grow in an environment of protectionism, as seems to be promised by the incoming U.S. administration.

While this book will most naturally be of interest to international lawyers, its clear, comprehensive and easily-accessible contents should also be useful to a wide range of other audiences. These might include diplomats and policy makers whose activities depend on an understanding of public international law and its associated institutions, or academics, for example political scientists, who will find within this work the public international law considerations that may impact their research or analysis of geopolitical conflicts. All such audiences may gain insights into the rules and application of public international law which will prove helpful in the development of their particular fields of expertise.

- Charles L. O. Buderi
Chair, Public International Law
Curtis, Mallet-Prevost, Colt & Mosle LLP
London and Dubai

CHAPTER 1
Introduction

I THE DEFINITION AND ORIGINS OF INTERNATIONAL LAW

International Law can be defined as the set of binding rules and principles that govern the relations and dealings of nations and international organizations with one another and with natural or juridical persons. The Restatement 3d of the Foreign Relations Law of the United States ("RFR") thus states that international law "consists of rules and principles of general application dealing with the conduct of states and of international organizations and with their relations *inter se*, as well as with some of their relations with persons, whether natural or juridical" (§ 101 RFR).

The origins of international law date back thousands of years, to peace treaties signed between kings and pharaohs and conventions ratified by city-sites. Among the earliest examples of international conventions are the peace treaties concluded between the Mesopotamian city-states of Lagash and Umma in approximately 3100 BCE. In the more recent era, international law took giant leaps forward with the writings of the Dutch jurist Hugo Grotius (1583-1645), whose *De jure belli ac pacis* (On the Law of War and Peace) and *Mare Liberum* (The Free Seas) laid the foundations for contemporary international law. The Peace of Westphalia of 1648, which put an end to the Thirty Years War in the Holy Roman Empire and the Eighty Years' War (1568-1648), was yet another major development in the evolution of international law. It gave rise to the birth of modern nation-states, which looked to international law to govern trade and political relations.

II PUBLIC VERSUS PRIVATE INTERNATIONAL LAW

Public international law concerns itself with questions of rights between several nations and some questions of rights between nations and the citizens or subjects of other nations. Private international law, in contrast, governs the activities of and relations between natural and juridical persons when they cross national borders.

Private international law involves such areas as trade and commerce, finance and banking, trusts and estates and family law matters, including international child abduction between private litigants when a foreign element is present. In these cases, conflict of law provisions must be invoked in order to determine: (i) which jurisdiction has competence to hear a case; and (ii) which jurisdiction's laws are to be applied by the court hearing the case.

According to Anthony Aust, the major difference between public and private international law is that while public international law seeks to lay out a regime of supernational norms that govern issues having foreign elements, private international law is a body of domestic legal rules that are used to determine which laws should be applied when such a case having foreign elements arises. While true (public) international law is a system of positive international legal instruments, private international law is merely domestic *conflict of laws*. Thus, organizations such as HCPIL, UNIDROIT and UNCITRAL that seek to harmonize states' domestic laws in a variety of areas ranging from conflict of laws to international trade law fall within private international law (conflict of laws), and organizations such as the WTO that write international laws binding on member states fall within public international law, as they do not deal with states' domestic laws strictly speaking.

Public international law, which is often referred to simply as "international law," is the main subject of this treatise. Private international law will only be mentioned in passing.

III SUBJECTS OF INTERNATIONAL LAW

A Overview

The subjects of international law are thus: (i) states; (ii) international organizations; (iii) juridical persons; and (iv) natural persons. All of these subjects bear the rights and responsibilities of international law.

States have historically been the primary subjects of public international law, which developed to regulate states as a result of state interaction, particularly in times of war. The laws of war developed because of the mutual interests of states to regulate the use of force in wartime and to create a legal framework to mitigate the risk of the emergence of war.

Both natural and juridical persons are also subjects of international law. The natural person has increasingly become accepted as an independent actor subject to and benefiting from international law. Although natural persons are not parties to international law, they may bear rights and duties emanating from international law. Juridical persons—whether corporations or other business associations or registered non-governmental organizations, such as charities—similarly may bear rights and responsibilities under international law.

Finally, international organizations are subjects of international law that are comprised either solely or primarily of states. Examples of international organizations include the United Nations, the European Union and the Organization of American States.

B Individuals in the International Order

1 Overview

Traditionally, the subjects of international law have been states. However, there is a growing trend whereby international law also applies to natural persons (individuals) and legal persons (such as corporations), all of which increasingly hold rights and obligations under international law. Historically, such rights and obligations could only be enforced through states. Today, there are numerous treaties between states that enable individuals to bring suits before international tribunals and domestic laws that enable residents (both citizens and resident aliens) to file claims against states for torts or other wrongful acts.

However, only states and, increasingly, international organizations, have full legal personality under international law. Individuals only have legal personality in the international order to the extent that states allow them. For example, individual victims of violations of international criminal law may refer crimes to their state, which may, in turn, refer the case to the International Criminal Court if the state is a party to the Rome Statute (Article 13(a) SICC).

In this section, we explore the extent to which international law has enabled non-state actors (other than international organizations) to serve as subjects and objects in the international legal order.

2 Examples of Individuals in the International Order

Individuals may serve as subjects in the international order who may enforce their rights in national and international courts or who may be called to account for breaching their duties and responsibilities under international law. Among the examples of individuals in the international order, we may point to:

- *Domestic law*. Individuals as subjects of tort law against their states of residence (in the case of aliens) (e.g., ATCA) or as individuals who can be sued civilly under domestic law for the violation of international law (e.g., ATCA).
- *International human rights law*. Perhaps more than in any other area of international law, individuals have standing as subjects with rights under international human rights law and may file claims against states under, *inter alia*, the American Convention on Human Rights, the European Convention on Human Rights, the International Covenant on Civil and Political Rights through the Human Rights Committee ("HRC"), etc.
- *International criminal law*. In venues such as the International Criminal Court ("ICC") or in ad hoc tribunals, such as the International Criminal Tribunal for the former Yugoslavia ("ICTY"), which has jurisdiction over both state and

non-state actors, individuals may be prosecuted under international criminal law.

IV INTERSECTION OF THE BRANCHES OF INTERNATIONAL LAW

Although the principles and customs of international law date back many centuries, the codification of international law is a relatively new phenomenon. Some of this codification, such as the Vienna Convention on the Law of Treaties, codifies principles that are already accepted in customary international law. Other developments in international law are innovative. For example, the Charter of the International Military Tribunal laid down principles that were at the time novel, such as the principle that persons may be individually responsible for violations of international law.

The development and codification of international law are welcomed by many as bringing light to principles that otherwise have been uncertain. At the same time, because it is relatively new, there has been a great deal of overlap among the various branches of international law. For example, a crime may be classified as an international crime if it has an international dimension. If it is a crime that violates an individual's basic right, it may be classified as a human rights violation. If the same crime is committed in a systematic and organized fashion against civilians in a time of armed conflict, it may be considered a war crime in violation of international humanitarian law, as well as a human rights violation and an international crime. Thus, international institutions such as the International Criminal Court ("ICC") may be responsible for overseeing cases that fall not only into the category of international criminal law but also international human rights law and international humanitarian law.

CHAPTER 2

International Organizations and International Law

I INTRODUCTION

An international organization is a body created by a treaty with a permanent institutional structure whose membership consists either exclusively or in large part of states. The treaty is the constituent instrument of the organization. Although the main subject of international law has traditionally been the state, international law has evolved in the last century to include international and regional organizations. International organizations are subjects of international law because they have duties and rights under international law and can make international law.

One cannot understand international law without understanding the international organizations that make, apply and enforce international law. Among these organizations, we can consider the United Nations, the European Union, NATO and many others. Several of these organizations, such as the UN, OAS and EU, have their own legal arms that deal with issues ranging from international trade to human rights.

II THE UNITED NATIONS

A Overview of the United Nations

At the conclusion of World War I, the Treaty of Versailles was signed in 1919 between Germany and the Allied Powers to establish peace between them and to create the League of Nations. However, because the Treaty required Germany to accept sole responsibility for causing the war, to make substantial territorial concessions and to pay reparations deemed by many economists to be excessive, the Treaty was later largely ignored by Germany. The peace would ultimately collapse, and the Treaty would be used by radical factions in Germany to win support for a nationalist cause that eventually gave rise to the Nazi Party and to World War II.

After the failure of the Treaty of Versailles and the League of Nations during World War II, the United Nations was founded in 1945 to maintain peace and security, develop friendly relations among nations, achieve international cooperation in solving international problems and be a center for harmonizing the actions of the nations and attaining their common ends. The U.N. has been the locus for the development of binding laws and advisory standards, such as the Universal Declaration of Human Rights and has established various organizations for the promulgation of rules ranging from labor to intellectual property standards. Among these organizations are the ILO, the World Health Organization, the World Intellectual Property Organization, the International Telecommunication Union, UNESCO, the World Trade Organization and the International Monetary Fund.

B Charter of the United Nations

1 Overview of the Charter

The Charter of the United Nations ("U.N. Charter" or "Charter"), together with the Statute of the International Court of Justice ("SICJ"), is the principal legal instrument of the U.N. It was signed on 26 June 1945, in San Francisco, by the representatives of 50 nations at the conclusion of the United Nations Conference on International Organization and came into force on 24 October 1945. The Charter has been promulgated in order to achieve the U.N.'s goals of attaining peace and security, friendly relations among nations and international cooperation. It has been adhered to by virtually all states; the few remaining non-member states have acquiesced to the principles established in the Charter.

2 Preamble of the Charter

The Charter consists of a Preamble and a series of articles grouped into chapters. The preamble consists of three parts:

(1) *an outline of the purposes for the establishment of the UN:* to save succeeding generations from the scourge of war; to affirm fundamental human rights and human dignity; to establish justice and respect for the rule of law; and to promote social progress and better standards of life;
(2) *a covenant among member states that agree to:* practice tolerance; unite strength to maintain peace and security; ensure that armed force not be used except in the common interest; and promote international economic and social progress; and
(3) a declaration that the governments of the peoples of the U.N. have agreed to the Charter.

3 *Body of the Charter*

The body of the Charter consists of 19 chapters as follows:

- *Chapter I.* Sets forth the purposes and principles of the United Nations and provisions for the maintenance of international peace and security.
- *Chapter II.* Defines the criteria for membership in the United Nations, stating that the U.N. is "open to all other peace-loving states which accept the obligations contained in the present Charter and, in the judgment of the Organization, are able and willing to carry out these obligations" (Article 4.1 Charter).
- *Chapters III-V.* Describe the organs of the U.N. with specific attention given to the General Assembly and Security Council.
- *Chapter VI.* Deals with the pacific settlement of disputes and the Security Council's power to investigate and mediate disputes (Chapter VI).
- *Chapter VII.* Outlines the Security Council's power to take action in disputes through imposing sanctions to interrupt "economic relations and of rail, sea, air ... and the severance of diplomatic relations" (Article 41 Charter) or "operations by air, sea, or land forces of Members of the United Nations" (Article 42 Charter), thus authorizing the use of military force in cases involving threats to and breaches of the peace and acts of aggression. For further treatment, *see* "U.N. Collective Security Measures," *infra*.
- *Chapter VIII.* Makes possible regional arrangements for maintaining peace and security within their own regions.
- *Chapters IX and X.* Lay out a framework for international economic and social cooperation and establish ECOSOC, which oversees this framework.
- *Chapters XI-XIII.* A declaration regarding non-self-governing territories and an outline of the international trusteeship system, which oversaw decolonization.
- *Chapters XIV-XV.* Description of the ICJ and U.N. Secretariat and their respective powers and roles. *See supra*, "Legal Institution: the International Court of Justice" for a full description of the ICJ and the SICJ.
- *Chapters XVI-XVII.* Miscellaneous provisions and transitional security arrangements related to World War II for integrating the U.N. with established international law.
- *Chapters XVIII-XIX.* The Charter amendment and ratification processes and signature by respective member governments.

C Principal Non-legal Organs

The U.N. is comprised of six principal organs: (1) the General Assembly, (2) the Security Council, (3) ECOSOC, (4) the Trusteeship Council, (5) the Secretariat, and (6) the International Court of Justice. In this section, we will examine the first five organs. In the following section, we will examine the International Court of Justice.

1 *The General Assembly (Chapter IV Charter)*

a Overview

The U.N. General Assembly ("UNGA"), the main deliberative body of the U.N., is composed of delegates from all member states. The decisions of the General Assembly largely mandate the activities and direction of the U.N. each year. These decisions are generally issued by majority vote, although there are certain issues, such as the admission of new members to the United Nations, that require the vote of a majority of two-thirds of the members present and voting (Article 18 Charter).

Apart from approval of budgetary matters regarding the allotment and collection of dues, the resolutions of the General Assembly are not binding on U.N. members. The General Assembly may make recommendations on any matters within the scope of the U.N., except matters of peace and security under the consideration of the Security Council. The General Assembly may also adopt conventions, such as the 1948 Genocide Convention, that states are free to adopt and ratify. These conventions become binding sources of law on the member states that sign and ratify them.

Although the resolutions of the General Assembly are not legally binding per se, states sometimes express their opinions about the status of customary international law through declarations and recommendations of the General Assembly, and this may, in turn, shape the content of customary international law. Furthermore, as will be mentioned below, the resolutions and declarations of international organizations such as the U.N. may constitute international "soft law."

b Structure and Organization

The General Assembly works through six Main Committees: First (Disarmament & security); Second (Economic & financial); Third (Social, humanitarian & cultural); Fourth (Decolonization); Fifth (Administrative & budgetary); and Sixth (Legal).

Organs subsidiary to the General Assembly include UNCTAD, UNDP, UNEP, UNFPA, UNHCR, UNHSP (UN-Habitat), UNICEF, UNITAR and WFP.

2 *Security Council (Chapter V Charter)*

The Security Council has primary responsibility for the maintenance of international peace and security. It has the ability to make decisions that are legally binding on member states. Under the U.N. Charter, members of the U.N. agree to "accept and carry out the decisions of the Security Council in accordance with the present Charter" (Article 25 Charter). They thus agree that the decisions of the Security Council will be legally binding on them and on all other members.

Under Article 103 of the Charter, if there is a conflict "between the obligations of the Members of the United Nations under the present Charter and their obligations under any other international agreement, their obligations under the present Charter shall prevail." Therefore, if the Security Council adopts policies contrary to states' other treaty obligations, states are required to abrogate these other treaty obligations.

Each member of the Security Council has one vote (Article 27.I Charter). Decisions are made by the following majorities:

- *Procedure.* Decisions on procedural matters are made by an affirmative vote of *nine members* (Article. 27.II Charter).
- *All other matters.* Decisions on all other matters are made by an affirmative vote of *nine members*, including the *concurring votes of the permanent members* (i.e., such decisions may not be vetoed by the permanent members), provided that, in decisions under Chapter VI (Pacific Settlement of Disputes), and under paragraph 3 of Article 52 (pacific settlement of local disputes through regional arrangements or regional agencies), a party to a dispute shall abstain from voting (Article 27.III Charter).

3 Economic and Social Council (Chapter X Charter)

The Economic and Social Council ("ECOSOC") coordinates the economic and social work of the United Nations and its specialized agencies and institutions. Voting in ECOSOC is by simple majority, with each member holding one vote.

4 Trusteeship Council (Chapters XII-XIII Charter)

The TC was established in 1945 to provide international supervision for 11 Trust Territories placed under the administration of seven member states in order to adequately prepare them for self-governance. When these Trust Territories had attained self-government by 1994, the work of the TC had been completed.

5 Secretariat (Chapter XV Charter)

The Secretariat is the managerial body that carries out the day-to-day activities of the organization by servicing other organs and executing various tasks, such as peacekeeping administration and preparing studies.

D Legal Institution: International Court of Justice

1 Overview

The International Court of Justice ("ICJ") was established by the Charter of the U.N. in June 1945 and began its work in 1946 as the "principal judicial organ of the United Nations" (Article 92 Charter). It is governed by the Statute of the International Court of Justice ("SICJ"), which is an integral part of the Charter. As the only one of the six principal U.N. organs not located in New York, the ICJ is seated in The Hague. The

Court's stated objective is to settle in accordance with international law legal disputes submitted to it by states.

Although international law may regulate *some* of the relations between states and natural or juridical persons or international organizations and natural or juridical persons, the jurisdiction of the ICJ is limited to hearing only those cases in which all of the parties are states (Article 34.1 SICJ). Thus, non-state actors, including international organizations and individual and juridical persons, may not sue or be sued by states before the ICJ. Among the cases handled by the ICJ are the application and interpretation of international treaties and conventions, environmental issues and border and law of the sea disputes between state actors. The ICJ may also hear international criminal and humanitarian law cases when all of the parties to a dispute are states, as was the case of the Bosnian genocide case (*Bosnia and Herzegovina v. Serbia and Montenegro*, case 91) that the Court heard in 2006.

The ICJ is governed by Chapter XIV of the Charter (Articles 92-96) as well as by the SICJ, which is an integral part of the United Nations Charter that we examine below.

2 *Provisions of the U.N. Charter with Respect to the ICJ*

a *Peaceful Resolution of Disputes*

The Charter establishes in its second Article that "All Members ... shall fulfill in good faith the obligations assumed by them in accordance with the present Charter [and] settle their international disputes by peaceful means" (Article 2 Charter). Article 33 further requires parties to any dispute whose continuance is likely to endanger international peace and security to "seek a solution by negotiation, enquiry, mediation, conciliation, arbitration, judicial settlement, resort to regional agencies or arrangements, or other peaceful means of their own choice" (Article 33 Charter). When such disputes arise, the Security Council may, at any stage of a dispute, "recommend appropriate procedures or methods of adjustment" (Article 36.1 Charter). In making such recommendations, the Security Council should "take into consideration that legal disputes should as a general rule be referred by the parties to the International Court of Justice in accordance with the provisions of the Statute of the Court" (Article 36.3 Charter).

b *Open to All States*

The ICJ is the widest-reaching court in the international arena, as it is potentially open to all states. All members of the U.N. are *ipso facto* parties to the SICJ and agree to comply with the decision of the ICJ in any case to which they are parties. Furthermore, a "state which is not a Member of the United Nations may become a party to the Statute of the International Court of Justice on conditions to be determined in each case by the General Assembly upon the recommendation of the Security Council" (Article 93 Charter).

c Enforcement of Judgments

Each member of the U.N. "undertakes to comply with the decision of the International Court of Justice in any case to which it is a party" (Article 94.1 Charter). Because U.N. members are obligated to obey decisions of the ICJ, the ICJ decisions have the power of binding law among parties to a dispute. If any party to a case fails to perform the obligations imposed by an ICJ judgment, the other party may have recourse to the Security Council, which may "make recommendations or decide upon measures to be taken to give effect to the judgment" (Article 94.2 Charter).

However, a decision of the ICJ "has no binding force except between the parties and in respect of that particular case" (Article 59 SICJ). If a state intervenes in a case before the ICJ, "the construction given by the judgment will be equally binding upon" that state (Article 63.2 SICJ).

d Advisory Opinions

As discussed under "Types of Cases Handled by the ICJ," *infra*, the General Assembly or Security Council may, under Article 96 of the U.N. Charter, request the ICJ to give an advisory opinion on any legal question. Other organs of the U.N. and specialized agencies authorized by the General Assembly may also request advisory opinions of the ICJ on legal questions arising within the scope of their activities. Articles 65 to 68 of the SICJ are dedicated to the procedural aspects for requesting advisory opinions and for the issuance thereof.

3 The Statute of the ICJ

The SICJ establishes the ICJ as "the principal judicial organ of the United Nations" that is "constituted and shall function in accordance with the provisions of the present Statute" (Article 1 SICJ). The Statute is comprised of 70 articles divided into five chapters:

(1) Organization of the Court (Articles 2-33 SICJ).
(2) Competence of the Court (Articles 34-38 SICJ).
(3) Procedure (Articles 39-64 SICJ).
(4) Advisory opinions (Articles 65-68).
(5) Amendment (Articles 69-70 SICJ).

Under the Statute, the ICJ is to apply international conventions, international custom, the general principles of law "recognized by civilized nations," and "judicial decisions and the teachings of the most highly qualified publicists of the various nations, as subsidiary means for the determination of rules of law" (Article 38.1 SICJ). However, the application of these conventions and other legal sources "shall not prejudice the power of the Court to decide a case *ex aequo et bono* [*Lat.*, "according to the right and good" or "from equity and conscience"], if the parties agree thereto"

(Article 38.2 SICJ). The Court may thus make a legal ruling based both on law as well as equity.

4 *Jurisdiction*

a Cases Referred to the ICJ on an Ad Hoc Basis (Article 36.1 SICJ)

The SICJ establishes jurisdiction of the ICJ over "all cases which the parties refer to it" (Article 36.1 SICJ). The ICJ thus has jurisdiction over those cases that states agree to bring before it. In this way, states may agree to the jurisdiction of the ICJ in specific matters without conferring jurisdiction to the ICJ over all of their disputes.

b Compromissory Clause (Article 36.1 SICJ)

The SICJ further states that the jurisdiction of the Court comprises "all matters specially provided for in the Charter of the United Nations or in treaties and conventions in force" (Article 36.1 SICJ). This applies to states parties to a convention (e.g., the Genocide Convention) that submits to the jurisdiction of the Court any questions of interpretation or application.

c State Recognition of ICJ Compulsory Jurisdiction (Article 36.2 SICJ)

In addition, the SICJ declares in Article 36.2 as follows:

> The states parties to the present Statute may at any time declare that they recognize as compulsory *ipso facto* and without special agreement, in relation to any other State accepting the same obligation, the jurisdiction of the Court in all legal disputes concerning: a. the interpretation of a treaty; b. any question of international law; c. the existence of any fact which, if established, would constitute a breach of an international obligation; d. the nature or extent of the reparation to be made for the breach of an international obligation.

Thus, if any two states have made this recognition, the ICJ will hold compulsory jurisdiction between them over any legal question arising under one of the four categories. States may withdraw their declaration to compulsory jurisdiction if they give reasonable notice (defined by the ICJ as six months in *Nicaragua v. United States of America* (ICJ)). Furthermore, their declarations "may be made unconditionally or on condition of reciprocity on the part of several or certain states, or for a certain time" (Article 36.3 SICJ). When a state makes such reservations, it is the ICJ that makes the final decision as to whether the Court has jurisdiction in the event that a dispute arises regarding the same (Article 36.6 SICJ).

At the time of this writing, 66 states have deposited with the Secretary-General declarations recognizing ICJ compulsory jurisdiction.[1,2]

d *Carryover Jurisdiction from the Permanent Court of International Justice*

Finally, Article 37 of the Statute of the ICJ states that "Whenever a treaty or convention in force provides for reference of a matter to a tribunal to have been instituted by the League of Nations, or to the Permanent Court of International Justice, the matter shall, as between the parties to the present Statute, be referred to the International Court of Justice" (Article 37 SICJ). Thus, if a state granted jurisdiction to the Permanent Court of International Justice to govern certain legal matters, this jurisdiction is carried over to the ICJ with respect to these matters.

e Forum Prorogatum

Article 38.5 of the 1978 Rules of Court of the International Court of Justice bases jurisdiction on the consent "yet to be given." The Rule states that "[w]hen the applicant State proposes to found the jurisdiction of the Court upon a consent thereto yet to be given or manifested by the State against which such application is made, the application shall be transmitted to that State. It shall not however be entered in the General List ... unless and until the State against which such application is made consents to the Court's jurisdiction ..." The precept was successfully used by Djibouti and Congo against France, but when Argentina invoked *forum prorogatum* against the U.S. in 2014, the U.S. did not respond. Yet even in cases where the respondent state does not

1. The states that accepted ICJ compulsory jurisdiction are as follows: Australia (22 March 2002); Austria (19 May 1971); Barbados (1 August 1980); Belgium (17 June 1958); Botswana (16 March 1970); Bulgaria (21 June 1992); Cambodia (19 September 1957); Cameroon (3 March 1994); Canada (10 May 1994); Costa Rica (20 February 1973); Cote d'Ivoire (29 September 2001); Cyprus (3 September 2002); Democratic Republic of the Congo (8 February 1989); Denmark (10 December 1956); Djibouti (2 September 2005); Dominica, Commonwealth of (31 March 2006); Dominican Republic (30 September 1924); Egypt (22 July 1957); Estonia (31 October 1991); Finland (25 June 1958); Gambia (22 June 1966); Georgia (20 June 1995); Germany (30 April 2008); Greece (10 January 1994); Guinea, Republic of (4 December 1998); Guinea-Bissau (7 August 1989); Haiti (4 October 1921); Honduras (6 June 1986); Hungary (22 October 1992); India (18 September 1974); Japan (9 July 2007); Kenya (19 April 1965); Lesotho (6 September 2000); Liberia (20 March 1952); Liechtenstein (29 March 1950); Luxembourg (15 September 1930); Madagascar (2 July 1992); Malawi (12 December 1966); Malta (2 September 1983); Mauritius (23 September 1968); Mexico (28 October 1947); Netherlands (1 August 1956); New Zealand (23 September 1977); Nicaragua (24 September 1929); Nigeria (30 April 1998); Norway (25 June 1996); Pakistan (13 September 1960); Panama (25 October 1921); Paraguay (25 September 1996); Peru (7 July 2003); Philippines (18 January 1972); Poland (25 March 1996); Portugal (25 February 2005); Senegal (2 December 1985); Slovakia (28 May 2004); Somalia (11 April 1963); Spain (20 October 1990); Sudan (2 January 1958); Suriname (31 August 1987); Eswatini (Swaziland) (26 May 1969); Sweden (6 April 1957); Switzerland (28 July 1948); Togo (25 October 1979); Uganda (3 October 1963); United Kingdom of Great Britain and Northern Ireland (5 July 2004); Uruguay (28 January 1921).
2. "Declarations Recognizing the Jurisdiction of the Court as Compulsory," *International Court of Justice:* Jurisdiction, available at <http://www.icj-cij.org/jurisdiction/index.php?p1=5&p2=1&p3=3>.

appear, the invocation of *forum prorogatum* carries with it an important public relations component, as it puts the respondent state on the defensive regarding alleged breaches of international law.

5 *Types of Cases Handled by the ICJ*

a *Contentious Disputes Between States*

The ICJ principally handles the resolution of contentious disputes between member states. Yet before the ICJ can adjudicate a contentious dispute, its jurisdiction must be established. The Charter states that "All Members of the United Nations are *ipso facto* parties to the Statute of the International Court of Justice" (Article 93 Charter). However, neither the Charter nor the SICJ states that the ICJ holds jurisdiction over *all* disputes between member states. Rather, jurisdiction must be based on the consent of all of the parties on one of the jurisdictional bases discussed above.

b *Advisory Opinions*

As discussed under "Provisions of the U.N. Charter with Respect to the ICJ," *supra*, the General Assembly or Security Council may request the ICJ to give an advisory opinion on any legal question. Other organs of the U.N. and specialized agencies authorized by the General Assembly may also request advisory opinions of the ICJ on legal questions arising within the scope of their activities. Articles 65 to 68 of the SICJ are dedicated to the procedural aspects for requesting advisory opinions and for the issuance thereof. Under Article 68, the ICJ shall "be guided by the provisions of the present Statute which apply in contentious cases to the extent to which it recognizes them to be applicable."

Article 66 of the 1986 Vienna Convention on the Law of Treaties between States and International Organizations or between International Organizations (VCLTSIO) provides additional guidance on ICJ legal opinions:

- if a state is a party to a dispute to which one or more international organizations are parties, the state may request the General Assembly, the Security Council or the competent organ of an international organization that is a party to the dispute and is authorized in accordance with Article 96 of Charter to request an advisory opinion of the ICJ in accordance with Article 65 of the SICJ (Article 66(b) VCLTSIO);
- if the U.N. or an international organization that is authorized in accordance with Article 96 of the Charter is a party to the dispute, it may request an advisory opinion of the ICJ (66(c) VCLTSIO);
- if an international organization other than those referred to in Article 66(c) VCLTSIO is a party to the dispute, it may, through a U.N. Member State, follow the procedure specified in Article 66(b) VCLTSIO (Article 66(d) VCLTSIO);

- the advisory opinion given to a state, the U.N. or an international organization pursuant to Article 66(b)-(d) "shall be accepted as decisive by all the parties to the dispute concerned" (Article 66(e) VCLTSIO).

III THE COUNCIL OF EUROPE

A Overview

The Council of Europe was founded in 1949 to work toward the integration of democratic development, freedom, the rule of law and human rights throughout Europe. Perhaps the most well-known of the conventions of the Council of Europe is the European Convention for the Protection of Human Rights and Fundamental Freedoms (colloquially known as the "European Convention on Human Rights," "ECHR"), which was drafted in 1950 and entered into force on 3 September 1953.

The Council of Europe currently has 47 member states comprising approximately 800 million citizens, from Portugal on the western flank to Russia on the eastern flank. In addition to member states, five states—Canada, Japan, Mexico, the United States and the Holy See—have observer status with the Council of Europe. They can participate in the Committee of Ministers and all intergovernmental committees and may voluntarily contribute financially to the activities of the Council of Europe.

B Member States

As of 2019, the Council of Europe has 47 member states, with Montenegro being the latest to join. Article 4 of the Council of Europe Statute specifies that membership is open to any European country, provided they meet specific democratic and human rights standards. Almost all of the European states have acceded to the Council of Europe, though Belarus, the Holy See (Vatican City), Kazakhstan, and some states with limited international recognition have not joined.

Observer status was created as an option for non-European democracies willing to contribute to democratic transitions in Europe. Canada, Japan, Mexico, the U.S., and Vatican City (the Holy See) hold observer status with the Council of Europe. Observer status enables them to participate in the Committee of Ministers and all intergovernmental committees and to voluntarily contribute financially to the activities of the Council of Europe.

In 2009, the Parliamentary Assembly established "Partner for democracy" status for institutional cooperation with parliaments of non-member states in neighboring regions wishing to be supported by the Parliamentary Assembly in democratic transitions. Interested states can become Partners for democracy if they commit to embracing pluralist democracy, the rule of law, respect for human rights and fundamental freedoms, and other Council of Europe values.

The parliaments of Morocco (as of June 2011), Kyrgyzstan (as of April 2014) and the Palestinian National Council (as of October 2011) have been accorded Partner for democracy status.

C Legal Institution: European Court of Human Rights

1 Overview

The Council of Europe has vested the European Court of Human Rights ("ECtHR"), based in Strasbourg, France, with the power to hear cases involving the ECHR. Every state joining the Council of Europe must accede to the ECHR and agree to submit to the ECtHR's compulsory jurisdiction for cases submitted by its individual nationals or foreign residents alleging human rights abuses in contravention of the ECHR.

The ECtHR, as a supranational court, provides legal recourse of last resort for individuals whose human rights have been violated by a contracting party to the ECHR. Before bringing suit to the ECtHR, individuals must have exhausted the domestic legal proceedings that would have been capable of providing an adequate remedy for the breach of their rights under the ECHR.

2 Jurisdiction

The ECtHR has jurisdiction to decide complaints ("applications") submitted by individuals and states concerning violations of the ECHR. It cannot take up a case *motu proprio*. The person, group or non-governmental organization submitting the complaint ("the applicant") does not have to be a citizen or resident of a state party to the ECHR in order to bring a claim. However, complaints submitted to the ECtHR must concern violations of the ECHR that were allegedly committed by a state party to the ECHR and that directly and significantly affected the applicant.

As of 1 August 2018, the ECtHR also has advisory jurisdiction. Under Protocol 16 to the ECHR, which entered into force on August 1, the highest domestic courts in the states that are a party to the Protocol may request advisory opinions from the ECtHR on questions of interpretation of the ECHR and its Protocols.

IV THE EUROPEAN UNION

A Overview

The European Union (E.U.) was created after World War II to reduce trade barriers and increase cooperation among European nations. Through the European Commission, it has created significant bodies of legislation in a wide variety of areas, including environmental law, commercial law, labor law, the law of the sea, air and space law, monetary law and immigration law.

B Legal Institution: European Court of Justice

The European Court of Justice (ECJ) is the highest court in the European Union in matters of E.U. law. Established in 1952 and based in Luxembourg, the Court is tasked with interpreting E.U. law and ensuring its equal application across all E.U. member states. It is composed of one judge per Member State and normally hears cases in panels of 3, 5, or 13 judges.

V NORTH ATLANTIC TREATY ORGANIZATION

A Overview

The North Atlantic Treaty Organization (NATO) is an international organization headquartered in Brussels and created in 1949 by the North Atlantic Treaty for the purpose of international collective security. As of 2010, NATO has 28 members: Albania, Belgium, Bulgaria, Canada, Croatia, Czech Republic, Denmark, Estonia, France, Germany, Greece, Hungary, Iceland, Italy, Latvia, Lithuania, Luxembourg, Netherlands, Norway, Poland, Portugal, Romania, Slovakia, Slovenia, Spain, Turkey, the United Kingdom and the United States.

The North Atlantic Treaty sets out the resolve of the parties to "safeguard the freedom, common heritage and civilization of their peoples, founded on the principles of democracy, individual liberty and the rule of law [and to] to promote stability and well-being in the North Atlantic area."

B The Use of Force under Article 5 of the North Atlantic Treaty

NATO was designed to be consistent in its purpose and functions with the obligations of U.N. member states contracted under the U.N. Charter. In the North Atlantic treaty, the parties recommit to "refrain in their international relations from the threat or use of force in any manner inconsistent with the purposes of the United Nations" (Article 1 NAT).

Within this framework, Article 5 of the North Atlantic Treaty recognizes the legitimacy of the use of force for the purpose of individual or collective self-defense under the U.N. Charter. The parties agree that (Article 5 NAT):

- "an armed attack against one or more of them in Europe or North America shall be considered an attack against them all"; and
- "if such an armed attack occurs, each of them, in exercise of the right of individual or collective self-defense recognised by Article 51 of the Charter of the United Nations, will assist the Party or Parties so attacked by taking forthwith, individually and in concert with the other Parties, such action as it deems necessary, including the use of armed force, to restore and maintain the security of the North Atlantic area."

VI THE ORGANIZATION OF AMERICAN STATES

A Overview

The Organization of American States ("OAS") is an international organization based in Washington, DC comprised of the 35 independent nations of the Americas. The Charter of the OAS ("COAS") creating the organization was adopted by the nations of the Americas at the Ninth International Conference of American States in Bogotá, Colombia, in April 1948. Entering into force in 1951, the COAS sets out to achieve for its member nations "an order of peace and justice, to promote their solidarity, to strengthen their collaboration and to defend their sovereignty, their territorial integrity and their independence" (Article 1 COAS).

B Legal Instruments

1 American Declaration of the Rights and Duties of Man (1948)

The American Declaration of the Rights and Duties of Man ("ADRDM") was adopted by the nations of the Americas at the meeting that created the OAS in 1948. For a full discussion on the ADRDM, *see* "American Declaration of the Rights and Duties of Man (1948)" in Chapter 7, "Human Rights and Related Topics," *infra.*

2 American Convention on Human Rights (1969)

The ADRDM has been largely superseded by the more detailed American Convention on Human Rights ("ACHR") (Pact of San José). For a full discussion on the ACHR, *see* "American Convention on Human Rights (1969)" in Chapter 7, "Human Rights and Related Topics," *infra.*

3 Inter-American Democratic Charter (2011)

The Inter-American Democratic Charter (IADC) was adopted on 11 September 2001 by a special session of the OAS General Assembly held in Lima. It is an inter-American instrument aiming to *strengthen and uphold democracy* in OAS member nations. The Charter is binding on all of the active OAS member states.

The *raison d'être* of the IADC is the affirmation of the importance of democracy in stability and development and the defense and preservation of democratic institutions. In its recitals, the IADC affirms that the "participatory nature of democracy in our countries in different aspects of public life contributes to the consolidation of democratic values and to freedom and solidarity in the Hemisphere."

Title I, Democracy and the Inter-American System, proclaims that the peoples of the Americas "have a right to democracy and their governments have an obligation to promote and defend it" (Article 1 IADC). Subsequent titles discuss Democracy and Human Rights (Title II), Democracy, Integral Development and Combating Poverty (Title III), Strengthening and Preservation of Democratic Institutions (Title IV), Democracy and Electoral Observation Missions (Title V) and Promotion of a Democratic Culture (Title VI).

C Legal Institutions: Inter-American Commission on Human Rights and Inter-American Court of Human Rights

1 *Overview*

The bodies responsible for overseeing compliance with the ACHR are the Inter-American Commission on Human Rights ("IACHR") and the Inter-American Court of Human Rights ("IACtHR"). The IACHR was created by the OAS in 1959 to promote the respect and defense of human rights in the Americas by investigating individual petitions alleging violations of the ADHR and resolving petitions in a collaborative way acceptable to both parties. Any person, group of persons or NGO may present a petition to the Commission alleging violations or failure to prevent violations by one of the OAS member states of the rights protected in the ADRDM or in the ACHR. The petitions presented to the Commission must show that the victim has exhausted the available domestic remedies.

The parties then exchange briefs, and the Commission prepares a report including its conclusions and also generally its recommendations to the state concerned. The Commission gives the state a period of time to resolve the situation and to comply with its recommendations. Upon the expiration of this period of time, the Commission may either prepare a second report with recommendations that the state is to implement or it may take the case to the IACtHR.

2 *Jurisdiction*

The IACHR and IACtHR were created by the OAS in 1979 to enforce and interpret provisions of the ACHR. They also have jurisdiction to enforce provisions of the ADRDM against OAS member states. The IACtHR may hear and make decisions on human rights cases referred to it by IACHR and may also issue advisory opinions on matters of legal interpretation brought by OAS bodies or member states.

As discussed further under "American Convention on Human Rights (1969)" in Chapter 7, "Human Rights and Related Topics," *infra*, 11 of the 35 OAS member states, including Canada, Cuba, the Republic of Trinidad and Tobago, and the United States, have not ratified the ACHR. The IACHR does not therefore have jurisdiction to accept complaints of alleged violations by these 11 nations of human rights set forth in the ACHR.

However, OAS member states not parties to the ACHR are subject to the jurisdiction of the IACHR to receive and examine complaints of alleged violations of human rights set forth in the ADRDM based upon the ratification by those states of the OAS Charter. Article 20 of the IACHR Statute states that the IACHR has the following powers over OAS member states that are not parties to the ACHR:

- to pay particular attention to the observance of the human rights referred to in Articles I, II, III, IV, XVIII, XXV, and XXVI of the ADRDM; and

- to examine communications submitted to it to address the government of any Member State, not a party to the ACHR, for information deemed pertinent by the IACHR and to make recommendations to it in order to bring about more effective observance of fundamental human rights.

Consistent with this framework, the United States and other states that have not ratified the ACHR are subject to the IACHR's jurisdiction for alleged violations of the ADRDM.[3]

VII THE ORGANISATION OF THE ISLAMIC CONFERENCE

A Overview

The Organisation of Islamic Cooperation ("OIC"), formerly the Organisation of the Islamic Conference, is an intergovernmental organization established in September 1969 consisting of 57 member states spread over four continents. Founded to safeguard and protect the interests of the Muslim world, it is the world's second-largest intergovernmental organization after the U.N.

B Agreement on Promotion, Protection and Guarantee of Investments

The OIC's Agreement on Promotion, Protection and Guarantee of Investments among the member states of the Organisation of the Islamic Conference (the "OIC Investment Agreement") was opened for signature by Resolution 7/12-E of the Twelfth Islamic Conference of Foreign Ministers held in Baghdad, Iraq, in June 1981 and entered into force in September 1986.

The OIC Agreement requires each host state to allow investors the right to resort to its national judicial systems to complain against measures adopted by the state authorities or to contest the extent of the conformity of such measures with the provisions of the host state's regulations and laws or to complain against the non-adoption by the host state of a measure that is in the interest of the investor. Investors may file claims before national courts or arbitral tribunals, but once having chosen a forum, they lose the right of recourse to the other forum (Article 16). Article 17 of the OIC Agreement provides for the mechanisms of conciliation and arbitration for the peaceful settlement of disputes.

In *Hesham al-Warraq v. Indonesia*, a UNCITRAL Tribunal held that the Agreement for the promotion, protection and guarantee of investments among OIC member states allows for state-to-state and state-investor arbitration through ad hoc arbitration.

3. *See also*, "The Inter-American Commission on Human Rights: How Can It Be Utilized in a Capital Case?" *The International Justice Project*, IACHR Information, pp. 1-2.

VIII LEAGUE OF ARAB STATES

A Overview

The League of Arab States, commonly referred to as the "Arab League," was founded in Cairo in 1945 by Egypt, Iraq, Lebanon, Saudi Arabia, Syria and Jordan (then Transjordan) to draw the relations between the member states closer. Later, in 1945, Yemen joined. The League of Arab States is headquartered in Cairo.

B Institutions

The Arab League seeks to coordinate collaboration between member states. Most of its activity revolves around economic integration. Among Arab League institutions to this end are the Arab League Educational, Cultural and Scientific Organization ("ALECSO") and the Council of Arab Economic Unity ("CAEU"), which facilitate political and economic programs. Among the documents issued by the Arab League is the Joint Arab Economic Action Charter, which sets forth principles for economic activities in the region.

C State-Investor Relations and the Arab Investment Court

1 Overview

The Unified Agreement for the Investment of Arab Capital in the Arab States ("Arab Investment Agreement" or "Agreement") was signed in Amman, Jordan, during the Eleventh Arab Summit Conference in 1980 and entered into force in 1981. All of the Arab League's 22 member states—with the exception of Algeria and the Comoros—have ratified the Unified Agreement. The Arab Investment Agreement defines the investor as an Arab natural or legal person who owns capital invested in the territory of an Arab state of which the Arab person is not a national.

An amendment to the Arab Investment Agreement was signed by Iraq, Jordan, Kuwait, Oman and Palestine in January 2013. In 2016, the Amended Arab Investment Agreement entered into force between the ratifying states. The Arab Investment Agreement continues to govern investment guarantees and protections in the Arab states that did not ratify the Amended Arab Investment Agreement.

2 Arab Investment Court

Disputes arising from the application of the Arab Investment Agreement may be settled by way of conciliation, arbitration or recourse to an Arab Investment Court (Article 25 Agreement). Article 1 of the Annex of the Arab Investment Agreement discusses conciliation, while Article 2 of the Annex covers arbitration.

Chapter VI of the Arab Investment Agreement provides the regulations governing the Arab Investment Court, which is seated in Cairo with jurisdiction to settle investment disputes and adjudicate claims between Arab governments, corporations and individuals from Arab states. The Court's internal rules were adopted by the General Assembly of the Court during its first session in 1986. The AIC is composed of at least five serving judges, each with a different Arab nationality, which must not be the same nationality as either of the parties to the conflict.

The Court, which was established in 1985, was inactive until 2003 when a Saudi company, Tanmiah for Consultancy Management & Marketing, filed a claim against the Tunisian government for damages surrounding the execution of sponsorship for the 2001 Mediterranean Games. The Court issued its decision in 2004, ruling in favor of the Tunisian government. In the following years, disputes have been filed against other Arab governments, including the United Arab Emirates and Egypt.

Judgments rendered by the AIC are final and are enforceable in each of the contracting states in the same way as a judgment delivered by their national courts.

D Member States

As of 2023, the following 22 states are Arab League members: Algeria, Bahrain, Comoros, Djibouti, Egypt, Iraq, Jordan, Kuwait, Lebanon, Libya, Mauritania, Morocco, Oman, Palestine, Qatar, Saudi Arabia, Somalia, Sudan, Syria, Tunisia, United Arab Emirates and Yemen.

The following ten of the Arab League's 22 states are also members of the African Union: Algeria, Comoros, Djibouti, Egypt, Libya, Mauritania, Morocco, Somalia, Sudan and Tunisia.

IX ANDEAN COMMUNITY

A Overview

The Andean Community is a customs union comprising Bolivia, Colombia, Ecuador and Peru. The trade bloc, headquartered in Lima, Peru, came into being in 1969 with the signing of the Cartagena Agreement.

At its height, membership of the Andean Community comprised six nations. Chile withdrew its membership in 1976, and Venezuela withdrew in 2006.

B Legal Institution: Court of Justice of the Andean Community

The Andean Community has vested authority in the Court of Justice of the Andean Community, based in Quito, Ecuador, for the purpose of hearing cases alleging the violation of Andean trade, labor, intellectual property and industrial property law.

X AFRICAN UNION

A Overview

The African Union ("AU") was founded in 2002 in order to accelerate political and socioeconomic integration in Africa; to promote and defend African common positions on issues of interest to the continent; to achieve peace and security on the continent and to promote democratic institutions, good governance and human rights. The AU is comprised of 55 members.

The AU is the successor to the Organization of African Unity ("OAU"), which was established in 1963 to promote the unity and solidarity of the African states, act as a collective voice for Africa and eradicate all forms of colonialism.

B Legal Institutions

1 African Court on Human and Peoples' Rights

The African Court on Human and Peoples' Rights was formed to ensure the protection of human and peoples' rights in Africa and complement and reinforce the work of the African Commission on Human and Peoples' Rights. The Court, which is based in Arusha, Tanzania, was established by Article 1 of the Protocol to the African Charter on Human and Peoples' Rights on the Establishment of an African Court on Human and Peoples' Rights, which was adopted in 1998 by the OAU in Ouagadougou, Burkina Faso and came into force in 2004 after being ratified by more than 15 countries.

The following 30 states have ratified the Protocol: Algeria, Benin, Burkina Faso, Burundi, Cameroon, Chad, Côte d'Ivoire, Comoros, Republic of the Congo, Gabon, The Gambia, Ghana, Kenya, Libya, Lesotho, Mali, Malawi, Mozambique, Mauritania, Mauritius, Nigeria, Niger, Rwanda, Sahrawi Arab Democratic Republic, South Africa, Senegal, Tanzania, Togo, Tunisia and Uganda.

The Court has jurisdiction to hear cases submitted by NGOs and individuals. It hears cases and disputes concerning the interpretation and application of the African Charter on Human and Peoples' Rights and any other human rights instrument ratified by states parties. The Court has both contentious and advisory jurisdiction.

2 The African Court of Justice and Human Rights

a Overview

As mentioned above, the *Protocol to the African Charter on Human and Peoples' Rights on the Establishment of an African Court on Human and Peoples' Rights* came into force in 2004 after being ratified by more than 15 countries.

At the 2008 African Union Summit in Sharm El Sheikh, Egypt, heads of state and government signed the *Protocol on the Statute of the African Court of Justice and Human Rights*. The purpose of this Protocol was to establish the African Court of

Justice and Human Rights, a merger of the African Court on Human and Peoples' Rights with the still non-existent African Court of Justice. As of 18 June 2020, eight countries ratified the Protocol on the Statute of the African Court of Justice and Human Rights, out of 15 needed for its entry into force. Therefore, the African Court of Justice and Human Rights has not yet become operational.

b *Expanded International Criminal Jurisdiction under the Malabo Protocol*

On 27 June 2014, the *Protocol on Amendments to the Protocol on the Statute of the African Court of Justice and Human Rights* (the "Malabo Protocol") was adopted by the AU. The Malabo Protocol provides for the inclusion of criminal jurisdiction within the remit of the proposed African Court of Justice and Human Rights. If the Malabo Protocol comes into effect, the African Court of Justice and Human Rights would become the first regional court with international criminal jurisdiction to try the following 14 crimes: genocide, crimes against humanity, war crimes, the crime of aggression, piracy, terrorism, trafficking in persons, trafficking in drugs, trafficking in hazardous wastes, mercenarism, the crime of unconstitutional change of government, corruption, money laundering and illicit exploitation of natural resources. In essence, the international criminal law section of the African Court of Justice and Human Rights will serve as an African regional criminal court, operating in a manner akin to the ICC but with a geographically limited remit.

As of 2023, the African Court of Justice and Human Rights has not yet become operational and the Malabo Protocol has not yet come into effect. While 15 states have signed the Malabo Protocol, none have ratified it.

3 *Timeline*

Following is a timeline of critical dates for the African Court of Justice and Human Rights:

- 1998: The African Court on Human and Peoples' Rights was established by Article 1 of the *Protocol to the African Charter on Human and Peoples' Rights on the Establishment of an African Court on Human and Peoples' Rights.*
- 2004: The Protocol to the African Charter on Human and Peoples' Rights on the Establishment of an African Court on Human and Peoples' Rights came into force after being ratified by more than 15 countries.
- 2008: Heads of state and government at the African Union Summit in Sharm El Sheikh, Egypt, signed the *Protocol on the Statute of the African Court of Justice and Human Rights* for the merger of the African Court on Human and Peoples' Rights with the still non-existent African Court of Justice.
- 2014: The *Protocol on Amendments to the Protocol on the Statute of the African Court of Justice and Human Rights (the "Malabo Protocol")* was adopted by the AU on 27 June 2014, providing for the inclusion of criminal jurisdiction within the remit of the proposed African Court of Justice and Human Rights. If the

Malabo Protocol goes into effect, the African Court of Justice and Human Rights would become the first regional court with international criminal jurisdiction.

- 2020: Eight countries ratified the Protocol on the Statute of the African Court of Justice and Human Rights as of 18 June 2020, out of 15 needed for its entry into force. Therefore, the African Court of Justice and Human Rights has not yet become operational.
- 2023: 15 states have signed the Malabo Protocol, but none have ratified it. Therefore, it has not yet come into effect. Even if the African Court of Justice and Human Rights were to become operational, it would not have jurisdiction over international crimes until the Malabo Protocol comes into effect.

CHAPTER 3
Sources of International Law

I INTRODUCTION

The Statute of the ICJ recognizes the following four sources of international law that apply to disputes submitted to it (Article 38 SICJ):

a. international conventions, whether general or particular, establishing rules expressly recognized by the contesting states;
b. international custom, as evidence of a general practice accepted as law;
c. the general principles of law recognized by civilized nations;
d. ... judicial decisions and the teachings of the most highly qualified publicists of the various nations, as subsidiary means for the determination of rules of law.

II INTERNATIONAL TREATIES

The most important sources of international law are international treaties and conventions, which, under Article 38(a) of the SICJ, establish "rules expressly recognized by the contesting states." These multilateral agreements govern the interaction of nations, multinational businesses, or non-governmental organizations.

A Overview

A treaty can be defined as a bilateral or multilateral agreement between states, between states and international organizations, or between international organizations that is governed by and binding under international law. According to the VCLT, treaties may be "embodied in a single instrument or in two or more related instruments" (Article 2(1)(a) VCLT). Treaties are generally in written form, and the VCLT includes the written form of treaties as part of their definition (Article 2(1)(a) VCLT), yet under customary international law, treaties do not necessarily need to be written.

Treaties are a source of international obligation for those states that agree to be bound by them. A unilateral law that governs the relations of a state with other states or that defines a state's foreign policies is not, however, a treaty if it is not binding on one or more other states or international organizations.

B "Treaty," "Convention" and "Agreement" as Synonyms

The designation of a treaty as such is not an essential element of the agreement. A treaty may thus be titled "convention," "agreement," or any other term that denotes the same, while still falling into the definition of a treaty.

C Binding Force of Treaties

That treaties are binding on those states that agree to be bound by them is a general principle of law and is also established by international custom. States that agree to be bound by a treaty are known as "parties" to the treaty. States that sign a treaty are known as "signatories," and are not bound by a treaty until the state has agreed to be bound (usually through ratifying the treaty) and the treaty has entered into force.

To give further weight to the binding nature of treaties on parties to them, the VCLT establishes in its 26th Article (*pacta sunt servanda*) that "Every treaty in force is binding upon the parties to it and must be performed by them in good faith" (Article 26 VCLT). The VCLT is binding on the 111 states parties to the convention, and other nations, such as the United States and France, which have not ratified the VCLT, are bound by their respective treaties under international custom and under the general principles of law, which consider the breach of a valid treaty to be a breach of international law. Thus, the breach of a provision of the VCLT by a state that has not ratified the VCLT would only be considered a breach of international law if the provision of the VCLT being breached were also a provision of international custom or of the general principles of law.

D Vienna Convention on the Law of Treaties

1 Consent to Be Bound by Treaties

The Vienna Convention on the Law of Treaties ("VCLT") both codifies existing customary international law and adds to it. Signed in Vienna in 1969 and entering into force in 1980, it applies to treaties between states. Under the Convention, once a state consents to be bound to a treaty and a treaty enters into force, the state becomes a party bound by the treaty (Article 2(1)(g) VCLT). Consent to be bound by a treaty may be expressed "by signature, exchange of instruments constituting a treaty, ratification, acceptance, approval or accession, or by any other means if so agreed" (Article 11 VCLT).

The Convention goes on to explain the various ways that a state may express its intent to ratify, to be bound by, and to accede to a treaty. In processes with both a signature and ratification, the signature demonstrates the intent to ratify but not necessarily consent to be bound (Article 12 VCLT). Ratification is the act whereby a state expresses its consent to be bound (Article 14 VCLT), and in those cases where a state has not signed a treaty and the treaty is no longer open for signature, the state may "accede" to the treaty, whereby the state expresses its consent to be bound by the treaty (Article 15 VCLT).

2 *Obligations That Arise Between Signature and Ratification of a Treaty*

In the period between a state's signing a treaty and the ratification of the treaty, or between the ratification of a treaty by a state and the entry into force of a treaty, the signatory or ratifying state may not undertake any actions that defeat the object and purpose of the treaty (Article 18 VCLT). Some argue that this should not be construed to prohibit a state from unsigning a treaty that it no longer intends to ratify and that if the state unsigns a treaty, it is no longer prohibited from taking actions that may defeat the object or purpose of the treaty. Other sources argue that a state cannot unsign a treaty once it has signed it; it must first ratify the treaty and then withdraw from it.

3 *Interpretation of Treaties*

a *Overview*

"A treaty shall be interpreted in good faith in accordance with the ordinary meaning to be given to the terms of the treaty in their context and in the light of its object and purpose" (Article 31.1 VCLT). This context comprises:

- any agreement relating to the treaty which was made between all the parties in connection with the conclusion of the treaty; and
- any instrument which was made by one or more parties in connection with the conclusion of the treaty and accepted by the other parties as an instrument related to the treaty (Article 31.2 VCLT).

Recourse may be had to supplementary means of interpretation, including the preparatory work of the treaty (*travaux préparatoires*) and the circumstances of its conclusion, in order to confirm the meaning of the treaty (Article 32 VCLT).

b *Textual, Intent-based and Teleological Approaches to Treaty Interpretation*

The three primary approaches to treaty interpretation are as follows:

- Text of the Treaty. The first approach looks to the actual text of the agreement and the words used. This approach has been characterized as the "objective approach" by publicists of the law.

- Intention of the Parties. The second looks to the intention of the parties adopting the agreement to resolve ambiguities in the text. This approach has been characterized as the "subjective approach" by publicists of the law.
- Teleological Approach. The final approach to treaty interpretation looks to the object and purpose of the treaty being interpreted. The meaning of any treaty provision is measured against the backdrop of such purpose. This has the effect of underlining the role of the judge, who will often be called upon to define the object and purpose of the treaty, where such object and purpose is not explicitly laid out by the treaty itself.

Effective treaty interpretation in most cases requires adopting from all three of these approaches, which are encompassed in the Vienna Convention, which refers to the text of the treaty, as well as its object and purpose, which must be interpreted in good faith. Article 31 requires that a treaty "be interpreted in good faith in accordance with the ordinary meaning to be given to the terms of the treaty in their context and in the light of its object and purpose" (Article 31.1 VCLT).

c *Supplementary Means of Interpretation, Including* Travaux Préparatoires

The Vienna Convention allows judges and arbitrators interpreting treaties to take into account the *travaux préparatoires* (preparatory work) and other contextual circumstances in order to confirm the meaning of treaties. Article 32 stipulates as follows:

Recourse may be had to supplementary means of interpretation, including the preparatory work of the treaty and the circumstances of its conclusion, in order to confirm the meaning resulting from the application of article 31, or to determine the meaning when the interpretation according to article 31:

(a) leaves the meaning ambiguous or obscure; or
(b) leads to a result which is manifestly absurd or unreasonable.

4 ***Reservations***

The Convention allows states to formulate reservations when signing, ratifying, accepting, approving or acceding to a treaty unless (Article 19 VCLT):

(a) the reservation is prohibited by the treaty;
(b) the treaty provides that only specified reservations, which do not include the reservation in question, may be made; or
(c) in cases not falling under sub-paragraphs (a) and (b), the reservation is incompatible with the object and purpose of the treaty.

5 *Invalidity, Termination, Suspension of and Withdrawal from Treaties*

a *Overview*

Treaties may be held invalid for a variety of reasons, ranging from a state representative's incompetence to conclude a treaty to fraud, corruption, duress or coercion (Articles 46-52 VCLT). Similarly, a treaty is void if, at the time of its conclusion, it conflicts with peremptory norms of general international law (*jus cogens*) (Article 53 VCLT).

b *Breach*

A treaty may be terminated or suspended as a consequence of its breach. A material breach of a bilateral treaty by one of the parties entitles the other to invoke the breach as a ground for terminating the treaty or suspending its operation (Article 60.1 VCLT).

The material breach of a multilateral treaty by one of the parties entitles the other parties by unanimous agreement to suspend the operation of the treaty or to terminate it in relation between themselves and the defaulting state or between all the parties. A material breach of a multilateral treaty by one of the parties also entitles a party affected by the breach to invoke the breach as a ground for suspending the operation of the treaty in whole or in part in the relations between itself and the defaulting state and entitles any party other than the defaulting state to "invoke the breach as ground for suspending the operation of the treaty in whole or in part with respect to itself if the treaty is of such a character that the material breach of its provisions by one party radically changes the position of every party with respect to the further performance of its obligations under the treaty" (Article 60.2 VCLT).

A material breach may consist of: "(a) a repudiation of the treaty not sanctioned by the present Convention; or (b) the violation of a provision essential to the accomplishment of the object or purpose of the treaty" (Article 60.3 VCLT).

The decision of a state not to suspend or revoke a treaty that has been materially breached does not impair its ability to seek other means of compensation or reparation, including seeking damages or submitting to international arbitration.

c *Withdrawal*

The termination of a treaty or the withdrawal of a party may take place (Article 54 VCLT):

(a) in conformity with the provisions of the treaty; or
(b) at any time by consent of all the parties after consultation with the other contracting States.

III CUSTOMARY INTERNATIONAL LAW

A Definition

Article 38(b) of the SICJ defines customary international law as "evidence of a general practice accepted as law." Customary international law may be defined according to the following two elements:

(i) a consistent and recurrent state practice developed over time ("state practice"); that is
(ii) undertaken out of a sense of legal obligation ("*opinio juris*").

In this manner, the Restatement 3d of the Foreign Relations Law of the United States defines customary international law as resulting "from a general and consistent practice of states followed by them from a sense of legal obligation" (§ 102(2) RFR). This general and consistent practice is often referred to as "state practice." The sense of legal obligation is referred to as *opinio juris*.

As the ICJ declared in the *Continental Shelf case (Libya v. Malta)*, 1985 ICJ 13 (3 June), this state practice, together with the *opinio juris* of states, forms the substance of customary law.

B Formation

Although customary international law does not have to be universal, it must be widely enough practiced among states to qualify as "general" and "consistent" before it can serve as a source of the law. Widespread departure from customary international law may be an indication of the evolution of customary international law; if enough states adopt new practices, customary law may change and adopt the new practices as custom, even if these practices initially violate the customary international law in place at the time.

Historically, customary international law has been the most important source of international legal obligations. Legal instruments, such as the VCLT, have been seen by some states as a mere restatement or codification of customary law.

We can determine the content of customary international law by looking to various sources, including the jurisprudential of international tribunals, the practices of international organs and states' domestic laws and military and administrative practices.

C Binding Nature

Nations typically defer to customary international law when passing judgments on international legal questions. References to customary international law can be found in legal opinions and in the writings of publicists of the law. The U.S. Supreme Court, for example, in *The Paquete Habana*, a 1900 case, held as follows:[4]

> International law is part of our law, and must be ascertained and administered by the courts of justice of appropriate jurisdiction as often as questions of right depending upon it are duly presented for their determination. For this purpose, *where there is no treaty and no controlling executive or legislative act or judicial decision, resort must be had to the customs and usages of civilized nations*, and, as evidence of these, to the works of jurists and commentators, not for the speculations of their authors concerning what the law ought to be, but for trustworthy evidence of what the law really is.
>
> At the present day, *by the general consent of the civilized nations of the world and independently of any express treaty or other public act*, it is an established rule of international law that coast fishing vessels, with their implements and supplies, cargoes and crews, unarmed and honestly pursuing their peaceful calling of catching and bringing in fresh fish, are exempt from capture as prize of war. And this rule is one which prize courts, administering the law of nations, are bound to take judicial notice of, and to give effect to, in the absence of any treaty or other public act of their own government in relation to the matter.
>
> (emphasis added).

D Reservations and Objection: Persistent Objectors

If, during the development of a new rule of customary international law, a state repeatedly publicly announces its opposition to the rule, then the "persistent objector" will not be legally bound by the rule when it crystallizes into customary law. This legal exemption will last as long as the state continues to object, unless the customary international law develops the status of *jus cogens* (a peremptory norm of general international law). If enough states object to the practice, then it will not evolve into customary international law. If, however, a small group of states objects to the practice, then they may develop their own special custom, which may be binding on them but not on other nations, which would be bound by the customary law that they implicitly or tacitly accepted.

E *Jus Cogens* Norms and *Erga Omnes* Obligations as Part of Customary International Law

1 Overview

Jus cogens refers to the legal status that certain international crimes reach, while *erga omnes* refers to the legal implications arising out of a crime's reaching *jus cogens* status. According to some commentators, *jus cogens* norms produce *erga omnes* obligations (*obligatio erga omnes*).

4. *The Paquete Habana*, 175 U.S. 677, 677 (1900).

2 *Jus Cogens* Norms

Some customary international law rises to the status of *jus cogens* (or *ius cogens*), or non-derogable peremptory legal norms, which are also referred to as "peremptory norms of general international law," whereas other customary international law may only be binding on states that accept the law as binding. A *jus cogens* norm is a fundamental, overriding principle of international law from which no derogation is permitted. It is also known as a "peremptory norm of general international law," which is defined by the VCLT as "a norm accepted and recognized by the international community of States as a whole as a norm from which no derogation is permitted and which can be modified only by a subsequent norm of general international law having the same character" (Article 53 VCLT). Under the VCLT, "[a] treaty is void if, at the time of its conclusion, it conflicts with a peremptory norm of general international law" (Article 53 VCLT). Examples of *jus cogens* norms include prohibitions on genocide, torture, slavery, human trafficking, crimes against humanity, and aggression.

When customary international law is comprised of *jus cogens*, no derogation is ever permitted. Any laws contravening such international standards are deemed null and void. Examples include prohibitions on violations of international humanitarian law, including genocide, crimes against humanity, war crimes and aggression. Whereas such prohibitions have traditionally been governed by customary international law, most recently, they have become part of international treaties, including the Geneva Conventions on the protection of persons in armed conflicts.

3 Erga Omnes *Obligations*

A wrongful act is deemed to be *erga omnes* ("toward all") if it harms everyone and not merely the injured party. The ICJ referred to *erga omnes* obligations in its judgment of 5 February 1970 in *Barcelona Traction, Light and Power Company, Limited (Belgium v. Spain)* (1962-1970). The ICJ commented on a category of international *erga omnes* obligations, which are owed by states to the international community as a whole and are intended to protect and promote the basic values and common interests of all. The ICJ referenced the "obligations of the state toward the international community as a whole," in whose protection all states have a "legal interest" and which are thus "the concern of all states." Specifically, the ICJ enumerated four *erga omnes* obligations:

- the outlawing of acts of aggression;
- the outlawing of genocide;
- protection from slavery; and
- protection from racial discrimination.

The ICJ concluded:[5]

5. *Barcelona Traction, Light and Power Company (Belgium v. Spain)*, 1970 ICJ Rep. 3 (1970), p. 32, para. 33.

> When a State admits into its territory foreign investments or foreign nationals, whether natural or juristic persons, it is bound to extend to them the protection of the law and assumes obligations concerning the treatment to be afforded them. These obligations, however, are neither absolute nor unqualified. In particular, an essential distinction should be drawn between the obligations of a State towards the international community as a whole, and those arising vis-à-vis another State in the field of diplomatic protection. By their very nature the former are the concern of all States. In view of the importance of the rights involved, all States can be held to have a legal interest in their protection; they are obligations *erga omnes*.

IV GENERAL PRINCIPLES OF LAW

Article 38(c) of the SICJ defines "general principles of law recognized by civilized nations" as a source of international law. However, there is no consensus as to what constitutes these general principles. For many writers, the general principles of law are an affirmation of natural law principles that are used to test the validity of positive law. They may also be used as gap fillers by international courts when there is no applicable treaty provision or rule of customary international law. The courts may attempt to ascertain general principles of law by finding commonalities among well-developed legal systems in the world (controversially referred to by the SICJ as the principles of law of "civilized nations"). These general principles may include both principles of law as well as principles of equity.

Examples of well-developed and nearly universal general principles of law include the notion that a contract to which assent was given through coercion or duress is null and void; that states are not permitted to interfere in the domestic affairs of other sovereign states; and that an injured party is entitled to remedy as a result of another party's tort.

In the area of commercial contracts, the UNIDROIT Principles of International Commercial Contracts are considered to be a written expression of general principles of international commercial law. Contracts governed by the UNIDROIT Principles often include a clause whereby issues not covered by the UNIDROIT Principles are governed by "generally accepted principles of international commercial law."

V JUDICIAL DECISIONS AND TEACHINGS

A Overview

The "judicial decisions and the teachings of the most highly qualified publicists of the various nations" serve as a "subsidiary means for the determination of rules of law" (Article 38(d) SICJ).

Judicial decisions and teachings are not themselves a source of law, but they help bring to light the substantive content of the law. Furthermore, judicial decisions issued by the ICJ are only binding "between the parties and in respect of that particular case" (Article 59 SICJ). Yet, while judicial decisions and the analyses of experts are binding only with respect to the parties and issues of a particular case, they may also be helpful in determining what the law is.

B Distinction Between the Sources That Create Law and the Subsidiary Means of Determining the Law

While there is no formal doctrine of precedent in international law, "the articulation of principles by the ICJ or other international adjudicators, can clarify customary international law and treaty provisions. Decisions of regional and domestic tribunals, notably supreme courts, may also be used by decision-makers when determining the requirements of customary international law."[6]

A distinction can be made between the first three sources of public international law under Article 38 of the SICJ (conventions, custom and general principles of law) and the subsidiary means for the determination of rules of law under Article 38(d) of the SICJ:

> the decision, or the textbook, will not assert that the rule stated is law because the judge or the author has stated it; it will be so stated because the judge or the author considers that it derives from one of the three principal sources indicated in paragraphs (a) to (c) of Article 38. The first three sources of Article 38 are formal sources; those of paragraph (d) are material rather than formal sources, but material sources having a special degree of authority ...
>
> ... even where a court creates law in the sense of developing, adapting, modifying, filing gaps, interpreting or even branching out in a new direction, the decision must be seen to emanate reasonably and logically from existing and previously ascertainable law. A court has no purely legislative competence.'[7]

C Binding Nature of ICJ Decisions Between the Parties to a Case

Importance must attach to judicial decisions that purport to apply international law, even though decisions of the ICJ are formally binding only between the parties to a dispute. There is no formal *stare decisis doctrine*, as known in common law systems, in public international law, that establishes binding precedent. In international law, international courts are not obliged to follow previous decisions, although they almost always take into account previous decisions.[8]

However, the ICJ frequently uses its previous decisions as authority in later cases. Other tribunals follow precedent as a matter of principle rather than as a matter of law, since judicial consistency is the most obvious means of avoiding accusations of bias.

6. Martin Dixon, Robert McCorquodale and Sarah Williams, *Cases and Materials on International Law*, Oxford University Press (Oxford, 2011), p. 20 (citing Hilary Charlesworth and Christine Chinkin, *The Boundaries of International Law: A Feminist Analysis*, Manchester University Press (Manchester, 2000)).
7. Hugh Thirlway, *The Sources of International Law*, Oxford University Press, 2nd Ed. (Oxford, 2019), pp. 131-132.
8. Peter Malanczuk, *Akehurst's Modern Introduction to International Law*, Routledge (1997), p. 51 (citing Volker Röben, *Le Precedent dans la jurisprudence de la Cour Internationale*, German Yearbook of International Law *32* (1989), pp. 382-407).

Moreover, it has been suggested that at least with respect to the law of the sea, maritime delimitation law was judge-made rather than based on customary international law:

> in connection with the jurisprudence of the Court on maritime delimitation ... that the tendency of the Court is to follow and apply earlier decisions rather than to investigate the practice of States supposedly creative of custom had led to a situation in which it might be said that maritime delimitation law was judge made law rather than customary law.[9]

D Judicial Decisions as a Subsidiary Means for the Determination of the Law

Many ICJ decisions, including the *Reparation for Injuries* case,[10] the *Genocide* case[11] and the *Fisheries* case,[12] have introduced innovations into international law which have subsequently won general acceptance. The impact of decisions of national courts on the content and role of international law should not be underestimated; the *Pinochet* cases in the U.K. have had considerable impact on principles of sovereign immunity. However, while it may appear that judges are applying international law, they are in fact applying national legal precepts.

In the case concerning the Arrest Warrant of 11 April 2000, the ICJ examined whether the immunities of a Foreign Minister can protect him when he is accused of war crimes or crimes against humanity. In this connection, it referred to "those few decisions of national higher courts, such as the House of Lords or the French Court of Cassation" relevant to the matter. However, this reference was made in the context of the Court's examination of "State practice" pointing to the existence or otherwise of a rule in "customary international law." This approach emphasizes the essentially "subsidiary" nature of judicial decisions, whether of international tribunals or municipal courts, for the determination of the law.[13]

9. Martin Dixon, Robert McCorquodale and Sarah Williams, *Cases and Materials on International Law*, Oxford University Press (Oxford, 2011), p. 20 (citing Hugh Thirlway, *British Yearbook of International Law 116* (2005), p. 116).
10. *Reparations for Injuries Suffered in Service of U.N.*, Advisory Opinion, ICJ Reports (11 April 1949), p. 174 (leading judicial authority on the personality of international organizations).
11. *Reservations to the Convention on the Prevention and Punishment of the Crime of Genocide*, Advisory Opinion, ICJ Reports (28 May 1951), 15, p. 29 (a state that has made a reservation that has been objected to by one or more of the parties to the Genocide Convention but not by others, can be regarded as a party to the Convention if the reservation is compatible with the object and purpose of the Convention).
12. *United Kingdom v. Norway* (the *Fisheries* case), ICJ Reports (18 December 1951), 116, p. 138 (in the Fisheries case (minor inconsistencies (a small amount of practice which goes against the rule in question) do not prevent the creation of a customary rule).
13. Hugh Thirlway, *The Law and Procedure of the International Court of Justice: Fifty Years of Jurisprudence, Volume II*, Oxford University Press (Oxford, 2013).

E Writings of the Most Highly Qualified Publicists

While the Statute of the ICJ includes among its sources "the teachings of the most highly qualified publicists of the various nations," the Statute does not define what constitutes a "highly qualified publicist." In a multicultural world, identifying the teachings of writers which are the most authoritative is no longer likely to lead to easy universal acceptance. This has led to debates and discussion as to whether the sources used as subsidiary means for the determination of rules of law sufficiently represent diverse cultures and legal systems, and whether international law is truly international.[14]

The practice of the ICJ is not to cite the views of scholars in decisions, though legal representatives before the Court frequently refer to publicists in their arguments. Individual judges, in their dissenting or concurring opinions, have on occasion cited the works of publicists of international law. The ICJ historically "avoided quoting scholarly publications, despite the justification for doing so offered by Article 38; the Chamber judgment in the *Land, Island and Maritime Frontier* case (mentioning Oppenheim, Lauterpacht, and Gidel) seemed to signal a relaxation of this policy, but the example has not been followed in subsequent cases."[15]

VI INTERNATIONAL DECLARATIONS

A As "Soft Law"

States may make declarations, such as the UDHR, which are not legally binding. Such declarations are considered to be international "soft law": although they are not legally binding, they may influence states by placing political, rather than legal, pressure on their actions. Such declarations may also be effective when states are uncertain as to whether other states are ready to undertake the commitment of submitting to binding laws, and they may serve as intermediate steps toward the formation of future treaties or other legal instruments.

International declarations are not enumerated in Article 38 of the Statute of the ICJ as a source of international law. They therefore constitute soft law, that is, guidelines of conduct that are neither binding norms of law nor completely irrelevant political maxims. Soft law often emerges in a grey zone between law and politics where states agree to certain principles, but do not yet wish to bind themselves legally. Yet soft law principles may nonetheless acquire considerable strength in structuring international conduct in practice. For example, if ratified by enough states and practiced by them out of a sense of legal obligation, international declarations can become sources of, or at least reflect, binding customary international law.

A high level of preparation and often intense negotiations take place before declarations at international conferences are issued. While Article 38 of the Statute of

14. *See, e.g.*, Anthea Roberts, *Is International Law International?* Oxford University Press (Oxford, 2017).
15. High Thirlway, *The Sources of International Law*, 2nd Ed. (2019), pp. 131-132.

the ICJ denies the status of formally binding law to international declarations, such declarations, including resolutions of international organizations and international codes of conduct," have an important impact on the "realities of contemporary international law making."[16]

While international declarations are not law per se, "they may be evidence of existing law or formative of the *opinio juris* or state practice,"[17] which generates customary international law. In addition, "widespread acceptance of a soft law instrument will tend to legitimise conduct and make it harder to sustain the legality of opposing positions."[18]

Soft law can be distinguished from the subsidiary sources of law (judicial decisions and teachings of the most qualified publicists of international law). Unlike judicial decisions, soft law is never legally binding, and unlike the teachings of publicists, the objective of soft law is not to determine what the law is or to clarify the content of the law. Soft law exists outside of the world of legal obligations in the world of norms, recommendations and general guidance at the international level.

B Resolutions of International Organizations

While resolutions of the U.N. General Assembly are generally non-binding, resolutions regulating the internal affairs of the U.N., such as elections to various committees, create situations that members of the U.N. may not disregard. Moreover, resolutions approving budgetary matters regarding the allotment and collection of dues are binding on U.N. member states.

U.N. General Assembly resolutions may in some cases have normative value. As noted in the ICJ's *Nuclear Weapons Advisory Opinion*, U.N. General Assembly resolutions may provide evidence of the current state of the law and provide valuable guidance as to the meaning and interpretation of legal texts. Moreover, such resolutions may contribute to the development of customary international law. U.N. General Assembly resolutions "can, in certain circumstances, provide evidence important for establishing the existence of a rule or the emergence of *opinio juris*. To establish whether this true of a given General Assembly resolution, it is necessary to look at its content and the conditions of its adoption ... [A] series of resolutions may show the gradual evolution of the *opinio juris* required for the establishment of a new rule."[19] In each case, the circumstances surrounding the resolution should be considered before according any legal significance to it.

16. Martin Dixon, Robert McCorquodale and Sarah Williams, *Cases and Materials on International Law*, Oxford University Press (Oxford, 2011), p. 20 (citing Hilary Charlesworth and Christine Chinkin, *The Boundaries of International Law: A Feminist Analysis*, Manchester University Press (Manchester, 2000)).
17. Alan Boyle and Christine Chinkin, *The Making of International Law*, Oxford University Press (Oxford, 2007), p. 212.
18. *Ibid.*
19. *Legality of the Threat or Use of Nuclear Weapons*, Advisory Opinion, ICJ Reports (8 July 1996), p. 70.

CHAPTER 4

States and Governments in the International Order

I OVERVIEW

We begin by highlighting an important distinction between "states" and "governments." States are bearers of rights and responsibilities under international law; governments represent them. As a general rule, a change in government does not affect the international obligations of the state.

In the past 50 years, there has been a rapid increase in the number of recognized states. This is evidenced by the vast increase in members of the UN. When the U.N. was formed in 1945, it had only 51 member states; today, it has 193 members.[20] This increase can be attributed to a variety of causes, among which we may list decolonization and the breakup of states such as the USSR, Yugoslavia, Czechoslovakia and Ethiopia (with Eritrea breaking away).

The breakup of states occurs through dissolution or secession. In the case of dissolution, an existing state implodes and becomes two or more new states (e.g., Yugoslavia and Czechoslovakia). In secession, part of an existing state breaks away to become a new state (e.g., the breakaway of Eritrea from Ethiopia), with the new state holding the right to govern its own citizens, enter into treaties, join international organizations, or be a state party to an ICJ case.

20. For a list of U.N. Member States and their dates of admission, *see* "Member States of the United Nations," available at <https://www.un.org/en/about-us/member-states>. Territories that may become fully recognized as U.N. Member States in the future include Kosovo and Palestine (the latter currently having the status of "non-member observer State" under General Assembly Resolution A/67/L.28).

II CRITERIA FOR STATEHOOD

Although the distinction has narrowed recently, there are two traditional theories that provide guidance as to the legal recognition of an entity's sovereignty in the international community: (i) the declaratory theory; and (ii) the constitutive theory.

A Objective Test under the Declaratory Theory

1 *Montevideo Convention on the Rights and Duties of States*

The declaratory theory (also referred to as the "declarative theory" in some sources) is the prevailing theory for the recognition of state sovereignty. It holds that an entity is recognized as a state when it satisfies four objective criteria for statehood laid out in the Montevideo Convention on the Rights and Duties of States. At the Seventh International Conference of American States, where the Montevideo Convention was codified, U.S. President Franklin D. Roosevelt and Secretary of State Cordell Hull declared the Good Neighbor Policy, which emphasized cooperation and trade rather than military intervention in the affairs of inter-American states. The International Conference was convened to provide criteria to facilitate the ability of former colonial states to achieve international legal personality as nation-states, with most delegations at the International Conference of American States consisting of independent states that had only recently emerged from colonialism.

The Montevideo Convention was signed on 26 December 1933, and subsequently ratified by the following 17 states: Brazil, Chile, Colombia, Costa Rica, Cuba, Dominican Republic, Ecuador, El Salvador, Guatemala, Haiti, Honduras, Mexico, Nicaragua, Panama, Paraguay, United States and Venezuela.

2 *Criteria for Statehood*

Article 1 of the Montevideo Convention sets out the criteria for statehood as follows:

- *Permanent Population*. The size is incidental, but what is important is that the population not consist of seasonal inhabitants or people simply passing through.
- *Defined Territory*. The size of the territory is incidental, but the state must consider itself to have exclusive authority over some defined territory. The borders of this territory may be disputed, yet the government must hold to a fixed position.
- *Effective Government*. There must be a government with effective control over the territory, though there are times when states are recognized even though there is a civil war and no single entity is in effective control of the whole territory (e.g., Somalia). This is due to states' reluctance to revoke their long-standing recognition of other states that have been established by the

international community just because they have been thrust into the misfortune of civil war. Doing so would generate international legal uncertainty and instability.
- *Capacity to Enter into Relations with Other States*. The state must be able to enter into relations with other states. Examples of such relations include the establishment of diplomatic missions and the conclusion of bilateral treaties.

Under the declaratory theory, an entity is deemed a state based on these four criteria, regardless of its recognition as a state by other states.

B State Recognition under the Constitutive Theory

Under the constitutive theory, an entity is not a state unless it is recognized as a state by the international community. Recognition is thus the mechanism by which entities become states. "Recognition" refers to the formal acknowledgement by other states that an entity is a state. This recognition implies a political decision, one that each country takes of its own accord and volition. In this way, the constitutive theory is based on a legal construct and is usually invoked by entities when a majority of the international community recognizes them as states.

Recognition has important consequences. It grants effective title to territory as well as title to assets or other property that may be held abroad. It also bolsters the claim to statehood based on the declaratory theory.

Individual states may condition recognition of new states on certain criteria, above and beyond those that comprise the declaratory theory. For example, the European Community (the predecessor to the E.U.) conditioned its recognition of new states of the Eastern bloc on their commitments to human rights and nuclear non-proliferation.

C The Declaratory Theory as the More Widely Accepted Test

1 The Constitutive Theory Deprives Unrecognized States of International Legal Protection

The declaratory theory provides the more widely accepted and prevalent test for state recognition under international law. There are many reasons for this, to which we now turn.

If the constitutive theory is applied, states can be deprived of their rights under international law if other states do not accord to them state recognition. States can therefore flout international law and the rights of self-determination and non-interference by simply arguing that they do not recognize another entity as a state. On this basis, a state can invade another state and argue that no rights were violated because the invader does not recognize the victim as a state. States can circumvent the prohibition on the crime of aggression by arguing that they have adopted a political decision to deny state recognition.

The *Institut de Droit International* has addressed this concern in its 1936 Resolutions concerning the Recognition of New States and New Governments, declaring that the existence of new states with all connected legal effects "is not affected by the refusal of one or more States to recognize."[21] The declaratory theory overcomes this shortfall by looking to statehood based on the de facto on-the-ground situation, regardless of whether other states have conferred recognition.

2 *State Practice Points to the Declaratory Theory as the Dominant Theory*

Professor Malcolm Shaw, in the 5th Edition of his treatise, *International Law*, characterizes the declaratory theory as the dominant theory of state recognition. He writes:

> Practice over the last century ... does point to the declaratory approach as the better of the two theories. States which for particular reasons have refused to recognize other states, such as in the Arab world in Israel and the USA in certain communist nations, rarely contend that the other party is devoid of powers and obligations before international law and exists in a legal vacuum. The stance is rather that rights and duties are binding upon them and that recognition has not been accorded for primarily political reasons. If the constitutive theory were accepted it would mean, for example, in the context of the former Arab non recognition of Israel, that the latter was not bound by international law rules of non aggression and non intervention ...
>
> Of course, if an entity, while meeting the conditions of international law as to statehood, went totally unrecognized, this would undoubtedly hamper the exercise of its rights and duties, especially in view of the absence of diplomatic relations, but it would not seem in law to amount to a decisive argument against statehood itself. For example, the charter of the organization of American states adopted at Bogota in 1948 notes in its survey of the fundamental rights and duties of states that 'the political existence of this state is independent of recognition by other states. Even before being recognized the state has the right to defend its integrity and independence'.[22]

Moreover, the declaratory theory is largely reflective of customary international law. It is the only theory of statehood that has been codified in an international convention. It is binding upon at least the 17 states parties to the Montevideo Convention, namely: Brazil, Chile, Colombia, Costa Rica, Cuba, Dominican Republic, Ecuador, El Salvador, Guatemala, Haiti, Honduras, Mexico, Nicaragua, Panama, Paraguay, U.S. and Venezuela. To the extent the declaratory theory is reflective of customary international law, it is also binding upon the wider international community, with the exception of persistent objectors.

A range of leading international law scholars have argued that the four criteria of the Montevideo Convention are reflective of customary international law and, as such, states are obliged under customary international law to confer recognition to entities that fulfill the four criteria. Among these scholars are Rose Parfitt, who, in Anne Orford and Florian Hoffman's edited volume, *The Oxford Handbook of the Theory of International Law*, states as follows:

21. Institut de Droit International, "Resolutions concerning the Recognition of New States and New Governments," Cambridge University Press (Cambridge, 1936).
22. Malcolm Shaw, *International Law*, Cambridge University Press (5th Ed., 2003), pp. 370-71.

> the passage of the four 'Montevideo' criteria into customary international law marked the beginning of the end both for the constitutive theory and for the so-called "standard of civilization" upon which it relied.[23]

Other leading international law scholars who adopt this view include Antonio Cassesse[24] and James L. Brierly.[25]

Former ICJ judge James Crawford, in *The Creation of States in International Law*, a key source on the issue of state recognition, characterizes the criteria in the Montevideo Convention as "the best known formulation of the basic criteria for statehood." He affirms that state practice recognizes statehood based on the factual qualities of the state and how a state interacts with other states (all criteria subsumed into the Montevideo criteria). He writes:

> Modern state practice suggests statehood exists as a matter of both internal and external factors: internal being the factual qualities of a state, and external being how a state interacts with other states.[26]

How a state interacts with other states depends on whether that state has the capacity to enter into relations with other states. If it does not, then the entity is not a state. It is not a state because it does not fulfill the criteria of the Montevideo Convention and, lacking the capacity to enter into relations with other states, it is unable to achieve recognition by other states as a state.

3 *The Problem of Partial Recognition under the Constitutive Theory*

The constitutive theory is further weakened by the problem that may arise when some, but not all, states recognize an entity as a state. Can a state exist for some states but not for others? "Partial" statehood does not exist in the international legal order and the constitutive theory does not provide an answer to this anomaly.

The declaratory theory of statehood avoids this problem because it is based on objective criteria (for example, either a state has a defined territory or it doesn't, regardless of what states say about this). The constitutive theory, in contrast, is based on subjective political determinations by states, which may change from time to time as governments change and the political winds blow in a different direction. This can lead to impossible results. For example:

23. Rose Parfitt, "Theorizing recognition and personality," in Anne Orford and Florian Hoffman (eds.), *The Oxford Handbook of the Theory of International Law*, Oxford University Press (Oxford, 2016).
24. *See* Antonio Cassesse, *International Law*, OUP (2nd Ed., 2005), p. 74.
25. *See* James Leslie Brierly, *The Law of Nations: An Introduction to the International Law of Peace*, Clarendon Press, 5th Ed. (Oxford, 1955), pp. 129 and 132.
26. James Crawford, *The Creation of States in International Law*, Oxford University Press, 2nd Ed. (Oxford, 2007), pp. 4-5.

> if "State A" gains recognition from only a few other states, State A cannot simultaneously hold statehood (because of the states that recognize it) and lack statehood (because of the states that do not recognize it).[27]

This conundrum can be avoided by applying the declaratory theory of statehood.

4 *The Declaratory Theory Takes into Account the Constitutive Theory as Its Fourth Prong*

The declaratory theory is the superior test because it takes into account and embeds the constitutive theory into its own four-pronged test: An entity cannot be a state under the declaratory theory unless it has the capacity to enter into relations with other states, but an entity cannot enter into relations with other states unless other states recognize that entity as a state. Therefore, whether or not the constitutive theory is applied, an entity cannot be said to be a state if, as a result of non-recognition by other states, it has been unable to enter into international relations.

D Reconciling the Declaratory and Constitutive Theories

The declaratory and constitutive theories of statehood are not necessarily irreconcilable. There is an intermediary position that holds that once an entity fulfills the criteria of the declaratory theory, it exists as a state and other states are obligated to confer recognition to the entity as a state. This is the position adopted by former ICJ Judge Hersch Lauterpacht, who wrote the following in his classic 1944 essay, "Recognition of States in International Law":

> A State exists as a subject of international law—as a subject of international rights and duties—as soon as it "exists" as a fact, that is, as soon as it fulfils the conditions of statehood as laid down in international law. Recognition merely declares the existence of that fact.[28]

Lauterpacht then affirmed that once a state fulfills the declaratory criteria, other states are obligated to accord recognition. In his essay, he went on to express the following:

> To recognize a community as a State is to declare that it fulfills the conditions of statehood as required by international law. If these conditions are present, existing States are under the duty to grant recognition. In the absence of an international organ competent to ascertain and authoritatively to declare the presence of requirements of full international personality, States already established fulfill that function in their capacity as organs of international law.[29]

27. Major Ryan M. Fisher, "Defending Taiwan: Collective Self-Defense of a Contested State," 32(1) Article 3 *Florida Journal of International Law* (2020), p. 114.
28. Hersch Lauterpacht, "Recognition of States in International Law," 53 *Yale Law Journal* (June 1944), p. 423.
29. Hersch Lauterpacht, "Recognition of States in International Law," 53 *Yale Law Journal* (June 1944), p. 385.

E Number of Recognized Sovereign States

1 *Sovereign States Recognized by the International Community*

There are 194 sovereign states recognized by the international community: the 193 U.N. member states[30] and Vatican City (the Holy See). While Vatican City is an independent state with its own population, territory, government and ability to enter into relations with other states, it has chosen to remain an observer rather than a member of the global body.

For a list of recognized states within the international community, *see* the Appendix "Recognized Sovereign States and Their Memberships."

2 *Disputed States*

In addition to these 193 states, there are a handful of territories whose sovereignty is disputed. Kosovo and Taiwan are two such territories.

a Kosovo

While there are at the time of writing 71 states, in addition to Taiwan, the Cook Islands and Niue, recognize Kosovo as a state. However, there are approximately 89 that have implicitly or explicitly denied Kosovo's statehood. Thus, although the ICJ, in its *Advisory opinion on Kosovo's declaration of independence* (2010), held that Kosovo's unilateral declaration of independence does not violate international law, the status of Kosovo as an independent state under the constitutive theory is as of yet uncertain.

b Palestine

General Assembly Resolution A/67/L.28 on the Status of Palestine at the United Nations upgraded the Palestinian Authority's status at the United Nations from a "permanent observer entity" to a "non-member observer State." The Resolution was adopted on 29 November 2012. An overwhelming majority of states (73% of those present) voted in favor of Resolution a/67/L.28, with 138 in favor, 9 against, and 41 abstentions.

The upgrade in Palestine's status at the United Nations under Resolution A/67/L.28 does not necessarily equate to full-fledged membership in the international community. The recognition of statehood is a rather complex area of international law

30. The most recent members to the United Nations family are Switzerland (190th member, 10 September 2002), Timor-Leste (191st member, 27 September 2002), Montenegro (192nd member, 28 June 2006) and South Sudan (193rd member, 14 July 2011). For a list of U.N. Member States and their dates of admission, *see* "Member States of the United Nations," available at < https://www.un.org/en/about-us/member-states > . Territories that may become recognized as U.N. Member States in the future include Kosovo, Southern Sudan and Palestine.

subject to competing tests and theories, namely, the declaratory theory and constitutive theory, which are discussed under "Criteria for Statehood" on p. 79, *supra*.

c *Sahrawi Arab Democratic Republic*

The Sahrawi Arab Democratic Republic is a partially recognized state that claims the non-self-governing territory of Western Sahara, the easternmost fifth of which it controls. It maintains diplomatic relations with 40 U.N. states and is a full member of the African Union.

d *Taiwan*

Taiwan stands in a similar position. While it has its own population, defined territory, effective government and ability to enter into relations with other countries (Taiwan has, in several countries, established bureaus for cultural and economic affairs similar to embassies), its status as an independent country has largely been disputed, and China uses its Security Council veto, which was transferred from the Republic of China to the People's Republic of China in 1971, to ensure that no resolutions recognizing Taiwan as an independent state are passed. Thus, although Taiwan fulfills the criteria for statehood, it is not to be considered a sovereign, independent state under the constitutive theory because most states have not recognized Taiwan as a state. As of the date of this writing, 12 states recognize Taiwanese statehood.

e *Case in Contrast: East Timor*

East Timor (Timor-Leste) was colonized by Portugal from the 16th century. In 1975, East Timor declared its independence from Portugal but was later invaded and occupied by Indonesia that same year. In 1999, Indonesia relinquished control of East Timor, following the United Nations-sponsored act of self-determination.

Unlike Kosovo and Taiwan, East Timor meets the criteria for statehood under the constitutive theory. As evidenced by its membership at the U.N., East Timor is recognized by the international community as an independent state.

F Special Cases

1 *Vatican City*

The Lateral Pacts were signed in 1929 between Pietro Gasparri, representing the Holy See and Benito Mussolini, representing Italy. The Pacts contained the Treaty of Conciliation, where Italy recognized "the sovereignty of the Holy See in international matters" (Article 2 Conciliation Treaty). In order to assure this sovereignty, the Treaty of Conciliation created Vatican City as an independent state under the dominion and sovereign jurisdiction of the Holy See. Although Vatican City is the state, its delegates are sent on behalf of and represent the Holy See. For example, the mission to the U.N. is known as the "Permanent Observer Mission of the Holy See to the United Nations," not as the mission of Vatican City. The state should be viewed as the support structure that guarantees that the Holy See may realize its mission with autonomy.

Some argue that Vatican City cannot validly be considered a state because it lacks a permanent population (apart from church functionaries existing to support the Holy See). However, Vatican City exists as a state under the constitutive theory of state recognition because the international community and international organizations recognize Vatican City's claims to be an independent state.

2 *Sovereign Military Order of Malta*

The Sovereign Military Order of Malta (also known as the Knights of Malta; not to be confused with the Republic of Malta) is a Catholic lay religious order, traditionally of military and chivalrous nature. The Sovereign Military Order of Malta is headquartered in Rome, Italy, but is widely considered a sovereign subject of international law. The Italian Court of Cassation recognized the international personality of the Order in 1935.

Following the loss of Christian territories of the Holy Land to Muslims, the Order operated from Rhodes and later from Malta, over which it was sovereign. Although the Order was ejected from Malta by Napoleon, the Order has survived and continues to claim sovereignty under international law. The Order maintains diplomatic relations with states in Europe, Asia, Africa and South America and has been granted permanent observer status with the United Nations.[31]

III RECOGNITION OF GOVERNMENTS

Three legal doctrines are used to inform whether a new government will be recognized as legitimate by other states: the traditional approach, which is the most widely accepted, the Tobar doctrine and the Estrada doctrine.

A Traditional Approach (Effective Control Doctrine)

Under the traditional approach, states consider four factors in deciding whether to recognize a government: (i) the effectiveness of control; (ii) stability and permanence; (iii) ability and willingness to fulfill obligations; and (iv) popular support (i.e., the acquiescence of the people to the government). The rationale behind these elements is to ensure that a new government is internally stable before being recognized by and entering into relations with other states that imply obligations and responsibilities.

Because the elements applied to the recognition of new governments under the traditional approach revolve around the effective control of the government over the

31. *See* the Permanent Observer Mission of the Order of Malta to the United Nations in New York, available at <http://www.un.int/orderofmalta>.

state and its land and people, the traditional approach is often referred to as the effective control doctrine.

B Tobar Doctrine (Doctrine of Legitimacy)

Under the Tobar doctrine, also known as the doctrine of legitimacy, states will not recognize governments that come into power as a consequence of a *coup* or a revolution against the government, at least until the people recognize and accept the new government. States that follow this approach will accept a new government when a *coup* is accompanied by democratic legitimacy, evidenced by, for example, a democratic vote confirming the new government or passing a new constitution reorganizing the state's decision-making processes.

Over the past decade, the United States and other countries have spent a great deal of resources discussing the importance of democratic governance, and the OAS has adopted significant resolutions in this spirit. The Tobar doctrine signifies a new trend in the past decade whereby states withhold their recognition of new governments where such governments take power in a manner contrary to basic principles of democracy. Accordingly, the U.N., in some cases, will not allow a government to take a seat at the U.N. when the government was not democratically installed.

C Estrada Doctrine (Automatic Recognition of All Governments)

The Estrada doctrine, named after the former Mexican Secretary of Foreign Relations, was created by the Mexican government, though Mexico no longer follows this approach. A state that follows the Estrada doctrine automatically recognizes all governments in all circumstances and refrains from making any determination as to the legitimacy of new governments, even those that came into power by extra-constitutional means.

Under the Estrada doctrine, when a new government comes to power (through constitutional or extra-constitutional means), the relations between the state and third-party states remain unchanged. This is to prevent third-party states from passing judgment on the internal affairs of other states or embarrassing states that recognize governments with abusive human rights records, thus permitting them to avoid the perception that they approve or condone the acts of the government being recognized.

IV JURISDICTION

Questions of jurisdiction in civil matters are generally resolved by applying conflict of laws rules. The issue becomes important in international law when the assertion of jurisdiction by a state affects foreign nationals.

It is a general principle of law that states may exercise jurisdiction over nationals with whom they have sufficient contacts. It may be a general principle of law that states may exercise jurisdiction over subject matters when the ties to a subject matter are sufficiently close to override the interests of a competing state.

A Territorial Principle

The primary basis for jurisdiction is a state's territory: States may legislate and apply legislation within their territories, unless treaties provide otherwise. This principle allows states to apply their legislation to any individual located within their territory, whether they are nationals or aliens.

The courts of a state may adjudicate any legal or factual issues when the case or controversy arises in the state's own territory.

B Nationality Principle

A second basis for jurisdiction is nationality: a state may regulate the activities of both its nationals located in the home state as well as its nationals located abroad. Most states have laws that require that their nationals who commit crimes abroad be tried at home, and to this end, extradition treaties have been established.

V TERRITORY

A Territorial Expansion Through Cession, Prescription and *Terra Nullius*

One of the fundamental elements of a sovereign state is a defined territory subject to the exclusive jurisdiction and governance of the state. The territory of a state may be expanded through:

- *Cession*. Territory may be validly transferred between states via voluntary transfers.
- *Prescription*. A state acquires title to a territory by practicing uncontested sovereignty thereon over an uninterrupted period of time.
- *Terra nullius*. States may obtain title to land not under the sovereignty or control of any state—*terra nullius* (*Lat.*, "the land of no one")—through the occupation thereof, with some limitations (*see, e.g.*, the Antarctic Treaty System).

The *Island of Palmas Case* between the United States and the Netherlands at the Permanent Court of Arbitration (1928), one of the most highly influential precedents dealing with island territorial conflicts, recognized cession and prescription as valid means of transferring territory between states.

B Inadmissibility of Territorial Expansion Through the Use of Force

Under modern international law, military conquest is not a valid means of territorial expansion. Title to territory cannot be acquired through the use of force alone; express or implied consent is a prerequisite before international recognition of title to conquered territory will be conferred.

This principle was confirmed by U.N. Security Council Resolution 242 of 1967, which emphasized the "inadmissibility of the acquisition of territory by war and the need to work for a just and lasting peace in which every state in the area can live in security." The Resolution, adopted within the context of the 1967 Six-Day Arab-Israeli War, called for Israel's withdrawal from the territories occupied in the War.

C Jurisdiction of the International Court of Justice over Territorial Disputes

The ICJ, acting under its contentious jurisdiction, may hear and resolve territorial dispute cases, as it did in *Botswana v. Namibia* (1999), ruling in favor of Botswana's claim over Sedudu Island.

VI LEGALITY OF THE USE OF FORCE (*JUS AD BELLUM*)

A Origins of the Legal Use of Force under International Law

1 Overview

Since ancient times, world cultures have explored the political, philosophical and religious grounds of just war and the legality of the use of force. The ninth-century BC Indian epic *Mahabharata*, exploring the concept of *dharma-yuddha*, or "righteous war," observes that war is to be waged only as a last resort. In his essay *De Officiis* ("On Duties"), Cicero argued in the first century BC that the "only excuse, therefore, for going to war is that we may live in peace unharmed."[32] In the fifth century, St. Augustine argued that there should be no shame in the use of force to maintain or reestablish justice. St. Thomas Aquinas, who, building on the foundation laid down by Augustine, set forth the conditions of just war.

Contemporary international law draws a distinction between *jus ad bellum*, laws that regulate recourse to the use of armed force, and *jus in bello*, the rules governing the conduct of war once armed hostilities have commenced. For the purpose of this section, the origins of the first category of laws will be examined. For a discussion of *jus in bello*, *see* the following chapter, which deals with international humanitarian law (the law of armed conflict).

32. Marcus Tullius Cicero and Walter Miller (tr), *De officiis (On Moral Duties)*, Harvard University Press (1913) 17, para. 1.11.35.

2 *Foundations in Christian Just War Theory*

a *The First Three Centuries*

Christian involvement in the affairs of the state was limited during the first centuries of the Church. There were some Christians in civil service (consider the Christians within "Caesar's household" referenced by St. Paul (Php 4:22)) and in military service (both John the Baptist and Jesus ministered to soldiers (Luke 3:14; Mat 8:5-8) and the centurion Cornelius was use to bring the Gospel to the Gentiles (Acts 10:35-48)). However, Christians, like other minorities in the early Roman Empire, faced persecution by the Roman government. The extent to which Christians were involved with civil government was generally limited to praying for the emperor (1Tim 2:1-2). A Christian's association with the military and support of the Empire's oppression of other Christians would have been incongruous.

The first centuries of Christianity were thus marked by pacifism with respect to military service and the use of violence. Origen (c. 184-253) said that Christians "do not go forth as soldiers." Tertullian (c. 160-c. 225) wrote that only "*without* the sword can the Christian wage war: for the Lord has abolished the sword" (*see* Mat 26:52). Clement of Alexandria (c. 150-c. 215) wrote that "he who holds the sword must cast it away" and "if one of the faithful becomes a soldier he must be rejected by the Church, for he has scorned God."

b *Constantine's Conversion (312)*

Much of this changed with Constantine's conversion to Christianity in 312 AD. After Constantine's conversion, Christianity became the official religion of the Roman Empire. Military service was no longer associated with the brutal oppression and killing of Christians on behalf of a pagan Empire. Defending the Empire from northern invasions took on new meaning and was not deemed to be inconsistent with the Gospel of peace, particularly when war was being waged in order to maintain peace or reestablish justice.

This shift in position is reflected in the writings of early Church fathers and councils. The Council of Arles (314) stated that to forbid the state "the right to go to war was to condemn it to extinction." St. Athanasius of Alexandria (293-373) wrote:

> Although one is not supposed to kill, the killing of the enemy in time of war is both a lawful and praiseworthy thing. This is why we consider individuals who have distinguished themselves in war as being worthy of great honors and indeed public monuments are set up to celebrate their achievements. It is evident, therefore, that at one particular time and under one set of circumstances, an act is not permissible, but when time and circumstances are right, it is both allowed and condoned (*The Letter of St. Athanasius to Amun*).

Shortly thereafter, Christian theologians, starting with St. Augustine, began formulating a Christian just war theory.

c St. Augustine (354-430)

For Augustine of Hippo, war was a necessary consequence of human sin and evil. God therefore instituted civil government to punish evil (Rom 13:4). Civil leaders are to use force to defend the innocent when all other forms of peaceful intervention fail. Armies are raised not to oppress and maraud but to protect the weak and establish law, order, and justice. Augustine concedes that any system of worldly justice will ultimately be marred by the effects of sin, yet conscientious Christians are to seek justice that reflects the perfect justice that we will witness in the hereafter.

Augustine observes that if Christianity "forbade war altogether, those who sought salutary advice in the Gospel would rather have been counseled to cast aside their arms and to give up soldiering altogether. On the contrary, they were told: 'Do violence to no man ... and be content with your pay.' If he commanded them to be content with their pay, he did not forbid soldiering" (Thomas Aquinas, *Summa Theologica*, II-II, q. 40 a.1 (quoting Augustine)).

It would seem that Augustine's justification of the legitimacy of war is contrary to Jesus' teaching to not "resist evil" and to "turn the other cheek" (Mat 5:39). Yet Augustine argues that Jesus teaches the law of grace that governs the kingdom of God, which is "within you" (Luke 17:21). While the law of grace is to govern man's interior spiritual life of the kingdom of God, Christians are also subject to another, worldly kingdom, which is governed by the law of justice "for your own good" (Rom 13:4).

While the Christian is to love and forgive his enemy on the spiritual level, according to the law of grace, he is nonetheless to seek justice (Mic 6:8). For example, if a Christian is assaulted and robbed, he is to first forgive his "enemy." But he is not to eschew justice; rather, he is to actively seek it. This may take on many forms, such as seeing to the criminal's arrest and punishment by the civil authorities, thus furthering the state's divinely-appointed purpose of punishing evil (Rom 13:4). This is not inconsistent with loving his "enemy" or visiting or ministering to him while he is in prison.

One thus sees in Augustine's work a dichotomy between the kingdom of God and the kingdoms of the world. He argues that Christ's injunction to "turn the other cheek" applies only to the interior life. A just war is, according to Augustine, one that seeks to punish evildoers in the spirit of Romans 13:4 and reestablish peace, order and the rule of law. War can then be said for Augustine to be an instrument of peace.

d St. Thomas Aquinas (1225-1274)

St. Thomas Aquinas built upon the just war foundation developed by Augustine and introduced the concept of the common good as a necessary element in the legality of war. To be legitimate, a military must, when carrying out the use of force, have as its goal the defense of the public good, which includes the right to worship God. Soldiers are therefore instruments of the civil authority instituted by God, which guarantees civil order and stability.

Aquinas then lays down his conditions for just war, which must be waged: (i) by a legitimate authority; (ii) with a just cause; and (iii) with a right intention. This theory, over the centuries, came to incorporate other elements, including the exhaustion of all non-violent options and a reasonable prospect of success, further elaborated below.

e *Modern Church Views*

i The Catholic Church

The Benedictine Monks of Solesmes, France, provide a succinct overview of the Catholic Church's teaching on the use of force in *Just War at the Service of the Divine Precept of Peace*, which observes that:[33]

> [P]eace can have recourse to force. However, force, in itself, is incapable of restoring peace, since peace is the fruit of the union of justice and charity. Some enemies of justice cannot be led to accept the necessary conditions for peace without the use of force. The importance of a certain good justifies entirely its defense by force against an unjust aggression.

The *Catechism of the Catholic Church* has expanded Aquinas' three just war conditions (legitimate authority, just cause, and right intention) and expanded his list with four additional conditions. Today, the Catholic Church requires a war to meet the following seven criteria in order for it to be classified as "just:"[34]

- *Legitimate authority*. It must be waged by a legitimate civil authority (i.e., a state, in accordance with Romans 13), not individuals or groups who do not constitute an authority sanctioned by whatever the society deems legitimate.
- *Just cause*. The cause must be just (i.e., defense of the innocent against an armed attack, redressing an injury, punishing evil, restoring territory unjustly seized).
- *Right intention*. The central intention of the war must be reestablishing a just peace (as opposed to conquest, expanding territory, spreading the seeds of revolt or acquiring power or material possessions).
- *Last resort*. All non-violent options must be exhausted before the use of force is justified.
- *Reasonable prospect of success*. Deaths and injury incurred in a war not having a reasonable chance of success are not morally justifiable.
- *Proportionality*. The use of arms must not produce evils graver than the evil to be eliminated; the peace established by the war must be preferable to the peace that would have prevailed had the war not been fought.
- *Grave damage from the aggressor*. The damage inflicted on the people under the control of the legitimate authority must be lasting, grave and certain.

33. Moines de Solesmes, *La Paix Internationale*, Desclée (Paris, 1956), Vol. I, 20.
34. Notably, all of these criteria except for the seventh one, grave damage from the aggressor, are included in the ICISS's Principles for Military Intervention, discussed under "Responsibility to Protect ('R2P')," *infra*.

ii Protestant Churches

While Catholic just war theory is perhaps the most developed and precise statement of the justification of war among the various Christian denominations, it is not universally accepted by Christian churches. Many churches have their own traditions or reject just war theory altogether, believing war to be incompatible with Jesus' prohibition on resisting evildoers (Mat 5:39) and St. Paul's teaching to never "repay anyone evil for evil" (Rom 12:17).

While some Christians reject the use of force under any circumstances, the World Council of Churches' "Ecumenical Call to Just Peace" (2011) perhaps best captures the views of most Protestant Christians. The statement calls for non-violent resistance, the transformation of conflict and just peace toward "God's purpose for humanity and all creation" (Cl. 12) but recognizes that there are "extreme circumstances where, as the last resort and the lesser evil, the lawful use of armed force may become necessary" (Cl. 22).

Nonetheless, there are certain Protestant churches that continue to reject the use of force under *any* circumstances. Mennonites, for example, believe Christ's teachings to "love your enemies" and "do good to those who hate you" (Mat 5:44), prevent them from participating in military campaigns against other countries. The Quakers, also committed to non-violence, have declared that "the spirit of Christ which leads us into all Truth will never move us to fight and war against any man with outward weapons, neither for the kingdom of Christ, nor for the kingdoms of the world" (*A Declaration from the harmless and innocent people of God, called Quakers*, 1660).

iii Eastern Orthodox Church

There is no ethical teaching for just war in the writings of the Greek Orthodox Church fathers. War, even in unavoidable circumstances, is deemed an "evil," albeit a lesser of evils in certain circumstances. According to Fr. Stanley Harakas, the Greek Fathers never elaborate on a just war theory and instead take a pro-peace stance on the question of war.

St. John Chrysostom (347-407), bishop of Constantinople, for example, distinguishes between Christians, who are "not permitted forcibly to correct the failings of those who sin" and the civil authorities, who, "when they have captured malefactors under the law, show their authority to be great and prevent them even against their will from following their own devices." Christians, in contrast, are to make the wrong-doer better "by persuasion," not "by force" (St. John Chrysostom, "On the Priesthood").

The Eastern Orthodox Church, while recognizing that war may be a necessary consequence of man's fall, always considers war and the taking of human life to be "an objective evil, even when done in the pursuit of a 'just cause'" (Fr. Paul O'Callaghan, "Peace and War in The Eastern Orthodox Church," *Messenger*, December 2002). The Ecumenical Patriarch of the Orthodox Christian Church, Bartholomew I, in his 22 October 1999 address in Novi Sad, Serbia, said:

> War and violence are never means used by God in order to achieve a result ... [I]n a few specific cases, the Orthodox Church forgives an armed defense against oppression and violence. However, as a rule, peaceful resolution of differences and peaceful cooperation are more pleasing to God and more beneficial to humankind.
>
> War and violence breed hatred and revenge, leading to an endless cycle of evil until opponents completely annihilate each other. For this reason St. Paul exhorts us, "Do not be overcome by evil, but overcome evil with good" (Rom 12:21).

For the Orthodox Church, war, while an objective evil, may be permitted by applying *economia*, or dispenzation, to the strict principles of *akrievia* embodied in canon law. Like divorce, war is permitted not because it is good but because of the frailty of human nature. When the Eastern Orthodox Church forgives the use of armed force, such use of force is never deemed "just," "moral" or "justified," though it may be excused and forgiven in light of postlapsarian human weakness.

iv Conclusion

While the view of the Catholic Church, as summarized above, offers general guidance as to Christian just war theory, it does not speak for the diversity of views contained in the Orthodox and Protestant Churches and particularly for those churches absolutely committed to the principles of pacifism and insist that war, by its very nature, can never be just.

3 *Jus ad Bellum and Jus in Bello under Grotius' Natural Law Paradigm*

The seventeenth-century Dutch philosopher and theologian Hugo Grotius has been credited as having laid down the foundations for international law, which in the following centuries would become customary international law and codified treaties governing the conduct of states in armed conflict. Grotius discussed the philosophy of war at length in his treatise *De jure belli ac pacis* ("On the Law of War and Peace"), published in 1625, which advances a system of principles of natural law, whereby what is "just" is consistent with the nature of a society of rational beings. He holds these principles to be binding on all people and nations regardless of local custom and then goes on to outline the circumstances under which war may be justly executed. The book is divided into three parts, as follows:

(1) *Book I: General conception*. Offers a conception of war and natural justice, arguing that there are some circumstances in which war is justifiable.
(2) *Book II: Jus ad bellum (justice in the resort to war)*. Describes three "just causes" for war: self-defense, reparation of injury and punishment. Grotius considers a wide variety of circumstances under which these causes apply.
(3) *Book III: Jus in bello (justice in the conduct of war)*. Enumerates the rules governing the conduct of war once it has begun. Grotius argues that all parties to war are bound by such rules, whether or not their cause is just.

For the purpose of this section, we discuss modern codified international law with respect to Grotius' Book II, that is, the principles that apply when resorting to force is legal under international law.

B Prohibition on the Use of Force: The Principles of Sovereignty and Non-interference

1 Historic Approach: War as the Prerogative of States

Historically, war was the prerogative of states. States could resort to war whenever they deemed a dispute between them to be irreconcilable. War was not prohibited, and even if it was, no sovereign entity existed that could enforce such a prohibition.

2 Prohibition of War in the Twentieth Century

In the early twentieth century, states moved away from war as a legitimate means of resolving disputes. They progressively began drafting and adopting conventions that outlawed resorting to armed violence as a result of disputes. In 1907, states adopted the Hague Convention (II) for the Limitation of Employment of Force for Recovery of Contract Debts. Two decades later, the Kellogg-Briand pact was concluded in 1928 to prohibit the use of war to resolve "disputes or conflicts of whatever nature or of whatever origin they may be."

In the devastating aftermath of World War II, the international community came together to formally codify the prohibition on the use of force. The U.N. Charter became the codification of the *jus ad bellum* rules. Under the Charter, war was no longer the prerogative of sovereign states, as it had previously been under international law. Rather, the Charter granted sovereign nations an absolute right to independence and territorial integrity. Moreover, it imposed on states a duty to "settle their international disputes by peaceful means in such a manner that international peace and security and justice, are not endangered" (Article 2.3 Charter).

Today, both customary international law as well as the U.N. Charter recognize the territorial integrity and independence of states and prohibit military force from interfering with this integrity. The Charter states that "All Members shall refrain in their international relations from the threat or use of force against the territorial integrity or political independence of any state, or in any other manner inconsistent with the Purposes of the United Nations" (Article 2.4 Charter).

C Exceptions to the Prohibition on the Use of Force

Chapter VII of the U.N. Charter permits only two exceptions to these blanket prohibitions. The use of force is only permitted when acting pursuant to: (i) U.N. collective security measures (Article 42 Charter); or (ii) self-defense (Article 51 Charter).

1 *Use of Force as a Chapter VII Collective Security Measure (Article 42 Charter)*

The first exception involves the right of the Security Council to employ the use of force in order to secure peace.

a Determination of a Threat to Peace (Article 39 Charter)

The first step in employing force to secure peace is for the Security Council to determine the existence of a threat to or breach of the peace or an act of aggression. In such a case, it is to make recommendations or decide what measures are to be taken "to maintain or restore international peace and security" (Article 39 Charter).

b Measures Not Involving the Use of Armed Force (Articles 40-41 Charter)

In order to prevent an aggravation of the situation, the Security Council may:

- issue injunctions upon the parties concerned by calling upon them to "comply with such provisional measures as it deems necessary or desirable" (Article 40 Charter); and
- decide what measures not involving the use of armed force, including "complete or partial interruption of economic relations and of rail, sea, air, postal, telegraphic, radio, and other means of communication, and the severance of diplomatic relations," are to be employed to give effect to the Security Council's decisions (Article 41 Charter).

c The Use of Armed Force (Article 42 Charter)

i Overview

If these measures are inadequate or ineffective, the Security Council may pass a resolution to take military action "by air, sea, or land forces as may be necessary to maintain or restore international peace and security" (Article 42 Charter). To this end, all U.N. members are to make available to the Security Council "armed forces, assistance and facilities, including rights of passage" (Article 43 Charter).

ii Regional Arrangements

The Security Council shall, when appropriate, utilize regional arrangements or agencies "for enforcement action under its authority. But no enforcement action shall be taken under regional arrangements or by regional agencies without the authorization of the Security Council, with the exception of measures against any enemy state," which is in turn defined as a "state that during the Second World War had been an enemy of any signatory" of the Charter (Article 53 Charter). Thus, even a regional organization such as NATO must act with authorization from the Security Council prior to undertaking a military act.

iii Historical Development of Article 42 Interventions

The references to "threats to international peace and security" throughout Chapter VII of the U.N. Charter have historically been interpreted as military invasions of states against other states. However, in the post-Cold War environment, states acting through the Security Council have taken an expansive view of "threats to international peace and security" to encompass not only military invasions but also threats arising from violations of human rights and humanitarian law. "If in 1945 the founders of the U.N. had been primarily concerned to enable the USSC to prevent another world war, after the Cold War the major preoccupation of the Security Council concerned, most of the time, intranational violence with international implications."[35] In the post-Cold War era, Article 42 has rarely been invoked in response to an invasion of one state against another, with Iraq's 1990 invasion of Kuwait being a rare exception.

2 *Use of Force in Chapter VII Self-Defense (Article 51 Charter)*

a Overview

The second exception is the use of force pursuant to states' inherent right to self-defense. Defensive military acts may be taken by states as a last resort under the U.N. Charter, which states that "nothing in the present Charter shall impair the inherent right of individual or collective self-defense" (Article 51 Charter). However, such acts may *only* be undertaken as a last resort "if an armed attack occurs against a Member of the United Nations" (Article 51 Charter). This right to act in self-defense is also embedded in customary international law.

The Charter imposes certain requirements and restrictions on the right to act in self-defense, namely:

- The Charter only permits the right to act in self-defense "*until* the Security Council has taken measures necessary to maintain international peace and security" (Article 51 Charter), that is, until the Security Council actually acts.
- Measures taken by members in the exercise of self-defense must be "immediately reported to the Security Council" (Article 51 Charter). The Security Council will determine if the action falls within the right of self-defense, or it may appoint another U.N. organ to do so.

The use of force against an aggressor must be proportionate; states must limit the magnitude, scope, and duration of the use of force to that level of force reasonably

35. David Forsythe, "The UN Security Council and Human Rights: Promising Developments, Persistent Problems," 13(2) *Journal of Human Rights* (2014), p. 126 available at <https://doi.org/10.1080/14754835.2014.886945>.

necessary to counter an attack. For example, if an aggressor state threatens the use of force using small arms, the victim state may not respond with a nuclear attack.

b *Anticipatory Self-Defense: The* Caroline *Case*

In the 1837 *Caroline* case, a vessel was being used by private American citizens to provide support to Canadian independence movement rebels against British forces in Canada. The British forces entered the United States and set fire to the vessel, destroying it. The destruction of the Caroline outraged civilians on both sides of the U.S.-Canadian border. The British claimed that they attacked the Caroline in self-defense. United States Secretary of State Daniel Webster responded that the employment of force might have been justified by the necessity of self-defense but that, in the present circumstances, no such necessity existed. He negotiated with Alexander Baring, 1st Baron Ashburton, who argued that the British were excused for their act under the circumstances but nonetheless apologized for the incursion on United States territory.

The negotiation between Webster and Baring gave rise to a principle of international law that holds that a state may only engage in *anticipatory self-defense* when it can show "a necessity of self-defense, instant, overwhelming, leaving no choice of means, and no moment for deliberation." A state does not need to suffer an actual armed attack before it may take defensive action. This principle has since formed a part of customary international law. Known as "anticipatory self-defense," the doctrine, which extends beyond the black letter language of Article 51, justifies the use of force in anticipation of an "imminent" armed attack. Under this doctrine, a state does not need to wait until it is attacked before it may employ armed force; it may act in anticipatory self-defense when doing so is both necessary and proportional.

It is important to note that the principle of anticipatory self-defense under the *Caroline* case is separate and distinct from the doctrine of "preemptive strike" propagated by United States President George W. Bush. The doctrine of "preemptive strike" involves a more aggressive use of preventative force that is controversial, not commonly accepted, and deemed to be illegal under international law by a significant number of scholars.

D Consent

In addition to the use of force as a Chapter VII collective security measure (Article 42 Charter) and in Chapter VII self-defense (Article 51 Charter), consent provides a legal basis for the use of force. However, consent is not an "exception" to the principle of non-interference because there can be no "interference" in the internal affairs of a state when that state has authorized a third state's use of force within its territory. Moreover, while Chapter VII collective security measures and self-defense normally act as a basis for the use of force in international armed conflict, consent normally falls within the context of non-international armed conflicts.

E Contemporary Context of Cyberattacks

1 *Overview*

Cyberattacks are attempts by hackers to damage or destroy computer information systems, networks, systems or personal computer devices. Cyberattacks generally originate from anonymous sources that steal, alter or destroy specified targets by hacking into systems. Within the context of government-to-government attacks, cyberattacks are often referred to as cyber warfare or cyberterrorism. Within this context, a growing number of commentators hold that cyberattacks that are tantamount to the use of force trigger a right to respond in self-defense through the use of force.

2 *The* Tallinn Manual

The *Tallinn Manual on the International Law Applicable to Cyber Warfare*, commonly referred to as the *Tallinn Manual*, is an academic study on how international law applies to cyber conflicts and cyber warfare. The *Tallinn Manual* was written between 2009 and 2012 at the invitation of the Tallinn-based NATO Cooperative Cyber Defence Centre of Excellence by an international group of 20 experts and was published by Cambridge University Press in 2013.

The original *Tallinn Manual*, which was published in 2013, addressed cyber operations that violate the prohibition of the use of force, entitle states to exercise their right of self-defense or occur during armed conflict. The original manual was revised and published in 2017 as the *Tallinn Manual 2.0*, expanding the original edition with considerations of the rules of international law governing cyber incidents that states encounter on a day-to-day basis that fall below the thresholds of the use of force or armed conflict. The *Tallinn Manual* is currently being revised with a view to publish an update, the *Tallinn Manual 3.0*.

3 *Cyberattacks as Acts of Aggression in the* Tallinn Manual

a *Cyberattacks as a "Use of Force"*

To qualify as a crime of aggression under the Rome Statute, an act must constitute a use of "armed force" by a state against the sovereignty, territorial integrity or political independence of another state or in any other manner inconsistent with the Charter of the U.N. In addition, the act must constitute a manifest violation of the Charter of the U.N.

The *Tallinn Manual 2.0* states as follows with respect to the use of force:

Rule 10—Prohibition of Threat or Use of Force

> A cyber operation that constitutes a threat or use of force against the territorial integrity or political independence of any State, or that is in any other manner inconsistent with the purpose of the United Nations, is unlawful.
>
> Rule 11—Definition of Use of Force
>
> A cyber operation constitutes a use of force when its scale and effects are comparable to non-cyber operations rising to the level of a use of force.

The definition in the *Tallinn Manual* makes clear that cyber operations can constitute a use of force. Therefore, a cyberattack by one state against another could potentially constitute a violation of Article 2.4 of the U.N. Charter, which prohibits "the threat or use of force against the territorial integrity or political independence of any state, or in any other manner inconsistent with the Purposes of the United Nations."

b Cyberattacks as "Armed Attacks"

A cyberattack could constitute an act of aggression under the Rome Statute if the cyberattack's "use of force" constitutes "armed force." The *Tallinn Manual 2.0* discusses the distinction between a "use of force" and an "armed attack," articulating the two alternative positions addressed below.

i A Use of Force Constitutes an Armed Attack Based on Its Gravity

Under the first position, a use of force constitutes an armed attack if it crosses a threshold of gravity. The Group of Experts characterizes an "armed attack" as a more severe form of a use of force, one that triggers the right to self-defense:

> In determining whether an act constitutes a "use of force," it is useful to consider the notion of "armed attack," which is the threshold at which a State may lawfully use force in self-defence (Rule 13). In the *Nicaragua* Judgment, the International Court of Justice distinguished the "most grave" forms of the "use of force" (those constituting an "armed attack" for the purposes of the law of self-defense) from other less grave forms. The International Group of Experts agreed, therefore, that any cyber operation which rises to the level of an "armed attack" in terms of scale and effects pursuant to Rule 13, and which is conducted by or otherwise attributed to a State, qualifies as a "use of force."[36]

On this basis, it can be concluded that a cyberattack that constitutes a "use of force," based on its scale and effects, could also constitute an "armed attack" for purposes of the crime of aggression, depending on the gravity of the attack.

ii Uses of Force Are Interchangeable with Armed Attacks

The Group of Experts articulates a contrary position, which equates a "use of force" with an "armed attack," treating them interchangeably:

---

36. Michael N. Schmitt (ed.), *Tallinn Manual 2.0 on the International Law Applicable to Cyber Operations*, Cambridge University Press (Cambridge, 2017), pp. 48-49, para. 6.

> [T]he distinction between the two concepts is either so narrow as to be insignificant or nonexistent. This position, articulated by the United States after the *Nicaragua* decision, asserts that any illegal use of force can qualify as an armed attack triggering the right of self-defense; there is no gravity threshold distinguishing illegal uses of force from armed attacks. On this view, no gap exists between an unlawful use of force and an armed attack.[37]

The commentary to Rule 11 goes on to discuss the criteria for determining when a cyberattack constitutes an armed attack. It draws on the same criteria that it cites for determining when a cyberattack constitutes a use of force; one must examine the "scale and effects" of the attack:

> In discussions regarding the appropriate threshold for a use of force, the International Group of Experts took notice of the *Nicaragua* Judgment. In that case, the International Court of Justice stated that 'scale and effects' are to be considered when determining whether particular actions amount to an 'armed attack' (Rule 13). The Experts found the focus on scale and effects to be an equally useful approach when distinguishing acts that qualify as uses of force from those that do not.[38]

Under this second position, a cyberattack could constitute both a use of force and an armed attack based on an analysis of its scale and effects.

iii Conclusion: Cyberattacks Could Constitute "Armed" Attacks

Regardless of which position one adopts, it is clear that a cyberattack, on its own, could constitute an "armed attack" for purposes of the crime of aggression and that triggers the existence of an armed conflict and the right of self-defense of the victim state.

VII CONTEMPORARY CHALLENGES TO STATE SOVEREIGNTY

A Responsibility to Protect ("R2P")

1 Introduction to State Sovereignty

Military intervention in a foreign state has traditionally been an affront to one of the original general principles of law—state sovereignty. However, there are cases where invading a foreign state is justified, such as when such military action is necessary for a state's self-defense or when it is justified as retaliation after an attack.

It is unclear whether there is a duty to infringe on a foreign state's sovereignty for humanitarian purposes, such as protecting the foreign state's population against crimes at the hands of the state (*see* "The Development of the Responsibility to Protect Doctrine," *infra*, for further discussion).

37. *Ibid.*, p. 49, para. 7.
38. *Ibid.*, p. 47, para. 1.

2 *Affirmative Duty to Act under International Treaties*

Multiple international treaties codify an affirmative duty to act or a duty to rescue.

a Genocide Convention (1948)

Some international treaties codify a clear duty to act within certain contexts. For example, the Convention on the Prevention and Punishment of the Crime of Genocide ("CPPG") creates an affirmative duty to protect. For further detail and discussion, *see* "Affirmative Duty to Act" under "Convention on the Prevention and Punishment of the Crime of Genocide (1948)," *infra*.

b Geneva Conventions (1949)

As discussed under "State Responsibility to 'Respect and Ensure Respect,'" *infra*, Article 1, common to the four Geneva Conventions of 1949, requires states parties to "*respect* and to *ensure respect* for the present Convention *in all circumstances*" (emphasis added). Therefore, states have an affirmative duty to not only respect, but also to ensure the respect of international humanitarian law. Moreover, no derogation is permitted from these duties, which apply "in all circumstances." The duty to "ensure respect" of the Geneva Conventions effectively means that states not involved in an armed conflict must call upon states that *are* involved in the armed conflict to ensure that they respect the rules.

Moreover, the Geneva Conventions "grave breaches" Articles (Article 49 GC I; Article 50 GC II; Article 129 GC III; Article 146 GC IV) create affirmative duties that require states parties to enact legislation necessary to provide effective penal sanctions for persons who have committed grave breaches of the Conventions and search for perpetrators and bring them before its own courts for prosecution or extradite them to other states for prosecution.

c International Covenant on Civil and Political Rights (1966)

Similarly, the International Covenant on Civil and Political Rights ("ICCPR") requires that states agree not only to refrain from violating basic rights such as the right to life (Article 6 ICCPR), freedom of thought, conscience and religion (Article 18 ICCPR) and freedom of expression (Article 19 ICCPR), but also that they ensure the protection of these rights from other member states' violations (Article 2(3) ICCPR). Under Sub-Clauses (a), (b) and (c) of Article 2(3) of the ICCPR, states parties to the ICCPR undertake:

> (a) To *ensure that any person whose rights or freedoms as herein recognized are violated shall have an effective remedy*, notwithstanding that the violation has been committed by persons acting in an official capacity.

(b) To ensure that any person claiming such a remedy *shall have his right thereto determined by competent judicial, administrative or legislative authorities*, or by any other competent authority provided for by the legal system of the state, and to develop the possibilities of judicial remedy.
(c) To ensure that the competent authorities *shall enforce such remedies when granted.*

The ICCPR thus not only prohibits states parties from violating civil and political rights but also requires them to act to ensure the protection of these rights. It thus incorporates an affirmative duty to act.

d United Nations Convention on the Law of the Sea (1982)

Under the United Nations Convention on the Law of the Sea (1982) ("UNCLOS"), every state party shall (Article 98.1 UNCLOS):

> require the master of a ship flying its flag, in so far as he can do so without serious danger to the ship, the crew or the passengers:
>
> (a) to render assistance to any person found at sea in *danger of being lost*;
> (b) to proceed with all possible speed to the *rescue of persons in distress*, if informed of their need of assistance, in so far as such action may reasonably be expected of him;
> (c) after a collision, to *render assistance* to the other ship, its crew and its passengers and, where possible, to inform the other ship of the name of his own ship, its port of registry and the nearest port at which it will call.

UNCLOS further requires every coastal state to "promote the establishment, operation and maintenance of an adequate and effective search and rescue service regarding safety on and over the sea and, where circumstances so require, by way of mutual regional arrangements cooperate with neighbouring States for this purpose" (Article 98.2 UNCLOS).

e Convention Against Torture and Other Cruel, Inhuman or Degrading Treatment or Punishment (1984)

It has been suggested in international jurisprudence that the Convention against Torture and Other Cruel, Inhuman or Degrading Treatment or Punishment (1984) creates an obligation on states to try or prosecute alleged torturers and that this obligation has an *erga omnes* ("toward all") character.[39]

39. *Questions relating to the Obligation to Prosecute or Extradite (Belgium v. Senegal)*, ICJ Reports (20 July 2012), para. 103.

3 *The Development of the Responsibility to Protect Doctrine*

a *Overview*

Given the experience of the twentieth century, which saw countless episodes of genocide, war crimes, crimes against humanity and crimes of aggression go unpunished by the international community, a series of states and international organizations have come to recognize an emerging principle of international law designed to protect citizens from egregious violations of international law at the hands of their own states. The United Nations 2005 World Summit declared that "there can be no development without security, no security without development, and neither without the universal application and protection of human rights" and called for "the acceptance of a universal principle of the *responsibility to protect civilian populations from crimes against humanity when Governments are unwilling or unable to do so.*"[40] This increasingly recognized yet controversial doctrine came to be known as the Responsibility to Protect ("R2P") doctrine.

Under this doctrine, the international community has a duty to intervene when a people suffers from egregious acts of violence at the hands of their state or as a result of their state's inability or unwillingness to protect its people. In such cases, the R2P doctrine demands that the duty of the international community to protect the population trump the principle of sovereignty of the state in question.

b *Controversy of Doctrine*

In a 2000 address to the United Nations, Secretary-General Kofi Annan recognized the inherent conflict between state sovereignty and the new, emerging R2P doctrine, which undermines state sovereignty. Acknowledging the atrocities of the previous decade, he asked: "if humanitarian intervention is, indeed, an unacceptable assault on sovereignty, how should we respond to a Rwanda, to a Srebrenica—to gross and systematic violations of human rights that offend every precept of our common humanity?"[41]

The R2P doctrine, which holds that states have a duty to intervene in foreign humanitarian crises, even without Security Council authorization, remains deeply controversial. Most prominently, the doctrine was used to justify NATO's 1999 military intervention in Kosovo. There, Russia vetoed United Nations collective security action under the U.N. Charter, yet NATO nonetheless undertook military action. Some observers agreed that NATO's actions were legitimate and justified under international

40. "The 2005 World Summit: An Overview," High Level Plenary Meeting, United Nations Information Service (2005), available at <https://unis.unvienna.org/pdf/Overview_Summit_22July.pdf>.
41. Eve Massingham, "Military intervention for humanitarian purposes: does the Responsibility to Protect doctrine advance the legality of the use of force for humanitarian ends?," 91(876) *International Review of the Red Cross* (December 2009), p. 804 available at <https://doi.org/10.1017/s1816383110000068>.

law, though they may not have been technically compliant with the black letter of the law.[42]

c *International Commission on Intervention and State Sovereignty*

In response to Kofi Annan's 2000 address to the United Nations, the Canadian government formed the International Commission on Intervention and State Sovereignty ("ICISS"). In December 2001, ICISS concluded that when the state is unable or unwilling to fulfill its sovereign responsibility, "it becomes the responsibility of the international community to act in its place." On this basis, intervention does not contradict the principle of sovereignty but rather complements it in situations in which the state fails to meet its responsibility.[43]

ICISS came to the conclusion that four prerequisites are required to invoke a responsibility to protect foreign citizens from their government through military intervention. Under the Principles for Military Intervention, a military intervention must fulfill the following criteria:[44,45]

(1) The Just Cause Threshold
   - "To be warranted, there must be serious and irreparable harm occurring to human beings, or imminently likely to occur";

(2) The Precautionary Principles
   - Right intention: "The primary purpose of the intervention, whatever other motives intervening states may have, must be to halt or avert human suffering";

---

42. David Forsythe, "The UN Security Council and Human Rights: Promising Developments, Persistent Problems," 13(2) *Journal of Human Rights* (2014), p. 128 available at <https://doi.org/10.1080/14754835.2014.886945> ("According to an international commission established by the Canadian government, the NATO air strikes were said to be morally legitimate even if not 'technically' legal").
43. Mehrdad Payandeh, "With Great Power Comes Great Responsibility? The Concept of the Responsibility to Protect Within the Process of International Lawmaking," 35 *Yale Journal of International Law* (2009), p. 473 (quoting *Int'l Comm'n on Intervention & State Sovereignty, the Responsibility to Protect* (2001) at 2.29).
44. Gareth Evans et al., *The Responsibility to Protect: Report of the International Commission on Intervention and State Sovereignty*, International Development Research Centre (Ottawa, 2001), XII-XIII.
45. For a comparison of the conditions for a just war under the *Catechism of the Catholic Church* and the ICISS Guidelines, see "Just War Theory under the *Catechism of the Catholic Church* and the ICISS Guidelines Combined" in the Appendices, *infra*.

    Notably, all six of these elements fall within the Catholic Church's requirements for a war to be classified as "just." According to the *Catechism of the Catholic Church*, the following elements apply:

    - Right intention.
    - Last resort.
    - Proportionality.
    - Reasonable prospect of success.
    - Legitimate authority.
    - Just cause.
    - Grave damage from the aggressor (the damage inflicted on the people under the control of the aggressor must be lasting, grave and certain).

- Last resort: "Military intervention can only be justified when every non-military option for the prevention or peaceful resolution of the crisis has been explored, with reasonable grounds for believing lesser measures would not have succeeded";
- Proportional means: "The scale, duration and intensity of the planned military intervention should be the minimum necessary to secure the defined human protection objective";
- Reasonable prospects: "There must be a reasonable chance of success in halting or averting the suffering which has justified the intervention, with the consequences of action not likely to be worse than the consequences of inaction";

(3) Right Authority
- "There is no better or more appropriate body than the United Nations Security Council to authorize military intervention for human protection purposes ...
- "Security Council authorization should in all cases be sought prior to any military intervention action being carried out. Those calling for an intervention should formally request such authorization, or have the Council raise the matter on its own initiative, or have the Secretary-General raise it under Article 99 of the U.N. Charter ...
- "The Security Council should take into account in all its deliberations that, if it fails to discharge its responsibility to protect in conscience-shocking situations crying out for action, concerned states may not rule out other means to meet the gravity and urgency of that situation—and that the stature and credibility of the United Nations may suffer thereby."

(4) Operational Principles
- A. Clear objectives; "clear and unambiguous mandate at all times; and resources to match";
- B. Common military approach among involved partners, including unity of command;
- C. Acceptance of limitations, incrementalism and gradualism in the application of force;
- D. Rules of engagement which fit the operational concept are precise, reflect the principle of proportionality, and adhere to international humanitarian law;
- E. Acceptance that force protection cannot become the principal objective; and
- F. Maximum coordination with humanitarian organizations.

Although the responsibility for maintaining international peace and security is vested in the U.N. Security Council of the U.N. (Article 24.I Charter), the ICISS report cautiously approached the question of intervening with single state or coalition military forces without Security Council approval, invoking a duty to protect. The ICISS stated that, on the one hand, "there will be damage to the international order if the Security Council is bypassed." On the other hand, there will be "damage to that order if human beings are slaughtered while the Security Council stands by."

The ICISS thereby cautioned the Security Council that single states or coalitions might undertake action under the R2P doctrine if the Security Council fails to act.[46]

46. Payandeh, *supra* (quoting *Int'l Comm'n on Intervention & State Sovereignty, the Responsibility to Protect* at 6.37).

B Humanitarian Intervention

Humanitarian intervention may be a new and emerging standard under customary international law. Like responsibility to protect, it should be seen as a possible exception to Article 2.4 of the U.N. Charter. However, unlike responsibility to protect, which can be seen as compatible with U.N. Charter Chapter VII action, humanitarian intervention is often discussed as an alternative justification for the intervention in another state's affairs absent U.N. Security Council authorization and based on moral and humanitarian grounds. It is thus a developing, albeit controversial, justification for action.

Humanitarian intervention has, to an extent, watered down the principle of non-intervention and respect for state sovereignty in circumstances in which a state is unable or unwilling to avert a humanitarian catastrophe or is itself responsible for the catastrophe or for large-scale human rights violations of its own citizens.

There is a fine line in the distinction between humanitarian intervention and responsibility to protect. The latter can be seen as having a more aggressive posture vis-à-vis state sovereignty than responsibility to protect. In practice, however, the two are often incorrectly interchangeably used.

C The "Unwilling or Unable" Standard for Self-Defense against Non-state Actors

In some contemporary contexts, non-state actors launch armed attacks from within the territory of "host" states. Some scholars maintain that when such host states are "unwilling or unable" to deal with the non-state actors who are launching the armed attacks, cross-border attacks against the actors are permitted without the consent of the host states. In *War, Aggression and Self-Defence*, for example, Yoram Dinstein writes that a state is "entitled to enforce international law extra-territorially if and when [the other state] is unable or unwilling to prevent repetition of that armed attack."[47] Some scholars argue that such cross-border attacks into a host state require the victim state to meet a higher burden of proof in demonstrating the criteria that trigger that state's right to the use of force in self-defense.

The "unwilling or unable" standard for self-defense against non-state actors should not be viewed as a third exception to Article 2.4 Charter non-interference in the internal affairs of states. Rather, it should be viewed in parallel with Article 51 Charter self-defense, the only difference being that while Article 51 is silent on the question of whether a host state may be attacked for the acts of a non-state actor within its borders, the "unwilling or unable" standard affirms that it may.

As of the time of this writing, the following ten nations have explicitly endorsed the "unwilling or unable" standard: Australia, Canada, Czech Republic, Germany, Israel, The Netherlands, Russia, Turkey, the United Kingdom and the United States.[48]

47. Yoram Dinstein, *War, Aggression and Self-Defence*, Cambridge University Press, 5th Ed. (New York, 2011), p. 272.
48. Elena Chachko and Ashley Deeks, "Who is on Board with 'Unwilling or Unable'?" International Law, *Lawfare* (10 October 2016).

CHAPTER 5
International Human Rights Law

I INTRODUCTION

A General Overview

One phenomenon that has led to rapid developments in international law and the structure of the international legal system is the *increased* and *nearly universal* recognition of the protection of human rights as a proper concern of international law, beginning first with the Universal Declaration of Human Rights and later with multiple U.N. and regional treaties that proliferated in the 1960s and 1970s, including the International Covenant on Civil and Political Rights (1966); the International Covenant on Economic, Social and Cultural Rights (1966); Convention on the Elimination of All Forms of Racial Discrimination (1966); and the Convention on the Elimination of All Forms of Discrimination against Women (1979).

B Human Rights Law and the Principle of Non-intervention

It is a principle of customary international law that states and international organizations may not interfere or intervene in matters within the domestic jurisdiction of other states. This principle is enshrined in the Charter, which states: "Nothing contained in the present Charter shall authorize the United Nations to intervene in matters which are essentially within the domestic jurisdiction of any state or shall require the Members to submit such matters to settlement under the present Charter" (Article 2.7 Charter).

Under this historic principle, state acts with respect to purely domestic affairs have traditionally been shielded by immunity in the international arena. This has been the case even when state acts violate the rights of the state's own people. International law historically only applied when *foreign* nationals fall victim to the crimes of a state.

After WWII, however, this changed. Due to the atrocities committed in the war, the Allied Powers made a firm commitment not to allow the German and Japanese authorities responsible for war crimes, including those who committed such crimes against their own citizens, to go free under the principle of non-intervention. To do so would be a miscarriage of justice. Under this exception to the principle of non-intervention, the International Military Tribunal and IMTFE were established to try the war crimes of Nazi Germany and Imperial Japan.

Practice thus departed from precedent with the establishment of these military tribunals. Since then, in cases involving the most egregious crimes, international human rights law has ignored the principle of non-intervention. Under current practice, states are obliged under their human rights treaties to respect the rights of both their own citizens as well as aliens within their borders, and other states or international organizations may intervene to ensure that these rights are respected if a state fails to insure them. The Charter incorporates this premise when articulating an exception to the general rule of sovereignty: the principle of non-intervention "shall not prejudice the application of enforcement measures under Chapter VII [of the Charter]" (Article 2.7 Charter).

II UNIVERSALITY OF INTERNATIONAL HUMAN RIGHTS STANDARDS

A Historical Background

Western democracies have long held that human rights standards are universally valid. *The English Declaration of Rights and Liberties of the Subject* enumerated "rights and liberties" that were deemed to be "ancient" rather than limited to a particular epoch. The United States *Declaration of Independence* held as "self-evident" truths that all men are "created equal" and endowed with rights to "life, liberty, and the pursuit of happiness." The *French Declaration of the Rights of Man* and of the Citizen defined man's rights to "liberty, property, security and resistance to oppression" as "natural, unalienable, and sacred rights" established by unchanging natural law principles "under the auspices of the Supreme Being."

These instruments are seen by many commentators as precursors to the Universal Declaration of Human Rights ("UDHR"), which the international community has repeatedly affirmed as an expression of binding, universal rights. U.N. General Assembly Resolution 60/1 of 16 September 2005, for example, affirmed states' "solemn commitment" to protect human rights in accordance with the UDHR and held that the "universal nature of these rights and freedoms is beyond question." While states repeatedly affirm the universal nature of human rights, some question whether rights are truly universal.

B First- and Second-Order Rights

1 *Natural Law Principles*

One finds, across time and culture, shared core beliefs that exist on a moral and ethical level that transcends national systems. These core beliefs encompass principles of justice, mercy, good faith and veracity. One finds, for example, a law of general beneficence common to various cultures and ancient religious traditions:[49]

> "Speak kindness ... show good will." (Babylonian. *Hymn to Samaš. ERE* v. 445)
> "Men were brought into existence for the sake of men that they might do one another good." (Roman. Cicero, *De Off.*, I. vii)
> "Man is man's delight." (Old Norse. *Hávamál* 47)
> "He who is asked for alms should always give." (Hindu. Janet, i. 7)
> "When the people have multiplied, what next should be done for them? The Master said, Enrich them. Jan Ch'iu said, When one has enriched them, what next should be done for them? The Master said, Instruct them." (Ancient Chinese. *Analects*, xiii. 9)
> "What good man regards any misfortune as no concern of his?" (Roman. Juvenal xv. 140)
> "I am a man: nothing human is alien to me." (Roman. Terence, *Heaut. Tim.*)
> "Love thy neighbour as thyself ... Love the stranger as thyself" (Ancient Jewish. Leviticus 19:18, 33, 34)
> "Do to men what you wish men to do to you." (Christian. Matt. 7:12)

Similarly, the African concept of "*ubuntu*," which encompasses respect for human dignity, compassion, and justice, has permeated African societies from before the era of modern human rights instruments.[50]

2 *Inherent, Universal First-Order Rights*

a *Overview*

Human rights based on natural law principles that transcend culture include the rights to life, equality and human dignity, and prohibitions of genocide, crimes against humanity, torture and slavery, which are incompatible with life, quality and dignity. These rights are both universal and inherent:

- As universal rights, they are held by all people at all times. They are not dependent on one's race, ethnicity, nationality, religion or membership in a particular social or economic group. Rather, they are based on the "equal moral status" of all individuals."[51]

---

49. Compiled in "Appendix-Illustrations of the *Tao*," in C.S. Lewis, *The Abolition of Man*, HarperOne (2015), p. 83.
50. *See* Desmond Tutu, "Who we are: Human uniqueness and the African spirit of Ubuntu," available at <https://www.youtube.com/watch?v=0wZtfqZ271w#t=162>.
51. Samantha Besson, "Justifications," in Daniel Moeckli et al. (eds.), *International Human Rights Law*, Oxford University Press (2018), p. 32.

- As inherent rights, all people enjoy them simply by virtue of their being human. They are thus "inalienable rights, because being or not being human usually is seen as an inalterable fact of nature, not something that is either earned or can be lost."[52] Human rights are not dependent on any individual's achievements; they are not earned by working hard, achieving success or being born into a particular socioeconomic group. They are freely enjoyed by all people equally.

While first-order rights are universal, they may be subject to differing expressions. For example, the Cairo Declaration on Human Rights in Islam (1990) expresses many of the same principles enshrined in the UDHR, such as the rights to life (Article 2) and property (Article 15) and prohibitions on slavery and colonization (Article 11), but others, given the Islamic context, vary. *See* "Cairo Declaration on Human Rights in Islam (1990)," *infra*, for a discussion.

b *Evidence of Universal First-Order Rights*

Starting with the principle of equal status and universal rights in the moral realm, societies build legal frameworks to protect human rights in the political realm.[53] To determine the substantive content of universal first-order rights, we must look to universally adopted human rights declarations and treaties, which enunciate "particular principles, aspirations and ideals of universal and enduring significance."[54] These human rights instruments "do not legislate human rights; they 'recognize' them and build upon that recognition," which assumes the human rights' "preexistence in some other moral or legal order."[55] Where they have been universally adopted, they serve as evidence of first-order universal rights.

The Charter of the U.N. ("Charter"), for example, has been adopted by 193 states,[56] making it one of the most universally adopted treaties in history. The Charter states that one of its purposes is to promote "respect for human rights and for fundamental freedoms for all without distinction as to race, sex, language, or religion" (Article 1.3 Charter). This is reemphasized in Article 55, which declares that "the United Nations shall promote ... universal respect for and observance of, human rights and fundamental freedoms for all without distinction as to race, sex, language, or religion" (Article 55 Charter). That the whole of the international community came together to express a commitment to these rights is evidence that they constitute first-order universal standards outside of national legal systems.

---

52. Jack Donnelly, "The Relative Universality of Human Rights," 29 *Human Rights Quarterly* (2007), pp. 282-283 available at <https://doi.org/10.1353/hrq.2007.0016>.
53. Samantha Besson, "Justifications," in Daniel Moeckli et al. (eds.), *International Human Rights Law*, Oxford University Press (Oxford, 2018), pp. 33-34.
54. *Adela Chiminya Tachiona v. Mugabe*, 234 F. Supp. 2d 401 (S.D.N.Y., 2002), at 409.
55. Louis Henkin (ed.), *The International Bill of Rights*, Columbia University Press (1981), pp. 12, 15.
56. The only recognized sovereign State that is not a member to the U.N. is the Holy See (Vatican City), which is a U.N. permanent observer.

3 *Distinguishing Second-Order Rights*

First-order rights are a very special set of extraordinary, basic, inherent interests that are held at all times by all people "simply because one is human."[57] Yet, not all human rights can be said to be first-order rights. Important cultural and political differences exist with respect to second-order relative rights, allowing for "a form of universalism that also allows substantial space for important (second-order) claims of relativism."[58] For example, whether a person has a right to demand that the collective community provide, at the community's expense, an education, housing, or clean water is not the subject of first-order rights but of second-order rights subject to political preference.

One finds differences across cultures as to whether such rights should be recognized. For example, philosophical considerations as to whether the individual as *homme* or as the communal *citoyen* is the proper subject of the social contract may lead to the recognition of economic rights.[59] Similarly, politics may play a factor, as was the case of the international community's split when negotiating the ICCPR and ICESCR in the 1960s, with some nations fearing that the recognition of social rights would be a first step toward certain people groups declaring independence.[60] Yet even with this split as to second-order rights, one finds first-order rights common to even the ICCPR and ICESCR, both of which prohibit discrimination and uphold equality and other first-order rights.

C Critiques

1 *Universalism: Abuse and Arrogance*

Some criticize universalism for its abusive effects, including justifying violence. Jochen von Bernstorff observed that "recent Western interventions in Kosovo (1999), Afghanistan (2001), and Iraq (2003) all had in common that their official justifications made ample references to the negative human rights record of the invaded country."[61] Yet the question of whether violence is the proper response to a state that allegedly engaged in acts of genocide (e.g., Bosnia), shelters terrorists (e.g., the Islamic Emirate of Afghanistan) or harbors prohibited weapons (e.g., Iraq) is a separate question of whether universal rights exist on a moral plane in the first place.

---

57. Donnelly, p. 282.
58. *Ibid.*, p. 301.
59. *See, e.g.*, Karl Marx, *On the Jewish Question*, Grapevine (1843, republished in 2023) ("the so-called rights of man, the *droits de l'homme* as distinct from the *droits du citoyen*, are nothing but the rights of a member of civil society ... separated from other men and from the community").
60. *See* Andrew Clapham, *Human Rights: A Very Short Introduction*, Oxford University Press (2015), p. 51.
61. Jochen von Bernstorff, "The Changing Fortunes of the Universal Declaration of Human Rights: Genesis and Symbolic Dimensions of the Turn to Rights in International Law," 19(5) *European Journal of International Law* (2008), p. 921 available at <https://doi.org/10.1093/ejil/chn069>.

Others accuse universalism of "having a bad side–arrogance."[62] However, regardless of whether the imposition of universal standards can be offensive or viewed as arrogant, states have a duty, by the very treaties to which they have acceded, to uphold and defend non-derogable rights and prohibit violations, such as genocide. Yet others argue that the idea of universal human rights is exploited for political purposes and that states only comply with their human rights obligations when it is in their interest to do so. Here, it would be necessary to point out that "almost all nations observe almost all principles of international law and almost all of their obligations almost all the time."[63] While violations of law attract attention, the "daily, sober loyalty of nations to the law and their obligations is hardly noted."[64]

2 *Cultural Relativism: Confusing Clear Standards*

Rejecting universalism brings with it grave dangers. To embrace cultural relativism and rely on norms or practices that conflict with universal rights diminishes standards, confuses clear rules and creates a sense that international human rights law is just one of many sets of norms. Cultural relativism may lead to the assertion that societal practices that fall short of universal standards must be tolerated, leading to the "danger of inaction or indifference."[65] This may result in the denial of the rights of minority groups or women on the basis of religious practice or local tradition, which can, in turn, perpetuate violence.

D Conclusion

On the basis of the foregoing, we can conclude that human rights are universal, though they may be expressed in different cultural terms and may be accompanied by second-order rights specific to a particular cultural or political context. While first-order rights are always non-derogable, second-order rights tolerate a degree of variance based on local context, provided they do not conflict with universal first-order rights.

III SOURCES OF INTERNATIONAL HUMAN RIGHTS LAW

Because human rights law is primarily treaty-based, states not party to human rights treaties are not bound by them. However, treaties that have been universally or nearly universally adopted may become sources of customary international law binding even over groups that have not formally accepted their terms.

62. *See* Marie-Bénédicte Dembour, "Critiques," in Daniel Moeckli et al. (eds.), *International Human Rights Law*, Oxford University Press (2018), p. 52.
63. Louis Henkin, *How Nations Behave*, Columbia University Press (1979), p. 47.
64. *Ibid.*
65. Dembour, pp. 51-52.

Human rights law is also partially contained in non-codified customary international law as well as in non-binding international declarations. It may also be contained in general principles of law.

In the domestic sphere, human rights, often termed "civil rights," are governed by statutes or by constitutional guarantees, as is the case of England, the United States and France.

A Origins of Human Rights Law in Domestic Law: The Case of the Common Law

Human rights have developed, first in domestic law, from as early as the English *Magna Carta*, which is widely accepted to be the "mother document" of human rights instruments. In response to abuses under King John's tyrannical rule and application of the principle *Rex Lex* ("the king is the law"), English barons revolted and forced the King to sign the *Magna Carta* in 1215 to protect citizens' rights under the principle of the rule of law (*Lex Rex*—the law is king). The *Magna Carta* established the right of the Church to be free from the interference of the king, the protection of private property, habeas corpus, due process in civil and criminal proceedings and taxation by consent.

From the *Magna Carta* came other developments in English law that would ultimately have an international influence in nations such as the United States and France. With tensions under King Charles I rising, the Upper and Lower Houses of Parliament eventually conditioned their cooperation with Charles in raising taxes on the king's signing of the *1628 Petition of Right*, which was drawn up by Edward Coke to protect rights, including taxation only with representation and the prohibition of arbitrary imprisonment. It also protected the rule of law and petitioned the king to remove stationed soldiers and mariners who obliged the citizens to receive them into their homes. The Glorious Revolution in England gave way to the Declaration of Rights and Liberties of the Subject, which would in 1689 be enacted as a statute entitled the "Bill of Rights," which echoed many of the elements of the Petition of Right in 1628 under King Charles, such as the prohibition of taxation without representation and of standing armies in times of peace. The list of enumerated rights also set limitations on royal power.

The English Bill of Rights foreshadowed and, to an extent, inspired the American Bill of Rights, which was introduced to the first United States Congress in 1789 as a series of legislative articles and came into effect as Constitutional Amendments in 1791 through the process of ratification by three-fourths of the states. The United States Bill of Rights, among its other provisions, limits the powers of the federal government, guarantees freedom of religion, freedom of speech and of the press, free assembly and free association, the right to bear arms, the right to a speedy trial with an impartial jury, the right not to be forced to testify against oneself and due process under law and reserves for the people any rights not specifically enumerated in the Constitution.

The French model, in some ways, follows this same tradition. In France, the Declaration of the Rights of Man and of the Citizen, adopted in 1791, serves as a bill of rights that defines man's rights to "liberty, property, security and resistance to oppression." It called for the destruction of aristocratic privileges, the restriction of the monarchy and popular sovereignty with all citizens taking part. Freedom of speech and the press were declared, arbitrary arrests were outlawed, and the rights of man were held to be universally valid at all times and in all places. The French Declaration of the Rights of Man and of the Citizen is seen by many as a precursor to the U.N.'s Universal Declaration of Human Rights.

B United Nations Treaties and Conventions

1 *United Nations Charter (1945)*

The Charter states that one of the purposes of the U.N. is to achieve "international co-operation in ... promoting and encouraging respect for human rights and for fundamental freedoms for all without distinction as to race, sex, language, or religion" (Article 1.3 Charter). This is reemphasized in Article 55, which declares that "the United Nations shall promote ... universal respect for and observance of, human rights and fundamental freedoms for all without distinction as to race, sex, language, or religion" (Article 55 Charter). However, because the only concrete human right expressly mentioned in the Charter is non-discrimination ("distinction as to race, sex, language, or religion"), members of the U.N. came together to draft the UDHR (*see supra*), which more clearly defines the human rights to be protected in the international order. The UDHR, because it is not binding, in turn gave rise to two other instruments: the International Covenant on Civil and Political Rights and the International Covenant on Economic, Social and Cultural Rights (*see infra*), both binding instruments.

2 *Convention on the Prevention and Punishment of the Crime of Genocide (1948)*

a *Overview*

The Convention on the Prevention and Punishment of the Crime of Genocide (the "Genocide Convention" or "CPPG") was adopted by the U.N. General Assembly on 9 December 1948, just one day before the adoption of the Universal Declaration of Human Rights.

b *Definition of Genocide*

The Convention, which entered into force in 1951, defines genocide in its Article II as:

> any of the following acts committed with intent to destroy, in whole or in part, a national, ethnical, racial or religious group, as such:
>
> (a) killing members of the group;
> (b) causing serious bodily or mental harm to members of the group;

(c) deliberately inflicting on the group conditions of life calculated to bring about its physical destruction in whole or in part;
(d) imposing measures intended to prevent births within the group;
(e) forcibly transferring children of the group to another group.

It is important to note that under this definition, the application of the Genocide Convention is not predicated on the existence of an armed conflict.

c *Individual Criminal Responsibility*

Article 4 of the Genocide Convention establishes the obligation to punish not only "rulers" or "public officials" who commit genocide but also "private individuals." The article states:

> Persons committing genocide or any of the other acts enumerated in article III shall be punished, whether they are constitutionally responsible rulers, public officials or private individuals.

Article 6 gives both domestic and international tribunals competence to try offenders.

d *Dispute Resolution Through the International Court of Justice*

Disputes between states parties to the Genocide Convention relating to the interpretation, application or fulfilment of the Convention, including those relating to the responsibility of a state for genocide or for any of the other acts enumerated in Article III (genocide, conspiracy to commit genocide, direct and public incitement to commit genocide, attempt to commit genocide and complicity in genocide), are to be submitted to the International Court of Justice at the request of any of the parties to the dispute (Article III CPPG).

e *Affirmative Duty to Act*

The Genocide Convention is an example of a human rights instrument that creates an affirmative duty to act. It requires not only that states parties refrain from the crime of genocide but also that they "undertake to prevent and to punish" genocide (Article I CPPG) and further pledge "to grant extradition in accordance with their laws and treaties in force" of persons charged with genocide (Article VII CPPG). The ICJ thus found in the Bosnian Genocide Case (*Bosnia and Herzegovina v. Serbia and Montenegro*) (2007) that Belgrade breached international law by failing to prevent the 1995 genocide in the town of Srebrenica (of the political entity Republika Srpska, within

Bosnia and Herzegovina) and for failing to try or transfer to the ICTY those accused of genocide, thus violating its obligations under the Genocide Convention.[66]

f *States Parties*

The Genocide Convention was opened for signature in 1948. As of 2023, 152 states have ratified or acceded to the treaty. One state, the Dominican Republic, has signed but not ratified the Convention.

The following are states parties to the Convention: Afghanistan, Albania, Algeria, Andorra, Antigua and Barbuda, Argentina, Armenia, Australia, Austria, Azerbaijan, Bahamas, Bahrain, Bangladesh, Barbados, Belarus, Belgium, Belize, Benin, Bolivia, Bosnia and Herzegovina, Brazil, Bulgaria, Burkina Faso, Burundi, Cambodia, Canada, Cape Verde, Chile, China, Colombia, Comoros, Costa Rica, Ivory Coast, Croatia, Cuba, Cyprus, Czech Republic, Democratic People's Republic of Korea (North Korea), Democratic Republic of the Congo, Denmark, Dominica, Ecuador, Egypt, El Salvador, Estonia, Ethiopia, Fiji, Finland, France, Gabon, Gambia, Georgia, Germany, Ghana, Greece, Guatemala, Guinea, Guinea-Bissau, Haiti, Honduras, Hungary, Iceland, India, Iran, Iraq, Ireland, Israel, Italy, Jamaica, Jordan, Kazakhstan, Kuwait, Kyrgyzstan, Laos, Latvia, Lebanon, Lesotho, Liberia, Libya, Liechtenstein, Lithuania, Luxembourg, Malaysia, Maldives, Mali, Malta, Mauritius, Mexico, Moldova, Monaco, Mongolia, Montenegro, Morocco, Mozambique, Myanmar, Namibia, Nepal, Netherlands, New Zealand, Nicaragua, Nigeria, Norway, Pakistan, Palestine, Panama, Papua New Guinea, Paraguay, Peru, Philippines, Poland, Portugal, North Macedonia, Republic of

66. The decision against Serbia and Montenegro was not framed exclusively as an Art. I failure to act; the International Court of Justice also examined whether Serbia and Montenegro had also committed genocide as defined under Art. II of the Convention. The Court concluded that the 1995 massacre of over 7,000 Bosnian Muslim men in the town of Srebrenica (of the political entity Republika Srpska, within Bosnia and Herzegovina) was an act that satisfied the *actus reus* requirement of sub-clauses (a) and (b) of Art. II of the Convention (killing members of a group and causing serious bodily or mental harm to members of the group, respectively). The Court also found that the Serbian forces acted with the requisite "intent to destroy ... a national, ethnical, racial or religious group," as required by Art. II. Therefore, the Court found that both elements of Art. II (*actus reus* and intent) were met and the Srebrenica massacre therefore constituted genocide, as defined under the Convention.

    However, the Srebrenica genocide was committed by members of the army of Republika Srpska (the "VRS"), which was separate and distinct from Serbia. The Court concluded there was nothing that could justify concluding that acts of genocide committed in Srebrenica were perpetrated by "persons or entities" having the status of organs of the Federal Republic of Yugoslavia ("FRY") (as Serbia and Montenegro was known at the time) under its internal law, as then in force. Nothing suggested that the FRY army took part in the massacres or that the political leaders of the FRY had a hand in preparing, planning or in any way carrying out the massacres. The Court found evidence of direct or indirect participation by the official army of the FRY, along with the Bosnian Serb armed forces, in military operations in Bosnia and Herzegovina in the years prior to the events at Srebrenica. It was not, however, shown that there was any such participation in relation to the Srebrenica genocide. Further, neither the Republika Srpska, nor the VRS (its army) were *de jure* organs of the FRY, since none of them had the status of organ of that State under its internal law.

    Therefore, Serbia and Montenegro was not held responsible for the Srebrenica genocide. Rather, Belgrade breached the Genocide Convention by failing to prevent the Srebrenica genocide.

Korea (South Korea), Romania, Russia, Rwanda, Saint Vincent and the Grenadines, San Marino, Saudi Arabia, Senegal, Serbia, Seychelles, Singapore, Slovakia, Slovenia, South Africa, Spain, Sri Lanka, Sudan, Sweden, Switzerland, Syria, Tajikistan, Tanzania, Togo, Tonga, Trinidad and Tobago, Tunisia, Turkey, Uganda, Ukraine, United Arab Emirates, United Kingdom, United States, Uruguay, Uzbekistan, Venezuela, Vietnam, Yemen and Zimbabwe.

3 Convention Relating to the Status of Refugees (1951)

The Convention Relating to the Status of Refugees ("Refugee Convention" or "CRSR") was adopted in 1951 in Geneva by the United Nations Conference of Plenipotentiaries on the Status of Refugees and Stateless Persons and entered into force in 1954. For a full discussion, *see* "Convention Relating to the Status of Refugees" under "Refugee Law," *infra*.

C Nine Core International Human Rights Treaties

1 The International Covenant on Civil and Political Rights (ICCPR) (1966) and the International Covenant on Economic, Social and Cultural Rights (ICESCR) (1966)

a Overview and Comparison

The International Covenant on Civil and Political Rights ("ICCPR") and the International Covenant on Economic, Social and Cultural Rights ("ICESCR") are two international treaties that aim at converting the non-binding provisions of the UDHR into binding treaty provisions. Together with the UDHR, the ICCPR and ICESCR have come to constitute the so-called "International Bill of Human Rights."

Because the USSR and the United States were unable to agree as to the rights that should be enumerated (the U.S. argued that economic and social rights do not exist, while the USSR wished to codify them), two separate treaties resulted. Unlike the UDHR, which took only a few years to draft because it was not binding, the drafting of the ICCPR and the ICESCR took 18 years.

Unlike the ICESCR, which the U.S. signed but did not ratify, the ICCPR was signed and ratified by both the U.S. and the USSR.

b International Covenant on Civil and Political Rights (1966)

i Overview

The ICCPR, which came into effect on 23 March 1976, is similar to a global "bill of rights." It undertakes to protect the wide range of civil and political rights, including a right to life (Article 6 ICCPR), prohibitions on torture (Article 7 ICCPR) and slavery (Article 8 ICCPR), prohibitions on arbitrary arrest or detention (Article 9.1 ICCPR), a right to trial within a reasonable time of arrest or detainment (Article 9.3 ICCPR) and to freedom of thought, conscience, and religion (Article 18 ICCPR), as well as freedom of expression (Article 19 ICCPR).

The ICCPR requires states not only to agree to not violate these rights but also to ensure the rights by protecting them from other member states' violations (Article 2(3) ICCPR). It thus incorporates an affirmative duty to act. To guarantee these rights, each state party to the ICCPR is required (Article 2(3) ICCPR):

> (a) To ensure that any person whose rights or freedoms as herein recognized are violated shall have an effective remedy, notwithstanding that the violation has been committed by persons acting in an official capacity.
> (b) To ensure that any person claiming such a remedy shall have his right thereto determined by competent judicial, administrative or legislative authorities, or by any other competent authority provided for by the legal system of the state and to develop the possibilities of judicial remedy.
> (c) To ensure that the competent authorities shall enforce such remedies when granted.

ii Due Process Rights

Article 9 of the ICCPR establishes baseline due process rights. It provides as follows:[67]

> 1. Everyone has the right to liberty and security of person. No one shall be subjected to *arbitrary arrest or detention.* No one shall be deprived of his liberty except on such grounds and in accordance with such procedure as are established by law.
> 2. Anyone who is arrested shall be informed, at the time of arrest, *of the reasons for his arrest and shall be promptly informed of any charges against him.*
> 3. Anyone arrested or detained on a criminal charge shall be brought *promptly before a judge or other officer* authorized by law to exercise judicial power and shall be entitled to *trial within a reasonable time or to release.* It shall not be the general rule that persons awaiting trial shall be detained in custody, but release may be subject to guarantees to appear for trial, at any other stage of the judicial proceedings, and, should occasion arise, for execution of the judgement.
> 4. Anyone who is deprived of his liberty by arrest or detention shall be entitled to take proceedings before a court, in order that that court *may decide without delay on the lawfulness of his detention* and order his release if the detention is not lawful.
> 5. Anyone who has been the victim of unlawful arrest or detention shall have an enforceable right to compensation.

iii Prohibition of *Ex Post Facto* Laws

Article 15.1 of the ICCPR prohibits the conviction of any criminal offence "on account of any act or omission which did not constitute a criminal offence, under national or international law, at the time when it was committed." Article 15.1 also prohibits a

67. Article 9 ICCPR.

heavier penalty than the one that was applicable at the time when the criminal offence was committed from being imposed.

iv Extraterritorial Application

The ICCPR provides that each state party "undertakes to respect and to ensure to all *individuals within its territory and subject to its jurisdiction* the rights recognized in the present Covenant" (Article 2.1 ICCPR). While it is clear that the ICCPR establishes a binding commitment to respect human rights law within the territories of states parties, states differ as to whether the commitment applies outside of this territory:

- The U.S. adopts the approach that it is only bound to apply the provisions of the ICCPR to individuals who are both physically located within its territory and subject to its jurisdiction.
- However, other nations claim that the provisions apply to both individuals within the territory of states parties and to individuals subject to the jurisdiction or control of states parties, regardless of whether these individuals are physically located within the territory of the states in question.

Under this latter interpretation, a state would be bound to apply the provisions of the ICCPR to individuals located in the territories occupied by ICCPR states parties as well as to persons detained by states parties outside of the territory of such states. It is the view that has been adopted by the ICCPR Human Rights Committee, including with respect to Israel's responsibility for human rights abuses in the Occupied Territories[68] and the U.S.'s responsibility over detainees in Guantánamo Bay, Cuba.[69]

The Human Rights Committee's 2004 "power or effective control" standard establishes jurisdiction according to the relationship between the state party and the individual under the control of the state. General Comment No. 31 provides that a state party "must respect and ensure the rights laid down in the Covenant to anyone within the power or effective control of that State Party, even if not situated within the territory of the State Party."[70]

The interpretation adopted has the potential to impact the means by which a state party undertakes military operations. Under the U.S. view, the ICCPR has no direct impact on battlefield operations; U.S. forces would be constrained only by the law of armed conflict and applicable U.S. domestic law and policies. However, under the extraterritorial view, states parties must apply the ICCPR's due-process-like police protections and limit the use of force to self-defense only, thereby restricting states' use of force beyond the restrictions imposed by the law of armed conflict.

68. U.N. Human Rights Committee, Concluding Observations of the Human Rights Committee: Israel, CCPR/C/ISR/CO/3 (3 September 2010).
69. U.N. Human Rights Committee, Concluding Observations: US, CCPR/C/USA/CO/3 (15 September 2006).
70. U.N. Human Rights Committee, General Comment No. 31: The Nature of the General Legal Obligation Imposed on States Parties to the Covenant, 80th Sess., 1 10, U.N. Doc. CCPR/C/2 1/Rev. 1/Add. 13 (26 May 2004).

v States Parties

The vast majority of states in the international community are parties to the ICCPR. As of 2018, there are 74 signatories and 172 states parties. The following states have signed but have not yet ratified the Convention: the People's Republic of China, Comoros, Cuba, Nauru, Palau and Saint Lucia. The U.S. ratified the ICCPR in 1992.

The following states have neither signed nor ratified the ICCPR: Antigua and Barbuda, Bhutan, Brunei, Burma (Myanmar), Kiribati, Malaysia, Micronesia, Oman, Saint Kitts and Nevis, Saudi Arabia, Singapore, Solomon Islands, South Sudan, Tonga, Tuvalu, United Arab Emirates, and Vatican City.

vi Optional Protocol

Because there are no specified enforcement mechanisms in the ICCPR, states parties drafted an optional protocol that allows for complaints against violating states to be brought before the 18-member HRC, a human rights treaty body based at the U.N.'s New York headquarters during its spring session and at the U.N. Office in Geneva during its summer and fall sessions. The HRC holds the power to: (i) review reports on compliance submitted by states parties to the ICCPR and issue its "Observations"; (ii) issue "General Comments" on the implementation of the ICCPR; and (iii) under the (First) Optional Protocol to the ICCPR, the HRC may consider petitions from individuals claiming to be victims of violations of the ICCPR by a state party to the Convention if the individuals have exhausted the available domestic remedies. The HRC may study the matter and then send its views to the petitioner and to the state, but its views are not binding and only hold the weight of the "views" of the Committee.

c *International Covenant on Economic, Social and Cultural Rights (1966)*

i Overview

The ICESCR took effect on 3 January 1976 and includes a series of economic rights, including the right to work and join trade unions. States parties agree to the "progressive realization" of these rights. There is thus an affirmative obligation to *take steps* "to the maximum of its available resources" toward the progressive realization of these rights.

The rights and freedoms guaranteed by the ICESCR include the right to just and favorable conditions of work (Article 7 ICESCR), to social security (Article 9 ICESCR), to an adequate standard of living (Article 11 ICESCR), to enjoyment of the highest standard of physical and mental health (Article 12 ICESCR) and to free education (Article 13 ICESCR).

The U.N. Committee on Economic, Social and Cultural Rights ("CESCR") monitors implementation of the ICESCR.

ii States Parties

As of 2018, there are 71 signatories and 169 states parties to the ICESCR. Four countries—Comoros, Cuba, Palau and the U.S.—have signed, but not ratified, the ICESCR. States that neither signed nor ratified the ICESCR include Botswana, Haiti, Malaysia, Myanmar (Burma), Mozambique, Oman, Pakistan, Saudi Arabia, the United Arab Emirates and Western Sahara.

2 *International Convention on the Elimination of All Forms of Racial Discrimination (1965)*

a Overview

The International Convention on the Elimination of All Forms of Racial Discrimination ("ICERD") is a U.N. convention that was adopted in 1965 and entered into force on 4 January 1969. It commits its members to the elimination of racial discrimination and the promotion of understanding among all races.

The Convention includes an individual complaints mechanism, making it enforceable against its parties. The human rights treaty body charged with monitoring and implementing the Convention is the Committee on the Elimination of Racial Discrimination ("CERD"), which in many ways parallels the mechanisms and procedures of the HRC.

The International Court of Justice has also affirmed the extraterritorial protection of human rights under the ICERD. In *Georgia v. Russian Federation*, for example, the Court "applied the 'effective control' standard for determining jurisdiction under human rights treaties" as it relates to the ICERD.[71]

b States Parties

The ICERD has 88 signatories and 180 states parties, as follows: Afghanistan, Albania, Algeria, Andorra, Angola, Antigua and Barbuda, Argentina, Armenia, Australia, Austria, Azerbaijan, Bahamas, Bahrain, Bangladesh, Barbados, Belarus, Belgium, Belize, Benin, Bhutan, Bolivia, Bosnia and Herzegovina, Botswana, Brazil, Bulgaria, Burkina Faso, Burundi, Cabo Verde, Cambodia, Cameroon, Canada, Central African Republic, Chad, Chile, China, Colombia, Comoros, Congo, Costa Rica, Côte d'Ivoire, Croatia, Cuba, Cyprus, Czech Republic, Democratic Republic of the Congo, Denmark, Djibouti, Dominica, Dominican Republic, Ecuador, Egypt, El Salvador, Equatorial Guinea, Eritrea, Estonia, Eswatini, Ethiopia, Fiji, Finland, France, Gabon, Gambia, Georgia, Germany, Ghana, Greece, Grenada, Guatemala, Guinea, Guinea-Bissau, Guyana, Haiti, Holy See, Honduras, Hungary, Iceland, India, Indonesia, Iran, Iraq, Ireland, Israel, Italy, Jamaica, Japan, Jordan, Kazakhstan, Kenya, Kuwait, Kyrgyzstan,

71. Oona A. Hathaway et al., "Human Rights Abroad: When Do Human Rights Treaty Obligations Apply Extraterritorially?" 43 *Arizona State Law Journal* (2011), p. 415.

Lao People's Democratic Republic, Latvia, Lebanon, Lesotho, Liberia, Libya, Liechtenstein, Lithuania, Luxembourg, Madagascar, Malawi, Maldives, Mali, Malta, Marshall Islands, Mauritania, Mauritius, Mexico, Monaco, Mongolia, Montenegro, Morocco, Mozambique, Namibia, Nauru, Nepal, Netherlands, New Zealand, Nicaragua, Niger, Nigeria, North Macedonia, Norway, Oman, Pakistan, Palau, Panama, Papua New Guinea, Paraguay, Peru, Philippines, Poland, Portugal, Qatar, Republic of Korea, Republic of Moldova, Romania, Russian Federation, Rwanda, San Marino, Sao Tome and Principe, Saudi Arabia, Senegal, Serbia, Seychelles, Sierra Leone, Singapore, Slovakia, Slovenia, Solomon Islands, Somalia, South Africa, Spain, Sri Lanka, St. Kitts and Nevis, St. Lucia, St. Vincent and the Grenadines, State of Palestine, Sudan, Suriname, Sweden, Switzerland, Syrian Arab Republic, Tajikistan, Thailand, Timor-Leste, Togo, Tonga, Trinidad and Tobago, Tunisia, Turkey, Turkmenistan, Uganda, Ukraine, United Arab Emirates, United Kingdom, United Republic of Tanzania, United States of America, Uruguay, Uzbekistan, Venezuela, Viet Nam, Yemen, Zambia, Zimbabwe.[72]

3 *Convention on the Elimination of All Forms of Discrimination Against Women (1979)*

a Overview

The Convention on the Elimination of All Forms of Discrimination against Women ("CEDAW") is an international convention that was adopted by the U.N. General Assembly in 1979 and entered into force in 1981. It is often described as an "international bill of human rights for women."

The implementation of the Convention is monitored by the Committee on the Elimination of Discrimination against Women (also "CEDAW Committee"), which parallels the mechanisms and procedures of the HRC.

b Reproductive Rights

While CEDAW does not explicitly require states parties to protect a right of women to an abortion, the Convention devotes substantial attention to women's reproductive rights and implicitly or indirectly supports a right to abortion. The Preamble states that "the role of women in procreation should not be a basis for discrimination." Article 16.1(e) protects women's rights to: "decide freely and responsibly on the number and spacing of their children and to have access to the information, education and means to enable them to exercise these rights." Article 10(h) guarantees women's "[a]ccess to specific educational information to help to ensure the health and well-being of families, including information and advice on family planning."

72. For a full list of states parties, *see* available at <https://treaties.un.org/Pages/ViewDetails.aspx?src=TREATY&mtdsg_no=IV-2&chapter=4&lang=en>.

c States Parties

CEDAW is a nearly universally adopted convention, with 189 states parties and only six U.N. member states that have not ratified it as of 2019: Iran, Palau, Somalia, Sudan, Tonga, and the United States. Of these states, two have signed but not ratified the Convention (the United States in 1980[73] and Palau in 2011).

4 *Convention Against Torture and Other Cruel, Inhuman or Degrading Treatment or Punishment (1984)*

a Overview

The Convention against Torture and Other Cruel, Inhuman or Degrading Treatment or Punishment (1984) (the "Convention against Torture") was adopted by the U.N. General Assembly in New York on 10 December 1984 (resolution 39/46) and went into effect in 1987. The Convention against Torture was initiated soon after the adoption of the Declaration on the Protection of All Persons from Being Subjected to Torture and Other Cruel, Inhuman or Degrading Treatment or Punishment (the "Torture Declaration") by the General Assembly on 9 December 1975 (resolution 3452 (XXX)).

b Definition and Prohibition of Torture

Article 1.1 of the Convention defines torture as:

> any act by which severe pain or suffering, whether physical or mental, is intentionally inflicted on a person for such purposes as obtaining from him, or a third person, information or a confession, punishing him for an act he or a third person has committed or is suspected of having committed, or intimidating or coercing him or a third person, or for any reason based on discrimination of any kind, when such pain or suffering is inflicted by or at the instigation of or with the consent or acquiescence of a public official or other person acting in an official capacity. It does not include pain or suffering arising only from, inherent in, or incidental to, lawful sanctions.

Article 2 creates an absolute prohibition on torture, as follows:

> 1. Each State Party shall take effective legislative, administrative, judicial or other measures to prevent acts of torture in any territory under its jurisdiction.
> 2. No exceptional circumstances whatsoever, whether a state of war or a threat of war, internal political instability or any other public emergency, may be invoked as a justification of torture.
> 3. An order from a superior officer or a public authority may not be invoked as a justification of torture.

73. Religiously conservative senators in the United States have opposed CEDAW on the basis that it is unnecessary, subjects the U.S. to the whims of an international agency, advocates for reproductive rights and enforces gender-neutral work rules.

c *Affirmative Duty to Act*

Article 5.1 of the Convention against Torture requires each state party to take measures as may be necessary to establish its jurisdiction over torture in the following cases:

(a) when the offences are committed in any territory under its jurisdiction or on board a ship or aircraft registered in that state;
(b) when the alleged offender is a national of that state;
(c) when the victim is a national of that state if that state considers it appropriate.

In addition, each state party must "take such measures as may be necessary to establish its jurisdiction over such offences in cases where the alleged offender is present in any territory under its jurisdiction and it does not extradite him" (Article 5.2).

d *Extraterritorial Application*

The Convention against Torture applies an "effective control" standard for the extraterritorial application of human rights. The Convention holds that each "State Party shall take effective legislative, administrative, judicial or other measures to prevent acts of torture in any territory under its jurisdiction."[74] The dispositive criterion is not whether an individual is located within the borders of a state party but rather whether the individual is in a territory under a state party's jurisdiction (i.e., control). The Committee against Torture made this position clear in its Concluding Observations on the report submitted by the Macau Special Administrative Region. The Committee recommended that Macau "establish full jurisdiction over torture crimes committed extraterritorially," without limiting jurisdiction to only torture "if the conduct in question was criminal under both Macau law and the law of the state in whose territory the conduct occurred."[75]

e *Disputes Before the International Court of Justice*

Any dispute between two or more states parties concerning the interpretation or application of the Convention that cannot be settled through negotiation shall, at the request of one of them, be submitted to arbitration. If, within six months from the date of the request for arbitration, the parties are unable to agree on the form of the arbitration, any one of them may refer the dispute to the International Court of Justice, which will hold jurisdiction to resolve the dispute (Article 30.1). Each State may, at the time of signature, ratification or accession to the Convention, declare that it does not

74. Article 2.1 Convention against Torture.
75. Oona A. Hathaway et al., "Human Rights Abroad: When Do Human Rights Treaty Obligations Apply Extraterritorially?" 43 *Arizona State Law Journal* (2011), pp. 417-418.

consider itself bound by the referral to disputes to the International Court of Justice (Article 30.2).

f *States Parties*

The Convention against Torture entered into force on 26 June 1987 following its ratification by 20 States. As of 2022, there are 173 states parties. The United States is a state party to the Convention against Torture but not to the 2002 Optional Protocol.

g Erga Omnes *Obligations*

It has been suggested that the Convention against Torture creates an obligation on states to try or prosecute alleged torturers and that this obligation has an *erga omnes* ("toward all") character.[76]

5 *Indigenous and Tribal Peoples Convention (1989)*

The Indigenous and Tribal Peoples Convention ("ITPC"), an ILC Convention adopted in 1989 and entering into force in 1991, sets out to guarantee the rights of indigenous peoples, adopt international standards for indigenous peoples with a view to removing the assimilationist orientation of earlier standards and guarantee indigenous peoples the right to control their own institutions, ways of life and economic development, while maintaining and developing their "identities, languages and religions, within the framework of the States in which they live" (Preamble).

6 *Convention on the Rights of the Child (1989)*

a *Overview*

The U.N. Convention on the Rights of the Child ("CRC") is a human rights treaty setting out the civil, political, economic, social and cultural rights of children, defined as any person under the age of 18 unless an earlier age of majority is recognized by a country's law. The Convention was adopted in 1989 and became effective in 1990. Its two optional protocols were adopted in 2000.

The Convention and its protocols are monitored by the U.N. Committee on the Rights of the Child ("CRC Committee"), which is composed of members from countries around the world. Once a year, the Committee submits a report to the U.N. General Assembly, which also hears a statement from the CRC Committee Chair and the General Assembly adopts a Resolution on the Rights of the Child.

---

76. *Questions relating to the Obligation to Prosecute or Extradite (Belgium v. Senegal)*, ICJ Reports (20 July 2012), para. 103.

b States Parties

The CRC enjoys the overwhelming support of the international community, with 196 states parties (some with stated reservations), with Somalia and South Sudan ratifying the Convention in 2015. The U.S., the Cook Islands, the Holy See, Niue, and the State of Palestine are not states parties.

The U.S. signed the Convention in 1995, but never ratified it. The U.S. was concerned that the Convention undermines U.S. sovereignty, threatens parental rights, undermines state rights, grants children rights not recognized in U.S. law, such as rights to leisure and to recreational activities (Article 31.1) and imposes upon states obligations such as encouraging the provision of opportunities for cultural, artistic, recreational and leisure activity (Article 31.2).

7 Convention on the Rights of Persons with Disabilities (2008)

a Overview

The U.N. Convention on the Rights of Persons with Disabilities is intended to protect the rights and dignity of persons with disabilities. States parties are required to promote, protect, and ensure the full enjoyment of human rights by persons with disabilities and ensure that they enjoy full equality under the law. It encapsulates the movement from viewing persons with disabilities as "objects" of charity, medical treatment, and social protection toward viewing them as "subjects" with rights who are capable of claiming those rights and making decisions for their lives based on their consent and who are active members of society.

The text was adopted by the U.N. General Assembly on 13 December 2006 and was opened for signature on 30 March 2007. It came into force on 3 May 2008 following ratification by the 20th state party.

b States Parties

As of 2018, it has 162 signatories and 177 states parties, which includes 172 states and the E.U. (which ratified it in 2010). The United States is not, however, a party. A 2012 United States Senate vote fell six votes short of the two-thirds required majority for ratification.

8 International Convention for the Protection of All Persons from Enforced Disappearance (2010)

a Overview

The U.N. International Convention for the Protection of All Persons from Enforced Disappearance ("ICPPED") was adopted by the U.N. General Assembly on 20 December 2006 and entered into force on 23 December 2010 to prevent forced disappearance.

The Convention defines an "enforced disappearance" as (Article 2):

> the arrest, detention, abduction or any other form of deprivation of liberty by agents of the State or by persons or groups of persons acting with the authorization, support or acquiescence of the State, followed by a refusal to acknowledge the deprivation of liberty or by concealment of the fate or whereabouts of the disappeared person, which place such a person outside the protection of the law.

The Convention places an absolute ban on enforced disappearance, which cannot be justified by "a state of war or a threat of war, internal political instability or any other public emergency" (Article 1).

b *States Parties*

As of 2022, there are 68 states parties and 44 state signatories to the ICPPED. The following are states parties: Albania, Argentina, Armenia, Austria, Belgium, Belize, Benin, Bolivia, Bosnia and Herzegovina, Brazil, Burkina Faso, Cambodia, Central African Republic, Chile, Colombia, Costa Rica, Croatia, Cuba, Czech Republic, Denmark, Dominica, Ecuador, Fiji, France, Gabon, Gambia, Germany, Greece, Honduras, Iraq, Italy, Japan, Kazakhstan, Lesotho, Lithuania, Luxembourg, Malawi, Mali, Malta, Mauritania, Mexico, Mongolia, Montenegro, Morocco, Netherlands, Niger, Nigeria, Norway, Oman, Panama, Paraguay, Peru, Portugal, Samoa, Senegal, Serbia, Seychelles, Slovakia, Slovenia, Spain, Sri Lanka, Sudan, Switzerland, Togo, Tunisia, Ukraine, Uruguay and Zambia.

The United States has neither signed nor ratified the Convention.

D Regional Treaties and Conventions

1 *Introduction*

In general, regional human rights systems complement and strengthen the international human rights system. Regional systems provide legal, judicial, and accountability measures and institutions that may not be available in the international human rights system. Many of these institutions have proven effective in promoting human rights at the regional level. For example, in the inter-American system, "states now accept responsibility in almost half of the contentious cases referred to the Inter-American Court. In response to Court-ordered reparations, states have paid monetary compensation to numerous victims and reformed national legislation, including the repeal of objectionable amnesty laws. States have apologized to victims in high-profile ceremonies, provided medical and psychological rehabilitation, reversed wrongful convictions, cleared criminal records, and trained national security forces in human rights."[77]

77. Thomas M. Antkowiak, "The Americas," in Daniel Moeckli et al. (eds.), *International Human Rights Law*, Oxford University Press (2018), p. 439.

As regional human rights courts confront new international human rights issues and issue jurisprudence on forced disappearances, extrajudicial killings, torture, and related issues of international law, other regional systems rely upon, refer to, and expand upon this jurisprudence, giving rise to an emerging jurisprudence of international human rights law. This interaction between regional systems results in an ever-growing body of judicial insights and precedents. In this way, regional human rights systems should be viewed as complementary to international human rights rather than as breakaway movements.

2 *European Convention on Human Rights (1950)*

a Overview

The European Convention on Human Rights ("ECHR"), formally known as the Convention for the Protection of Human Rights and Fundamental Freedoms, is an international treaty to protect human rights and fundamental freedoms in Europe. It was drafted in 1950 by the then-newly formed Council of Europe and entered into force on 3 September 1953. All 47 members of the Council of Europe are parties to the Convention.

b Extraterritorial Application

Under Article 1 of the ECHR, states parties "shall secure to everyone within their jurisdiction the rights and freedoms defined in Section I of this Convention." States are thus obligated to extend human rights protections not only to individuals contained within their territorial limits but rather to "everyone within their jurisdiction." This extraterritorial application was confirmed by the European Court of Human Rights ("ECtHR"), which held in *Loizidou v. Turkey*[78] and *Cyprus v. Turkey*[79] that the ECHR rights apply extraterritorially.

Issa v. Turkey[80] further cemented the position of the ECtHR in holding that the ECHR is applicable not only within the territories of states parties to the ECHR but also extraterritorially when a state party has effective control. *Issa* involved the claim that shepherds that were captured by Turkish soldiers in norther Iraq were unlawfully killed. The ECtHR held that if the shepherds had been under the effective control of Turkey at the time of the alleged violations, then they would be "within the jurisdiction of Turkey (and not that of Iraq, which is not a Contracting State ...)."[81] "This argument renders the issue of 'legal space' irrelevant when a contracting state is in fact exercising 'effective control' over any area anywhere in the world."[82] However, the ECtHR in

78. (1997) 23 EHRR 513.
79. (2002) 35 EHRR 30.
80. (2005) 41 EHRR 27.
81. *Ibid.*, para. 74.
82. Daniel Moeckli et al. (eds.), *International Human Rights Law*, Oxford University Press (2018), p. 121.

Al-Skeini v. United Kingdom subsequently found such extraterritorial jurisdiction to be "exceptional."[83] On this basis, the ECtHR concluded that the ECHR does not apply in extraterritorial armed conflicts unless a state party exercises "control and authority" over an individual or "effective control" over an area outside of its territory.[84] When "the State through its agents exercises control and authority over an individual, and thus jurisdiction, the State is under an obligation under Article 1 to secure to that individual the rights and freedoms under Section 1 of the Convention that are relevant to the situation of that individual."[85]

As a result of this extraterritorial application, states parties to the ECHR may not ascribe to the *lex specialis* principle with respect to the suspension of international human rights law in extraterritorial military operations on the basis that international humanitarian law displaces and takes precedence over international human rights law in such circumstances. Rather, states are obligated to adopt a parallel application approach where both humanitarian law and human rights law applies in such operations. Therefore, states must apply international human rights standards, including due-process standards, during detainee operations and respect other basic human rights, even in times of armed conflict. For example, the United Kingdom, unlike the United States and other states not subject to the ECHR, has no inherent authority to detain unprivileged belligerents unless permitted by local law.

Similarly, Council of Europe members are restricted with respect to status-based targeting in military operations. Whereas the United States can target a member of a declared hostile force based on his or her membership of that force, states parties to the ECHR may not. They must first wait for a hostile act or a demonstration of hostile intent before their right to act in self-defense is triggered. Their operational participation is therefore limited in the way that the operations of police forces are limited under local laws.

3 *American Convention on Human Rights (1969)*

a Overview

The American Convention on Human Rights ("ACHR" or "Pact of San José") was adopted by the nations of the Americas meeting in San José, Costa Rica, in 1969 and entered into force in 1978.

The ACHR sets out to guarantee a "system of personal liberty and social justice based on respect for the essential rights of man" (Preamble ACHR). It is implemented by the Inter-American Commission on Human Rights and the Inter-American Court of Human Rights, both of which are organs of the OAS that are responsible for overseeing compliance with the ACHR.

83. *Al-Skeini v. United Kingdom*, 53 EHRR 18 (2011), para 131.
84. *Ibid.*, para. 131.
85. *Ibid.*, para 137.

b Life at Conception

The ACHR provides that "[e]very person has the right to have his life respected. This right shall be protected by law and, in general, from the moment of conception. No one shall be arbitrarily deprived of his life" (Article 4.1 ACHR). The ACHR thus acts to restrict abortion in many cases.

c Extraterritorial Application

Like the ECHR, the ACHR does not limit its application to the territories of states parties. Its first Article provides that states parties "undertake to respect the rights and freedoms recognized herein and to ensure to all persons subject to their jurisdiction the free and full exercise of those rights and freedoms" (Article 1 ACHR). States parties are therefore bound to apply the human rights guarantees and protections of the ACHR to all persons in their jurisdiction, regardless of where such persons may be located. In *Coard et al. v. United States*,[86] the IACHR went a step further and extended this extraterritorial application to the American Declaration of the Rights and Duties of Man, which, unlike the ACHR, contains no jurisdictional clause. The IACHR thus found that the American Declaration applied to the U.S.'s actions in Grenada and found that "people could come within United States jurisdiction through the actions of United States agents, namely the United States military in Grenada."[87]

The IACHR repeated its holding in *Coard* with respect to the extraterritorial application of the American Declaration in *Alejandre v. Cuba*,[88] which involved the "shooting down of unarmed civilian aircraft by Cuban aircraft."[89] The Commission found that there was jurisdiction on the basis of "the relationship between the agents of Cuba and the victims in the circumstances at the time of the incident."[90]

The IACHR's *Report on Terrorism and Human Rights* (2002) reiterated this position. It stated that "the overriding significance of the principles of necessity, proportionality, humanity and non-discrimination in all circumstances in which states purport to place limitations on the fundamental rights and freedoms of persons *under their authority and control.*"[91] In other words, the factor that is controlling is not whether an individual is located within the territory of an OAS Member State; rather, what controls is whether such an individual is within the authority and control of the Member State.

86. *Coard et al. v. United States*, Case 10.951, Inter-American Commission on Human Rights, Report No 109/99 (29 September 1999).
87. Daniel Moeckli et al. (eds.), *International Human Rights Law*, Oxford University Press (2018), p. 124.
88. Armando Alejandre Jr., Carlos Costa, Mario De La Peña, And Pablo Morales, Complaint against Cuba, Case 11.589, Inter-American Commission on Human Rights Report No 86/99 (29 September 1999).
89. Daniel Moeckli et al. (eds.), *International Human Rights Law*, Oxford University Press (2018), p. 124.
90. *Ibid.*
91. *Report on Terrorism and Human Rights*, Inter-American Commission on Human Rights (2002), available at <http://hrlibrary.umn.edu/iachr/terrorism-index.html>.

d States Parties

At present, 24 of the 35 OAS member states have ratified the ACHR. Canada, Cuba, the Republic of Trinidad and Tobago and the United States are among the 11 member states that have not ratified the ACHR. The U.S. signed the ACHR in 1977 but did not ratify it, in part due to constitutional concerns as to the jurisdiction of the IACHR and the IACtHR.

4 African Charter on Human and Peoples' Rights (1981)

The African Charter on Human and Peoples' Rights ("African Charter"), also known as the "Banjul Charter," was adopted in June of 1981 by the 18th Assembly of Heads of State and Government of the OAU with the purpose of promoting and protecting human rights and basic freedoms in Africa. It emerged under the Organization of African Unity (the predecessor of the African Union) ("OAU"), which called for a committee of experts to draft a continent-wide human rights instrument. The draft was unanimously approved as the African Charter on Human and Peoples' Rights at the OAU's 1981 Assembly and entered into force on 21 October 1986.

The African Charter restates many of the provisions of the ICCPR and ICESCR. For example, in the arena of economic, social, and cultural rights, the African Charter recognizes the right to work (Article 15), the right to health (Article 16), and the right to education (Article 17). In some ways, the African Charter goes further than the ICCPR and the ICESCR by providing for certain rights, such as the right to development (Article 22), that are not explicitly recognized in the ICCPR and ICESCR. In addition, the African Charter recognizes groups' rights, with numerous references to "peoples' rights."

5 Protocol to the African Charter on Human and Peoples' Rights on the Rights of Women in Africa ("Maputo Protocol") (2005)

a Overview

The Protocol to the African Charter on Human and Peoples' Rights on the Rights of Women in Africa (also referred to as the "African Women's Protocol" or "Maputo Protocol") was adopted by the African Union in Maputo, Mozambique in July 2003 and went into force on 25 November 2005 following ratification by the required 15 member states of the African Union. It was adopted in the form of a protocol to the African Charter on Human and Peoples' Rights.

Following years of lobbying by African women's rights advocates for a document that would protect the rights of African women, the Maputo Protocol guarantees the right to take part in the political process, improved autonomy in reproductive health decisions, and an end to female genital mutilation, while promoting "social and political equality with men" (Preamble).

b *Provisions*

Much of the Maputo Protocol restates or expands upon provisions established in international human rights law. For example, Article 6 on marriage builds on many existing human rights instruments, including not only CEDAW but also the ICCPR and the Convention on the Consent to Marriage, Minimum Age of Marriage and Registration of Marriage. Article 6(h) restates CEDAW's provisions on the equal rights of women with men with respect to the nationality of their children.

In other ways, the Maputo Protocol expands upon the protections established in CEDAW. For example, "[w]ith the exception of article 6 on trafficking and exploitation of prostitution of women, CEDAW does not have any provisions pertaining to violence against women,"[92] whereas provisions on violence against women in the family, violence against women in the community and public violence, including violence against women in war and abuse of refugees, are discussed throughout the Maputo Protocol. The Maputo Protocol even goes as far as protecting women from "verbal violence," which very well may be "the first time that verbal violence against women has been recognized bin an international human rights instrument."[93]

Another of the Protocol's expansions over CEDAW is the requirement that states "take effective legislative and administrative measures to prevent the exploitation and abuse of women in advertising and pornography" (Article 18.m Protocol). CEDAW, in contrast, does not prohibit or reference pornography. Another innovation of the African Protocol is in its introduction of the "right to equal access to housing and to acceptable living conditions in a healthy environment" and the obligation that States "grant to women, whatever their marital status, access to adequate housing" (Article 16 Protocol).

The Maputo Protocol seeks to end harmful practices. States parties are required to "prohibit and condemn all forms of harmful practices which negatively affect the human rights of women and which are contrary to recognised international standards" (Article 5 Protocol). More specifically, states parties are required to prohibit, through legislative measures backed by sanctions, "all forms of female genital mutilation, scarification, medicalisation and para-medicalisation of female genital mutilation and all other practices in order to eradicate them" (Article 5 Protocol).

c *Departures of the Maputo Protocol from CEDAW*

The Maputo Protocol departs from CEDAW in several areas. For example, under Article 7, states parties shall ensure that "in case of separation, divorce or annulment of marriage, women and men shall have the right to an *equitable sharing* of the joint property deriving from the marriage" rather than a right to "equal" sharing. The Committee on the Elimination of All Forms of Discrimination against Women noted that "the terms equal and equity were not synonymous or interchangeable. It further

92. Fareda Banda, "Blazing a Trail: The African Protocol on Women's Rights Comes into Force," *Journal of African Law*, Vol. 50, Issue 1 (2006), p. 79.
93. *Ibid.*

noted that the aim of the Convention was the elimination of discrimination between men and women: 'and ensuring *de jure* and *de facto* equality between men and women. The Committee therefore recommends that the State party use the term "equality" henceforth.'"[94]

d States Parties

Of the 54 states in the African Union, 49 have signed the Maputo Protocol and 37 have ratified it as of 2019. Of the 17 states that have not ratified the Protocol, two states—Botswana and Egypt—have neither signed nor ratified it. The 15 remaining states—Algeria, Burundi, Central African Republic, Chad, Eritrea, Ethiopia, Madagascar, Mauritius, Niger, São Tomé and Príncipe, Sahrawi Arab Democratic Republic,[95] Somalia, South Sudan, Sudan, and Tunisia—have signed but not ratified the Protocol.

6 Arab Charter on Human Rights (2004)

a Overview

The Arab Charter on Human Rights ("Arab Charter") (2004) was initially drafted by the Arab League in 1994. No state ratified this initial version. An updated 2004 version came into force in 2008 after seven members of the League of Arab States ratified it. Today, there are 16 states parties, as discussed below.

b The Role of the Sharī'a

The Arab Charter reaffirms the principles contained in the U.N. Charter, the UDHR, and the ICCPR. The Preamble also reaffirms the Cairo Declaration on Human Rights in Islam (1990), which represents human rights within the context of the *Sharī'a*. The Charter recognizes traditional human rights, such as the right to liberty and security of persons, equality of persons before the law, protection of persons from torture and the right to property. However, Article 25 allows for restrictions on freedom of religion, the exercise of which "shall be governed by law."

c Due Process Rights

The Arab Charter guarantees the following due process rights:[96]

> 1. Everyone has the right to liberty and security of person. No one shall be subjected to arbitrary arrest, search or detention without a legal warrant.

94. *Ibid.*, pp. 77-78.
95. The Sahrawi Arab Democratic Republic is a partially recognized state that claims the non-self-governing territory of Western Sahara, the easternmost fifth of which it controls. It maintains diplomatic relations with 40 U.N. states and is a full member of the African Union.
96. Article 14 Arab Charter.

2. No one shall be deprived of his liberty except on such grounds and in such circumstances as are determined by law and in accordance with such procedure as is established thereby.
3. Anyone who is arrested shall be informed, at the time of arrest, in a language that he understands, of the reasons for his arrest and shall be promptly informed of any charges against him. He shall be entitled to contact his family members.
4. Anyone who is deprived of his liberty by arrest or detention shall have the right to request a medical examination and must be informed of that right.
5. Anyone arrested or detained on a criminal charge shall be brought promptly before a judge or other officer authorized by law to exercise judicial power and shall be entitled to trial within a reasonable time or to release. His release may be subject to guarantees to appear for trial. Pre-trial detention shall in no case be the general rule.
6. Anyone who is deprived of his liberty by arrest or detention shall be entitled to petition a competent court in order that it may decide without delay on the lawfulness of his arrest or detention and order his release if the arrest or detention is unlawful.

d *Incompatibility with International Human Rights Standards*

The Arab Charter has been criticized as falling short of international standards. For example, the U.N. High Commissioner for Human Rights, Louise Arbour, has stressed that the Charter is incompatible with international standards for women's, children's, and non-citizens' rights. She has stated that throughout the development of the Arab Charter, her office "shared concerns with the drafters about the incompatibility of some provisions with international norms and standards." These concerns included "the approach to death penalty for children and the rights of women and noncitizens. Moreover, to the extent that it equates Zionism with racism, we reiterated that the Arab Charter is not in conformity with General Assembly Resolution 46/86, which rejects that Zionism is a form of racism and racial discrimination."[97]

e *States Parties*

As of 2021, the following 16 states are parties to the Arab Charter on Human Rights: Algeria, Bahrain, Egypt, Iraq, Jordan, Kuwait, Lebanon, Libya, Mauritania, Palestine, Qatar, Saudi Arabia, Sudan, Syria, the United Arab Emirates and Yemen.

f *Enforcement Mechanism: Arab Court of Human Rights*

i Overview

One of the weaknesses of the Arab Charter of Human Rights is the absence of an enforcement mechanism. To fill this gap, the creation of an Arab Court of Human

97. "Arab rights charter deviates from international standards, says UN official," *UN News* (30 January 2008), available at <https://news.un.org/en/story/2008/01/247292-arab-rights-charter-deviates-international-standards-says-un-official>.

Rights to be formed by the Arab League was proposed in 2012, and the Arab League adopted a Statute of the Arab Court of Human Rights in 2014.

ii Criticisms of the Statute

The Statute was subject to sharp criticism. Concerns were raised regarding the inaccessibility of the Court, which allows complaints to be filed only by states parties and accredited NGOs rather than by aggrieved individuals, groups, and victims of human rights violations.[98] The Arab League was further criticized for drafting the Statute "without consulting with any civil society groups, despite their vast expertise in relevant issues, or any other stakeholders, despite several requests from civil society organizations to engage in the process."[99] The Statute has also been criticized for failing to "affirm and guarantee the obligation of states parties to ensure fully the protection of victims, witnesses and others that participate in proceedings, and ensure that no reprisals are taken against them."[100]

iii Entry into Force of the Statute

Notwithstanding these criticisms, a ministerial meeting of the League of Arab States approved the Statute for an Arab Court of Human Rights in September 2014. The Statute will "enter into force after seven of the member states have ratified it and deposited the instruments of ratification" and will be "operative one year after it has entered into force."[101] In 2016, Saudi Arabia became the first country to ratify the Statute. Bahrain expressed an interest to host the court.

iv Jurisdiction, Case Initiation, and Admissibility

When the Statute comes into force, the Arab Court of Human Rights "shall be established within the framework of the League of Arab States as an independent Arab judicial organ to reinforce the desire of the States Parties to implement their obligations regarding human rights and freedoms."[102] The Court will have jurisdiction "over all suits and conflicts resulting from the implementation and interpretation of the Arab

---

98. Konstantinos Magliveras and Gino Naldi, "The Arab Court of Human Rights," 29(2) *Revue québécoise de droit international* (2016) ("This is arguably its leading failing which undermines the whole project," p. 170).
99. "Proposed Arab Court of Human Rights: An Empty Vessel Without Substantial Changes to the Draft Statute," *Human Rights Watch* (6 June 2014), available at <https://www.hrw.org/news/2014/06/06/proposed-arab-court-human-rights-empty-vessel-without-substantial-changes-draft>.

    The entire process has been conducted behind closed doors and through opaque procedures that contravene basic principles of inclusive participation and transparency.
100. *The Arab Court of Human Rights: A Flawed Statute for an Ineffective Court*, International Commission of Jurists (Geneva 2015), p. 28.
101. Article 33 Statute.
102. Article 2 Statute.

Charter of Human Rights, or any other Arab convention in the field of Human Rights involving a member State."[103] However, the Court "may only look into facts that are committed after the entry into force of the Statute with regards to the State in question."[104] Cases are inadmissible in the following cases:[105]

(1) Non-exhaustion of local remedies in the respondent State by a final and definitive judgment according to the national legal regime.
(2) The case with the same subject matter has been filed before another regional human rights court.
(3) The case has been filed six months after the notification of the claimant of the definitive judgment.

The Statute allows for cases to be initiated only by states parties and accredited NGOs rather than by aggrieved individuals, groups, and victims of human rights violations. It provides:[106]

(1) The State Party whose citizen claims to be a victim of a human rights violation has the right to access the Court, provided that both the claimant State and the Defendant State are party to this Statute, or they have accepted the jurisdiction of the Court as determined by Article 20 of the Statute.
(2) State Parties can accept, when ratifying or acceding to the Statute or at any time later, that one or more NGOs that are accredited and working in the field of human rights in the State whose subject claims to be a victim of a human rights violation has access to the Court.

Moreover, the jurisdiction of the Court in human rights cases is not automatic in all cases of human rights violations of Arab League member states. Rather, Arab League members must become parties to the Statute or must otherwise declare "their acceptance of the Court's jurisdiction, whether in a specific case or in general."[107]

7 *Charter of Fundamental Rights of the European Union (2000)*

Adopted on 2 October 2000 and ratified on 7 December 2000, the Charter of Fundamental Rights of the European Union ("CFREU") serves as the E.U.'s bill of rights. It encapsulates civic, personal, economic and social rights of E.U. citizens and residents. Its content, which covers human dignity, justice, freedom, equality and child protection, is based on the rights captured in the constitutional and legal traditions of member countries, on the case law of the ECJ and on the ECHR and other international human rights agreements. Under the Charter, the E.U. must act and legislate consistently with the Charter. The E.U.'s courts will strike down E.U. legislation that contravenes it.

103. Article 16.1 Statute.
104. Article 17 Statute.
105. Article 18 Statute.
106. Article 19 Statute.
107. Article 20.1 Statute.

The CFREU was drafted by the European Convention and proclaimed on 7 December 2000 by the European Parliament, the Council of Ministers, and the European Commission. However, its legal status remained uncertain until the 1 December 2009 entry into force of the Treaty of Lisbon on 1 December 2009, which made the CFREU legally binding and gave it full legal effect.

E Customary International Law

As defined above, customary international law results from a general and consistent practice of states followed by them from a sense of legal obligation. Unlike treaties, which are binding only on states parties thereto, customary law is binding on all states.

Customary international law in the field of human rights develops primarily as a result of international treaties that are adopted by a large plurality of states, such that the practices contained therein become general and consistent binding practices in the international arena, as well as when international declarations are widely accepted and practiced by the international community. Some have argued, for example, that the UDHR, though it is a non-binding declaration, has, to some extent, evolved into a source of binding customary international law because of its wide acceptance and consistent and recurrent practice by states.

F International Declarations

1 American Declaration of the Rights and Duties of Man (1948)

a Overview

The American Declaration of the Rights and Duties of Man ("ADRDM") was adopted by the nations of the Americas at the same meeting that created the OAS in 1948—the Ninth International Conference of American States in Bogotá. It was the world's first international human rights instrument and predated the UDHR by approximately six months.

The ADRDM is comprised of a preface followed by two chapters: Chapter One on Rights, beginning with the right to life, liberty and security and progressing to the rights to equality before the law, religious freedom, expression and a host of other rights—and Chapter Two on Duties, laying out a series of duties to society and family. These duties include the duty to receive instruction, to vote, to obey the law, to serve the community, to cooperate with the state with respect to social security and welfare, to pay taxes, to work, and to refrain from political activities in other countries.

b Binding Nature of the Inter-American Declaration

Although declarations in international law are generally not binding, the jurisprudence of the Inter-American Court of Human Rights has suggested that the ADRDM is a source of binding international law for OAS member states. In Advisory Opinion OC-10/89 (14 July 1989), the Court held that the fact that:[108]

> the Declaration is not a treaty does not, then, lead to the conclusion that it does not have legal effect, nor that the Court lacks the power to interpret it within the framework of the principles set out above.

This could be interpreted to mean only that the ADRDM is binding to the extent that it assists in the interpretation of the American Convention on Human Rights, which is binding on states that have ratified it. However, the IACHR has held that the ADRDM constitutes a source of legal obligation even for OAS members that are not parties to the ACHR:[109]

> according to the well-established and long-standing jurisprudence and practice of the inter-American human rights system, the American Declaration is recognized as constituting a source of legal obligation for OAS member states, including those States that are not parties to the American Convention on Human Rights. These obligations are considered to flow from the human rights obligations of member states under the OAS Charter. Member states have agreed that the content of the general principles of the OAS Charter is contained in and defined by the American Declaration, as well as the customary legal status of the rights protected under many of the Declaration's core provisions.

c States Parties

The terms of the ADRDM are enforced against states parties to the OAS, including the 11 states (Canada, Cuba, the Republic of Trinidad and Tobago, the United States, and others) that have not ratified the ACHR.

2 Universal Declaration of Human Rights (1948)

a Overview

The Universal Declaration of Human Rights ("UDHR") was adopted by the U.N. General Assembly on 10 December 1948. Most sources consider the UDHR to be a non-binding resolution that sets forth a "common standard of achievement for all peoples and all nations" (Preamble UDHR). Other sources view it as an elaboration of the human rights provisions of the U.N. Charter and thus claim that it is binding through the Charter. Yet others, as mentioned above, consider it to be a source of binding customary international law.

---

108. *Interpretation of the American Declaration of the Rights and Duties of Man within the Framework of Article 64 of the American Convention on Human Rights*, Advisory Opinion, Inter-American Court of Human Rights, OC-10/89 (14 July 1989), para. 47.
109. *Jessica Lenahan (Gonzales) et al. v. United States of America*, Case 12.626 (2011), para. 115.

b States Parties

The UDHR was passed by a vote of 48 in favor, zero against and eight abstentions (Byelorussian SSR, Czechoslovakia, Poland, Ukrainian SSR, USSR, Yugoslavia, South Africa and Saudi Arabia). The following countries voted in favor of the Declaration: *Afghanistan*, Argentina, Australia, Belgium, Bolivia, Brazil, Burma, Canada, Chile, China, Colombia, Costa Rica, Cuba, Denmark, the Dominican Republic, Ecuador, *Egypt*, El Salvador, Ethiopia, France, Greece, Guatemala, Haiti, Iceland, India, *Iran*, *Iraq*, Lebanon, Liberia, Luxembourg, Mexico, Netherlands, New Zealand, Nicaragua, Norway, *Pakistan*, Panama, Paraguay, Peru, Philippines, Thailand, Sweden, *Syria*, *Turkey*, United Kingdom, United States, Uruguay and Venezuela.

3 Cairo Declaration on Human Rights in Islam (1990)

a Overview

The Cairo Declaration on Human Rights in Islam ("Cairo Declaration") is a declaration of the member states of the Organisation of Islamic Cooperation ("OIC") (known as the Organisation of the Islamic Conference prior to 28 June 2011) that was adopted in Cairo in 1990. The purpose of the Cairo Declaration is to provide "general guidance for Member States [of the OIC] in the Field of human rights."

The Cairo Declaration, which has been signed by 45 states, serves as a framework of the Islamic perspective on human rights and as an Islamic response to the UDHR of 1948. Accordingly, it affirms the *Sharīʿa* as its sole source. The Declaration states that "[a]ll the rights and freedoms stipulated in this Declaration are subject to the Islamic *Sharīʿa*" (Article 24 Cairo Declaration) and the "Islamic *Sharīʿa* is the only source of reference for the explanation or clarification of any of the articles of this Declaration" (Article 25 Cairo Declaration).

b Challenge to the Universality of International Human Rights

While the Cairo Declaration expresses some of the principles enshrined in the UDHR (e.g., the rights to life (Article 2) and property (Article 15) and the prohibitions on slavery and colonization (Article 11)), it clashes with international human rights law in some respects. For example:

- The Cairo Declaration prohibits "any form of pressure on man or to exploit his poverty or ignorance in order to force him to change his religion to another religion or to atheism" (Article 10). One may argue that this prohibition is not incompatible with freedom of religion since, strictly speaking, it prohibits only the forced conversion from a religion. Presumably, one is free to choose his religion or no religion at all so long as he is not compelled to do so. However, in practice, signatories interpret Article 10 as prohibiting non-Muslim proselytization and conversions from Islam to any other religion. Such acts are treated as crimes and, in many Muslim countries, are punishable by death.[110] Consequently, the Cairo Declaration has been criticized for falling "short of international human rights standards in not designating freedom of religion as 'a fundamental and non-derogable right.' This failure is potentially detrimental to not only to all non-Muslim citizens, but also to those who dissent from the officially imposed constructs of Islam."[111]

- Unlike the UDHR, which categorically establishes the "equal rights of men and women" (Preamble), the Cairo Declaration qualifies women's rights, stating that they are "equal to man *in human dignity*" (Article 6(a)) (emphasis added). This is distinct from full and unequivocal equality, as established in international human rights law. Moreover, the Cairo Declaration creates outright distinctions between the rights and duties of men and women: "The husband is responsible for the maintenance and welfare of the family" (Article 6(b)), and the woman "has her own rights to enjoy as well as duties to perform" (Article 6(a)).
- The Cairo Declaration makes 15 references to the Islamic *Sharī'a*, explicitly conditioning the enjoyment of rights on the provisions of Islamic law. In some ways, this leads to a disparity between universal human rights law and human rights as envisioned by the Cairo Declaration. For example, Islamic law provisions that grant women's testimony in court half the value of that of men's testimony undermine the due process rights of women as recognized in international treaties and customary international law. Where a discrepancy exists between international treaty rights and rights established in Islamic law, the Cairo Declaration defers to Islamic law.

Given these and other issues, the Cairo Declaration was criticized by the International Commission of Jurists when it was presented to the U.N. Commission on Human Rights in 1992.

IV THE INDIVIDUAL AS A SUBJECT OF INTERNATIONAL HUMAN RIGHTS LAW

A Overview

As mentioned in Chapter 1, international law may govern not only the relationships between states and international organizations *inter se* but it may also govern some of their relations with natural persons. Human rights law is one of the principal areas of international law that governs the relationships between states and individuals.

110. "Laws Criminalizing Apostasy," *The Law Library of Congress*, available at <https://www.loc.gov/law/help/apostasy/>.
111. Farhad Kazemi, "Perspectives on Islam and Civil Society," in Sohail H. Hashmi (ed.), *Islamic Political Ethics: Civil Society, Pluralism and Conflict*, Princeton University Press (Princeton, 2002), p. 50.

B Protections Afforded to the Individual

Individual victims of human rights, rather than the states corresponding to the victims' nationality, may, in some international legal institutions, file claims against the alleged violating states. As discussed under "Individuals in the International Order" in Chapter 1, individuals have standing to file claims against states under, *inter alia*, the American Convention on Human Rights, the European Convention on Human Rights, the International Covenant on Civil and Political Rights through the HRC, etc.

Some international courts, such as the ICC, do not permit individuals to file claims directly against states but offer individuals protection by permitting their states of nationality to refer cases to the ICC.

C Responsibilities Imposed on the Individual

Until recently, individuals were not seen as subjects or objects of international law. This changed beginning with the Nuremberg IMT and later with the IMT for the Far East, the ICTY, the ICTR and the ICC, which recognize the principle of individual criminal responsibility. For further discussion, *see* "Human Rights Violations by Individuals" under "Remedies within the International Framework" in section V ("Remedies for Human Rights Breaches"), *infra*.

V RELIGION AND HUMAN RIGHTS

Freedom of religion or belief intersects with many other areas of human rights, including the right to religiously neutral governance, gender equality, the right to education and freedom of expression. The ICCPR, ECHR and other treaties and international instruments make up the relevant normative framework.

A Freedom of Religion and Freedom to Change and Manifest One's Religion

International law guarantees freedom of religion or belief, the right to change one's religion or belief and the right to manifest one's religion or belief. These rights constitute both the *forum internum* (freedom of religion and to change one's religion) and *forum externum* (freedom to manifest one's religion).

1 Universal Declaration of Human Rights (Article 18.1)

The Universal Declaration of Human Rights guarantees freedom of religion as well as the freedom to manifest one's religion (Article 18.1):

> Everyone has the right to freedom of thought, conscience and *religion*; this right includes *freedom to change his religion or belief*, and freedom, either alone or in

community with others and in public or private, to manifest his religion or belief in teaching, practice, worship and observance.

This tripartite right encompasses three elements:

- *Freedom of religion*;
- Freedom to *change one's religion* (and, by analogy, freedom to be punished for what another deems to be "apostasy"); and
- Freedom to *manifest* one's religion.

2 *ICCPR (Article 18.1)*

Article 18.1 ICCPR guarantees the right to freedom of religion and the right to manifest one's religion:

> Everyone shall have the right to freedom of thought, conscience and religion. This right shall include freedom to have or to adopt a religion or belief of his choice, and freedom, either individually or in community with others and in public or private, to manifest his religion or belief in worship, observance, practice and teaching.

This language does not explicitly reference the right to change one's religion, as does Article 18.1 of the UDHR. However, the language in Article 18.2 of the ICCPR, which is discussed below, prohibits the coercion of a person "which would impair his freedom to have or to adopt a religion or belief of his choice," which implicitly encompasses the right to change one's religion or belief.

General Comment 22 of the Human Rights Committee (1993) has held that the right of Article 18.1 is intended to be broad and far-reaching. The OHCHR held that (paragraph 1):

> The right to freedom of thought, conscience and religion (which includes the freedom to hold beliefs) in article 18.1 is *far-reaching and profound*; it encompasses freedom of thought on all matters, personal conviction and the commitment to religion or belief, whether manifested individually or in community with others. The Committee draws the attention of states parties to the fact that the freedom of thought and the freedom of conscience are protected equally with the freedom of religion and belief. The fundamental character of these freedoms is also reflected in the fact that *this provision cannot be derogated from, even in time of public emergency*, as stated in article 4.2 of the Covenant.

Article 4.2 of the ICCPR, in turn, states that "[n]o derogation from articles 6, 7, 8 (paragraphs I and 2), 11, 15, 16 and 18 may be made under this provision."

3 *Religious Discrimination Declaration (Article 1.1)*

The Declaration on the Elimination of All Forms of Intolerance and of Discrimination Based on Religion or Belief ("Religious Discrimination Declaration"), passed on 25 November 1981, guarantees freedom of religion and the right to manifest one's religion as follows (Article 1.1):

> Everyone shall have the right to freedom of thought, conscience and religion. This right shall include freedom to have a religion or whatever belief of his choice, and freedom, either individually or in community with others and in public or private, to manifest his religion or belief in worship, observance, practice and teaching.

4 *European Convention on Human Rights (Article 9.1)*

The European Convention on Human Rights similarly guarantees freedom of religion and the right to change and manifest one's religion (Article 9.1):

> Everyone has the right to freedom of thought, conscience and religion; this right includes freedom to change his religion or belief and freedom, either alone or in community with others and in public or private, to manifest his religion or belief, in worship, teaching, practice and observance.

B Prohibition on Religious Coercion

1 *Overview and Three-Part Test*

Limitations on freedom of religion must meet a three-part test, must be non-discriminatory and must not destroy the essence of the right:

- the law must be clear as to what the limitation is so that accidental breach does not occur;
- the restriction must reflect a pressing social need in a democratic society; and
- the restriction must be proportional (i.e., the least restrictive method of achieving the pressing social need).

2 *ICCPR (Article 18.2)*

Article 18.2 of the ICCPR states that "[n]o one shall be subject to coercion which would impair his freedom to have or to adopt a religion or belief of his choice." This implies not only that one holds a right to freedom of religion or belief but that he or she shall be free to change and adopt a religion or belief of his choice.

In interpreting the ICCPR, General Comment 22 of the Human Rights Committee (1993) held that (paragraph 5):

> Article 18.2 *bars coercion* that would impair the right to have or adopt a religion or belief, including *the use of threat of physical force or penal sanctions to compel believers or non-believers to adhere to their religious beliefs and congregations*, to recant their religion or belief or to convert. Policies or practices having the same intention or effect, such as, for example, those restricting access to education, medical care, employment or the rights guaranteed by article 25 and other provisions of the Covenant, are similarly inconsistent with article 18.2.

3 *Religious Discrimination Declaration (Article 1.2)*

The Religious Discrimination Declaration similarly prohibits coercion. It states that (Article 1.2):

> No one shall be subject to coercion which would impair his freedom to have a religion or belief of his choice.

C Permitted Restrictions on the Manifestation of Religion: Public Order and Protecting the Rights of Others

1 *Overview*

The criteria prescribed for limitation on freedom of religion to be justifiable typically include the following three requirements:

- a prescription by law;
- a legitimate purpose, namely, protection of:
  - public safety, order, health or morals or the fundamental rights; and/or
  - the freedoms of others; and
- the proportionality test (i.e., the least restrictive means of achieving the purpose must be adopted; restrictions must not be so broad that they destroy freedoms).

2 **Forum Internum *and* Forum Externum**

The *forum internum* and *forum externum* sometimes intersect. For example, a Muslim woman's wearing a *hijāb* for religious reasons is a *forum externum* manifestation of a *forum internum* religious belief. Outside of religious belief, the mere action of wearing the *hijāb* would have no place in the freedoms discussed herein. However, when we are discussing *forum internum* beliefs not manifested with action or conduct, legal restrictions cannot be applied. The restrictions discussed herein can be applied to the *forum externum* only (i.e., restrictions on the right to manifest one's religion). This is because *forum internum* rights, including the right to be free from religious coercion, are absolute rights, in the same way that the rights to be free from torture or slavery are absolute rights.

3 *Normative Framework Establishing Public Order and Protecting the Rights of Others*

a ICCPR: Public Order and Protection of Rights of Others (Article 18.3)

While freedom of religion or belief (*forum internum*) is entitled to absolute protection, the manifestation of one's religion or beliefs (*forum externum*) may be subject to limitations. The right to manifest one's religion is thus a qualified right. However, states are restricted on the types of limitations that they may impose (Article 18.3 ICCPR):

> Freedom to manifest one's religion or beliefs may be subject only to such limitations as are prescribed by law and are necessary to protect *public safety, order, health,* or *morals* or the *fundamental rights and freedoms of others.*

Limitations of freedom of religion must thus be:

- prescribed by law; and
- necessary to protect public safety, order, health or morals (e.g., a limitation on a religious right to practice female genital mutilation, which poses a risk to public safety, order, and health) or the fundamental rights and freedoms of others (e.g., a limitation on the right of religious infant sacrifice, which infringes on the fundamental right to life of the infant).

The ICCPR provides parallel restrictions to freedom of expression in Article 19.3. These restrictions overlap with freedom of religion as it relates to freedom to manifest one's religion since such manifestation involves expression. Article 19.3 states as follows:

> The exercise of the rights provided for in paragraph 2 of this article carries with it special duties and responsibilities. It may therefore be subject to certain restrictions, but these shall only be such as are provided by law and are necessary:
>
> (a) For respect of the rights or reputations of others;
> (b) For the protection of national security or of public order (*ordre public*), or of public health or morals.

b *Religious Discrimination Declaration (Article 1.3)*

In this same manner, the Religious Discrimination Declaration permits limitations on one's religion or beliefs only to protect public safety, order, health or morals or as necessary to protect the rights of others. Article 1.3 states:

> Freedom to manifest one's religion or beliefs may be subject only to such limitations as are prescribed by law and are necessary to protect public safety, order, health or morals or the fundamental rights and freedoms of others.

c *European Convention on Human Rights (Article 9.2)*

The permitted restrictions in the European Convention on Human Rights are virtually identical to those found in the ICCPR and Religious Discrimination Declaration. The Convention states (Article 9.2):

> Freedom to manifest one's religion or beliefs shall be subject only to such limitations as are prescribed by law and are necessary in a democratic society in

> the interests of public safety, for the protection of public order, health or morals, or for the protection of the rights and freedoms of others.

D State-Religion Relationships: A Right to Religiously Neutral Governance?

With respect to establishing a state religion or ideology versus religiously neutral governance, international human rights law provides for the principles of non-impairment and non-discrimination. The Human Rights Committee is particularly concerned with:

- the protection of freedom of religion or belief for everyone;
- blasphemy laws;
- the status of minorities; and
- the protection of dissenters.

E Freedom of Expression

1 *Freedom of Opinion and Restrictions on Freedom of Expression (Article 19 ICCPR)*

The ICCPR establishes an absolute *forum internum* right to "hold opinions without interference" (Article 19.1 ICCPR). In addition, everyone has "the right to freedom of expression" (Article 19.2 ICCPR). However, like the right to manifest one's religion, which is a qualified right whose restrictions are set forth in Article 18.3, freedom of expression is a qualified right. The exercise of freedom of expression (Article 19.3 ICCPR):

> carries with it special duties and responsibilities. It may therefore be subject to certain restrictions, but these shall only be such as are provided by law and are necessary:
>
> (a) For respect of the rights or reputations of others;
> (b) For the protection of national security or of public order (*ordre public*), or of public health or morals.

The Article 19.3 restrictions on freedom of expression are largely parallel to the Article 18.3 restrictions on freedom to manifest one's religion. These restrictions can be summarized as follows:

- limitations that are necessary to protect national security, public order, public health or morals; and
- limitations that are necessary to protect the rights and reputations of others.

2 *Blasphemy Laws and the Tension of Freedom of Religion and Freedom of Expression*

a Overview

Some states have proposed that freedom of expression clashes with freedom of religion and that protecting the latter requires restricting the former. This has been the main premise behind anti-blasphemy laws or laws "combating defamation of religions." Some proponents of this view argue that freedom of religion encompasses not only the right to act in accordance with one's religion but also the right *not* to be exposed to criticism or to proselytism from other religions. On this basis, proponents of anti-blasphemy laws have attempted to prohibit speech that insults, criticizes or shows contempt toward others' religion.

b No Right of Religion Not to Be Offended

Such laws pose serious challenges to life in free, democratic societies. They undermine freedom of expression, a bedrock right in democratic states, in the name of shielding religions from criticism. However, religions hold no standing as rights bearers in international law. The traditional human rights approach protects human beings, not religions. It is the persons who practice religion—not the religions themselves—that hold religious rights. Yet these rights extend only to the freedom to act in accordance with one's religious beliefs. They do not extend to a right to be free from criticism, offense, insult or ridicule.

Laws seeking to prohibit free speech on the basis of protecting others' religious rights not to be offended or exposed to differing opinions or beliefs are facially invalid because no such right not to be offended or exposed exists under international law. This position has been expressed by Asma Jahangir, the former Special Rapporteur on freedom of religion or belief, who in 2006 stressed that freedom of religion "primarily confers a right to act in accordance with one's religion but does not bestow a right for believers to have their religion itself protected from all adverse comment."[112] She also pointed out that freedom of religion or belief "does not include the right to have a religion or belief that is free from criticism or ridicule."[113] Frank La Rue, the former Special Rapporteur on freedom of expression, argued that "for the right to freedom of thought, conscience and religion to be fully realized, robust examination and criticism of religion doctrines and practices—even in a harsh manner—must also be allowed."[114] On the basis of the foregoing, we can conclude that freedom of expression cannot be

112. Report of the Special Rapporteur on freedom of religion or belief, Asma Jahangir, and the Special Rapporteur on contemporary forms of racism, racial discrimination, xenophobia and related intolerance, Doudou Diène, further to Human Rights Council decision 1/107 on incitement to racial and religious hatred and the promotion of tolerance, A/HRC/2/3, para. 37.
113. *Ibid.*, para. 36.
114. Report of the Special Rapporteur on promotion and protection of the right to freedom of opinion and expression, A/67/357, para. 36.

curtailed because of the sensitivities of persons who do not wish for their religious beliefs to be challenged.

c *Freedom of Religion and Freedom of Expression Are Mutually Reinforcing*

Not only can we state that freedom of religion and freedom of expression do not collide, but we can go a step further and state that the two are *mutually reinforcing*. The right to manifest one's religion under Article 18.2 of the ICCPR can only truly be realized if states respect and protect Article 19.2 freedom of expression. Where freedom of expression is curtailed, so too is the right to distribute religious pamphlets, write about and publish one's religious beliefs, engage in missionary activities, proselytize and preach sermons from pulpits or in mosques. The full realization of freedom of religion is dependent on protecting the manifestation of one's religion, which is, in turn, dependent on freedom of expression. This is in line with Special Rapporteur Jahangir's observation that freedom of religion or belief "needs other human rights to be fully exercised, including the right to freedom of association or the right to freedom of expression."[115]

3 *Prohibition of Racial and Religious Hatred (ICCPR)*

At the same time, however, freedom of expression is not an absolute right. As with freedom to manifest one's religion, it can be subjected to lawful restrictions, provided such restrictions are for a proper purpose and are proportionate. Certain types of expression, including hate speech, are curtailed. Article 20 of the ICCPR specifically prohibits the following types of expression:

- propaganda for war;
- advocacy of national, racial or religious hatred *that constitutes incitement* to discrimination, hostility or violence.

The restriction on the expression of religious hatred is limited to only advocacy that "constitutes incitement to discrimination, hostility or violence." Expressions of religious hatred are thus not prohibited where they do not lead to such incitement.

It is important to note, however, that advocacy of national or racial hatred (as opposed to religious hatred) may be prohibited on the basis of the ICERD, even if it does *not* constitute incitement to discrimination, hostility or violence, as discussed further below.

4 *Prohibition of Ideas Based on Racial Superiority or Hatred (ICERD)*

Article 4 of ICERD requires states to condemn propaganda and organizations based on ideas of the superiority of one race (Article 4.I) and to (Article 4.I(a)):

115. A/HRC/2/3, para. 41.

> declare an offence punishable by law *all dissemination of ideas based on racial superiority or hatred, incitement to racial discrimination,* as well as all acts of violence or incitement to such acts against any race or group of persons of another colour or ethnic origin, and also the provision of any assistance to racist activities, including the financing thereof.

The provision thus requires states to criminalize the dissemination of ideas based on racial superiority, *regardless of whether such acts actually incite or involve violence.* In this way, the prohibition under ICERD is broader than that of the ICCPR, which is limited to advocacy that incites discrimination, hostility or violence. Article 4.I of the ICERD is a rare instance where the dissemination of ideas itself—regardless of whether such ideas incite unlawful conduct or undermine public order—is prohibited. Article 4 of the ICERD can thus be criticized as undermining the very essence of what it means to be a democratic society, where all ideas, regardless of how distasteful, can be disseminated, provided they do not threaten public safety, health or the fundamental rights and freedoms of others.

Given the breadth of the prohibition in Article 4.I, the U.S., when ratifying the ICERD, lodged the following reservation:[116]

> That the Constitution and laws of the United States contain extensive protections of individual freedom of speech, expression and association. Accordingly, the United States does not accept any obligation under this Convention, in particular under articles 4 and 7, to restrict those rights, through the adoption of legislation or any other measures, to the extent that *they are protected by the Constitution and laws of the United States.*

This reservation is in keeping with U.S. constitutional law, which recognizes a far-reaching freedom of expression rooted in the First Amendment of the American Bill of Rights. Free speech in the U.S. is protected, even if it encompasses speech advocating for racial superiority or hatred. However, the right guaranteed by the First Amendment does not extend to speech advocating illegal conduct when there is an imminent threat of lawless action. In *Brandenburg v. Ohio* (U.S. 1969), the U.S. Supreme Court held that the constitutional protections of free speech do not extend to speech that: (a) aims to incite imminent unlawful conduct and (b) is likely to produce such conduct.

However, it is important to bear in mind that the prohibition encompassed by Article 4 of the ICERD applies only to ideas relating to race, not to religion. While it is true that in some cases, race and religion intersect (e.g., where members of a particular religion largely derive from a particular ethnic group), in almost all cases, there are members of any particular religious class that do not share the same ethnicity or race. Therefore, the restriction of Article 4 of the ICERD cannot be said to carry over or apply to the sphere of religion.

This is a key distinction vis-à-vis the prohibition in Article 18.3 of the ICCPR, which explicitly applies to religion. Had Article 4 of the ICERD been a prohibition that encompassed the dissemination of ideas based on religious superiority, it would

116. Available at <https://treaties.un.org/Pages/ViewDetails.aspx?src=TREATY&mtdsg_no=IV-2&chapter=4&lang=en>.

potentially usher in the end of discourse in democratic societies as to religious doctrine and belief. Books and pamphlets critical of a religion or religious practices, apologetic materials setting out to prove the truth of a religion and lectures that criticize one religion and advocate for another would all be banned and criminalized as tending toward religious superiority. The drafters of ICERD thus limited the Article 4 restriction to ideas relating to race, color and ethnic origin.

F Gender Equality and Religion

The ICCPR requires states to respect freedom of thought and religion, permitting restrictions only in exceptional circumstances (Article 18.3):

> Freedom to manifest one's religion or beliefs may be subject only to such limitations as are prescribed by law and are necessary to protect public safety, order, health, or morals or the fundamental rights and freedoms of others.

The protections set forth in Article 18 are deemed to be non-derogable, even in cases of national emergency (Article 4 ICCPR). Moreover, the ICCPR provides that (Article 5.1):

> Nothing in the present Covenant may be interpreted as implying for any State, group or person any right to engage in any activity or perform any act *aimed at the destruction of any of the rights and freedoms recognized herein* or at their limitation to a greater extent than is provided for in the present Covenant.

The CEDAW requires that (Article 2):

> States Parties condemn discrimination against women in all its forms, agree to pursue by all appropriate means and without delay a policy of eliminating discrimination against women.

In practice, the realization of these rights can be challenging within the context of religion, particularly in the case of cultures that embrace religions or religious practices that presuppose unequal gender roles. This has led some commentators to conclude that there is an inherent clash between the full realization of both the rights of women and freedom of religion. This controversy has lead reformers in some religious traditions to reconsider the meaning of their sacred texts and to reinterpret them in light of modern ideas of women's equality.

G The State and Education

1 *Overview*

The right to education does not impose a complete ban on the state from interacting or cooperating with the church. In *Delgado Paez v. Colombia* (1990), the Human Rights Committee held that it was not a violation of Article 18 of the ICCPR for the state to allow the church to make decisions regarding religious instruction in schools, including how and who should teach.

International human rights law is silent on the question of the state's establishment of religion, but the Human Rights Committee's General Comment 22 requires: (i) non-impairment of the enjoyment of any of the rights under ICCPR; and (ii) non-discrimination (e.g., with respect to political office or economic opportunities).

2 *ICCPR (Article 18.4 ICCPR)*

Article 18.4 ICCPR protects the right of parents and legal guardians to ensure the religious education of their children. It provides as follows:

> The States Parties to the present Covenant undertake to have *respect for the liberty of parents* and, when applicable, legal guardians to ensure the religious and moral *education of their children in conformity with their own convictions.*

This rule is consistent with the holding in the U.S. Supreme Court case *Wisconsin v. Yoder* (U.S. 1972). The defendants were practitioners of the Amish faith whose religious values conflicted with those of the public school system. When the defendants, due to their religious beliefs, refused to comply with a Wisconsin law requiring all students under age 16 to attend school, they were convicted. The Court, requiring the government to show a *compelling state interest* in burdening the free exercise of religion, held that the laws were invalid under strict scrutiny. Reversal of the conviction was affirmed.

3 *Religious Discrimination Declaration (Article 5.1)*

The Religious Discrimination Declaration provides parental rights that parallel those of the ICCPR. The Declaration states as follows (Article 5.1):

> The *parents* or, as the case may be, the legal guardians of the child *have the right to organize the life within the family in accordance with their religion or belief* and bearing in mind the *moral education in which they believe the child should be brought up.*

At the same time, the Declaration guarantees the rights of children to education in accordance with the wishes of parents but based on the best interests of the child (Article 5.2):

> Every child shall enjoy the right to have access to education in the matter of religion or belief in accordance with the wishes of his parents or, as the case may be, legal guardians, and shall not be compelled to receive teaching on religion or belief against the wishes of his parents or legal guardians, the best interests of the child being the guiding principle.

VI MECHANISMS FOR GUARANTEEING HUMAN RIGHTS PROTECTION

A Human Rights Council

1 *Overview*

The U.N. Human Rights Council ("UNHRC") is the successor to the United Nations Commission on Human Rights. As a subsidiary body of the U.N. General Assembly, it is responsible for strengthening the promotion and protection of human rights around the globe. The Council was created by the U.N. General Assembly on 15 March 2006 with the main purpose of addressing situations of human rights violations and making recommendations on them.

2 *Human Rights Council Complaint Procedures*

The Human Rights Council's complaint procedures are as follows:

- the Special Procedures of the Human Rights Council, which involve independent human rights experts with mandates to report and advise on human rights from a thematic or country-specific perspective covering civil, cultural, economic, political, and social rights;[117]
- the Human Rights Council Complaint Procedure, which addresses consistent patterns of gross and reliably attested violations of human rights and fundamental freedoms. The complaint procedure addresses communications submitted by individuals, groups, or NGOs claiming to either be victims of human rights violations or to have direct, reliable knowledge of such violations. The Complaint Procedure is governed by Human Rights Council resolution 5/1, entitled "Institution-Building of the United Nations Human Rights Council" and adopted on 18 June 2007.[118]

3 *Universal Periodic Review*

a *Introduction*

The Universal Periodic Review ("UPR") of the Human Rights Council was established by General Assembly resolution 60/251 of 3 April 2006 to periodically examine the human rights performance of all 193 U.N. member states. The UPR is an innovation of the Human Rights Council that provides an opportunity for all states to declare the actions they have taken to improve human rights and overcome challenges to the protection of human rights in their countries. It is intended to complement the work of

117. *See* available at <https://www.ohchr.org/EN/HRBodies/SP/Pages/Welcomepage.aspx>.
118. *See* available at <https://www.ohchr.org/EN/HRBodies/HRC/ComplaintProcedure/Pages/HRCComplaintProcedureIndex.aspx>.

other human rights mechanisms, including the U.N. human rights treaty bodies. The Working Group on the UPR, which is composed of the HRC's 47 member states and is chaired by the HRC President, conducts country reviews.

b *Pre-Sessions*

UPR pre-review documentation consists of the following:

- Stakeholders Report, consisting of a summary of contributions submitted by national human rights institutions, regional organizations, and civil society groups. The Report, which should not exceed 5,350 words, is prepared by OHCHR and should summarize the views of various stakeholders, particularly civil society groups in countries such as the U.S. that do not have national human rights organizations.
- U.N. Compilation, consisting of information contained in treaty bodies, special procedures, and other United Nations entities reports. The Compilation, which is prepared by OHCHR, should not exceed 5,350 words.
- National Report, prepared by the country under review, ideally the result of consultations with relevant stakeholders. It should not exceed 10,700 words and should be submitted in one of the six official U.N. languages.

c *A Non-confrontational Approach*

i Problems with a Confrontational Approach

The non-confrontational approach of the UPR serves as a model of constructive engagement. Because the Commission on Human Rights never had enforcement powers, resolutions condemning states' human rights records had the effect of erecting walls of hostility and impeding dialogue without achieving improved human rights records. Scathing reports confronting nations on their human rights records are unlikely to have any impact in enlisting the nations' cooperation in reforming these records. Rather, confrontation results in backlash. Nations subjected to unwanted scrutiny put up defenses and point fingers back, accusing their accusers of imposing "western" values or undermining their sovereignty with hidden foreign agendas. This results in no real progress in addressing human rights abuses, particularly where confrontation and naming and shaming are exploited for political purposes. Additionally, governments accused of human rights violations might undertake reprisals against individuals, NGOs and national human rights institutes that cooperate with the U.N. and its human rights mechanisms. These issues can be avoided through a non-confrontational approach that elicits the voluntary cooperation of the state being scrutinized while avoiding divisiveness and polarization.

ii Non-Confrontation Is Not Silence

It may be argued that the non-confrontational approach equates to standing by silently in the face of gross violations of human rights, thereby propagating and perhaps even abetting in the commission of such violations. However, non-confrontation is not the same as standing by idly. One may report human rights violations and seek to correct them non-confrontationally through constructive engagement without standing by silently. It is possible to be just as engaged in promoting human rights and be more successful through a non-confrontational approach than in a confrontational style.

iii Circumstances Where Confrontation May Be Appropriate

At the same time, however, the approach of the UPR has its limits. A nation may not wish to cooperate with the international community in reforming its human rights record. A non-confrontational approach is thus only workable "where the state has a true desire to improve human rights enjoyment."[119] A further weakness of the UPR is that its reviews are only periodic. This makes it "unsuitable for urgent and chronic human rights concerns."[120] In such cases, the confrontational operating style of the former Commission on Human Rights, where states issue country-specific resolutions by a vote, may be better suited to "reforms to ameliorate the human rights violations" in specific situations.[121] However, neither a confrontational nor a cooperative approach is likely to lead to any results unless either the nation being scrutinized has a genuine will to reform or the agency undertaking the review is granted the power to enforce its resolutions and recommendations.

B Human Rights Treaty Bodies

1 Overview

There are nine principal international human rights treaties. Each of these has created a "human rights treaty body," or committee of experts, to monitor implementation of the treaty provisions by states parties. These treaty bodies, which are responsible for considering individual complaints or communications, are comprised of committees of independent experts. They receive secretariat support from the Human Rights Treaties Branch of the OHCHR. The nine human rights treaty bodies are as follows:

- the U.N. Human Rights Committee ("HRC"), perhaps the most prominent of human rights treaty bodies, monitors implementation of the ICCPR (1966) and its optional protocols;

119. Jane Connors, "United Nations," in Daniel Moeckli et al. (eds.), *International Human Rights Law*, Oxford University Press (2018), p. 377.
120. *Ibid.*
121. Felice D. Gaer, "A Voice Not an Echo: Universal Periodic Review and the U.N. Treaty Body System," *Human Rights Law Review*, Vol. 7, Issue 1 (2007), pp. 129-130.

- the Committee on Economic, Social and Cultural Rights ("CESCR") monitors implementation of the ICESCR (1966);
- the Committee on the Elimination of Racial Discrimination ("CERD") monitors implementation of the International Convention on the Elimination of All Forms of Racial Discrimination (1965);
- the Committee on the Elimination of Discrimination against Women ("CEDAW") monitors implementation of the Convention on the Elimination of All Forms of Discrimination against Women (1979) and its optional protocol (1999);
- the Committee Against Torture ("CAT") monitors implementation of the Convention against Torture and Other Cruel, Inhuman or Degrading Treatment (1984);
- the Committee on the Rights of the Child ("CRC") monitors implementation of the Convention on the Rights of the Child (1989) and its optional protocols (2000);
- the Committee on Migrant Workers ("CMW") monitors implementation of the International Convention on the Protection of the Rights of All Migrant Workers and Members of Their Families (1990);
- the Committee on the Rights of Persons with Disabilities ("CRPD") monitors implementation of the International Convention on the Rights of Persons with Disabilities (2006); and
- the Committee on Enforced Disappearance ("CED") monitors implementation of the International Convention for the Protection of All Persons from Enforced Disappearance (2006).

One mechanism that almost all human rights treaty bodies have is requiring states to periodically submit reports explaining how they are working to fulfill the terms of the respective treaty. After the submission, the treaty bodies give the reports "concluding observations." While these observations may serve as important leverage in the international arena, states are not required to act on them.

2 Complaints Procedures

In addition to the complaint procedures of the Human Rights Council (*see* "Human Rights Council Complaint Procedures," *supra*), the human rights treaty body system offers the following procedures for bringing complaints of violations of human rights treaties:

- individual communications;
- state-to-state complaints; and
- inquiries.

a *Individual Communications*

i Overview

The nine human rights treaty bodies (HRC, CERD, CAT, CEDAW, CRPD, CED, CMW, CESCR, and CRC) may, under certain conditions, consider individual complaints or communications submitted by individuals. However, not all treaty body-based complaint mechanisms have entered into force; at this time, only eight of them (HRC, CERD, CAT, CEDAW, CRPD, CED, CESCR, and CRC) permit individual complaints or communications to be submitted by individuals under certain conditions:[122]

- the Human Rights Committee ("HRC") may consider individual communications alleging violations of the rights set forth in the ICCPR by states parties to the First Optional Protocol to the ICCPR;
- the Committee on Elimination of Discrimination against Women ("CEDAW") may consider individual communications alleging violations of the Convention on the Elimination of All Forms of Discrimination against Women by states parties to the Optional Protocol to the Convention on the Elimination of Discrimination against Women;
- the Committee against Torture ("CAT") may consider individual complaints alleging violations of the rights set out in the Convention against Torture and Other Cruel, Inhuman or Degrading Treatment or Punishment by states parties who have made the necessary declaration under Article 22 of the Convention;
- the Committee on the Elimination of Racial Discrimination ("CERD") may consider individual petitions alleging violations of the International Convention on the Elimination of All Forms of Racial Discrimination by states parties who have made the necessary declaration under Article 14 of the Convention;
- the Committee on the Rights of Persons with Disabilities ("CRPD") may consider individual communications alleging violations of the Convention on the Rights of Persons with Disabilities by states parties to the Optional Protocol to the Convention;
- the Committee on Enforced Disappearances ("CED") may consider individual communications alleging violations of the International Convention for the Protection of All Persons from Enforced Disappearance by states parties who have made the necessary declaration under Article 31 of the Convention;
- the Committee on Economic, Social and Cultural Rights ("CESCR") may consider individual communications alleging violations of the International Covenant on Economic, Social and Cultural Rights by states parties to the Optional Protocol to the International Covenant on Economic, Social and Cultural Rights;

122. *See* "Human Rights Bodies—Complaints Procedures," U.N. Office of the High Commissioner for Human Rights (2019), available at <https://www.ohchr.org/EN/HRBodies/TBPetitions/Pages/HRTBPetitions.aspx#inquiries>.

- the Committee on the Rights of the Child ("CRC") may consider individual communications alleging violations of the Convention on the Rights of the Child or its first two Optional Protocols (the Optional Protocol on the Sale of Children, Child Prostitution and Child Pornography ("OPSC") and the Optional Protocol on the Involvement of Children in Armed Conflict ("OPAC")) by State Parties to the third Optional Protocol on a Communications Procedure ("OPIC").

The individual complaint mechanism of the Committee on Migrant Workers (CMW) has not yet entered into force.

ii Complaint Procedure

A complaint may be lodged with a Committee against a state:

- that is party to the treaty in question providing for the rights which have been allegedly violated;
- that accepted the Committee's competence to examine individual complaints, either through ratification or accession to an Optional Protocol (in the case of ICCPR, CEDAW, CRPD, ICESCR and CRC) or by making a declaration to that effect under a specific article of the Convention (in the case of CERD, CAT, CED and CMW).

Complaints may also be brought by third parties on behalf of individuals, provided they have given their written consent. However, a third party may bring a case without such consent in certain cases, such as when a person is imprisoned without access to the outside world. In such cases, the author of the complaint should state clearly why such consent cannot be provided.

b Interstate Complaints

Several of the human rights treaties permit states parties to complain to the relevant treaty body about alleged violations of the treaty by another State party, as follows:[123]

> CAT, CMW, CED, ICESCR and CRC: Article 21 CAT, article 74 CMW, article 32 CED, article 10 of the Optional Protocol to ICESCR, and article 12 of the Optional Protocol (on a communications procedure) to the Convention on the Rights of the Child set out a procedure for the relevant Committee itself to consider complaints from one State party which considers that another State party is not giving effect to the provisions of the Convention. This procedure applies only to states parties who have made a declaration accepting the competence of the Committee in this regard.
>
> CERD, HRC and CRC: Articles 11-13 ICERD, articles 41-43 ICCPR set out a more elaborate procedure for the resolution of disputes between states parties over a State's fulfilment of its obligations under the relevant Convention/Covenant

123. *Ibid.*

through the establishment of an ad hoc Conciliation Commission. The procedure normally applies to all states parties to ICERD, but applies only to states parties to the ICCPR and CRC which have made a declaration accepting the competence of the relevant Committees in this regard.

c *Inquiries*

Upon receipt of "reliable information on serious, grave or systematic violations by a State party of the conventions they monitor," the following Committees may, "on their own initiative, initiate inquiries if they have received reliable information containing well-founded indications of serious or systematic violations of the conventions in a State party":[124]

- the Committee against Torture (Article 20 CAT);
- the Committee on the Elimination of Discrimination against Women (Article 8 of the Optional Protocol to CEDAW);
- the Committee on the Rights of Persons with Disabilities (Article 6 Optional Protocol to CRPD);
- the Committee on Enforced Disappearances (Article 33 of CED);
- the Committee on Economic;
- Social and Cultural Rights (Article 11 of the Optional Protocol to ICESCR) and the Committee on the Rights of the Child (Article 13 of the Optional Protocol (on a communications procedure) to the CRC).

However, inquiries may only be conducted with respect to states parties that have recognized the competence of the relevant Committee to accept inquiries.

C Domestic Guarantees

1 *National Human Rights Institutions*

a *Overview*

"Too often, the decisions and recommendations of international legal bodies charged with protecting human rights are ignored by states unable or unwilling to implement them."[125] Without a national enforcement authority to enforce rights, human rights advocates are left to depend on the good will of states to comply with their obligations. However, as Thucydides skeptically but aptly remarked, the "strong do what they can and the weak suffer what they must,"[126] often with little regard for the law.

124. *Ibid.*
125. Christian M. de Vos, *From Rights to Remedies: Structures and Strategies for Implementing International Human Rights Decisions*, Open Society Foundations (2013), p. D.
126. Oona A. Hathaway, "Do Human Rights Treaties Make a Difference?" 111.8 Yale Law Journal 1935 (2002), p. 1937-38.

This is where national human rights institutions ("NHRIs") can play an important role. Ensuring there are effective domestic mechanisms and independent national bodies, such as NHRIs, is an indispensable element in implementing international human rights law. Without NHRIs, states may flout their international human rights obligations with impunity, given the absence of an accountability mechanism. The Vienna Declaration and Program of Action ("VDPA") mentions NHRIs as institutions vital in "creating conditions whereby each individual can enjoy universal human rights and fundamental freedoms."[127] The VDPA highlights the "constructive role" of NHRIs in promoting and protecting human rights, noting their "advisory capacity to competent authorities, their role in remedying human rights violations, in the dissemination of human rights information, and education in human rights."[128]

The Hungarian case of *A.S. v. Hungary* is illustrative. When the U.N. Committee on the Elimination of Discrimination against Women ruled against Hungary in the case of *A.S. v. Hungary*, for example, "it took more than three years to ensure that the government implemented the committee's decision. The struggle of Ms. A.S. to achieve justice—through a maze of domestic courts, executive ministries, and the Hungarian legislature—highlights the challenges involved in ensuring that states live up to their legal obligations."[129] The presence of an effective NHRI adhering to the Paris Principles, including mechanisms to guarantee independence and pluralism, would have assisted in the execution of Hungary's human rights obligations without causing Ms. A.S. to navigate through mazes of bureaucracy over eight years before she was compensated for the abuse of her rights.

"Although states must implement the decisions of human rights courts and treaty bodies, national institutions can serve as implementation facilitators—assisting in the process of developing remedial legislation and monitoring the execution of judgments on the ground."[130] The presence of NHRIs or ombudsmen offices can "draw attention to deficient implementation, if they are independent and have high quality staff. National institutions and ombudsmen can also bring unique pressure to bear in linking the implementation of judgments to compliance with human rights norms more generally."[131] Without an NHRI that implements the Paris Principles, the implementation of human rights will be severely weakened with a protection framework that is, at best, anemic.

b *The Case of the United States*

In a 1 June 2015 statement posted by the U.S. Mission to the OSCE entitled "National Human Rights Institutions (NHRI)," the U.S. acknowledged that it does not have an NHRI, but it has:

127. VDPA, para. 34.
128. *Ibid.*, para. 36.
129. Christian M. de Vos, *From Rights to Remedies: Structures and Strategies for Implementing International Human Rights Decisions*, Open Society Foundations (New York, 2013), p. D.
130. *Ibid.*, p. 21.
131. *Ibid.*

multiple complementary protections and mechanisms to reinforce our ability to guarantee respect for human rights, including through our independent judiciary at both federal and state levels and numerous state and local human rights institutions. More than 140 state and local governments within the United States have civil rights or human rights agencies or commissions, many of which participate in the International Association of Official Human Rights Agencies. Over the last several years, the federal government has increased its engagement with state, local, tribal, and territorial governments on our human rights obligations through outreach to state governors and attorneys general and participation in state-sponsored training and events.

Additionally, in 2012, the U.S. Government created the Equality Working Group, co-chaired by the Departments of State and Justice, to enhance the government's domestic implementation of our international human rights obligations and commitments relating to non-discrimination and equal opportunity. This mechanism creates additional opportunities for federal agencies to work together to combat discrimination in their relevant areas of expertise, facilitate the sharing of best practices, and engage with civil society and other stakeholders.

2 *Domestic Law*

a *Overview*

International human rights law may be binding on states through not only treaties and customary international law but also domestic law.

b *The Leahy Amendment*

In the United States, for example, federal legislation such as the Leahy[132] Amendment establishes vetting requirements on the basis of human rights records as a precondition for the funding, equipping, and training of foreign forces by the U.S.

The annual Department of Defense Appropriations Act explains how "Leahy Vetting" applies to the military of the United States. The Department of Defense may not "train, equip, or fund" any foreign force if there is credible information that any *member* of the foreign unit has committed any gross violation of human rights. The restriction applies to particular units rather than to nationwide armed forces. Therefore, the Department of Defense may exclude a particular unit with a record of gross human rights violations from funding while providing funds to other units within the same nation.

Before any training, equipping or funding may occur, the military must vet the foreign unit and submit a list of names to the relevant U.S. embassy, which may either delay, support or cancel it altogether.

132. Pronounced "la' he."

VII REMEDIES FOR HUMAN RIGHTS BREACHES

A Domestic Remedies

1 Human Rights Violations by Individuals

The judiciary systems of most nations recognize a cause of action in tort against violators of human rights. Such causes of action will generally take the form of intentional torts such as assault, battery, false imprisonment, trespass to chattels or intentional infliction of emotional distress.

In addition, where human rights violations also constitute crimes (e.g., murder, rape, arson, etc.), the victim may normally press charges through a public prosecutor seeking the imprisonment or other applicable punishment of the alleged criminal actor.

2 Human Rights Violations by States

Some nations allow their residents to bring suit against them in their own domestic courts for civil rights abuses and other wrongs committed by the state or by state actors. Such suits are brought under some form of legislation whereby the state partially waives its immunity to be sued and permits human rights violations (often called "civil rights abuses") to be heard against the state or its agents in its courts. Such legislation may include protection from discrimination, hate crimes, damage to property or violations of other rights. (For specific examples of national legislations that permit citizens to sue the state or state actors in cases alleging not only human rights abuses but ordinary torts and criminal cases as well, *see* Chapter 8—State Responsibility and Immunities from Jurisdiction, "Partial Waivers of Sovereign Immunity in Domestic Courts," below).

As a further protection of human rights provided under domestic laws, we may consider asylum laws. Most countries are parties to the CRSR and thus have incorporated asylum laws into their domestic legislation that permit resident aliens to remain in the country if the aliens can show that persecution due to race, nationality, religious affiliation, political views or social group membership would result in the resident's home country if he or she were to return. For further treatment on this topic, *see* "Refugee Law," below.

B Remedies Within the International Framework

A variety of remedies under international law are available for victims of human rights breaches. The remedies depend to a large extent on whether a state or individual committed the violation: States may be required to pay compensation to victims or to change domestic law; individuals may be required to pay a fine or may face criminal penalties, such as imprisonment. In either case, international treaties normally require individuals to have exhausted the domestic remedies available before bringing suit in the international forum (*see, e.g.*, Article 41(1)(c) ICCPR). This requirement is, however, waived if it can be shown that doing so would be unreasonable, ineffective, or the remedy inadequate.

1 *Human Rights Violations by Individuals*

a International Criminal Tribunals and Individual Responsibility

Until recently, individuals were not seen as subjects or objects of international law, but this has changed beginning with the Nuremberg IMT and later with the IMT for the Far East, both of which tried and convicted a number of state actors for violations of international law, making it clear that it is individuals, not nations, that commit violations of international humanitarian and human rights law.

For a full discussion, *see* "Individual Criminal Responsibility of State Actors and Non-State Actors," in Chapter 7, International Criminal Law, *infra.*

b Universal Jurisdiction

Universal jurisdiction is a concept under international law that allows national courts to try cases involving the most egregious crimes that are considered *jus cogens* crimes that trigger *obligatio erga omnes* ("obligations toward all") (e.g., genocide, crimes against humanity, torture and piracy). The principle allows the courts of any nation to try nationals of any other nation without the consent of the accused or of his nation. This is an exception to the general rule that requires the consent of sovereign nations to have their nationals tried by international or foreign courts.

For a full discussion, *see* "Universal Jurisdiction," in Chapter 7, International Criminal Law, *infra.*

2 *Human Rights Violations by States*

The various human rights regimes have established monitoring mechanisms that are capable of providing varying degrees of redress to victims. The focus of such mechanisms is the responsibility of the state and its obligation to make reparations for human rights violations suffered by victims. Such reparations may encompass a range of measures, including amendment of domestic law, prosecution of perpetrators and rehabilitation and compensation of victims.

a Human Rights Treaty Bodies

States may be called to account for violations of human rights by human rights treaty bodies, such as the HRC, which are created by human rights treaties to implement and enforce the provisions contained therein. These bodies may receive complaints by individuals or groups of individuals alleging violations of human rights norms by states or by state actors. The human rights treaty bodies may investigate these complaints, make their views known and recommend to states how shortfalls with respect to human rights should be addressed.

b *International Courts*

When domestic remedies are unavailable or when they have been exhausted, the allegedly injured party may sometimes find recourse in international tribunals. Some of these tribunals, such as the Inter-American Court of Human Rights, are open to individuals, groups of individuals, or NGOs. They generally require the petitioner to show that all domestic remedies have been exhausted before allowing the case to move forward in their courts.

Like domestic remedies, international remedies are only open to citizens or residents of those states that allow their citizens or residents to sue the states in international tribunals (universal jurisdiction, as discussed above, is an exception to this general rule, as it allows the courts of any nation to try nationals of any other nation without that nation's consent). This partial waiver of sovereign immunity is usually achieved through international treaties among nations agreeing to create an international forum for hearing human rights abuse cases, such as the European Court of Human Rights. Only states parties to the treaties may be sued.

For examples of such treaties, we may point to the American Convention on Human Rights, which allows individuals to bring petitions to the Inter-American Commission on Human Rights for human rights violations by OAS member states of the ADRDM or the ACHR. The Commission may, in turn, refer the case to the Inter-American Court of Human Rights for adjudication. This is similarly the case of the European Convention on Human Rights, which allows individuals to bring cases to the European Court of Human Rights for human rights violations by states parties.

VIII BUSINESS AND HUMAN RIGHTS

A Businesses as Subjects of International Law

While states are the primary subjects of international law, natural and juridical persons are also subjects of international law. Juridical persons—whether corporations or other business associations or registered non-governmental organizations, such as charities—similarly may bear rights and responsibilities under international law.

Businesses are increasingly seen as subjects of international law. For example, the United Nations Convention on the Law of the Sea ("UNCLOS") (1982) establishes guidelines for businesses and the management of marine natural resources. One of the guiding principles governing the administration of international environmental law is the "polluter pays" principle, which is the basis for resolving transboundary environmental disputes established in the *Trail Smelter Arbitration* (1941). It holds that a business that is responsible for pollution is liable for the clean-up costs.

Some national jurisdictions have promulgated legislation that not only requires business organizations to respect human rights but also criminalizes business organizations that violate international law, including international humanitarian law. Amendments made to the Norwegian Penal Code in 2008, for example, include international crimes that are extended to corporations. Under the amended Penal Code, corporations may be held criminally liable for war crimes.[133]

Other jurisdictions limit the liability of corporations for violations of international human rights law to civil damages. In the US, for example, corporations may be held civilly liable for violations of international human rights law under the Alien Tort Claims Act (28 USC 1350) ("ATCA," also known as the "Alien Tort Statute"), which provides US federal courts jurisdiction to hear claims brought "by an alien for a tort only, committed in violation of the law of nations or a treaty of the United States."[134] The Statute is routinely invoked by human rights advocates in claims against multinational corporations.

In 2021, for example, the US Supreme Court decided *Nestlé USA Inc. v. Doe et al.*, Docket No. 19-416,[135] which involved allegations of forced labor and child labor on the basis of the Statute. Plaintiffs claimed that they were former child slaves who were forced to work on plantations in Côte d'Ivoire and that defendants Nestlé USA, Inc. and Cargill, Inc. facilitated abuses of international human rights law. The Court decided in favor of Nestlé and Cargill, but only because the alleged forced labor and child labor took place in Ivory Coast, outside of the territorial scope of the ATCA. Although the case was decided in favor of the defendants, it nonetheless demonstrates the potential civil liability that multinational corporations may face if they have inadequate human rights implementation policies and supply chain audit mechanisms in place.

B Legal Instruments and Guiding Principles

Legal instruments and guiding principles governing business and human rights include the following:

- the U.N. Guiding Principles on Business and Human Rights;
- the OECD Guidelines for Multinational Enterprises;
- the ILO Tripartite Declaration of Principles Concerning Multinational Enterprises and Social Policy;
- the OAS American Convention on Human Rights;
- European Union Directive 2014/95/EU; and
- the ASEAN Human Rights Declaration.

133. Simon O'Connor, "Corporations, international crimes and national courts: a Norwegian view," 887 *International Review of the Red Cross* (September 2012), available at <https://international-review.icrc.org/articles/corporations-international-crimes-and-national-courts-norwegian-view>; <https://doi.org/10.1017/s1816383113000544>.
134. 28 U.S. Code § 1350—Alien's action for tort.
135. *Nestle USA Inc. v. Doe et al*, Docket No. 19-416 (decided 17 June 2021), available at <https://www.supremecourt.gov/opinions/20pdf/19-416_i4dj.pdf>.

C U.N. Special Representative of the Secretary-General on Human Rights and Transnational Corporations and Other Business Enterprises

1 Overview

U.N. Commission on Human Rights Resolution E/CN.4/RES/2005/69, dated 20 April 2005, mandated the U.N. Secretary-General to appoint a U.N. Special Representative of the Secretary-General on human rights and transnational corporations and other business enterprises. The Special Representative was mandated to:

- identify and clarify standards of corporate responsibility and accountability for transnational corporations and other business enterprises with regard to human rights;
- elaborate on the role of states in effectively regulating and adjudicating the role of transnational corporations and other business enterprises with regard to human rights;
- research and clarify the implications for transnational corporations and other business enterprises of concepts such as "complicity" and "sphere of influence";
- develop materials and methodologies for undertaking human rights impact assessments of the activities of transnational corporations and other business enterprises;
- compile a compendium of best practices.

In 2005, the U.N. Secretary-General appointed Mr. John Ruggie as the Special Representative on human rights and transnational corporations and other business enterprises. In his final report under the 2005-2011 mandate, the Special Representative proposed a "Protect, Respect and Remedy" Framework that comprised three principles:

(i) protect: the state duty to protect against human rights abuses by third parties, including businesses;
(ii) respect: the corporate responsibility to respect human rights (i.e., to act with due diligence to avoid infringing on the rights of others); and
(iii) remedy: the need for greater access by victims to effective remedies.

The Special Representative's mandate concluded in June 2011.

2 U.N. Guiding Principles on Business and Human Rights

On 16 June 2011, the Human Rights Council, in resolution A/HRC/RES/17/4, endorsed the U.N. Guiding Principles on Business and Human Rights, a set of guidelines for states and companies to prevent, address and remedy human rights abuses committed in business operations. The Guiding Principles provide a global standard to implement the "Protect, Respect and Remedy" Framework and prevent and address the risk of adverse impacts on human rights resulting from business activity.

The Guiding Principles outline steps that states can take to encourage business respect for human rights, provide a blueprint for businesses to know and show that they respect human rights, and reduce the risk of causing or contributing to human rights violations. They set forth benchmarks for state stakeholders to assess business respect for human rights. They are organized under three pillars:

(1) The state duty to *protect* human rights;
(2) The corporate responsibility to *respect* human rights; and
(3) Access to *remedies*.

D Promoting Human Rights and Environmental Stewardship as Company Policy

Businesses have a variety of tools at their disposal for promoting human rights and environmental stewardship as core company principles. In particular, businesses may participate in the U.N. Guiding Principles Reporting Framework, self-report through the Business & Human Rights Resource Center, adopt global human rights policies and environmental protection policies and ensure that their global supply chains commit to comply with such policies.

1 *U.N. Guiding Principles Reporting Framework*

The U.N. Guiding Principles Reporting Framework provides guidance for companies to report on how they respect human rights. It consists of a series of questions for businesses to confirm that their operations respect human rights and to show others the progress they are making. The Reporting Framework provides implementation guidance for companies that are reporting and assurance guidance for internal auditors and external assurance providers.

The Reporting Framework is a joint initiative of the Shift Project, a non-profit consultancy founded by former U.N. Special Representative on Business and Human Rights John Ruggie, and Mazars, an accounting company. The Reporting Framework is based specifically on the framework John Ruggie created as U.N. Special Representative, but it is not formally affiliated with the U.N. It provides participants with a questionnaire that can be completed in accordance with reporting principles. It also offers participants implementation guidance that addresses each question of the Reporting Framework and states its objective, supporting guidance, relevant information, citations from the U.N. Guiding Principles on Business and Human Rights and cross-reference points to other reporting initiatives.

2 *Business & Human Rights Resource Centre*

The Business & Human Rights Resource Centre ("BHRRC") works to advance human rights in business while eradicating abuse and seeking accountability. The BHRRC works to build corporate transparency, strengthen corporate accountability and empower advocates.

The BHRRC maintains a database of companies that have adopted human rights policies or business codes of conduct.[136] The BHRRC routinely invites companies to respond to allegations of misconduct raised by civil society. This process encourages companies to publicly address human rights concerns and provides the public with both the allegations and the company's comments in full while increasing transparency. Response rates for each company are indicated in the company profile of each company featured on the site.

Many companies report on compliance with and breaches of their internal policies and voluntarily disclose shortcomings with respect to business practices that may infringe on human rights, workplace health and safety norms or environmental stewardship. While self-reporting promotes some degree of accountability, some critics argue that because reporting is voluntary, it lacks verification and enforcement mechanisms, thereby limiting its value. However, such policies can ensure that the employees and affiliates of multinational companies aspire to a uniform transnational human rights standard and set an expectation of global compliance with baseline ethics standards.

The BHRRC is a registered charity in England & Wales. In addition, it is registered as a 501(c)(3) non-profit organization in the U.S. While the BHRRC is a depository for business and human rights materials, including U.N. documents, the BHRRC has no formal U.N. affiliation.

3 *Human Rights Risks Relating to Supply Chains*

Human rights violations are an inherent risk that may arise indirectly within a company's global supply chains. Such violations may relate to the rights of employees working within those supply chains and the impacts of such supply chains on the environment. Such supply chains can include property leases, catering and cleaning services, recruitment agencies, vendors of IT equipment and other goods and outsourced business process services.

Companies with global operations face a risk that their impact on local communities and the environment may adversely impact human rights through their supply chains. This risk can be mitigated by appropriately vetting local vendors, undertaking due diligence on local partners and ensuring that local vendors, service providers and partners commit to comply with all applicable local laws and the principles enshrined in companies' human rights policies.

136. The database is available at <https://old.business-humanrights.org/en/company-policy-statements-on-human-rights> accessed 14 May 2021.

Multinational companies can further mitigate risk by ensuring that their supply chains adopt business and human rights policies at least as rigorous as the companies' own policies or codes. In addition, companies may go a step further by implementing annual or biannual training on their local supply chain partners to ensure that they understand, respect and ensure respect of universal human rights standards in their local operations.

E Adoption of Business and Human Rights Policies

1 Overview

Human rights policies are becoming increasingly common among multinational companies that seek to demonstrate their leadership in the areas of ethics, transparency, environmental stewardship, workplace safety, indigenous rights and the rule of law. Just as regional human rights treaties vary from one region to another, the specific provisions of human rights policies vary from one location to another. What may be culturally accepted in one country may not be in another. Very often, the rights deemed to be central in the dominant culture of a multinational company's headquarters tend to inform the content of the company's human rights policy globally.

2 Policy Names

Human rights policies can go by various names, including, simply "Human Rights Policy" or "Human Rights Charter." Some industry sectors tend to vary the names of their policies. Law firms might adopt a "Human Rights and Rule of Law Charter." Energy companies might adopt a "Human Rights, Environment, Health and Safety Charter."

3 Baseline Provisions of Human Rights Policies

Regional differences aside, company human rights policies generally include, as a baseline minimum, the following provisions:

- respect for the human rights of company employees, including the right to just and favorable working conditions, physical integrity, workplace safety, privacy and family life, and to freedom from harassment and bullying in the workplace;
- a covenant to protect the right of employees to be free from discrimination on the basis of nationality, race, gender or any other protected class, regardless of employees' location, function, role or seniority within the company;
- respect for the right of employees to express their opinions or their faith in the workplace;

- a commitment to environmental stewardship and to comply with applicable local, national and international norms relating to environmental protection and preservation;
- a commitment to act in accordance with national and international standards of business transparency and integrity and to combat bribery and corruption at all levels of the company and among companies' agents and assigns;
- support for the rule of law and for the institutions, processes and frameworks that ensure the resolution of disputes and accountability, predictability and justice in governing economic transactions and social relations and resolving disputes;
- a covenant to combat human trafficking and eradicate modern slavery in all its forms and to report incidences of the same to local authorities when discovered among supply chains;
- a requirement for local agents, vendors, service providers and partners to comply with companies' business and human rights policies or adopt their own polices having similar baseline standards.

4 *Sample Language*

For sample language that can be included in human rights policies, *see* "Human Rights Policies: Sample Language" in the Appendices, *infra*.

F Modern Slavery Statements

In addition to the above, companies should consider whether they are required to publish a modern slavery statement under section 54 (Transparency in Supply Chains) of the UK Modern Slavery Act 2015. A commercial organization is required to publish an annual statement if all the criteria below apply:

- it is a "body corporate" or a partnership, wherever incorporated or formed;
- it carries on a business, or part of a business, in the UK;
- it supplies goods or services; and
- it has an annual turnover of GBP 36 million or more.

Business organizations that have a demonstrable business presence in the UK and meet the other criteria should publish an annual statement. Factors that should be considered by companies when determining whether the UK Modern Slavery Act applies to them include, but are not limited to, the following:

- they have UK offices;
- they provide service or support functions in the UK;
- they receive income in the UK; and
- they have other visible UK business presence, such as a website.

CHAPTER 6

International Humanitarian Law: The Law of Armed Conflict

I INTRODUCTION

A Limiting Human Suffering in the Chaos of War

1 *Overview*

War is an inherently chaotic clash of wills between two or more forces where violence is employed to achieve political goals. As a large-scale endeavor that leads to the destruction of both life and property, war inevitably results in the loss of innocent life. The intensive interaction of armed forces during war with two or more sides actively working to disrupt one another's functioning gives rise to chaos and collateral damage, including unintended consequences on civilians and civilian objects that may not be readily foreseeable at the time of military operations.

This chaos gives rise to uncertainty in military operations, which in turn demands an approach to war that seeks to limit unnecessary human suffering. In an attempt to prevent this suffering and to uphold the principles of humanity, virtually all human civilizations have sought to govern military conduct via rules of engagement, laws of war, and moral, religious, and ethical codes.

2 *The Martens Clause*

a *Expression in Treaties from 1899 to 1980*

The principle of humanity that international humanitarian law seeks to uphold is expressed in the so-called "Martens Clause" contained in the Preamble of Hague Convention (II) of 1899 with Respect to the Laws and Customs of War on Land and its annex: Regulations concerning the Laws and Customs of War on Land. The Martens Clause, which was proposed by F. F. de Martens, the Russian delegate to the Hague Peace Conference, states as follows:[137]

> Until a more complete code of the laws of war is issued, the High Contracting Parties think it right to declare that *in cases not included in the Regulations adopted by them*, populations and belligerents remain under the protection and empire of the principles of international law, as they result from the usages established between civilized nations, from the laws of humanity, and the requirements of the public conscience.

Hague Convention (IV) of 1907 respecting the Laws and Customs of War on Land contains a somewhat different expression of the Martens Clause. It states (changes emphasized in italics):

> Until a more complete code of the laws of war has been issued, the High Contracting Parties deem it expedient to declare that, in cases not included in the Regulations adopted by them, the *inhabitants* and the belligerents remain under the protection and the rule of the principles of the *law of nations*, as they result from the usages established *among* civilized *peoples*, from the laws of humanity, and the *dictates* of the public conscience.

Additional Protocol I phrases the Martens Clause as follows (changes emphasized in italics):[138]

> *In cases not covered by this Protocol or by other international agreements, civilians and combatants* remain under the protection and authority of the principles of *international law* derived from *established custom*, from the *principles of humanity* and from the dictates of public conscience.

Additional Protocol II further abbreviates the Clause as follows:[139]

> Recalling that, in cases not covered by the law in force, the human person remains under the protection of the principles of humanity and the dictates of the public conscience.

The Clause was also paraphrased in Resolution XXIII of the Tehran Conference on Human Rights of 1968. It was restated with slight variations in the Preamble to the

137. The original French of the Martens Clause states as follows:

> "En attendant qu'un code plus complet des lois de la guerre puisse être édicté, les Hautes Parties Contractantes jugent opportun de constater que, dans les cas non compris dans les dispositions réglementaires adoptées par Elles, les populations et les belligérants restent sous *la sauvegarde* et sous *l'empire des principes du droit des gens*, tels qu'ils résultent des usages établis entre nations civilisées, des lois de l'humanité et des exigences de la conscience publique." *See* available at <https://ihl-databases.icrc.org/applic/ihl/dih.nsf/Article.xsp?action=openDocument&documentId=AF4868EA2C79EA8EC12563BD002B95CF>.

138. Article 1.2 AP I.
139. Preamble AP II.

Convention on Conventional Weapons (1980) and is cited in various national military manuals, including those of the United States.[140]

b *Content*

The Martens Clause requires that in cases not covered by the law in force, persons remain under the protection of the principles of international law as they result from:

- the practices ("usages") established between civilized nations;
- the principles of humanity; and
- the dictates of the public conscience.

The Martens Clause:[141]

> has ancient antecedents rooted in natural law and chivalry. It is articulated in strong language, both rhetorically and ethically, which goes a long way toward explaining its resonance and influence on the formation and interpretation of the law of war and international humanitarian law.

B Defining International Humanitarian Law

The International Committee of the Red Cross ("ICRC") defines international humanitarian law ("IHL") as "a set of rules which seek, for humanitarian reasons, to limit the effects of armed conflict."[142] Also known as the "law of war," the "law of armed conflict," or "*jus in bello*," international humanitarian law is a set of non-derogable legal norms governing the protection of civilians and members of armed forces during wars, armed conflicts and military occupations.

The respect of international humanitarian law is of paramount importance not only for ensuring compliance with binding international norms that protect civilians in armed conflict but also for avoiding the loss of support of local populations by being perceived as employing weapons and tactics that cause unnecessary human suffering.

C Origins

As discussed earlier, with respect to the legality of the use of force, the law of war can be said to have originated with the Dutch jurist Hugo Grotius (1583-1645), whose writings established the basis of international law based on natural law. In his treatise *De jure belli ac pacis libri tres* (*On the Law of War and Peace: Three books*), Grotius

140. U.S. Department of the Army, *The Law of Land Warfare* (Field Manual No. 27-10 (1956), para. 6; U.S. Department of the Air Force, *International Law-The Conduct of Armed Conflict and Air Operations*, 1-7(b), AFP No. 110-31 (1976).
141. Theodor Meron, "The Martens Clause, Principles of Humanity, and Dictates of Public Conscience," 94(1) *American Journal of International Law* (2000), pp. 78, 79 available at <https://doi.org/10.2307/2555232>.
142. "What is International Humanitarian Law?" Advisory Service on International Humanitarian Law, ICRC (July 2004), p. 1.

advances a system of principles of natural law, whereby what is "just" is consistent with the nature of a society of rational beings.

As discussed earlier, Grotius' treatise is divided into three parts, as follows:

(i) *Book I: General conception*. Offers a conception of war and natural justice, arguing that there are some circumstances in which war is justifiable.
(ii) *Book II: Jus ad bellum (justice in the resort to war)*. Describes three "just causes" for war: self-defense, reparation of injury and punishment; Grotius considers a wide variety of circumstances under which these causes apply.
(iii) *Book III: Jus in bello (justice in the conduct of war)*. Enumerates the rules governing the conduct of war once it has begun. Grotius argues that all parties to war are bound by such rules, whether or not their cause is just.

For the purpose of this section, we discuss modern codified international law with respect to Grotius' Book III, that is, the principles that apply to the conduct of war when conflict has already commenced. This branch of international law, known as international humanitarian law, has four purposes:

- limit the *damages, casualties and other consequences* of conflict;
- protect combatants and civilians from *unnecessary suffering*;
- guarantee the *fundamental rights* of combatants and civilians; and
- prevent the *escalation of conflict*.

D International Humanitarian Law as Customary International Law and Non-derogable *Jus Cogens*

1 *Common Article 1 to the Geneva Conventions of 1949*

As discussed under "Common Article 1: Respecting the Conventions in All Circumstances," *infra*, Article 1, common to the four Geneva Conventions of 1949, requires states parties to "*respect* and to *ensure respect* for the present Convention *in all circumstances*" (emphasis added). Therefore, states have an affirmative duty to not only respect, but also to ensure the respect of international humanitarian law. Moreover, no derogation is permitted from these duties, which apply "in all circumstances." The duty to "ensure respect" of the Geneva Conventions effectively means that states not involved in an armed conflict must call upon states that *are* involved in the armed conflict to ensure that they respect the rules.

2 *International Jurisprudence*

In *Legality of the Threat or Use of Nuclear Weapons, Advisory Opinion, ICJ Reports 1996*, p. 226, the ICJ observed that international humanitarian law reflects non-derogable customary international law and *jus cogens*:[143]

143. *Legality of the Threat or Use of Nuclear Weapons*, Advisory Opinion, ICJ Reports (8 July 1996), p. 258, para. 79.

> 79. It is undoubtedly because a great many rules of humanitarian law applicable in armed conflict are so fundamental to the respect of the human person and "elementary considerations of humanity" as the Court put it in its Judgment of 9 April 1949 in the *Corfu Channel* case (ICJ Reports 1949, p. 22), that the Hague and Geneva Conventions have enjoyed a broad accession. Further *these fundamental rules are to be observed by all States whether or not they have ratified the conventions that contain them, because they constitute intransgressible principles of international customary law.*

In the Advisory Opinion, the ICJ went on to state that the principal conventions of international humanitarian law reflect customary international law:[144]

> 80. The Nuremberg International Military Tribunal had already found in 1945 that the humanitarian rules included in the Regulations annexed to the Hague Convention IV of 1907 "were recognized by all civilized nations and were regarded as being declaratory of the laws and customs of war" (Trial of the Major War Criminals, 14 November 1945-1 October 1946, Nuremberg, 1947, Vol. 1, p. 254).
>
> 81. The Report of the Secretary-General pursuant to paragraph 2 of Security Council resolution 808 (1993), with which he introduced the Statute of the International Tribunal for the Prosecution of Persons Responsible for Serious Violations of International Humanitarian Law Committed in the Territory of the Former Yugoslavia since 1991, and which was unanimously approved by the Security Council (resolution 827 (1993)), stated:
>
>> In the view of the Secretary-General, the application of the principle *nullum crimen sine lege* requires that the international tribunal should apply rules of international humanitarian law which are beyond any doubt part of customary law ...
>>
>> The part of conventional international humanitarian law which has beyond doubt become part of international customary law is the law applicable in armed conflict as embodied in: the Geneva Conventions of 12 August 1949 for the Protection of War Victims; the Hague Convention (IV) Respecting the Laws and Customs of War on Land and the Regulations annexed thereto of 18 October 1907; the Convention on the Prevention and Punishment of the Crime of Genocide of 9 December 1948; and the Charter of the International Military Tribunal of 8 August 1945.

The ICJ further held that the codification of international humanitarian law, as found in the Geneva Conventions and the other principal humanitarian treaties, reflects "the most universally recognized humanitarian principles." The ICJ held:[145]

> 82. The extensive codification of humanitarian law and the extent of the accession to the resultant treaties, as well as the fact that the denunciation clauses that existed in the codification instruments have never been used, have provided the international community with a *corpus* of treaty rules the great majority of which had already become customary and which reflected the most universally recognized humanitarian principles. These rules indicate the normal conduct and behaviour expected of States.

144. *Ibid.*, p. 258, paras. 80-81.
145. *Ibid.*, para. 82.

Finally, the ICJ noted that "[i]t has been maintained in these proceedings that these principles and rules of humanitarian law are part of *jus cogens* as defined in Article 53 of the Vienna Convention on the Law of Treaties of 23 May 1969."[146] On this basis, we can conclude that international humanitarian law bears a *jus cogens* character. Therefore, states may not derogate the provisions of international humanitarian law, which remain mandatory when states are engaged in armed conflict. These norms are binding upon even states that have not ratified or have objected to the Geneva Conventions or other treaties that govern armed conflict.

This character of non-derogability is one of the characteristics of international humanitarian law that distinguishes it from international human rights law. As one scholar has remarked, a "major difference which enhances protection is the non-derogability of international humanitarian law."[147]

E State Responsibility to "Respect and Ensure Respect"

While the ICRC is regarded as the "guardian" of the Geneva Conventions and other treaties that constitute international humanitarian law, it cannot enforce international humanitarian law or serve as a judge. These functions belong to states parties to international treaties, which are required to respect international humanitarian law, ensure the respect of international humanitarian law and punish those responsible for "grave breaches" of the Geneva Conventions in accordance with their treaty obligations, customary international law and other commitments as discussed below.

1 *Customary International Law*

The requirement to respect and ensure the respect of international humanitarian law is customary. Rule 144 of the ICRC's *Customary International Humanitarian Law* states as follows:

> Rule 144. Ensuring Respect for International Humanitarian Law *Erga Omnes*
>
> States may not encourage violations of international humanitarian law by parties to an armed conflict. They must exert their influence, to the degree possible, to stop violations of international humanitarian law.

2 *Judicial Decisions*

In the *Nicaragua* case (Merits) (1986), the ICJ held that the duty to respect and ensure respect derived from the Geneva Conventions and from "general principles of humanitarian law to which the Conventions merely give specific expression." The ICJ concluded, therefore, that the U.S. was "under an obligation not to encourage persons

146. *Ibid.*, para. 83.
147. Michael Bothe, "The Status of Captured Fighters in Non-International Armed Conflict," in Christian Tomuschat et al. (eds.), *The Right to Life*, Brill (2010), p. 211.

or groups engaged in the conflict in Nicaragua to act in violation of the provisions of Article 3 common to the four 1949 Geneva Conventions."[148]

3 *International Declarations*

After the Geneva Conventions were adopted, rules were adopted to require those engaged in armed conflict to respect international humanitarian law and to ensure the respect of international humanitarian law. The U.N. Security Council and the U.N. General Assembly have interpreted common Article 1 to involve obligations beyond those of the parties to the conflict. In a resolution adopted in 1990, the U.N. Security Council called on states parties to Geneva Convention IV to ensure respect by Israel for its obligations in accordance with common Article 1.[149] The U.N. General Assembly has also adopted resolutions restating the obligation of states parties to Geneva Convention IV to ensure respect of the treaty.[150] In the Final Declaration adopted by the International Conference for the Protection of War Victims in 1993, the participants committed "to respect and ensure respect for international humanitarian law in order to protect the victims of war" and urged all states to "ensure the effectiveness of international humanitarian law and take resolute action, in accordance with that law, against States bearing responsibility for violations of international humanitarian law with a view to terminating such violations."[151] Moreover, the Draft Articles on the Responsibility of States for Internationally Wrongful Acts provide that "a State which aids or assists another State in the commission of an internationally wrongful act by the latter is internationally responsible for doing so."[152]

F Interaction of International Humanitarian Law and Human Rights Law

1 *Overview*

In some ways, international humanitarian law can be viewed as a set of specialized human rights regulations that apply during war and armed conflict. There is therefore some question among legal theorists as to whether human rights law continues to apply in times of armed conflict or whether, in such cases, international humanitarian law applies exclusively.

148. *Military and Paramilitary Activities in and against Nicaragua (Nicaragua v. United States of America), Merits*, Judgment, ICJ Reports (27 June 1986), p. 114, para. 220.
149. U.N. Security Council, Res. 681 (20 December 1990).
150. *See, e.g.*, U.N. General Assembly Resolution 32/91 (13 December 1977) and U.N. General Assembly Resolution 37/123 (16 December 1982).
151. Part II, Final declaration of the International Conference for the Protection of War Victims (1 September 1993).
152. Article 16 DARS.

2 *Traditional (Minority) "Displacement" Approach:* **Lex Specialis**

The traditional approach, which is a minority approach, holds that international human rights law only applies in times of peace and international humanitarian law, being the more specialized set of rules, substitutes human rights law in times of war. This view conforms to the legal principle known as *lex specialis*, from the Latin *lex specialis derogat legi generali*, meaning "the more specific law has precedence over the more general law." Under this doctrine, where two laws govern the same factual situation, the law governing a specific subject matter (*lex specialis*) overrides the law governing general matters (*lex generalis*).

3 *Modern "Complementarity" Approach*

a *Within State Borders: Parallel Application View*

The modern approach holds that ordinary human rights regulations continue to operate even when international humanitarian law is applicable. In such cases, unless human rights laws are derogated by treaty or otherwise, they apply in addition to international humanitarian law, informing and even filling in the gaps left by international humanitarian law. For example, in a state where domestic law prohibits racial discrimination by state actors (a human rights provision that is often called a "civil right" within the domestic context), citizens of that state continue to enjoy the right to be free from discrimination even if their country is in the midst of civil war unless such rights are derogated by law. This therefore means that state actors within the military are bound not only by international humanitarian law but also by human rights law.

b *Outside State Borders: Doctrinal Differences with Respect to the Extraterritorial Application*

Under the modern view of parallel application, there is a consensus that states are *always* bound by international humanitarian law, whether an armed conflict is of an international or non-international character. That is, even when a military crosses a state border, it is under a continuing obligation to respect the Geneva Conventions and other provisions of international humanitarian law.

There is no such consensus with respect to the extraterritorial application of human rights law. Thus, if a military crosses a state border, some commentators would argue that the military would be under a continuing obligation to respect its state's human rights law. Others argue that the state's human rights law applies only within the state's territory.

Despite these varied opinions, there is some consensus based on modern cases that suggest that human rights law continues to apply extraterritorially in at least two circumstances, namely, if a state party exercises:[153]

153. *Al-Skeini v. United Kingdom*, 53 EHRR 18 (2011), para 131.

(i) "control and authority over an individual"; or
(ii) "effective control of an area outside [its] national territory" (e.g., at a foreign military base or installation, such as Guantanamo Bay).

In each of these cases, the state must continue to respect human rights law over the area or individual over which it exercises control, even if such area or individual is located outside of its territory.

4 *Position of the United States*

The U.S. courts have not yet confronted the question of whether the ICCPR and Convention against Torture apply to the U.S. government extraterritorially, but the executive branch "has at times suggested that the United States' commitments under these human rights agreements do not apply when the United States acts overseas."[154] Under this view, the U.S. adopts the traditional *lex specialis* approach with respect to the application of human rights law.

However, with respect to certain human rights treaties, the U.S. takes the opposite approach, holding that even in times of war, human rights continue to apply. For example, in 2014, the Obama administration shifted to an "unequivocal yes" on the following issues under the Convention against Torture: "whether the ban on cruel, inhuman, and degrading treatment applies to actions outside U.S. borders, and whether the [Convention against Torture] applies in war."[155] Under this view, the U.S. is, at least in theory, opposed to any form of torture, even in military installations located outside of U.S. territory.

Moreover, the U.S. Department of State has articulated that the U.S. position has shifted from a "displacement" view (only international humanitarian law applies on the battlefield) to a "complementarity" view (both international humanitarian law and human rights law apply), although the U.S. continues to maintain that international humanitarian law remains the primary body of law in military operations. The trend toward accepting the application of human rights law on the battlefield may eventually result in the application by the U.S. of international human rights treaties to which it is

154. Oona A. Hathaway et al., "Human Rights Abroad: When Do Human Rights Treaty Obligations Apply Extraterritorially?" 43 *Arizona State Law Journal* (2011), p. 393 (citing the Letter from the Permanent Representative of the U.S. to the U.N. and Other International Organizations in Geneva, to the Office of the High Commissioner for Human Rights (31 January 2006), reprinted as Annex II to the U.N. High Commission on Human Rights, Report of the Chairman of the Working Group on Arbitrary Detention et al. on the Situation of Detainees at Guantánamo Bay, U.N. Doc. E/CN.4/2006/120 (27 February 2006) ("The United States has made clear its position that . . . the International Covenant on Civil and Political Rights, by its express terms, applies only to 'individuals within its territory and subject to its jurisdiction.'") as well as other sources, including John B. Bellinger, III, U.S. Department of State, Opening Remarks, U.S. Meeting with U.N. Committee Against Torture (May 5, 2006) ("As a general matter, countries negotiating the Convention [Against Torture] were principally focused on dealing with rights to be afforded to people through the operation of ordinary domestic legal processes")).

155. *See* Ryan Goodman and Eric Messinger, "U.N. Committee Criticizes U.S. Record on Torture, Praises U.S. on Extraterritorial Reach of Treaty" *Just Security* (28 November 2014), available at < https://www.justsecurity.org/17837/un-committee-torture-concluding-observations-united-states >.

a party, such as the ICCPR, in military operations, indicating a shift away from the traditional *lex specialis* approach.

5 *Summary of the Application of IHRL and IHL*

<table>
<tr><th></th><th colspan="2">In Times of Peace</th><th colspan="2">Armed Conflict within State Boarders</th><th colspan="2">Extraterritorial Armed Conflict</th></tr>
<tr><th></th><th>IHRL</th><th>IHL</th><th>IHRL</th><th>IHL</th><th>IHRL</th><th>IHL</th></tr>
<tr><td>Traditional View</td><td>✓</td><td>☒</td><td>☒</td><td>✓</td><td>☒</td><td>✓</td></tr>
<tr><td>Modern View</td><td>✓</td><td>☒</td><td colspan="2">✓</td><td>☒[156]</td><td>✓</td></tr>
<tr><td>U.S. View</td><td>✓</td><td>☒</td><td colspan="4">Gradual shift from “displacement” view to “complementarity” view[157]</td></tr>
</table>

II DETERMINING WHETHER AN ARMED CONFLICT EXISTS

A Origins of the Existence of Armed Conflict under International Law

Historically, international law defined “war” as a contest between two or more states that either declared or accepted that they were in a state of armed struggle. Determining the existence of a state of war required a careful examination of the statements, declarations and other expressions of state leaders rather than an examination of de facto on-the-ground facts.

The case *Kawasaki Kisen Kabushiki Kaisha of Kobe v. Bantham Steamship Co., Ltd.* (1939)[158] challenged this approach, elevating the de facto on-the-ground situation over the strictly formal definition under international law. The Court held that war existed between China and Japan despite the fact that no declaration of war had been made and despite the fact that diplomatic relations between China and Japan had not been severed. The word “war” in the charterparty at issue “was not to be given a technical meaning based on principles of international law, but its ordinary common sense meaning.”[159] The Court's reasoning was based on the absurd results that would arise if states could be allowed to shirk their responsibilities under the laws of war by simply refusing to formally recognize a state of armed conflict that existed between them as “war.” In this way, the Court elevated the de facto existence of armed conflict over the official pronouncements of states.

156. The modern view holds that IHRL generally does not apply in extraterritorial armed conflict, unless a state has effective control over an area outside of its territory or over an individual.
157. However, the U.S. continues to maintain that international humanitarian law remains the primary body of law in military operations.
158. *Kawasaki Kisen Kabushiki Kaisha of Kobe v. Bantham Steamship Co., Ltd.*, 2 K.B. 544, Court of Appeal (1939).
159. *Ibid.*

Just ten years later, in keeping with the spirit of *Kawasaki Kisen Kabushiki Kaisha of Kobe*, the international community adopted the Geneva Conventions of 1949, which embraced a set of rules that based the existence of armed conflict not on what states say but on what they do. A declaration of war is no longer necessary to trigger the application of the law of armed conflict. The law of armed conflict now applies to all cases of any "armed conflict which may arise between two or more of the High Contracting Parties, even if the state of war is not recognized by one of them" under common Article 2 of the Geneva Conventions and in "the case of armed conflict not of an international character occurring in the territory of one of the High Contracting Parties" under common Article 3, regardless of what states actually declare. This introduced a conceptual revolution, replacing the historic formalistic concept of war based on state declarations with the post-Geneva Conventions concept of the law of armed conflict, which is based on the existence of an international or non-international armed conflict.

B Disparate Rules for International and Non-international Armed Conflict

While the Geneva Conventions of 1949 state that they apply to "armed conflict which may arise between two or more of the High Contracting Parties"[160] and that common Article 3 applies to "armed conflict not of an international character occurring in the territory of one of the High Contracting Parties,"[161] the Geneva Conventions themselves never define the term "armed conflict." To determine when an armed conflict subject to the provisions of the Geneva Conventions exists, we must turn to customary international law.

The position of customary international law is most clearly expressed in the 1995 Decision of the Appeals Chamber of the ICTY in *Prosecutor v. Dusko Tadić*. The ICTY sought to define when armed conflict exists for the purpose of both international and non-international armed conflict. The Tribunal held:[162]

> On the basis of the foregoing, we find that an armed conflict exists whenever there is a resort to armed force between states or protracted armed violence between governmental authorities and organized armed groups or between such groups within a State.

The foregoing holding establishes disparate standards when determining whether an international versus a non-international armed conflict exists:

- In the first standard, armed conflict exists whenever there is a "resort to armed force between states" (without distinction as to whether such armed force is protracted or crosses a particular threshold). This scenario has come to be

160. Common Art. 2, Geneva Conventions of 1949.
161. Common Art. 3, Geneva Conventions of 1949.
162. *Prosecutor v. Dusko Tadić*, IT-94-1AR72, ICTY Appeals Chamber, Decision (2 October 1995), para. 70.

called "international armed conflict" in international jurisprudence and in the teachings and writings of the publicists of international law.[163]
- In the second standard, non-international armed conflict exists whenever there is "protracted armed violence between governmental authorities and organized armed groups or between such groups within a State" (note that such armed violence must be "protracted"). This scenario has come to be called "non-international armed conflict" in international jurisprudence and in the teachings and writings of international law.[164]

This view is in accordance with the principles of customary international humanitarian law.

C International Armed Conflict

1 Overview

Common Article 2 of the Geneva Conventions states:

> the present Convention shall apply to all cases of declared war or of any other armed conflict which may arise between two or more of the High Contracting Parties, even if the state of war is not recognized by one of them.
>
> The Convention shall also apply to all cases of partial or total occupation of the territory of a High Contracting Party, even if the said occupation meets with no armed resistance.

Therefore, in order for hostilities to qualify as an international armed conflict, the following elements must be met:

- there must be a declared war;[165] or
- there must be armed conflict, *and* it must be between at least two states (or by a state and a non-state armed group controlled by a state, as discussed later); or
- there must be a partial or total occupation of the territory of a state party.

2 "One Shot One Prisoner" Rule

Unlike the determination of the existence of a non-international armed conflict, whose existence involves the application of factor-based tests, in international armed

163. *See, e.g.*, "How is the Term 'Armed Conflict' Defined in International Humanitarian Law?" International Committee of the Red Cross (ICRC) Opinion Paper (March 2008), pp. 2-3, available at < https://www.icrc.org/en/doc/assets/files/other/opinion-paper-armed-conflict.pdf >.

164. *Ibid.*, pp. 3-5.

165. The declaration of war should be by one state against another in order to trigger the application of Common Art. 1 and the law of international armed conflict. Common Art. 1 is not referring to situations in which politicians declare war in a rhetorical sense (e.g., where a politician declares a "war on drugs") or use the rhetoric of war in informational campaigns against other states, but without formally issuing a declaration of war through applicable legal channels.

conflicts, the employment of *any* level of force between states technically triggers the existence of the conflict. Under the ICRC "one shot one prisoner" view, an international armed conflict exists when just a single shot is fired between states or a single prisoner of war is taken.

D Non-international Armed Conflict

1 *Factors to Determine the Existence of a Non-international Armed Conflict*

The existence of a non-international armed conflict, in contrast, involves the application of factor-based tests.

a *Pictet Factors: Organized and Effective Military Forces*

Under the Pictet[166] Factors, the following are used when determining whether a conflict qualifies as a non-international armed conflict:

- *organized* military force;
- subject to some *authority*;
- *control* of territory;
- respect of the *law of war*;
- whether a state responds with *regular armed forces.*

In his *Commentaries* on armed conflict, Jean Pictet wrote that a formal declaration of war was not required to trigger a non-international armed conflict.

b *Threshold of Intensity and Organization of the Parties*

i *Prosecutor v. Dusko Tadić* (1995 and 1997)

In *Prosecutor v. Dusko Tadić* (1995), the ICTY acknowledged that the following elements are applicable for determining whether violence rises to the level of a non-international armed conflict, thus triggering common Article 3 of the Geneva Conventions: (i) the protracted nature of the violence (later interpreted to mean "intensity," as discussed below); and (ii) organization of the parties to the conflict (to distinguish from lesser forms of violence, such as banditry, rioting, or individual terrorist activities).[167]

Two years later, the Trial Chamber in *Prosecutor v. Dusko Tadić* (1997) further fleshed out the 1995 standard as follows:[168]

166. Jean Pictet (1914-2002) was one of the main authors of the *Commentary on the Geneva Conventions of 12 August 1949*.
167. *Prosecutor v. Dusko Tadić*, IT-94-1-AR72, ICTY Appeals Chamber, Decision (2 October 1995).
168. *Prosecutor v. Dusko Tadić*, IT-94-1-T, ICTY Trial Chamber (7 May 1997), para. 562.

> The test applied [to confirm] the existence of an armed conflict for the purposes of the rules contained in Common Article 3 focuses on two aspects of a conflict; the intensity of the conflict and the organization of the parties to the conflict. In an armed conflict of an internal or mixed character, these closely related criteria are used solely for the purpose, as a minimum, of distinguishing an armed conflict from banditry, unorganized and short-lived insurrections, or terrorist activities, which are not subject to international humanitarian law.

This rule is largely considered to be reflective of customary international law.

ii *Prosecutor v. Ramush Haradinaj* (2008); Defining "Intensity"

In *Prosecutor v. Ramush Haradinaj et al.*, the ICTY defined "intensity" for the purpose of determining when internal disturbances rise to the level of armed conflict. The ICTY stated that:[169]

> Trial Chambers have relied on indicative factors relevant for assessing the "intensity" criterion, none of which are, in themselves, essential to establish that the criterion is satisfied. These indicative factors include the number, duration and intensity of individual confrontations; the type of weapons and other military equipment used; the number and calibre of munitions fired; the number of persons and type of forces partaking in the fighting; the number of casualties; the extent of material destruction; and the number of civilians fleeing combat zones. The involvement of the U.N. Security Council may also be a reflection of the intensity of a conflict.

c *Meaning of "Organized" Armed Group*

Non-state entities must fulfil certain criteria in order to form a party to a non-international armed conflict. Such entities must be collective entities with the ability to ensure respect for basic humanitarian norms and the capacity to engage in sufficiently intense violence.[170] The ICTY held that for an armed group to be considered organized, "it would need to have some hierarchical structure and its leadership requires the capacity to exert authority over its members."[171] This means that superior members must command and exert authority over subordinates.

Factors to be taken into account when determining whether a non-state entity qualifies as an organized armed group include:

- the presence of a command structure;
- the existence of disciplinary rules and mechanisms within the group;

169. *Prosecutor v. Ramush Haradinaj, Idriz Balaj and Lahi Brahimaj*, IT-04-84-T, ICTY Trial Chamber, Judgment (3 April 2008), para. 49.
170. Tilman Rodenhäuser, *Organizing Rebellion: Non-state Armed Groups under International Humanitarian Law, Human Rights Law, and International Criminal Law*, Oxford University Press (2018), pp. 61 ff.
171. *Prosecutor v. Boškoski and Tarčulovski*, Case No. IT-04-82-T, ICTY, Judgment (10 July 2008), para. 195.

- the ability to ensure compliance with the law of non-international armed conflict;
- the operational capacity to plan, coordinate and carry out military operations and sufficiently intense violence;
- the logistical capacity to procure, transport and distribute arms; and
- the ability to speak with one voice and negotiate and conclude peace accords and other agreements.

d Violence That Does Not Rise to the Level of Armed Conflict

Acts of violence that do not reach the threshold required for the application of the law of armed conflict remain in the exclusive domain of domestic criminal law. Professor Leslie C. Green's *The contemporary law of armed conflict* clarifies this point as follows:[172]

> [A]cts of violence committed by private individuals or groups which are regarded as acts of terrorism, brigandage, or riots which are of a purely sporadic character are outside the scope of such regulation and remain subject to national law or specific treaties relating to the suppression or punishment of terrorism. Such acts occurring during an international armed conflict may amount to war crimes or grave breaches of the Geneva Conventions or Protocol I and render those responsible liable to trial under the law of armed conflict.

In further support of this point, Additional Protocol II, which applies to non-international armed conflict, states that it does not apply to "riots, isolated and sporadic acts of violence and other acts of similar nature," which are deemed to be "internal disturbances and tensions" rather than non-international armed conflicts (Article 1.2 Additional Protocol II).

2 "Spillover Conflicts" and Other Non-international Armed Conflicts with International Elements

If an internal armed conflict spills over into other states (e.g., as was the case of the Somalian conflict) or involves cross-border operations (e.g., as is the case of Colombia-Venezuela border area conflicts by armed groups), the conflict is deemed to be a "spillover" conflict. Such a conflict retains its characterization as a non-international armed conflict that is subject to common Article 3 of the Geneva Conventions, despite its international dimension, in the same way, that a conflict would retain its characterization as a non-international armed conflict if a third state or multinational force intervened alongside the government against rebel groups (e.g., as the U.S. did in Afghanistan).

172. Leslie C. Green, *The contemporary law of armed conflict*, Juris Publishing, Manchester University Press (2000), p. 56.

However, if state actors of two or more distinct states confront one another, the armed conflict would be deemed an "internationalized non-international armed conflict" that triggers the application of common Article 2 rather than common Article 3, as discussed further below.

E Internationalized Non-international Armed Conflicts

A non-international armed conflict that becomes "internationalized" is treated as an international armed conflict subject to common Article 2 of the Geneva Conventions and the entire panoply of international law that applies to international armed conflicts. There are three ways that a non-international armed conflict can become internationalized:

1 Additional Protocol I Armed Conflicts

Additional Protocol I applies to international armed conflicts and to certain types of non-international armed conflicts that meet the criteria of Article 1.4. When such conflicts meet the criteria, they are treated as international conflicts subject to the entire range of the law of armed conflict rather than as non-international armed conflicts subject only to common Article 3 of the Geneva Conventions. Article 1.4 of Additional Protocol I states that it applies to armed conflicts:

> in which peoples are fighting against colonial domination and alien occupation and against racist régimes in the exercise of their right of self-determination, as enshrined in the Charter of the United Nations and the Declaration on Principles of International Law concerning Friendly Relations and Co-operation among States in accordance with the Charter of the United Nations.

However, Additional Protocol I does not automatically apply to such conflicts. Rather, the authority representing a people engaged against a state party must address a unilateral declaration to the depositary of the Protocol. Under Article 96.3 of Additional Protocol I:

> The authority representing a people engaged against a High Contracting Party in an armed conflict of the type referred to in Article 1, paragraph 4, may undertake to apply the Conventions and this Protocol in relation to that conflict by means of a unilateral declaration addressed to the depositary. Such declaration shall, upon its receipt by the depositary, have in relation to that conflict the following effects:
>
> a) the Conventions and this Protocol are brought into force for the said authority as a Party to the conflict with immediate effect;
> b) the said authority assumes the same rights and obligations as those which have been assumed by a High Contracting Party to the Conventions and this Protocol; and
> c) the Conventions and this Protocol are equally binding upon all Parties to the conflict.

This scenario will only apply in non-international armed conflicts that take place in the territories of states parties to Additional Protocol I.

The only time that this scenario applied was in the armed conflict in Western Sahara. The Polisario Front made a unilateral declaration in June 2015 on behalf of the people of Western Sahara that it undertook to apply the 1949 Geneva Conventions and Additional Protocol I to the conflict between it and the Kingdom of Morocco.

2 *Recognition of Belligerency*

a Overview

The recognition of belligerency is defined as:[173]

> the declaration, express or implied, that hostilities waged between two communities, of which one is not or, possibly, both are not sovereign States, are of such character and scope as to entitle the parties to be treated as belligerents engaged in a war in the sense ordinarily attached to that term by international law.

When a state recognizes belligerency, it acknowledges that the magnitude of the insurgency is such that it would be appropriate to treat the insurgent as a belligerent enemy state subject to the full panoply of the law of war.[174] The recognition of belligerency gives the contesting parties the right to be "treated as if they are engaged in a war waged by two sovereign States."[175]

The recognition of belligerency has:[176]

> developed as customary international law, its origin dating back to the period before World War I. The purpose of such recognition is to bring the laws of war, in particular the rules of humanitarian law in armed conflict into operation for an internal armed conflict.

b Triggering the Application of the Law of War

Prior to the 1949 Geneva Conventions, there was no subpart of the law of war that applied to internal or non-international armed conflicts, as common Article 3 does in the modern era. If a state recognized belligerency, it would apply the entire panoply of the law of war rather than a subpart of the law of war that specifically governed internal

173. Hersch Lauterpacht, *Recognition in International Law*, Cambridge University Press (Cambridge, 1947), p. 175.
174. For example, as the Union had done with respect to the Confederacy during the American Civil War.
175. Hersch Lauterpacht, *Recognition in International Law*, Cambridge University Press (Cambridge, 1947), p. 175.
176. Rüdiger Wolfrum and Christianne E. Philipp, "The Status of the Taliban: Their Obligations and Rights under International Law," *Max Planck Yearbook of United Nations Law*, UNYB 6 (2002), p. 578.

armed conflicts. This has the effect of bringing into application "the major part of international humanitarian law ... to a non-international armed conflict."[177]

In recognizing belligerency, the state brought into application the law of war to the non-international armed conflict, granting to insurgents the protection of the international law of war that normally would not apply to them and thereby "chang-[ing] the legal situation under international law."[178]

c *Implicit Recognition of Belligerency*

It is not necessary to explicitly recognize belligerency in order to trigger the application of the law of war. "The recognition of a group as a belligerent party may be declared explicitly or implicitly."[179] Unlike the recognition of states and governments, recognition of belligerency "does not, as a rule, take place by means of a formal declaration to that effect."[180] It can occur either through an express declaration or through the "pursuance of an attitude of neutrality identical with that obtaining in ordinary wars—an attitude of which the essence is impartiality of treatment and submission to measures of interference necessitated by the conduct of the war."[181]

Examples of implicit recognition of belligerency abound. British practice shows numerous instances in which "belligerent rights [were] granted in part or in full" without a formal proclamation of neutrality or belligerency.[182] The United States' recognition of belligerency has almost always been implicit. For example, "[d]uring the revolutions in South America directed against the Spanish rule there was no express recognition of belligerency by means of a proclamation of neutrality."[183] In contrast, the United States' refusal to recognize belligerency is almost always express.[184]

A prominent example of an implicit recognition of belligerency occurred during the American Civil War. The Union sought to treat the conflict with the Confederate States of America ("CSA") as an insurgency rather than as hostilities subject to the law of war. In order to avoid explicitly recognizing the belligerency of the CSA, the Union never officially declared war. However, in the *Prize Cases*,[185] the U.S. Supreme Court held that a formal declaration of war was not necessary to trigger the law of war or to recognize belligerency. Rather, the analysis was to examine the "magnitude" of the

177. "Recognition of belligerency," in *How Does Law Protect in War?* ICRC, 3rd ed., available at <https://casebook.icrc.org/a_to_z/glossary/recognition-belligerency>.
178. Herbert W. Briggs, *The Law of Nations: Cases, Documents, and Notes*, Appleton-Century-Crofts, 2nd Ed. (1952), pp. 991-92.
179. Rüdiger Wolfrum and Christianne E. Philipp, "The Status of the Taliban: Their Obligations and Rights under International Law," *Max Planck Yearbook of United Nations Law*, UNYB 6 (2002), p. 578.
180. Hersch Lauterpacht, *Recognition in International Law*, Cambridge University Press (Cambridge, 1947), p. 177.
181. *Ibid.*
182. *Ibid.*, p. 180.
183. *Ibid.*, p. 181.
184. *Ibid.*, p. 182.
185. *Prize Cases*, 67 U.S. 635 (1862).

conflict.[186] The Court concluded that the "present civil war between the United States and the so-called Confederate States has such character and magnitude as to give the United States the same rights and powers which they might exercise in the case of a national or foreign war."[187] The Supreme Court also held that President Lincoln's "proclamation of blockade is itself official and conclusive evidence to the Court that a state of war existed which demanded and authorized a recourse [to the use of a degree of force demanded by the crisis]."[188] Recognition was thus "expressed by implication in the Presidential proclamation of a blockade of some of the ports in the disaffected States."[189]

d Use of the Recognition of Belligerency in the Modern Era

The recognition of belligerency was routinely invoked during the nineteenth century, including, perhaps most notably, during the American Civil War. It was also used in the late 1970s to recognize the Sandinista National Liberation Front (FSLN), which ousted the dictatorship of Anastasio Somoza in Nicaragua.[190] In the modern era, however, the recognition of belligerency has largely fallen into desuetude. However, it could still be invoked by states to internationalize internal armed conflicts.

3 *State "Overall Control" over Non-state Armed Groups (*Tadić*)*

Finally, a non-international armed conflict becomes internationalized when a third-party state exercises "overall control" over a non-state armed group engaged in an armed conflict against another state.

a Overall Control Test

Under *Prosecutor v. Dusko Tadić*, an international armed conflict exists if a foreign state exercises "overall control" (i.e., "overall political and military authority")[191] over an organized armed group or an armed non-state actor's military activity "not only by equipping and financing the group, but also by co-ordinating or helping in the general planning of military activity."[192] To internationalize a conflict, a foreign state must thus

186. *See* Kevin Jon Heller, "The Civil War and the Blockade of Gaza (a Response to Posner)," *OpinioJuris* (4 June 2010), available at <http://opiniojuris.org/2010/06/04/eric-posners-incomplete-editorial-on-the-blockade-of-gaza>.
187. *Prize Cases*, 67 U.S. 635 (1862).
188. *Ibid.*, 67 U.S. 635, 670 (1862).
189. Hersch Lauterpacht, *Recognition in International Law*, Cambridge University Press (Cambridge, 1947), p. 178.
190. Hernando Salazar, "Colombia: beligerancia polémica," BBCMundo.com (18 January 2008), available at <http://news.bbc.co.uk/hi/spanish/latin_america/newsid_7196000/7196558.stm> ("el Frente Sandinista de Liberación Nacional (FSLN), que derrocó a la dictadura de Anastasio Somoza en Nicaragua, obtuvo el reconocimiento de beligerancia a finales de la década de 1970 por parte de algunos países, entre ellos Colombia").
191. *Prosecutor v. Dusko Tadić*, IT-94-1-A, ICTY Appeals Chamber (15 July 1999), para. 160.
192. *Ibid.*, para. 131.

equip, finance and coordinate (or help) the general planning of the organized armed group's or armed non-state actor's military activity.[193]

b *Effective Control Test*

The overall control test is often confused with the effective control test. However, the effective control test, which establishes a higher threshold of control, applies to questions of state responsibility rather than to the internationalization of an armed conflict. In the *Case Concerning Military and Paramilitary Activities in and against Nicaragua (Nicaragua v. United States of America)*, the ICJ held that state responsibility is triggered when a state exercises effective control over a non-stage armed group. Specifically, state responsibility requires that a state *direct* or *enforce* the perpetration of humanitarian law breaches.[194] To establish state responsibility for breaches of international humanitarian law, training, arming, equipping, financing, supplying, or otherwise encouraging, supporting, and aiding, absent directing and enforcing the perpetration of humanitarian law breaches are insufficient for meeting the effective control test. The overall control test, in contrast, requires only that a state coordinate or help the general planning of an organized armed group or armed non-state actor's military activity, not that a state provides specific or direct instructions or direct or enforce breaches of humanitarian law. The overall control test is therefore less stringent than the effective control test.

c *Reconciling the Two Tests*

The ICTY, in the *Tadić* Appeals Chamber decision, recognized the important distinction between the overall control test and the effective control test. "Effective control," including activities that are "specifically imposed, requested or directed by the State,"[195] is not necessary to internationalize a conflict. However, effective control is relevant to "State responsibility rather than individual criminal responsibility."[196] The *Tadić* Appeals Chamber held that "the armed forces of the Republika Srpska were to be regarded as acting under the overall control of and on behalf of the FRY" and, therefore, "the armed conflict in Bosnia and Herzegovina between the Bosnian Serbs and the central authorities of Bosnia and Herzegovina must be classified as an international armed conflict."[197]

The ICJ, reinforcing the position of the ICTY *Tadić* decision, held in the Genocide case (*Bosnia and Herzegovina v. Serbia and Montenegro*)[198] that the overall control test

193. *See generally Prosecutor v. Dusko Tadić*, IT-94-1-A, ICTY Appeals Chamber (15 July 1999), paras. 88-162.
194. *Case Concerning the Military and Paramilitary Activities in and Against Nicaragua* (*Nicaragua v. United States of America*), 1986 ICJ 14 (27 June 1986), p. 14.
195. *Prosecutor v. Dusko Tadić*, IT-94-1-A, ICTY Appeals Chamber (15 July 1999), para. 122.
196. *Ibid.*, para. 70.
197. *Ibid.*, para. 162.
198. *Application of the Convention on the Prevention and Punishment of the Crime of Genocide (Bosnia and Herzegovina v. Serbia and Montenegro)*, Case 91, ICJ (26 February 2007), p. 43.

and effective control test deal with distinct areas of the law and are therefore not self-contradictory:

- "Overall control" is used to determine whether an international armed conflict exists under international humanitarian law; and
- "Effective control" is applicable when determining whether non-state actors' breaches of international humanitarian law are attributable to a state under the law of state responsibility.

III PRINCIPLES OF INTERNATIONAL HUMANITARIAN LAW

War is a contest of clashing wills where fear, passion and grief are ever-present realities. Since emotion can affect the conduct of war and decisions that are taken, international humanitarian law developed to provide a set of principles and clear guidelines to limit the effects of armed conflict on civilian populations and civilian objects and reduce human suffering.

A Introduction: Military Necessity and Humanitarian Imperative

International humanitarian law seeks to strike a delicate balance between military necessity and humanitarian imperative. It is for this reason that international humanitarian law is also known as the "law of armed conflict"; both humanitarian as well as military considerations make up its core provisions. International humanitarian law therefore sets standards for the humanitarian treatment of victims and prisoners of war, seeks to limit the effects of armed conflict on civilians and restricts the means and methods of warfare.

B Protection of Persons

1 Distinction (Discrimination)

a Overview

The principle of distinction is arguably the most important of the core principles of international humanitarian law. Rule 1 of the ICRC's *Customary International Humanitarian Law* defines the principle as follows:

> The parties to the conflict must at all times distinguish between civilians and combatants. Attacks may only be directed against combatants. Attacks must not be directed against civilians.

In its *Advisory Opinion on the Legality of the Threat or Use of Nuclear Weapons* (1996), the International Court of Justice held that the principle of distinction is:[199]

199. *Legality of the Threat or Use of Nuclear Weapons*, Advisory Opinion, ICJ Reports (8 July 1996), p. 257, available at <https://www.icj-cij.org/docket/files/95/7495.pdf>.

> aimed at the protection of the civilian population and civilian objects and establishes the distinction between combatants and non-combatants; states must never make civilians the object of attack and must consequently never use weapons that are incapable of distinguishing between civilian and military targets.

Following this framework, states may not intentionally target civilians and civilian objects. However, civilians may lose their protected status if a party fails to separate civilians and civilian objects from military targets. Similarly, civilian objects such as places of worship, schools, hospitals and dwellings may lose their protected status if they become tools for military action.

b Normative Background

The principle of distinction, which is sometimes referred to as the principle of discrimination, was first articulated in the 1868 St. Petersburg Declaration, which states:

> the only legitimate object which States should endeavour to accomplish during war is to weaken the military forces of the enemy.

Article 25 of the Regulations Respecting the Laws and Customs of War on Land Annexed to Hague Convention IV of 1907 restates the principle of distinction as follows:

> The attack or bombardment, by whatever means, of towns, villages, dwellings, or buildings which are undefended is prohibited.

Article 26 of the Hague Regulations states:

> The officer in command of an attacking force must, before commencing a bombardment, except in cases of assault, do all in his power to warn the authorities.

Article 27 further states:

> In sieges and bombardments all necessary steps must be taken to spare, as far as possible, buildings dedicated to religion, art, science, or charitable purposes, historic monuments, hospitals, and places where the sick and wounded are collected, provided they are not being used at the time for military purposes.
>
> It is the duty of the besieged to indicate the presence of such buildings or places by distinctive and visible signs, which shall be notified to the enemy beforehand.

Seventy years later, Additional Protocol I set forth the principle of distinction as follows (Article 48 AP I):

> In order to ensure respect for and protection of the civilian population and civilian objects, the Parties to the conflict shall at all times *distinguish between the civilian population and combatants* and between *civilian objects and military objectives* and accordingly shall direct their operations only against military objectives.

c Military Objective: Nature, Location, Purpose, Use

The goal of military necessity is to identify and achieve *lawful military objectives* that accomplish the conflict's aims and swift termination. In this spirit, Additional Protocol I limits attacks to military objectives, which are defined as (Article 52 AP I):

> those objects which by their nature, location, purpose or use make an effective contribution to military action and whose total or partial destruction, capture or neutralization, in the circumstances ruling at the time, offers a definite military advantage.

United States policy accepts this definition, which is incorporated in its military manuals, as legally binding. Under Joint Publication 3-60, Joint Targeting, lawful military objectives are defined as objects that "by their *nature, location, purpose, or use* make an effective contribution to military action and whose total or partial destruction, capture, or neutralization, under the circumstances ruling at that time, offers a definite military advantage."[200] Examples of military objectives include facilities in which combatants are billeting and production sites for armaments and other military equipment.

The ICRC Commentary to Additional Protocol I defines "nature, location, purpose, or use" as follows (636-637):

- Nature includes "all objects used directly by the armed forces," such as weapons, fortifications and other military equipment;
- Location includes an object or site "which is of special importance for military operations in view of its location," such as a territory on high ground;
- Purpose is "concerned with the intended future use of an object," such as a site where a military base may be constructed in the near future;
- "Use" is "concerned with [the object's] present function," such as a hospital being used as a warehouse for military equipment. "Dual-use facilities" are those that serve both civilian and military purposes, such as a power plant that produces electricity for both the civilian and military realms. These may be targeted after a careful balancing of military advantage against collateral damage caused.[201]

Some have taken a broad view as to what constitutes a military objective whose "total or partial destruction, capture, or neutralization" would offer a definite military advantage." Certainly, this is the case of non-state armed groups that target civilian objects based on the principle that the destruction of such objectives would offer a definite military advantage by undermining the morale of the nation against which they are at war. While such a view is in clear tension with the principle of distinction, it is

200. Joint Publication 3-60, Joint Targeting (U.S.), para. A.4.b.
201. Once a civilian object is converted to military use, it loses its civilian protection and may be lawfully targeted as a military objective.

not a view exclusive to non-state armed groups. The primary object of the Combined Bomber Offensive laid down in the Casablanca directive of 21 January 1943 was:[202]

> the progressive destruction and dislocation of the German military, industrial and economic systems and the undermining of the morale of the German people to a point where their capacity for armed resistance is fatally weakened.

d *Indiscriminate Attacks*

Additional Protocol I prohibits indiscriminate attacks, which are defined as (Article 51.4 AP I):

- those which are not directed at a specific military objective;
- those which employ a method or means of combat that cannot be directed at a specific military objective; or
- those which employ a method or means of combat whose effects cannot be limited as required by the Protocol.[203]

Examples of indiscriminate attacks include (Article 51.5 AP I):

- an attack "by bombardment by any methods or means which treats as a single military objective a number of clearly separated and distinct military objectives located in a city, town, village or other area containing a similar concentration of civilians or civilian objects" (Article 51.5(a) AP I); and
- an attack that "may be expected to cause incidental loss of civilian life, injury to civilians, damage to civilian objects, or a combination thereof, which would be excessive in relation to the concrete and direct military advantage anticipated" (Article 51.5(b) AP I).

e *Combatants: Definition and Distinction Between Lawful and Unlawful Combatants*

i Definition

"Combatant" is a term of art that describes the legal status of an individual engaging in hostilities in an international armed conflict and who has the right to engage in such hostilities. The definition of "combatant" is found in Article 43.2 of Additional Protocol I,[204] which states:

---

202. Arthur Travers Harris and Sebastian Cox, *Despatch on War Operations: 23 February 1942, to 8 May 1945*, Routledge (1995), p. 196.
203. The U.S., which is not a state party to AP I, has adopted a more expansive view of this third prong to permit the use of cluster munitions and nuclear arms.
204. The U.S. signed Additional Protocol I on 12 December 1977, but due to fundamental policy disagreements, never ratified it.

> *Members of the armed forces of a Party to a conflict* (other than medical personnel and chaplains covered by Article 33 of the Third Convention) are combatants, that is to say, they have the right to participate directly in hostilities.

Rule 3 of the ICRC's *Customary International Humanitarian Law* study indicates that this definition of "combatant" in Additional Protocol I is customary international law and that "No official contrary practice was found" (p. 12). On this basis, we may conclude that under customary international law, in order to qualify as a "combatant," an individual must be a member of the armed forces of a state party to a conflict and must have the right to directly participate in hostilities.

ii Lawful and Unlawful Combatants

(1) ICRC Position

The ICRC does not distinguish between "lawful" and "unlawful" combatants or "privileged" and "unprivileged" combatants. In the ICRC's view, members of the armed forces of a state party to a conflict (other than medical personnel and chaplains covered by Article 33 of the Third Convention) are combatants, regardless of whether they undertake acts that might forfeit their combatant privileges. Civilians who directly take part in hostilities remain civilians and do not take on the status of a lawful or unlawful "combatant."

(2) U.S. Position

The U.S. position, in contrast, distinguishes between lawful and unlawful combatants.

(a) Lawful Combatants

Lawful combatants are those that fall under the criteria of Article 4A of Geneva Convention III for combatants, namely:

- Article 4A(1) members of the armed forces of a party to the conflict, as well as members of militias or volunteer corps forming part of such armed forces;
- Article 4A(2) members of other militias and members of other volunteer corps, including those of organized resistance movements, belonging to a Party to the conflict and operating in or outside their own territory, even if this territory is occupied, provided that such militias or volunteer corps, including such organized resistance movements, fulfil the following conditions:[205]
  - (a) that of being commanded by a person responsible for his subordinates;
  - (b) that of having a fixed distinctive sign recognizable at a distance;
  - (c) that of carrying arms openly;
  - (d) that of conducting their operations in accordance with the laws and customs of war.

205. This provision was intended to cover the French *Partisans* (the French Resistance) during World War II.

- Article 4A(3) members of regular armed forces who profess allegiance to a government or an authority not recognized by the detaining power; and
- Article 4A(6) *levée en masse*.

(b) Unlawful Combatants

In the U.S. view, unlawful combatants (often referred to as "unprivileged enemy belligerents")[206] can be any of the following:

- Combatants who would otherwise be privileged but have forfeited the combatant privilege by breaching the laws and customs of war (e.g., by feigning surrender or killing enemy prisoners of war).[207]
- Spies (members of an armed force who engage in spying behind enemy lines), mercenaries (soldiers hired to serve in a foreign army), child soldiers, and civilians who directly participate in hostilities and do not fall into one of the categories of combatants listed in Article 4A of Geneva Convention III.[208] Such individuals are sometimes referred to as "guerillas" or "terrorist fighters."

---

206. The term "enemy belligerent" derives from *Ex Parte Quirin*, 317 U.S. 1 (1942), a U.S. Supreme Court case that upheld the jurisdiction of a U.S. military tribunal over the trial of eight German saboteurs who, "being enemies of the United States and acting for ... the German Reich, a belligerent enemy nation, secretly and covertly passed, in civilian dress, contrary to the law of war, through the military and naval lines and defenses of the United States ... and went behind such lines, contrary to the law of war, in civilian dress ... for the purpose of committing ... hostile acts, and, in particular, to destroy certain war industries, war utilities and war materials within the United States." 317 U.S. 1, 2 (1942). The case has been cited as a precedent for trials of unprivileged "enemy belligerents" by U.S. military commissions.

    The Military Commissions Act of 2009 defines "unprivileged enemy belligerent" as follows:

    > The term "unprivileged enemy belligerent" means an individual (other than a privileged belligerent) who—
    > (A) has engaged in hostilities against the United States or its coalition partners;
    > (B) has purposefully and materially supported hostilities against the United States or its coalition partners; or
    > (C) was a part of Al Qaeda at the time of the alleged offense under this chapter.

    10 U.S.C. § 948a(B)(7).

    The Military Commissions Acct defines "privileged belligerent," in contrast, as follows:

    > The term "privileged belligerent" means an individual belonging to one of the eight categories enumerated in Article 4 of the Geneva Convention Relative to the Treatment of Prisoners of War.

    10 U.S.C. § 948a(B)(6).
207. In the view of the ICRC, such individuals are nonetheless deemed to be combatants; the illegal acts make them susceptible to prosecution for war crimes, but they do not impact the combatant privilege.
208. According to the ICRC, which does not distinguish between lawful and unlawful combatants, such individuals are deemed to be civilians, because they do not fall into any of the combatant categories under Art. 4A of Geneva Convention III. Therefore, for the ICRC, a civilian who directly participates in hostilities is deemed to be a civilian. In the U.S. view, in contrast, he is deemed to be an unlawful combatant or unprivileged enemy belligerent.

The concept of "unlawful combatants" is not a formal category established by the Geneva Conventions. Rather, the Geneva Conventions, as interpreted by the ICRC, permit only two categories of individuals in times of war:

- (1) members of armed forces. This includes the following sub-categories:
  - (1.a) combatants; and
  - (1.b) non-combatants (i.e., members of armed forces who do not have a right to directly participate in hostilities—namely, medical personnel and chaplains, per Rule 3 of the ICRC's *Customary International Humanitarian Law* study and Article 43.2 AP I);
- (2) civilians (i.e., non-members of armed forces).

The concept of "unlawful combatants" as a third category is established by U.S. state doctrine, which defines detainees captured in the Global War on Terror as "unlawful combatants." These individuals, many of whom are detained at Guantánamo Bay, enjoy neither prisoner of war status nor civilian rights, such as the right to civilian trials. The U.S. argues that they do not hold the privileges afforded to combatants because they do not qualify under any of the combatant categories under Article 4A of Geneva Convention III, and they do not hold the rights and protections afforded to civilians, which they forfeited by directly participating in hostilities.

f *Lawful Targeting*

i Groups that May Be Lawfully Targeted

Combatants, with the exception of those who fall *hors de combat* (e.g., they become wounded or are taken prisoner), and civilians directly participating in hostilities may be lawfully targeted. Combatants *hors de combat*, non-combatants and civilians not directly participating in conflict may *not* be lawfully targeted.

The following list summarizes the three groups (non-combatants, civilians and enemy personnel *hors de combat*) that may not be lawfully targeted:

- Non-combatants:
  - Medical personnel exclusively engaged in the provision of medical care (Article 24 GC I).
  - Chaplains (Article 24 GC I).
- Civilians who are not members of any armed force or group and who do not directly participate in hostilities, including:
  - Personnel of national Red Cross societies and other recognized relief societies (GC I, Article 26) and of neutral countries (GC I, Article 27).
  - Civilian medical and religious personnel (Article 15 AP I).
  - Journalists, who are protected as "civilians" as long as they take no action adversely affecting their civilian status (Article 79 AP I). This rule is deemed to be customary international law by the U.S.
- Enemy personnel *hors de combat*, including:
  - Prisoners of war (Article 4 GC III; Article 23(c), (d) HC IV).

- The wounded and sick in the field and at sea (Article 12 GC I; Article 12 GC II).
- Enemy personnel who have surrendered (deemed by many scholars to mean ceasing resistance and placing themselves at the captor's discretion and control).
- Parachutists (crewmen of a disabled aircraft, as distinct from paratroopers, who are presumed to be on a military mission and may be targeted), who under Additional Protocol I, "shall be given the opportunity to surrender before being made the object of attack" (Article 42 AP I).
- Auxiliary medical personnel of the armed forces ("Members of the armed forces specially trained for employment, should the need arise, as hospital orderlies, nurses or auxiliary stretcher-bearers, in the search for or the collection, transport or treatment of the wounded and sick") (Article 25 GC I).

ii Status-Based and Conduct-Based Determinations

The determination as to whether a person qualifies as a lawful target can be status-based or conduct-based.

(1) Status-Based "Continuous Combat Function"

Combatants of a declared hostile force may be attacked without any showing of hostility based on their status. The U.S. includes persons belonging to hostile, non-state armed groups as status-based lawful targets. The ICRC would refer to such individuals as civilian members of organized armed groups who hold a "continuous combat function." They cease to be civilians and can thus be attacked by virtue of their status. Unlike civilians who directly participate in hostilities, who can only be targeted for such time as they directly participate in hostilities, civilians with a continuous combat function can always be targeted.

In this spirit, recommendation VII ("Temporal scope of the loss of protection") of the ICRC's *Interpretive Guidance on Direct Participation in Hostilities under International Humanitarian Law* states as follows:[209]

> Civilians lose protection against direct attack for the duration of each specific act amounting to direct participation in hostilities, whereas members of *organized armed groups* belonging to a non-State party to an armed conflict cease to be civilians (see above II), and lose protection against direct attack, for as long as they assume *their continuous combat function.*

Recommendation II ("The concept of civilian in non-international armed conflict"), for its part, states as follows:[210]

209. Nils Melzer, *Interpretive Guidance on the Notion of Direct Participation in Hostilities under International Humanitarian Law*, ICRC (Geneva, 2009), p. 70.
210. *Ibid.*, p. 27.

> For the purposes of the principle of distinction in non-international armed conflict, all persons who are not members of State armed forces or organized armed groups of a party to the conflict are civilians and, therefore, entitled to protection against direct attack *unless and for such time as they take a direct part in hostilities*. In non-international armed conflict, organized armed groups constitute the armed forces of a non-State party to the conflict and consist only of individuals whose continuous function it is to take a direct part in hostilities ("continuous combat function").

Because the ICRC *Interpretative Guidance* views continuous combat function fighters within the context of non-international armed conflict, Geneva Convention III does not apply, and such fighters are not considered to be prisoners of war if captured and can thus be criminally charged for their actions.

(2) Conduct-Based

(a) Overview

Hostile conduct may justify attacks on those who commit such acts or demonstrate hostile intent. Such conduct can be comprised of either:

- hostile acts; or
- hostile intent.

In either case, the conduct in question authorizes a response of self-defense on the battlefield against actors that do not have the status of a declared hostile force.

(b) Direct Participation of Civilians in Hostilities

(i) Overview

The Geneva Conventions only protect civilians "unless and for such time as they take a direct part in hostilities" (Article 51.3 AP I). Therefore, once they take a direct part in hostilities and for as long as they do so, they forfeit their protection from attack and may be targeted by enemy forces. Once they cease their direct participation in hostilities, their protection is restored.

(ii) The Revolving Door Fighter

Individuals who constantly shift between engagement and disengagement in direct participation in hostilities are known as "revolving door fighters." The ICRC position is that directly participating in hostilities does not transform civilians into combatants; while combatants may always be targeted, civilians may only be targeted while directly participating in hostilities.

In the ICRC view, the "revolving door" of civilian protection is an integral part of international humanitarian law that:[211]

211. *Ibid.*, pp. 70-71.

> prevents attacks on civilians who do not, at the time, represent a military threat. In contrast to members of organized armed groups, whose continuous function it is to conduct hostilities on behalf of a party to the conflict, the behaviour of individual civilians depends on a multitude of constantly changing circumstances and, therefore, is very difficult to anticipate. Even the fact that a civilian has repeatedly taken a direct part in hostilities, either voluntarily or under pressure, does not allow a reliable prediction as to future conduct. As the concept of direct participation in hostilities refers to specific hostile acts, IHL restores the civilian's protection against direct attack each time his or her engagement in a hostile act ends. Until the civilian in question again engages in a specific act of direct participation in hostilities, the use of force against him or her must comply with the standards of law enforcement or individual self-defence.

Some critics raise issues with the prohibition on targeting so-called revolving door fighters when they are not directly participating in hostilities. On the one hand, "a civilian who took a direct part in hostilities once, or sporadically, but detached himself from them (entirely, or for a long period) is not to be harmed. On the other hand, the 'revolving door' phenomenon, by which each terrorist has 'horns of the alter' (1 Kings 1:50) to grasp or a 'city of refuge' (Numbers 35:11) to flee to, to which he turns in order to rest and prepare while they grant him immunity from attack, is to be avoided .... In the wide area between those two possibilities, one finds the 'gray' cases, about which customary international law has not yet crystallized."[212]

(iii) Distinguishing General Participation in a War Effort from Direct Participation in Hostilities

The original ICRC Commentary to Additional Protocol I distinguished general participation in the war effort from direct participation in hostilities. The Commentary states:[213]

> There should be a clear distinction between *direct participation in hostilities* and *participation in the war effort*. The latter is often required from the population as a whole to various degrees ... In fact, in modern conflicts, many activities of the nation contribute to the conduct of hostilities, directly or indirectly; even the morale of the population plays a role in this context.

(iv) Functional Scope of "Direct Participation"

There are currently several debates underway attempting to circumscribe the functional scope of the definition of "direct participation" as an effective contribution to the use of lethal force. Traditionally, taking a "direct part" in hostilities meant carrying a weapon on a battlefield.

According to the Commentary on the Additional Protocols to the Geneva Conventions, direct participation must be "likely to *cause actual harm* to the personnel and

212. "Israel: Practice Relating to Rule 6. Civilians' Loss of Protection from Attack," IHL Database: Customary IHL available at <https://ihl-databases.icrc.org/customary-ihl/eng/docs/v2_cou_il_rule6>.

213. Yves Sandoz et al. eds., *Commentary on the Additional Protocols of June 1977 to the Geneva Conventions of 12 August 1949*, ICRC (Geneva, 1987), p. 619.

equipment of the enemy armed forces."[214] Thus, while throwing a stone at an armored vehicle would not qualify as "direct participation," throwing the same stone at a soldier would qualify because of the likelihood of causing the soldier harm.

(v) View of the ICRC

The modern view of direct participation in hostilities has been broadened to include any effective contribution to the use of lethal force. The ICRC view involves a test that involves the following elements:

- An act that meets the following criteria:
  - *threshold of harm*. The act must be likely to adversely affect the military operations or military capacity of a party to an armed conflict or, alternatively, to inflict death, injury, or destruction upon persons or objects protected against direct attack;
  - *direct causation*. A direct causal link between the act and the harm likely to result from the act or from a coordinated military operation of which the act constitutes an integral part must exist; and
  - *belligerent nexus*. There must be specific intent for an act to cause the required threshold of harm in support of a party to the conflict and to the detriment of the opposition.
- Timing. Preparing for the execution of the act and deployment to and the return from the location of its execution are integral parts of the act.

Under this test, direct participation does not include the following:

- supporting an armed group by providing financial support;
- working in a weapon-manufacturing factory;
- participation in rationing efforts;
- participating in the dissemination of propaganda or support of enemy governments;
- the provision of administrative or logistical support to forces not deployed in hostile territory;
- Paying taxes or buying war bonds.

(vi) Expansive View of the United States

The U.S. has adopted a more expansive view of direct participation in hostilities based on a factor test. Direct participation "includes certain acts that are an integral part of combat operations or that *effectively and substantially contribute* to an adversary's ability to *conduct or sustain* combat operations" (§ 5.8.3 LoWM).

(3) Cessation and Restoration of Protection

Some acts, such as firing a weapon at a soldier, meet the definition of direct participation in hostilities and justify a response by deadly force. When a civilian

214. *Ibid.*, p. 619.

desists from such acts and expresses that he or she is no longer willing or able to engage in combat, the protected status is restored.

iii Challenges in Modern Warfare

Developments in modern warfare present special challenges to the application of the principle of distinction. For example, in modern warfare, the line between direct participants in hostilities, who may be targeted, and civilians, who must be protected, is blurred when such civilians provide material support to direct participants.

Difficult cases further arise as conduct becomes more indirect and further removed geographically or temporally from actual hostilities, giving rise to the question of what conduct constitutes direct participation.

Further issues arise when transnational non-state actors engage in military actions in territories whose governments are unable or unwilling to respond. In such cases, actors illegally use civilian populations and objects to conduct or conceal their attacks as a war tactic, failing to distinguish themselves and thereby putting civilian populations at risk.

2 *Proportionality with Respect to Civilian Losses*

a Overview

Under Additional Protocol I, an attack violates the principle of proportionality if it (Article 51.5(b) AP I):

> may be expected to cause *incidental loss* of civilian life, injury to civilians, damage to civilian objects, or a combination thereof, which would be *excessive* in relation to the concrete and direct military advantage anticipated.

In this spirit, those who plan military operations must take into consideration the extent of civilian destruction and probable casualties that will result and, to the extent consistent with *military necessity*, seek to *avoid or minimize such casualties* and destruction. While civilian losses must be proportionate to the military advantages sought, this principle must be consistent with the allowable risk to the attacking force; the attacker need not expose himself to excessive risk merely in order to minimize civilian losses.

b Incidental Loss of Life or Injury and Collateral Damage

The law recognizes that unavoidable collateral damage, including the death and injury of civilians and the destruction of civilian property, may occur during military operations. Commanders must consider such losses before and during military operations to determine whether the expected loss of civilian life or injury to civilians and damage to civilian objects incidental to the attack would be excessive in relation to the expected military advantage anticipated from the attack.

C Means and Methods of Warfare

1 Introduction

a Means and Methods of Warfare as Distinct from the Protection of Persons

While the principles of distinction and proportionality govern who must be protected or may be lawfully targeted, the principles dealing with the means and methods of warfare govern the following:

- means of warfare: the weapons used in battle (e.g., small arms projectiles, landmines, incendiaries and chemical, biological, and nuclear weapons); and
- methods of warfare: how warfare is conducted, including the tactics of fighting.

b Overview of the Principles of Military Necessary and Humanity

Parties to a conflict and members of their armed forces do not have an unlimited choice of means and methods of warfare. Employing weapons or methods of warfare of a nature that causes unnecessary losses (in violation of the principle of military necessity) or excessive or unnecessary suffering (in violation of the principle of humanity) is prohibited.

2 Military Necessity

a Overview

Military necessity permits the application of only that degree of regulated force required for the partial or complete submission of the enemy with the least expenditure of *life, time* and *resources*. While many treaties have acknowledged the role of military necessity, the principle arises predominantly from customary international law.

b Elements

Military necessity requires belligerents to meet the following elements in their military operations:

(i) a military *requirement* to undertake a certain measure, which;
(ii) is indispensable to achieve a military objective and a swift termination to a conflict; and
(iii) is not forbidden elsewhere by the laws of armed conflict.

In this vein, the U.S. Department of Defense defines the principle of military necessity as:[215]

> the principle that justifies the use of all *measures needed to defeat the enemy* as quickly and efficiently as possible that are *not prohibited* by the law of war.

A commander must thus articulate a military requirement, select an action or measure to achieve the military requirement and ensure that neither the requirement nor the measure violates the laws of armed conflict.

c *The Concept of Kriegraison: Military Necessity as a Justification of Violations of International Humanitarian Law*

Under the concept of Kriegraison,[216] acts violating international humanitarian law are justified if they meet the principle of necessity. However, in order for a certain measure to meet the principle of necessity, one of the elements that must be met is that the measure not be forbidden by the laws of armed conflict. Therefore, military necessity cannot justify violations of international humanitarian law. Thus, the doctrine *Kriegsraison geht vor Kriegsmanier* (roughly, "necessity in war overrides the manner of warfare"), articulated by the Prussian general and military theorist Carl Philipp Gottfried von Clausewitz, is an invalid defense of the violation of the principle of necessity.

3 *Humanity (Unnecessary Suffering)*

a *Overview*

International humanitarian law limits the right of parties to a conflict to adopt means of injuring their enemy. Also known as the "principle of unnecessary suffering" or the "principle of superfluous injury," the principle of humanity requires military forces to *refrain from inflicting gratuitous violence on the enemy and prohibits the employment of any degree of force that causes unnecessary loss and excessive suffering*. It thus serves as a counterbalance against the principle of military necessity.

Rule 70 of the ICRC's *Customary International Humanitarian Law* ("Weapons of a Nature to Cause Superfluous Injury or Unnecessary Suffering") summarizes the principle of humanity as follows:

> The use of means and methods of warfare which are of a nature to cause superfluous injury or unnecessary suffering is prohibited.

As articulated by the ICRC, the principle applies to both means and methods of warfare, which means that it could potentially prohibit not only weapons that per se

215. Office of General Counsel, U.S. Department of Defense, *Department of Defense Law of War Manual* (2015), para. 2.2.
216. Sometimes rendered as "Kreigraison."

create unnecessary suffering but also the use of otherwise permitted weapons if they are employed in a way that produces unnecessary suffering, as well as methods of war such as starvation and sexual violence.

The principle of humanity establishes three requirements to ensure the legality of weapons (*means*) and the tactics by which weapons are employed (*methods*). Military personnel:

- must not use arms that civilized societies recognize as per se causing unnecessary suffering (e.g., projectiles filled with glass);
- must scrupulously observe treaty or customary limitations on weapons use (e.g., prohibitions on the use of chemical weapons); and
- must not improperly use otherwise lawful weapons in a manner calculated to cause unnecessary suffering.

b *Historic Approach: The 1868 Declaration of St. Petersburg*

The principle of humanity was articulated as early as 1868 by the Declaration of St. Petersburg Renouncing the Use, in Time of War, of Explosive Projectiles under 400 Grammes Weight. The Declaration prohibits the use of "any projectile of a weight below 400 grams, which is either explosive or charged with fulminating or inflammable substances." Such projectiles would, on impact, explode in the human flesh, creating superfluous injury. Because heavier projectiles would kill on impact, they were not prohibited by the Declaration, which was designed to minimize unnecessary suffering. The Declaration holds that the only legitimate object of war is the "weaken[ing of] the military forces of the enemy," but "this object would be exceeded by the employment of arms which uselessly aggravate the sufferings of disabled men, or render their death inevitable."

c *Prohibited Weapons (Means of Warfare)*

A weapon would be deemed to cause unnecessary suffering if it inevitably (in its normal use) has a particular effect and the injury it causes is disproportionate to the military necessity for that effect. This act of balancing cannot be conducted in isolation; rather, the weapon's effects must be weighed in light of comparable, lawful weapons or munitions in use on the battlefield.

Various international treaties regulate and restrict the use of specific weapons on the basis of the principle of humanity. For example, Protocol (I) of the Convention on Conventional Weapons (1980), discussed below, prohibits the use of any weapon whose *primary effect* is to injure by fragments or fragmentation that escape detection by X-rays in the human body. Protocol (IV) of the Convention on Conventional Weapons, also discussed below, restricts the use of weapons specifically designed to cause permanent blindness to unenhanced vision.

d *Prohibited Tactics (Methods of Warfare)*

The principle of humanity limits the ability of parties to a conflict to employ certain tactics of warfare. By way of example, prohibited tactics include gender-based violence and perfidy, as further discussed under "V. Means and Methods: Hague Law," below.

D Honor

Ideals of culture, honor, religion, and chivalry have historically helped define battlefield norms. Today, these ideals form the principle of honor, which seeks to provide fairness in offensive and defensive operations and provides "a foundation for obligations that help enforce and implement the law of war or special agreements between belligerents during armed conflict."[217] The principle of honor requires parties to "comply with the law of war in good faith" and "refrain from taking advantage of its opponent's adherence to the law by falsely claiming the law's protections."[218]

E Application

1 ***Case Study: Grdelica Bridge Strikes***

a *Overview*

In 1999, NATO was engaged in Operation Allied Force against the Federal Republic of Yugoslavia (FRY). On 12 April 1999, U.S. aircraft fired two missiles that hit a passenger train while it was passing across a railway bridge in the Grdelica gorge in Serbia. Between 20 to 60 civilians were killed or declared missing.

b *Legality of Killings*

The Yugoslav government and some NGOs characterized the attack as a violation of humanitarian law, particularly since the second missile strike occurred after the train had been struck the first time.

General Wesley Clark, the Supreme Allied Commander Europe (SACEUR) at the time, defended the pilot who fired the missiles. He stated that during the first missile strike, while the pilot stared at the target on the bridge, he saw the train come into his field of vision "at the very last instant with less than a second to go." He could not divert the bomb, which was locked on its target. With respect to the second strike, he stated that the pilot targeted the "other end of the bridge from where the train had

217. Office of General Counsel, U.S. Department of Defense, *Department of Defense Law of War Manual* (2015), para. 2.6.2.1.
218. *Ibid.*, paras. 2.6.2.1-2.6.2.2.

come," by the time the bomb got close to the bridge, it was covered with smoke and clouds that obscured the pilot's vision. He explained that:[219]

> at the last minute, again in an uncanny accident, the train had slid forward from the original impact and parts of the train had moved across the bridge, and so that by striking the other end of the bridge he actually caused additional damage to the train.

Amnesty International stated that the attack:[220]

> appears to have violated Article 57 of Protocol I which requires an attack to "be cancelled or suspended if it becomes clear that the objective is a not a military one ... or that the attack may be expected to cause incidental loss of civilian life ... which would be excessive in relation to the concrete and direct military advantage anticipated."

The International Criminal Tribunal for the former Yugoslavia ("ICTY") established a committee in May 1999 to determine whether violations of international humanitarian law had been committed. In its final report to the ICTY's Prosecutor, the committee took the view that the attack met the principles of distinction and proportionality:[221]

> It is the opinion of the committee that the bridge was a legitimate military objective. The passenger train was not deliberately targeted. The person controlling the bombs ... targeted the bridge and, over a very short period of time, failed to recognize the arrival of the train while the first bomb was in flight. The train was on the bridge when the bridge was targeted a second time and the bridge length has been estimated at 50 meters ... It is the opinion of the committee that the information in relation to the attack with the first bomb does not provide a sufficient basis to initiate an investigation. The committee has divided views concerning the attack with the second bomb in relation to whether there was an element of recklessness in the conduct of the pilot or WSO. Despite this, the committee is in agreement that, based on the criteria for initiating an investigation ..., this incident should not be investigated.

Although the committee was divided on whether the aircrew had behaved recklessly, it recommended that the Prosecutor not investigate the Grdelica Bride strikes.

2 Principles Matrix

The following matrix presents four scenarios, each of which violates one of the four principles of international humanitarian law:

---

219. "Press Conference by Jamie Shea and General Wesley Clark," NATO (13 April 1999) available at <https://www.nato.int/kosovo/press/p990413a.htm>.
220. "'Collateral Damage' or Unlawful Killings? Violations of the Laws of War by NATO during Operation Allied Force," Amnesty International (7 May 2000).
221. "Final Report to the Prosecutor by the Committee Established to Review the NATO Bombing Campaign Against the Federal Republic of Yugoslavia," United Nations International Criminal Tribunal for the Former Yugoslavia (2000), para. 62.

Scenario	*Distinction*	*Proportionality*	*Military Nec.*	*Humanity*
Bombing a neighborhood inhabited by civilians is necessary for the submission of the enemy. The incidental loss to civilian life is not excessive in relation to the military advantage anticipated. The bombs will cause the immediate death of both civilians and combatants without prolonged injury or suffering.	☒	✓	✓	✓
The bombardment of a city is necessary for the submission of the enemy and will result in a concrete and direct military advantage. The bombs will cause the immediate death of both civilians and combatants without prolonged injury or suffering. However, mostly civilians will perish, and their death is excessive in relation to the military advantage anticipated.	✓	☒	✓	✓
A bombardment targets an abandoned military installation and will not result in the death or injury of combatants or civilians. The installation plays no current role and will play no future role in the conflict. The bombardment is not required for the partial or complete submission of the enemy.	✓	✓	☒	✓

Scenario	*Distinction*	*Proportionality*	*Military Nec.*	*Humanity*
The use of chemical weapons against combatants is necessary for the submission of the enemy, and it will not impact civilian life or objects, but it will lead to excessive suffering.	✓	✓	✓	☒

IV PROTECTION OF PERSONS: GENEVA LAW

A Overview

The Geneva Conventions comprise four treaties and three Additional Protocols. Prior to the first Geneva Convention of 1864, only customary law applied to the conduct of states at war. It was only with the first Geneva Convention that the rules of armed conflict were codified. Prior to the Convention, the nations' customs and traditions governing the conduct of war varied among states or were temporary.

B Conventions Preceding the 1949 Geneva Conventions

The governments of Europe and America came together in 1864 to establish rules governing conduct during warfare. The resulting Convention of 1864 was replaced by the Geneva Conventions of 1906, 1929 and 1949, all of which expanded the original and added provisions relating to war at sea, prisoners of war and civilians. The original treaties continued to have binding force only between those countries that did not ratify the later treaties.

1 Geneva Convention of 1864 for the Wounded in Armies in the Field

After the termination of the Geneva Conference of 1863, the Swiss Federal Council invited the governments of Europe and America to a diplomatic conference to adopt a convention for the amelioration of the condition of the wounded in war. The conference adopted a treaty comprised of ten articles—the Convention for the Amelioration of the Condition of the Wounded in Armies in the Field (Geneva, 1864), which provides relief to the sick and the wounded without distinction as to nationality. The wounded and sick must be collected and cared for by the party that has them in its power, and this protection was extended to medical personnel, establishments, transports and equipment.

The Geneva Convention of 1864 established the neutrality of medical personnel and medical establishments and units. The following distinctive signs were established as signs of protection:

- the red cross;
- the red crescent;
- the red lion and sun on a white ground.

The 1864 Convention had 57 states parties. It ceased to have effect in 1966 when the Republic of Korea, the last party to the 1864 Convention that had not acceded to a later Convention, acceded to the 1949 Conventions.

2 *Geneva Convention of 1906 for the Wounded and Sick in Armies in the Field*

Several proposals were made after 1864 to revise the Geneva Convention of 1864. A conference was convened at Geneva in 1868 to adapt the principles of the 1864 Convention to sea warfare, but the additional articles were not ratified. The 1899 Hague Peace Conference proposed a special conference for the revision of the Geneva Convention of 1864, and this resulted in a 1906 Conference attended by 35 states that adopted the Geneva Convention for the Amelioration of the Condition of the Wounded and Sick in Armies in the Field of 6 July 1906. This new Convention replaced the 1864 Convention between the contracting states.

With 33 articles rather than 10, the 1906 Convention is more detailed than the 1864 Convention and adds additional provisions for wounded and sick soldiers while changing some provisions. For example, Article 6 of the 1906 Convention provided for the duty to repatriate the wounded who are unfit for further service.

The Geneva Convention of 1906 had 52 states parties and 5 states signatories.

3 *Geneva Convention of 1929 for Prisoners of War*

Provisions relating to the treatment of prisoners of war are contained in the 1899 and 1907 Hague Regulations. Due to their imprecision, the ICRC drafted a convention that would complete these Hague Regulations by including a prohibition of reprisals and collective penalties, the organization of prisoners' work and prisoners' designation of representatives. The Diplomatic Conference of Geneva adopted the Convention relative to the Treatment of Prisoners of War on 27 July 1929, containing 97 articles and an Annex model draft agreement concerning the direct repatriation or accommodation in a neutral country of prisoners of war for reasons of health.

C Geneva Conventions of 1949

1 *Introduction*

a *General Overview*

The pre-1949 Geneva Conventions are all concerned primarily with combatants rather than with civilians. The events of World War II showed the disastrous consequences of the absence of a treaty protecting civilians in wartime. Thus, in 1949, the preceding three Conventions were revised, and a fourth Convention was adopted to provide for the protection of civilians from the consequences of war. The results were the four Geneva Conventions, dated 12 August 1949, dealing with the treatment and protection of persons—both combatants and civilians—during armed conflict.

The Geneva Conventions deal with the following issues:

- protection for the wounded, the shipwrecked and civilians in and around war zones;
- the rights of those captured during a military conflict and rules for the treatment of civilian internees; and
- the status and treatment of protected persons, including civilian populations in occupied territory and provisions on humanitarian relief for these populations.

b *States Parties*

The 1949 Geneva Conventions have been ratified, in whole or with reservations, by all 194 internationally recognized sovereign states,[222] all of which, with the exception of the Holy See (Vatican City), are members of the U.N.[223] These 194 states include South Sudan, a U.N. Member State that acceded to the Geneva Conventions in 2012.

In addition to these 194 states, the quasi-sovereign Cook Islands ratified the Geneva Conventions, thus bringing the total number of states parties to the Geneva Conventions to 195.

2 *Articles Common to the Four Geneva Conventions of 1949*

Articles 1 to 3 and 9 are common to the four Geneva Conventions of 1949. Moreover, several Articles, including Article 10, are substantially similar to one another across the four Conventions.

222. See "Internationally Recognized Sovereign States," in the Appendices, for the full list of these 194 States.
223. The Holy See is a U.N. permanent observer.

a Common Article 1: Respecting the Conventions in All Circumstances

As discussed under "State Responsibility to 'Respect and Ensure Respect,'" *supra*, Article 1, common to the four Geneva Conventions of 1949, requires states parties to "*respect* and to *ensure respect* for the present Convention *in all circumstances*" (emphasis added). Therefore, states have an affirmative duty to not only respect, but also to ensure the respect of international humanitarian law. Moreover, no derogation is permitted from these duties, which apply "in all circumstances." The duty to "ensure respect" of the Geneva Conventions effectively means that states not involved in an armed conflict must call upon states that *are* involved in the armed conflict to ensure that they respect the rules.

b Common Article 2: Application of the Conventions in International Conflicts

Under common Article 2 of the Geneva Conventions, the Conventions apply to:

> all cases of declared war or of any other armed conflict which may arise between two or more of the High Contracting Parties, even if the state of war is not recognized by one of them [as well as to] all cases of partial or total occupation of the territory of a High Contracting Party.

Furthermore, in a conflict between three or more powers, "although one of the Powers in conflict may not be a party to the present Convention, the Powers who are parties thereto shall remain bound by it in their mutual relations." If a non-party to the Convention accepts and applies the provisions of the Conventions, the states parties "shall furthermore be bound by the Convention" in relation to the non-party (Article 2 GC I-IV).

c Common Article 3: Application of the Conventions in Non-international Armed Conflicts

i Overview

The Geneva Conventions also codify the rules of engagement in non-international (domestic) armed conflict. Common Article 3 is the first express codification of law "[i]n the case of armed conflict not of an international character occurring in the territory of one of the High Contracting Parties." Such conflict includes civil wars, civil insurrections and internal armed conflicts.

ii Application to Both Government Forces and Non-state Actors

In non-international armed conflicts, common Article 3 imposes duties and obligations on "each Party to the conflict." The article therefore expressly binds both *government forces* as well as *non-state actors*, such as rebel and dissident forces.

Common Article 3, as well as Additional Protocol II, which also binds non-state armed groups, are frequently criticized on the basis that they apply to groups that never gave consent to the applicable terms. Non-state actors are thus required to submit to provisions that they never had an opportunity to negotiate. Therefore, unlike governments, which may escape the application of treaty law by simply not ratifying treaties, non-state actors are placed under treaties with no opportunity to register reservations or avoid the application of treaty law or customary international law by repeatedly and publicly announcing opposition to the rule in question.

In response to this criticism, some advocates of common Article 3 and Additional Protocol II argue that, as a matter of principle, states may enter into treaties that are binding not only on their governments but also on the actors that are within their jurisdiction. Therefore, in the same way that a government may issue criminal law that applies to criminals who may or may not consent to the application of the law, so too may governments ratify treaties imposing obligations on non-state armed groups, whether or not such groups consent to the treaties or had the opportunity to participate in the negotiation, formation and ratification of the treaty.

iii Rules

Common Article 3 establishes fundamental rules from which no derogation is permitted and whose violation gives rise to individual rather than state liability. It is like a mini-Convention within the Geneva Conventions as it contains the essential rules of the Conventions compressed down to roughly one-half of a page and applied to conflicts of a domestic character.

(1) Protections Afforded to Persons Taking No Part in Hostilities

It applies to *all persons* "taking no active part in the hostilities," including soldiers who have "laid down their arms" (surrendered) or those placed *hors de combat* due to "sickness, wounds, detention, or any other cause" (Article 3(1) GC I-IV). It protects them from the following:

- violence, murder, inhumane treatment and torture;
- taking of hostages;
- outrages upon personal dignity, including degrading treatment; and
- the passing of sentences and the carrying out of executions through unfair trials or without "previous judgment pronounced by a regularly constituted court affording all the judicial guarantees which are recognized as indispensable by civilized peoples" (Article 3(1) GC I-IV).[224]

224. As an important reminder, this provision *applies only in the case of non-international armed conflicts*. In the case of international armed conflicts, States may judge prisoners of war by special military courts (*see* Part III of Chapter III of Geneva Convention III).

(2) Protections Afforded to the Wounded and the Sick

Common Article 3 further requires that the wounded, the sick, and the shipwrecked shall be collected and cared for and permits impartial humanitarian bodies such as the ICRC to offer their services to the parties to the conflict. It calls on the parties to the conflict to endeavor to bring all or part of the Geneva Conventions into force through special agreements. Common Article 3 further holds that the application of these rules does not affect the legal status of the parties to the conflict (Article 3(2) GC I-IV).

d Common Article 9: No Obstacle to the Humanitarian Activities of the Red Cross

Common Article 9 provides that the provisions of the Geneva Conventions "constitute no obstacle to the humanitarian activities which the International Committee of the Red Cross or any other impartial humanitarian organization may, subject to the consent of the Parties to the conflict concerned, undertake for the protection of wounded and sick, medical personnel and chaplains, and for their relief."

e Articles Addressing Educating the Public on International Humanitarian Law

Each of the Geneva Conventions includes language that mandates that states parties disseminate the Geneva Conventions and educate the public on international humanitarian law. The "High Contracting Parties undertake, in time of peace as in time of war, to disseminate the text of the present Convention as widely as possible in their respective countries, and, in particular, to include the study thereof in their programmes of military and, if possible, civil instruction, so that the principles thereof may become known" (Article 47 GC I; Article 48 GC II; Article 127 GC III; Article 144 GC IV).[225]

f Articles Addressing Grave Breaches

Each of the Geneva Conventions also includes language that establishes the grave breaches regime, discussed under "D. Grave Breaches," below.

225. These articles vary only in their characterization of the entire population to which principles of international humanitarian law should become known (i.e., "to the entire population, in particular to the armed fighting forces, the medical personnel and the chaplains," as in Art. 47 GC I and Art. 48 GC II versus "to all their armed forces and to the entire population" in Art. 127 GC III or "to the entire population" in Art. 144 GC IV).

3 *Geneva Convention I for the Wounded and Sick in the Field*

a Overview

Containing 64 articles, Geneva Convention I for the Amelioration of the Condition of the Wounded and Sick in Armed Forces in the Field sought to protect wounded and sick soldiers on land during war. It extends protection to wounded or sick combatants, to those who provide care and to items protected by distinctive emblems in common Article 2 international armed conflicts.

Convention (I) also contains two annexes containing a draft agreement relating to hospital zones and a model identity card for medical and religious personnel.

b Distinctive Symbols: The Emblems

i The Red Cross, Red Crescent, and Red Lion and Sun

The following distinctive symbols were previously established by and in use since the Geneva Convention of 1864:

- the red cross;
- the red crescent; and
- the red lion and sun on a white ground.

The Red Cross symbol was never intended to be a religious symbol associated with Christianity.[226] Rather, it is based on the Swiss flag with the colors inverted (a red cross on a white background rather than a white cross on a red background). However, Muslim countries, sensitive to the association of the symbol of the cross with Christianity, moved to create a symbol based on a red crescent rather than a red cross.

The Red Lion and Sun Society of Persia (and later Iran) was admitted to the International Red Cross and Red Crescent Movement in 1923, following its establishment in 1922. However, the Red Crescent came to replace the Red Lion and Sun following the establishment of the Islamic Republic of Iran in 1979.

ii The Red Crystal

In addition, the red crystal ("Third Protocol Emblem," previously referred to as the "red diamond") was created under Additional Protocol III, which was adopted on 8 December 2005 and entered into force on 14 January 2006. Israel's relief agency, Magen David Adom, uses the red crystal with a red Star of David inside of it.

226. In November 1889, the Swiss Federal Council published a "communication regarding the federal coat of arms," detailing the history of the use of the Swiss cross since the fifteenth century. The Federal Council communicated that "our heraldic cross is not a mathematical figure, but at the same the Christian cross symbol and the field sign of the Old Confederacy." *See* "Flag of Switzerland," available at <https://en.wikipedia.org/wiki/Flag_of_Switzerland>.

iii The Distinctive Flag of Geneva Convention I

The distinctive flag of Geneva Convention I is to be hoisted only over such medical units and establishments as are entitled to be respected under the Convention, and only with the consent of the military authorities. In mobile units, as in fixed establishments, it may be accompanied by the national flag of the party to the conflict to which the unit or establishment belongs (Article 42 GC I).

c *Respect and Protection of Medical and Religious Personnel*

i Overview

Geneva Convention I, as well as Geneva Convention II and Geneva Convention IV, provide special protections for medical and religious personnel. These protections are codified as follows:

- Articles 24-26 of Geneva Convention I.
- Article 36 of Geneva Convention II.
- Article 20 of Geneva Convention IV.

Medical and religious personnel receive special protections in the sense that states parties to a conflict may not interfere with their work. Moreover, such personnel are given special rights of movement.

ii General Provisions

(1) Medical Personnel, Medical Staff and Chaplains

The following shall be respected and protected in all circumstances (Article 24 GC I):

- medical personnel exclusively engaged in the search for, or the collection, transport or treatment of the wounded or sick, or in the prevention of disease;
- staff exclusively engaged in the administration of medical units and establishments; and
- chaplains attached to the armed forces.

(2) Specially Trained Members of the Armed Forces

The following persons shall likewise be respected and protected if they are carrying out these duties at the time when they come into contact with the enemy or fall into his hands (Article 25 GC I): members of the armed forces specially trained for employment as hospital orderlies (hospital attendants), nurses or auxiliary stretcher-bearers, in the search for or the collection, transport or treatment of the wounded and sick.

(3) Staff of Red Cross Societies and Other Voluntary Aid Societies

The staff of National Red Cross Societies and other voluntary aid societies, duly recognized and authorized by their governments, who may be employed on the same duties as the Article 24 medical personnel, are placed on the same footing as the personnel named in Article 24, provided that the staff of such societies are subject to military laws and regulations. Each state party shall notify the other, before actually employing them, the names of the societies which it has authorized, under its responsibility, to render assistance to the regular medical service of its armed forces (Article 26 GC I).

iii Specific Provisions

(1) Wounded and Sick Combatants

Members of the armed forces who are wounded or sick shall be respected and protected in all circumstances (Article 12.I GC I). Only urgent medical reasons will authorize priority in the order of treatment to be administered (triage) (Article 12.III GC I).

At all times, and particularly after an engagement, parties to conflicts shall "take all possible measures to search for and collect the wounded and sick, to protect them against pillage and ill-treatment, to ensure their adequate care, and to search for the dead and prevent their being despoiled" (Article 15.I GC IV).

(2) Medical Personnel

Under Geneva Convention I, "[m]edical personnel exclusively engaged in the search for, or the collection, transport or treatment of the wounded or sick, or in the prevention of disease, staff exclusively engaged in the administration of medical units and establishments … shall be respected and protected in all circumstances" (Article 24 GC I).

The standard of respect and protection to be accorded to such personnel is that of humane treatment; they are to be treated by enemy forces as such forces would treat their own personnel. Geneva Convention I does not permit any "adverse distinction founded on sex, race, nationality, religion, political opinions, or any other similar criteria" (GC I, Article 12).

Although medical personnel may carry small arms for the purpose of self-defense, they are not deemed to be combatants under the Geneva Conventions. Like that of chaplains, the status of medical personnel upon capture under Geneva Convention I is retained personnel, *not* prisoners of war.

The staff of National Red Cross Societies and other voluntary aid societies recognized and authorized by their governments are granted the same protections as the medical personnel named in Article 24, provided they are "exclusively engaged" (Article 24 GC I) in their humanitarian role and are subject to military laws and regulations (Article 26 GC I).

(3) Medical Units and Establishments

Medical establishments and mobile medical units "[m]ay in no circumstances be attacked" and "shall at all times be respected and protected by the Parties to the conflict" (Article 19 GC I) unless they are used to commit acts harmful to the enemy (Article 21 GC I) (e.g., storing munitions, sheltering combatants, etc.). Protection may cease only after a due warning has been given, naming a reasonable time limit and after such warning has remained unheeded (Article 21 GC I).

The authorities should ensure that medical establishments and units are, as far as possible, situated away from military objectives in such a manner that attacks against such objectives do not imperil their safety (Article 19 GC I). Additional Protocol I further prohibits the use of medical units to shield military objectives from attack (Article 12 AP I).

(4) Medical Transportation

Medical vehicles must be properly marked in order to claim protection. They forfeit their protection if engaged in "acts harmful to the enemy" (Article 21 GC I). While medical aircraft must be properly marked, their protection ultimately depends upon agreement between the parties to a conflict. Flights over an enemy or over enemy-occupied territory are prohibited unless an agreement provides otherwise.

Under Additional Protocol I, three overflight regimes are established:

(i) *Land controlled by friendly forces*. No agreement is required, though notice is recommended;
(ii) *Contact Zone (disputed area)*. Absolute protection requires an agreement;
(iii) *Land or sea controlled by the enemy (Article 27 AP I)*. Medical aircraft is protected while flying over land or sea areas controlled by the enemy, provided that "prior agreement to such flights has been obtained from the competent authority of that adverse Party" (Article 27.1 AP I).

iv Armlets Bearing the Distinctive Emblem

Medical and religious personnel, staff of National Red Cross Societies and of other voluntary aid societies "shall wear, affixed to the left arm, a water-resistant armlet bearing the distinctive emblem, issued and stamped by the military authority" (Article 40 GC I).

4 *Geneva Convention II for the Wounded, Sick and Shipwrecked at Sea*

Geneva Convention II for the Amelioration of the Condition of Wounded, Sick and Shipwrecked Members of Armed Forces at Sea protects wounded, sick and shipwrecked military personnel at sea during war. It replaced The Hague Convention of 1907 for the Adaptation to Maritime Warfare of the Principles of the Geneva Convention. Its content closely follows the first Geneva Convention, but its 63 articles specifically apply to war at sea by protecting, for example, hospital ships. It has one annex containing a model identity card for medical and religious personnel.

5 *Geneva Convention III for the Treatment of Prisoners of War*

Geneva Convention III relative to the Treatment of Prisoners of War replaced the Prisoners of War Convention of 1929. With 143 articles, it provides more detail than the 1929 Convention did.

a Application to International Armed Conflicts

Geneva Convention III, with the exception of common Article 3, applies to international armed conflicts only. A detained person can thus only benefit from the protections offered to Geneva Convention III prisoners of war if he is captured in an international armed conflict. In a non-international armed conflict, he or she will be treated as an unprivileged belligerent, subject to the capturing power's authority. In some cases, the detained person may be imprisoned and tried as an ordinary criminal in domestic courts. In other cases, special mechanisms may be established to investigate and prosecute the detained person. In the United States, for example, captured enemy belligerents are tried by military commissions established by the Military Commissions Act of 2009.

b Categories of Detainees

Detained persons fall under three main categories:

i Prisoners of War (Combatants)

There are two types of combatants:

- lawful combatants (who enjoy prisoner of war status upon their detention); and
- unprivileged belligerents (recognized as a class under U.S. law but not under customary international law).

As discussed further below, only lawful combatants, contractors (Article 4A(4) GC III) and crewmembers (Article 4A(5) GC III) are entitled to the status of prisoners of war and the accompanying protections accorded thereto. U.S. policy does not grant prisoner of war status to individuals it deems to be "unlawful" combatants.

ii Retained Personnel (Non-combatants)

While retained by a detaining power with a view to assisting prisoners of war, medical personnel and chaplains are not deemed to be prisoners of war; rather, they are given the status of retained personnel. However, they must receive, as a minimum, the benefits and protection of GC IV and must be granted "all facilities necessary to provide for the medical care of, and religious ministration to prisoners of war" (Article 33.I GC III). They shall (Article 33.II GC III):

> continue to exercise their medical and spiritual functions for the benefit of prisoners of war, preferably those belonging to the armed forces upon which they depend, within the scope of the military laws and regulations of the Detaining Power and under the control of its competent services, in accordance with their professional etiquette.

Non-combatant medical personnel and chaplains are permitted to carry small arms to use in self-defense without compromising or losing their status as retained personnel. However, if they abuse their protected status and employ their arms against an enemy in an offensive manner, they may lose their protected status and may be lawfully targeted and treated as prisoners of war.

Retained personnel can only be required to perform their medical and spiritual functions. They may not be compelled to carry out any work other than that concerned with their medical or religious duties. If no such work is available, the retained personnel must be released (Article 33-38 GC III).

iii Civilian Internees

(1) Overview

Civilians are not members of the armed forces and are therefore neither combatants nor non-combatants. In a sense, they are non-combatants because they do not perform a combat role in hostilities. However, to avoid any confusion with respect to the use of "non-combatant" as a term of art to refer to members of armed forces in a non-combatant role, namely, medical personnel and chaplains (i.e., retained personnel in the event of capture), we use the term "civilian internees" to refer to non-members of the armed forces of a party to a conflict that are captured and detained.

(2) Civilians Entitled to Prisoner of War Status

There are two categories of persons who, while in a technical sense are deemed to be civilians because they are not members of armed forces, are nevertheless given the status of prisoners of war under Geneva Convention III:

- Article 4A(4) persons who accompany the armed forces without actually being members thereof (e.g., contractors);
- Article 4A(5) members of crews, including masters, pilots and apprentices, of the merchant marine and the crews of civil aircraft of the Parties to the conflict, who do not benefit by more favorable treatment under any other provisions of international law.

As discussed further below, while these civilians are given the status of prisoners of war, they are not deemed to be combatants.

(3) Treatment of Civilian Internees

Part III ("Status and Treatment of Protected Persons") of Geneva Convention IV, in section IV, sets forth the regulations for the treatment of internees.

(a) General Protections

Geneva Convention IV establishes that the Parties to a conflict shall not intern protected persons, except in accordance with the following provisions (Article 79 GC IV):

- Article 41: Should the power, in whose hands protected persons may be, consider the measures of control mentioned in Geneva Convention IV to be inadequate, it may not have recourse to any other measure of control more severe than that of *assigned residence* or *internment*.
- Article 42: The internment or placing in assigned residence of protected persons may be ordered *only if the security of the detaining power makes it absolutely necessary*.
- Article 43: Any protected person who has been interned or placed in assigned residence shall be entitled to have such action *reconsidered as soon as possible* by an *appropriate court or administrative board* designated by the detaining power for that purpose.

(b) Judicial Protections

Geneva Convention IV further establishes a series of judicial protections that govern the following in cases of occupation:

- the *internment* or *imprisonment* of protected persons who commit an offence (Article 68 GC IV); and
- the *assigned residence* or *internment* of protected persons for imperative reasons of security of an occupying power, which must include a right of appeal and periodical review (Article 78 GC IV).

For further details, *see* "Internment, Imprisonment, Assigned Residence, the Death Penalty" under "Section III: Provisions for Occupied Territories," *infra*.

c *Categories of Prisoners of War*

i Overview

Geneva Convention III defines prisoners of war as persons who have "fallen into the power of the enemy" and belong to one of the following eight enumerated categories (Article 4A GC III):[227]

227. Note: The language enumerating the categories of persons protected as prisoners of war in Art. 4A of Geneva Convention III is virtually identical to the Geneva Convention I Art. 13 language

(1) members of the armed forces of a party to the conflict, as well as members of militias or volunteer corps forming part of such armed forces (*combatant prisoners of war*) (Article 4A(1) GC III);

(2) members of other militias and members of other volunteer corps, including those of organized resistance movements, belonging to a party to the conflict and operating in or outside their own territory, provided that such militias or volunteer corps:

  (a) are *commanded by a person responsible* for his subordinates;

  (b) have a *fixed distinctive sign* (insignia) recognizable at a distance [normally worn on a uniform, though a uniform on its own normally meets the standard];

  (c) *carry arms openly*;

  (d) conduct their operations in *accordance with the laws and customs of war* (*combatant prisoners of war*) (Article 4A(2) GC III).

(3) members of regular armed forces who profess allegiance to a government or an authority not recognized by the detaining power (*combatant prisoners of war*) (Article 4A(3) GC III);

(4) persons who accompany the armed forces without actually being members thereof, such as civilian members of military aircraft crews, war correspondents (journalists), or supply contractors, provided that they have *received authorization* from the armed forces which they accompany, who shall provide them for that purpose with an *identity card* similar to the annexed model (*non-combatant prisoners of war*) (Article 4A(4) GC III);

(5) members of crews, including masters, pilots and apprentices, of the *merchant marine and the crews of civil aircraft* of the Parties to the conflict, who do not benefit by more favorable treatment under any other provisions of international law (*non-combatant prisoners of war*) (Article 4A(5) GC III); and

(6) inhabitants of a non-occupied territory, who on the approach of the enemy, spontaneously take up arms to resist the invading forces without having had time to form themselves into regular armed units (i.e., in the sense provided under sub-clauses 4A(1) and 4A(2)), provided they carry arms openly and respect the laws and customs of war (the "*levée en masse*" category) (*combatant prisoners of war*) (Article 4A(6) GC III).

In addition, the following are likewise treated as prisoners of war under Geneva Convention III:

(7) "Persons belonging, or having belonged, to the armed forces of the occupied country, if the occupying Power considers it necessary by reason of such allegiance to intern them, even though it has originally liberated them while hostilities were going on outside the territory it occupies, in particular where such persons have made an unsuccessful attempt to rejoin the armed forces to

enumerating the categories of the wounded and sick and the Geneva Convention II Art. 13 language enumerating the categories of the wounded, sick and shipwrecked at sea.

which they belong and which are engaged in combat, or where they fail to comply with a summons made to them with a view to internment" (Article 4B(1) GC III).

(8) "The persons belonging to one of the categories enumerated in the present Article, who have been received by neutral or non-belligerent Powers on their territory and whom these Powers are required to intern under international law, without prejudice to any more favourable treatment which these Powers may choose to give and with the exception of Articles 8, 10, 15, 30, fifth paragraph, 58-67, 92, 126 and, where diplomatic relations exist between the Parties to the conflict and the neutral or non-belligerent Power concerned, those Articles concerning the Protecting Power. Where such diplomatic relations exist, the Parties to a conflict on whom these persons depend shall be allowed to perform towards them the functions of a Protecting Power as provided in the present Convention, without prejudice to the functions which these Parties normally exercise in conformity with diplomatic and consular usage and treaties" (Article 4B(2) GC III).

ii Cases of Doubt

Article 5 of GC III establishes what is colloquially referred to as the "Article 5 Tribunal," which adjudicates whether a detainee qualifies as a prisoner of war in cases of doubt. Under Article 5:

> Should any doubt arise as to whether persons, having committed a belligerent act and having fallen into the hands of the enemy, belong to any of the categories enumerated in Article 4, such persons shall enjoy the protection of the present Convention until such time as their status has been determined by a competent tribunal.

The Convention creates a presumption of prisoner of war status if there is "any doubt" as to a detainee's status. Unless a detaining power is confident beyond a shred of doubt that a detainee does not qualify as a prisoner of war, the detainee is to be presumed a prisoner of war until a competent tribunal determines otherwise.

d Protection and Rights of Prisoners of War

i Combatant Immunity

Combatant immunity is a term implied but not expressly referenced in Geneva Convention III. It refers to the immunity of prisoners of war from trial for lawful wartime acts. It does *not*, however, exempt prisoners of war from trial for war crimes.

Of the six groups entitled to prisoner of war status under Article 4A of Geneva Convention III, only four are entitled to full combatant immunity:

- Article 4A(1) members of the armed forces of a party to the conflict, as well as members of militias or volunteer corps forming part of such armed forces;
- Article 4A(2) members of other militias and members of other volunteer corps belonging to a party to the conflict, provided that they fulfill four conditions;[228]
- Article 4A(3) members of regular armed forces who profess allegiance to a government or an authority not recognized by the detaining power; and
- Article 4A(6) *levée en masse.*

The following are civilians entitled to prisoner of war status that do not receive combatant immunity, though they may carry small arms for the purpose of *self-defense*:

- Article 4A(4) persons who accompany the armed forces without actually being members thereof (e.g., contractors); and
- Article 4A(5) members of crews (e.g., pilots).

Article 4A(4) persons who accompany the armed forces and Article 4A(5) members of crews may be prosecuted for wartime acts if they use their arms to attack enemy forces.

ii Rights While in Captivity (Articles 17-90 GC III)

(1) In General

Geneva Convention III delineates the conditions and places of captivity of prisoners of war, particularly with regard to the relief they receive and their labor, financial resources and payment of a fair working rate. Among the enumerated rights are as follows:

- the right to be humanely treated at all times and free from violence, insult or public curiosity. Any unlawful act or omission by the detaining power causing death (including murder) or seriously endangering the health of a prisoner of war in its custody is prohibited and is a serious breach of Geneva Convention III;[229]
- the right to cleanliness and healthfulness,[230] to an adequate infirmary and appropriate diet[231] and medical inspections held at least once a month;[232]
- the right to send and receive letters and cards.[233]

The Convention further established the principle of repatriating prisoners of war immediately upon the cessation of hostilities.

228. They must (i) be commanded by a person responsible for his subordinates; (ii) have a fixed distinctive sign recognizable at a distance; (iii) carry arms openly; and (iv) conduct their operations in accordance with the laws and customs of war.
229. Article 13 GC III.
230. Article 29 GC III.
231. Article 30 GC III.
232. Article 31 GC III.
233. Article 71 GC III.

(2) Prohibition of Torture or of Compelling the Disclosure of Information (Article 17 GC III)

Every prisoner of war, when questioned, "is bound to give only his surname, first names and rank, date of birth, and army, regimental, personal or serial number, or failing this, equivalent information."[234] A detaining power may not use any form of coercion to extract information from a prisoner of war. Geneva Convention III states that:[235]

> No physical or mental torture, nor any other form of coercion, may be inflicted on prisoners of war to secure from them information of any kind whatever. Prisoners of war who refuse to answer may not be threatened, insulted, or exposed to unpleasant or disadvantageous treatment of any kind.

(3) Relations of Prisoners of War with the Exterior (Articles 69-77 GC III)

Section V of Part III of Geneva Convention III (Articles 69-77) governs relations of prisoners of war with the exterior and requires that the detaining party permit prisoners of war to correspond with their family members and inform them of their capture, address and state of health:[236]

> Immediately upon capture, or not more than one week after arrival at a camp, even if it is a transit camp, likewise in case of sickness or transfer to hospital or to another camp, every prisoner of war shall be enabled to write direct to his family, on the one hand, and to the Central Prisoners of War Agency provided for in Article 123, on the other hand, a card similar, if possible, to the model annexed to the present Convention, informing his relatives of his capture, address and state of health.

(4) Labor and Work Conditions (Article 49 GC III)

Protected persons may be compelled to work only to the same extent as nationals of the state party to the conflict in whose territory they are. If protected persons are of enemy nationality, they may only be compelled to do work which is normally necessary to ensure the feeding, sheltering, clothing, transport, and health of human beings and which is not directly related to the conduct of military operations.

A detaining power may utilize the labor of prisoners of war "who are physically fit, taking into account their age, sex, rank and physical aptitude, and with a view particularly to maintaining them in a good state of physical and mental health."[237]

Non-commissioned officers who are prisoners of war shall only be required to do supervisory work. Those not so required may ask for other suitable work which shall, so far as possible, be found for them.[238] If officers or persons of equivalent status ask

234. Article 17.I GC III.
235. Article 17.IV GC III.
236. Article 70 GC III.
237. Article 49, para. 1 GC III.
238. Article 49, para. 2 GC III.

for suitable work, it shall be found for them, so far as possible, but they *may in no circumstances be compelled to work*.[239]

(5) Financial Resources (Article 60 GC III)

Detaining powers must grant prisoners of war a monthly advance of pay, the amount of which is to be fixed by conversion into the currency of the detaining power, of the following amounts:[240]

> Category I: Prisoners ranking below sergeants: eight Swiss francs.
> Category II: Sergeants and other non-commissioned officers, or prisoners of equivalent rank: twelve Swiss francs.
> Category III: Warrant officers and commissioned officers below the rank of major or prisoners of equivalent rank: fifty Swiss francs.
> Category IV: Majors, lieutenant-colonels, colonels or prisoners of equivalent rank: sixty Swiss francs.
> Category V: General officers or prisoners of war of equivalent rank: seventy-five Swiss francs.

iii Penal and Disciplinary Sanctions (Articles 82-105 GC III)

(1) In General (Articles 82-88 GC III)

Prisoners of war must be subject to the same laws, regulations and orders in force in the armed forces of the detaining power.[241] If any law, regulation or order of the detaining power declares acts committed by a prisoner of war to be punishable, whereas the same acts would not be punishable if committed by a member of the forces of the detaining power, such acts may entail disciplinary punishments only.[242] With respect to sentencing, prisoners of war may not be sentenced by the military authorities and courts of the detaining power to any penalties except those provided for in respect of members of the armed forces of the detaining power who have committed the same acts.[243] The following acts are forbidden:[244]

> Collective punishment for individual acts, corporal punishment, imprisonment in premises without daylight and, in general, any form of torture or cruelty.

(2) Disciplinary Sanctions (Articles 89-90 GC III)

The disciplinary punishments applicable to prisoners of war are as follows:[245]

239. Article 49, para. 3 GC III.
240. Article 60 GC III.
241. Article 82.I GC III.
242. Article 82.II GC III.
243. Article 87.I GC III.
244. Article 87.III GC III.
245. Article 89 GC III.

(1) A fine which shall not exceed 50 percent of the advances of pay and working pay which the prisoner of war would otherwise receive under the provisions of Articles 60 and 62 during a period of not more than thirty days.
(2) Discontinuance of privileges granted over and above the treatment provided for by the present Convention.
(3) Fatigue duties not exceeding two hours daily.
(4) Confinement.

The duration of any single punishment may not exceed 30 days. This maximum of 30 days may not be exceeded, even if the prisoner of war is answerable for several acts at the same time when he is awarded punishment, whether such acts are related or not.[246]

(3) Judicial Proceedings against Prisoners of War (Articles 99-108 GC III)

The judicial proceedings instituted against prisoners of war are dealt with in Part III of Chapter III (Articles 99-108 GC III), which prohibits trying or sentencing any prisoner of war under any *ex post facto* law.[247] Unlike common Article 3, which applies only to non-international conflicts and prohibits "the passing of sentences and the carrying out of executions without previous judgment pronounced by a regularly constituted court affording all the judicial guarantees,"[248] Article 102 implies that such guarantees are not required if they are not the detaining state's custom with regard to members of its own armed forces:

> A prisoner of war can be validly sentenced only if the sentence has been *pronounced by the same courts according to the same procedure as in the case of members of the armed forces of the Detaining Power.*

Thus, in countries such as the United States, where members of the armed forces may be tried by special courts-martial (military courts), prisoners of war are not entitled to civilian trials and all of their guarantees. At the same time, GC III requires that the prisoner of war have access to a "defense by a qualified advocate or counsel of his own choice, to the calling of witnesses and ... to the services of a competent interpreter."[249]

iv Release and Repatriation (Articles 118-119 GC III)

At the close of hostilities, prisoners of war must be released and repatriated without delay after the cessation of active hostilities, with the costs of repatriation equitably apportioned between the detaining power and the power on which the prisoners depend.[250]

246. Article 90 GC III.
247. Article 99 GC III.
248. Article 3(1)(d) GC III.
249. Article 105 GC III.
250. Article 118 GC III.

Moreover, repatriation shall be effected in conditions similar to those laid down in Articles 46 to 48 (Transfer of Prisoners of War after their Arrival in Camp) of Geneva Convention III, which require under Article 46 that the transfer of prisoners of war be effected humanely and in conditions not less favorable than those under which the forces of the detaining power are transferred.[251]

Moreover, "[p]risoners of war against whom criminal proceedings for an indictable offence are pending may be detained until the end of such proceedings, and, if necessary, until the completion of the punishment. The same shall apply to prisoners of war already convicted for an indictable offence."[252]

e Model Regulations and Identity Cards

The five annexes of Geneva Convention III contain various model regulations, model identity and other cards.

6 Geneva Convention IV for the Protection of Civilian Persons in Time of War

a Overview

Perhaps the most fundamental norm of international humanitarian law today is contained in Geneva Convention IV relative to the Protection of Civilian Persons in Time of War, which prohibits states from directly targeting civilians in military attacks.

Taking into account the experience of WWII, where civilians were systematically targeted in both internal as well as international conflicts, the fourth Convention was drafted and adopted with the purpose of protecting a defined group of civilians from arbitrary action by the enemy. Geneva Convention IV thus contains provisions regarding the general protection of populations against the consequences of war and promulgates regulations governing the status and treatment of protected persons. The Fourth Convention is supplementary to the provisions of the Hague Regulations of 1907 (Article 154 GC IV).

The three annexes of the Fourth Convention contain a model agreement on hospital and safety zones, model regulations on humanitarian relief, and model cards.

b Definition of "Civilians"

Geneva Convention IV does not specifically define "civilian." However, Article 50 of AP I states that a "civilian" is any person who does not belong to:

- One of the categories of persons referred to in the following clauses of Geneva Convention III:

251. Article 119.I GC III.
252. Article 119.V GC III.

  - Article 4A(1) members of the armed forces of a party to the conflict, as well as members of militias or volunteer corps forming part of such armed forces;
  - Article 4A(2) members of other militias and members of other volunteer corps belonging to a party to the conflict, provided that they fulfill four conditions;[253]
  - Article 4A(3) members of regular armed forces who profess allegiance to a government or an authority not recognized by the detaining power;
  - Article 4A(6) *levée en masse*.
- Article 43 of AP I: the armed forces of a Party to a conflict, which consist of all organized armed forces, groups and units which are under a command responsible to that Party for the conduct of its subordinates, even if that Party is represented by a government or an authority not recognized by an adverse Party.

In case of doubt whether a person is a civilian, that person is to be considered a civilian.[254]

c Organization of Provisions and Protections Accorded

i Overview

In Pictet's Commentary to Geneva Convention IV, he wrote that a person is a "legal subject within a state and the provisions concerning the protection of civilians in time of war take no account of disputes which may exist between the State and its own citizens" (p. 372). In this vein, Geneva Convention IV, with the exception of the 14 Articles in the Whole Population provisions of Part II, does not apply to the relationship between a state and its own nationals.

ii Part I General Provisions

(1) Overview

Part I of Geneva Convention IV lays out general provisions, including common Articles 1, 2, 3 and 9 to the Geneva Conventions.

(2) Definition of Part III Protected Persons

(a) Overview and Elements

Article 4 of Geneva Convention IV defines protected persons who receive the Part III protections as follows:

253. They must (i) be commanded by a person responsible for his subordinates; (ii) have a fixed distinctive sign recognizable at a distance; (iii) carry arms openly; and (iv) conduct their operations in accordance with the laws and customs of war.
254. Article 50.1 AP I.

> those who, at a given moment and in any manner whatsoever, find themselves, in case of a conflict or occupation, in the hands of a Party to the conflict or Occupying Power of which they are not nationals.

There are thus two elements to qualify as a "protected person" (Article 4 GC IV):

- there must be an international armed conflict (otherwise, only common Article 3 with respect to non-international armed conflicts rather than Geneva Convention IV would apply); and
- the persons must find themselves in the hands of a party to the conflict or occupying power of which they are not nationals (i.e., they are aliens in the territory of a party to a conflict or they are persons living in a territory occupied by a power of which they are not nationals).

(b) Exceptions

Protected persons are not (Article 4 GC IV):

- nationals of a state not party to Geneva Conventions (Article 4.II GC IV);
- nationals of a neutral state who find themselves in the territory of a belligerent state while the state of which they are nationals has normal diplomatic representation in the state in whose hands they are (Article 4.II GC IV);[255]
- nationals of a co-belligerent state (an ally) in a belligerent state while the state of which they are nationals has normal diplomatic representation in the state in whose hands they are (Article 4.II GC IV);[256] and
- Persons protected by one of the other three Geneva Conventions (i.e., members of armed forces protected by Geneva Convention I or II or prisoners of war protected by Geneva Convention III) (Article 4.IV GC IV).

(c) Narrow Application

The scope of Part III protected persons is thus narrow. Article 4 of Geneva Convention IV recognizes that the provisions of Part II of the Convention (whole populations, which are discussed below) are "wider in application" than the narrow definition granted in Article 4 for "protected persons." A civilian who does not qualify as a protected person under Geneva Convention IV will qualify for the whole population protections under Geneva Convention IV.

---

255. In the case of an occupation where the occupying power disrupts the diplomatic relations between a neutral state and the state in which nationals of the neutral state are located, the nationals of the neutral state will be deemed to be protected persons. This is nearly always the case in occupations, since the occupying power shuts down the embassies of the occupied state.
256. *See* the above note with respect to occupations. In nearly all cases, an occupation will disrupt all of the diplomatic relations between the occupied state and all other states. Therefore, the exception with respect to nationals of co-belligerent states (and neutral states, as mentioned above) will not apply. Rather, these individuals will be deemed to be protected persons.

iii Part II General Protection of Whole Populations Against Certain Consequences of War

(1) Overview

The provisions of Part II cover "the whole of the populations of the countries in conflict, without any adverse distinction based, in particular, on race, nationality, religion or political opinion" (Article 13 GC IV). By "whole of the populations," Part II of Geneva Convention IV is not restricting its application to the whole of the populations that are nationals of the countries in conflict; rather, it applies to the whole of populations that are physically located in the countries in conflict, regardless of their nationality.

(2) Protections Accorded

The protections accorded to the whole population in the 14 articles of Part II (Articles 13 to 26) include:

- hospitals and safety zones;[257]
- neutral zones/neutralized zones intended to shelter from the effects of war;[258]
- particular protection and respect for the wounded and sick, as well as the infirm and expectant mothers;[259]
- striving to conclude local agreements for the removal from besieged or encircled areas of vulnerable persons and for the passage of ministers, medical personnel, and medical equipment;[260]
- respect and protection of civilian hospitals,[261] unless they are used to commit, outside their humanitarian duties, acts harmful to the enemy;[262]
- respect and protection of persons regularly and solely engaged in the operation and administration of civilian hospitals, including the personnel engaged in the search for, removal and transporting of and caring for wounded and sick civilians, the infirm and maternity cases;[263]
- respect and protection of convoys of vehicles or hospital trains or specially provided vessels on sea, conveying wounded and sick civilians, the infirm, and maternity cases;[264]
- respect of aircraft exclusively employed for the removal of wounded and sick civilians, the infirm, and maternity cases or the transport of medical personnel and equipment;[265]

257. Article 14 GC IV.
258. Article 15 GC IV.
259. Article 16 GC IV.
260. Article 17 GC IV.
261. Article 18 GC IV.
262. Article 19 GC IV.
263. Article 20 GC IV.
264. Article 21 GC IV.
265. Article 22 GC IV.

- free passage of all consignments of medical and hospital stores and objects necessary for religious worship intended only for civilians of another state party,[266] subject to certain restrictions;[267]
- protection of children under 15 who are orphaned or are separated from their families, who are not to be left to their own resources, and the entrustment of their education to persons of a similar cultural tradition;[268]
- communication and correspondence of all persons in the territory of a party to the conflict or in a territory occupied by it with their families;[269]
- facilitation of inquiries made by family members dispersed owing to the war, with the object of renewing contact with one another and of meeting.[270]

iv Part III Status and Treatment of "Protected Persons"

In addition to the Part II general protection of populations against certain consequences of war, "protected persons," as defined in Article 4, Part I of Geneva Convention IV, receive the Part III Status and Treatment protections, which are comprised of the following:

(1) Section I: Provisions Common to All Protected Persons

The section I provisions are common to the territories of the parties to the conflict and to occupied territories.

Protected persons are entitled, in all circumstances, to respect for their persons, honor, family rights, religious convictions and practices, manners and customs. They must at all times be humanely treated and protected against all acts of violence or threats thereof and against insults and public curiosity. Women are especially protected against rape, enforced prostitution and any form of indecent assault (Article 27 GC IV). The taking of hostages is prohibited (Article 34 GC IV).

In addition to section I, the section II Provisions for Aliens *or* the section III Provisions for Occupied Territories, discussed below, apply to protected persons.

(2) Section II: Provisions for Aliens in the Territory of a Party to the Conflict

(a) Overview

The section II provisions for aliens in the territory of a party to the conflict apply only to protected persons located in a belligerent state, that is, nationals of an enemy located in the territory of a party to the conflict (e.g., Japanese who were located in the U.S. during World War II). This protected class is granted the right to leave the belligerent state as well as the right to humane treatment during internment and the right to employment. They may not be compelled to work to support military operations.

266. Article 23.I GC IV.
267. Article 23.II GC IV.
268. Article 24 GC IV.
269. Article 25 GC IV.
270. Article 26 GC IV.

Article 44 of GC IV goes as far as prohibiting detaining powers from treating refugees who do not, in fact, enjoy the protection of any government "as enemy aliens exclusively on the basis of their nationality *de jure* of an enemy State."

(b) Detainment

Examples of the protections include the following:

- Article 41: Should the power, in whose hands protected persons may be, consider the measures of control mentioned in Geneva Convention IV to be inadequate, it may not have recourse to any other measure of control more severe than that of *assigned residence* or *internment*.
- Article 42: The internment or placing in assigned residence of protected persons may be ordered only if the *security* of the detaining power makes it *absolutely necessary*.
- Article 43: Any protected person who has been interned or placed in assigned residence shall be entitled to have such action reconsidered *as soon as possible by an appropriate court or administrative board* designated by the detaining power for that purpose. If the internment or placing in assigned residence is maintained, the court or administrative board shall periodically, and at least twice yearly, give consideration to his or her case, with a view to the favorable amendment of the initial decision, if circumstances permit.

(3) Section III: Provisions for Occupied Territories

For a discussion of the protections accorded in belligerent occupation under section III of Part III of Geneva IV, *see* section E.2, "Protections Accorded under Geneva Convention IV," below.

(4) Section IV: Internment Provisions

(a) Overview

Section IV provisions apply if the protected person is interned in enemy territory of a Party or in an occupied territory. The protections that are afforded are distinct from those granted to prisoners of war, who, with the exception of Article 4A(4) GC III persons who accompany the armed forces and Article 4A(5) GC III members of crews, are considered to be non-civilian combatants.

Throughout the duration of their internment, members of the same family must be lodged together in the same place of internment, except when separation of a temporary nature is necessitated for reasons of employment or health or for the purposes of enforcement of penal and disciplinary sanctions. The detaining Party must, when possible, accommodate the internees according to their nationality, language and customs.[271] The detaining Party must place at the disposal of interned persons premises suitable for the holding of religious services.[272]

(b) Penal and Disciplinary Sanctions

The disciplinary punishments applicable to internees are as follows:

(1) A fine which shall not exceed 50 percent of the wages which the internee would otherwise receive under the provisions of Article 95 during a period of not more than 30 days.
(2) Discontinuance of privileges granted over and above the treatment provided for by Geneva Convention IV.
(3) Fatigue duties, not exceeding two hours daily, in connection with the maintenance of the place of internment.
(4) Confinement.

In no case shall disciplinary penalties be inhuman, brutal or dangerous for the health of internees. The duration of any single punishment shall in no case exceed a maximum of 30 consecutive days, even if the internee is answerable for several breaches of discipline when his case is dealt with, whether such breaches are connected or not.[273]

In legal proceedings, the provisions of Articles 71 to 76 with respect to occupation shall apply, by analogy, to proceedings against internees who are in the national territory of the detaining power.[274]

v Part IV Execution of the Convention

Part IV of Geneva Convention IV establishes the general and final provisions concerning the execution of the Convention.

D Grave Breaches

1 Overview

Articles 49 GC I, 50 GC II, 129 GC III, and 146 GC IV contain nearly identical language[275] establishing the grave breaches regime of the Geneva Conventions. They state as follows:

271. Article 82 GC IV.
272. Article 86 GC IV.
273. Article 119 GC IV.
274. Article 126 GC IV.
275. The language is identical in the four Geneva Conventions, except for the last paragraph in Art. 129 of Geneva Convention III, which states "of the present Convention" rather than "of the Geneva Convention relative to the Treatment of Prisoners of War of 12 August 1949."

> The High Contracting Parties undertake to enact any legislation necessary to provide effective penal sanctions for persons committing, or ordering to be committed, any of the grave breaches of the present Convention defined in the following article.
>
> Each High Contracting Party shall be under the obligation to search for persons alleged to have committed, or to have ordered to be committed, such grave breaches and shall bring such persons, regardless of their nationality, before its own courts. It may also, if it prefers, and in accordance with the provisions of its own legislation, hand such persons over for trial to another High Contracting Party concerned, provided such High Contracting Party has made out a prima facie case.
>
> Each High Contracting Party shall take measures necessary for the suppression of all acts contrary to the provisions of the present Convention other than the grave breaches defined in the following Article.
>
> In all circumstances, the accused persons shall benefit by safeguards of proper trial and defence, which shall not be less favourable than those provided by Article 105 and those following, of the Geneva Convention relative to the Treatment of Prisoners of War of 12 August 1949.

States parties to the Geneva Conventions are thus required to respect international humanitarian law, ensure the respect of international humanitarian law, search for persons alleged to have committed "grave breaches" of the Geneva Conventions and bring such persons, regardless of their nationality, before their own courts or extradite them for trial in another state (Article 49-50 GC I; Article 50-51 GC II; Article 129-30 GC III; Article 146-47 GC IV). If breaches of the Geneva Conventions are perpetrated against protected persons, all states have an obligation to find the perpetrators and bring them to justice.

2 *Definition of "Grave Breaches"*

Geneva Conventions I and II define grave breaches as follows (Article 50 GC I; Article 51 GC II, emphasis added):

> any of the following acts, if committed against persons or property protected by the Convention: wilful killing, torture or inhuman treatment, including biological experiments, wilfully causing great suffering or serious injury to body or health, and extensive destruction and appropriation of property, *not justified by military necessity and carried out unlawfully and wantonly.*

Geneva Conventions III and IV slightly modify this definition. Geneva Convention III tailors the definition to the treatment of prisoners of war as follows (Article 130 GC III, emphasis added):

> any of the following acts, if committed against persons or property protected by the Convention: wilful killing, torture or inhuman treatment, including biological experiments, wilfully causing great suffering or serious injury to body or health, *compelling a prisoner of war to serve in the forces of the hostile Power,* or wilfully depriving a prisoner of war of the rights of fair and regular trial prescribed in this Convention.

Geneva Convention III is the only one of the Geneva Conventions that does not include the caveat "not justified by military necessity and carried out unlawfully and wantonly" as part of the definition of "grave breaches."

Geneva Convention IV tailors the definition to the protection of civilians as follows (Article 147 GC IV, emphasis added):

> any of the following acts, if committed against persons or property protected by the present Convention: wilful killing, torture or inhuman treatment, including biological experiments, wilfully causing great suffering or serious injury to body or health, *unlawful deportation or transfer or unlawful confinement of a protected person*, compelling a protected person to serve in the forces of a hostile Power, or *wilfully depriving a protected person of the rights of fair and regular trial prescribed in the present Convention, taking of hostages* and extensive destruction and appropriation of property, not justified by military necessity and carried out unlawfully and wantonly.

3 *Obligations of States*

a Overview

The Geneva Conventions "grave breaches" Articles (Article 49 GC I; Article 50 GC II; Article 129 GC III; Article 146 GC IV) create affirmative duties that require states parties to:

- Enact Legislation
  - "*enact any legislation necessary to provide effective penal sanctions* for persons committing, or ordering to be committed, any of the grave breaches of the present Convention";
- Search for Perpetrators
  - "*search for persons* alleged to have committed, or to have ordered to be committed, such grave breaches";
- Trial
  - "*bring such persons, regardless of their nationality,* before its *own courts*"; or, if it prefers,
- Extradition
  - "in accordance with the provisions of its own legislation, *hand such persons over for trial to another High Contracting Party* concerned, provided such High Contracting Party has made out a prima facie case."

With respect to "all acts contrary to the provisions of the present Convention other than the grave breaches," states parties are required only to "take measures necessary for [their] suppression" (Article 129.III GC IV). Unlike grave breaches of the Geneva Conventions, which require states parties to enact legislation, search for perpetrators and bring violators to trial or extradite them, states have discretionary power to decide how to "suppress" violations of the Conventions other than grave breaches, without being directed as to how they must suppress such violations.

b Mandatory Universal Jurisdiction

The grave breaches regime of the Geneva Conventions is a landmark development in international law as it is the first time that universal jurisdiction is empaneled on a mandatory rather than a voluntary basis. In instances other than grave breaches of the Geneva Conventions (e.g., in cases of piracy or crimes against humanity not having nexus to armed conflict or the Geneva Conventions), states have a right rather than an obligation to invoke universal jurisdiction.[276]

4 *Application to Non-international Armed Conflicts*

In *Prosecutor v. Dusko Tadić* (1999), the ICTY Appeals Chamber held that the "requirement that the conflict be international for the grave breaches regime to operate pursuant to Article 2 of the Statute has not been contested by the parties."[277] The Appeals Chamber therefore did not consider that question. However, the Appeals Chamber did hold that grave breaches did not necessarily require violations by state actors; non-state armed groups could be held liable for such violations. Therefore, even non-state armed groups that have not formally accepted the terms of the Geneva Conventions may be prosecuted for war crimes that constitute "grave breaches" of the Geneva Conventions. This rule is largely considered to be part of customary international law with respect to non-international armed conflicts.

E Belligerent Occupation

1 *Definition of Occupation: Invasion and Firm Control*

Article 42 of the Annex to Hague Convention IV of 1907 states that "[t]erritory is considered occupied when it is *actually placed* under the authority of the hostile army" (emphasis added). An occupation is thus an *invasion* of a territory followed by *firm control* over that territory. It does not matter whether the occupying state declares such control to be an occupation. On the other hand, a declaration is not necessary to legally establish an actual occupation; whether an invasion occurs that is followed by firm control is a question of fact that does not require a proclamation. Therefore, a proclamation of occupation absent firm control is not in fact an occupation, and an invasion followed by firm control is an occupation regardless of whether a proclamation of occupation is made.

This is in accordance with Article 43 of the Annex to Hague Convention IV of 1907, which states that when the authority of the legitimate power has "*in fact passed*

276. Rule 157 of the ICRC's Customary International Humanitarian Law provides that "[s]tates have the *right* to vest universal jurisdiction in their national courts over war crimes"; unlike in the grave breaches regime of the Geneva Conventions, invoking universal jurisdiction is a right rather than an obligation under customary international law. *Customary International Humanitarian Law*, Vol. I, ICRC, Cambridge University Press (Cambridge, New York, 2009), Rule 157.
277. *Prosecutor v. Dusko Tadić*, IT-94-1-A, ICTY Appeals Chamber (15 July 1999), para. 4.

into the hands of the occupant, the latter shall take all the measures in his power to restore, and ensure, as far as possible, public order and safety ..." The key is thus a question of whether control has "in fact" passed into the hands of the occupying power. Once an occupation through firm control is achieved, it terminates upon the loss of control or relinquishment of territorial authority.

Because an occupation is temporary, sovereignty is not transferred to the occupying power. In order for sovereignty to transfer, an international agreement (e.g., a peace treaty) is required.

2 *Protections Accorded under Geneva Convention IV*

a *Overview*

In addition to the provisions applicable to whole populations and the section I Provisions Common to All Protected Persons, the section II Provisions for Aliens, which are discussed above, *or* the section III Provisions for Occupied Territories, discussed herein, apply to protected persons.

b *General Protections Afforded*

The protections afforded to protected persons in occupied territories include:

- the right to leave the territory (aliens);
- the prohibition against forced transfers; and
- protections for children and property.

In addition, the occupying power must ensure the provision of food, medical care and public health and must permit relief consignments and maintain existing penal laws.

c *Internment, Imprisonment, Assigned Residence, the Death Penalty*

i Penal Sanctions, Internment and Imprisonment

The penal provisions enacted by the occupying power shall not come into force before they have been published and brought to the knowledge of the inhabitants in their own language. The effect of these penal provisions shall not be retroactive.[278]

Protected persons who commit an offence may be interned or imprisoned for offences solely intended to harm the occupying power. Article 68 of GC IV states:

> Protected persons who commit an offence which is solely intended to harm the occupying power, but which does not constitute an attempt on the life or limb of members of the occupying forces or administration, nor a grave collective danger,

278. Article 65 GC IV.

> nor seriously damage the property of the occupying forces or administration or the installations used by them, shall be liable to *internment or simple imprisonment*, provided *the duration of such internment or imprisonment is proportionate to the offence committed.* Furthermore, internment or imprisonment shall, for such offences, be the *only measure* adopted for depriving protected persons of liberty.

ii Regular Trials

No sentence shall be pronounced by the competent courts of the occupying power except after a regular trial.[279] Where in occupied territory, an individual protected person is detained as a spy or saboteur, or as a person under definite suspicion of activity hostile to the security of the occupying power, such person shall, in those cases where absolute military security so requires, be regarded as having forfeited rights of communication under the present Convention. In such cases, persons shall nevertheless be treated with humanity and, in case of trial, "shall not be deprived of the rights of fair and regular trial prescribed by the present Convention."[280]

The requirement of a regular trial "introduces into the law of war a fundamental notion of justice as it is understood in all civilized countries."[281] The requirement of a regular trial is:[282]

> so important that it also finds expression, as has been seen, in Article 3, which prohibits at all times and in all cases whatsoever "the passing of sentences and the carrying out of executions without previous judgment pronounced by a regularly constituted court, affording all the judicial guarantees which are recognized as indispensable by civilized peoples."

The requirement of a fair and regular trial is so fundamental and indispensable that "wilfully depriving a protected person of the rights of fair and regular trial" is deemed to be a grave breach of Geneva Convention IV.[283]

iii Death Penalty

The death penalty may be imposed on a protected person in cases of espionage, serious acts of sabotage or intentional offences which have caused the death of one or more persons. Article 68 of GC IV provides as follows:

> The penal provisions promulgated by the Occupying Power in accordance with Articles 64 [requiring that the penal laws of the occupied territory remain in force] and 65 [requiring that the penal provisions enacted by the occupying power not come into force before they have been published and brought to the knowledge of the inhabitants in their own language] *may impose the death penalty* on a protected person only in cases where the person is guilty of *espionage*, of serious

279. Article 71 GC IV.
280. Article 5 GC IV.
281. Jean Pictet (ed.), *Commentary to Geneva Convention (IV) Relative to the Protection of Civilian Persons in Time of War*, ICRC (1960), p. 353.
282. *Ibid.*, p. 354.
283. Article 147 GC IV.

> acts of *sabotage* against the military installations of the Occupying Power or of intentional offences which have *caused the death of one or more persons*, provided that such offences were *punishable by death under the law of the occupied territory* in force before the occupation began.

iv Assigned Residence and Internment

Assigned residence and internment are authorized if necessary for imperative reasons of security. Article 78 of GC IV states:

> If the Occupying Power considers it necessary, for *imperative reasons of security*, to take safety measures concerning protected persons, it may, at the most, subject them to *assigned residence* or to *internment*. Decisions regarding such assigned residence or internment shall be made according to a *regular procedure* to be *prescribed by the occupying power in accordance with the provisions of Geneva Convention IV* and such procedure shall include the right of appeal and is subject to periodical review, *if possible every six months*, by a competent body set up by the occupying power.

d Obligation of States and Occupying Powers to Permit Humanitarian Assistance

i Part II General Rule in All Cases: Requirement of State Consent (Article 23 GC IV)

Part II of Geneva Convention IV requires states parties to "allow the free passage of all consignments of medical and hospital stores and objects necessary for religious worship intended only for civilians of another High Contracting Party, even if the latter is its adversary. It shall likewise permit the free passage of all consignments of essential foodstuffs, clothing and tonics intended for children under 15, expectant mothers and maternity cases" (Article 23.I GC IV).

However, a state party may refuse to allow the free passage of consignment in cases in which it believes (Article 23.II GC IV):

- that the consignments may be diverted from their destination;
- that the control may not be effective; or
- that a definite advantage may accrue to the military efforts or economy of the enemy through the substitution of the above-mentioned consignments for goods which would otherwise be provided or produced by the enemy or through the release of such material, services or facilities as would otherwise be required for the production of such goods.

Therefore, as a general rule, states' consent is a required prerequisite to humanitarian organizations' access to civilian populations.

ii Part III Specific Rule in Cases of Occupation: Affirmative Duty to Consent (Article 59 GC IV)

The general rule articulated above changes in cases of occupied territories. In such cases, an occupying power is under an affirmative duty to consent to the relief schemes directed at the civilian population of the occupied territory if the occupying power is unable or unwilling to provide humanitarian supplies itself. Article 59 of Geneva Convention IV states that in cases in which "the whole or part of the population of *an occupied territory is inadequately supplied*, the Occupying Power shall agree to relief schemes on behalf of the said population, and shall facilitate them by all the means at its disposal" (Article 59 GC IV). Therefore, unlike the general rule enunciated in Article 23, which permits states to refuse the free passage of consignments and aid convoys, Article 59 imposes on occupying powers an affirmative duty to consent to the entry of impartial, neutral humanitarian organizations to tend to the protection of civilian populations of an occupied territory if the occupying power is not, on its own, providing humanitarian supplies. In addition to this obligation, an occupying power remains obligated to "take all the measures in his power to restore, and ensure, as far as possible, public order and safety, while respecting, unless absolutely prevented, the laws in force in the country" (Article 43 Annex of HC IV).[284]

The Article 59 requirement applies only to schemes that provide for emergency, life-saving relief, such as "the provision of consignments of foodstuffs, medical supplies and clothing" (Article 59 GC IV). An occupying power is not therefore required to admit humanitarian organizations that may engage in human rights protection, social development or other forms of non-emergent assistance not directly linked to the survival of civilian populations.

e *The Wall Case*

i Application of International Humanitarian Law

In the 2004 *ICJ advisory opinion on Legal Consequences of the Construction of a Wall in the Occupied Palestinian Territory* (the Wall Case), the ICJ held that international humanitarian law (the Regulations annexed to the Fourth Hague Convention of 1907 and Geneva Convention IV) apply to the Palestinian territories that before 1967 lay to the east of the 1949 "Green Line" and international human rights law (ICCPR, ICESCR, U.N. Convention on the Rights of the Child) apply in the Occupied Palestinian Territory. The ICJ was not required to conclude that Palestine was a state or a "High Contracting Party" in order to trigger the application of Geneva Convention IV; rather, the fact that Israel occupied Jordanian territory was a sufficient basis for the application of the Convention.

284. This could involve, by way of example, the obligation of an occupier to permit electricity and fuel to pass into the occupied territory. For a general discussion, *see Jaber Al-Bassiouni & Others v. Prime Minister of Israel & Minister of Defence*, H.C.J. 9132/07 (judgment of 30 January 2008).

The ICJ held that:[285]

> the Fourth Geneva Convention is applicable in any occupied territory in the event of an armed conflict arising between two or more High Contracting Parties. Israel and Jordan were parties to that Convention when the 1967 armed conflict broke out. The Court accordingly finds that that Convention is applicable in the Palestinian territories which before the conflict lay to the east of the Green Line and which, during that conflict, were occupied by Israel, there being no need for any enquiry into the precise prior status of those territories.

ii Violations of International Law: De Facto Annexation and Impediment of Right to Self-Determination

The ICJ found several violations of both international humanitarian law and international human rights law and concluded that "the Israeli settlements in the Occupied Palestinian Territories (including East Jerusalem) have been established in breach of international law" (p. 184, paragraph 120).

The ICJ noted (p. 184, paragraph 121):

> the assurance given by Israel that the construction of the wall does not amount to annexation and that the wall is of a temporary nature ..., [but] it nevertheless cannot remain indifferent to certain fears expressed to it that the route of the wall will prejudge the future frontier between Israel and Palestine, and the fear that Israel may integrate the settlements and their means of access. The Court considers that the construction of the wall and its associated régime create a '*fait accompli*' on the ground that could well become permanent, in which case, and notwithstanding the formal characterization of the wall by Israel, it would be tantamount to *de facto* annexation."

The route of the Wall entailed "a risk of further alterations to the demographic composition of the Occupied Palestinian Territory resulting from the construction of the wall inasmuch as it is contributing ... to the departure of Palestinian populations from certain areas." Furthermore, the Wall "severely impedes the exercise by the Palestinian people of its right to *self-determination*, and is therefore a breach of Israel's obligation to respect that right" (*Ibid.*, p. 184, paragraph 122).

The ICJ further concluded (pp. 189-190, paragraphs 132-135):

> 132. From the information submitted to the Court, particularly the report of the Secretary-General, it appears that the construction of the wall has led to the destruction or requisition of properties under conditions which contravene the requirements of Articles 46 and 52 of the Hague Regulations of 1907 and of Article 53 of the Fourth Geneva Convention.
>
> 133. That construction, the establishment of a closed area between the Green Line and the wall itself and the creation of enclaves have moreover imposed *substantial restrictions on the freedom of movement* of the inhabitants of the Occupied Palestinian Territory (with the exception of Israeli citizens and those assimilated thereto) ...

285. *Legal Consequences of the Construction of a Wall in the Occupied Palestinian Territory* (the Wall Case), Advisory Opinion, ICJ Reports (9 July 2004), p. 177, para. 101.

> 134. To sum up, the Court is of the opinion that the construction of the wall and its associated régime impede the liberty of movement of the inhabitants of the Occupied Palestinian Territory (with the exception of Israeli citizens and those assimilated thereto) as guaranteed under Article 12, paragraph 1, of the International Covenant on Civil and Political Rights …
>
> 135. The Court would observe, however, that the applicable international humanitarian law contains provisions enabling account to be taken of military exigencies in certain circumstances.

3 *Treatment of Property During Occupation*

During an occupation, public property may be seized (Article 53.I HC IV):

> An army of occupation can only take possession of cash, funds, and realizable securities which are strictly the property of the State, depots of arms, means of transport, stores and supplies, and, generally, all movable property belonging to the State which may be used for military operations.

In addition, private *munitions de guerre* can be confiscated (Article 53.II HC IV):

> All appliances, whether on land, at sea, or in the air, adapted for the transmission of news, or for the transport of persons or things, exclusive of cases governed by naval law, depots of arms, and, generally, all kinds of munitions of war, may be seized, even if they belong to private individuals, but must be restored and compensation fixed when peace is made.

Moreover, the occupying power may act as an administrator and usufructuary of public goods. This has been the basis on which some occupants have continued to extract natural resources from the territories they have occupied. Article 55 of the Annex of Hague Regulation IV of 1907 states:

> The occupying State shall be regarded only as administrator and usufructuary of public buildings, real estate, forests, and agricultural estates belonging to the hostile State, and situated in the occupied country. It must safeguard the capital of these properties, and administer them in accordance with the rules of usufruct.

4 *Post-Conflict Governance and Transformative Occupation*

a *Obligation to Ensure Public Order and Safety*

Article 43 of the Annex to Hague Convention IV of 1907 serves as the "constitution" of belligerent occupation. It states as follows:

> The authority of the legitimate power having in fact passed into the hands of the occupant, the latter shall take all the measures in his power to *restore, and ensure*, as far as possible, *public order and safety*, while respecting, unless absolutely prevented, the laws in force in the country.

States are thus required to take measures to ensure "public order and safety." The authentic French version provides a much broader concept than the English. It states as follows:

> [l]'autorité du pouvoir légal ayant passé de fait entre les mains de l'occupant, celui-ci prendra toutes les mesures qui dépendent de lui en vue de rétablir et d'assurer, autant qu'il est possible, *l'ordre et la vie publics* en respectant, sauf empêchement absolu, les lois en vigueur dans le pays.

In the French, the occupant is to ensure not only public order and safety but public order and public life (*l'ordre et la vie publics*), which could include social and economic aspects of public life.

In addition, Article 43 opens up the possibility of changing laws in force in a country. However, as discussed below, this could lead to what is known as a "transformative occupation," which, as discussed below, is presumed to be impermissible under international law.

b *Transformative Occupation*

A transformative occupation is a situation in which an occupying power makes changes to the legal or political infrastructure of an occupied territory, including where such changes accord with the rebuilding of a post-conflict state along democratic lines. In such occupations, the stated purpose is to change states that have failed or have been subject to tyrannical rule.

c *Presumption against Changing Penal Laws in an Occupied Territory*

There is a presumption *against* the legitimacy of transformative occupations that change the laws in place of an occupying territory. Article 43 of the Annex to Hague Convention IV of 1907 serves as the "constitution" of belligerent occupation. It states that when the authority of the legitimate power has "in fact passed into the hands of the occupant," the occupant must respect, "unless absolutely prevented, the laws in force in the country."

Similarly, under Article 64.I of Geneva Convention IV, the occupying power is required to maintain the penal laws of the occupied territory in force, with the exception that they may be repealed or suspended by the occupying power in cases where:

- they constitute a *threat to the occupying power's security* (e.g., a law that grants persons in the occupied territory the right to bear arms); or
- they constitute an *obstacle to* (i.e., are inconsistent with) *the application of Geneva Convention IV* (e.g., they oppress certain groups or infringe on the rights of persons protected by the Convention).

Subject to the latter consideration and to *the necessity for ensuring the effective administration of justice*, the tribunals of the occupied territory shall continue to function in respect of all offences covered by the penal laws (Article 64.II GC IV).

d Introduction of Additional Provisions

The occupying power may, however, subject the population of the occupied territory to provisions which are essential to enable the occupying power to (Article 64.III GC IV):

- fulfil its *obligations under Geneva Convention IV*;
- maintain the *orderly government* of the territory;
- *ensure the security* of the occupying power, of the members and property of the occupying forces or administration and of the establishments and lines of communication used by them.

F Additional Protocols to the Geneva Conventions (1977 and 2005)

1 Introduction to Additional Protocols I and II of 1977

a Overview

Two Additional Protocols to the 1949 Geneva Conventions were adopted in 1977 to strengthen the protection of victims of international and non-international armed conflicts:

- Additional Protocol to the Geneva Conventions of 12 August 1949 and Relating to the Protection of Victims of *International Armed Conflicts* ("AP I"), 8 June 1977 (entry into force 7 December 1979); and
- Additional Protocol to the Geneva Conventions of 12 August 1949 and Relating to the Protection of Victims of *Non-International Armed Conflicts* ("AP II"), 8 June 1977 (entry into force 7 December 1979).

Additional Protocol I, dealing with international armed conflicts, is thorough and detailed, while Additional Protocol II, dealing with non-international armed conflicts, is brief.

The Protocols place limits on the conduct of states during hostilities with respect to both areas of international humanitarian law—the weapons and methods of war, as well as the protection of persons. The Additional Protocols thus act as a merger between the Hague Conventions and the Geneva Conventions.

b Position of the United States

The U.S. signed Additional Protocols I and II on 12 December 1977, but it has not yet ratified either of them. The U.S. has fundamental disagreements with Additional Protocol I. Its principal concern is with the broadened definition of international armed conflict under Article 1.4, which includes armed conflicts in which peoples are fighting *against colonial domination* and *alien occupation* and against *racist régimes* in the exercise of their right of self-determination. A further issue that the U.S. takes with Additional Protocol I is with the definition of armed forces of a Party to the conflict under Article 43 (which fails to adopt the four criteria of Article 4 of Geneva Convention III and specifically excludes the requirement of "having a fixed distinctive sign recognizable at a distance" under Article 4A(2)(b) of Geneva Convention III).

The U.S. supports Additional Protocol II in policy. However, while President Reagan and President Obama have urged the ratification of Additional Protocol II, the U.S. Senate has not yet done so.

Under the Vienna Convention on the Law of Treaties ("VCLT"), in the period between a state's signing a treaty and the ratification of the treaty, the state may not undertake any actions that defeat the object and purpose of the treaty (Article 18 VCLT). The U.S. has not ratified the VCLT, but it considers many of the provisions of the VCLT to be customary international law. As the U.S. has not unsigned Additional Protocols I and II, it should refrain from taking actions that defeat the object or purpose of the Protocol.

2 *Additional Protocol I (1977): International Armed Conflicts*

Additional Protocol I, dated 8 June 1977, entered into force on 7 December 1979.

a *Scope of Application*

Additional Protocol I applies in the situations referred to in common Article 2 (i.e., international armed conflicts) (Article 1.3 AP I). However, the scope of application of Additional Protocol I is broader than that of common Article 2. Additional Protocol I applies to (Article 1.4 AP I):

> armed conflicts in which peoples are fighting *against colonial domination* and *alien occupation* and against *racist régimes* in the exercise of their right of self-determination, as enshrined in the Charter of the United Nations and the Declaration on Principles of International Law concerning Friendly Relations and Co-operation among States in accordance with the Charter of the United Nations.

b *Protections of Persons Who Directly Participate in Hostilities*

i Article 45 Protections of Persons Having Taken Part in Hostilities and Not Entitled to Prisoner-of-War Status

Article 45.3 of Additional Protocol I sets forth protections for persons having taken part in hostilities but who are not entitled to prisoner of war status. This includes, for example, civilians who directly participate in hostilities but who do not fulfill the conditions set forth by Article 4A(2) of Geneva Convention III. Article 45 of Additional Protocol I states as follows:

> Any person who has taken part in hostilities, who is not entitled to prisoner-of-war status and who does not benefit from more favourable treatment in accordance with the Fourth Convention shall have the right at all times to the protection of Article 75 of this Protocol. In occupied territory, any such person, unless he is held as a spy, shall also be entitled, notwithstanding Article 5 of the Fourth Convention, to his rights of communication under that Convention.

ii Article 75 Fundamental Guarantees

(1) Overview

Article 75 of AP I ("Fundamental guarantees"), in turn, provides basic due process rights that in many ways restate those of Geneva Convention III with respect to prisoners of war, but unlike Geneva Convention III, it does not predicate its application on an individual's fulfilling the criteria for enjoying prisoner of war treatment. Rather, it provides a baseline standard of treatment applicable to all detained persons "who do not benefit from more favourable treatment under the Conventions or under this Protocol" (Article 75.1 AP I). It states:

> 1. ... persons who are in the power of a Party to the conflict and who do not benefit from more favourable treatment under the Conventions or under this Protocol shall be treated humanely in all circumstances and shall enjoy, as a minimum, the protection provided by this Article without any adverse distinction based upon race, colour, sex, language, religion or belief, political or other opinion, national or social origin, wealth, birth or other status, or on any other similar criteria.
>
> ...
>
> 2. The following acts are and shall remain prohibited at any time and in any place whatsoever, whether committed by civilian or by military agents:
>   a) violence to the life, health, or physical or mental well-being of persons, in particular:
>   i) murder;
>   ii) torture of all kinds, whether physical or mental;
>   iii) corporal punishment; and
>   iv) mutilation;
>   b) outrages upon personal dignity, in particular humiliating and degrading treatment, enforced prostitution and any form of indecent assault;
>   c) the taking of hostages;
>   d) collective punishments; and
>   e) threats to commit any of the foregoing acts.
> 3. Any person arrested, detained or interned for actions related to the armed conflict *shall be informed promptly, in a language he understands, of the reasons why these measures have been taken. Except in cases of arrest or detention for penal offences, such persons shall be released with the minimum delay possible and in any event as soon as the circumstances justifying the arrest, detention or internment have ceased to exist.*
> 4. *No sentence may be passed and no penalty may be executed on a person found guilty of a penal offence related to the armed conflict except pursuant to a conviction pronounced by an impartial and regularly constituted court respecting the generally recognized principles of regular judicial procedure, which include the following:*

a) the procedure shall provide for *an accused to be informed without delay of the particulars of the offence alleged against him* and shall afford the accused before and during his trial all necessary rights and means of defence;
b) no one shall be convicted of an offence except on the basis of individual penal responsibility;
c) no one shall be accused or convicted of a criminal offence on account of any act or omission which did not constitute a criminal offence under the national or international law to which he was subject at the time when it was committed; nor shall a heavier penalty be imposed than that which was applicable at the time when the criminal offence was committed; if, after the commission of the offence, provision is made by law for the imposition of a lighter penalty, the offender shall benefit thereby;
d) anyone charged with an offence is presumed innocent until proved guilty according to law;
e) anyone charged with an offence shall have the right to be tried in his presence;
f) no one shall be compelled to testify against himself or to confess guilt;
g) anyone charged with an offence shall have the right to examine, or have examined, the witnesses against him and to obtain the attendance and examination of witnesses on his behalf under the same conditions as witnesses against him;
h) no one shall be prosecuted or punished by the same Party for an offence in respect of which a final judgment acquitting or convicting that person has been previously pronounced under the same law and judicial procedure;
i) anyone prosecuted for an offence shall have the right to have the judgment pronounced publicly; and
j) a convicted person shall be advised on conviction of his judicial and other remedies and of the time-limits within which they may be exercised.

...

6. *Persons who are arrested, detained or interned for reasons related to the armed conflict shall enjoy the protection provided by this Article until final release, repatriation or re-establishment, even after the end of the armed conflict.*
7. *In order to avoid any doubt concerning the prosecution and trial of persons accused of war crimes or crimes against humanity, the following principles shall apply:*
   a) persons who are accused of such crimes should be submitted for the purpose of prosecution and trial in accordance with the applicable rules of international law; and
   b) any such persons who do not benefit from more favourable treatment under the Conventions or this Protocol shall be accorded the treatment provided by this Article, whether or not the crimes of which they are accused constitute grave breaches of the Conventions or of this Protocol.

(2) As Customary International Law

Article 75 of Additional Protocol I has largely been accepted as a restatement of customary international humanitarian law. This has been the position of the United States, in particular. The Obama Administration made the following statements confirming the United States' position that Article 75 reflects a legal obligation (*opinio juris*) on the United States:[286]

> Article 75 is a provision of the treaty that is consistent with our current policies and practice and is one that the United States has historically supported ... The U.S. Government will therefore choose out of a sense of legal obligation to treat the principles set forth in Article 75 as applicable to any individual it detains in an international armed conflict, and expects all other nations to adhere to these principles as well.

Some commentators have argued that President Obama's statement reflects more than just *opinio juris*; it reflects the substance of customary international law itself.[287] Regardless of this, the United States government is now bound by Article 75 because of the statement by President Obama directly asserting the legal obligation:[288]

> almost certainly has the force of a binding "unilateral act" and has the effect of committing the United States to apply Article 75 as a matter of law in all applicable circumstances, despite the fact that the Senate has not provided its constitutionally mandated advice and consent.

c *Espionage*

Among the elements of international armed conflicts that Additional Protocol I governs is espionage, defined as acting clandestinely (or on false pretenses) in order to obtain information for transmission back to friendly territory. The gathering of intelligence while in military uniform is not deemed espionage because it is not undertaken covertly.[289],[290]

---

286. "Fact Sheet: New Actions on Guantanamo and Detainee Policy," Office of the Press Secretary, The White House (7 March 2011), available at <https://obamawhitehouse.archives.gov/the-press-office/2011/03/07/fact-sheet-new-actions-guant-namo-and-detainee-policy>.

287. John B. Bellinger III, the former Legal Adviser for the U.S. Department of State and the National Security Council during the George W. Bush administration, has disputed the view that the Obama's administration states that Art. 75 is custom. He wrote:

> It is also important to note that [the Obama] Administration has not concluded that Article 75 already constitutes "customary international law." This would have required the Administration to determine that almost all the states in the world accept Article 75 as a legally binding obligation, which would have been difficult to do. Instead, the Administration has announced that it will "choose out of a sense of legal obligation to treat the principles set forth in Article 75 as applicable to any individual detained in an international armed conflict, and expects all other nations to adhere to these principles as well." In other words, the Administration is saying (appropriately, in my view) that it will lead by example by attempting to create customary international law through state practice.

John B. Bellinger III, "Obama's Announcements on International Law," *Lawfare* (8 March 2011), available at <https://www.lawfareblog.com/obamas-announcements-international-law>.

288. Eric Talbot Jensen, "Presidential Pronouncements of Customary International Law as an Alternative to the Senate's Advice and Consent," *Brigham Young University Law Review*, Vol. 2015, Issue 6 (December 2015), p. 1,540.

289. *See* Art. 46.2 AP I.

While espionage is not a violation of international humanitarian law, there is no protection under the Geneva Conventions for acts of espionage. A captured spy is treated as a spy under the laws of the capturing nation rather than as a prisoner of war under Geneva Convention III.[291]

Reaching friendly lines immunizes the spy for past acts of espionage, though the spy can be prosecuted for any violations of international humanitarian law that he committed. Upon later capture as a lawful combatant after he has rejoined the armed forces to which he belongs, the former spy cannot be tried for past acts of espionage.[292]

d *Refugees*

Under Article 73 of Additional Protocol I, refugees must be regarded as protected persons in all circumstances and without any adverse distinction.

e *States Parties*

Additional Protocol I has been ratified by 174 states. Three states—the Islamic Republic of Iran, Pakistan and the U.S.—signed both Additional Protocols I and II on 12 December 1977 but have not ratified either one. In 2009, Afghanistan acceded to both Additional Protocols I and II. In 2010, Iraq acceded to Additional Protocol I.[293]

The following are states parties to Additional Protocol I: Afghanistan, Albania, Algeria, Angola, Antigua and Barbuda, Argentina, Armenia, Australia, Austria, Bahamas, Bahrain, Bangladesh, Barbados, Belarus, Belgium, Belize, Benin, Bolivia, Bosnia and Herzegovina, Botswana, Brazil, Brunei Darussalam, Bulgaria, Burkina Faso, Burundi, Cabo Verde, Cambodia, Cameroon, Canada, Central African Republic, Chad, Chile, China, Colombia, Comoros, Congo, Cook Islands, Costa Rica, Côte d'Ivoire, Croatia, Cuba, Cyprus, Czech Republic, Democratic People's Republic of Korea,

290. *See also Osman Bin Haji Mohamed Ali and Another v. Public Prosecutor*, Judicial Committee of the Privy Council (U.K.), Appeal No. 20 of 1967 (29 July 1968) by special leave from a 1966 judgment of the Federal Court of Malaysia, dismissing the appeals of the first appellant, Osman Bin Haji Mohamed Ali, and the second appellant, Harun Bin Said alias Tahir, against their 1965 conviction in the High Court of Singapore of murder and affirming the death sentences passed on the appellant. The Court held that two Indonesians that had committed an act of war while in Singapore were not prisoners of war with combatant immunity because they were not dressed in uniform ("under international law it is clear that the appellants, if they were members of the Indonesian armed forces, were not entitled to be treated on capture as prisoners of war under the Geneva Convention when they had landed to commit sabotage and had been dressed in civilian clothes both when they had placed the explosives and lit them and when they were arrested. In their opinion Chua J. and the Federal Court were right in rejecting the appellants' plea on this ground").
291. Article 46.1 AP I.
292. *See* Art. 46.4 AP I.
293. "Protocol Additional to the Geneva Conventions of 12 August 1949, and relating to the Protection of Victims of International Armed Conflicts (Protocol I), 8 June 1977," *International Committee of the Red Cross*, available at <https://ihl-databases.icrc.org/applic/ihl/ihl.nsf/States.xsp?xp_viewStates=XPages_NORMStatesParties&xp_treatySelected=470>.

Democratic Republic of the Congo, Denmark, Djibouti, Dominica, Dominican Republic, Ecuador, Egypt, El Salvador, Equatorial Guinea, Estonia, Eswatini, Ethiopia, Fiji, Finland, France, Gabon, Gambia, Georgia, Germany, Ghana, Greece, Grenada, Guatemala, Guinea, Guinea-Bissau, Guyana, Haiti, Holy See, Honduras, Hungary, Iceland, Iraq, Ireland, Italy, Jamaica, Japan, Jordan, Kazakhstan, Kenya, Kuwait, Kyrgyzstan, Lao People's Democratic Republic, Latvia, Lebanon, Lesotho, Liberia, Libya, Liechtenstein, Lithuania, Luxembourg, Madagascar, Malawi, Maldives, Mali, Malta, Mauritania, Mauritius, Mexico, Micronesia (Federated States of), Monaco, Mongolia, Montenegro, Morocco, Mozambique, Namibia, Nauru, Netherlands, New Zealand, Nicaragua, Niger, Nigeria, North Macedonia, Norway, Oman, Palau, Palestine, Panama, Paraguay, Peru, Philippines, Poland, Portugal, Qatar, Republic of Korea, Republic of Moldova, Romania, Russian Federation, Rwanda, Saint Kitts and Nevis, Saint Lucia, Saint Vincent and the Grenadines, Samoa, San Marino, Sao Tome and Principe, Saudi Arabia, Senegal, Serbia, Seychelles, Sierra Leone, Slovakia, Slovenia, Solomon Islands, South Africa, South Sudan, Spain, Sudan, Suriname, Sweden, Switzerland, Syrian Arab Republic, Tajikistan, Timor-Leste, Togo, Tonga, Trinidad and Tobago, Tunisia, Turkmenistan, Uganda, Ukraine, United Arab Emirates, United Kingdom of Great Britain and Northern Ireland, United Republic of Tanzania, Uruguay, Uzbekistan, Vanuatu, Venezuela, Viet Nam, Yemen, Zambia, and Zimbabwe.

3 *Additional Protocol II (1977): Non-international Armed Conflicts*

a *Overview*

Whereas common Article 3 of the Geneva Conventions was the first codification of the rules of non-international conflict, Additional Protocol II was the first international treaty devoted exclusively to non-international armed conflicts. It is a very brief treaty of only 28 articles that largely reflect custom. It was ratified in the three decades following the adoption of the 1949 Geneva Conventions, which witnessed an increase in the number of non-international armed conflicts. Such conflicts included wars of national liberation in which states engaged in hostilities against non-state actors. Additional Protocol II was adopted to establish rules governing conduct in such non-international armed conflicts.

b *Criteria for the Application of Additional Protocol II*

i National Borders; Responsible Command; Control over Territory (Article 1.1 AP II)

Unlike common Article 3, which applies to non-international armed conflicts generally, Additional Protocol II applies to non-international armed conflicts only when certain threshold criteria are met, namely (Article 1.1 AP II):

- armed conflicts that take place in the territory of a High Contracting Party between its armed forces and a dissident armed force or other organized armed group;
- the armed group is under responsible command; and
- the armed group exercises such control over a part of its territory to enable it to carry out sustained and concerted military operations and to implement Additional Protocol II.

ii Non-application to Internal Disturbances (Article 1.2 AP II)

Additional Protocol II does not, however, apply to "riots, isolated and sporadic acts of violence and other acts of similar nature," which are deemed to be "internal disturbances and tensions" rather than non-international armed conflicts (Article 1.2 Additional Protocol II).

For a discussion of jurisdiction that examined the threshold of violence required to trigger the application of international humanitarian law (*Prosecutor v. Dusko Tadić* and *Prosecutor v. Ramush Haradinaj*), *see* "Factors to Determine the Existence of a Non-International Armed Conflict," *supra*.

c *Protections*

Additional Protocol II provides a series of fundamental protections to persons in armed conflict, including:

- the right to humane treatment (Part II);
- protection of the wounded, sick and shipwrecked (Part III); and
- protection of the civilian population (Part IV).

In particular, Additional Protocol II provides certain fundamental judicial guarantees. Under Article 6.2:

> No sentence shall be passed and no penalty shall be executed on a person found guilty of an offence except pursuant to a conviction pronounced by a court offering the *essential guarantees of independence and impartiality*. In particular:
>
> a) the procedure shall provide for an accused to be *informed without delay of the particulars of the offence alleged against him* and shall afford the accused before and during his trial all necessary rights and means of defence;
> b) no one shall be convicted of an offence except on the basis of individual penal responsibility;
> c) no one shall be held guilty of any criminal offence on account of any act or omission which *did not constitute a criminal offence, under the law, at the time when it was committed*; nor shall a heavier penalty be imposed than that which was applicable at the time when the criminal offence was committed; if, after the commission of the offence, provision is made by law for the imposition of a lighter penalty, the offender shall benefit thereby;
> d) anyone charged with an offence is presumed innocent until proved guilty according to law;

e) anyone charged with an offence shall have the right to be tried in his presence;
f) no one shall be compelled to testify against himself or to confess guilt.

d As Reflective of Customary International Law

The Appeals Chamber of the ICTY held that although Additional Protocol II is not universally recognized as part of customary law, "[m]any provisions of this Protocol can now be regarded as declaratory of existing rules or as having crystallised emerging rules of customary law or else as having been strongly instrumental in their evolution as general principles."[294] Moreover, the core principles of Additional Protocol II, including prohibitions on violence toward persons taking no active part in hostilities, hostage taking, degrading treatment, and punishment without due process of law, are reflected in Common Article 3 of the 1949 Geneva Conventions and therefore form part of customary international law.

The U.S., which signed Additional Protocol II, supports Additional Protocol II in the policy. However, it has not yet ratified it.

e Amnesty

Additional Protocol II encourages a policy of broad amnesties as a means of restoring civil society at the conclusion of non-international armed conflicts. It provides as follows (Article 6.5 AP II):

> At the end of hostilities, the authorities in power shall endeavour to grant the broadest possible amnesty to persons who have participated in the armed conflict, or those deprived of their liberty for reasons related to the armed conflict, whether they are interned or detained.

Rule 159 of the ICRC's *Customary International Humanitarian Law* provides amnesties as a customary rule in non-international armed conflicts. However, unlike Additional Protocol II, which grants broad amnesties to "persons who have participated in the armed conflict, or those deprived of their liberty for reasons related to the armed conflict," the ICRC study excludes persons "suspected of, accused of or sentenced for war crimes" from receiving amnesty. Rule 159 states:

> At the end of hostilities, the authorities in power must endeavour to grant the broadest possible amnesty to persons who have participated in a non-international armed conflict, or those deprived of their liberty for reasons related to the armed conflict, with the exception of persons suspected of, accused of or sentenced for war crimes.

The commentary clarifies that this rule is "a norm of customary international law applicable in non-international armed conflicts" (p. 611).

---

294. *Prosecutor v. Dusko Tadić*, IT-94-1AR72, ICTY Appeals Chamber, Decision (2 October 1995), para. 117.

f States Parties

Additional Protocol II has been ratified by 168 states. As mentioned above, the Islamic Republic of Iran, Pakistan and the U.S. have signed both Additional Protocols I and II on 12 December 1977 but have not ratified either one. In 2009, Afghanistan acceded to both Additional Protocols I and II. Iraq has not acceded to Additional Protocol II.[295]

The following are states parties to Additional Protocol II: Afghanistan, Albania, Algeria, Antigua and Barbuda, Argentina, Armenia, Australia, Austria, Bahamas, Bahrain, Bangladesh, Barbados, Belarus, Belgium, Belize, Benin, Bolivia, Bosnia and Herzegovina, Botswana, Brazil, Brunei Darussalam, Bulgaria, Burkina Faso, Burundi, Cabo Verde, Cambodia, Cameroon, Canada, Central African Republic, Chad, Chile, China, Colombia, Comoros, Congo, Cook Islands, Costa Rica, Côte d'Ivoire, Croatia, Cuba, Cyprus, Czech Republic, Democratic Republic of the Congo, Denmark, Djibouti, Dominica, Dominican Republic, Ecuador, Egypt, El Salvador, Equatorial Guinea, Estonia, Eswatini, Ethiopia, Fiji, Finland, France, Gabon, Gambia, Georgia, Germany, Ghana, Greece, Grenada, Guatemala, Guinea, Guinea-Bissau, Guyana, Haiti, Holy See, Honduras, Hungary, Iceland, Ireland, Italy, Jamaica, Japan, Jordan, Kazakhstan, Kenya, Kuwait, Kyrgyzstan, Lao People's Democratic Republic, Latvia, Lebanon, Lesotho, Liberia, Libya, Liechtenstein, Lithuania, Luxembourg, Madagascar, Malawi, Maldives, Mali, Malta, Mauritania, Mauritius, Micronesia (Federated States of), Monaco, Mongolia, Montenegro, Morocco, Mozambique, Namibia, Nauru, Netherlands, New Zealand, Nicaragua, Niger, Nigeria, North Macedonia, Norway, Oman, Palau, Palestine, Panama, Paraguay, Peru, Philippines, Poland, Portugal, Qatar, Republic of Korea, Republic of Moldova, Romania, Russian Federation, Rwanda, Saint Kitts and Nevis, Saint Lucia, Saint Vincent and the Grenadines, Samoa, San Marino, Sao Tome and Principe, Saudi Arabia, Senegal, Serbia, Seychelles, Sierra Leone, Slovakia, Slovenia, Solomon Islands, South Africa, South Sudan, Spain, Sudan, Suriname, Sweden, Switzerland, Tajikistan, Timor-Leste, Togo, Tonga, Trinidad and Tobago, Tunisia, Turkmenistan, Uganda, Ukraine, United Arab Emirates, United Kingdom of Great Britain and Northern Ireland, United Republic of Tanzania, Uruguay, Uzbekistan, Vanuatu, Venezuela, Yemen, Zambia, and Zimbabwe.

4 *Additional Protocol III (2005): Additional Distinctive Emblem*

a Overview

Additional Protocol to the Geneva Conventions of 12 August 1949 and Relating to the Adoption of an Additional Distinctive Emblem ("AP III") was adopted on 8 December 2005 and entered into force on 14 January 2006. It created an additional emblem—"a red frame in the shape of a square on edge on a white ground—commonly referred to

295. "Protocol Additional to the Geneva Conventions of 12 August 1949, and relating to the Protection of Victims of Non-International Armed Conflicts (Protocol II), 8 June 1977," *International Committee of the Red Cross*, available at < https://ihl-databases.icrc.org/applic/ihl/ihl.nsf/States.xsp?xp_viewStates = XPages_NORMStatesParties&xp_treatySelected = 475 > .

as the red crystal." The Red Crystal is intended to provide a further option and has the same international status as its Red Cross and Red Crescent equivalents.

b States Parties

Additional Protocol III has been ratified by 73 states, including the U.K. and the U.S. A total of 23 states have signed but have not ratified Additional Protocol III.

G Special Protections

1 Overview

Special protections grant heightened protection status in addition to general protection from attack to certain categories of persons and objects based on their vulnerability or the special role they play during armed conflict. Under most circumstances, special protections are lost when a specially protected person directly participates in hostilities or a specially protected object is misused. Special protections are distinguishable from general protections because they require additional elements beyond status that must be met for the special protections to be triggered.

2 Persons Out of Combat (Hors de Combat)

These are persons out of combat or "outside the fight." Under Rule 47 of the ICRC's *Customary International Humanitarian Law*, a person hors de combat is: "(a) anyone who is in the power of an adverse party; (b) anyone who is defenceless because of unconsciousness, shipwreck, wounds or sickness; or (c) anyone who clearly expresses an intention to surrender; provided he or she abstains from any hostile act and does not attempt to escape." Persons out of combat also include parachutists and auxiliary medical personnel of the armed forces.

3 Prisoners of War

Combatants who have fallen into the hands of the enemy become prisoners of war in accordance with GC III. In some circumstances, civilians (i.e., contractors (Article 4A(4) GC III) and crewmembers (Article 4A(5) GC III)) may also receive prisoner of war protections. Prisoner of war protections apply from the time a person falls into the power of the enemy until their final release or repatriation at the cessation of hostilities. In cases of doubt, they are to be treated as prisoners of war until a competent tribunal makes a final status determination. Prisoners of war are granted a host of protections relating to combatant immunity, special rules relating to labor and work conditions, judicial proceedings, and a series of rights (to humane treatment, prohibitions against torture, etc.).

4 *Parlementaires*

Parlementaires are combatant representatives of warring forces sent to negotiate terms or ceasefires with the opposing side or to collect casualties. Parlementaires receive special protection under Hague Regulation IV. Fighting must cease to the extent necessary to ensure the safety of parlementaires. To receive this special protection, parlementaires must carry a white flag and, at the conclusion of their mission, they must be allowed to rejoin their own forces.

5 *Medical and Religious Personnel Attached to the Armed Forces (Non-combatants)*

a *Overview*

Geneva Convention I, as well as Geneva Convention II and Geneva Convention IV, provide special protections for medical and religious personnel. States parties to a conflict may not interfere with the work of medical and religious personnel. Moreover, such personnel are given special rights of movement. The following shall be respected and protected in all circumstances:[296]

- medical personnel exclusively engaged in the search for, or the collection, transport or treatment of the wounded or sick, or in the prevention of disease;
- staff exclusively engaged in the administration of medical units and establishments; and
- chaplains attached to the armed forces.

b *Detainment as Retained Personnel*

Geneva Convention III provides that "[m]embers of the medical personnel and chaplains while retained by the Detaining Power with a view to assisting prisoners of war, *shall not be considered as prisoners of war*. They shall, however, receive as a minimum the benefits and protection of the present Convention, and shall also be granted all facilities necessary to provide for the medical care of, and religious ministration to prisoners of war" (emphasis added).[297]

c *Special Protections of Medical Personnel*

Medical personnel that fall into the hands of the adverse party become retained personnel entitled to release unless they are needed, in which case they are entitled to the same protections as prisoners of war and must be allowed to continue performing their medical duties.

296. Article 24 GC I.
297. Article 33 GC III.

However, combatants trained as part-time orderlies, nurses, or stretcher-bearers who are engaged in the search for, collection, transport, or treatment of the wounded and sick enjoy this protection only while they are engaged in these activities. Upon capture, these combatants become prisoners of war but may continue to perform their trained functions as required.

d *Special Protections of Chaplains*

Religious personnel, such as chaplains in the armed forces, also are entitled to special protection. If captured, they are given the status of retained personnel and may continue performing their duties when they fall into the hands of the adverse party. They must distinguish themselves by wearing armlets, headgear, or clothing with the Red Cross, Red Crescent, or Red Crystal emblems.

6 ***Civilians in the Hands of the Adverse Party***

Members of the civilian population may find themselves particularly vulnerable and in need of protection beyond those guaranteed by the prohibition of adverse treatment and the general protection against attack. These special protections are discussed in GC IV.

Civilians in the hands of an adverse party are to be treated humanely and protected against "all acts of violence or threats thereof and against insults and public curiosity" (Article 27 GC IV). This situation often arises during an occupation or when civilians are present during the outbreak of a conflict.

7 ***Women and Children***

a *In General*

The Geneva Conventions accord special protections to women and children. For example:

- "Children under fifteen years, pregnant women and mothers of children under seven years shall benefit by any preferential treatment to the same extent as the nationals of the State concerned" (Article 38 GC IV).
- The parties to a conflict shall endeavor during the course of hostilities to "conclude agreements for the release, the repatriation, the return to places of residence or the accommodation in a neutral country of certain classes of internees, in particular children, pregnant women and mothers with infants and young children" (Article 132 GC IV).

b *Women*

Several provisions issue heightened protection to women. Under Geneva Convention I, "[w]omen shall be treated with all consideration due to their sex. The Party to the conflict which is compelled to abandon wounded or sick to the enemy shall, as far as military considerations permit, leave with them a part of its medical personnel and material to assist in their care" (Article 12 GC I).

With respect to female prisoners of war:

- "Women shall be treated with all the regard due to their sex and shall in all cases benefit by treatment as favourable as that granted to men" (Article 14 GC III).
- "In any camps in which women prisoners of war, as well as men, are accommodated, separate dormitories shall be provided for them" (Article 26 GC III).
- "In any camps in which women prisoners of war are accommodated, separate conveniences shall be provided for them" (Article 29 GC III).
- "Women prisoners of war undergoing disciplinary punishment shall be confined in separate quarters from male prisoners of war and shall be under the immediate supervision of women" (Article 97 GC III).

With respect to female civilians:

- Women are to be especially protected "against any attack on their honor, in particular against rape, enforced prostitution, or any form of indecent assault" (Article 27 GC IV).
- Civilian women detainees "shall be confined in separate quarters and shall be under the direct supervision of women" (Article 76 GC IV).
- "Whenever it is necessary, as an exceptional and temporary measure, to accommodate women internees who are not members of a family unit in the same place of internment as men, the provision of separate sleeping quarters and sanitary conveniences for the use of such women internees shall be obligatory" (Article 85 GC IV).
- "Women internees undergoing disciplinary punishment shall be confined in separate quarters from male internees and shall be under the immediate supervision of women" (Article 124 GC IV).
- Female prisoners of war are to be housed in separate facilities, and their sex should also be taken into account in other aspects of detention.
- Pregnant women or mothers with dependent infants are to be given special priority in situations of arrest and detention.

With respect to international criminal law, the Rome Statute criminalizes sexual violence, including outrages against personal dignity, rape, sexual slavery, enforced prostitution, forced pregnancy, and enforced sterilization.

c *Children*

Geneva Convention IV affords the following protections to children:

- In times of peace, states parties to Geneva Convention IV and, after the outbreak of hostilities, the parties to the conflict "may establish in their own territory and, if the need arises, in occupied areas, hospital and safety zones and localities so organized as to protect from the effects of war, wounded, sick and aged persons, children under fifteen, expectant mothers and mothers of children under seven" (Article 14 GC IV).
- The Parties to the conflict shall endeavor to "conclude local agreements for the removal from besieged or encircled areas, of wounded, sick, infirm, and aged persons, children and maternity cases, and for the passage of ministers of all religions, medical personnel and medical equipment on their way to such areas" (Article 17 GC IV).
- The parties to a conflict "shall take the necessary measures to ensure that children under fifteen, who are orphaned or are separated from their families as a result of the war, are not left to their own resources, and that their maintenance, the exercise of their religion and their education are facilitated in all circumstances" (Article 24 GC IV).

Additional Protocol I provides that "[c]hildren shall be the object of special respect and shall be protected against any form of indecent assault" (Article 77.1 AP I). "The Parties to the conflict shall take all feasible measures in order that children who have not attained the age of fifteen years do not take a direct part in hostilities and, in particular, they shall refrain from recruiting them into their armed forces. In recruiting among those persons who have attained the age of fifteen years but who have not attained the age of eighteen years, the Parties to the conflict shall endeavour to give priority to those who are oldest" (Article 77.2 AP I). If, despite the provisions of Article 77, a child is recruited into the armed forces or an organized armed group, he or she may be subject to attack. Moreover, a child who directly participates in hostilities is subject to attack, even if he or she is not a member of the armed forces.

"If arrested, detained or interned for reasons related to the armed conflict, children shall be held in quarters separate from the quarters of adults, except where families are accommodated as family units" (Article 77.4 AP I). In addition, the imposition of the death penalty on persons under 18 years of age is prohibited (Article 77.5 AP I).

V MEANS AND METHODS: HAGUE LAW

A Hague Conventions (1899, 1904, and 1907)

The Hague Conventions are a group of international treaties aimed at regulating the conduct of war and limiting certain types of military technology. The Conventions were adopted in the 1899 and 1907 Hague conferences.

1 *Hague Conventions of 1899 on the Laws and Customs of War*

The Conventions adopted on 29 July 1899 at the 1899 Hague Conference are as follows:

- Final Act of the International Peace Conference (states signatory—27).
- Hague Convention (I) for the Pacific Settlement of International Disputes (creating the Permanent Court of Arbitration, "with the object of facilitating an immediate recourse to arbitration for international differences" (Article 20)).
- Hague Convention (II) with Respect to the Laws and Customs of War on Land and its annex: Regulations concerning the Laws and Customs of War on Land (states parties—49). The Preamble contains the famed "Martens Clause," which was discussed above.
- Hague Convention (III) for the Adaptation to Maritime Warfare of the Principles of the Geneva Convention of 22 August 1864 (states parties—49).
- Declaration (IV, 1), to Prohibit, for the Term of Five Years, the Launching of Projectiles and Explosives from Balloons and Other Methods of Similar Nature (states parties—24; states signatory—2).
- Declaration (IV, 2) concerning Asphyxiating Gases (states parties—31).
- Declaration (IV, 3) concerning Expanding Bullets (states parties—31).

2 *Hague Convention of 1904 on Hospital Ships*

The Hague Convention for the Exemption of Hospital Ships, in Time of War, from The Payment of all Dues and Taxes Imposed for the Benefit of the State of 21 December 1904 had 31 states parties and 1 state signatory.

3 *Hague Conventions of 1907 on the Laws and Customs of War*

a *Overview*

The Conventions adopted on 18 October 1907 at the 1907 Hague Conference are as follows (those with continuing validity are in bold italics):

- Final Act of the Second Peace Conference (states signatory—44).
- Hague Convention I for the Pacific Settlement of International Disputes.
- Hague Convention II for the Limitation of Employment of Force for Recovery of Contract Debts.
- Hague ***Convention III relative to the Opening of Hostilities*** (states parties—34; states signatory—17).
- Hague ***Convention IV respecting the Laws and Customs of War on Land and its annex: Regulations Concerning the Laws and Customs of War on Land*** (states parties—35; states signatory—15).
- Hague ***Convention V respecting the Rights and Duties of Neutral Powers and Persons in Case of War on Land*** (states parties—32; states signatory—17).

- Hague Convention VI Relating to the Status of Enemy Merchant Ships at the Outbreak of Hostilities (states parties—29; states signatory—19).
- Hague Convention VII Relating to the Conversion of Merchant Ships into Warships (states parties—32; states signatory—16).
- Hague ***Convention VIII relative to the Laying of Automatic Submarine Contact Mines*** (states parties—27; states signatory—17).
- Hague ***Convention IX concerning Bombardment by Naval Forces in Time of War*** (states parties—35; states signatory—16).
- Hague Convention X for the Adaptation to Maritime Warfare of the Principles of the Geneva Convention (states parties—33; states signatory—16).
- Hague Convention XI relative to certain Restrictions with regard to the Exercise of the Right of Capture in Naval War (states parties—31; states signatory—17).
- Hague Convention XII relative to the Creation of an International Prize Court (states parties—1; states signatory—31).
- Hague Convention XIII concerning the Rights and Duties of Neutral Powers in Naval War (states parties—28; states signatory—18).
- Declaration XIV Prohibiting the Discharge of Projectiles and Explosives from Balloons (states parties—20; states signatory—12).

b *Hague Convention IV of 1907*

Perhaps the most important of the Hague Conventions of 1907 is Convention (IV) respecting the Laws and Customs of War on Land and its Annex ("HC IV"). The Annex is comprised of Regulations concerning the Laws and Customs of War on Land. These regulations establish the *principle of humanity* (also known as the principle of unnecessary suffering), which prohibits the employment of any degree of force that is not necessary for the purposes of military mission accomplishment and causes unnecessary losses or excessive suffering. Article 22 sets out this principle when it states that "the right of belligerents to adopt means of injuring the enemy is not unlimited" (Article 22 HC IV), and Article 23 follows up by making the following acts specifically forbidden:

(a) To employ poison or poisoned weapons;
(b) To kill or wound treacherously individuals belonging to the hostile nation or army;
(c) To kill or wound an enemy who, having laid down his arms, or having no longer means of defense, has surrendered at discretion;
(d) To declare that no quarter will be given;
(e) To employ arms, projectiles, or material calculated to cause unnecessary suffering;
(f) To make improper use of a flag of truce, of the national flag or of the military insignia and uniform of the enemy, as well as the distinctive badges of the Geneva Convention;
(g) To destroy or seize the enemy's property, unless such destruction or seizure be imperatively demanded by the necessities of war;

(h) To declare abolished, suspended, or inadmissible in a court of law the rights and actions of the nationals of the hostile party. A belligerent is likewise forbidden to compel the nationals of the hostile party to take part in the operations of war directed against their own country, even if they were in the belligerent's service before the commencement of the war (Article 23 HC IV).

B Geneva Protocol to the Hague Conventions of 1899 and 1907 (1925)

The Protocol for the Prohibition of the Use in War of Asphyxiating, Poisonous or other Gases, and of Bacteriological Methods of Warfare, often called the "Geneva Protocol" and at times the "1925 Chemical Weapons Treaty," is a protocol to the Hague Conventions of 1899 and 1907. It prohibits the use of chemical and biological weapons in *international armed conflicts*. Signed at Geneva on 17 June 1925, it entered into force on 8 February 1928.

The Geneva Protocol prohibits the use of asphyxiating and poisonous gases and of "all analogous liquids, materials or devices" as well as of "bacteriological methods of warfare." The Treaty is complemented by the 1972 Biological Weapons Convention and the 1993 Chemical Weapons Convention.

The 1972 Biological Weapons Convention supplements the 1925 Geneva Protocol and prohibits the production, stockpiling, and use of biological and toxin weapons. The U.S. renounced the use of all biological and toxin weapons (DoD Law of War Manual, paragraph 6.9).

C Other Conventions

A range of other conventions and protocols covering a range of conventional weapons, chemical weapons, landmines, laser weapons, cluster munitions and the protection of children in armed conflict has been adopted by the international community.

1 Biological Weapons Convention (1972)

a Overview

The Convention on the Prohibition of the Development, Production and Stockpiling of Bacteriological (Biological) and Toxin Weapons and on their Destruction, often referred to as the "Biological Weapons Convention," was opened for signature in 1972 and entered into force on 26 March 1975.

The Biological Weapons Convention supplements the 1925 Geneva Protocol, which prohibits the use of chemical and biological weapons. The states parties to the Biological Weapons Convention are prohibited from developing, producing, stockpiling and using biological and toxin weapons.

b States Parties

A total of 187 states may become members of the Biological Weapons Convention. These states consist of the 193 U.N. member states as well as Vatican City, Palestine and the quasi-independent Cook Islands and Niue. The Convention was initially ratified by 22 governments and currently has 183 states parties, including Palestine. Four states—Egypt, Haiti, Somalia and Syria—have signed but have not yet ratified the Convention. Ten states—Chad, Comoros, Djibouti, Eritrea, Israel, Kiribati, Micronesia, Namibia, South Sudan and Tuvalu—have neither signed nor ratified the Convention. In ratifying the Convention, the U.S. renounced the use of all biological and toxin weapons.

2 Convention on Certain Conventional Weapons (1980)

a Overview

The U.N. Convention on Prohibitions or Restrictions on the Use of Certain Conventional Weapons Which May be Deemed to be Excessively Injurious or to Have Indiscriminate Effects (Geneva, 10 October 1980), as amended on 21 December 2001, is colloquially known as the "Inhumane Weapons Convention" or the "Convention on Conventional Weapons" ("CCW"). As its title suggests, the CCW seeks to prohibit or restrict the use of conventional weapons considered to be excessively injurious or to have indiscriminate effects.

b States Parties

As of 2016, 123 states have ratified or acceded to the treaty, the most recent being Ivory Coast on 25 May 2016. The United States signed the CCW on 8 April 1982 and ratified it on 24 March 1995. The following five states have signed but have not yet ratified the treaty: Afghanistan, Egypt, Nigeria, Sudan and Vietnam.

c Prohibitions under the Five Protocols

Through its five Protocols, the Convention prohibits the use of weapons of which the primary effect is to injure by fragments that are not detectable in the human body by X-rays, non-detectable anti-personnel mines and booby-traps and other devices, making civilians the object of attack by incendiary weapons and laser weapons specifically designed to cause permanent blindness. It also requires parties to a conflict to take measures to reduce dangers posed by explosive remnants of war. The Convention contains the following Protocols:

- *Protocol (I) on Non-Detectable Fragments* (adopted on 10 October 1980, in Geneva; 111 states parties). It prohibits the use of any weapon whose primary effect is to injure by fragments or fragmentation that escape detection by X-rays in the human body.

- *Protocol (II) on Prohibitions or Restrictions on the Use of Mines, Booby-Traps and Other Devices* (adopted on 10 October 1980, in Geneva; 94 states parties). It restricts landmines and booby-traps and deals with marking minefields and removing mines at the end of a conflict:
  - With respect to booby-traps, Protocol (II) provides guidelines in Article 7, prohibiting booby-traps and other devices "which are in any way attached or associated with" internationally recognized protective emblems (e.g., the red cross, red crescent, or red crystal), medical facilities, children's toys and objects of a religious nature. In this way, the Protocol prohibits perfidy.
  - The U.S. and a number of other countries amended the Protocol on 3 May 1996 to require anti-personnel landmines ("APL") outside marked minefields to self-detonate within a limited time and to forbid non-detectable APLs. The U.S. ratified the Amended Protocol on 24 May 1999.
- *Protocol (III) on Prohibitions or Restrictions on the Use of Incendiary Weapons* (adopted on 10 October 1980, in Geneva; 108 states parties). It restricts incendiary weapons in certain instances, including the use of air-delivered incendiary weapons on military objectives located within concentrations of civilians.
- *Protocol (IV) on Blinding Laser Weapons* (adopted on 13 October 1995, in Vienna; 98 states parties). It restricts the use of weapons specifically designed to cause permanent blindness to unenhanced vision.
- Protocol (V) on Explosive Remnants of War (adopted on 28 November 2003 in Geneva; 69 states parties). It sets out obligations and best practices for the clearance of explosive remnants of war, addresses some aspects of the use of cluster bombs, and requires states parties to clear areas under their control of unexploded ordnance when feasible.

3 *Chemical Weapons Convention (1993)*

a *Overview*

The 1993 Convention on the Prohibition of the Development, Production, Stockpiling and Use of Chemical Weapons and their Destruction, colloquially known as the "Chemical Weapons Convention" ("CWC"), entered into force on 29 April 1997. It bans the use of all chemical weapons "as a method of warfare."

Under Article I, states parties agree to never develop, produce, stockpile, transfer, use, or engage in military preparations to use chemical weapons. It requires parties to agree to destroy chemical stockpiles and not "use riot control agents as a method of warfare" (Article I.5 CWC).

b Relationship with the 1925 Geneva Gas Protocol

The Convention complements the 1925 Geneva Gas Protocol, which deals with international armed conflicts, but is different in some respects:

- Whereas the 1925 Protocol allows parties to reserve their right to use chemical weapons in response to a "first use" against them, the 1993 Convention does not allow such reservations.
- Whereas the 1925 Protocol applies only to international armed conflicts, the 1993 Convention applies to both international and non-international armed conflicts.

c States Parties

As of 2021, the Convention has 193 states parties. All but the following four U.N.-recognized states have ratified or acceded to the Convention:

- Israel signed the Convention in 1993 but has not yet ratified it.
- the Democratic People's Republic of Korea (North Korea), Egypt and South Sudan have neither signed nor ratified the Convention.

Somalia acceded to the Convention in May of 2013, followed by Syria in September of 2013 and Angola in September of 2015. Burma, which signed the Convention in 1993, ratified it in 2015.

d As Customary International Law

The Convention has been so widely adopted by states that the prohibition on the use of chemical weapons is considered customary international law. The ICRC's study on international humanitarian law provides as follows:[298]

> State practice establishes this rule as a norm of customary international law applicable in both international and non-international armed conflicts.

In effect, the prohibition on the use of chemical weapons applies to both states and non-state actors, including those who are not parties to the Convention.

4 *Ottawa Convention ("Mine Ban Treaty") (1997)*

a Overview

The Convention on the Prohibition of the Use, Stockpiling, Production and Transfer of Anti-Personnel Mines and on their Destruction (1997), colloquially known as the

298. Jean-Marie Henckaerts and Louise Doswald-Beck, *Customary International Humanitarian Law*, Vol. I, ICRC, Cambridge University Press (Cambridge, New York, 2009), Rule 74, p. 259.

"Ottawa Treaty" or the "Mine Ban Treaty" ("MBT"), completely bans all anti-personnel mines, including "smart" landmines that self-destruct or self-deactivate at the end of a conflict. It does not, however, restrict states parties with respect to anti-tank or anti-tank with anti-handling device mines.

b *States Parties*

At present, 162 states, including Canada and the United Kingdom, are parties to the Mine Ban Treaty. The U.S. withdrew from negotiations in September of 1997 and declined to sign the Treaty when other countries would not allow exceptions for the use of "smart mines" or for anti-personnel landmines in Korea. For further discussion, *see* "Mines" under "Use of Specific Weapons," *infra*.

D Means of Warfare: The Use of Specific Weapons

1 Overview

The means of warfare refers to the weapons used in battle (e.g., small arms projectiles, landmines, incendiaries and chemical, biological and nuclear weapons).

Under Additional Protocol I (Article 36):

> In the study, development, acquisition or adoption of a new weapon, means or method of warfare, a High Contracting Party is under an obligation to determine whether its employment would, in some or all circumstances, be prohibited by this Protocol or by any other rule of international law applicable to the High Contracting Party.

This includes a calculus as to whether the weapons: (i) are intended to cause unnecessary suffering; (ii) are inherently indiscriminate; and (iii) fall within a class of specifically prohibited weapons.

2 Nuclear Weapons

There is a presumption that nuclear weapons are prohibited by international law, but they are not prohibited per se by custom or conventions. In paragraph 35 of its Advisory Opinion on the Legality of the Threat or Use of Nuclear Weapons (1996), the ICJ recognized the destructive character of nuclear weapons. The Court observed as follows:[299]

> The Court ... notes that nuclear weapons are explosive devices whose energy results from the fusion or fission of the atom. By its very nature, that process, in nuclear weapons as they exist today, releases not only immense quantities of heat and energy, but also powerful and prolonged radiation. According to the material

299. *Legality of the Threat or Use of Nuclear Weapons*, Advisory Opinion, ICJ Reports (8 July 1996), pp. 243-44, para. 35.

> before the Court, the first two causes of damage are vastly more powerful than the damage caused by other weapons, while the phenomenon of radiation is said to be peculiar to nuclear weapons. These characteristics render the nuclear weapon *potentially catastrophic*. The destructive power of nuclear weapons *cannot be contained in either space or time*. They have the potential to *destroy all civilization and the entire ecosystem of the planet*.

In light of this potential for widespread destruction, many treaties have been adopted that restrict the proliferation and deployment of nuclear weapons. However, "they have not resulted in a treaty of general prohibition of the same kind as for bacteriological and chemical weapons" (pp. 248-249, paragraph 58). Rather, they restrict the acquisition, manufacture and possession of nuclear weapons, the deployment of nuclear weapons in Antarctica, outer space, and the seabed and ocean floor and the testing of nuclear weapons. On this basis, the ICJ held by 11 votes to three that (p. 266, paragraph 105):

> There is in neither customary nor conventional international law any comprehensive and universal prohibition of the threat or use of nuclear weapons as such.

In a split vote of seven votes to seven, by the President's casting vote, the ICJ held that the threat or use of nuclear weapons would:

> generally be contrary to the rules of international law applicable in armed conflict, and in particular the principles and rules of humanitarian law. However, in view of the current state of international law, and of the elements of fact at its disposal, the Court cannot conclude definitively whether the threat or use of nuclear weapons would be lawful or unlawful in an extreme circumstance of self-defence, in which the very survival of a state would be at stake.

The ICJ thus could not definitively conclude whether the threat or use of nuclear weapons would be lawful in such extreme circumstances, thereby leaving the question to individual state interpretation.[300] Certainly, what could be stated is that the use of nuclear weapons against a city populated with civilians would necessarily contravene international humanitarian law, namely, the principle of distinction.

3 *Mines*

a *Legal Overview*

Protocol II of the 1980 Convention on Conventional Weapons deals with Prohibitions or Restrictions on the Use of Mines, Booby-Traps and Other Devices (adopted on 10 October 1980 in Geneva). It restricts landmines and booby-traps and deals with marking minefields and removing mines at the end of a conflict. The U.S. and a number of other countries amended the Protocol on 3 May 1996 to require anti-personnel

300. The United States does not deem the threat or use of nuclear weapons to be a per se violation of international humanitarian law.

landmines ("APL") outside marked minefields to self-detonate within a limited time and to forbid non-detectable APLs.

The 1997 Ottawa Treaty completely bans all anti-personnel mines, including "smart" landmines that self-destruct or self-deactivate at the end of a conflict. It does not, however, restrict states parties with respect to anti-tank or anti-tank with anti-handling device mines.

b *Position of the United States*

The U.S. withdrew from Ottawa Treaty negotiations in September of 1997 and declined to sign the Convention when other countries would not allow exceptions for the use of "smart mines" that self-deactivate as well as anti-personnel landmines in Korea. This would have required the removal of U.S. minefields along the Korean border, which the U.S. views as a major deterrent to an attack by the Democratic People's Republic of Korea (North Korea).

The United States has committed to eliminate persistent ("dumb") landmines of all types from its arsenal and maintains that it only stockpiles persistent landmines in fulfillment of treaty obligations to the Republic of Korea.

c *Summary Tables*

The following tables summarize the positions of the Ottawa Convention, Protocol (II) of the Conventional Weapons Convention and U.S. policy with respect to the use of anti-personnel mines, anti-tank mines and "dumb" and "smart" mines:

	Anti-Personnel Landmines	
	In Korea	*Outside of Korea*
Position of U.S. Policy	Permitted	Banned
Position of the Ottawa Convention	Banned	
Position of Conventional Weapons Convention Protocol (II)	Restricted; requires minefields to be marked and requires removing mines at the end of conflicts; as amended, requires anti-personnel landmines outside marked minefields to self-detonate within a limited time and forbids non-detectable APLs.	

	All Other Mines (Anti-Tank Mines, Anti-Tank with Anti-Handling Device Mines, etc.)	
	Dumb	*Smart*
Position of U.S. Policy	Banned	Permitted
Position of the Ottawa Convention	Not discussed	

	All Other Mines (Anti-Tank Mines, Anti-Tank with Anti-Handling Device Mines, etc.)	
	Dumb	*Smart*
Position of Conventional Weapons Convention Protocol (II)	Restricted; requires minefields to be marked and removing mines at the end of conflicts; as amended, requires anti-personnel landmines outside marked minefields to self-detonate within a limited time and forbids non-detectable APLs.	

4 *Cluster Munitions*

a *Overview*

Cluster munitions are explosive weapons that release or eject many small explosive bomblets designed to kill enemy personnel, disperse chemical or biological weapons or destroy vehicles, runways, air defense radars, armor, artillery or power transmission lines.

b *Convention on Cluster Munitions (2008)*

i Overview

Since the bomblets or submunitions dispense over a relatively large area and a small percentage typically fail to detonate, they may create an unexploded ordinance ("UXO") hazard. They may further pose risks to civilians both during attacks and afterwards. As a result, cluster munitions have been prohibited by the Convention on Cluster Munitions, which was signed on 3 December 2008 and went into force on 1 August 2010.

ii States Parties

As of 2016, the Convention on Cluster Munitions has been signed by 108 states and ratified or acceded to by 100 states. A number of countries that produce or stockpile significant quantities of cluster munitions, including China, Russia, the United States, India, Israel, Pakistan and Brazil, have opposed the Convention.

5 *Phosphorus*

Since World War II, many nations have employed phosphorous weapons in war. There is, however, some question as to whether its use contravenes international humanitarian law. Answering this question is not as straightforward as it may seem. Nothing in the Hague Conventions, Additional Protocols I, II and III to the Geneva Conventions,

Convention on Certain Conventional Weapons, Chemical Weapons Convention or the Ottawa Convention prohibits the use of phosphorous weapons per se. One may argue that phosphorus is an incendiary weapon,[301] the use of which would be controlled but not prohibited, or a poison or gas or a chemical weapon, the use of which would be banned under treaty law, but this question has no clear legal answer and is subject to interpretation. For example, the Hague Regulations, while prohibiting the use of poison weapons, contain no definition of "poison."

With respect to the Chemical Weapons Convention, there is a possibility to construe phosphorus as a chemical weapon. However, the weapon is not strictly banned by the Convention. Yet an argument can be made that if a weapon is designed that takes advantage of phosphorus's toxic properties, then its use would be banned as a "chemical weapon" under the Convention. If, in contrast, phosphorus is merely being used to create a smoke screen or to clear fortified areas or entrenchments of enemy personnel, then it would not be banned as a chemical weapon under the Convention.

The general consensus is that the use of white phosphorus violates international humanitarian law when the principles of military necessity, humanity and proportionality with respect to civilian losses or distinction (discrimination) are violated (i.e., the attacker employs the use of phosphorous weapons in civilian areas employing the toxic characteristics of the weapon and causing excessive collateral casualties among protected civilians). This requires the careful analysis of many factors before drawing any definitive conclusion. Where white phosphorus is merely used to create a smoke screen in an open field to screen the vision of the enemies and provide a force with a visual cover, its use would *not* be illegal per se.

6 *Riot Control Agents*

a *Overview*

The Chemical Weapons Convention (1993) requires states parties not to "use riot control agents as a method of warfare" (Article I.5 CWC).

b *View of the United States*

The United States views riot control agents ("RCAs") as having a "transient" effect and not as incapacitating agents prohibited by the Convention. Therefore, the U.S. does not consider the use of RCAs in war to be a "method of warfare" that is prohibited by the Chemical Weapons Convention. Other nations disagree with this interpretation, arguing that Article I.5 of the Chemical Weapons Convention imposes a blanket ban on RCAs as a "method of warfare," regardless of whether they have a transient or incapacitating effect.

301. U.S. Department of Defense policy does not consider white phosphorous to be an incendiary weapon.

Some United States officials retort that because the ban on RCAs applies only when they are used as a "method of warfare," the use of RCAs with a transient effect by the United States is not employed as a method of warfare and therefore does not contravene the Chemical Weapons Convention. Rather, U.S. policy is to restrict RCAs to defensive uses to save lives.

These uses by U.S. troops are governed by four documents, discussed below. In order to determine which documents apply, it is necessary to determine whether the U.S. is currently engaged in armed conflict.

- If engaged in armed conflict: The use of RCAs is governed by the CWC and Executive Order 11850, which requires presidential approval before use (normally granted in the form of Rules of Engagement) and only allows for the use of RCAs in armed conflicts in defensive military modes to save lives, such as in controlling riots, dispersing civilians where the enemy uses them to mask or screen an attack, rescue missions (e.g., for escaping PoWs) and for police actions in rear areas. U.S. policy does not permit the use of RCAs as offensive modes of attack, even where an enemy is using civilians as human shields.
- If not engaged in armed conflict: The use of RCAs is governed by Chairman of the Joint Chiefs of Staff Instruction ("CJCSI") 3110.07C and tangentially by the Senate's resolution of advice and consent to the CWC.

E Methods of Warfare: The Tactics of Fighting

1 *Overview*

The methods of warfare refer to how warfare is conducted, including the tactics of fighting, such as tricking the enemy through ruses, treachery/perfidy (feigning surrender and misuse of Red Cross, Red Crescent or cultural property symbols), assassination, and espionage. The following rules are of particular importance:

- It is prohibited to make improper use of a flag of truce, of the national flag or of the military insignia and uniform of the enemy, as well as the distinctive badges of the Geneva Convention (Article 23(f) HR IV; Article 39 AP I). However, this is not intended to affect the existing generally recognized rules of international law applicable to espionage or to the use of flags in the conduct of armed conflict at sea Article 39.3 AP I).
- The improper use of certain signs is prohibited (Art 24 HR IV; Article 37, 39 AP I).
- The attack on undefended cities, towns and villages is prohibited (Article 25 HR IV; Article 59 AP I).
- Persons and objects cannot be used to shield military operations (Article 51.7 AP I).
- The seizure and destruction of enemy property is prohibited unless it is "necessary" (Article 23(g) HR IV).

2 *Perfidy and Ruses of War*

a Perfidy

Perfidy is a method of warfare that is prohibited under both Article 37(1) of Additional Protocol I and Article 23(b) of the Regulations Concerning the Laws and Customs of War on Land, annexed to Hague Convention (IV) of 1907, respecting the Laws and Customs of War on Land. Additional Protocol I states that it is prohibited to:[302]

> kill, injure or capture an adversary by resort to perfidy. Acts inviting the confidence of an adversary to lead him to believe that he is entitled to, or is obliged to accord, protection under the rules of international law applicable in armed conflict, with intent to betray that confidence, shall constitute perfidy. The following acts are examples of perfidy:
>
> a) the feigning of an intent to negotiate under a flag of truce or of a surrender;
> b) the feigning of an incapacitation by wounds or sickness;
> c) the feigning of civilian, non-combatant status; and
> d) the feigning of protected status by the use of signs, emblems or uniforms of the United Nations or of neutral or other States not Parties to the conflict.

b Ruses of War

Additional Protocol I contrasts perfidy, which is prohibited, with ruses of war, which are "not prohibited." Additional Protocol I defines ruses of war as:[303]

> acts which are intended to mislead an adversary or to induce him to act recklessly but which infringe no rule of international law applicable in armed conflict and which are not perfidious because they do not invite the confidence of an adversary with respect to protection under that law. The following are examples of such ruses: the use of camouflage, decoys, mock operations and misinformation.

A prominent example of the use of ruses was during World War II when the Allies used inflatable rubber tanks and decoy ships to mislead the Nazis into believing the Allies would invade Norway rather than cross the English Channel and invade Normandy.

c Capturing Enemy Vessels and Other Equipment

Like ruses of war, capturing enemy equipment, including aircraft, vessels and vehicles, is permitted.[304] Once captured, such equipment may be used by the armed forces that possess the equipment.

302. Article 37(1) Additional Protocol I.
303. Article 37(2) Additional Protocol I.
304. Some commentators refer to capturing as "hijacking" or "stealing" of enemy equipment.

3 *Cultural and Religious Heritage and Property*

a *Protections under Customary International Law*

Customary international humanitarian law requires parties to both international and non-international armed conflict to both respect and protect cultural heritage and religious property. Under Rule 38 of the ICRC's *Customary International Humanitarian Law*, each party to a conflict must respect cultural property:

A. Special care must be taken in military operations to avoid damage to buildings dedicated to religion, art, science, education or charitable purposes and historic monuments unless they are military objectives.
B. Property of great importance to the cultural heritage of every people must not be the object of attack unless imperatively required by military necessity.

Under Rule 40 of the ICRC's *Customary International Humanitarian Law*, each party to a conflict must protect cultural property:

A. All seizure of or destruction or wilful damage done to institutions dedicated to religion, charity, education, the arts and sciences, historic monuments and works of art and science is prohibited.
B. Any form of theft, pillage or misappropriation of, and any acts of vandalism directed against, property of great importance to the cultural heritage of every people is prohibited.

Civilian cultural property may not be made the object of attack unless it qualifies as a military objective. This customary international rule applies in both international and non-international armed conflicts.[305] The Rome Statute reinforces this provision. It stresses that "intentionally directing attacks against buildings dedicated to religion, education, art, science or charitable purposes, historic monuments, hospitals and places where the sick and wounded are collected, provided they are not military objectives," qualifies as a war crime in both international armed conflict (Article 8.2.b.ix SICC) and non-international armed conflict (Article 8.2.e.iv SICC). The Statute of the ICTY contains a similar provision. It prohibits the "seizure of, destruction or wilful damage done to institutions dedicated to religion, charity and education, the arts and sciences, historic monuments and works of art and science" as violations of the laws and customs of war over which the Tribunal has jurisdiction.[306]

305. Jean-Marie Henckaerts and Louise Doswald-Beck, *Customary International Humanitarian Law*, Vol. I, ICRC, Cambridge University Press (Cambridge, New York, 2009), p. 127 (for Rule 38) and p. 133 (for Rule 40).
306. Article 3(d) Statute of the ICTY.

b *Protections under Conventional Law*

i Hague Regulations (1907)

The Annex to Hague Convention IV of 1907 prohibits the destruction or wilful damage of institutions of a religious, charitable or educational character and subjects such destruction or damage to legal proceedings. Article 56 of the Annex provides as follows:

> The property of municipalities, that of institutions dedicated to religion, charity and education, the arts and sciences, even when State property, shall be treated as private property.
>
> All seizure of, destruction or wilful damage done to institutions of this character, historic monuments, works of art and science, is forbidden, and should be made the subject of legal proceedings.

ii Convention for the Protection of Cultural Property in Armed Conflict (1954)

(1) Overview

The Convention for the Protection of Cultural Property in the Event of Armed Conflict, done at The Hague on 14 May 1954, entered into force on 7 August 1956) and has 133 states parties. The Convention protects cultural property, which is defined as (Article 1):

(a) movable or immovable property of great importance to the cultural heritage of every people, such as monuments of architecture, art or history, whether religious or secular; archaeological sites; groups of buildings which, as a whole, are of historical or artistic interest; works of art; manuscripts, books and other objects of artistic, historical or archaeological interest; as well as scientific collections and important collections of books or archives or of reproductions of the property defined above;

(b) buildings whose main and effective purpose is to preserve or exhibit the movable cultural property defined in sub-paragraph (a) such as museums, large libraries and depositories of archives, and refuges intended to shelter, in the event of armed conflict, the movable cultural property defined in sub-paragraph (a);

(c) centers containing a large amount of cultural property as defined in sub-paragraphs (a) and (b), to be known as "centers containing monuments."

(2) Protections

The Convention requires states parties to (Article 4.1):

> respect cultural property situated within their own territory as well as within the territory of other High Contracting Parties by refraining from any use of the

> property and its immediate surroundings or of the appliances in use for its protection for purposes which are likely to expose it to destruction or damage in the event of armed conflict; and by refraining from any act of hostility, directed against such property.

(3) Military Necessity Exception

The exception to the mandate to protect cultural property revolves around the principle of military necessity (Article 4.2):

> The obligations mentioned in paragraph 1 of the present Article may be waived only in cases where military necessity imperatively requires such a waiver.

iii Additional Protocol I (1977)

Under Additional Protocol I, which applies to international armed conflict, certain cultural property, cultural objects and places of worship receive special protections. Article 53 states:

> Without prejudice to the provisions of the Hague Convention for the Protection of Cultural Property in the Event of Armed Conflict of 14 May 1954, and of other relevant international instruments, it is prohibited:
>
> a) to commit any acts of hostility directed against the historic monuments, works of art or places of worship which constitute the cultural or spiritual heritage of peoples;
> b) to use such objects in support of the military effort;
> c) to make such objects the object of reprisals.

4 *Protection of the Environment*

Protections for the environment are found in the following sources of international law:

a Convention on the Prohibition of Military or Any Hostile Use of Environmental Modification Techniques (1976)

The United Nations Convention on the Prohibition of Military or Any Hostile Use of Environmental Modification Techniques (10 December 1976) ("ENMOD") entered into force on 5 October 1978 with a view to prohibiting the use of environmental modification as a weapon in armed conflict. It states as follows (Article 1.1 ENMOD):

> Each State Party to this Convention undertakes not to engage in military or any other hostile use of environmental modification techniques having *widespread, long-lasting or severe effects* as the means of destruction, damage or injury to any other State Party.

"Long-lasting" has been interpreted as lasting for a period of months.
ENMOD has 48 signatories and 78 states parties as of 2019.

b *Additional Protocol I*

Unlike ENMOD, which seeks to prohibit the use of environmental modification as a weapon in armed conflict, Additional Protocol I seeks to protect the environment as a victim of armed conflict. Article 35.3 states:

> It is prohibited to employ methods or means of warfare which are intended, or may be expected, to cause widespread, long-term and severe damage to the natural environment.

Long term has been interpreted in the commentaries to mean a period of decades. Unlike in ENMOD, the criteria in Additional Protocol I (widespread, long-term and severe) are cumulative. Article 55 of Additional Protocol I further states:

> 1. Care shall be taken in warfare to protect the natural environment against widespread, long-term and severe damage. This protection includes a prohibition of the use of methods or means of warfare which are intended or may be expected to cause such damage to the natural environment and thereby to prejudice the health or survival of the population.
> 2. Attacks against the natural environment by way of reprisals are prohibited.

c *Customary International Law*

The ICRC's *Customary International Humanitarian Law* represents a fusion of the ENMOD rule, which seeks to prohibit the use of the environment as a weapon, and Additional Protocol I, which seeks to protect the environment as a victim of armed conflict. Rule 45 of the ICRC's study states:

> The use of methods or means of warfare that are intended, or may be expected, to cause widespread, long-term and severe damage to the natural environment is prohibited. Destruction of the natural environment may not be used as a weapon.

5 ***Starvation***

a *Starvation of Civilians*

Starvation of civilians as a method of warfare is prohibited (Article 54.1 AP I; Article 14 AP II). Additional Protocol I provides an absolute prohibition on attacks against objects indispensable to the survival of the civilian population (Article 54.2 AP I):

> It is prohibited to attack, destroy, remove or render useless objects indispensable to the survival of the civilian population, such as foodstuffs, agricultural areas for the production of foodstuffs, crops, livestock, drinking water installations and supplies and irrigation works, for the specific purpose of denying them for their sustenance value to the civilian population or to the adverse Party, whatever the motive, whether in order to starve out civilians, to cause them to move away, or for any other motive.

Article 14 of Additional Protocol II similarly provides a blanket prohibition of the starvation of civilians:

> Starvation of civilians as a method of combat is prohibited. It is therefore prohibited to attack, destroy, remove or render useless, for that purpose, objects indispensable to the survival of the civilian population, such as foodstuffs, agricultural areas for the production of foodstuffs, crops, livestock, drinking water installations and supplies and irrigation works.

This is reinforced by Rule 53 of the ICRC's *Customary International Humanitarian Law*, which states, "The use of starvation of the civilian population as a method of warfare is prohibited," and Rule 54, which states, "Attacking, destroying, removing or rendering useless objects indispensable to the survival of the civilian population are prohibited."

However, in international armed conflicts, Article 54.5 provides an exception that pierces the absolutism of Article 54.2 blanket prohibition. It states:

> In recognition of the vital requirements of any Party to the conflict in the defence of its national territory against invasion, derogation from the prohibitions contained in paragraph 2 may be made by a Party to the conflict within such territory under its own control where required by imperative military necessity.

b *Starvation of Combatants*

When targeting members of the armed forces, the use of starvation as a method of warfare is not strictly prohibited. This has been the case since the time of the Lieber Code, which held that "War is not carried on by arms alone. It is lawful to starve the hostile belligerent, armed or unarmed so that it leads to the speedier subjection of the enemy" (Article 17). In this same vein, Article 54.3 of Additional Protocol I states that the prohibition of starvation as a method of warfare:

> shall not apply to such of the objects covered by it as are used by an adverse Party:
>
> a) as sustenance solely for the members of its armed forces; or
> b) if not as sustenance, then in direct support of military action, provided, however, that in no event shall actions against these objects be taken which may be expected to leave the civilian population with such inadequate food or water as to cause its starvation or force its movement.

F **Sexual Violence**

Sexual violence is prohibited as a means and method of warfare under both treaty law and customary international law.

1 *Prohibition of Sexual Violence under Customary International Law*

Under Rule 93 of the ICRC's *Customary International Humanitarian Law*, "[r]ape and other forms of sexual violence are prohibited" in both international and non-international armed conflicts. The earliest written codes governing conduct in war, including the Lieber Code,[307] recognized the prohibition of rape as a method of warfare.

2 *Prohibition of Sexual Violence under Treaty Law*

a *International Armed Conflict*

Hague law and Geneva law do not explicitly prohibit conflict-related sexual violence and sexual and gender-based violence. However, they uphold principles of human dignity and family honor. With reference to international armed conflict:

- Article 46 of the Annex to Hague Convention IV of 1907 states that "[f]amily honour and rights, the lives of persons, and private property, as well as religious convictions and practice, must be respected." The term "family honour" has been broadly construed to include a protection against rape and forced prostitution.
- Half a century later, this principle was brought forward explicitly in Geneva Convention IV of 1949, which states that "[w]omen shall be especially protected against any attack on their honour, in particular against *rape, enforced prostitution, or any form of indecent assault*" (Article 27.2 GC IV).
- Additional Protocol I provides similar protection: "Women shall be the object of special respect and shall be protected in particular against rape, forced prostitution and any other form of indecent assault" (Article 76.1 AP I).

Several provisions of the Geneva Conventions issue heightened protection to women. Under Geneva Convention I, "[w]omen shall be treated with all consideration due to their sex. The Party to the conflict which is compelled to abandon wounded or sick to the enemy shall, as far as military considerations permit, leave with them a part of its medical personnel and material to assist in their care" (Article 12 GC I).

With respect to female prisoners of war:

- "Women shall be treated with all the regard due to their sex and shall in all cases benefit by treatment as favourable as that granted to men" (Article 14 GC III).

307. Article 44 Lieber Code (1863) ("All wanton violence committed against persons in the invaded country, all destruction of property not commanded by the authorized officer, ... all rape, wounding, maiming, or killing of such inhabitants, are prohibited under the penalty of death, or such other severe punishment as may seem adequate for the gravity of the offense").

- "In any camps in which women prisoners of war, as well as men, are accommodated, separate dormitories shall be provided for them" (Article 26 GC III).
- "In any camps in which women prisoners of war are accommodated, separate conveniences shall be provided for them" (Article 29 GC III).
- "Women prisoners of war undergoing disciplinary punishment shall be confined in separate quarters from male prisoners of war and shall be under the immediate supervision of women" (Article 97 GC III).

With respect to female civilians:

- Civilian women detainees "shall be confined in separate quarters and shall be under the direct supervision of women" (Article 76 GC IV).
- "Whenever it is necessary, as an exceptional and temporary measure, to accommodate women internees who are not members of a family unit in the same place of internment as men, the provision of separate sleeping quarters and sanitary conveniences for the use of such women internees shall be obligatory" (Article 85 GC IV).
- "Women internees undergoing disciplinary punishment shall be confined in separate quarters from male internees and shall be under the immediate supervision of women" (Article 124 GC IV).
- Female prisoners of war are to be housed in separate facilities, and their sex should also be taken into account in other aspects of detention.

b *Non-international Armed Conflict*

With reference to non-international armed conflict, common Article 3 to the Geneva Conventions and Additional Protocol II, both of which largely reflect customary international law, prohibit sexual violence:

- Common Article 3 forbids "violence to life and person," "cruel treatment" and "outrages upon personal dignity, in particular humiliating and degrading treatment";
- Additional Protocol II, which largely reflects custom, prohibits "at any time and in any place whatsoever … rape, enforced prostitution and any form of indecent assault" (Article 4.2 AP II).

3 *Sexual Violence as an International Crime*

The Rome Statute criminalizes sexual violence, including outrages against personal dignity, rape, sexual slavery, enforced prostitution, forced pregnancy, and enforced sterilization. It defines the following acts as crimes against humanity (Article 7.1(g) SICC):

> Rape, sexual slavery, enforced prostitution, forced pregnancy, enforced sterilization, or *any other form of sexual violence* of comparable gravity.

The Rome Statute defines the following acts as war crimes in *international* armed conflict (Article 8.2(b) SICC):

> Committing rape, sexual slavery, enforced prostitution, forced pregnancy ... enforced sterilization, or *any other form of sexual violence* also constituting a grave breach of the Geneva Conventions.

The Rome Statute defines these same acts as war crimes in *non-international* armed conflict (Article 8.2(e) SICC):

> Committing rape, sexual slavery, enforced prostitution, forced pregnancy ... enforced sterilization, and *any other form of sexual violence* also constituting a serious violation of article 3 common to the four Geneva Conventions.

4 *The Experience of Women in Armed Conflict*

a *Overview*

An emerging body of scholarship argues that international humanitarian law, in its current form, fails to adequately capture the experience of women in armed conflict. In *Women, Armed Conflict, and International Law*, Judith Gardam and Michelle Jarvis argue that "[t]he international community increasingly is recognising that the experience of women must be taken into account in determining which acts committed during armed conflict are recognised and prosecuted as crimes."[308] The authors contend that while existing international humanitarian law must be implemented more robustly, gaps in the law must be filled to address vulnerabilities that women face in war; "if there is no law, there can be no enforcement."[309] In the meantime, those who work in international humanitarian law, whether from international organizations, governments, academia or non-governmental organizations, can act now by improving dissemination and training in international humanitarian law and ensuring greater female participation in armed conflict decision-making.

b *Tokyo Women's Tribunal*

Various civil society organizations have pointed to the failure of the International Military Tribunal for the Far East to prosecute groups and individuals for rape or sexual slavery during World War II as an example of the inadequacy of international humanitarian law to address the experience of women in armed conflict. To remedy this failure, various women's groups and human rights organizations from across Asia organized a people's tribunal in 2000 known as the Women's International War Crimes

308. Judith Gardam and Michelle Jarvis, *Women, Armed Conflict, and International Law*, Kluwer Law International (2001), p. 179.
309. *Ibid.*, p. 253.

Tribunal on Japan's Military Sexual Slavery, also known as the Tokyo Women's Tribunal. The Tribunal met in December of 2000 and issued a judgment convicting the late Emperor Hirohito Showa, who, as leader of the country, was deemed ultimately responsible for the sexual slavery policy and World War II "comfort stations" for Japanese soldiers. The Tribunal, organized more than half a century after the trials of the International Military Tribunal for the Far East, was called on to apply the law at the time of World War II as it existed with respect to crimes against humanity.

5 *Issues in Prosecuting Conflict-Related Sexual Violence*

a Notions of "Honor" and Victim Stigma

One specialist in sexual and gender-based violence has remarked that framing conflict-related sexual violence as attacks against honor within the framework of social morality "fuels the shame and stigma associated with sexual violence." Rather than valorize survivors, it has the effect of contributing "to the perpetuation of the stigma attached to [sexual violence] and the disempowerment of survivors."[310]

Moreover, the conception of rape as more a matter of honor than a violent act "may explain the shame and ostracism experienced by many survivors of sexual violence crimes … [T]he fear of stigma is sometimes so strong that survivors will conceal the very fact of the assault from their families."[311]

b Proving Crimes of Sexual Violence

i Victim Testimony

Successful sexual violence prosecutions depend largely on effective contributions from victims. In some cases, victims may be reluctant to testify. Some may want to avoid reliving past trauma. Others distrust the justice system. Those who come from tight-knit communities may fear social ostracization. Male victims of sexual violence may feel particular stigma based on social norms and expectations of a strong masculine identity, thereby leading to underreporting of male sexual violence.[312]

To overcome these challenges, prosecutors must build relationships of trust with victims. Regular contact between prosecutors and victims prior to their testimony is often crucial to building these relationships. It is also helpful for prosecutors to explain the importance of the testimony and the reason courts need to hear the testimony in

310. Priya Gopalan, "Rejecting Notions of 'Honour' to Mitigate Stigma," *LSE Women, Peace and Security Working Paper Series*, 27/2021 (2021), p. 1.
311. Priya Gopalan, Daniela Kravetz and Aditya Menon, "Proving Crimes of Sexual Violence," in Serge Brammertz and Michelle Jarvis (eds.), *Prosecuting Conflict-Related Sexual Violence at the ICTY*, Oxford University Press (2016), p. 36.
312. *See* U.N. Special Representative of the Secretary-General on Sexual Violence in Conflict Situations, "Report on Workshop on Sexual Violence against Men and Boys in Conflict," July 2013 (New York).

detail.[313] It may be necessary for prosecutors to offer protective measures, such as the option for testifying in closed session or obtaining a confidentiality order, as discussed further below.

Evidentiary issues frequently arise in sexual violence cases, where it is commonly assumed that victims are unwilling to speak out due to the stigma associated with crimes of sexual violence. Such assumptions and stereotypes can create barriers that undermine evidence. However, in some cases, victims are willing to testify and may feel empowered when publicly speaking about their suffering.[314]

ii Other Evidence

Diversifying evidence by introducing non-victim witnesses and experts and documentary and forensic evidence mitigates the risk of having to withdraw charges if a victim opts not to testify.[315] Non-victim witness testimony can serve as important circumstantial evidence to prove crimes of sexual violence in the event a victim is unavailable to testify. Moreover, non-victim witness testimony can serve as powerful corroboration evidence when a victim witness is available to testify. In addition, expert testimony can be presented to bolster victim credibility or during sentencing to demonstrate "the impact of sexual violence crimes on victims, particularly where there is an absence of specific victim impact information."[316]

Documentary evidence, including reports by local authorities, armed forces or international observers, can be used to demonstrate the "occurrence and extent of sexual violence" charged in the indictment.[317] Documentary evidence can also be used to demonstrate that government or military officials had knowledge of crimes of sexual violence and did nothing to stop them. Finally, forensic evidence can be used to prove rape and other sexual violence, particularly where a victim was murdered. Moreover, it can be used to corroborate victim testimony.

iii Protective Measures

Protective measures may be necessary to protect victims and witnesses when a witness-centered approach to prosecution is adopted. Such protective measures include obtaining confidentiality orders or offering witnesses the option of testifying in closed session. However, closed testimony should not be overused lest it diminish the transparency of the proceedings.

313. Priya Gopalan, Daniela Kravetz and Aditya Menon, "Proving Crimes of Sexual Violence," in Serge Brammertz and Michelle Jarvis (eds.), *Prosecuting Conflict-Related Sexual Violence at the ICTY*, Oxford University Press (2016), p. 116.
314. *See Ibid.*, p. 111.
315. *Ibid.*, p. 150.
316. *Ibid.*, p. 152.
317. *Ibid.*, p. 155.

Other measures, such as the use of pseudonyms and image or voice distortion, may be implemented where witnesses wish to remain anonymous. In some cases, it may be necessary to request full anonymity of victims, though such requests must be balanced against the rights of the accused. It may also be possible to shield the view of a witness from the accused but not from defense counsel.

When a victim agrees to testify, it may be necessary to solicit the expertise of a victim's psychologist or a victim's counsel, who may be able to intervene if a witness begins to relive trauma while testifying.

G Reprisals

1 Introduction

It is necessary to first point out a distinction between two types of reprisals—armed reprisals and belligerent reprisals. The two are often used interchangeably and, as a result, confusion between the two often arises. However, the two concepts must not be conflated. Each is, in fact, a distinct legal concept, with armed reprisals falling with the *jus ad bellum* and belligerent reprisals falling within the *jus in bello*.

2 Armed Reprisals

An armed reprisal is a use of military force that follows an armed incident prior to the onset of hostilities. It is normally used as punishment, retaliation or revenge for an armed attack. It does not fit into the exception that allows the use of force for self-defense.

The concept of armed reprisals has historically been used as a justification for the use of force by one state against another where the use of force does not fit into the self-defense exception to the prohibition of the use of armed force. However, following the adoption of the U.N. Charter and the prohibition on the use of force imposed by Article 2.4 of the Charter,[318] armed reprisals are no longer legal. If a state cannot justify its use of force on the basis of self-defense (Article 51 U.N. Charter) or pursuant to a U.N. Security Council collective security measure (Article 42 U.N. Charter), then it may not use force against another state, even if such use of force is intended as punishment, revenge or retaliation for another state's unlawful use of force against it. Rather, the attacked state must be able to demonstrate that its use of force is in furtherance of its self-defense or that the use of force is authorized by a U.N. Security Council resolution.

318. Article 2.4 of the U.N. Charter states that "All Members shall refrain in their international relations from the threat or use of force against the territorial integrity or political independence of any state, or in any other manner inconsistent with the Purposes of the United Nations."

3 *Belligerent Reprisals*

a *Overview*

Belligerent reprisals are employed by states as an enforcement measure in reaction to the unlawful acts of an adversary. The *Naulilaa* case (*Portugal v. Germany*) (1949) defines reprisals as:[319]

> an act of self-help on the part of the injured states, responding after an unsatisfied demand to an act contrary to international law on the part of the offending State ... They would be illegal if a previous act contrary to international law had not furnished the reason for them. They aim to impose on the offending State reparation for the offense or the return to legality in avoidance of new offenses.

The ICRC defines a belligerent reprisal as:[320]

> an action that would otherwise be unlawful but that in exceptional cases is considered lawful under international law when used as an enforcement mechanism in reaction to unlawful acts of an adversary. In international humanitarian law there is a trend to outlaw belligerent reprisals altogether. Those that may still be lawful are subject [to] stringent conditions ....

Belligerent reprisals were traditionally the mechanism for ensuring compliance with the law and punishing violations of the law. In the modern era, states have largely abandoned reprisals as a law enforcement measure. Instead, states have embraced a system of penal repression instituted by the Geneva Conventions, including the grave breaches regime. This has been supplemented by the advent of international criminal courts, including the International Criminal Court and ad hoc and hybrid institutions charged with investigating and punishing war crimes and ending cultures of impunity.

b *Prohibition under Conventional Law*

The Geneva Conventions prohibit taking reprisals against persons in the power of a party to the conflict, including the wounded, sick and shipwrecked; medical and religious personnel; captured combatants; and civilian protected persons (alien civilians in the territory of a party to a conflict and civilians in occupied territory). Of note:

- Article 46 of Geneva Convention I states, "[r]eprisals against the wounded, sick, personnel, buildings or equipment protected by the Convention are prohibited."

319. *Responsabilité de L'allemagne a Raison des Dommages Causés dans les Colonies Portugaises du Sud de L'Afrique*, 8 Trib. Arb. Mixtes 409 (1928) (*Portugal v. Germany*) (The Naulilaa Case), reprinted in 2 Reports of International Arbitral Awards 1011 (1949).
320. Jean-Marie Henckaerts and Louise Doswald-Beck, *Customary International Humanitarian Law*, Vol. I, ICRC, Cambridge University Press (Cambridge, New York, 2009), Rule 145, p. 513.

- Article 47 of Geneva Convention II states, "[r]eprisals against the wounded, sick and shipwrecked persons, the personnel, the vessels or the equipment protected by the Convention are prohibited."
- Article 13 of Geneva Convention III states, "[m]easures of reprisal against prisoners of war are prohibited."
- Article 33 of Geneva Convention IV states, "[r]eprisals against protected persons and their property are prohibited."

In this same vein, Additional Protocol I prohibits reprisals as follows:

- Article 33 states that "[r]eprisals against the persons and objects protected by this Part are prohibited."
- Article 51.6 states that "[a]ttacks against the civilian population or civilians by way of reprisals are prohibited."
- Article 52.1 states that "[c]ivilian objects shall not be the object of attack or of reprisals."
- In addition, Article 53 (Protection of cultural objects and places of worship), Article 54 (Protection of objects indispensable to the survival of the civilian population), Article 55 (Protection of the natural environment) and Article 56 (Protection of works and installations containing dangerous forces) prohibit reprisals.

While the Geneva Conventions and Additional Protocol I provide blanket prohibitions on reprisals, they never define "reprisals." Therefore, to fully understand the nature and scope of the prohibition, we must look to customary international law.

c *Prohibition under Customary International Law and Exceptions*

i Non-international Armed Conflicts

Rule 148 of the ICRC's *Customary International Humanitarian Law* provides a blanket prohibition on reprisals on non-international armed conflicts:

> Parties to non-international armed conflicts do not have the right to resort to belligerent reprisals. Other countermeasures against persons who do not or who have ceased to take a direct part in hostilities are prohibited.

This general prohibition in non-international armed conflicts applies to *all* types of reprisals rather than only to reprisals on civilians and other protected persons.

ii International Armed Conflicts

(1) General Prohibition and Exception

Rule 145 of the ICRC's *Customary International Humanitarian Law* holds as follows:

> Where not prohibited by international law, belligerent reprisals are subject to stringent conditions.

Reprisals are thus deemed to be unlawful as a general rule. However, there is a narrow exception that permits reprisals. The following five conditions must be met in order for reprisals against permitted categories of persons and objects not to be unlawful:[321]

(1) *purpose of reprisals*. Reprisals may only be taken in reaction to a prior serious violation of international humanitarian law and only for the purpose of inducing the adversary to comply with the law. "Anticipatory" reprisals or "counter-reprisals" are not permissible;
(2) *measure of last resort*. Reprisals may only be carried out as a measure of last resort when no other lawful measures are available. According to the Draft Articles on State Responsibility, before taking countermeasures, an injured state must call on the responsible state to fulfill its obligations, notify the responsible state of any decision to take countermeasures and offer to negotiate with the state;
(3) *proportionality*. Reprisals must be proportionate to the violations they aim to stop;
(4) *decision at the highest level of government*. The decision to resort to reprisals must be taken at the highest political or military level of government and not by local commanders;[322] and
(5) *termination*. Reprisals must cease as soon as the adversary complies with the law.

(2) Prohibition of Reprisals against Civilians and Other Protected Persons

While the commentary to Rule 145 permits these narrow exceptions, Rule 146, in turn, provides a seeming blanket prohibition against protected persons. Rule 146 states:

> Belligerent reprisals against persons protected by the Geneva Conventions are prohibited.

Rule 146 appears to provide blanket protection to persons protected by the Geneva Conventions, namely the wounded and sick in armed forces in the field; wounded, sick and shipwrecked members of armed forces at sea; prisoners of war; and civilians. However, the commentary to Rule 146 undermines the universal nature of the prohibition. The ICRC's *Customary International Humanitarian Law* states:[323]

> The *trend* to ban reprisals against civilians during the conduct of hostilities was introduced in a U.N. General Assembly resolution adopted in 1970, which affirmed

321. *Ibid.*, Rule 145, p. 515-18.
322. *Kupreškić case*, ICTY, 2000.
323. Jean-Marie Henckaerts and Louise Doswald-Beck, *Customary International Humanitarian Law*, Vol. I, ICRC, Cambridge University Press (Cambridge, New York, 2009), p. 520 (emphasis added).

> the principle that "civilian populations, or individual members thereof, should not be the object of reprisals" as a basic principle for the protection of civilian populations in armed conflict.

The ICRC's study continues to state:[324]

> Because of existing contrary practice, albeit very limited, it is difficult to conclude that there has yet crystallised a customary rule specifically prohibiting reprisals against civilians during the conduct of hostilities. Nevertheless, it is also difficult to assert that a right to resort to such reprisals continues to exist on the strength of the practice of only a limited number of States, some of which is also ambiguous. Hence, there appears, at a minimum, *to exist a trend in favour of prohibiting such reprisals*. The International Criminal Tribunal for the former Yugoslavia, in its review of the indictment in the *Martić case* in 1996 and in its judgement in the *Kupreškić case* in 2000, found that there was such a prohibition already in existence, based largely on the imperatives of humanity or public conscience. These are important indications, consistent with a substantial body of practice now condemning or outlawing such reprisals.

The ICRC's reference to a "trend" rather than a "general practice" in favor of prohibiting reprisals against civilians implies that the prohibition has not yet reached the level of custom. It is necessary to point out that a trend is not the same as a consistent and recurrent state practice that, when accompanied by *opinio juris*, forms customary international law. A "trend" in favor of a practice simply means that a growing number of states accept the practice, even if the number of states in favor of the practice is relatively small. The state practice that is necessary to form customary international law does not need to be universal, but it must be widely enough practiced among states to qualify as general, consistent and recurring before it can serve as a source of the law. Therefore, the fact that the ICRC cited a mere "trend" in favor of prohibiting reprisals against civilians rather than a general practice is evidence of a gap that allows for the argument that, at least in some circumstances, reprisals against civilians are permitted.

VI COMMAND RESPONSIBILITY AND LIABILITY

A Command Responsibility

1 Precautions in Attack

Commanders must take constant care in military operations to spare the civilian population, civilians, and civilian objects[325] and to uphold the principles of international humanitarian law. Those who plan or decide upon an attack shall:[326]

324. *Ibid.*, p. 523 (emphasis added).
325. Article 57.1 AP I.
326. Article 57.2(a) AP I.

- do everything feasible to verify that the objectives to be attacked are neither civilians nor civilian objects and are not subject to special protection but are instead military objectives;
- take all feasible precautions in the choice of means and methods of warfare with a view to avoiding, and in any event to minimizing, incidental loss of civilian life, injury to civilians and damage to civilian objects; and
- refrain from deciding to launch any attack which may be expected to cause incidental loss of civilian life, injury to civilians, damage to civilian objects, or a combination thereof, which would be excessive in relation to the concrete and direct military advantage anticipated.

An attack must be cancelled or suspended if it becomes apparent that the objective is not a military one, is subject to special protection, or that the attack may be expected to cause civilian loss or damage excessive in relation to the military advantage anticipated.[327] Effective advance warning shall be given of attacks which may affect the civilian population (e.g., attacking a hospital being used to launch attacks) unless circumstances do not permit.[328]

2 *Responsibility for the Acts of Subordinates*

a *Overview*

Under customary international law, a commander may be criminally liable for the acts of his or her subordinates. The commonly agreed upon international *mens rea* standard is whether the commander "knew, or should have known" that his or her subordinates were violating international humanitarian law or international criminal law and whether the commander took reasonable measures to prevent and/or report and punish those violations.

b *Example: The Case of General Tomoyuki Yamashita*

Tomoyuki Yamashita was a Japanese Imperial Army general in the Philippines in WWII whose forces were responsible for extensive atrocities against civilians, internees and prisoners of war. In a prosecution brought by the IMT, General Yamashita raised the defense that he was unaware of the crimes being committed by his forces because the U.S. disrupted communications with his subordinates. The IMT rejected this defense and held that the crimes were so widespread that he "knew or should have known" of them.

327. Article 57.2(b) AP I.
328. Article 57.2(c) AP I.

B Commanders' Liability

1 *Judging Commanders for Breaching the Principle of Proportionality*

When committed willfully and causing death or serious injury to body or health, the following acts are deemed to be grave breaches of Additional Protocol I:[329]

- launching an indiscriminate attack affecting the civilian population or civilian objects *in the knowledge* that such attack will cause *excessive* loss of life, injury to civilians or damage to civilian objects; and
- launching an attack against works or installations containing dangerous forces *in the knowledge* that such attack will cause *excessive* loss of life, injury to civilians or damage to civilian objects.

2 *The Rendulic Rule's Objective and Subjective Standards for Commanders' Actions*

General Lothar Rendulic, an Austrian commander during World War II, was charged with ordering extensive destruction of civilian buildings and lands while retreating from an expected attack in a "scorched earth" campaign to deny use to the enemy. The Rendulic case presents a broad proposition regarding a commander's liability for mistakes in war. The Nuremberg International Military Tribunal observed that Rendulic's judgment may have been faulty but was not criminal: The conditions "as they appeared to the defendant at the time were sufficient upon which he could honestly conclude that urgent military necessity warranted the decision made."[330]

The Rendulic Rule is the contemporary standard by which commanders are judged. Under the Rule, a commander's *liability is based on the information reasonably available* to the commander at the time of his or her decision. The standard thus combines both a subjective standard (i.e., what the commander actually knew) and an objective standard (i.e., what information was reasonably available to the commander).

Under the Rendulic Rule, in judging a commander's actions, the requirement is thus for a commander to act reasonably, which involves both an objective and subjective analysis:

- objective: one must consider what a reasonable commander would do and whether the commander in question acted reasonably on the basis of the information reasonably available to determine whether a target was a military objective and that the incidental damage was not disproportionate;
- subjective: one must look at the situation as the commander saw it in light of the information he had gathered and that affected the commander's judgment.

329. Article 85.3 AP I.
330. *United States of America v. Wilhelm List, et al.* (Hostage Case), Nuremberg International Military Tribunal, Case No. 7 (1948), at 1,297.

C Liability of Subordinates Who Obey Unlawful Orders

The obedience of orders is generally not a defense under international law for the commission of war crimes. The Nuremberg Principles (1946) state that "any person who commits an act which constitutes a crime under international law is responsible thereafter and liable to punishment" and "the fact that a person acted pursuant to order of his Government or of a superior does not relieve him from responsibility under international law, provided a moral choice was in fact possible to him." The *U.S. Manual for Courts-Martial* (1969) states that homicide "committed in the proper performance of a legal duty" is justifiable, but not when the act is "manifestly beyond the scope of his authority, or the order is such that a man of ordinary sense and understanding would know it to be illegal."

CHAPTER 7
International Criminal Law

I INTRODUCTION AND DEFINITIONS

International criminal law deals with the prohibition and punishment of international crimes, which can be defined as internationally wrongful acts resulting from breaches by a state actor or a non-state actor of peremptory norms (*jus cogens*) so essential for the protection of the international community's fundamental interests that the breach is classified by the community as a crime. Examples of international crimes include war crimes, crimes against humanity, genocide, and aggression. Individuals may be held responsible for violations of international criminal law whether they are acting as state agents with a nexus to state action or as non-state actors with no such nexus.

II INTERNATIONAL CRIMES

A Overview

1 List of International Crimes

The international community has been very selective in defining acts that constitute international crimes—only the most egregious acts meet the definition. Ordinary crimes and even felonies in many jurisdictions, such as rape and murder, do not on their own constitute international crimes. Such acts must rise to a level of severity such that they breach peremptory norms (*jus cogens*) in order to qualify. This would be the case, for example, of systematic mass rapes and murders of a civilian population. In this way, the international community has agreed to include the following four acts within the definition of prosecutable international crimes:

(i) war crimes;
(ii) genocide;

(iii) crimes against humanity; and
(iv) aggression.

It is important to note that the international community has, to a large extent, opted against including within this list of crimes certain criminal acts, such as terrorism, that might be used by some states for political reasons to bring actions against the nationals of other states.

2 *The Varying Definitions of International Crimes*

Various international courts and ad hoc institutions have distinct definitions of international crimes. The earliest modern definitions derive from the Charter of the International Military Tribunal, but these definitions evolved with the establishment of later courts, including the International Criminal Tribunal for the former Yugoslavia ("ICTY") (1993), the International Criminal Tribunal for Rwanda ("ICTR") (1994) and, most recently, the International Criminal Court ("ICC") (2002). Because the Statute of the ICC ("SICC") is the most universally applicable, serves in some ways as a model for later ad hoc and hybrid tribunals and largely reflects customary international law, the definitions of international crimes presented herein rely heavily on the SICC as a reference.

However, it is important to note that some of the SICC's definitions vary across other tribunals. Moreover, some international tribunals have focused on crimes not included in the SICC. For example, the Special Tribunal for Lebanon ("STL") has within its jurisdiction the power to prosecute those responsible for acts of terrorism.

B War Crimes

War crimes are defined as "[s]erious violations of international humanitarian law."[331] The Rome Statute defines war crimes as follows:

- "Grave breaches of the Geneva Conventions of 12 August 1949."[332]
- "Other serious violations of the laws and customs applicable in international armed conflict, within the established framework of international law."[333]
- "In the case of an armed conflict not of an international character, serious violations of article 3 common to the four Geneva Conventions of 12 August 1949."[334]

The Rome Statute further provides an extensive list of war crimes falling within each of these three categories, including:

331. Jean-Marie Henckaerts and Louise Doswald-Beck, *Customary International Humanitarian Law*, Vol. I, ICRC, Cambridge University Press (Cambridge, New York, 2009), Rule 156, Chapter 44, p. 568.
332. Article 8.2(a) SICC.
333. Article 8.2(b) SICC.
334. Article 8.2(c) SICC.

(1) Grave breaches of the Geneva Conventions of 12 August 1949, namely, any of the following acts against persons or property protected under the provisions of the relevant Geneva Convention (i.e., the wounded in the field, the wounded, sick and shipwrecked at sea, prisoners of war, civilian persons in time of war):[335]
   (i) willful killing;
   (ii) torture or inhuman treatment;
   (iii) willfully causing great suffering or serious injury to body or health;
   (iv) extensive, unlawful, wanton and militarily unjustified destruction and appropriation of property;
   (v) compelling service in the forces of a hostile power;
   (vi) willful deprivation of the rights of fair and regular trial;
   (vii) unlawful deportation, transfer or confinement (forcible transfer);
   (viii) taking of hostages.

(2) Other serious violations of the laws and customs applicable in international armed conflict, including:[336]
   (i) intentionally directing attacks against the civilian population;
   (ii) intentionally directing attacks against civilian objects;
   (iii) intentionally directing attacks against personnel, installations, material, units or vehicles involved in a humanitarian assistance or U.N. peacekeeping mission entitled to protection under the international law of armed conflict;
   (iv) intentionally launching an attack in the knowledge that such attack will cause incidental loss of life or injury to civilians or damage to civilian objects or widespread, long-term and severe damage to the natural environment, which would be clearly excessive in relation to the concrete and direct overall military advantage anticipated;
   (v) attacking or bombarding, by whatever means, towns, villages, dwellings or buildings which are undefended and not military objectives;
   (vi) killing or wounding a combatant who, having laid down his arms or having no longer means of defence, has surrendered at discretion;
   (vii) making improper use of a flag of truce, of the flag or of the military insignia and uniform of the enemy or of the United Nations, as well as of the distinctive emblems of the Geneva Conventions, resulting in death or serious personal injury;
   (viii) transferring, directly or indirectly, by the Occupying Power of parts of its own civilian population into the territory it occupies, or the deportation or transfer of all or parts of the population of the occupied territory within or outside this territory;

335. Article 8.2(a) SICC.
336. Article 8.2(b) SICC.

(ix) intentionally directing attacks against buildings dedicated to religion, education, art, science or charitable purposes, historic monuments, hospitals and places where the sick and wounded are collected, provided they are not military objectives;
(x) employing poison or poisoned weapons;
(xi) employing asphyxiating, poisonous or other gases and all analogous liquids, materials or devices;
(xii) employing bullets which expand or flatten easily in the human body, such as bullets with a hard envelope which does not entirely cover the core or is pierced with incisions;
(xiii) committing rape, sexual slavery, enforced prostitution, forced pregnancy, as defined in Article 7, paragraph 2 (f), enforced sterilization, or any other form of sexual violence also constituting a grave breach of the Geneva Conventions;
(xvi) utilizing the presence of a civilian or other protected person to render certain points, areas or military forces immune from military operations;
(xv) intentionally directing attacks against buildings, materials, medical units and transport, and personnel using the distinctive emblems of the Geneva Conventions in conformity with international law.

(3) In the case of an armed conflict not of an international character, serious violations of Article 3 common to the four 12 August 1949 Geneva Conventions, including any of the following acts committed against persons taking no active part in the hostilities:[337]
(i) violence to life and person, i.e., murder of all kinds, mutilation, cruel treatment and torture;
(ii) committing outrages upon personal dignity;
(iii) taking of hostages;
(iv) passing of sentences and the carrying out of executions without previous judgment pronounced by a regularly constituted court, affording all judicial guarantees which are generally recognized as indispensable.

The London Charter gave the following examples of war crimes under the jurisdiction of the IMT: "murder, ill-treatment or deportation to slave labor or for any other purpose of civilian population of or in occupied territory, murder or ill-treatment of prisoners of war or persons on the seas, killing of hostages, plunder of public or private property, wanton destruction of cities, towns or villages, or devastation not justified by military necessity."[338]

337. Article 8.2(c) SICC.
338. Article 6(b) IMT.

C Crimes Against Humanity

1 *Overview*

Crimes against humanity are certain enumerated inhuman and odious acts committed as part of a systematic attack directed against any civilian population that constitutes grave humiliation or degradation or a serious attack on human dignity. The SICC enumerates a series of crimes, including murder, extermination, enslavement, deportation and forcible transfer, that constitute crimes against humanity when "committed as part of a widespread or systematic attack directed against any civilian population, with knowledge of the attack" (Article 7.1 SICC). "Attack directed against any civilian population" is, in turn, defined as "a course of conduct involving the multiple commission of acts ... against any civilian population, pursuant to or in furtherance of a State or organizational policy to commit such attack" (Article 7.2 SICC).

Any act of large-scale violence carried out in an organized fashion, such as the gathering together of hundreds of girls in a village to then be systematically raped and murdered, constitutes a crime against humanity.

2 *Elements*

The elements of crimes against humanity are as follows:

- the commission of any of the following enumerated *inhuman and odious acts*;
  - (a) murder;
  - (b) extermination;
  - (c) enslavement;
  - (d) deportation or forcible transfer of population;
  - (e) imprisonment or other severe deprivation of physical liberty in violation of fundamental rules of international law;
  - (f) torture;
  - (g) rape, sexual slavery, enforced prostitution, forced pregnancy, enforced sterilization, or any other form of sexual violence of comparable gravity;
  - (h) persecution against any identifiable group or collectivity on political, racial, national, ethnic, cultural, religious, gender as defined in paragraph 3, or other grounds that are universally recognized as impermissible under international law in connection with any act referred to in this paragraph or any crime within the jurisdiction of the Court;
  - (i) enforced disappearance of persons;
  - (j) the crime of apartheid;
  - (k) other inhumane acts of a similar character intentionally causing great suffering or serious injury to the body or to mental or physical health.
- committed as part of a *widespread or systematic attack* against any civilian population;

  - the enumerated act constitutes a crime against humanity when "committed as part of a *widespread or systematic attack* directed against any civilian population, with knowledge of the attack" (Article 7.1 SICC).
  - "Attack directed against any civilian population" is, in turn, defined as "a course of conduct involving the multiple commission of acts ... against any civilian population, pursuant to or in furtherance of a *State or organizational policy to commit such attack*" (Article 7.2 SICC).
- that constitutes grave humiliation or degradation or a serious attack on human dignity.

Any act of large-scale violence carried out in an organized fashion, such as the gathering together of hundreds of girls in a village to then be systematically raped and murdered, constitutes a crime against humanity.

3 *Distinguishing War Crimes from Crimes Against Humanity*

a *Historic Distinction*

International humanitarian law and the definition of war crimes have historically focused on protecting wounded or sick soldiers in the field or at sea, as well as prisoners of war. The focus was thus on the military, though civilian populations were also beneficiaries. The definition of crimes against humanity, in contrast, focuses on civilian populations that fall victim to systematic inhumane and odious acts.

The distinction between war crimes and crimes against humanity has historically been clear, particularly since the Conventions dealing with the protection of persons in armed conflicts preceding the 1949 Geneva Conventions (the Geneva Convention of 1864 for the Wounded in War; Geneva Convention of 1906 for the Wounded and Shipwrecked at Sea; and Geneva Convention of 1929 for Prisoners of War) explicitly dealt with military personnel only.

b *Current Overlap*

The universal adoption of the 1949 Geneva Conventions, and in particular Geneva Convention IV for the Protection of Civilian Persons in Time of War (1949), has changed the historic application of international humanitarian law to military personnel only; today, non-military personnel are a protected class of international humanitarian law.

As a result, there is now some overlap between crimes against humanity and war crimes. A crime against humanity, which systematically targets civilians, *will necessarily be a war crime if carried out during a time of armed conflict*. However, a crime against humanity that occurs in the absence of armed conflict (or before armed conflict) will not constitute a war crime.

For example, an attack on a village to gather together and systematically rape and murder hundreds of schoolgirls, with knowledge of the attack, constitutes a crime against humanity, whether or not it was committed within the context of an armed conflict. However, this same crime, if committed within an international armed conflict, would also constitute a war crime and a violation of Geneva Convention IV.

A war crime that constitutes a systematic attack against a civilian population (e.g., the systematic targeting of schools, hospitals and places of worship in a time of war) will necessarily constitute a crime against humanity. In contrast, the abuse of military prisoners or the intentional and knowing killing of wounded soldiers that have been placed *hors de combat* will not constitute a crime against humanity since it has as its target military personnel rather than civilians.

D Genocide

1 *Overview*

Genocide is defined under Article 6 of the Rome Statute and Article 2 of the Genocide Convention as any of the following acts committed on members of any *national, ethnical, racial* or *religious* group with the intent to destroy it, in whole or in part:

(a) killing members of the group;
(b) causing serious bodily or mental harm to members of the group;
(c) deliberately inflicting on the group conditions of life calculated to bring about its physical destruction in whole or in part;
(d) imposing measures intended to prevent births within the group;
(e) forcibly transferring children of the group to another group.

2 *Elements*

a Overview

The Polish-born U.S. jurist Raphael Lemkin coined the term "genocide" in his book *Axis Rule in Occupied Europe*, published in 1944. The term combines the Greek word γένος (*genos*), meaning "race," "kind" or "people," with the Latin suffix *-cide*, meaning "killing." The term, in its lay meaning, refers to the act of "killing" a race.

Article 6 of the ICC Statute and Article 2 of the Genocide Convention Genocide define genocide as any of the following acts committed on members of any *national, ethnical, racial* or *religious* group with the intent to destroy it, in whole or in part:

(a) killing members of the group;
(b) causing serious bodily or mental harm to members of the group;
(c) deliberately inflicting on the group conditions of life calculated to bring about its physical destruction in whole or in part;
(d) imposing measures intended to prevent births within the group;
(e) forcibly transferring children of the group to another group.

Unlike crimes against humanity and war crimes, the crime of genocide has no *chapeau* or contextual element. It can be committed in times of peace or in armed conflict, and it does not require systematic or widespread acts. What distinguishes it from other international crimes is the special intent element to destroy a protected group in whole or in part, which is further discussed below.

The ICC Elements of Crimes outline a series of elements for each of the five acts constituting genocide (killing, causing serious bodily or mental harm, inflicting on the group conditions of life calculated to bring about its physical destruction, imposing measures to prevent births and forcibly transferring children to another group). The elements for each type of genocide are identical, with the exception of the first element, which corresponds to each specific genocidal act. For example, the elements of genocide by killing are as follows:

Article 6 (a)

Genocide by killing

Elements

1. The perpetrator killed one or more persons.
2. Such person or persons belonged to a particular national, ethnical, racial or religious group.
3. The perpetrator intended to destroy, in whole or in part, that national, ethnical, racial or religious group, as such.
4. The conduct took place in the context of a manifest pattern of similar conduct directed against that group or was conduct that could itself effect such destruction.

In contrast, the elements for genocide by causing serious bodily or mental harm are as follows:

Article 6 (b)

Genocide by causing serious bodily or mental harm

Elements

1. The perpetrator caused serious bodily or mental harm to one or more persons.
2. Such person or persons belonged to a particular national, ethnical, racial or religious group.
3. The perpetrator intended to destroy, in whole or in part, that national, ethnical, racial or religious group, as such.
4. The conduct took place in the context of a manifest pattern of similar conduct directed against that group or was conduct that could itself effect such destruction.

b *Actus Reus*

i Prohibition of Physical or Biological Destruction

The Genocide Convention and customary international law, in general, prohibit only the physical or biological destruction of a human group. A perpetrator must commit any of the aforementioned acts on members of any *national, ethnical, racial* or *religious* group.

The term "destroy" encompasses only acts that amount to physical or biological genocide.[339] This is tantamount to "[t]he material destruction of a group either by physical and biological means and not the destruction of the national, linguistic, religious, cultural or other identity of a particular group."[340]

However, there has been some case law that has adopted a more liberal view of the *actus reus* element for genocide. In a Partial Dissenting Opinion in *The Prosecutor v. Radislav Krstić*, Judge Shahabuddeen held as follows:

> 55. Third, it was contended for the appellant that what happened in Srebrenica was a displacement and not a genocide. Displacement, in the sense of compulsory relocation, is a common feature of wars. According to one commentator, displacement is not genocide even if the consequence is dissolution of the group, a proposition on which I reserve my opinion where it is proven that, there being an initial listed act, the deliberate object of the relocation is to accomplish such a dissolution.
>
> 56. In support of his submission that displacement is not genocide, counsel for the appellant cited the fact that displacement is not listed in article 4(2) of the Statute as one of the means of perpetrating genocide, and he drew a contrast with article 5(d) which specifically sets out deportation as a crime against humanity ...
>
> 57. No doubt, mere displacement does not amount to genocide. But, in this case, there was more than mere displacement. The killings, together with a determined effort to capture others for killing, the forced transportation or exile of the remaining population, and the destruction of homes and places of worship, constituted a single operation which was executed with intent to destroy a group in whole or in part within the meaning of the chapeau to paragraph 2 of article 4 of the Statute. It was this combination of factors to which the Trial Chamber referred when it stated in paragraph 595 of its judgment that the "Bosnian Serb forces knew, by the time they decided to kill all of the military-aged men, that the combination of those killings with the forcible transfer of the women, children and elderly would inevitably result in the physical disappearance of the Bosnian Muslim population at Srebrenica."

ii Prohibited Acts

(1) Killing

Killing members of the protected group is identical to the crime of murder.[341] While the *actus reus* contains no numerical threshold, the scale of the killings can be an important indicator of the necessary special intent.[342] The killing does not necessarily need to be premeditated, but it must be intentional as opposed to resulting from involuntary or negligent behavior.

339. *Prosecutor v. Laurent Semanza*, ICTR-97-20-T, Trial Judgment (15 May 2003), para. 315.
340. *Prosecutor v. Juvenal Kajelijeli*, ICTR-98-44A-T, Trial Judgment (1 December 2003), para. 808.
341. *Prosecutor v. Radoslav Brdjanin*, IT-99-36-T, ICTY Trial Judgment (1 September 2004), paras. 381, 689; *Croatia v. Serbia*, Trial Judgment, ICJ Reports (3 February 2015), p. 3, para. 156.
342. *Prosecutor v. Radovan Karadžić et. al.*, IT-95-5/18-T, Trial Judgment (24 March 2016), para. 543.

(2) Serious Bodily or Mental Harm

Serious harm is such that the acts must "be such as to contribute to the physical or biological destruction of the group, in whole or in part."[343] Bodily or mental harm does not need to be permanent or irremediable, but it must be of such a serious nature as to *threaten the group's destruction in whole or in part*. The effects should be long-lasting. Serious mental harm, in particular, refers to "more than minor or temporary impairment of mental faculties such as the infliction of strong fear or terror, intimidation or threat."[344] However, the harm need not entail "permanent impairment."[345]

Causing "serious bodily or mental harm" includes "acts of torture, inhumane or degrading treatment, sexual violence including rape, interrogations combined with beatings threats of death, and harm that damages health or causes disfigurement or serious injury."[346]

Prisoners held in deplorable conditions and taken for execution, including those who survived, can suffer serious mental harm prior to the executions.[347] Within the *Srebrenica* cases before the ICTY, each of the Bosnian Muslim men targeted for killing was subjected to two of three genocidal acts: "the pre-anguish of death; death itself; and for the males who survived, the anguish of a botched execution."[348] The mental anguish of the women and girls whose fathers, husbands, sons and other male relatives were taken away and executed was ultimately recognized in the 2016 *Karadžić* Trial Judgment.[349]

---

343. *Croatia v. Serbia*, Trial Judgment, ICJ Reports (3 February 2015), p. 3, para. 157; *Prosecutor v. Zdravko Tolimir*, IT-05-88/2-A, ICTY Appeal Judgment (8 April 2015), para. 202 ("serious mental harm must be of such a serious nature as to contribute or tend to contribute to the destruction of all or part of the group").
344. *Prosecutor v. Athanase Seromba*, ICTR-01-66-A, ICTR Appeal Judgment, 12 March 2008, para. 46; *Prosecutor v. Radovan Karadžić*, IT-95-5/18-T, Trial Judgment, 24 March 2016, para. 2580-81 ("many detainees bore serious injuries, had visible wounds, were unable to walk or talk for days, and suffered long-term psychological and physical effects ... rape and other acts of sexual violence, involving serious abuses of a sexual nature").
345. *Prosecutor v. Zdravko Tolimir*, IT-05-88/2-A, ICTY Appeal Judgment (8 April 2015), para. 204.
346. *Prosecutor v. Radoslav Brdjanin*, IT-99-36-T, Trial Judgment (1 September 2004), para. 690.
347. *Prosecutor v. Zdravko Tolimir*, IT-05-88/2-T, Trial Judgment, 12 December 2012, para. 754-755 ("The Chamber finds that the group of men separated in Potocari and taken to the White House, as well as the group of men who surrendered or were captured from the column throughout 13 July, would have become aware at one stage or another of the real possibility that they would ultimately meet their death at the hands of Bosnian Serb Forces who were detaining them. It finds that the suffering of these men, in the days and hours before they were killed, amounted to serious bodily or mental harm ... As such, the Chamber finds that the harm inflicted upon them rises to the level of serious bodily and mental harm, a phrase which, the Chamber recalls, is understood to mean, inter alia, inhumane or degrading treatment, causing serious injury to members of the group"). *See also Prosecutor v. Zdravko Tolimir*, IT-05-88/2-A, ICTY Appeal Judgment, 8 April 2015, paras. 206-207.
348. Patricia Viseur Sellers, "*Genocide Gendered: The Srebrenica Cases*," Proceedings of the Ninth International Humanitarian Law Dialogs, The Fifth Annual Katherine B. Fite Lecture (30 August-1 September 2015).
349. *Prosecutor v. Radovan Karadžić*, IT-95-5/18-T, ICTY Trial Judgment (24 March 2016), para. 5664.

Despite some initial debate within the jurisprudence,[350] the ICTY has determined that, depending on the circumstances of a given case, forcible transfer may cause serious mental harm so as to constitute a prohibited act under Article II of the Genocide Convention.[351]

(3) Conditions Calculated to Bring About Physical Destruction

Inflicting conditions of life calculated to bring about the physical destruction of a group "capture[s] those methods of destruction that do not immediately kill the members of the group, but which, ultimately, seek their physical destruction."[352] Measures designed to bring about death slowly, whether they succeed or not, can satisfy this definition.[353] This "typically relate[s] to the deliberate withholding or taking away of the basic necessities of life over an extended period of time"[354] and has been recognized as including "deprivation of food, medical care, shelter or clothing, as well as lack of hygiene, systematic expulsion from homes, or exhaustion as a result of excessive work or physical exertion."[355]

In the ICJ's 2015 Judgment in *Croatia v. Serbia,* the Court indicated that rape could fall within Article II(c) of the Genocide Convention but noted, in the particular case before the Court, "it has not been shown that these occurrences [of rape] were on such a scale to have amounted also to inflicting conditions of life on the group that were capable of bringing about its physical destruction in whole or in part."[356]

The word "calculated" excludes any requirement of success; all that is required is that the measures be applied with the aim of bringing about the group's physical destruction. A "siege" deployed to cut off the necessities of life of a civilian population in a locality, combined with systematic targeting of the civilian population in a way that

350. *Prosecutor v. Radislav Krstić*, IT-98-33-T, ICTY Trial Judgment (2 August 2001), para 595. The Trial Chamber determined that the forcible transfer, mainly of women and children, from Srebrenica constituted credible evidence of the perpetrators' specific intent to commit genocide against the executed males and against those males who survived executions, but was not an act of genocide in and of itself. The Appeals Chamber upheld the Trial Chamber's determination in *Prosecutor v. Radislav Krstić*, IT-98-33-A, ICTY Appeal Judgment (19 April 2004), para 33.
351. *Prosecutor v. Vujadin Popović et al*, IT-05-88-T, ICTY Trial Judgment (10 June 2010), para. 846; *Prosecutor v. Zdravko Tolimir*, IT-05-88/2-A, ICTY Appeal Judgment (8 April 2015), para. 209.
352. *Prosecutor v. Zdravko Tolimir*, IT-05-88/2-A, ICTY Appeal Judgment (8 April 2015), para 228; *Croatia v. Serbia*, Trial Judgment, ICJ Reports (3 February 2015), p. 3, para. 161.
353. *Prosecutor v. Radovan Karadžić*, IT-95-5/18-T, Trial Judgment (24 March 2016), para. 2586 (while Article 4(2)(a) and (b) refer to acts causing a specific result (i.e., death and serious bodily or mental harm), Article 4(2)(c) concerns "those methods of destruction that do not immediately kill the members of the groups, but which, ultimately, seek their physical destruction," i.e., through slow death"); *Prosecutor v. Zdravko Tolimir*, IT-05-88/2-A, ICTY Appeal Judgment (8 April 2015), para. 233.
354. *Ibid.*, para. 234.
355. *Croatia v. Serbia*, Trial Judgment, ICJ Reports (3 February 2015), p. 3, para. 161.
356. *Bosnia Herzegovina v. Serbia and Montenegro*, ICJ Reports 2007 (26 February 2007), p. 43, paras. 362-364.

was demonstrative of an intent to physically destroy the population, could constitute an *actus reus*.[357]

(4) Prevention of Births

Imposing measures intended to prevent births does not require that the measures succeed, but the measures must be "intended" to achieve that aim. This could manifestly include not only "sexual mutilation, the practice of sterilization, forced birth control, separation of the sexes and prohibition of marriages" but also rape when "a woman of the said group is deliberately impregnated by a man of another group, with the intent to have her give birth to a child who will consequently not belong to its mother's group."[358]

In *Akayesu*, the Trial Chamber noted that "rape can be a measure intended to prevent births when the person raped refuses subsequently to procreate, in the same way that members of a group can be led, through threats or trauma, not to procreate."[359] Indeed, any form of sexual violence or enslavement, or measures committed with the intent of preventing, diminishing or destroying the capacity ... to procreate within the group, fall within this *actus reus*.[360] Such acts, by their nature, lead to the physical or biological destruction of the group.

(5) Forcibly Transferring Children

Forcibly transferring children from their own group to another may constitute biological destruction by preventing the existence of future generations of children in the group. The gravamen of this form of genocide is not, as such, the elimination of the child's affiliation with the group but obstructing "the group's capacity to renew itself" through subsequent generations.[361] However, unlike other *actus reus* elements for the crime of genocide, forcibly transferring children does not necessarily lead to the physical or biological destruction of the group. Moreover, the ICJ has suggested that forced pregnancy that leads to women being forced to give birth to children to be brought up as members of a group other than their own could satisfy the requirements of this *actus reus*.[362]

---

357. *Ibid.*, para. 328 (finding that the siege and the sniping and shelling of Sarajevo did not qualify as this form of *actus reus* because it did not demonstrate an intent to physically destroy the Bosnian population rather than terrorize them into fleeing).
358. *Prosecutor v. Jean-Paul Akayesu*, ICTR-96-4-T, Trial Judgment (2 September 1998), para. 507.
359. *Ibid.*, para. 508.
360. *Croatia v. Serbia*, Trial Judgment, ICJ Reports (3 February 2015), p. 3, para. 166 ("it is necessary that the circumstances of the commission of those acts, and their consequences, are such that the capacity of members of the group to procreate is affected. Likewise, the systematic nature of such acts has to be considered in determining whether they are capable of constituting the *actus reus* of genocide within the meaning of Article II (d) of the Convention").
361. *Croatia v. Serbia*, Trial Judgment, ICJ Reports (3 February 2015), p. 3, para. 136 ("As regards the forcible transfer of children of the group to another group within the meaning of Article II(e), this can also entail the intent to destroy the group physically, in whole or in part, since it can have consequences for the group's capacity to renew itself, and hence to ensure its long-term survival").
362. *Bosnia Herzegovina v. Serbia and Montenegro*, ICJ Reports 2007 (26 February 2007), p. 43, para. 367 ("The Respondent points out that Muslim women who had been raped gave birth to their babies in Muslim territory and consequently the babies would have been brought up not

c Mens Rea

i Overview

What sets genocide apart from war crimes and crimes against humanity is the specific intent ("*dolus specialis*") to eradicate, in whole or in part, a national, ethnical, racial or religious group. The target of destruction for the crime of genocide must be the group, *not* its members as individuals. Accordingly, victims of genocide must be deliberately targeted because of their real or perceived membership in one of the protected groups (national, ethnic, racial or religious).

ii Protected Groups

Four groups are protected under the Genocide Convention, as follows:

(1) National Group

A national group is "a collection of people who are perceived to share a legal bond based on common citizenship, coupled with reciprocity of rights and duties."[363]

(2) Ethnic Group

An ethnic group is "a group whose members share a common language or culture."[364] Unlike race, which is biologically based, ethnicity is largely a social construct. If two groups share the same race but speak different languages, they might have different ethnicities, and yet the same race.

(3) Racial Group

A racial group is "based on the hereditary physical traits often identified with a geographic region, irrespective of linguistic, cultural, national or religious factors."[365] Race is linked to biological factors, such as skin color and hair texture. The main racial groups include White/Caucasian, Hispanic/Latino, Black, Asian, Native American and Pacific Islander, and Middle Eastern/North African.

(4) Religious Group

A religious group is one "whose members share the same religion, denomination or mode of worship."[366]

---

by Serbs but, on the contrary, by Muslims. Therefore, in its view, it cannot be claimed that the children were transferred from one group to the other. The Court, on the basis of the foregoing elements, finds that the evidence placed before it by the Applicant does not establish that there was any form of policy of forced pregnancy, nor that there was any aim to transfer children of the protected group to another group within the meaning of Article II (e) of the Convention").

363. *Prosecutor v. Jean-Paul Akayesu*, ICTR-96-4-T, Trial Judgment (2 September 1998), para. 512.
364. *Ibid.*, para. 513.
365. *Ibid.*, para. 514.
366. *Ibid.*, para. 515.

iii Meaning of "In Whole or In Part"

A perpetrator need not intend to annihilate the entire targeted group. Genocide can be committed against only a part of the group as long as that part is identifiable (including within a geographically limited area) and "substantial."[367]

As mentioned above, there is no numeric threshold of victims necessary to establish genocide. However, to prove intent to destroy a protected group "in part," the part must be a *substantial part* of the group as a whole. The ICTY Appeals Chamber held the following:

> The aim of the Genocide Convention is to prevent the intentional destruction of entire human groups, and the part targeted must be significant enough to have an impact on the group as a whole ... In *Jelisic*, ... the Trial Chamber noted that, "[g]iven the goal of the [Genocide] Convention to deal with mass crimes, it is widely acknowledged that the intention to destroy must target at least a substantial part of the group." The same conclusion was reached by the *Sikirica* Trial Chamber: "This part of the definition calls for evidence of an intention to destroy a substantial number relative to the total population of the group." As these Trial Chambers explained, the substantiality requirement both captures genocide's defining character as a crime of massive proportions and reflects the Convention's concern with the impact the destruction of the targeted part will have on the overall survival of the group.[368]

iv Inference of Intent from Circumstances

The specific intent to destroy can be inferred from circumstances. The ICTY Trial Chamber held that the following factors, amongst others, can be used to infer intent:

(i) the extent of the actual destruction;
(ii) the existence of a state or organizational genocidal plan or policy;
(iii) the perpetration and/or repetition of other destructive or discriminatory acts committed as part of the same pattern of conduct; and
(iv) the utterances of the perpetrator.[369]

With respect to a state or organizational plan or policy, the existence of such a plan or policy is not required to prove genocide, but if there is a plan or policy that, if implemented, will promote genocidal conduct, it may provide evidence of the genocidal intent of those behind that plan or policy.[370]

The ICTY Appeals Chamber held that the "intent to destroy" can also be inferred from:

> the general context, the perpetration of other culpable acts systematically directed against the same group, the scale of atrocities committed, the systematic targeting

367. *Prosecutor v. Ignace Bagilishema*, ICTR-95-1A, ICTR Trial Judgment (7 June 2001), para. 64; *Prosecutor v. Laurent Semanza*, ICTR-97-20-T, Trial Judgment (15 May 2003), para. 316.
368. *Prosecutor v. Radislav Krstid*, IT-98-33-A, Appeal Judgment (19 April 2004), para. 8.
369. *Prosecutor v. Radoslav Brdjanin*, IT-99-36-T, Trial Judgment (1 September 2004), paras. 971-89.
370. *Prosecutor v. Radislav Krstid*, IT-98-33-A, Appeal Judgment (19 April 2004), para. 225.

> of victims on account of their membership of a particular group, or the repetition of destructive and discriminatory acts.[371]

3 *No Numeric Threshold*

There is no numeric threshold of victims necessary to establish genocide. ICTR jurisprudence has held that:

> The *actus reus* of genocide does not require the actual destruction of a substantial part of the group; the commission of even a single instance of one of the prohibited acts is sufficient, provided that the accused genuinely intends by that act to destroy at least a substantial part of the group.[372]

This holding can be read to mean that the killing of even a single individual is hypothetically sufficient to establish genocide. The *actus reus* element of genocide thus does not require the actual destruction of a group or of even a substantial part of such group.

In *Prosecutor v. Ndindabahizi*, the Trial Chamber held that the fact that only a single killing of a single person (Mr. Nors) did not negate the perpetrators' clear intent to destroy the Tutsi population of Kibuye and of Rwanda, in whole or in part, and that Mr. Nors' killers had committed genocide:

> 470. ... On the basis of these facts, the Chamber infers that, in killing Nors, the participants at this roadblock intended to destroy, in whole or in part, the Tutsi ethnic group.
>
> 471. The fact that only a single person was killed on this occasion does not negate the perpetrators' clear intent, which was to destroy the Tutsi population of Kibuye and of Rwanda, in whole or in part.[373]

Any of the acts that constitute genocide may be committed against one or more persons to constitute genocide, provided such acts were committed against a person or persons because of their membership in a protected group. "No acceptable rationale can justify why an individual murder, if committed with the intent to destroy a group 'in whole or in part', should not be qualified as genocide."[374]

A strictly textual reading of the Genocide Convention could lead to the conclusion that a single act is insufficient for purposes of meeting the *actus reus* element of genocide, since the language of the Convention refers to acts in the plural (e.g., "Killing members of the group"; "Causing serious bodily or mental harm to members of the group"; etc.). However, such an interpretation could lead to absurd consequences under certain circumstances. One scholar refers to the following hypothetical situation:

> a substantial part of a protected group is destroyed, the perpetrators all possessed the requisite special intent but each killed only one person. That would result in a

371. *Prosecutor v. Goran Jelisic*, IT-95-10- A, ICTY Appeals Judgment (5 July 2001), para. 47.
372. *Prosecutor v. John Mpambara*, ICTR-01-65-T, Trial Judgment (12 September 2006), para. 8.
373. *Prosecutor v. Ndindabahizi*, ICTR-2001-71-I, Trial Judgment (15 July 2004), paras. 470-71.
374. William Schabas, *Genocide in International Law*, Cambridge University Press (Cambridge, 2000), p. 234.

genocide where none of the perpetrators have actually committed the offense. *Mutatis mutandis*, the same applies to all other prohibited acts as well.[375]

Several countries have thus specified in their domestic legislation that prohibited acts committed against just one person can fulfill the *actus reus* element of genocide. Among these countries are Germany, Fiji, Italy and Uruguay.[376]

4 *Modes of Liability*

Article 3 of the Genocide Convention prohibits the following forms of participation in and crimes of genocide:

- genocide;
- conspiracy to commit genocide;
- direct and public incitement to commit genocide;
- attempt to commit genocide; and
- complicity in genocide.

E Aggression

1 *Overview*

Also termed "crime against peace," the crime of aggression is generally defined under customary international law and the Nuremberg Principles as the planning, preparation, initiation, or waging of any war in violation of international law, treaties, or agreements, including participation, conspiracy, or complicity in the same (*see* Nuremberg Principles VI and VII).

Article 8bis.1 of the Rome Statute, which entered into force on 17 July 2018 (the 20th anniversary of the Rome Statute), defines the crime of aggression as "the planning, preparation, initiation or execution, by a person in a position effectively to exercise control over or to direct the political or military action of a state, of an act of aggression which, by its character, gravity and scale, constitutes a manifest violation of the Charter of the United Nations." However, Article 15bis.5 limits the ICC's ability to exercise jurisdiction over the crime of aggression. It states: "In respect of a State that is not a party to this Statute, the Court shall not exercise its jurisdiction over the crime of aggression when committed by that State's nationals or on its territory."

2 *Elements under the Rome Statute*

The 2013 ICC Elements of Crimes provides the following elements of the crime of aggression under Article 8bis of the Rome Statute:

375. Tamás Hoffman, *The Crime of Genocide: Then and Now*, Brill (Leiden, 2022), § 3.4.
376. *Ibid.*, p. 75.

(1) The perpetrator planned, prepared, initiated or executed an act of aggression.
(2) The perpetrator was a person[377] in a position effectively to exercise control over or to direct the political or military action of the State which committed the act of aggression.
(3) The act of aggression—the use of armed force by a State against the sovereignty, territorial integrity or political independence of another State, or in any other manner inconsistent with the Charter of the United Nations—was committed.
(4) The perpetrator was aware of the factual circumstances that established that such a use of armed force was inconsistent with the Charter of the United Nations.
(5) The act of aggression, by its character, gravity and scale, constituted a manifest violation of the Charter of the United Nations.
(6) The perpetrator was aware of the factual circumstances that established such a manifest violation of the Charter of the United Nations.

Element 3 of the crime of aggression requires "the use of armed force by a State against the sovereignty, territorial integrity or political independence of another State, or in any other manner inconsistent with the Charter of the United Nations." According to the Council of Advisers' Report on the Application of the Rome Statute of the International Criminal Court to Cyberwarfare, the requirement of "armed force" can be satisfied through the use of any weapon, but attacks must be conducted "through kinetic methods of warfare." In other words, an attack that disables another state's military or economic infrastructure through a cyberattack or other means that does not use kinetic force would not qualify as an act of aggression. According to the Council of Advisers' Report on the Application of the Rome Statute of the International Criminal Court to Cyberwarfare:

> In discussing the meaning of the word "armed," the Council of Advisers agreed that any use of force regardless of the specific weapon used, would satisfy the use of "armed force" element for what constitutes an act of aggression under Article 8bis. The International Court of Justice in its advisory opinion about nuclear weapons makes clear that use of force may be accomplished "regardless of the weapons employed." There is no reason to treat the situation differently from equivalent attacks conducted through kinetic methods of warfare.[378]

Therefore, the attack of aggression under the Rome Statute requires that: (i) a weapon be used; and (ii) the attacks be conducted through kinetic methods of warfare.

377. With respect to an act of aggression, more than one person may be in a position that meets these criteria.
378. "The Council of Advisers' Report on the Application of the Rome Statute of the International Criminal Court to Cyberwarfare," Permanent Mission of Lichtenstein to the United Nations (August 2021), p. 10.

3 *Elements under Customary International Law*

a *The Nuremberg Principles as Customary International Law*

The Nuremberg Principles of the Nuremberg Charter, which have been reaffirmed in the statutes of international criminal tribunals, are widely considered to represent customary international law. U.N. General Assembly resolution 95 (I), adopted on 11 December 1946, affirmed the principles of international law recognized by the Charter of the Nuremberg Tribunal and the judgment of the Tribunal (the Nuremberg Principles). By "affirming" those principles, the General Assembly:

> intended to express its approval of and support for the general concepts and legal constructs of criminal law that could be derived from the IMT Charter and had been set out, either explicitly or implicitly, by the IMT. Translated into law-making terms, this approval and support meant that the world community had robustly set in motion the process for turning the principles at issue into general principles of customary law binding on member States of the whole international community.[379]

While the Nuremberg Principles were never formally adopted or rejected by the U.N. General Assembly, it would be appropriate to hold that "General Assembly resolution 95 (I) strongly contributed to giving the Nürnberg principles the customary law status they have today."[380]

b *Definition of "Crime Against Peace" under Nuremberg Principle VI*

Also termed "crime against peace," the crime of aggression under customary international law, as reflected in Principle VI of the Nuremberg Principles, is defined as follows:

> The crimes hereinafter set out are punishable as crimes under international law:
>
> (a) Crimes against peace:
> (i) Planning, preparation, initiation or waging of a war of aggression or a war in violation of international treaties, agreements or assurances;
> (ii) Participation in a common plan or conspiracy for the accomplishment of any of the acts mentioned under (i).

The Nuremberg Charter does not specifically define "war of aggression," but this term is generally understood to mean a military conflict waged without the justification of self-defense, usually for territorial gain and subjugation. The term "aggression" was defined in U.N. General Assembly Resolution 3314 on 14 December 1974 as follows:

---

379. Antonio Cassese, "Affirmation of the Principles of International Law recognized by the Charter of the Nürnberg Tribunal," Audiovisual Library of International Law, United Nations (June 2009).
380. *Ibid.*

> Aggression is the use of armed force by a State against the sovereignty, territorial integrity or political independence of another State, or in any other manner inconsistent with the Charter of the United Nations, as set out in this Definition.

However, the Nuremberg Charter also allows for a second, broader definition that does not specifically reference "war of aggression" or the use of "armed" force. That second definition refers to "war in violation of international treaties, agreements or assurances." It would seem that under this second, broader definition, acts of aggression that violate international treaties, including potentially cyberattacks and information warfare that violate the sovereignty of states, would constitute crimes against peace, regardless of whether they involve armed force.

This Nuremberg definition is thus wider than the definition adopted by the Rome Statute, as it includes the planning, preparation, initiation or waging of either a war of aggression or any war in violation of international treaties, agreements or assurances. Therefore, a war that violates a state's rights under an international human rights law treaty could constitute the crime of aggression under Nuremberg Principle VI. However, such a war would not qualify as a crime of aggression under the Rome Statute unless it was inconsistent with the Charter of the United Nations.

F Mental Element (*Mens Rea*)

1 *Overview*

Under Article 30 of the SICC, both intent and knowledge constitute the requisite *mens rea* for the commission of an international crime:

> Unless otherwise provided, a person shall be criminally responsible and liable for punishment for a crime within the jurisdiction of the Court only if the material elements are committed with intent and knowledge.

2 *Intent*

A person has intent where (Article 30.2 SICC):

(a) In relation to conduct, that person *means to engage in the conduct.*
(b) In relation to a consequence, that *person means to cause that consequence or is aware that it will occur in the ordinary course of events.*

3 *Knowledge*

"Knowledge" means "awareness that a circumstance exists or a consequence will occur in the ordinary course of events" (Article 30.3 SICC).

III CRIMINAL LIABILITY FOR INTERNATIONAL CRIMES

A Individual Criminal Responsibility of State and Non-state Actors

1 *Introduction: International Criminal Tribunals and Individual Responsibility*

Historically, individual actors were not seen as subjects or objects of international law. However, this changed beginning with the Nuremberg IMT and later with the IMT for the Far East, both of which tried and convicted a number of state actors for violations of international law, making it clear that individuals, not nations, commit violations of international humanitarian and human rights law. The 1947 Nuremberg IMT Judgment and Sentence held that:[381]

> the very essence of the [Nuremberg] Charter is that individuals have international duties which transcend the national obligations of obedience imposed by the individual state ... [C]rimes against international law are committed by men, not by abstract entities, and only by punishing individuals who commit such crimes can the provisions of international law be enforced.

In the 1990s, this concept was taken further with the ICTY and ICTR, which operated on the basis that even non-state individual actors could be held responsible for violations of international law (with the ICTY actually convicting a number of such actors). The ICTY Statute addresses individual criminal responsibility by holding individuals rather than states accountable for violations of international humanitarian law. Article 7 of the ICTY Statute states:

> 1. A person who planned, instigated, ordered, committed or otherwise aided and abetted in the planning, preparation or execution of a crime referred to in articles 2 to 5 of the present Statute, shall be *individually responsible* for the crime.
>
> ...
>
> 3. The fact that any of the acts referred to in articles 2 to 5 of the present Statute was committed by a subordinate *does not relieve his superior of criminal responsibility* if he *knew or had reason to know* that the subordinate was about to commit such acts or had done so and the superior *failed to take the necessary and reasonable measures* to prevent such acts or to punish the perpetrators thereof.
>
> 4. The fact that an accused person *acted pursuant to an order* of a Government or of a superior *shall not relieve him of criminal responsibility,* but may be considered in mitigation of punishment if the International Tribunal determines that justice so requires. [emphasis added]

In a similar fashion, U.N. Security Council Resolution 955 (1994), which created the ICTR, stated that persons committing violations of humanitarian law in Rwanda were individually responsible. Expressing its "grave concern at the reports indicating that genocide and other systematic, widespread and flagrant violations of international

381. *Ibid.*, p. 2; *see also* Robert Cryer, "International Criminal Law," in Daniel Moeckli et al. (eds.), *International Human Rights Law*, Oxford University Press (2018), p. 522.

humanitarian law have been committed in Rwanda,"[382] the Security Council determined it was necessary to assign individual criminal responsibility to bring justice to those individually responsible for such crimes. Article 6 of the Statue of the ICTR, incorporating language that is almost identical to that of Article 7 of the ICTY, states that:

> A person who planned, instigated, ordered, committed or otherwise aided and abetted in the planning, preparation or execution of a crime referred to in articles 2 to 4 of the present Statute, shall be *individually responsible* for the crime.

As yet another international criminal justice mechanism, we may point to the ICC, which potentially has worldwide jurisdiction against individual actors, provided the perpetrator is a national of a state party or if the persecutory act was committed on the territory of a state party or on a vessel or aircraft registered with a state party. The Statute of the ICC provides for individual criminal responsibility of not only state actors but also of non-state actors acting pursuant to an organizational policy to commit attacks, as discussed under "Individual Criminal Responsibility of Non-State Actors," *infra*.

2 *Individual Criminal Responsibility of State Actors*

State actors are those acting with a nexus to state action. Criminal responsibility may be placed on individual state actors under international law. As an example, we may consider the Nuremberg trials under the 1945 London Charter for the International Military Tribunal. At the time, individual criminal responsibility for violations of international law was a novel idea, yet the Nuremberg Tribunal held that "crimes against international law are committed by men, not by abstract entities and only by punishing individuals who commit such crimes can the provisions of international law be enforced."

On this basis, the International Military Tribunal prosecuted state individual actors for *war crimes*, *crimes against humanity* and *crimes against peace* (aggression). All of the defendants had a nexus with state action because they were Nazi officials or private industrialists with a link to Nazi state action.

The International Military Tribunal did not, however, address the question of whether international law could be violated by private non-state actors, such as members of militias, volunteer corps, organized resistance movements or organized armed groups not forming a part of or belonging to the armed forces of a state party to a conflict. This question came to be examined by subsequent international tribunals.

3 *Individual Criminal Responsibility of Non-state Actors*

With the increased recognition of non-state actors as violators of international law, there has been renewed and increasing interest in assigning responsibility and

382. U.N. Security Council Resolution 955 (1994), p. 1.

accountability to them for their acts. There has thus been a trend in both domestic as well as international law to find jurisdiction in cases brought against non-state actors.

a *Jurisdiction of Domestic Courts: The Case of* Kadic v. Karadzic *(U.S. 2d Cir. 1995)*

As an example of this trend, we can consider the case *Kadic v. Karadzic* (U.S. 2d Cir. Ct. App. 1995), where the U.S. Second Circuit Court examined the individual criminal responsibility of Radovan Karadžić, the President of Republika Srpska, one of the two administrative divisions of Bosnia and Herzegovina, and whether he could be sued civilly in the U.S. under the Alien Tort Claims Act ("ATCA"), which allows suit to be brought in U.S. federal courts by aliens for torts committed outside of the U.S. "in violation of the law of nations or a treaty of the United States" (28 USC 1350). By "law of nations," the statute refers to public international law comprised not only of international treaties but also customary international law and general principles of law. Most of the alleged violations of international law are international crimes. The court assumed that if these offenses are crimes under international law, they are also the basis of a civil suit brought under the ATCA.

The court dealt with the question of whether a private non-state actor could commit crimes against humanity, genocide, and war crimes. The Nuremberg Tribunal did not answer these questions because all of defendants were Nazi officials or private industrialists with a nexus to Nazi state action. In other words, they were private *state* actors rather than private *non*-state actors. The court held that crimes against humanity, genocide, and war crimes *can* be committed by private non-state actors:[383]

> We do not agree that the law of nations, as understood in the modern era, confines its reach to state action. Instead, we hold that certain forms of conduct violate the law of nations whether undertaken by those acting under the auspices of a state or only as private individuals.

The Court cited the Restatement 3d of the Foreign Relations Law of the U.S. in defending its position:

> "Individuals may be held liable for offenses against international law, such as piracy, war crimes and genocide." Restatement (Third) pt. II, introductory note. The Restatement is careful to identify those violations that are actionable when committed by a state, Restatement (Third) § 702, and a more limited category of violations of "universal concern," id. § 404, partially overlapping with those listed in section 702. Though the immediate focus of section 404 is to identify those offenses for which a state has jurisdiction to punish without regard to territoriality or the nationality of the offenders, cf. id. § 402(1)(a), (2), the inclusion of piracy and slave trade from an earlier era and aircraft hijacking from the modern era demonstrates that the offenses of "universal concern" include those capable of being committed by non-state actors.

383. Peter Baehr, *The Role of the Nation-State in the 21st Century: Human Rights, International Organizations and Foreign Policy*, Kluwer Law International (Cambridge, 1998), p. 58.

The appeals court thus reversed the district court's dismissal and permitted the case to move forward on the merits.

b *Accountability in International Courts*

i ICTY and ICTR

While the London Charter's definition of crimes against humanity could *potentially* apply to acts undertaken by non-state actors, the ICTY and ICTR conclusively established that international crimes could be committed by non-state actors. As discussed above, the ICTY actually convicted a number of non-state actors for crimes against humanity.

ii ICC

The ICC similarly allows prosecutions of individual non-state actors. In defining "crimes against humanity," the SICC requires that attacks directed against any civilian population involve a "course of conduct involving the multiple commission [of murder, extermination, enslavement, etc., mentioned in Article 7.1 SICC] against any civilian population, pursuant to or in furtherance of a state or *organizational policy* to commit such attack" (Article 7.2 SICC) (emphasis added). Thus, by including "organizational" policies in addition to "State" policies, the SICC contemplated acts by organizations, such as insurrection movements, armed non-state actors or other groups that may not have a clear nexus with state action.

B Modes of Liability

1 Commission

The Statutes of the U.N.-created or U.N.-affiliated international criminal tribunals impose individual criminal responsibility on any person who planned, instigated, ordered, aided and abetted or committed the crimes over which they have jurisdiction.[384] The commission of a crime requires proof that the accused "physically or directly perpetrated a crime or caused a culpable omission in violation of criminal law."[385] This perpetration can be performed "physically or otherwise directly, alone or jointly with others, in the material elements of the crime."[386] The *mens rea* is that the

384. *See* Art. 7 ICTY Statute ("A person who planned, instigated, ordered, committed or otherwise aided and abetted in the planning, preparation or execution of a crime ... shall be individually responsible for the crime"); Art. 6 ICTR Statute; Art. 6 SCSL Statute; Art. 3(a) STL Statute ("Committed, participated as accomplice, organized or directed others to commit"); Art. 29 ECCC Law.

385. *See Prosecutor v. Zdravko Tolimir*, IT-05-88/2, ICTY Trial Judgment (12 Dec 2012), para. 884. *Ibid.*

386. *Ibid.*

perpetrator acted with intent to commit the crime or possessed an awareness of the substantial likelihood that the crime would occur as a consequence of his conduct.

2 *Joint Criminal Enterprise*

The commission of an international crime includes "joint criminal enterprise" ("JCE"), which has the following variants:

- JCE I arises when all participants act pursuant to a common purpose that "amount[s] to or involve[s] the commission of a crime provided for in the Statute."[387] The minimum *actus reus* is making a "significant contribution" to the crimes within the common purpose.[388]
- JCE II is a slight variation of JCE I that involves the same requirements of *mens rea* and *actus reus*, but as performed through organized systems or institutions, such as the running concentration camps.[389]
- JCE III arises when participants have agreed on a common purpose involving the perpetration of a crime or crimes, but crimes are committed that fall outside of the scope of the common purpose, which are nevertheless a natural and foreseeable consequence of effectuating that common purpose.[390] Liability arises if "under the circumstances of the case, (i) it was *foreseeable* that such a crime might be perpetrated by one or other members of the group and (ii) the accused *willingly took that risk*."[391] This form of JCE III liability has been recognized as part of customary international law and applied in several cases before the ICTY,[392] and rejected as not part of customary international law at the ECCC.[393]

The ICC has not recognized JCE as a mode of liability. Instead, it has incorporated the concept of "co-perpetration,"[394] which adopts the following language, which is distinct from that adopted by the U.N.-backed tribunals:

---

387. *Prosecutor v. Momcilo Krajišnik*, IT-00-39-A, ICTY Appeal Judgment (17 March 2009), para. 704; *Prosecutor v. Dusko Tadić*, ICTY, IT-94-1-A, Appeal Judgment (15 July 1999), paras. 196-201.
388. *Prosecutor v. Radoslav Brđanin*, IT-99-36-A, ICTY Appeal Judgment (3 April 2007), para. 430.
389. *Prosecutor v. Dusko Tadić*, IT-94-1-A, ICYT Appeal Judgment (15 July 1999), paras 202-203.
390. *Ibid.*, para. 204; *Prosecutor v. Momcilo Krajišnik*, IT-00-39-T, Trial Judgment (27 September 2006), para. 882.
391. *Prosecutor v. Dusko Tadić*, IT-94-1-A, ICTY Appeal Judgment (15 July 1999), para. 228 (emphasis in original). *See also Prosecutor v. Marislov Kvočka et al.*, IT-98-30/1-A, ICTY Appeal Judgment (28 February 2005), para. 83.
392. *See, e.g., Prosecutor v. Milomir Stakić*, IT-97-24-A, ICTY Appeal Judgment (22 March 2006), para. 98; *Prosecutor v. Martić*, IT-95-11-T, ICTY Trial Judgment (12 June 2007), para. 435; *Prosecutor v. Jadranko Prlić et. al.*, IT-04-74-A, ICTY Appeal Judgment (29 November 2017), paras. 587, 591.
393. *Prosecutors v. Noun Chea et. al.*, 002/19-09-2007-ECCC/SC, ECCC Appeal Judgment (23 November 2016), para. 807 ("The Supreme Court Chamber finds that criminal liability based on making a contribution to the implementation of a common criminal purpose was, at the time relevant to the charges in the case at hand, limited to crimes that were actually encompassed by the common purpose").
394. Article 25(3)(a) ICC Statute.

> 3. In accordance with this Statute, a person shall be criminally responsible and liable for punishment for a crime within the jurisdiction of the Court if that person:
>
> (a) Commits such a crime, whether as an individual, jointly with another or through another person, regardless of whether that other person is criminally responsible

This language has been expressly rejected by the ICTY as not being part of customary international law.[395]

IV INTERNATIONAL CRIMINAL TRIBUNALS

A Introduction

1 *The Judicialization of Human Rights and Criminal Law*

The history of international, ad hoc, hybrid and domestic human rights and criminal courts and tribunals has had a checkered history. On the one hand, such institutions have established a clear message that violators of international criminal and human rights law will be brought to justice; on the other hand, they have, in many cases, been viewed with skepticism by local populations, who may see them as political tools to prosecute some actors while letting others go free. An effective approach to human rights advocacy demands that the judicialization of human rights should not be privileged over context-specific solutions for human rights. Rather, the two should work hand-in-hand as complementary elements of broader advocacy efforts to maximize human rights protection. Courts, as necessary institutions in the interpretation and enforcement of human rights law, should be used together with political and context-specific solutions in effecting human rights protection.

Within the international criminal and human rights sphere, judicialization can refer to the establishment of domestic or international tribunals and courts dealing with egregious violations of human rights, which, in many cases, involves violations of international criminal law. Judicialization may or may not represent the most effective approach to addressing human rights abuses. As discussed by Jane Stromseth, the establishment of international tribunals competes for "international funding and attention with struggling domestic justice systems" and may result in tensions and resentments.[396] At the same time, international tribunals, and in particular hybrid tribunals, have brought about a great deal of good to local judicial and human rights

395. *Prosecutor v. Milomir Stakić*, IT-97-24-A, ICTY Appeal Judgment (22 March 2006), para. 62 ("Upon a careful and thorough review of the relevant sections of the Trial Judgment, the Appeals Chamber finds that the Trial Chamber erred in conducting its analysis of the responsibility of the Appellant within the framework of "co-perpetratorship." This mode of liability, as defined and applied by the Trial Chamber, does not have support in customary international law or in the settled jurisprudence of this Tribunal, which is binding on the Trial Chambers").
396. Jane E. Stromseth, "Justice on the Ground: Can International Criminal Courts Strengthen Domestic Rule of Law in Post-Conflict Societies?," 1 *Hague Journal on the Rule of Law* (2009), p. 90 available at <https://doi.org/10.1017/s1876404509000876>.

protection systems. Hybrid tribunals such as the Special Court for Sierra Leone, the Special Panels for Serious Crimes in Dili District Court (East Timor) and the Extraordinary Chambers in the Courts of Cambodia bring to local communities a variety of benefits, allowing local staff to interact with international judges and prosecutors who impart best practices and ensure capacity-building and international standards in international criminal and human rights prosecutions.

In many cases, the judicialization of human rights via domestic, hybrid, ad hoc or international tribunals should be deployed along with context-specific solutions, such as national reconciliation campaigns. Particularly in post-conflict and transitional justice nations where civil society has been largely decimated by egregious violations of human rights, context-specific solutions may be a better means of addressing human rights abuses. In these nations, context-specific solutions such as truth commissions or amnesty may be more effective in achieving national healing and the restoration of civil society than prosecution via international and domestic tribunals.

In some ways, the question of context-specific solutions and the judicialization of human rights presents a false dichotomy; in reality, the two are interdependent. The establishment of international, ad hoc or hybrid tribunals cannot be divorced from the need to deploy political solutions. In the case of the genocides of the former Yugoslavia and Rwanda, for example, the judicialization of human rights and prosecution of their violations would have been avoided had the same political will that set up the ICTY and ICTR prevented the genocides, to begin with. The nations that pushed the U.N. Security Council to issue resolutions to establish the ICTY and ICTR were the very nations that failed to act to prevent the genocides to begin with.

B Overview of Permanent, Ad Hoc and Hybrid Institutions

Violations of international criminal law may be prosecuted by any of the following entities:

- the permanent ICC;
- ad hoc international courts, which may be:
  - created by select members of the international community, such as the Nuremberg International Military Tribunal or the International Military Tribunal for the Far East, which investigate and prosecute crimes within a certain territory and during a certain time; or
  - created by the U.N. Security Council, such as the International Criminal Tribunal for the former Yugoslavia and the International Criminal Tribunal for Rwanda;
- hybrid institutions that combine some of the elements of ad hoc courts created by individual states and ad hoc courts created by the U.N., as with the Special Court for Sierra Leone and the Special Tribunal for Lebanon. They are generally established in coordination between a national government and the U.N., though they can also be established under national legislation as domestic courts with international elements, such as foreign judges or prosecutors that participate in proceedings.

C The International Criminal Court

1 Overview

The International Criminal Court ("ICC"), based at The Hague, is the first permanent, treaty-based, international criminal court established to help end impunity for the perpetrators of serious crimes of concern to the international community. The ICC is an independent international organization and is not part of the United Nations system. Although the Court's expenses are funded primarily by states parties, it also receives voluntary contributions from governments, international organizations, individuals, corporations and other entities.

The Statute of the ICC ("Rome Statute") established and governs the ICC. It was adopted at a diplomatic conference in Rome in 1998 and entered into force in 2002, with operations beginning on 1 July 2002.

2 Subject Matter Jurisdiction

Under Article 5 of the Rome Statute, the ICC has subject matter jurisdiction over *genocide, crimes against humanity* and *war crimes* (Article 5.1 SICC). Moreover, on 15 December 2017, states parties to the Rome Statute agreed to activate the ICC's jurisdiction over the crime of *aggression*, granting an international tribunal jurisdiction to hold leaders criminally accountable for waging war for the first time since the Nuremberg International Military Tribunal and the International Military Tribunal for the Far East undertook this task at the close of WWII. For any crime to fall within the jurisdiction of the ICC, it must have been committed after 1 July 2002, when the SICC came into effect.

For a detailed treatment of the definitions and elements of the crimes under the SICC, *see* "International Crimes" above.

3 Personal Jurisdiction

a Cases Referred to the ICC by States Parties or Initiated by the ICC Prosecutor Proprio Motu

i Overview

In cases referred to the ICC by states parties or initiated by the ICC Prosecutor *proprio motu*, the ICC may exercise personal jurisdiction over the accused if one of the following preconditions is met:

- one or more of the following states are parties to the Rome Statute:
  - "The State on the territory of which the conduct in question occurred or, if the crime was committed on board a vessel or aircraft, the State of registration of that vessel or aircraft" (Article 12.2(a) SICC);

- "The State of which the person accused of the crime is a national" (Article 12.2(b) SICC; *see also* Article 12.1 SICC, which grants the ICC personal jurisdiction over the nationals of any State that becomes a party to the SICC); or
- one of the states mentioned in the preceding paragraph, if not party to the SICC, yet its acceptance is required under Article 12.2 SICC, that state, by declaration lodged with the Registrar, accepts "the exercise of jurisdiction by the Court with respect to the crime in question" (Article 12.3 SICC).

Therefore, the ICC may exercise jurisdiction in any of these cases:

- the crime was committed in the territory of an ICC Member State or on board a vessel or aircraft registered with a Member State (Article 12.2(a) SICC);
- the accused is a national of a state party to the Rome Statute (Article 12.2(b) SICC); or
- the state in question agrees to jurisdiction (Article 12.3 SICC).

ii Cases Partially Committed on the Territory of a State Party

A 2018 ICC Pre-Trial Chamber ruling held that the ICC may exercise jurisdiction over atrocities committed by nationals of a state not party to the Rome Statute in the territory of a state not party to the Rome Statute if the atrocities trigger a stream of refugees into the territory of an ICC state party. The ruling related to a request of the Prosecutor regarding the deportation of the Rohingya people from Myanmar (a non-state party) into the territory of Bangladesh (an ICC state party). The ICC Pre-Trial Chamber first distinguished between *deportation* (displacement across an international border) and *forcible transfer* (internal displacement within national borders), both of which are defined as crimes against humanity under Article 7.1.d of the Rome Statute. The Chamber then held that it may exercise jurisdiction if part of the crime of deportation was committed on the territory of a state party to the Rome Statute:[397]

> ... acts of deportation initiated in a State not Party to the Statute (through expulsion or other coercive acts) and completed in a State Party to the Statute (by virtue of victims crossing the border to a State) fall within the parameters of article 12(2)(a) of the Statute [jurisdiction for conduct committed on the territory of a state party to the Statute]. It follows that ... the Court has jurisdiction over the alleged deportation of members of the Rohingya people from Myanmar to Bangladesh, provided that such allegations are established to the required threshold.

The Myanmar precedent might open the door to ICC investigations of other crimes committed in non-states parties that trigger refugee influxes in states parties. The Guernica Centre for International Justice, for example, cited the 2018 ruling by the

397. Decision on the Prosecution's Request for a Ruling on Jurisdiction under Art. 19(3) of the Statute, ICC-RoC46(3)-01/18-37, Request Under Reg. 46(3) (6 September 2018), para. 73, available at <https://www.icc-cpi.int/CourtRecords/CR2018_04203.PDF>.

ICC Pre-Trial Chamber concerning jurisdiction over the situation involving the Rohingya as a precedent for investigating international crimes committed in Syria:[398]

> Although Myanmar was not a State Party to the Rome Statute, Bangladesh is, and therefore it was held that given that civilians were forcibly deported from Myanmar to Bangladesh, jurisdiction was conferred ... the situation concerning Syria, with reference to those civilians forcibly deported into Jordan, is akin to the situation considered in that ruling, in that although Syria is not a State Party, Jordan is, and therefore, jurisdiction is conferred ...
>
> Given the parallels to be drawn between the situation concerning the Rohingya in Bangladesh and Syrians in Jordan, we are hopeful the OTP will accept the argument that it has jurisdiction over certain crimes suffered by the Syrian civil population, including instances of Forced Deportation, Persecution, and Other Cruel and Inhumane Treatment.

Prosecuting the crime of deportation "enables the ICC to investigate, at a minimum, all perpetrators allegedly responsible for the crime under consideration without being forced to exempt any perpetrators from the outset, for example, on the basis of nationality."[399] However, if there is no direct intent for the crime of deportation, the ICC Prosecutor would need to prove "the severity of the coercive environment, the contribution and responsibility of those investigated, as well as the absence of genuine choice of the refugees."[400] It may be possible for the ICC prosecutor to demonstrate that some level of *dolus eventualis* would suffice to meet the *mens rea* element of the crime.

b Cases Referred to the ICC by the U.N. Security Council

It is important to note that Article 12.2 limits its applications to cases in which a crime is referred to the ICC Prosecutor by a state party (Article 13(a) SICC) or the prosecutor has initiated an investigation *proprio motu* (Article 13(c) SICC). Article 12.2 does *not* therefore apply to crimes referred to the prosecutor of the ICC by the Security Council acting under chapter VII of the Charter. In such cases referred to the prosecutor by the Security Council, the ICC may exercise jurisdiction (Article 13(b) SICC), regardless of whether the crime was committed in the territory or on board a vessel or aircraft of a Member State, the nationality of the accused and whether the state in question agrees to the jurisdiction. This was the case of the Security Council's referral of the situation in Darfur to the ICC prosecutor in 2005 and Libya in 2011.

398. The Guernica Centre for International Justice, "The Guernica Centre for International Justice Files Article 15 Communication with the ICC Office of the Prosecutor on the Situation in the Syrian Arab Republic, Press Release (4 March 2019), pp. 2-3, available at <https://perma.cc/GTY8-QQ79>.
399. Jörn Oliver Eiermann, "Investigating Nationals of States Not Party to the Rome Statute," *UCLA Journal of International Law and Foreign Affairs*, Vol. 24, No. 2 (2020), p. 258.
400. *Ibid.*, p. 269.

c *Summary*

The ICC may therefore exercise jurisdiction in any of these cases:

<table>
<tr><td rowspan="4">1.</td><td rowspan="4">State Referrals or Case Initiation by the Prosecutor
A state party has referred a case to the ICC Prosecutor (Article 13(a) SICC) or the prosecutor has initiated an investigation proprio motu (Article 13(c) SICC) and:</td><td>A. The crime was committed in the territory of a state party to the Rome Statute or on board a vessel or aircraft registered with a state party to the Rome Statute (Article 12.2(a) SICC);</td></tr>
<tr><td>B. The accused is a national of a state party to the Rome Statute (Article 12.2(b) SICC); or</td></tr>
<tr><td>C. The state in question agrees to jurisdiction (Article 12.3 SICC).</td></tr>
<tr><td>D. A crime is partially committed on the territory of a state party (e.g., where crimes trigger a stream of refugees into the territory of an ICC state party).</td></tr>
</table>

or

2.	*Security Council Referrals* The Security Council refers the case to the ICC Prosecutor (Article 13(b)).

4 *Issues of Admissibility; Principle of Complementarity*

a *Overview*

Article 1 of the Statute of the ICC establishes the principle of complementarity:

> An International Criminal Court ("the Court") is hereby established. It shall be a permanent institution and shall have the power to exercise its jurisdiction over persons for the most serious crimes of international concern, as referred to in this Statute, and shall be *complementary* to national criminal jurisdictions.

Complementarity refers to the fact that the ICC only acts if states have failed to genuinely carry out an investigation or prosecution. In this vein, Article 17 of the Statute of the ICC characterizes cases as inadmissible before the ICC when:

- the case is being investigated or prosecuted by a state which has jurisdiction over it, unless the state is unwilling or unable genuinely to carry out the investigation or prosecution. This is known as the "principle of complementarity";
- the case has been investigated by a state which has jurisdiction over it, and the state has decided not to prosecute the person concerned unless the decision resulted from the unwillingness or inability of the state genuinely to prosecute;

- the person concerned has already been tried for conduct which is the subject of the complaint, and a trial by the ICC is not permitted under Article 20.3 prohibiting retrials of individuals; or
- the case is not of sufficient gravity to justify further action by the ICC.

The principle of complementarity seeks to further three important policy objectives:

- to protect the accused if they have been prosecuted before domestic courts;
- to respect national sovereignty in the exercise of criminal jurisdiction; and
- to promote greater efficiency in avoiding the duplication of investigation and prosecution.

b *Case Study*

To demonstrate the principle of complementarity, one may consider the following hypothetical cases in which a state has committed 50 war crimes in an armed conflict:

i The State Is Investigating and Prosecuting All 50 War Crimes

As long as the prosecutions focus on the same perpetrators and substantially the same underlying conduct and, provided the prosecutions are genuine (not intended to shield the perpetrators from criminal liability), the ICC may not act.

ii The State Is Investigating and Prosecuting 20 of the War Crimes

In this case, the ICC could investigate the 30 war crimes that are not being investigated and prosecuted, subject to the requirements above with respect to the 20 war crimes that are being investigated, but likely would not do so if the state in question is already investigating 30 war crimes. This latter issue is a policy decision rather than a legal question.

iii The State Is Investigating and Prosecuting 1 of the War Crimes

The ICC could investigate the 49 war crimes not being investigated, subject to the requirements above with respect to the one war crime being investigated. If only one war crime were being investigated, the ICC Prosecutor may deem that the state is unwilling or unable genuinely to carry out the investigation or prosecution and may seek to initiate an investigation into all 50 war crimes.

iv The State in Question Is Investigating and Prosecuting a Corporation That Allegedly Financed and Provided Supplies for War Crimes, but None of the Direct Perpetrators Are Being Investigated

In this case, the ICC could investigate and prosecute the direct perpetrators of the war crimes. The ICC may also be able to investigate and prosecute the corporate officers and directors if they are not also being prosecuted along with the corporation.

v The State in Question Is Not Investigating or Prosecuting the 50 War Crimes, but Several European States Are Investigating and Prosecuting Them under Their Universal Jurisdiction Statutes

The ICC would be precluded from acting on any of the war crimes because they are being "investigated or prosecuted by a state which has jurisdiction" over them, regardless of the fact that the states in question are exercising universal jurisdiction. The basis for jurisdiction does not matter in terms of complementarity.

vi No State Is Investigating or Prosecuting the War Crimes, but a Regional Court Has Opened a Criminal Investigation

This hypothetical could come to fruition when the Malabo Protocol goes into effect and the African Court of Justice and Human Rights, a regional court with jurisdiction over international crimes, becomes operational. According to the black letter of the Rome Statute, the establishment of a regional criminal court investigating the crimes would not preclude the ICC from acting. The language of Article 17 of the Rome Statute is state-centric; it only precludes the ICC from acting if a case is being investigated or prosecuted by a "state" which has jurisdiction over it unless the state is unwilling or unable genuinely to carry out the investigation or prosecution. Article 17 makes no mention of an international tribunal or other international organization acting.

Alternatively, one can argue that when states come together to form an international tribunal or other international organization to investigate international criminal cases, the cases are, in fact, being investigated indirectly by states through the organizations they have formed to act on their behalf. These organizations are, in a sense, proxies of states. The fact that states are acting to promote accountability by establishing and funding international criminal mechanisms likely fulfills the requirement of states to genuinely carry out investigations and prosecutions, thereby making such cases inadmissible before the ICC.

However, this issue remains an open question that will ultimately need to be decided by a judicial ruling. Even if a judicial ruling held that such cases were admissible before the ICC, it is unlikely that the Office of the Prosecutor, given its limited resources, would pursue a case against the same suspects for substantially the same conduct if a regional court were genuinely investigating it.

5 *Case Initiation*

a Overview

Once one of the above preconditions leading to the jurisdiction of the ICC occurs, the Court may exercise competence if:

(a) a crime over which the ICC appears to have jurisdiction is referred to the prosecutor of the ICC by a state *party*, according to Article 14 SICC (Article 13.a SICC);
(b) a crime over which the ICC appears to have jurisdiction is referred to the prosecutor of the ICC by the *Security Council* acting under chapter VII of the Charter (Article 13.b SICC); or
(c) the *prosecutor* of the ICC has initiated an investigation *proprio motu* with respect to such a crime in accordance with Article 15 SICC on the basis of information received from individuals or organizations (Article 13.c SICC). In this case, the Prosecutor must submit to the Pre-Trial Chamber a request for authorization of an investigation, and the Pre-Trial Chamber must find a reasonable basis to proceed with an investigation (Article 15.2-.3 SICC).

Thus, individual victims of alleged international crimes may have their cases heard only if: (i) their state prosecutors refer the crimes to the prosecutor of the ICC; (ii) the Security Council refers the case to the ICC; or (iii) the prosecutor of the ICC initiates an investigation *propio motu*.

b The Case of Darfur

Acting under Chapter VII of the United Nations Charter, the Security Council referred the situation in Darfur since 1 July 2002 to the ICC Prosecutor by adopting Resolution 1593 (2005). Sudan protested by arguing that the preconditions of Article 12 SICC were not fulfilled since the alleged crimes took place in and the accused are from Sudan, which is not a state party to SICC. The ICC judges, however, took a more expansive reading of Article 12, which would only require Sudan to be a state party to the SICC if the crimes were referred to the ICC Prosecutor by a state party (Article 13.a SICC) or the prosecutor of the ICC has initiated an investigation *proprio motu* (Article 13.c SICC). However, because the crimes were referred to the prosecutor of the ICC by the Security Council acting under Chapter VII of the Charter (Article 13.b SICC), the preconditions of Article 12.2 did not apply, and nationals of Sudan, as a non-state party, could be prosecuted. The ICC judges concluded that the Security Council, acting out of its Chapter VII Charter powers, may refer such cases to the ICC regardless of the restrictions of Article 12.

6 Rights of the Accused

The SICC includes a long list of due process rights of the accused. These include, among other rights, the right to be present at the trial, to conduct the defense in person or through legal assistance of the accused's choosing, to have legal assistance assigned by the Court and without payment if the accused lacks sufficient means to pay for it, to confront witnesses against him, to remain silent (not to be compelled to testify or to confess guilt) and not to have imposed on him or her any reversal of the burden of proof or any onus of rebuttal (Article 67.1 SICC).

The ICC Prosecutor shall, as soon as practicable, "disclose to the defence evidence in the Prosecutor's possession or control which he or she believes shows or tends to show the innocence of the accused or to mitigate the guilt of the accused, or which may affect the credibility of prosecution evidence" (Article 67.2 SICC).

The right to a trial by jury is not set forth in the SICC. Rather, ICC trial verdicts and decisions are made by panels of three judges. This may be in part because of the impracticality of impaneling a jury to hear an international criminal case.

7 Applicable Penalties

Under the SICC, subject to review by the Court concerning the reduction of sentence, the Court may impose one of the following penalties (Article 77.1 SICC):

- imprisonment for a specified number of years, which may not exceed a maximum of 30 years; or
- a term of life imprisonment when justified by the extreme gravity of the crime and the individual circumstances of the convicted person.

In addition to imprisonment, the Court may order (Article 77.2 SICC):

- A fine under the criteria provided for in the Rules of Procedure and Evidence.
- A forfeiture of proceeds, property and assets derived directly or indirectly from that crime.

The maximum penalty that may therefore be imposed on a person convicted of genocide, crimes against humanity, war crimes, or the crime of aggression by the ICC is life imprisonment, a fine and a forfeiture of property derived from the crime.

8 No Ex Post Facto Law

Article 24 of the Rome Statute establishes the principle of non-retroactivity ratione personae. It states that "1. No person shall be criminally responsible under this Statute for conduct prior to the entry into force of the Statute [i.e., 2002]. 2. In the event of a change in the law applicable to a given case prior to a final judgement, the law more favourable to the person being investigated, prosecuted or convicted shall apply."

9 *Relationship with the United Nations*

As already mentioned, the ICC is an independent international organization that is not part of the U.N. system. It is legally and functionally independent from the U.N. However, the U.N. and ICC do enjoy a relationship of mutual support. A "Relationship Agreement between the International Criminal Court and the United Nations" governs the ICC's relations with the U.N. and allows cooperation with the U.N. in various areas, including the exchange of information and logistical support. The court reports to the U.N. each year on its activities and some meetings of the Assembly of States Parties are held at U.N. facilities. Furthermore, Article 13.b of the SICC allows the U.N. Security Council to refer to the court situations that would not otherwise fall under the court's jurisdiction, as was the case of the Security Council's referral of the situation in Darfur to the ICC Prosecutor.

10 *States Parties to the Rome Statute*

a States Parties

As of 2023, 123 states are parties to the Rome Statute and a further 38 states have signed the treaty but have not ratified it. The following are states parties to the Rome Statute: Afghanistan, Albania, Andorra, Antigua and Barbuda, Argentina, Australia, Austria, Bangladesh, Barbados, Belgium, Belize, Benin, Bolivia, Bosnia and Herzegovina, Botswana, Brazil, Bulgaria, Burkina Faso, Cambodia, Canada, Cape Verde, Central African Republic, Chad, Chile, Colombia, Comoros, Democratic Republic of the Congo, Republic of the Congo, Cook Islands, Costa Rica, Côte d'Ivoire, Croatia, Cyprus, Czech Republic, Denmark, Djibouti, Dominica, Dominican Republic, East Timor, Ecuador, El Salvador, Estonia, Fiji, Finland, France, Gabon, the Gambia, Georgia, Germany, Ghana, Greece, Grenada, Guatemala, Guinea, Guyana, Honduras, Hungary, Iceland, Ireland, Italy, Japan, Jordan, Kiribati, Kenya, Korea (Republic of), South, Latvia, Lesotho, Liberia, Liechtenstein, Lithuania, Luxembourg, Madagascar, Malawi, Maldives, Mali, Malta, Marshall Islands, Mauritius, Mexico, Moldova (Republic of), Mongolia, Montenegro, Namibia, Nauru, Netherlands, New Zealand, Niger, Nigeria, North Macedonia, Norway, Palestine, Panama, Paraguay, Peru, Poland, Portugal, Romania, Saint Kitts and Nevis, Saint Lucia, Saint Vincent and the Grenadines, Samoa, San Marino, Senegal, Serbia, Seychelles, Sierra Leone, Slovakia, Slovenia, South Africa, Spain, Suriname, Sweden, Switzerland, Tanzania, Tajikistan, Trinidad and Tobago, Tunisia, Uganda, United Kingdom, Uruguay, Vanuatu, Venezuela and Zambia.

b States That Withdrew from the Rome Statute

As of 2019, two states withdrew from the Rome Statute, pursuant to Article 127: Burundi and the Philippines.

c States That Signed but Did Not Ratify the Rome Statute

The 31 states that have signed but did not ratify the Rome Statute are as follows: Algeria, Angola, Armenia, Bahamas, The, Bahrain, Cameroon, Egypt, Eritrea, Guinea-Bissau, Haiti, Iran, *Israel*, Jamaica, Kuwait, Kyrgyzstan, Monaco, Morocco, Mozambique, Oman, *Russia*, São Tomé and Príncipe, Solomon Islands, *Sudan*, *Syria*, Thailand, Ukraine, United Arab Emirates, the *U.S.*, Uzbekistan, *Yemen* and Zimbabwe.

In 2002, the U.S., in a position shared with Israel and Sudan, after having signed the Rome Statute, withdrew its signature and indicated that it did not intend to ratify the treaty.

d States That Have Neither Signed nor Acceded to the Rome Statute

The 41 states that have neither signed nor acceded to the Statute are Azerbaijan, Belarus, Bhutan, Brunei, China, Cuba, Democratic People's Republic of Korea (North Korea), El Salvador, Equatorial Guinea, Ethiopia, India, Indonesia, Iraq, Kazakhstan, Kiribati, Laos, Lebanon, Libya, Malaysia, Mauritania, Federated States of Micronesia, Myanmar, Nepal, Nicaragua, Pakistan, Palau, Papua New Guinea, Qatar, Rwanda, Saudi Arabia, Singapore, Somalia, South Sudan, Sri Lanka, Eswatini (Swaziland), Togo, Tonga, Turkey, Turkmenistan, Tuvalu and Vietnam.

D Ad Hoc Tribunals

1 Nuremberg International Military Tribunal

The International Military Tribunal at Nuremberg ("IMT") was a court convened jointly by the victorious Allied governments (American, British, French and Soviet) in 1945 to adjudicate crimes against the Nazi regime. The Tribunal proceeded according to the laws and procedures set out by the London Charter of the International Military Tribunal ("London Charter" or "LC"), issued on 8 August 1945 and adjudicated the following crimes:

- *Crimes against peace (crimes of aggression)*. This was defined in the London Charter as the "planning, preparation, initiation or waging of a war of aggression, or a war in violation of international treaties, agreements or assurances, or participation in a common plan or conspiracy for the accomplishment of any of the foregoing" (Article 6(a) LC).
- *War crimes*. The London Charter defined war crimes as "violations of the laws or customs of war," also known as *jus in bello* or, in contemporary parlance, international humanitarian law, which regulates the conduct of war (Article 6(b) LC). For the specifics of these crimes, the Allies drew upon the customary laws of war, the Geneva Conventions of 1864, 1906 and 1929 and The Hague Conventions of 1899 and 1907 dealing with the methods and weapons of war. The court was granted jurisdiction to try "murder, ill-treatment or deportation

to slave labor or for any other purpose of civilian population of or in occupied territory, murder or ill-treatment of prisoners of war or persons on the seas, killing of hostages, plunder of public or private property, wanton destruction of cities, towns or villages, or devastation not justified by military necessity," all of which constitute violations of the laws of war (Article 6(b) LC).
- *Crimes against humanity.* These are enumerated inhuman and odious acts committed as part of a systematic attack against any civilian population. For the purposes of the International Military Tribunal, crimes against humanity included "murder, extermination, enslavement, deportation and other inhumane acts," as well as "persecutions on political, racial or religious grounds" (Article 6(c) LC). The Nazis were held responsible for crimes against humanity committed against their own citizens.

Genocide was not prosecuted because it had not, as of yet, been defined in the London Charter. The Convention on the Prevention and Punishment of the Crime of Genocide was concluded three years later in 1948.

2 *International Military Tribunal for the Far East*

At the conclusion of WWII, Asian countries victimized by Japanese aggression tried thousands of Japanese for war crimes in their own courts. As many as 900 Japanese were executed and many more were sentenced to life in prison.

In addition to these domestic courts, which found jurisdiction on the basis of crimes committed by the Japanese on the Asian nations' own territory or against their own people, the U.S. military established the International Military Tribunal for the Far East ("IMTFE"), also known as the Tokyo Trials or the Tokyo War Crimes Tribunal, to try the leaders of the Empire of Japan for the following crimes:

- "Class A" crimes, charging 28 Japanese military and political leaders in the highest decision-making bodies who participated in a joint conspiracy to start and wage war;
- "Class B" crimes, charging thousands of Japanese nationals who committed "conventional" atrocities or crimes against humanity;
- "Class C" crimes, charging thousands of Japanese for the planning, ordering, authorization, or failure to prevent such transgressions at higher levels of command.

The Charter of the IMTFE generally followed the model set by the Nuremberg Trials. Like the International Military Tribunal, the IMTFE charged defendants for crimes against humanity, conventional war crimes and crimes against peace (aggression).

3 *International Criminal Tribunal for the Former Yugoslavia ("ICTY")*

a *An Overview of the Yugoslav Conflict*

For an overview of the Yugoslav conflict, *see* "Overview of the Bosnian War" under "Human Rights Violations by States" in Chapter 7 "Human Rights and Related Topics."

b *Creation by the U.N. Security Council*

In the 1990s, violence in the Balkans was destabilizing the region. The international community chose to act quickly in 1993 through the Security Council in creating the International Criminal Tribunal for the former Yugoslavia ("ICTY,"),rather than through negotiating a treaty that could take a great deal of time and the enforcement of whose judgments states could avoid by refusing to ratify. In acting through a Chapter VII resolution, the Security Council was able to bind all U.N. members and move quickly in order to end a conflict threatening international peace. The ICTY was established as an international criminal tribunal in The Hague by Resolutions 808 (1993) and 827 (1993).

c *Location*

The ICTY was located in The Hague prior to its dissolution on 31 December 2017.

d *Jurisdiction*

The ICTY Statute grants jurisdiction to try the following crimes that occurred in the territory of the former Yugoslavia beginning in 1991: (i) *crimes against humanity*; (ii) *genocide*, which originated as a crime against humanity but now has its own distinct definition; and (iii) *war crimes*, including grave breaches of the Geneva Conventions as well as other violations of the laws of war based in either treaties or custom.

e *Convictions of Non-state Actors*

The ICTY played a pioneering role and set a precedent by convicting a number of non-state actors for crimes against humanity. Successful convictions of these political and military leaders were meant to bring justice to victims and deter others from committing such crimes in the future.

f *As an Ad Hoc Institution*

Like the ICTR, the ICTY is not considered to be a hybrid domestic/international court. Rather, it was created as an ad hoc tribunal as an organ of the U.N. Security Council.

4 *International Criminal Tribunal for Rwanda ("ICTR")*

a *An Overview of the Rwandan Civil War*

The Rwandan Civil War was a conflict between the Rwandan government and the rebel Rwandan Patriotic Front ("RPF") from 1990 to 1994. The War ostensibly ended on 4 August 1993, with the signing of the Arusha Accords, but was reignited with the assassination of Rwandan President Juvénal Habyarimana in April 1994, which triggered the Rwandan Genocide between the majority Hutus and the minority rebel Tutsis, leading to the deaths of approximately 800,000 Rwandans.

b *The Tribunal*

By Resolution 955 (1994), the U.N. Security Council established an ad hoc special international criminal tribunal in The Hague to prosecute those responsible for committing *genocide*, *crimes against humanity* and *war crimes* within the 1994 calendar year. Like the ICTY, the International Criminal Tribunal for Rwanda ("ICTR") was meant to bring justice to victims and to deter others from committing such crimes in the future.

The major difference between the ICTY and ICTR is that the Rwandan conflict was domestic, whereas the Yugoslavian conflict became international when Yugoslavia dissolved into several independent states. In both cases, the Security Council acted pursuant to its Chapter VII powers to create the ICTR to try the crimes that occurred in Rwanda. Only common Article 3 and Protocol 2 of the Geneva Conventions (relating to internal conflicts) apply, given the internal nature of the Rwandan conflict.

c *Location*

The ICTR is located in Arusha, northern Tanzania, with an office in Kigali, the capital of Rwanda, and an office in The Hague.

d *As an Ad Hoc Institution*

Like the ICTY, the ICTR is not considered to be a hybrid domestic/international court. Rather, it is an ad hoc tribunal as an organ of the U.N. Security Council.

5 *International Residual Mechanism for Criminal Tribunals*

a *Overview*

The Mechanism for International Criminal Tribunals ("MICT") (also known as the International Residual Mechanism for Criminal Tribunals) was established by Security Council Resolution 1966 on 22 December 2010 to carry out a number of functions of the

ICTY and ICTR, namely, continuing the "jurisdiction, rights and obligations and essential functions" of the Tribunals, including securing the arrest, transfer and prosecution of remaining fugitives still wanted for trial by the ICTR.

The functions, size and number of staff members of the MICT will diminish over time. The Security Council will review the progress of the work of the MICT in 2016 and every two years thereafter.

b *ICTY and ICTR Branches*

The MICT has one branch in Arusha, Tanzania, covering the functions inherited from the ICTR, and a second branch in The Hague, covering the functions inherited from the ICTY. The MICT began its operations as follows:

- 1 July 2012 for the ICTR branch.
- 1 July 2013 for the ICTY branch.

6 ***The International Criminal Court and Ad Hoc Tribunals Compared***

The main difference between the ICC and the ad hoc tribunals is that while the ad hoc tribunals are created as temporary tribunals with jurisdiction to try certain crimes that took place within a certain territory at a certain time, the ICC is a permanent institution that has much broader jurisdiction. The ICC may try any crime that is (Article 12.2-12.3 SICC):

- committed within the territory of any state party to the SICC or on board a vessel or aircraft if the vessel or aircraft was registered with a state party to the SICC;
- if the person accused is a national of a state party to the SICC;
- when the acceptance of a state not party to the SICC is a necessary precondition to the ICC's jurisdiction and that state accepts the ICC's jurisdiction with respect to the crime in question.

As a further difference between the ICC and the ad hoc tribunals, while the ICC was created by a multilateral treaty that binds only those states parties to it, the ICTY and ICTR were created by Security Council resolutions that are binding on all member states.

E Hybrid Institutions

Hybrid institutions are internationalized courts that share the characteristics of both domestic and international courts. They are based in the country in which the crimes are being investigated and are administered with local staff, though international (foreign) judges and prosecutors are often present to ensure that the institution applies international standards. There are several types, as follows:

- international institutions established in coordination between a national government and the U.N.;
- regional institutions established in coordination between a national government and a regional organization, such as the E.U.;
- national institutions established pursuant to national legislation and having international elements.

Each of these institutions is examined in turn, below:

(1) International Institutions: Sierra Leone, East Timor, Cambodia, Lebanon.

1 *Special Court for Sierra Leone*

a Overview

The Special Court for Sierra Leone ("SCSL") was an independent judicial body based in Freetown, the capital of Sierra Leone. The purpose of the Court was to try those who "bear the greatest responsibility for the commission of *crimes against humanity, war crimes* and *serious violations of international humanitarian law*, as well as *crimes under relevant Sierra Leonean law* within the territory of Sierra Leone since 30 November 1996," during the Sierra Leone 1991-2002 Civil War. The Court was set up in 2002 and began trials in 2004.

b Residual Special Court for Sierra Leone

In 2013, the SCSL became the first international criminal tribunal to complete its mandate and transition to a residual mechanism. The Residual Special Court for Sierra Leone was established by an agreement between the U.N. and the Government of Sierra Leone to oversee the continuing legal obligations of the SCSL (witness protection, supervision of prison sentences, administration of the SCSL archives, etc.) after the closure of the SCSL in 2013.

c Jurisdiction

The Court sought to bring justice for violations of international and Sierra Leonean law, including:

- crimes against humanity, such as:
  - the abduction and forced prostitution of young girls;
  - alleged practice of cannibalism by the Revolutionary United Front ("RUF") rebel army;

- war crimes (*common Article 3* of the Geneva Conventions and its Additional Protocol II, both of which deal with *conflicts not of an international nature*) and other serious violations of international humanitarian law, such as:
  - the enlistment of child soldiers by the government of Sierra Leone and by the RUF;
  - directing attacks against civilians;
  - the forcing of child soldiers to murder their parents;
  - cutting off the hands of captured soldiers by the RUF;
- certain serious violations of Sierra Leonean criminal law.

Among the indictees was former Liberian president Charles Taylor, who was heavily involved in the Sierra Leonean Civil War.

d Hybrid Institution

The Court is a hybrid institution in that it was formed following a 2002 request by Sierra Leone to the U.N. to set up a "special court" to address serious crimes that occurred during the 1991-2002 civil war. The U.N. continued to play a role in the functioning of the Court, with the Secretary-General appointing two of the three judges of the Trial Chamber, three of the five judges of the Appeals Chamber and the Prosecutor (after consultation with the government of Sierra Leone), as well as in the financing of the Court.

2 Special Panels for Serious Crimes in Dili District Court (East Timor)

a Overview

The Special Panels for Serious Crimes in Dili District Court (informally known as the "East Timor Tribunal") is a hybrid international-East Timorese tribunal that was created in 2000 by the United Nations Transitional Administration in East Timor ("UNTAET").

The Special Panels for Serious Crimes were created to try cases of "serious criminal offences" (e.g., genocide, war crimes, crimes against humanity, murder, sexual offences (including rape) and torture), which occurred in East Timor between 1 January and 25 October 1999. The Special Panels for Serious Crimes heard cases beginning in 2000 and concluded in 2006.

b Hybrid Institution

The Special Panels have many of the features of hybrid (mixed national-international) tribunals due to the presence of international prosecutors and judges and UNTAET's role in their creation.

3 *Extraordinary Chambers in the Courts of Cambodia*

a *Overview*

The Extraordinary Chambers in the Courts of Cambodia ("ECCC") (informally known as the "Cambodia Tribunal") is a court that was established in 2001 to try the most senior and most responsible members of the Khmer Rouge for serious violations of Cambodian criminal law, international humanitarian law and international conventions recognized by Cambodia, including *genocide, crimes against humanity* and *war crimes*, committed between 1975 and 1979.

b *Hybrid Institution*

The ECCC is a hybrid international-Cambodian court in that it was established as part of an agreement between the government of Cambodia and the U.N. The ECCC is independent of the U.N. and holds trials in Phnom Penh, Cambodia, using local (Cambodian) staff and local and foreign judges in order to apply international standards.

4 *Special Tribunal for Lebanon*

a *Mandate*

The mandate of the Special Tribunal for Lebanon ("STL") under Security Council Resolution 1664 of 29 March 2006 was to investigate and prosecute, under international law, criminal acts relating to the 14 February 2005 attack, pursuant to an agreement reached between the U.N. and the Republic of Lebanon. The United Nations Security Council, acting under Chapter VII of the Charter, endorsed the agreement on 30 May 2007 (SC Resolution 1757 (2007)).

b *Hybrid Institutions*

The STL is a hybrid institution in that it was formed when the Lebanese government in 2005 requested the U.N. to establish a tribunal to try those responsible for assassination and other killings. Following this request, the U.N. and Lebanese government signed an agreement establishing the STL in 2007, with the STL opening in the Netherlands in 2009. As a hybrid institution, the STL is composed of both Lebanese and international judges and staff.

c *Timeline of the Tribunal's Establishment*

The following timeline outlines the establishment of the Special Tribunal for Lebanon (STL):

i Assassination and U.N. Fact-Finding Mission (2005)

- 14 February 2005: Prime Minister Rafiq Hariri was assassinated, and 21 others were killed.
- March 2005: The U.N. Secretary-General sent a fact-finding mission to Beirut to enquire into the circumstances, causes and consequences of the attack. The group recommended the establishment of an independent international investigation into the attack.
- April 2005: The U.N. Security Council established the U.N. International Independent Investigation Commission ("UNIIIC") by Resolution 1595.
- 13 December 2005: Following a series of other bombings and killings in Lebanon, the Lebanese government requested the U.N. to establish a tribunal to try those responsible for the killings.

ii Establishing the STL under Resolution 1757 (2006-2007)

- 29 March 2006: The U.N. Security Council issued *Resolution 1664 (2006)*, establishing the mandate of the STL to investigate and prosecute criminal acts relating to the 14 February 2005 attack.
- 23 January 2007: The U.N. and Lebanese government signed an Agreement establishing the STL.
- 30 May 2007: The U.N. Security Council, acting under Chapter VII of the Charter, endorsed the Agreement with the Lebanese government and brought it into effect through *Resolution 1757 (2007)*.

iii The STL Begins Operations (2009)

- 1 March 2009: The STL opened in Leidschendam-Voorburg, near The Hague, with an office in Beirut and a Liaison Office in New York, as the first international court to try the crime of terrorism against a specific person.

d *Funding*

Voluntary contributions from states constitute 51% of the STL's budget; the remaining 49% is paid by the Lebanese government.

e *Organs*

The STL has four organs:

- *The Chambers*. Three distinct chambers constitute the STL's Chambers: (i) a Pre-Trial Chamber of one international judge; (ii) a Trial Chamber of three judges (one Lebanese and two international, plus two alternate judges); and (iii) an Appeals Chamber of five judges (two Lebanese and three international). The Presiding Judge of the Appeals Chamber is the President of the Tribunal.

- *The Office of the Prosecutor*. Led by an international Prosecutor, who is assisted by a Lebanese Deputy Prosecutor, the Office of the Prosecutor is responsible for prosecuting the persons responsible for the crimes falling within the STL's jurisdiction. The Prosecutor may decide to investigate, file indictments, prosecute or file appeals based on available evidence.
- *The Defence Office*. The STL is the first international hybrid tribunal to have an independent defense office responsible for protecting and promoting the rights of suspects and the accused (suspects that have been indicted). The Defence Office does not represent any suspect or accused. Rather, it coordinates a list of independent defense counsels that meet the standards of the court to represent the accused before the STL. The Defence Office is also responsible for training counsel and bringing them up to speed with the STL's Statute and Rules of Procedure and Evidence.
- *The Registry (also encompassing the Victims' Participation Unit)*. The Registry is akin to an executive office of the STL that handles the Tribunal's funds and administration. The Registrar, who heads up the Registry, has an external liaison and diplomatic function and secures the funds necessary for the Tribunal's functioning and oversees the *Victims and Witnesses Unit*, the *Victims' Participation Unit*, the *Court Management Services Section*, the *Language Services Section* and the *Safety and Security Section*. Moreover, the Registrar is responsible for fostering public understanding of the Tribunal and its work.

5 Regional Institutions: Kosovo, Senegal/Chad

a Kosovo Specialist Chambers and Specialist Prosecutor's Office

The Kosovo Specialist Chambers and Specialist Prosecutor's Office are temporary institutions seated in The Hague and established pursuant to an international agreement adopted between the Republic of Kosovo and the European Union and ratified by the Kosovo Assembly, a Constitutional Amendment and the Law on Kosovo Specialist Chambers and Specialist Prosecutor's Office with a mandate and jurisdiction over crimes against humanity, war crimes and other crimes under Kosovo law, which were commenced or committed in Kosovo between 1 January 1998 and 31 December 2000 by or against citizens of Kosovo or the Federal Republic of Yugoslavia.

The European Union Rule of Law Mission in Kosovo ("EULEX Kosovo" or "EULEX"), which supports Kosovo rule of law institutions on their path toward increased effectiveness, sustainability, multi-ethnicity and accountability in compliance with international human rights law, offers the Kosovo Specialist Chambers and Specialist Prosecutor's Office logistical and operational support.

b *Extraordinary African Chambers (Senegal/Chad)*

The Extraordinary African Chambers ("EAC") (*Chambres Africaines Extraordinaires*) is a tribunal established pursuant to an agreement between the African Union and Senegal with jurisdiction to try international crimes committed in Chad during the regime of former Chadian President Hissène Habré from 7 June 1982 to 1 December 1990. It began its operations in 2013 in Dakar, Senegal.

Several events led to the formation of the EAC. An Economic Community of West African States ("ECOWAS") Court of Justice decision held that trying Habré under Senegalese law would violate the principle of non-retroactivity because Senegal passed statutes on the crimes long after Habré's acts were committed. The Court held, however, that this defect would be overcome through a trial at a tribunal of an "international character." Belgium filed suit against Senegal at the ICJ, demanding that Senegal either prosecute or extradite Habré. However, Senegal and the AU wanted for the trial to occur in Africa rather than in Belgium. Senegal failed to extradite Habré, but also failed to try Habré in its domestic court due to political reasons and financial factors.

As a result of the ECOWAS Court of Justice decision and due to the potential of financial support, the AU and Senegal established the EAC by treaty. The EAC was situated in the Senegalese judicial system with an international judge from another African country in both the trial and appeal chambers. By "internationalizing" the tribunal, the trial was deemed not to offend the prohibition of trial by an *ex post facto* law since the crimes of which Habré was charged were already crimes under international law when Habré committed them.

6 ***Internationalized National Courts: Bosnia and Herzegovina***

a *Overview*

Internationalized national courts are national courts with international elements, such as foreign judges or prosecutors that participate in proceedings. Unlike international hybrid tribunals, which are established in coordination between national governments and the U.N., internationalized national courts are generally established pursuant to domestic legislation.

b *Court of Bosnia and Herzegovina*

The Court of Bosnia and Herzegovina ("Court of BiH") is a domestic court of the State of Bosnia and Herzegovina which includes international judges and prosecutors. Based in Sarajevo, the Court of BiH was established on 3 July 2002 by the Parliament of Bosnia and Herzegovina, with the Law on the Court of Bosnia and Herzegovina promulgated on 12 November 2000. The Court of BiH does not have a time-limited mandate.

The Court of BiH issues verdicts in accordance with the laws of the State of Bosnia and Herzegovina, including the Bosnia and Herzegovina Criminal Code and Criminal Procedure Code. Besides international judges and prosecutors who worked at the Court of BiH, the key functions of the Court are held by Bosnia and Herzegovina nationals. Trials are conducted in one of the official languages of Bosnia and Herzegovina, and convicted persons serve time in Bosnia and Herzegovina prisons.

The Court of BiH holds jurisdiction to try crimes laid down by the laws of BiH, including war crimes, organized crime, economic crime and corruption cases. The Court of BiH also holds administrative jurisdiction to adjudicate cases pertaining to the decisions issued by BiH institutions and other organizations in charge of public functions. Such decisions may involve, for example, the election laws of Bosnia and Herzegovina and property disputes related to the performance of public functions between the political divisions of Bosnia and Herzegovina.

c *Human Rights Chamber for Bosnia and Herzegovina*

i Introduction

Like ad hoc international criminal courts that are created from time to time to prosecute those responsible for international crimes, ad hoc judicial institutions are occasionally created to consider violations of human rights within a specific geographic region or specific to a particular conflict. The Human Rights Chamber for Bosnia and Herzegovina, which was created to consider violations of basic human rights and discrimination on the part of the state of Bosnia and Herzegovina following the Bosnian War, the Federation of Bosnia and Herzegovina or Republika Srpska, is one such institution.

ii Overview of the Bosnian War

The Bosnian War was an international armed conflict that took place from April 1992 to December 1995. The war began after the breakup of the Socialist Federal Republic of Yugoslavia in 1991 and the secessions of Croatia and Slovenia therefrom. The multi-ethnic Socialist Republic of Bosnia and Herzegovina passed a referendum for independence in 1992, but this referendum was rejected by the Bosnian Serbs who, supported by the Serbian government of Slobodan Milošević, mobilized their forces inside the Republic of Bosnia and Herzegovina. War soon broke out and was followed by the ethnic cleansing of the Muslim Bosniak and Croat populations, including a 1995 genocide in the town of Srebrenica (of the political entity Republika Srpska, within Bosnia and Herzegovina), indiscriminate shelling of civilian targets and systematic mass rape, mostly led by Serb and (to a lesser extent) Croat forces.

The war was waged between the forces of:

- The Republic of Bosnia, a country whose population is divided among Muslims, Orthodox Christians and Catholics;

- The forces of the self-proclaimed Bosnian Serb entity, "Republika Srpska," led and supplied by Serbia; and
- The forces of the self-proclaimed Bosnian Croat entity, "Croatian Republic of Herzeg-Bosnia," led and supplied by Croatia.

The war was concluded on 14 December 1995, with the signing of the General Framework Agreement for Peace in Bosnia and Herzegovina ("Dayton Peace Agreement"), which was reached at Wright-Patterson Air Force Base near Dayton, Ohio in November 1995 and signed in Paris in December 1995.

iii Overview of the Human Rights Chamber for Bosnia and Herzegovina

The Human Rights Chamber for Bosnia and Herzegovina served as a judicial body established in Bosnia and Herzegovina within Annex 6 of the Dayton Peace Agreement in order to ensure the protection of human rights of all peoples within Bosnia and Herzegovina following the Bosnian War.

(1) Violations Within the Chamber's Jurisdiction

The Human Rights Chamber operated between March 1996 and 31 December 2003 with the mandate to consider:

- alleged or apparent violations of human rights as provided in the European Convention for the Protection of Human Rights and Fundamental Freedoms and the Protocols thereto; and
- alleged or apparent discrimination arising in the enjoyment of the rights and freedoms provided for in the Convention and 15 other international agreements listed in the Appendix to Annex 6 of the Dayton Peace Agreement.

Such violations must have fallen within the responsibility of one of the Parties to Annex 6 of the Dayton Peace Agreement—i.e., one of the following:

- Bosnia and Herzegovina;
- The Federation of Bosnia and Herzegovina (one of the two political entities within Bosnia and Herzegovina); or
- The Republika Srpska (one of the two political entities within Bosnia and Herzegovina).

Particular priority was given to allegations of especially severe or systematic violations, as well as those founded on alleged discrimination on prohibited grounds.

(2) Victims with Standing

The Chamber received applications concerning such human rights violations directly from any of the following:

- any Party to Annex 6 of the Dayton Peace Agreement;

- any person, non-governmental organization or group of individuals claiming to be the victim of a violation by any Party;
- or any person, non-governmental organization or group of individuals acting on behalf of alleged victims who are deceased or missing.

(3) Current Status

The Human Rights Chamber's mandate expired on 31 December 2003. According to the Agreement Pursuant to Article XIV of Annex 6 to the General Framework Agreement for Peace in Bosnia and Herzegovina entered into in September 2003, the Human Rights Commission was established to operate within the Constitutional Court of Bosnia and Herzegovina throughout the 2004 calendar year to consider pending cases received by the Human Rights Chamber prior to 2004. Any new case received after 1 January 2004 is now decided by the Constitutional Court of Bosnia and Herzegovina.

V OTHER ACCOUNTABILITY MECHANISMS

A Universal Jurisdiction

1 Overview

Universal jurisdiction is a concept under international law that allows national courts to try cases involving the most egregious crimes that are considered *jus cogens* crimes that trigger *obligatio erga omnes* ("obligations towards all") (e.g., genocide, crimes against humanity, torture and piracy). The principle allows the courts of any nation to try nationals of any other nation without the consent of the accused or of his nation. This is an exception to the general rule that holds that sovereign nations must consent to have their nationals tried by international or foreign courts.

2 Universal Jurisdiction in Customary International Law

a With Respect to Armed Conflict

The right of states to exercise universal jurisdiction to try serious breaches of international humanitarian law is established in customary international law. Rule 157 of the ICRC's *Customary International Humanitarian Law* provides that:

> States have the right to vest universal jurisdiction in their national courts over war crimes.

The ICRC's commentary provides that this is a rule applicable not only to international armed conflict but to non-international armed conflict as well (p. 604):

> State practice establishes this rule as a norm of customary international law with respect to war crimes committed in both international and non-international armed conflicts.

As discussed below, the grave breaches regime of the Geneva Conventions establishes universal jurisdiction in times of armed conflict. International criminal jurisprudence declares that this jurisdiction is beyond members of state armed forces; members of non-state actors may also answer for violations of international humanitarian law through universal jurisdiction.

b With Respect to Breaches of International Law in Times of Peace

State practice dating back over centuries even suggests that universal jurisdiction has been exercised by states for grave breaches of international law, including in cases having no link to armed conflict. There is therefore a basis in customary international law that extends universal jurisdiction to crimes that may be committed in times of peace, such as genocide and crimes against humanity.

3 Overlap with the "Grave Breaches" Regime of the Geneva Conventions

As discussed in further detail under "Grave Breaches" in Chapter 6, International Humanitarian Law: The Law of Armed Conflict, *supra*, the "grave breaches" regime of the Geneva Conventions establishes the basis for exercising universal jurisdiction in cases of armed conflict. The grave breaches regime is the first time that universal jurisdiction is empaneled on a mandatory rather than a voluntary basis. States parties to the Geneva Conventions are obligated to respect international humanitarian law, ensure the respect of international humanitarian law, search for persons alleged to have committed "grave breaches" of the Geneva Conventions *and bring such persons, regardless of their nationality, before their own courts or extradite them for trial in another state* (Article 49-50 GC I; Article 50-51 GC II; Article 129-30 GC III; Article 146-47 GC IV). Geneva Conventions I to IV thus establish a basis for universal jurisdiction in cases of international armed conflict.

Unlike the grave breaches regime, which applies only to grave breaches of the Geneva Conventions, universal jurisdiction is applicable to crimes outside of the context of armed conflict (e.g., genocide, crimes against humanity, torture and piracy that may be committed in times of peace). Moreover, universal jurisdiction as a concept predates the grave breaches regime and the Geneva Conventions as a whole.

4 Challenges

There are many challenges that universal jurisdiction faces as a mechanism for international criminal justice. It is, by its nature, a voluntary mechanism that leads to "hit and miss justice" based on the will of states to prosecute actors where crimes have no direct nexus to the state in question. Very often, the actors who are prosecuted are low-level officials who left the states in which international crimes were committed.

In many cases, they are officials who defected from the governments, armed forces, militias or organized armed groups that committed atrocities. Very often, commanders and high-ranking government officials do not travel to a territory where they can be detained and tried for international crimes.

5 *Countries That have Invoked Universal Jurisdiction*

Some notable countries that have invoked universal jurisdiction include the following.

a Belgium

In 1993, Belgium passed its Law of Universal Jurisdiction, which allows it to prosecute defendants accused of certain violations of the 1949 Geneva Conventions and 1977 Additional Protocols, regardless of where such crimes were committed.[401] In 1999, the law was amended to add crimes against humanity, as defined in the Rome Statute, and genocide, as defined in the 1948 Genocide Convention.[402] In 2001, four Rwandan citizens were convicted and given sentences from 12 to 20 years' imprisonment for their involvement in the Rwandan genocide. The Belgian courts were soon confronted by a rapid succession of cases against Israeli, Palestinian, and U.S. officials.

In 2003, U.S. Defense Secretary Donald Rumsfeld threatened to pull NATO's headquarters out of Brussels unless Belgium revoked legislation giving its courts jurisdiction to prosecute foreigners for alleged war crimes committed anywhere in the world due to a fear that U.S. civilian and military officials could be arrested and tried for war crimes while in Belgium. Belgium's once robust universal jurisdiction statute became anemic overnight after the U.S. made this threat. Belgium restricted its universal jurisdiction to cases in which the accused is Belgian or is present in Belgium. In 2003, Belgium repealed its Law of Universal Jurisdiction and now has a law on extraterritorial jurisdiction with restrictions similar to those in the corresponding laws of most other European countries.

Belgium has restricted its law in three critical ways:[403]

(1) universal jurisdiction was replaced by a required link to Belgium with respect to the nationality or residence of the plaintiff or accused, thereby defeating the true "universality" of Belgium's jurisdiction;

401. *Loi du 16 juin 1993 relative à la répression des infractions graves aux Conventions internationales de Genève du 12 août 1949 et aux Protocoles I et II du 8 juin 1977, additionnels à ces Conventions*, 16 June 1993, *Moniteur Belge* (5 August 1993).
402. *See* Steven R. Ratner, "Belgium's War Crimes Statute: A Postmortem," 97(4) *American Journal of International Law* (2003), p. 889 available at <https://doi.org/10.2307/3133687>.
403. *Ibid.*, p. 891.

(2) leading foreign governmental officials were recognized as immune from prosecution while they were in office, and immunity from arrest was granted to all persons on official visits; and
(3) the role of the public prosecutor was expanded only if the victim was Belgian.

Cases relating to victims of human rights abuses outside of Belgium may proceed if:[404]

(1) the requisite tie to Belgium is present;
(2) the other states with a link to the crime do not have an independent system of justice; and
(3) the accused is not an immunized governmental official specified in the law, but rather, is another kind of governmental official or is a former official or has always been a private citizen.

b Spain

The Spanish courts have jurisdiction over crimes committed by Spaniards or foreign citizens outside Spain when such crimes constitute genocide, terrorism, or any other crime that, according to international treaties or conventions, must be prosecuted in Spain. On the basis of universal jurisdiction, various cases have been heard in the Spanish courts, including:

- a 2003 case in which a Spanish judge imprisoned a former Argentine naval officer on charges of-genocide and terrorism;
- a 2006 Spanish High Court case in which seven former Chinese officials were alleged to have participated in genocide in Tibet; and
- complaints lodged in 2009 against senior Israeli political and military officials alleging a targeted killing attack in Gaza in 2002.

While Spanish law provides for the principle of universal jurisdiction, the scope of universal jurisdiction in Spain has been limited following legislative reforms adopted in 2009 and 2014. In its original formulation, article 23, paragraph 4, of Organic Act No. 6/1985 of 1 July on the Judiciary ("Organic Act No. 6/1985") recognized the jurisdiction of Spanish courts over offences committed by Spanish nationals or foreigners outside Spanish territory, where those acts are classified as genocide, terrorism, piracy or unlawful seizure of aircraft, counterfeiting of foreign currency, crimes related to prostitution, trafficking in psychotropic, toxic or narcotic drugs or any other crime which should be prosecuted in Spain pursuant to an international treaty or agreement.

However, Organic Act No. 1/2009, for the first time, limited the scope of Article 23, paragraph 4, of Organic Act No. 6/1985 by establishing that there must be a link with Spain, which had not previously been stipulated (except with regard to the offence

404. *Ibid.*

of female genital mutilation), and by introducing the principle of subsidiarity. The jurisdiction of the Spanish courts thus became dependent on the existence of a link with Spain. This could be established through the presence of a perpetrator on Spanish territory, the Spanish nationality of the victims or any other "relevant link" with Spain.

c *Germany*

In February 2019, the German authorities arrested Anwar Raslan, a former colonel in a Syrian intelligence service who entered Germany in July 2014, and Eyad al-Gharib, a former Syrian secret police officer who entered Germany in April 2018. In April 2020, both men went on trial in Germany on charges of crimes against humanity committed in the early days of the Syrian civil war. In February 2021, Eyad al-Gharib was convicted and sentenced to four and a half years in prison for aiding and abetting crimes against humanity for his role in arresting and transporting protesters to an interrogation center known for torture. The conviction in Germany marks the first case of universal jurisdiction invoked against a Syrian official for grave crimes. The trial of Anwar Raslan resulted in a conviction for crimes against humanity in January 2022.

B Where No International Tribunal Is Created: The Case of Syria

1 Independent Institution on Missing Persons in Syria (2023)

On 26 June 2023, U.N. General Assembly Resolution A/77/L.79 created a new mechanism for investigating missing persons in Syria, the Independent Institution on Missing Persons in the Syrian Arab Republic ("IIMPSAR"). The Institution was established after 12 years of conflict and violence, with at least 100,000 people reported to be missing.

U.N. General Assembly Resolution A/77/L.79, which established the Institution "to ensure the right of families to know the fate and whereabouts of their missing relatives and receive adequate support," stated in part that the General Assembly:

> Decides to establish, under the auspices of the United Nations, the Independent Institution on Missing Persons in the Syrian Arab Republic, to clarify the fate and whereabouts of all missing persons in the Syrian Arab Republic and to provide adequate support to victims, survivors and the families of those missing, in close cooperation and complementarity with all relevant actors ...
>
> Also decides that the Independent Institution shall have a structural element that ensures the full and meaningful participation and representation of victims, survivors and the families of missing persons in the Syrian Arab Republic in its operationalization and work ....

In addition, the Resolution requests the U.N. as a whole to cooperate fully with the Independent Institution and to promptly respond to any requests, including access to information, documentation and any other forms of assistance necessary to carry out its mandate.

2 *The International, Impartial and Independent Mechanism ("IIIM") (2016)*

a *Establishment*

The International, Impartial and Independent Mechanism to Assist in the Investigation and Prosecution of Persons Responsible for the Most Serious Crimes under International Law Committed in the Syrian Arab Republic since March 2011 ("IIIM" or "Mechanism") was established by the U.N. General Assembly on 21 December 2016 to cooperate with the Independent International Commission of Inquiry on the Syrian Arab Republic ("CoI") and to:[405]

> collect, consolidate, preserve and analyse evidence of violations of international humanitarian law and human rights violations and abuses and to prepare files in order to facilitate and expedite fair and independent criminal proceedings, in accordance with international law standards, in national, regional or international courts or tribunals that have or may in the future have jurisdiction over these crimes, in accordance with international law.

The IIIM represents the first time the U.N. General Assembly established a "pre-tribunal body with a prosecutorial standard for collecting evidence for future tribunals."[406]

b *Mandate: Gathering Evidence and Preparing Cases for Prosecution*

IIIM is neither a prosecutor's office nor a court, but it holds a quasi-prosecutorial function in that it collects and analyses information and evidence of international crimes committed in Syria to assist criminal proceedings in national, regional or international courts or tribunals that have or may, in the future, have jurisdiction over such crimes. The IIIM seeks to support accountability processes aimed at bringing about justice for the victims of serious international crimes.

The mandate of the IIIM is divided into two prongs, as per its Terms of Reference:

A. To collect, consolidate, preserve and analyse evidence of violations of international humanitarian law and human rights violations and abuses; and
B. To *prepare files* in order to *facilitate and expedite* fair and independent criminal proceedings, in accordance with international law standards, in national, regional or international courts or tribunals that have or may in the future have jurisdiction over these crimes, in accordance with international law. This prong is divided into two sub-prongs:
   1. Preparation of Files. On the basis of the documentation and evidence of violations and abuses that it has collected, consolidated, preserved and

405. "General Assembly Takes Action on Second Committee Reports by Adopting 37 Texts," United Nations (21 December 2016), available at <https://www.un.org/press/en/2016/ga11880.doc.htm>.
406. Ayana Bowman, "Reframing Sexual and Gender-Based Violence: Proposed Practices for an International Tribunal in Syria," 34(1) *Temple International & Comparative Law Journal* (2019), p. 165, available at <https://ssrn.com/abstract=3611264>.

analysed, the Mechanism shall prepare files focusing on the criminal conduct of the persons responsible, regardless of their affiliation. The files shall include relevant information, documentation and evidence in the Mechanism's possession, both inculpatory and exculpatory, pertaining to the imputable crimes and to the mode or modes of criminal liability recognized under international law.

2. Sharing Information with Courts and Tribunals to Facilitate and Expedite Fair and Independent Criminal Proceedings. The IIIM shall share information with national, regional or international courts or tribunals that have or may in the future have jurisdiction over these crimes in order to facilitate and expedite fair and independent criminal proceedings, provided the jurisdictions respect international human rights law and standards, including the right to a fair trial, and where the application of the death penalty would not apply. The Mechanism shall adopt procedures and methods of work further regulating the sharing of information to facilitate and expedite fair and independent criminal proceedings, considering the requirements for security of information.

c *Standards and Procedural Requirements*

The IIIM shall:[407]

> adopt procedures, in accordance with international criminal law standards, to collect, consolidate, preserve and analyse documentation and evidence and shall prepare files to facilitate and expedite fair and independent criminal proceedings, with a view to best supporting criminal justice proceedings before a ... national, regional or international courts or tribunals that apply a variety of criminal procedures and standards of legal proof. These procedures shall be based on international law and standards, notably the *right to a fair trial and other due process provisions* under international human rights law, as well as on the *jurisprudence, procedural standards and best practices of the international criminal tribunals.*

All materials produced or obtained by the IIIM and its work products and analyses shall be classified as strictly confidential, in line with the U.N. policy on information sensitivity, classification and handling under ST/SGB/2007/6.[408]

d *Structure and Composition*

The IIIM is headed by a senior judge or prosecutor with extensive experience in criminal investigations and prosecutions and a deputy with extensive experience in international criminal justice and knowledge of international law. They are to recruit a secretariat composed of the following:[409]

> impartial and experienced professional and administrative staff, with expertise in the following areas, among others: international criminal law, human rights law,

407. *Terms of Reference*, Int'l, Impartial & Indep. Mechanism, para. 17, available at <https://iiim.un.org/terms-of-reference-of-iiim>.
408. *Ibid.*
409. *Ibid.*

> international humanitarian law, criminal investigation and prosecution, the *military*, forensic matters, including in particular digital forensics, forensic pathology and forensic imagery, witness and victim protection, sexual and gender-based crimes and violence, children's rights and crimes against children.
>
> In appointing members of the secretariat, due consideration shall be given to the representation of *different legal traditions* and *gender balance* and to appointing staff with the necessary *language skills* and *regional expertise*.

e Lack of Syrian Support

Unlike other international tribunals, the IIIM was established over Syria's opposition to the IIIM as an infringement of its national sovereignty. Syria's representative to the U.N. argued that:[410]

> The establishment of the proposed mechanism was a flagrant interference in the internal affairs of a Member State, undermining the legal jurisdictions of national authorities and organs as well as national reconciliation efforts undertaken by his Government, thus constituting a direct threat to a political solution in Syria.

f Technology for Sorting and Analyzing Evidence

The IIIM is different from other international criminal mechanisms in that it intends to rely upon new technology, including artificial intelligence, to synthesize and organize evidence, including many terabytes of video evidence:[411]

> If approaching the material without such software, and instead simply using human employees and once relied upon [IT], they would be forced to be extremely selective about which cases they choose to document [which would lead to impartiality concerns]. "It's not something that you can support with IT in the traditional way of having IT that can find stuff for you," Marchi-Uhel concludes.
>
> Nevertheless, artificial intelligence will not replace human intelligence but will be used alongside human analysis. The software is vital in going through the huge amount of video material and doing a first-step sorting. The standard is not taking every single piece of material into account but going through huge amounts of material and being able to understand what is relevant and what needs further assistance or documentation.

3 *Independent International Commission of Inquiry on the Syrian Arab Republic (2011)*

The Independent International Commission of Inquiry on the Syrian Arab Republic was established by the U.N. Human Rights Council in 2011 to investigate human rights

410. Nicolas Goeglin, "UN General Assembly Adopts a Resolution Establishing an International Investigation Mechanism in Syria on Grave Violations of Humanitarian Law and Human Rights," *Derecho Internacional* (2016) <dipublico.org>.
411. Interview with Catherine Marchi-Uhel (28 February 2018), reported in Deanna Rafla-Yuan, "The IIIM on Syrian War Crimes: What It Does and Doesn't Do," *Journal of Global Rights and Organizations* (2018-2019), p. 69.

violations during the Syrian Civil War and establish the facts and circumstances that may amount to violations and crimes and, where possible, to identify those responsible to be held accountable with a future prosecution of Syrian civil war criminals. The Commission of Inquiry has interviewed more than 6,000 victims and witnesses, produced over 20 reports and prepared several examples of war crimes and crimes against humanity.

4 *Complementarity of the International, Impartial and Independent Mechanism and the Commission of Inquiry*

The IIIM and the Commission of Inquiry on the Syrian Arab Republic are complementary. While the Commission of Inquiry focuses on directly collecting information, publicly reporting recent broad patterns of violations, abuses and emblematic incidents and making recommendations, the IIIM primarily builds on the information collected by others, including the Commission, by collecting, consolidating, preserving and analyzing evidence and preparing files to facilitate and expedite fair and independent criminal proceedings in national, regional or international courts or tribunals. The mandates of the IIIM and the Commission are also complementary in that the Commission must *publicly report on its findings*, while the IIIM focuses on *collecting, consolidating, preserving and analyzing documentation and evidence* and preparing files for future prosecution.[412]

C Reinforcing Domestic Accountability Mechanisms: The Case of UNITAD in Iraq

1 *Overview*

The United Nations Investigative Team for Accountability of Da'esh/ISIL ("UNITAD") is an agency established by the U.N. Secretary-General pursuant to Security Council resolution 2379 (2017), according to which it was mandated to support domestic efforts to hold ISIL (Da'esh) accountable by collecting, preserving and storing evidence in Iraq of acts that may amount to war crimes, crimes against humanity and genocide committed by the terrorist group ISIL (Da'esh) in Iraq.

2 *Organs*

a Head of the Investigative Team

The Investigative Team is led by a Special Adviser to the Secretary-General who possesses extensive experience in the conduct of investigations and prosecution of

412. *Terms of Reference*, International, Impartial & Independent Mechanism, para. 30, available at <https://iiim.un.org/terms-of-reference-of-iiim>.

criminal cases and a proven record of independence, impartiality and a commitment to upholding justice, accountability, human rights and gender equality.

b Office of Field Investigations ("OFI")

The Office of Field Investigations ("OFI") collects, preserves and assesses evidence of ISIL crimes for the purpose of creating criminal dossiers for use by Iraqi national courts and by third countries at their request. The OFI ensures that international best practices are upheld in carrying out its investigative mandate.

The Chief of the OFI ensures the effective direction and management of investigative activities, with the support of the Heads of the Field Investigations Units ("FIUs") and the Sexual and Gender-Based Violence and Crimes Against Children Unit ("SGBVCU," also referred to as the "Gender and Children Unit").

c Office of Analysis and Evidence

The Office of Analysis and Evidence ("OAE") collects, stores and preserves evidence and prepares analyses for its stakeholders, most notably the Government of Iraq and third-party countries that request such analyses. It focuses on preserving and delivering evidence to the highest international standards, conducting interviews, taking witness testimony and acquiring forensic materials.

d Witness Protection Unit

UNITAD has adopted a victim-centered approach in its activities that seeks to avoid any further harm to witnesses as part of the collection of testimonial evidence. UNITAD has developed working practices and methods for interviewing victims of CRSV, GSBV and violence against children.

e Office of National Engagement and Support

The Office of National Engagement and Support ("ONES") provides strategic advice to UNITAD's leadership regarding engagement of the Investigative Team with the Iraqi government. ONES provides advice and information to UNITAD's leadership regarding UNITAD's engagement with religious groups, NGOs, experts and Iraqi communities. ONES also works with the Public Information Office to ensure that UNITAD engages key national stakeholders and Iraqi civil society.

f Security

The Security section provides professional safety and security services and support to UNITAD staff, delegates and visitors while working in close coordination with the Iraqi government and the U.N. Department of Safety and Security in Iraq.

CHAPTER 8
Refugee Law

I INTRODUCTION

A Overview

After World War II, the international community was faced with the task of organizing thousands of displaced persons. There was a concerted effort to ensure that the atrocities committed during the war would never be repeated, and part of this was achieved by adopting the Universal Declaration of Human Rights ("UDHR") (1948). In order to secure the fundamental human rights of refugees, the Office of the U.N. High Commissioner for Refugees ("UNHCR") was established in 1950. Headquartered in Geneva, Switzerland, the agency is mandated with the task of supervising international conventions providing for the protection of refugees. The main principle behind UNHCR and refugee law, in general, is to provide surrogate international protection for an individual where national protection of his fundamental rights has failed.

B Applying for Refugee Status Versus Asylee Status

UNHCR does not deal with the intake process of those who have already left their countries of residence. Such individuals may be welcomed by third-party host states as asylees under local asylum laws. For example, the U.S. permits any person who is already in the U.S. or is entering the U.S. to apply to remain in the U.S. as an asylee. Under U.S. legal criteria, the applicant must show that he has a reasonable fear of persecution because of race, religion, nationality, membership in a particular social group or political opinion if forced to return to his country of last residence. Other states may apply a different set of criteria when evaluating whether to grant the right of asylum within its territory.

II CONVENTION RELATING TO THE STATUS OF REFUGEES (1951)

A Introduction

1 *The U.N. High Commissioner for Refugees (1950) and the Refugee Convention (1951)*

a *The U.N. High Commissioner for Refugees (1950)*

UNHCR was established in 1950 by U.N. General Assembly Resolution 428 (V) of 14 December 1950. Resolution 428 (V) adopted the Statute of UNHCR, which delineates the mandate of UNHCR as being (Article 1 Annex Statute of UNHCR) (emphasis added):

> providing international protection, under the auspices of the United Nations, to refugees who fall within the scope of the present Statute and of *seeking permanent solutions for the problem of refugees* by assisting governments and, subject to the approval of the governments concerned, private organizations to facilitate the *voluntary repatriation* of such refugees, or their *assimilation within new national communities*. In the exercise of his functions, more particularly when difficulties arise, and for instance with regard to any controversy concerning the international status of these persons, the High Commissioner shall request the opinion of an advisory committee on refugees if it is created.

The primary mission of UNHCR is thus to promote the protection of refugees by assisting governments and private partner organizations in seeking durable solutions for refugee problems. The role of UNHCR varies greatly from country to country, depending on several factors, including whether:

- There exists national legislation protecting the rights of refugees and national agencies or NGOs acting as refugee administrators.
- UNHCR is the primary refugee administrator or is even welcomed in the host country as an international presence.

While UNHCR does provide assistance and aid to refugees, its first priority is to advocate for the rights of refugees in host countries. It also encourages the development of national legislation that recognizes the rights of refugees and leads to a fair administration of those rights by national refugee agencies.

UNHCR may support refugees at the request of states or the U.N. itself.

b *The Refugee Convention (1951)*

In 1951, in Geneva, the United Nations Conference of Plenipotentiaries on the Status of Refugees and Stateless Persons convened under General Assembly resolution 429 (V) of 14 December 1950. On 28 July 1951, the Conference of Plenipotentiaries approved the Convention Relating to the Status of Refugees ("Refugee Convention" or "CRSR"), also referred to as the "Geneva Convention of 1951." The CRSR entered into force in 1954.

c Comparison

The CRSR is a legal instrument that lays out the human rights of refugees, while UNHCR is an agency with a mandate to promote durable solutions to refugee crises. The CRSR is central to the activities of UNHCR by defining who is a refugee, setting out their rights and outlining the responsibilities of the international community in applying refugee protections.

2 Refugee Protocol and States Parties

The CRSR was amended by the Protocol Relating to the Status of Refugees ("Refugee Protocol") in 1967. With 148 states parties to either the CRSR or the Refugee Protocol (145 are party to the CRSR and 3 are party to the Protocol only), the principles contained in the Convention and its Protocol now form part of customary international law.[413,414]

The following are the 145 states parties to the CRSR (which, in addition to the three states parties to the 1967 Protocol only—Cape Verde, United States of America and Venezuela), make up a total of 148 states parties to either the CRSR or the 1967 Protocol): Afghanistan, Albania, Algeria, Angola, Antigua and Barbuda, Argentina, Armenia, Australia, Austria, Azerbaijan, Bahamas, Belarus, Belgium, Belize, Benin,

413. Following are the 145 states parties to the CRSR (which, in addition to the three states parties to the 1967 Protocol only (Cape Verde, United States of America and Venezuela), make up a total of 148 states parties to either the CRSR or the 1967 Protocol): Afghanistan, Albania, Algeria, Angola, Antigua and Barbuda, Argentina, Armenia, Australia, Austria, Azerbaijan, Bahamas, Belarus, Belgium, Belize, Benin, Bolivia (Plurinational State of), Bosnia and Herzegovina, Botswana, Brazil, Bulgaria, Burkina Faso, Burundi, Cambodia, Cameroon, Canada, Central African Republic, Chad, Chile, China, Colombia, Congo, Costa Rica, Côte d'Ivoire, Croatia, Cyprus, Czech Republic, Democratic Republic of the Congo, Denmark, Djibouti, Dominica, Dominican Republic, Ecuador, Egypt, El Salvador, Equatorial Guinea, Estonia, Ethiopia, Fiji, Finland, France, Gabon, Gambia, Georgia, Germany, Ghana, Greece, Guatemala, Guinea, Guinea-Bissau, Haiti, Holy See, Honduras, Hungary, Iceland, Iran (Islamic Republic of), Ireland, Israel, Italy, Jamaica, Japan, Kazakhstan, Kenya, Kyrgyzstan, Latvia, Lesotho, Liberia, Liechtenstein, Lithuania, Luxembourg, Madagascar, Malawi, Mali, Malta, Mauritania, Mexico, Monaco, Montenegro, Morocco, Mozambique, Namibia, Nauru, Netherlands, New Zealand, Nicaragua, Niger, Nigeria, Norway, Panama, Papua New Guinea, Paraguay, Peru, Philippines, Poland, Portugal, Republic of Korea, Republic of Moldova, Romania, Russian Federation, Rwanda, Samoa, Sao Tome and Principe, Senegal, Serbia, Seychelles, Sierra Leone, Slovakia, Slovenia, Solomon Islands, Somalia, South Africa, Spain, St. Kitts and Nevis, St. Vincent and the Grenadines, Sudan, Suriname, Eswatini (Swaziland), Sweden, Switzerland, Tajikistan, North Macedonia, Timor-Leste, Togo, Trinidad and Tobago, Tunisia, Turkey, Turkmenistan, Tuvalu, Uganda, Ukraine, United Kingdom of Great Britain and Northern Ireland, United Republic of Tanzania, Uruguay, Yemen, Zambia, Zimbabwe.

414. Jordan, Lebanon and Syria, which hold some of the largest refugee populations in the world (mainly Palestinian, though more recently, Iraqi and Syrian), are among the States that are not party to the CRSR or its Protocol.

Bolivia (Plurinational State of), Bosnia and Herzegovina, Botswana, Brazil, Bulgaria, Burkina Faso, Burundi, Cambodia, Cameroon, Canada, Central African Republic, Chad, Chile, China, Colombia, Congo, Costa Rica, Côte d'Ivoire, Croatia, Cyprus, Czech Republic, Democratic Republic of the Congo, Denmark, Djibouti, Dominica, Dominican Republic, Ecuador, Egypt, El Salvador, Equatorial Guinea, Estonia, Ethiopia, Fiji, Finland, France, Gabon, Gambia, Georgia, Germany, Ghana, Greece, Guatemala, Guinea, Guinea-Bissau, Haiti, Holy See, Honduras, Hungary, Iceland, Iran (Islamic Republic of), Ireland, Israel, Italy, Jamaica, Japan, Kazakhstan, Kenya, Kyrgyzstan, Latvia, Lesotho, Liberia, Liechtenstein, Lithuania, Luxembourg, Madagascar, Malawi, Mali, Malta, Mauritania, Mexico, Monaco, Montenegro, Morocco, Mozambique, Namibia, Nauru, Netherlands, New Zealand, Nicaragua, Niger, Nigeria, Norway, Panama, Papua New Guinea, Paraguay, Peru, Philippines, Poland, Portugal, Republic of Korea, Republic of Moldova, Romania, Russian Federation, Rwanda, Samoa, Sao Tome and Principe, Senegal, Serbia, Seychelles, Sierra Leone, Slovakia, Slovenia, Solomon Islands, Somalia, South Africa, Spain, St. Kitts and Nevis, St. Vincent and the Grenadines, Sudan, Suriname, Eswatini (Swaziland), Sweden, Switzerland, Tajikistan, North Macedonia, Timor-Leste, Togo, Trinidad and Tobago, Tunisia, Turkey, Turkmenistan, Tuvalu, Uganda, Ukraine, United Kingdom of Great Britain and Northern Ireland, United Republic of Tanzania, Uruguay, Yemen, Zambia, Zimbabwe.

Jordan, Lebanon and Syria, which hold some of the largest refugee populations in the world (mainly Palestinian, though more recently, Iraqi and Syrian), are among the states that are not party to the CRSR or its Protocol. Iraq, too, has long been a host to many refugees but is not a state party to the CRSR.

B Definition of "Refugee"

1 Overview

Dozens of definitions of the term "refugee" are in effect within various jurisdictions."[415] Perhaps the closest to a universal definition of the term "refugee" can be found in Article 1 of the Refugee Convention, which establishes the five criteria integral to the definition of refugee status. Under Article 1 of the Convention, as modified by Article 1.2 of the Protocol,[416] a refugee is any person who (Article 1.A(2) CRSR):

> owing to well-founded fear of being persecuted for reasons of race, religion, nationality, membership of a particular social group or political opinion, is *outside the country of his nationality* and is unable, or owing to such fear, is unwilling to

415. Andrew Shacknove, "Who Is a Refugee?," 95(2) *Ethics The University of Chicago Press Journals* (January 1985), p. 275 available at <https://doi.org/10.1086/292626>.
416. Article 1.2 of the Protocol removes the geographical and time limitations written into the original Refugee Convention ("As a result of events occurring before I January 1951 ..."). The Protocol states that "[f]or the purpose of the present Protocol, the term 'refugee' shall, except as regards the application of paragraph 3 of this article, mean any person within the definition of article I of the Convention as if the words 'As a result of events occurring before 1 January 1951 and ...' and the words '... as a result of such events', in article 1 A (2) were omitted."

> avail himself of the protection of that country; or who, not having a nationality and being outside the country of his former habitual residence as a result of such events, is unable or, owing to such fear, is unwilling to return to it.

There are thus three key elements to the definition of a "refugee" under the CRSR:

- the person must be *outside the country* of his nationality or habitual residence (i.e., an international border must have been crossed);
- the reason for the person's displacement is a *well-founded fear of persecution*;
- the fear must be based on reasons of:
  - race;
  - nationality;
  - religion;
  - political opinion; or
  - membership of a particular social group.

This definition is not, however, universal in the absolute sense of the term. Several regional conventions have expanded the definition by including persons compelled to leave their country owing to generalized violence and aggression (*see, e.g.*, "Organization of African Unity Convention (1969)" and "Cartagena Declaration (1984)" under "Regional Conventions," *infra*).

Article 1 also sets forth a series of exceptions to the general definition of "refugee" provided above. Even if there is a well-founded fear of persecution for reasons of race, religion, nationality, membership of a social group or political opinion, the following individuals may not seek refugee status:

- an individual who (1) has voluntarily re-availed himself of the protection of the country of his nationality; (2) having lost his nationality, has voluntarily reacquired it; (3) has acquired a new nationality and enjoys the protection of the country of his new nationality; (4) has voluntarily re-established himself in the country which he left or outside which he remained owing to fear of persecution; or (5) can no longer, because the circumstances in connection with which he has been recognized as a refugee have ceased to exist, continue to refuse to avail himself of the protection of the country of his nationality or is able to return to the country of his former habitual residence (Article 1.C CRSR);
- persons who are at present receiving from organs or agencies of the U.N. other than UNHCR protection or assistance (Article 1.D CRSR);
- a person who is recognized by the competent authorities of the country in which he has taken residence as having the rights and obligations which are attached to the possession of the nationality of that country (Article 1.E CRSR);
- any person with respect to whom there are serious reasons for considering that: (a) he has committed a crime against peace, a war crime, or a crime against humanity; (b) he has committed a serious non-political crime outside the country of refuge prior to his admission to that country as a refugee; or (c)

he has been guilty of acts contrary to the purposes and principles of the U.N. (Article 1.F CRSR).

2 *Refugees Versus Internally Displaced Persons*

Internally displaced persons ("IDPs") are individuals who have had to leave their homes due to persecution or natural disaster but who are still within their countries of residence. Because they have never crossed an international border, they cannot be considered to be "refugees." Nonetheless, UNHCR has a mandate to work with IDPs. No treaty governs the protections to be afforded to IDPs, but some guidelines on their treatment and protection exist.

C Refugees Versus Asylum Seekers

Refugees must be distinguished from asylum seekers, with whom they are frequently confused.[417] An "asylum seeker" is a person who has claimed asylum under the Refugee Convention on the grounds of a well-founded fear of persecution if she is returned to her country of origin on account of race, nationality, religion, political belief or membership of a particular social group. She remains an asylum seeker for as long as her application for asylum is pending. Once her application for asylum is approved, she becomes a refugee.

UNHCR defines the term "asylum seeker" as follows:[418]

> An asylum seeker is an individual who is seeking international protection. In countries with individualized procedures, an asylum seeker is someone whose claim has not yet been finally decided on by the country in which he or she has submitted it. Not every asylum seeker will ultimately be recognized as a refugee, but every refugee is initially an asylum seeker.

A refugee, in contrast, is a person who has fled their country of origin and is unable or unwilling to return because of a well-founded fear of being persecuted because of their race, religion, nationality, membership of a particular social group or political opinion.

Under U.S. law, a person can only qualify as an "asylee" if he is already present in the U.S. or is seeking admission at a port of entry. A "refugee," in contrast, is an asylum seeker whose application or subsequent appeal against initial refusal has been successful.

In some legal systems, including that of the U.S., the term "refugee" may also refer more broadly to a person fleeing generalized violence or conflict without necessarily fearing persecution, as defined in Article 1.A(2) of the Refugee Convention.

---

417. *See* Anthony Aust, *Handbook of International Law*, Cambridge University Press (2d Ed., 2010), p. 172.
418. "UNHCR Glossary," UNHCR Global Appeal, U.N. High Commissioner for Refugees (2013), available at <https://www.unhcr.org/50a9f81ca.pdf>, p. 118.

D Rights of Refugees and Obligations of States Parties

1 Overview

The CRSR defines the rights of individuals who are granted asylum and the responsibilities of nations that grant asylum. The basic principle under the Convention is that refugees should be granted no less favorable treatment than similarly situated foreign residents under the law of their host countries.

2 Refugee Rights

The CRSR is, in many ways, a human rights convention in that it seeks to provide protection in the form of securing refugees' human rights. The CRSR provides such persons the right of asylum in states parties to the CRSR as well as a host of other rights. States parties to the Convention are obliged to guarantee the following refugee rights, among others:

- Intellectual property rights, including copyrights, patents and trademarks, that are accorded in refugees' countries of habitual residence (Article 14 CRSR).
- Right of association (Article 15 CRSR).
- Access to courts (Article 16. CRSR).
- Favorable conditions for gainful wage-earning and self-employment and for the practice of the liberal professions (Articles 17, 19 CRSR).
- Welfare, including housing (Article 21 CRSR), public education (Article 22 CRSR) and access to public relief and assistance (Article 23 CRSR).

3 Obligations of States Parties

States parties to the CRSR are under the following duties, among others:

- Prohibition of discrimination as to the admission of refugees on the basis of race, religion, or country of origin.
- Prohibition of expulsion or return (the principle of "non-refoulement") (Article 33 CRSR).
- Cooperation "with the Office of the United Nations High Commissioner for Refugees, or any other agency of the United Nations which may succeed it, in the exercise of its functions and shall in particular facilitate its duty of supervising the application of the provisions of [the] Convention" (Article 35 CRSR).
- Communication "to the Secretary-General of the United Nations the laws and regulations which they may adopt to ensure the application of [the] Convention" (Article 36 CRSR).

E Non-refoulement

1 General Rule

While refugees are entitled to the same basic human rights as everyone else, the particular right held by refugees is the right of *non-refoulement*. The principle of *non-refoulement* is a non-derogable right that grants refugees protection against forcible return to territories where their life or freedom would be in danger. This principle places an absolute obligation on states parties not to return refugees to countries in which their lives or freedom would be in danger. The CRSR states that "no Contracting State shall expel or return ("refouler") a refugee in any manner whatsoever to the frontiers of territories where his life or freedom would be threatened on account of his race, religion, nationality, membership of a particular social group or political opinion" (Article 33(1) CRSR). Because the treaty applies in situations where the individual's "life or freedom *would be* threatened" (emphasis added), the standard is an objective one that does not take into account the individual's perception as to whether his life or liberty would be threatened.

2 Application

In practice, this means that once an asylum seeker arrives at immigration control at an airport or seaport to claim refugee status, he should not be turned away. Nor should he be required to leave while his application is pending, provided he makes a prima facie claim.

The principle of *non-refoulement* is violated when any one of the following three elements is met:

- asylum seekers are rejected at a border when they have no possibility of obtaining asylum elsewhere;
- refugees are deported from their country of asylum to a territory where their life, liberty or physical security may be in danger; or
- refugees are forcibly returned to their country of origin where they fear persecution or are sent to a third-party country whence they may be deported to their country of origin.

3 Exceptions

The principle of *non-refoulement* is widely accepted as a part of customary international law that is binding even on states not party to the CRSR. However, there are exceptions to its practice. *Non-refoulement* does not apply when there are "reasonable grounds for regarding as a danger to the security" of the state of refuge or when the refugee has "been convicted by a final judgment of a particularly serious crime [and] constitutes a danger to the community of that country" (Article 33(2) CRSR). The refugee may also be expelled from the state of refuge "on grounds of national security or public order" (Article 32.1 CRSR). However, the state of refuge may be inhibited by practicing this right if relevant provisions to another treaty to which it is a party apply. For example, under Article 3 of the Convention against Torture and Other Cruel, Inhuman or Degrading Treatment (1984), the state may be prevented from returning the person to another state if there are grounds to believe that he would be in danger of torture.

F Refugees Unlawfully in the Country of Refuge

It is not necessary for individuals claiming refugee status to lawfully enter the state where they make their refugee claim: "The Contracting States shall not impose penalties, on account of their illegal entry or presence, on refugees who, coming directly from a territory where their life or freedom was threatened ... enter or are present in their territory without authorization, provided they present themselves without delay to the authorities and show good cause for their illegal entry or presence" (Article 31(1) CRSR).

III THE REFUGEE FRAMEWORK

A "Refugee Protection": A Debate over Definition

1 *Traditional Definition: Advocating for Durable Solutions*

The CRSR does not provide a definition of "protection" with respect to its interventions on behalf of refugees in the same what that it provides a definition of "refugee." The UNHCR Statute does, however, define the protection that falls under the competence of the High Commissioner. It states as follows:[419]

> The High Commissioner shall provide for the protection of refugees falling under the competence of his Office by:
>
> (a) Promoting the conclusion and ratification of international conventions for the protection of refugees, supervising their application and proposing amendments thereto;
>
> ...
>
> (c) Assisting governmental and private efforts to promote *voluntary repatriation* or *assimilation* within new national communities;
>
> (d) Promoting the admission of refugees, not excluding those in the most destitute categories, to the territories of states;
>
> (e) Endeavouring to obtain permission for refugees to transfer their assets and especially those necessary for their *resettlement*.

Paragraph 8 of the UNHCR Statute thus highlights the three traditional durable solutions that should be made available to refugees: repatriation, assimilation (local integration) and resettlement to third-party countries.

419. UNHCR Statute, para. 8.

2 *Expanded Definition: Advocating for Durable Solutions as well as Providing Assistance*

According to UNHCR, its "international protection function, as derived from its Statutes and the 1951 Convention relating to the Status of Refugees, has evolved steadily over the past five decades. It began almost as a surrogate for consular and diplomatic protection and has now expanded to include ensuring the basic rights of refugees and their physical safety and security." Thus, for UNHCR, "refugee protection" covers the full gamut of activities through which refugees' rights are secured, including not only advocacy in the search for durable solutions but also assistance in the sense of providing for basic needs. This is further made clear by the working definition of protection adopted by the UNHCR Department of International Protection, which holds that protection including not only realizing the right to assistance but also implementing durable solutions. In its Checklist for UNHCR Staff, UNHCR states that protection:

> encompasses all activities aimed at ensuring the enjoyment, on equal terms of the rights of women, men, girls and boys of concern to UNHCR in accordance with the letter and spirit of the relevant bodies of law [including] interventions by states or UNHCR on behalf of asylum seekers and refugees to ensure that their rights, security, and welfare are recognized and safeguarded in accordance with international standards. Such interventions will, amongst others, be deemed to: ensuring respect for the principle of *non-refoulement*; promoting admission to safety and access to fair procedures for the determination of refugee status; upholding humane standards of treatment; *realizing the right to assistance and services*; promoting non-discrimination, and the implementation of *durable solutions* (Designing Protection Strategies and Measuring Progress: Checklist for UNHCR Staff, Department of International Protection, UNHCR, 2002).

Thus, under UNHCR's expanded definition, protection includes the full gamut of activities through which refugees' rights may be secured. Such activities may include assistance, but protection is not necessarily limited to assistance and may comprise other activities, such as the implementation of durable solutions.

B The Three Traditional Durable Solutions

The international refugee legal framework provides refugees with three traditional durable solutions, which, in principle, are subject to the choice of refugees on the basis of the principle of voluntariness.

1 *Voluntary Repatriation (to the First Country)*

While it is not always possible, the solution most often preferred is voluntary repatriation. This solution involves the return of the refugee to the country of origin once the threat to freedom and safety has been eliminated. Repatriation must be a voluntary decision by the refugee. It is the responsibility of the international community to provide the refugee with clear and accurate information regarding the situation in their country of origin.

2 *Local Integration (in the Second Country)*

The refugee framework's second durable solution is local integration, whereby a host nation adjacent to a refugee-producing nation absorbs the refugee population into its own population. Local integration in the host nation remains one of the primary durable solutions, but host nations are under no obligation to absorb refugee populations. If they do, refugees are granted the full rights of foreign residents and are assimilated into the local community with access to jobs, education, healthcare and basic services. If host nations are unable or unwilling to integrate refugees into their societies, then the refugees normally wind up living in refugee camps or living illegally in urban centers until another durable solution becomes available.

3 *Resettlement (to a Third Country)*

Resettlement is a means by which several countries can share the responsibility of protecting refugees rather than placing the entire burden on countries adjacent to refugee-producing nations. There are 17 states with resettlement programs: Argentina, Australia, Benin, Brazil, Burkina Faso, Canada, Chile, Denmark, Finland, Iceland, Ireland, Netherlands, New Zealand, Norway, Sweden, the United Kingdom and the United States. The resettlement programs move refugees from a host nation to a third nation, where they are granted permanent residence.

Each nation with a resettlement program sets the conditions for resettlement and the number of refugees that it accepts annually. For example, in 2011, the U.S. accepted approximately 75,000 refugees, about half of which were from the Middle East, and many of these Iraqi refugees were displaced in the Iraq War and will return to Iraq when the situation stabilizes. In the U.S., as in many other countries with resettlement programs, the number of refugees accepted changes on an annual basis.

C Temporary Settlements for Refugees: Refugee Camps

There is a wide variety of refugee camps across the world. Generally, refugee camps can be divided into two types: formal refugee camps run by UNHCR and informal refugee camps, which are generally referred to as "informal tented settlements" and have no affiliation with UNCHR. For example, in Lebanon, which is not a state party to the CRSR or its Protocol, government policy has prohibited establishing formal refugee camps in response to the influx of Syrian refugees. However, informal tented settlements have spontaneously sprung up throughout the country, and in particular in the Beqaa Valley. In this chapter, the term "refugee camp" refers to the formal camps run by UNCHR and "informal tented settlement" refers to the spontaneous settlements having no affiliation with UNHCR.

UNHCR refugee camps are a significant component of the refugee regime. In the camps, refugees are identified and registered and wait for a "durable solution" to materialize. Humanitarian aid earmarked for refugees is distributed in the camps, which become a means of serving the refugees with educational services, healthcare, food, water and temporary shelter, all while maintaining control of the population until a long-term solution is identified.

Owing to a variety of factors, including a dislike of confinement at refugee camps, work opportunities, and food and medical treatment, many refugees choose to depart from refugee camps and move to the urban centers of the host nation. This presents many challenges, both for refugees and for the refugee administration. Urban refugees tend to move more often, making it difficult for refugee agency caseworkers to keep track of them. They are also vulnerable in urban settings because they may be mistaken by local authorities as illegal immigrants as opposed to refugees with a right to employment. Urban refugees often settle in areas with limited access to education, health services and low quality housing and may need to address hostility from urban residents who do not distinguish them from growing numbers of unwelcome economic migrants.

Refugee Camps such as this one in northern Jordan are born when the international community is unable to achieve a durable solution to a refugee crisis. Such camps are intended to provide temporary shelter to refugees, but some camps have been in existence for decades.

Source: Photograph by the author, using Canon A3100 IS (standard lens).

D Partners in the Refugee Administrative System

1 *National Agencies*

UNHCR's goal is that each nation would have national legislation, agencies and procedures to address refugees and administer refugee protections. Such institutions comprise a key element of the refugee framework.

For many countries, the agency that addresses refugee status determination and administration is the same agency that handles immigration. Such agencies are normally located within a Ministry of Foreign Affairs. In the U.S., for example, refugee affairs are handled by the Office of Refugee Resettlement, which falls under the U.S. Department of Health and Human Services, and United States Citizenship and Immigration Services ("USCIS"), a component of the United States Department of Homeland Security ("DHS").

In some cases, non-governmental organizations work as national refugee agencies in addressing refugee rights and administering their protections. Examples include national Refugee Councils, which exist in the United Kingdom, Australia and France, among other jurisdictions.

2 *Non-governmental Organizations*

When a country has an immigration office but no national legislation, agencies or procedures to address local refugees, UNHCR will often step in as the primary agency of refugee administration. When a country has such legislation or agencies in place, UNHCR often works in a supportive role in tandem with national agencies.

In both cases, NGOs often play a role in refugee administration and fill the gaps between UNHCR and national agencies. NGOs may work in any of the following areas:

- distribution of services;
- refugee status determination ("RSD"); or
- advocacy for legislating refugee protections.

Together with national agencies, NGOs may participate in complete or partial refugee administration parallel to that of UNHCR.

E The Palestinian Refugee Framework: United Nations Relief and Works Agency

1 *Overview*

Two refugee agencies exist within the U.N. framework. Up to this point, we have been discussing UNHCR. Prior to the 1950 establishment of UNHCR, the United Nations Relief and Works Agency for Palestine Refugees in the Near East ("UNRWA") was established in 1949 to provide relief and jobs on public works projects to 652,000 Arabs who fled or were expelled from Israel during the Arab-Israeli War. Today, it provides relief and aid in the form of education, healthcare, social services and emergency aid to 5 million Palestinian refugees and their descendants living in the West Bank, the Gaza Strip, Jordan, Lebanon and Syria.

With over 32,000 staff, UNRWA is the largest U.N. organization. The overwhelming majority of UNRWA staff (more than 30,000) are filled by Palestinians, thus fulfilling the organization's mandate to provide jobs as well as relief services.

2 *Mandate: Protection and Assistance until a Durable Solution is Available*

UNRWA has a very narrow and distinct mandate when compared to UNHCR. Its mandate is to provide limited protection and assistance for Palestinian refugees, who are operationally defined by UNRWA as "persons whose normal place of residence was Palestine between June 1946 and May 1948, who lost their homes and livelihood as a result of the 1948 Arab-Israeli conflict." This definition also includes the decedents of those identified as Palestinian refugees.

Under U.N. General Assembly Resolution 302 (IV), which established UNRWA, the only acceptable durable solution available to Palestinian refugees is repatriation. Palestinian refugees have generally not assimilated into their host nations. Rather, they have been born and live in refugee camps run by UNRWA, which provides education, healthcare and, in many cases, jobs.

3 *Funding*

Since funding of the UNRWA is voluntary, not assessed, UNRWA must actively seek funding from donors. The UNRWA private partnership unit (Partnerships Division) works to support the organization from a financial perspective.

IV REGIONAL CONVENTIONS

Among the regional conventions and declarations that add to or otherwise modify the Refugee Convention are as follows:

- the 1966 Bangkok Principles on Status and Treatment of Refugees adopted at the Asian-African Legal Consultative Committee in 1966;
- the 1969 *OAU Convention* Governing the Specific Aspects of Refugee Problems in Africa;
- the 1984 *Cartagena Declaration* on Refugees for Latin America;
- the 1976 Council of Europe's Recommendation 773 on the Situation of de facto Refugees; and
- the 2004 European Union's Council Directive on minimum standards for the qualification and status of third-country nationals and stateless persons as refugees or as persons who otherwise need international protection and content of the protection granted.

Two of the more prominent regional instruments, the Organization of African Unity Convention and the Cartagena Declaration, are discussed further below.

A Organization of African Unity Convention (1969)

The 1969 OAU Convention Governing the Specific Aspects of Refugee Problems in Africa ("OAU Refugee Convention") is a regional treaty largely based on the CRSR but, in some respects, expanded its sphere of protection, particularly in the area of generalized violence. It adds to the CRSR definition "any person compelled to leave his/her country owing to external *aggression, occupation, foreign domination* or *events seriously disturbing public order* in either part or the whole of his country of origin or nationality" (Article 1.2), thus waiving the requirement of genuine persecution due to race, religion, nationality, membership of a particular social group or political opinion.

B Cartagena Declaration on Refugees (1984)

The 1984 Cartagena Declaration on Refugees was adopted by several Latin American governments in 1984. Like the OAU Refugee Convention, the Declaration enlarges the CRSR's concept of refugee and includes "persons who have fled their country because their lives, safety or freedom have been threatened by generalized violence, foreign aggression, internal conflicts, massive violation of human rights or other circumstances which have seriously disturbed public order" (§ III.3 CDR). Although the Declaration is not legally binding, most Latin American States apply the expanded definition as a matter of practice, and some have incorporated the definition into their domestic law.

CHAPTER 9

State Responsibility and Immunities from Jurisdiction

I SOVEREIGN IMMUNITY

A Introduction

Sovereign states are generally immune from legal jurisdiction. As a general rule, they cannot be civilly sued or criminally prosecuted. This is based on the old adage, "the king can do no wrong," taken from the common law tradition. However, states may waive part or all of this immunity by consenting to be sued or prosecuted in certain cases. This is normally done through the approval of statutes that recognize causes of action that may be brought in the state's courts to try the sovereign for some alleged wrong attributable to the sovereign.

B Restrictive Sovereign Immunity for State Conduct of a Commercial Nature

Whether or not states have partially waived sovereign immunity through statutes that recognize causes of action that may be brought against them, many states recognize the doctrine of *restrictive state immunity*, where a state may be sued when it has engaged in a purely commercial transaction. This doctrine emerged during the early twentieth century in response to the increased participation of state governments in international trade.

Western nations, adopting restrictive sovereign immunity, distinguished between *acta jure imperii* (state conduct of a public or governmental nature), for which immunity was granted, and *acta jure gestionis* (state conduct of a commercial or private nature), for which immunity was not granted. Given the uncertainty of the distinction between these two classes, many common law jurisdictions developed national immunity legislation.[420]

C Waivers of Sovereign Immunity

1 International Courts and Tribunals

States' partial waiver of sovereign immunity can increasingly be found in international law, where states willingly grant international courts or tribunals the right to try them for injuries allegedly attributable to state conduct. For example, the ICJ may try any case under international law to which two states have agreed to confer jurisdiction. Numerous examples of the granting of jurisdiction to foreign courts can be found in regional organizations, such as the Council of Europe, to which acceding states must agree to grant jurisdiction to the ECtHR for human rights cases initiated by their nationals or residents.

2 Domestic Courts

As discussed in the Remedies section of Chapter 7, "Human Rights and Related Topics" (*see supra*), some nations also allow their residents or other claimants to bring suit against them in their own domestic courts for civil rights violations, torts and other wrongs committed by the state or by state actors. Such suits are brought under legislation whereby the state allows itself to be sued under certain circumstances. As mentioned above, this legislation, especially in common law countries, often allows citizens to sue the state or state actors for civil rights abuses (e.g., discrimination), but it may also extend to ordinary torts or even criminal law.[421]

For example, in the U.S., federal district courts may under the Federal Torts Claims Act hear "civil actions on claims against the United States, for money damages, accruing on and after 1 January 1945, for injury or loss of property, or personal injury or death caused by the negligent or wrongful act or omission of any employee of the Government while acting within the scope of his office or employment, under circumstances where the United States, if a private person, would be liable to the claimant in accordance with the law of the place where the act or omission occurred" (28 USC § 1346(b)(1)). Similarly, the U.S. allows federal district courts as a venue for "any other civil action or claim against the United States, not exceeding USD 10,000 in amount, founded either upon the Constitution, or any Act of Congress, or any regulation of an executive department, or upon any express or implied contract with

420. Lee M. Caplan, "State Immunity, Human Rights and *Jus Cogens*," 97 *The American Journal of International Law* (2003), p. 743 available at <https://doi.org/10.2307/3133679>.
421. In the case of criminal law, the ability to sue a state actor often arises not from a waiver of sovereign immunity, but from the fact that a state actor was not acting in an official capacity and thus not as an "arm" of the sovereign. Sovereign immunity thus would not apply in the first place. The actor could be prosecuted by the state or civilly sued by an individual as an ordinary citizen.

the United States, or for liquidated or unliquidated damages in cases not sounding in tort" (28 USC § 1346(a)(2)). The U.S. district courts may thus be used as venues for some human rights violations (e.g., for a discrimination suit against a federal employer), as well as for actions in tort (e.g., negligence) and breach of express or implied contracts.

One can find similar examples in civil law countries. For example, in Spain, the public administration can be held liable for injuries suffered by Spanish citizens attributable to the state. This principle is known as the *responsabilidad patrimonial de la administración pública.*

II DIPLOMATIC IMMUNITY

A Diplomatic Missions: An Overview

Most countries having diplomatic relations establish permanent diplomatic missions in one another's countries, but some, due mostly to financial constraints, do not. Some states that do not have many mutual interests choose for only one of the nations to establish a presence in the other nation or for the two nations to conduct their diplomatic relations via their missions to an international organization, such as the U.N. Whatever the arrangement, diplomatic missions are viewed as arms of the sovereign and the rules discussed above apply to them, albeit with the caveats discussed below.

B Diplomatic Immunity

1 Overview

There are 183 members of the 1961 Vienna Convention on Diplomatic Relations ("VCDR"). The treaty has been so widely-accepted that it has become a source of customary international law authoritative even for the few remaining non-member states.

2 Blanket Immunity from Arrest and Detention

The VCDR grants diplomatic mission staff the privileges and immunities necessary for them to carry out their work. Article 29 provides in part: "The person of a diplomatic agent shall be inviolable. He shall not be liable to any form of arrest or detention." Diplomats thus have complete immunity from criminal prosecution in their receiving states.

3 Immunity from Civil and Administrative Jurisdiction and Exceptions

Diplomats also enjoy immunity from civil and administrative jurisdiction in all matters that touch the diplomatic agent's function as a diplomat. Article 31(1) outlines the three cases in which immunity from civil and administrative jurisdiction does not apply:

- a real action relating to private immovable property situated in the territory of the receiving state, unless the diplomat holds it on behalf of the sending state for the purposes of the mission;
- an action relating to succession in which a diplomatic agent is involved as executor, administrator, heir or legatee as a private person and not on behalf of the sending state;
- an action relating to any professional or commercial activity exercised by the diplomatic agent in the receiving state outside his official functions (Article 31(1) VCDR).

4 *Time and Other Limitations*

The law of the receiving state cannot be applied to the immune person for as long as the immunity lasts and is not waived by the sending state. Because the immunity derives from the sovereignty of the state, diplomats cannot waive immunity on their own behalf. The immunity only lasts as long as the individual remains a diplomat. Thereafter, he may be prosecuted by the receiving state for crimes committed within its territory.

Diplomatic immunity does not mean that the immune person is exempt from the laws of his own state. If a serious crime is committed by the immune person, the sending state may recall the immune person back to the sending state to be prosecuted at the sending state. In addition, it may waive his immunity on his behalf, thereby allowing him to be prosecuted by the receiving state (Article 32 VCDR).

In any event, even with the diplomatic privileges in place, the host nation may "at any time and without having to explain its decision, notify the sending state that the head of the mission or any member of the diplomatic staff of the mission is *persona non grata* or that any other member of the staff of the mission is not acceptable" (Article 9 VCDR). Under such circumstances, the sending state must either recall the person concerned or terminate his functions with the mission.

C Other Diplomatic Protections and Guarantees

In addition to these provisions, the Vienna Convention holds the premises of a diplomatic mission (e.g., the embassy) to be inviolate; the host country may only enter with the permission of the head of the mission (Article 22 VCDR), and it provides for the "free communication between the diplomats of the mission and their home country" and protections of the diplomatic bag (Article 27 VCDR).

D Consular Privileges and Immunities

Because consular officials do not intervene in political matters to the same extent that diplomatic agents do, they are not permitted the same degree of immunity from jurisdiction as diplomats. Their privileges and immunities are governed by the 1963 Vienna Convention on Consular Relations ("VCCR").

Article 40 VCCR provides that "The receiving State shall treat consular officers with due respect and shall take all appropriate steps to prevent any attack on their person, freedom or dignity." They are not liable to arrest or detention pending trial, "except in the case of a grave crime and pursuant to a decision by the competent judicial authority" (Article 41 VCCR). If, however, criminal proceedings are instituted against him, the consular officer "must appear before the competent authorities," and the proceedings must be conducted "in a manner which will hamper the exercise of consular functions as little as possible" (Article 41 VCCR). Consular immunity from judicial and administrative jurisdiction applies to consular officials for acts performed in the exercise of consular functions. It does not apply to civil actions arising out of a contract concluded by a consular official in which he did not contract as an agent of the sending state or to civil actions by a third party for damage arising from an accident in the receiving state caused by a vehicle, vessel or aircraft (Article 43 VCCR).

III PRIVILEGES AND IMMUNITIES OF THE UNITED NATIONS

A Overview

Article 105 of the U.N. Charter states that the U.N. "shall enjoy in the territory of each of its Members such privileges and immunities as are necessary for the fulfilment of its purposes." These privileges and immunities are extended to "Representatives of the Members of the United Nations and officials of the Organization ... for the independent exercise of their functions in connexion with the Organization" (Article 105 Charter). Article 105 goes on to state that the General Assembly may make "recommendations with a view to determining the details of the application of [these privileges and immunities] or may propose conventions to the Members of the United Nations for this purpose" (Article 105 Charter).

Within this context, the U.N. General Assembly adopted the 1946 Convention on the Privileges and Immunities of the United Nations and the 1947 Convention on Privileges and Immunities of the Specialized Agencies.

B Convention on the Privileges and Immunities of the United Nations (1946)

1 Overview

Just as the VCDR grants diplomatic mission staff privileges and immunities, the Convention on the Privileges and Immunities of the United Nations ("CPIUN"), passed by the General Assembly on 13 February 1946, grants U.N. mission staff the privileges and immunities necessary for them to carry out their work. It requires U.N. member states to grant privileges and immunities to the UN, its assets and officials. As of August 2013, it has been ratified by 160 of the 193 U.N. member states.[422]

2 *Privileges and Immunities Granted to the United Nations and Its Personnel*

a *Juridical Personality (Article I CPIUN)*

The CPIUN begins by extending to the U.N. juridical personality with the capacity to: (a) contract; (b) acquire and dispose of immovable and movable property; and (c) institute legal proceedings (Article I, § 1 CPIUN).

b *Property and Assets (Article II CPIUN)*

The CPIUN then discusses a series of provisions relating to U.N. property and assets, which are immune from:

- "[L]egal process except insofar as in any particular case it has expressly waived its immunity" (Article II, §§ 2 CPIUN);
- "[S]earch, requisition, confiscation, expropriation and any other form of interference" (Article II, § 3 CPIUN); and
- direct taxes (excluding public utility services); customs duties and prohibitions and restrictions on imports and exports in respect of articles imported or exported for official U.N. use and of U.N. publications (Article II, § 7 CPIUN).

422. Following are the 160 states parties to the CPIUN: Afghanistan, Albania, Algeria, Angola, Antigua and Barbuda, Argentina, Armenia, Australia, Austria, Azerbaijan, Bahamas, Bahrain, Bangladesh, Barbados, Belarus, Belgium, Belize, Bolivia (Plurinational State of), Bosnia and Herzegovina, Brazil, Brunei Darussalam, Bulgaria, Burkina Faso, Burundi, Cambodia, Cameroon, Canada, Central African Republic, Chile, China, Colombia, Congo, Costa Rica, Côte d'Ivoire, Croatia, Cuba, Cyprus, Czech Republic, Democratic Republic of the Congo, Denmark, Djibouti, Dominica, Dominican Republic, Ecuador, Egypt, El Salvador, Estonia, Ethiopia, Fiji, Finland, France, Gabon, Gambia, Georgia, Germany, Ghana, Greece, Guatemala, Guinea, Guyana, Haiti, Honduras, Hungary, Iceland, India, Indonesia, Iran (Islamic Republic of), Iraq, Ireland, *Israel*, Italy, Jamaica, Japan, *Jordan*, Kazakhstan, Kenya, Kuwait, Kyrgyzstan, Lao People's Democratic Republic, Latvia, *Lebanon*, Lesotho, Liberia, Libya, Liechtenstein, Lithuania, Luxembourg, Madagascar, Malawi, Malaysia, Mali, Malta, Mauritius, Mexico, Federated States of Micronesia, Monaco, Mongolia, Montenegro, Morocco, Mozambique, Myanmar, Namibia, Nepal, Netherlands, New Zealand, Nicaragua, Niger, Nigeria, Norway, Pakistan, Panama, Papua New Guinea, Paraguay, Peru, Philippines, Poland, Portugal, Qatar, Republic of Korea, Republic of Moldova, Romania, Russian Federation, Rwanda, San Marino, Senegal, Serbia, Seychelles, Sierra Leone, Singapore, Slovakia, Slovenia, Somalia, South Africa, Spain, Sri Lanka, St. Lucia, Sudan, Sweden, Switzerland, *Syrian Arab Republic*, Tajikistan, Thailand, North Macedonia, Togo, Trinidad and Tobago, Tunisia, Turkey, Turkmenistan, Uganda, Ukraine, United Arab Emirates, United Kingdom of Great Britain and Northern Ireland, United Republic of Tanzania, United States of America, Uruguay, Venezuela (Bolivarian Republic of), Vietnam, Yemen, Zambia, Zimbabwe.

c *Diplomatic Communications (Article III CPIUN)*

The CPIUN extends diplomatic immunity to U.N. official communications, which are to enjoy treatment not less favorable than that that accorded to "to any other Government including its diplomatic mission" (Article III, § 9 CPIUN) and to correspondence by courier or in bags (the diplomatic bag or pouch), which "shall have the same immunities and privileges as diplomatic couriers and bags" (Article III, § 10 CPIUN).

d *Representatives of U.N. Members, Officials and Experts (Articles IV-VI CPIUN)*

Functional immunity is extended to:

- representatives (or delegates) of U.N. member states to the principal and subsidiary U.N. organs and to U.N. conferences (Article IV CPIUN);
- officials, whose categories are to be specified by the Secretary-General. They are immune from legal process in respect of words spoken or written and acts performed in their official capacity, are exempt from taxation with respect to their U.N. salaries and may import duty-free furniture and effects at the time of first taking up their post in the country in question (Article V, § 18 CPIUN). These rights may be waived by the Secretary-General if immunity would impede the course of justice (Article V, § 20 CPIUN); and
- experts performing missions for the UN, where such privileges and immunities are necessary for the independent exercise of their functions during the period of their missions (Article VI, § 22 CPIUN).

e *Laissez-Passer (Article VII CPIUN)*

States must recognize *laissez-passers* issued by the U.N. to its officials and must accept them as valid travel documents (Article VII, § 24 CPIUN).

f *Dispute Settlement (Article VIII CPIUN)*

Modes of settlement of disputes arising out of disputes of a private character, including contracts to which the U.N. is a party, and those involving U.N. officials enjoying immunity are subject to the provisions made by the U.N. to settle the same (Article VIII, § 29 CPIUN).

C **Convention on Privileges and Immunities of the Specialized Agencies (1947)**

The Convention on Privileges and Immunities of the Specialized Agencies ("CPISA") was adopted by General Assembly resolution 179 (II) on 21 November 1947 to extend privileges similar to those granted to the U.N. to the U.N. specialized agencies, which are defined as the autonomous organizations working within the U.N. and one another through the ECOSOC coordinating mechanism at the intergovernmental level and through the Chief Executives Board for coordination at the inter-secretariat level. The CPISA has been ratified by 125 of the 193 U.N. member states,[423] thus extending privileges and immunities to the U.N. specialized agencies, which currently number 15 (FAO, ICAO, IFAD, ILO, IMF, IMO, ITU, UNESCO, UNIDO, UNWTO, UPU, WHO, WIPO, WMO and the World Bank Group).

IV IMMUNITY OF GOVERNMENT OFFICIALS

A Historic Immunity Principle

Historically, heads of state and government held immunity from prosecution, particularly while still holding office. The finding of head of state immunity by Belgium's *Cour de Cassation*, for example, is representative of this historic approach. In the early years of Belgium's universal jurisdiction statute, multiple cases were filed against sitting heads of state and government including against Israeli Prime Minister Ariel Sharon and former Israeli Army chief of staff Amos Yaron. However, on 12 February 2003, the Belgian *Cour de Cassation* held that under customary international law, sitting heads of state and government hold immunity from prosecution. The *Cour de Cassation*, finding the immunity of sitting heads of state and government to be a principle of customary international law, "dismissed the case against Sharon but allowed the investigation against Yaron to proceed. The tribunal left open the possibility that Sharon could be tried after he left office."[424]

Today, a number of states accept Belgium's position, whereby domestic courts do not have jurisdiction to try acting heads of state and government for alleged crimes. For example, in October 2011, Australian national Jegan Waran filed charges in the Melbourne Magistrates Court for war crimes and crimes against humanity allegedly

423. Following are the 125 states parties to the CPISA: Albania, Algeria, Angola, Antigua and Barbuda, Argentina, Australia, Austria, Bahamas, Bahrain, Barbados, Belarus, Belgium, Bosnia and Herzegovina, Botswana, Brazil, Bulgaria, Burkina Faso, Cambodia, Cameroon, Central African Republic, Chile, China, Côte d'Ivoire, Croatia, Cuba, Cyprus, Czech Republic, Democratic Republic of the Congo, Denmark, Dominica, Ecuador, Egypt, El Salvador, Estonia, Fiji, Finland, France, Gabon, Gambia, Georgia, Germany, Ghana, Greece, Guatemala, Guinea, Guyana, Haiti, Honduras, Hungary, Iceland, India, Indonesia, Iran (Islamic Republic of), Iraq, Ireland, Italy, Jamaica, Japan, *Jordan*, Kenya, Kuwait, Lao People's Democratic Republic, Latvia, Lesotho, Libya, Lithuania, Luxembourg, Madagascar, Malawi, Malaysia, Maldives, Mali, Malta, Mauritius, Mongolia, Montenegro, Morocco, Mozambique, Nepal, Netherlands, New Zealand, Nicaragua, Niger, Nigeria, Norway, Pakistan, Paraguay, Philippines, Poland, Portugal, Qatar, Republic of Korea, Republic of Moldova, Romania, Russian Federation, Rwanda, San Marino, Senegal, Serbia, Seychelles, Sierra Leone, Singapore, Slovakia, Slovenia, South Africa, Spain, St. Lucia, Sweden, Switzerland, Thailand, North Macedonia, Togo, Tonga, Trinidad and Tobago, Tunisia, Uganda, Ukraine, United Arab Emirates, United Kingdom of Great Britain and Northern Ireland, United Republic of Tanzania, Uruguay, Uzbekistan, Vanuatu, Zambia, Zimbabwe.

424. *See* Steven R. Ratner, "Belgium's War Crimes Statute: A Postmortem," 97 *American Journal of International Law* (2003), 888, p. 890 available at <https://doi.org/10.2307/3133687>. Israel, vehemently protesting the action, withdrew its ambassador to Belgium.

committed by Mahinda Rajapaksa, the President of Sri Lanka. The suit claimed that civilian targets were bombed in 2009, and thousands of civilians were killed in the Sri Lankan Civil War. Mr. Waran alleged that he "witnessed Sri Lankan military forces deliberately attacking clearly marked civilian infrastructure such as hospitals"[425] and that civilians were targeted. Concluding that allowing the case to proceed would constitute a breach of international law, which prohibits the arrest and detention of acting heads of state on the basis of head of state immunity, former Australian Attorney-General Robert McClelland refused to allow the case to move forward.[426]

In contrast, when in 2004, the Center for Justice and Accountability ("CJA"), a San Francisco-based not-for-profit law firm, filed a civil lawsuit against LTG Mohammed Ali Samatar,[427] Somalia's former prime minister, on behalf of Somali survivors of violations of human rights law, the U.S. District Court in Virginia allowed the case to move forward. The case, which involved allegations that Somali nationals had been summarily executed, disappeared, tortured, abducted, arbitrarily detained or kept in solitary confinement for extended periods, was allowed to move forward as the case was brought in 2004 after Samatar had left the Office of Prime Minister in 1990, whereas the case against President Rajapaksa was brought in 2011 when he was actively serving as the president of Sri Lanka.

B ICJ Position: Immunity Before National, but Not International Tribunals

Under the contemporary majority view, regardless of their immunity before national courts, heads of state may only be prosecuted by international courts, provided such courts have jurisdiction. This view was reflected in the ICJ's *Case Concerning the Arrest Warrant of 11 April 2000 (Democratic Republic of the Congo v. Belgium)* (the *Arrest Warrant* case). The ICJ issued a judgment on 14 February 2002 finding that the issuance by Belgium of an arrest warrant of 11 April 2000 against Abdulaye Yerodia Ndombasi, the Congo's incumbent Minister for Foreign Affairs, failed to respect the immunity from criminal jurisdiction and the inviolability enjoyed by the Congo under international law. The ICJ ordered Belgium to cancel the arrest warrant. However, while holding that an arrest warrant by a national jurisdiction violated the principle of immunity, the ICJ recognized that a sitting or former head of state or government official could be prosecuted by international courts:

> an incumbent or former Minister for Foreign Affairs may be subject to criminal proceedings before certain international criminal courts, where they have jurisdiction. Examples include the International Criminal Tribunal for the former Yugoslavia, and the International Criminal Tribunal for Rwanda, established

425. "No war crimes case against Sri Lanka leader," *ABC News* (25 October 2011), available at <https://www.abc.net.au/news/2011-10-25/mcclelland-sri-lanka-decision/3600104>.
426. *See* Anna Hood and Monique Cormier, "Prosecuting International Crimes in Australia: The Case of the Sri Lankan President," 13(1) *Melbourne Journal of International Law* (June 2022).
427. The defendant's name is correctly transliterated from Arabic into English as "Samatar," but "Samantar" is used in the lawsuit and CJA press releases.

> pursuant to Security Council resolutions under Chapter VII of the United Nations Charter, and the future International Criminal Court created by the 1998 Rome Convention. The latter's Statute expressly provides, in Article 27, paragraph 2, that "[i]mmunities or special procedural rules which may attach to the official capacity of a person, whether under national or international law, shall not bar the Court from exercising its jurisdiction over such a person."[428]

C Minority View Rejecting the Immunity Principle

A minority of contemporary scholars, rejecting the ICJ position, deny that immunity exists as a customary international law principle, at least with respect to international crimes. These scholars argue that both sitting heads of state and former heads of state can be prosecuted for international crimes both in international and national jurisdictions. One scholar has argued that "sitting head-of-state immunity with regard to international crimes simply does not exist, be it before national courts or international ones."[429]

V STATE RESPONSIBILITY

A Generally

1 Overview

The laws of state responsibility govern when and how a state is held responsible for a breach of its international obligations. They determine when an obligation has been breached and the legal consequences of that violation. In this way, they are "secondary" rules that address basic issues of responsibility and remedies available for breach of "primary" or substantive rules of international law.

For example, the rules relating to the *use of armed forces* are primary rules of international law; the rules determining *whether a state breached these rules*—the laws of state responsibility—are secondary rules that provide a framework to define injury, claims and remedies. The rules *governing state responsibility* establish: (i) the conditions for an act to qualify as internationally wrongful; (ii) the circumstances under which actions of officials, private individuals and other entities may be attributed to the state; (iii) general defenses to liability; and (iv) the consequences of liability.

The Draft Articles on the Responsibility of States for Internationally Wrongful Acts ("DARS"), colloquially known as the "Draft Articles on State Responsibility," were adopted by the ILC in 2001 as an attempt to summarize and codify the customary international legal rules for state responsibility. It is non-binding declaration that serves as evidence of customary international law.

---

428. *Case Concerning the Arrest Warrant of 11 April 2000 (Democratic Republic of the Congo v. Belgium)* (the *Arrest Warrant* case), Judgment, ICJ Reports (14 February 2002), pp. 25-26.
429. Miguel Lemos, "The ICC as a 'Tool' of the United Nations Security Council and the 'Absurdity' of Head of State Immunity with Regard to International Crimes," 32 *Indiana International and Comparative Law Review* (2022), p. 316 available at <https://doi.org/10.18060/26523>.

2 *Definition and Elements*

a *Overview*

Under the Draft Articles, "every internationally wrongful act of a State entails the international responsibility of that State" (Article 1 DARS). By "wrongful act," DARS signals not only acts but also omissions (*see, e.g.*, Article 2). An act *or omission* of a state is an internationally wrongful act when it (Article 2 DARS):

- "(a) Is attributable to the State under international law; and
- "(b) Constitutes a breach of an international obligation of the State" (e.g., the breach of a treaty or the violation of another state's territory).

b *Attributable Conduct*

Breaches of international obligations are attributable to a state when the state acts through people with a mantle of authority exercising the state's power. Such breaches may also include injurious acts committed by a state's *internal organ* or by a *person* or *entity* exercising governmental authority, even if such a person or entity "exceeds its authority or contravenes instructions," so long as it was acting in an official capacity (Article 7 DARS). Injurious acts are also considered breaches of states' international obligations when committed by persons acting under the instructions, direction, or control of the state (Article 8 DARS).

A state is further responsible for conduct not attributable to a state if and to the extent that the state later "*acknowledges* and *adopts* the conduct in question as its own" (Article 11 DARS). This was the case of the Iran Hostages Case, in which students took over the American embassy in Iran, and the new Islamic government of Iran ratified the takeover after it occurred. In the *United States Diplomatic and Consular Staff in Tehran case* (*United States of America v. Iran* (1982)), the ICJ held that although the Islamic government did not have any connection to the takeover, the conduct could be attributed to the government because of the government's ratification thereof. The Court held that "the militants, authors of the invasion and jailers of the hostages, had now become agents of the Iranian State for whose acts the State itself was internationally responsible."

A state act or omission is not, however, internationally wrongful if conducted with another state's consent (Article 20 DARS), if it "constitutes a lawful measure of self-defense taken in conformity with the Charter of the United Nations" (Article 21 DARS), is a permitted countermeasure taken by a state injured by the wrongful act of another state in order to pressure the other state into compliance with its obligations (Article 22 DARS), resulted from force majeure (Article 23 DARS), a situation of distress requiring the act in order to save lives (Article 24 DARS), or a situation of necessity whereby the act is required to safeguard an "essential interest" of the state and no essential interest of a third state is impaired (Article 25 DARS). None of these exceptions is to imply that a state is excused from the wrongfulness of an act that contravenes peremptory norms of general international law (Article 26 DARS).

Furthermore, states are not responsible for conduct of a non-state character, such as acts or omissions of private persons, criminals, or terrorist networks, if such conduct is not supported or endorsed by the state. In a similar vein, a state is not responsible for the acts of unsuccessful insurgents who retain non-state status. However, if insurgents are successful, they attain state status and become responsible for actions undertaken during their insurgency.

3 *Preconditions to Legal Adjudication*

Two preconditions must be met before a suit can be brought against a state for injury to a non-citizen under international law—(i) *bond of nationality*; and (ii) *exhaustion of remedies*—in accordance with the following framework:

- *Bond of nationality.* The claim is not brought in accordance with applicable rules relating to the nationality of claims (Article 44(a) DARS). A state raising a claim against another state for injury to its nationals must show that those harmed are nationals with bona fide links to the state under the applicable provisions of international law.
- *Exhaustion of local remedies.* The claim is one to which the rule of exhaustion of local remedies applies, and any available and effective local remedy has not been exhausted (Article 44(b) DARS). If the injury is one over which the injuring state's courts have local jurisdiction, then before claiming state responsibility, the injured party or parties must bring suit and exhaust any other applicable local remedies unless doing so can be shown to be ineffective. For example, before a state could raise a claim against the U.S. for state responsibility, the injured parties would need to first adjudicate the claim under the U.S. Alien Tort Claims Act, which grants U.S. federal courts jurisdiction to hear claims by aliens.

State responsibility claims are thus inadmissible when a state has failed to show that those harmed are its nationals or when local remedies were not exhausted.

4 *Reparation*

Full reparation in the form of "restitution, compensation and satisfaction, either singly or in combination," is required of a state for an injury caused by its internationally wrongful act (Article 34 DARS). Restitution refers to the restoration of the situation existing before the wrongful act was committed (Article 35 DARS). When this is not possible or is unreasonably burdensome, the state must make compensation for the damage (Article 36 DAR) or, when this is not possible, satisfaction for the injury. Satisfaction may take the form of "an acknowledgement of the breach, an expression of regret, [or] a formal apology" (Article 37 DARS).

5 *International Crimes*

Since the end of WWII, individuals have been held responsible for international crimes such as torture, genocide and aggression. This has been the policy of international criminal tribunals beginning with the IMT and the IMTFE and, more recently, the ICTY, ICTR and SLSC, all of which tried individuals, not states, for international crimes. The ICC follows this approach.

There was thus a great outcry when the ILC, in its 1996 Draft on State Responsibility, suggested that states can be held responsible for international crimes. In addition to how such acts could attach to a state and not to individual actors, a series of questions relating to the definitions of such crimes arose.

The 2001 DARS left out this divisive question but includes a chapter in Part Two on "Serious breaches of obligations under peremptory norms of general international law." When such breaches are committed, all states are under an obligation to "cooperate to bring to an end [to any such breaches] through lawful means" (Article 41 DARS). Presumably, this would include states' rights to invoke universal jurisdiction in trying the actors involved.

6 *Implementation*

When invoking a state's responsibility, the injured state must give notice of its claim to the injuring state. The injured state may indicate what form reparation should take in repairing the injury (Article 43 DARS). In the event the injuring state fails to make reparations, the injured state may take countermeasures comprised of "the non-performance for the time being of international obligations of the State" against the injuring state in order to induce it to comply with its obligations (Article 49 DARS).

B Injury to Aliens

1 *Overview*

Traditionally, when an alien was injured by another state because the claim belonged to the state of the alien's citizenship, the state of the alien's citizenship brought the claim on behalf of the alien against the injuring state. If reparations were paid to the state of the victim's nationality, that state was not required to pay the individual since it was the state's claim.

Today, however, individual aliens may file claims against states for injuries attributable to the states when certain elements are met. Such claims fall under the regime of state responsibility to aliens. This legal regime is distinct from the general regime of state responsibility: while the law of state responsibility is a framework that provides a structure to define injury, claims and remedies, state responsibility for injury to aliens is a substantive part of international law that has its own laws. Thus, whereas the general regime of state responsibility is comprised of secondary laws, the regime of state responsibility to aliens is comprised of primary (substantive) norms.

2 *Standard of Treatment Applied to Foreign Nationals*

Regarding the standard of treatment that should be applied to foreign nationals, two views are available: the objective view and the equality of treatment view.

a Objective View

Under the majority objective view, states should adhere to an objective minimum standard that gives rise to responsibility for human rights violations, personal rights violations and property rights or economic interest violations that require states to protect non-citizens to the best of their ability.

b Equality of Treatment View

Developing countries simply may lack the resources to carry out this minimum standard of treatment. This is why, in many Latin American countries, the minority equality of treatment view is held: a state fulfills its duty toward foreign nationals when it gives them the same treatment as it does to its own citizens. This is because many Latin American countries have a low standard of treatment for their own citizens and do not wish to have to apply a higher standard to non-citizens.

3 *Elements*

As discussed above, state responsibility lies for injuries attributable to a state's act or omission when it: (i) is attributable to the state; and (ii) is in violation of the state's international obligations (Article 2 DARS). This same rule, which applies under many states' national legislations for injuries caused to their own citizens, applies as a principle under international law to wrongful acts by states to aliens within their territories. The legal regime outlined above regarding what constitutes state attribution also applies herein.

4 *Property Rights of Foreign Nationals: State Expropriation*

Under the Restatement of the Foreign Relations Law, state expropriation of land historically assigned responsibility to a state if it takes property of a national of another state that: (i) is not for a public purpose; or (ii) is discriminatory; or (iii) is not justly compensated. Compensation is just if it is an amount equivalent to the value of the property and is paid at the time of the taking or within a reasonable time thereafter (RFR § 712).

U.N. General Assembly Resolution 1803 (1962) and the Charter of Economic Rights and Duties of States (1974) are both statutes concerning takings. Resolution 1803 follows traditional takings law by holding that states must follow existing international law when taking property and that "*just*" compensation "*must*" be paid to the person from whom the land is taken. The Charter of Economic Rights and Duties of States requires compensation controversies to be settled using the "domestic law of the nationalizing State and by its tribunals"—not by international law—and holds that "*appropriate*" compensation "*should*" be paid to the person from whom the land is taken. The U.S. prefers the approach of Resolution 1803.

CHAPTER 10

International Environmental Law and Related Topics

I INTRODUCTION

International environmental law operates to regulate the interaction of humanity with the environment. It seeks to reduce the impact of human activity on the natural environment. Environmental law draws from and is influenced by principles of environmentalism, including ecology, conservation, stewardship, responsibility and sustainability.

From an economic perspective, environmental laws may be understood as concerned with the preservation of resources from exhaustion.

II GUIDING PRINCIPLES

Some of the guiding principles governing the development and administration of international environmental law include:

- *Duty to Warn.* There is a duty to promptly warn other states of environmental damages to which they may be exposed.
- *Principle of good neighborliness.* This is set out, for example, in Principle 21 of the Stockholm Declaration.
- *Polluter pays principle.* Basis for resolving transboundary environmental disputes was established in the *Trail Smelter Arbitration* (1941).
- *The precautionary principle.* If an action has a suspected risk of causing harm to the environment, in the absence of scientific consensus that the action is harmful, the burden of proof that it is not harmful falls on those acting.
- *The principle of sustainable development.* Development must be planned and administered in ways that are sustainable.

- *Environmental procedural rights*. Rules should be instituted granting civil society access to justice, information and participation (*see* Principle 10 of the 1992 Rio Declaration).

III WORLD SUMMITS AND TREATIES

The issues governed by environment law, including pollution control, global warming, the dangers of nuclear substances and resource conservation, are global in nature and reach across borders. They cannot be effectively tackled without international cooperation. Recognizing the common interest of all nations to establish policies for sustainable development, the international community has come together to

A United Nations Conference on the Human Environment (1972)

The United Nations Conference on the Human Environment, informally known as the "Stockholm Conference," was a U.N. conference convened in Stockholm in 1972 and attended by representatives of 113 countries, 19 intergovernmental agencies and more than 400 intergovernmental and non-governmental organizations. In addition to founding UNEP to oversee U.N. environmental programs, the Conference produced the following documents:

- *Declaration of the United Nations Conference on the Human Environment*, informally known as the "Stockholm Declaration," contains 26 principles concerning the human environment and development. It seeks to preserve and enhance the environment and enjoin states from causing environmental damage to other states or areas beyond their jurisdiction.
- *Action Plan*, containing 109 recommendations.
- *Resolution Convening of a Second United Nations Conference on the Human Environment*, recommending the General Assembly to convene a second U.N. Conference on the Human Environment.

B World Commission on Environment and Development (1983)

The World Commission on Environment and Development (WCED), informally known as the "Brundtland Commission," was convened by the U.N. in 1983 to address concerns about the deterioration of the human environment and natural resources and its consequences on economic and social development. The Commission was established by U.N. General Assembly Resolution 38/161 in 1983. The Commission published a report, *Our Common Future*, which searches for international multilateralism and interdependence in the search for sustainable development.

C Vienna Conference on Ozone Layer Depletion (1985)

The Vienna Conference on ozone layer depletion was convened in Vienna in 1985 when a hole in the ozone layer in the South Pole was detected. The international community drafted and adopted the Vienna Convention for the Protection of the Ozone Layer (1985), which entered into force in 1988 as a framework for international efforts to protect the ozone layer.

The Convention does not include legally binding reduction goals for the use of chlorofluorocarbons ("CFCs"), the main ozone-depleting chemical agents; these are laid out in the accompanying Montreal Protocol on Substances that Deplete the Ozone Layer, informally known as the "Montreal Protocol," which was opened for signature in 1987 and entered into force in 1989. There are currently 196 states parties.

D United Nations Conference on Environment and Development (1992)

1 *Overview*

The United Nations Conference on Environment and Development ("UNCED") (1992), better known as the "Earth Summit" or "Earth Summit 1992," was an international environmental summit attended by representatives of 172 governments, including 108 heads of state or government and 2,400 representatives of NGOs and 17,000 people at the parallel NGO "Global Forum," with Consultative Status. The Earth Summit addressed systematic scrutiny of patterns of production, especially of toxic or poisonous materials; alternative sources of energy to replace the use of fossil fuels linked to climate change; new reliance on public transportation systems in order to reduce vehicle emissions, pollution and congestion in cities; and water scarcity.

2 *Resulting Treaties and Protocols*

The Earth Summit resulted in the following treaties and protocols:

a The Convention on Biological Diversity

Informally known as the "Biodiversity Convention," this binding treaty was opened for signature at the Earth Summit in 1992 and entered into force in 1993. It made a start toward redefinition of money supply measures that did not inherently encourage destruction of natural eco-regions and so-called uneconomic growth.

b U.N. Framework Convention on Climate Change ("UNFCCC")

Also known as the "Climate Change Convention," this binding convention was adopted in 1992 and entered into force in 1994 with 192 parties. As of May 2011, UNFCCC has 194 parties comprised of the following:

- 191 of the 193 U.N. member states (all but Andorra, which is an observer);
- the E.U.; and
- the Cook Islands and Niue (quasi-sovereign countries in the South Pacific in free association with New Zealand).

In addition, Andorra and the Holy See are observers of the UNFCCC.

The UNFCCC seeks to stabilize greenhouse gas concentrations in the atmosphere at a level that would prevent interference with the climate system. The Convention is best known for leading to the Kyoto Protocol, adopted in 1997 (entering into force in 2005) to limit greenhouse gas emissions. It currently has 191 states parties (the U.S. signed but did not ratify the Protocol; Afghanistan, Andorra and Vatican City have neither signed nor ratified it). The UNFCCC, together with the Kyoto Protocol, build on the efforts of the Montreal Protocol in limiting the emission of greenhouse gases.

c *Indigenous Peoples Agreement*

Another agreement that resulted from the Earth Summit was an agreement not to "carry out any activities on the lands of indigenous peoples that would cause environmental degradation or that would be culturally inappropriate."

3 ***Resulting Declarations***

The Earth Summit also produced the following non-binding documents:

- *Rio Declaration on Environment and Development*. Informally known as the "Rio Declaration," it established 27 principles intended to guide sustainable development around the world.
- *Agenda 21*. A U.N. action plan that outlines strategies for cleaning up the environment and encouraging environmentally sound development. Work on the text began in 1989, and 178 governments voted to adopt the program at the Earth Summit.
- *Statement of Principles on Forests*. Formally known as the "Non-Legally Binding Authoritative Statement of Principles for a Global Consensus on the Management, Conservation and Sustainable Development of All Types of Forests," and informally as the "Forest Principles," it was produced at the Earth Summit to preserve the world's tropical rainforests and recommends that nations monitor the impact of development on their forests and limit the damage done to them.

The Green Cross International was founded at the Earth Summit to follow up on the Summit's work.

E World Summit on Sustainable Development (2002)

Informally known as "Earth Summit 2002" or "Rio + 10," the World Summit on Sustainable Development ("WSSD") was convened in Johannesburg to discuss sustainable development by the United Nations. The Summit gathered a number of leaders from business and non-governmental organizations and led to the following agreements:

- Johannesburg Declaration.
- *Johannesburg Plan of Implementation*, as an action plan.
- Johannesburg, 27 August: an agreement was made to restore the world's depleted fisheries for 2015.

IV REGIONAL REGULATION: THE EUROPEAN UNION

The E.U. Regulation on Registration, Evaluation, Authorization and Restriction of Chemicals (REACH), dated 18 December 2006, entered into force in 2007 with a phased implementation planned over the next decade. REACH addresses the production and use of chemical substances as well as their potential impacts on health and the environment. At 849 pages, it is among the most complex in the E.U.'s history and is the strictest law to date regulating chemical substances and will affect industries globally.

REACH applies to chemical substances manufactured and marketed in or imported into the EEA, whether on their own, in preparations/formulations, or in finished products. REACH imposes restrictions on the manufacturing, marketing and use of certain hazardous substances in the EEA. Its key objective is to place the burden of proving the safety of existing and new chemical substances on the EEA market onto the industry through data submission. The main obligations established under REACH are as follows:

- to register with the European Chemicals Agency certain substances manufactured in, or imported into, the EEA by specific deadlines (depending on import or manufacture volume thresholds and substance hazard profile) in order to legally market substances within the EEA (known in REACH as "no data, no market");
- to communicate up and down the supply chain in relation to substance safety and risk management measures;
- to cooperate with competitors in submitting joint registration dossiers; and
- to apply for and obtain authorization for defined uses of hazardous substances identified as of very high concern in order to progressively substitute these substances with less dangerous ones.

V U.N. ENVIRONMENTAL PROGRAMME

The United Nations Environment Programme ("UNEP"), headquartered in Nairobi, was founded in 1972 at the U.N. Conference on the Human Environment to coordinate the development of environmental policy consensus by keeping the global environment under review and bringing emerging issues to the attention of governments and the international community for action. It is governed by U.N. General Assembly resolution 2997 (XXVII) (1972) and subsequent amendments adopted at UNCED in 1992; the Nairobi Declaration on the Role and Mandate of UNEP; and the Malmö Ministerial Declaration of 31 May 2000. UNEP has played a significant role in developing international environmental conventions, promoting environmental science and information, working on the development and implementation of policy with national governments and regional institutions, working in conjunction with environmental NGOs and funding and implementing environmentally related development projects.

VI NUCLEAR NON-PROLIFERATION

The international legal instruments governing nuclear non-proliferation are as follows:

- *The Treaty Banning Nuclear Weapon Tests in the Atmosphere, in Outer Space and Under Water ("Nuclear Test Ban Treaty")* (1963). Prohibits all test detonations of nuclear weapons except underground. It was signed in August 1963 and entered into force in September 1963. Most countries are states parties; China, the Democratic People's Republic of Korea (North Korea), France and Saudi Arabia are among those states that are not.
- *Treaty on the Non-Proliferation of Nuclear Weapons (the Non-Proliferation Treaty)* (1968). A treaty that aims to control the spread of nuclear weapons. As of 2016, 191 states have become parties to the treaty, though the Democratic People's Republic of Korea (North Korea), which acceded in 1985, announced its withdrawal in 2003 following detonation of nuclear devices in violation of core obligations. Four U.N. member states are not states parties: India, Israel, Pakistan and South Sudan, which was founded in 2011.
- *Comprehensive Nuclear Test Ban Treaty* (1996). A proposed treaty to prohibit all testing of nuclear weapons in all environments, including underground, underwater, in the atmosphere, on land and in space. It currently has 182 signatories and 153 ratifications. It will enter force when 44 states enumerated in Annex 2 ratify the treaty. At present, 35 Annex 2 states have ratified the treaty, and the following 9 have not: China, the Democratic People's Republic of Korea (North Korea), Egypt, Indonesia, India, Iran, Israel, Pakistan and the United States (the U.S. Senate in 1999 refused to ratify the treaty).

CHAPTER 11

The Law of the Sea, Air and Space

I LAW OF THE SEA

A Overview

The law of the sea deals principally with issues involving the exploitation, ownership and use of the sea as both a means of communication and as a reservoir of resources. The law has developed gradually through customs embedded in state practices over the centuries, and the twentieth century saw the codification of much of this custom in the Law of the Sea Conventions of 1958 and 1982. These deal with the competing rights and responsibilities of coastal states and foreign states with respect to territorial and contiguous seas, exclusive economic zones, continental shelves and the high seas.

B Legal Instruments

1 Four Conventions of the Law of the Sea of 1958

In 1956, the U.N. held its first Conference on the Law of the Sea ("UNCLOS I") in Geneva. UNCLOS I resulted in four treaties concluded in 1958:

- *Convention on the Territorial Sea and Contiguous Zone ("GCTS")*. It confirmed coastal states' right to claim a territorial sea, over which their sovereignty extends and sets out the principles by which the limits of the territorial sea may be determined. However, it did not specify the breadth of the territorial sea. The Convention also established the concept of the contiguous zone, in which the coastal state enjoys limited jurisdiction for enforcing customs, fiscal, sanitary and immigration laws.
- *Convention on the Continental Shelf*. It incorporated then-existing rules and created new rules.

- *Convention on the High Seas*. Unlike the other three 1958 Geneva Conventions, which created new rules, it generally declares "established principles of international law" (Preamble).
- *Convention on Fishing and Conservation of Living Resources of the High Seas*. It incorporated the existing rules and created new rules.

2 *United Nations Convention on the Law of the Sea (1982)*

Whereas the second Conference on the Law of the Sea ("UNCLOS II") of 1960 failed to produce any new agreements, the third United Nations Conference on the Law of the Sea ("UNCLOS III"), which took place from 1974 through 1982, resulted in the United Nations Convention on the Law of the Sea ("UNCLOS"), colloquially known as the "Law of the Sea Convention." UNCLOS was concluded and signed in 1982 and entered into force in 1994, a year after Guyana became the sixtieth state to sign the treaty. With 320 articles and 9 annexes, the Convention defines the rights and responsibilities of nations in their use of the world's oceans and establishes guidelines for businesses and the management of marine natural resources. It formed an international framework for law over all ocean space, its uses and resources and established the International Tribunal for the Law of the Sea ("ITLS") and the International Seabed Authority. At present, 158 countries and the European Community have joined the Convention.

C Maritime Zones of Jurisdiction

The following provisions apply to the various maritime zones over which coastal states hold jurisdiction. Determinations of the breadth and locations of the internal waters, territorial sea, contiguous zones, exclusive economic zones and continental shelves explained herein apply not only to coasts of coastal states but to their islands as well.

1 *Internal Waters*

Internal waters are the inland lakes, rivers and ports located within the boundaries of a state. They are classified as appertaining to the land territory of the coastal state. There is no right to innocent passage of other states.

Ships of foreign states are under the jurisdiction of the coastal state when in the state's internal waters. The coastal state is sovereign over these waters and is fully entitled to enforce its laws against foreign marine ships. It has jurisdiction over the ship and events occurring thereon. However, if the ship is a warship, it is immune from enforcement without the authorization of the captain or of the flag state, as military vessels are viewed as arms of the sovereignty of the flag state. However, the coastal state may require such vessels to leave immediately.

2 *Territorial Sea*

a *Breadth and Methods for Drawing Baselines*

The territorial sea is located not more than "12 nautical miles, measured from baselines" determined in accordance with UNCLOS (Article 3 UNCLOS). The baseline is usually the low-water mark—the location of the coastline at low tide.

There are three methods for drawing baselines:

- *Normal method*. The normal baseline for measuring the width of the territorial sea is the "low-water line along the coast as marked on large-scale charts officially recognized by the coastal State" (Article 5 UNCLOS).
- *Reefs*. "In the case of islands situated on atolls or of islands having fringing reefs, the baseline for measuring the breadth of the territorial sea is the seaward low-water line of the reef, as shown by the appropriate symbol on charts officially recognized by the coastal State" (Article 6 UNCLOS).
- *Straight baselines*. When the coastline is deeply indented and cut into or has a fringe island in its immediate vicinity (e.g., the case of Chile), straight baselines joining appropriate points may be used (Article 7.1 UNCLOS).

When a coast is marked by a bay, it is accepted practice that a straight baseline from which to determine the breadth of the territorial sea may be drawn across the mouth of the bay. However, under UNCLOS, "If the distance between the low-water marks of the natural entrance points of a bay does not exceed 24 nautical miles, a closing line may be drawn between these two low-water marks and the waters enclosed thereby shall be considered as internal waters" (Article 10.4 UNCLOS). Otherwise, a straight baseline of 24 miles may be drawn "within the bay in such a manner as to enclose the maximum area of water that is possible with a line of that length" (Article 10.5 UNCLOS). However, this provision does not apply to so-called historic bays (bays whose waters are treated by the coastal state as internal in light of historic rights and general acquiescence) or in cases in which straight baselines are applied (Article 10.6 UNCLOS).

Where the coasts of two states are opposite or adjacent to each other, neither of the two states is entitled (absent agreement to the contrary or historic or special circumstances) "to extend its territorial sea beyond the median line, every point of which is equidistant from the nearest points on the baselines from which the breadth of the territorial seas of each of the two States is measured" (Article 15 UNCLOS).

b *Rights of States and Innocent Passage*

States have full sovereignty over their territorial seas. They possess the exclusive right to fish in their territorial seas, exploit their seabed resources and regulate the airspace above (cabotage). Certain powers of arrest over merchant ships exist in the territorial seas, with the exception of international straits, such as the Strait of Hormuz, linking the Gulf of Oman and the Persian Gulf, or the English Channel, which hold more favorable rules toward foreign ships.

Foreign merchant vessels have the right to innocent passage in the coastal state's territorial sea. Passage is innocent "so long as it is not prejudicial to the peace, good order or security of the coastal State" (Article 19.1 UNCLOS). As a basic principle, the foreign ship, in order to enjoy the right of innocent passage while in the coastal state's territorial sea, may not engage in any activity not having a direct bearing on passage. UNCLOS specifically enumerates the following activities, all of which are considered prejudicial to the coastal state, as prohibited: any threat or use of force against the sovereignty, territorial integrity or political independence of the coastal state; any exercise or practice with weapons; any act aimed at collecting information to the prejudice of the defense or security of the coastal state; any act of propaganda aimed at affecting the defense or security of the coastal state; the launching, landing or taking on board of any aircraft or military device; the loading or unloading of any commodity, currency or person contrary to the laws and regulations of the coastal state; acts of willful and serious pollution; fishing; research or survey activities; acts aimed at interfering with systems of communication of the coastal state (Article 19.2 UNCLOS). Western powers hold that the right to innocent passage extends to warships, but third-world countries disagree.

Coastal states may exercise criminal jurisdiction to arrest any person or to conduct any investigation in connection with any crime committed on board a foreign ship passing through its territorial sea, but Article 27.1 UNCLOS limits this right to the following cases only:

(a) if the consequences of the crime extend to the coastal state;
(b) if the crime is of a kind to disturb the peace of the country or the good order of the territorial sea;
(c) if the assistance of the local authorities has been requested by the master of the ship or by a diplomatic agent or consular officer of the flag state; or
(d) if such measures are necessary for the suppression of illicit traffic in narcotic drugs or psychotropic substances.

The coastal state should not stop or divert the passing ship in order to exercise civil jurisdiction in relation to a person on board the ship (Article 28 UNCLOS).

3 *Contiguous Zone*

The contiguous zone is a zone contiguous to a coastal state's territorial sea. Article 33.1 UNCLOS permits the coastal state to exercise the control necessary to:

(a) prevent infringement of its customs, fiscal, immigration or sanitary laws and regulations within its territory or territorial sea;
(b) punish infringement of the above laws and regulations committed within its territory or territorial sea.

The contiguous zone may extend up to 24 nautical miles from the baselines from which the breadth of the territorial sea is measured (Article 33.2 UNCLOS). Whereas under the 1958 GCTS, this zone formed a part of the high seas, at present it forms part of the exclusive economic zone.

4 *Exclusive Economic Zone*

The exclusive economic zone is located up to 200 nautical miles from the baselines used to measure the territorial sea (Article 57 UNCLOS). The exclusive economic zone grants the coastal state sovereign rights for the purpose of exploring and exploiting, conserving and managing both the living and non-living natural resources of the waters superjacent to the seabed and of the seabed and its subsoil and with regard to other activities for the economic exploitation and exploration of the zone, such as the production of energy from the water, currents and winds (Article 56.1(a) UNCLOS). The exclusive economic zone also entitles the coastal state to jurisdiction with regard to: "(i) the establishment and use of artificial islands, installations and structures; (ii) marine scientific research; (iii) the protection and preservation of the marine environment; (c) other rights and duties provided for in [UNCLOS]" (Article 56.1(b) UNCLOS).

5 *Continental Shelf Zone*

a Definition and Limits

In geology, the continental shelf refers to the ledge that projects from the continental landmass into the deep sea, connecting one to the other. Compared to the deep sea, which reaches thousands of meters of depth, the continental shelf, before falling away into the deep sea, is relatively shallow, usually at less than 200 meters deep. In terms of how far it projects from the coast, the figures vary widely. While in some coastal states, the continental shelf may be within the territorial sea, in others, it may protrude many hundreds of miles from the coast. For example, in Chile, the continental shelf is within the territorial sea and in California, it is only 5 miles from the coastline. In contrast, the entire North Sea is situated above a continental shelf.

Because of the rich natural resources, including oil and gas and fishing, available in the continental shelf zones, the rights to continental shelves have been highly sought after by states and have thus fallen under the regulations of the law of the sea conventions. Under UNCLOS, the continental shelf of a coastal state is defined as "the seabed and subsoil of the submarine areas that extend beyond its territorial sea throughout the natural prolongation of its land territory to the outer edge of the continental margin" (Article 76.1 UNCLOS). If the outer edge of the continental margin does not extend beyond 200 nautical miles from the baselines from which the territorial sea is measured (as in the case of Chile and the west coast of the U.S.), then the shelf will automatically be considered under UNCLOS to be located at 200 nautical miles from the baselines (Article 76.1 UNCLOS). Otherwise, its location is determined by its natural geological formation. However, even in this latter case, the outer limits of the continental shelf may not extend beyond 350 nautical miles from the baselines used to measure the territorial sea or 100 nautical miles from the 2,500-meter isobath (a line connecting the depth of 2,500 meters) (Article 76.5 UNCLOS).

b *Rights of the Coastal State*

The coastal state exercises over the continental shelf sovereign rights for the purpose of exploring it and exploiting its natural resources, defined as the mineral and other non-living resources of the seabed and subsoil and living *sedentary* organisms (organisms which, at the harvestable stage, either are immobile on or under the seabed or are unable to move except in constant physical contact with the seabed or the subsoil). This right is exclusive in the sense that no one may undertake these activities without the express consent of the coastal state (Article 77 UNCLOS). However, the rights of the coastal state over the continental shelf "do not affect the legal status of the superjacent waters or of the air space above those waters" (Article 78.1 UNCLOS).

6 *High Seas*

a *Definition*

The high seas are defined under UNCLOS as "all parts of the sea that are not included in the exclusive economic zone, in the territorial sea or in the internal waters of a state, or in the archipelagic waters of an archipelagic State" (Article 86 UNCLOS). The high seas are located beyond the continental shelf boundary, over the deep seabed.

b *Freedoms*

As a general rule, the high seas are open, and with the exception of the doctrines of recognition, acquiescence and prescription, no state "may validly purport to subject any part of the high seas to its sovereignty" (Article 89 UNCLOS). Freedom of the high seas comprises, subject to limitations, freedom of navigation; freedom of overflight; freedom to lay submarine cables and pipelines; freedom to construct artificial islands and other installations; freedom of fishing; and freedom of scientific research (Article 87.1 UNCLOS). UNCLOS further requires that these rights be "exercised by all States with due regard for the interests of other States in their exercise of the freedom of the high seas, and also with due regard for the rights under this Convention with respect to activities in the Area" (Article 87.2 UNCLOS). The high seas may only be used for peaceful purposes (Article 88 UNCLOS); nuclear testing or military exercises are prohibited.

As a general rule, under the principle of freedom of navigation on the high seas, coastal states may not stop foreign-flagged vessels. However, in the case of hot pursuit, if the coastal state has been pursuing a vessel and the pursuit commenced in the coastal state's internal or archipelagic waters, territorial sea, or contiguous zone, the coastal state may pursue the vessel even if the vessel crosses into the high seas if the pursuit has not been interrupted (Article 111.1 UNCLOS). This right ceases "as soon as the ship pursued enters the territorial sea of its own State or of a third State" (Article 111.3 UNCLOS).

D Protection and Preservation of the Marine Environment

Part XII of UNCLOS establishes the obligation of states to protect and preserve the marine environment. This obligation comprises the duty of states parties to prevent, reduce and control pollution of the marine environment (Article 194 UNCLOS); to minimize to the extent possible pollution from vessels and to undertake measures for preventing accidents and dealing with emergencies, ensuring the safety of operations at sea and preventing intentional and unintentional discharges (Article 194(b) UNCLOS); and not to transfer damage or hazards or transform one type of pollution into another (Article 195 UNCLOS).

E Jurisdiction and Enforcement of Law

On the high seas, ships are subject to international law and to the law of the state whose flag they are carrying (the "flag state"), which corresponds to the nationality of the ship. There must be a "genuine link" between the ship and the flag state (Article 91 UNCLOS), which enforces both international law and its own law.

F Legal Institutions

1 International Tribunal for the Law of the Sea

The International Tribunal for the Law of the Sea ("ITLS") is an intergovernmental organization seated in Hamburg, Germany, that was created by the mandate of the Third United Nations Conference on the Law of the Sea ("UNCLOS III") and established by UNCLOS. The ITLS has authority to settle disputes between its 155 member states.

2 International Seabed Authority

The International Seabed Authority ("ISA") is an independent treaty body created by UNCLOS to organize and control all mineral-related activities in the international seabed area beyond the limits of national jurisdiction. It issues licenses to states to exploit the resources of the deep seabed beyond the limits of national jurisdiction and is responsible for the regulation of seabed mining. Based in Kingston, Jamaica, the ISA is funded by a tax issued on continental shelf exploration.

II AIR LAW

A Regulatory Framework

Air law, also known as "aviation law," conventionally refers to that body of laws concerning civil aviation. It is sometimes broadly also used to refer to any law involving the use of the air (e.g., those governing radio transmissions), but in this text, only the conventional definition will be used.

Because of the international character of aviation, a large part of air law is comprised of international conventions. One of the earliest legal instruments to this effect was the Convention Relating to the Regulation of Aerial Navigation, colloquially known as the "Paris Convention," which was signed by 27 states in 1919 to deal with a host of aerial issues, including certificates of airworthiness of aircraft, the certification and licensing of pilots, admission to air navigation above foreign territories and departure and landing rules. The Paris Convention recognizes the exclusive sovereignty of each state over airspace above its territory without prejudice to innocent passage by foreign aircraft. Moreover, it extends to aircraft the principle of nationality, whereby each aircraft must be registered with a state.

Today's basic framework for aviation law is established by the Chicago Convention on International Civil Aviation, commonly referred to as the "Chicago Convention" (CC). The Convention has undergone nine revisions since its 1947 entry into force. The most recent revision took place in 2006. The treaty was signed in 1944 by 52 states at Chicago's International Civil Aviation Conference, which also led to the adoption of the International Air Services Transit Agreement, where freedom to fly across the territory of a state without landing and freedom to land for non-traffic purposes was established. As for the Chicago Convention, the principle of the "complete and exclusive sovereignty" of each state over airspace above its territory is reaffirmed (Article 1 CC) and various rules of airspace, aircraft registration, pilot licensing, radio navigation aids and safety, are set forth. Today, the Convention counts 188 states parties.

The Convention also established the International Civil Aviation Organization ("ICAO"), a specialized agency that seeks to promote security through cooperative aviation regulation. In October of 1947, within 6 months of its birth, ICAO became a specialized ECOSOC agency. It is mandated with the planning and development of international air navigation and regulation.

B Air Carrier Liability

Under the 1929 Warsaw Convention for the Unification of Certain Rules Relating to International Carriage by Air, informally known as the "Warsaw Convention," the owner or operator of a carrier was made liable for any injury, death, or property damage by the carrier.

The Convention for the Unification of Certain Rules for International Carriage, colloquially known as the "Montreal Convention," was adopted in 1999 by a Diplomatic meeting of the member states of the International Civil Aviation Organization to amend important provisions of the 1929 Warsaw Convention's regime concerning compensation for the victims of air disasters. The Convention protects passengers by introducing a two-tier liability system and by facilitating the swift recovery of proven damages without the need for litigation. Air carriers under the Convention are strictly liable for proven damages up to 100,000 Special Drawing Rights ("SDRs") (an IMF reserve currency equivalent) or USD 138,000 per passenger at the time of its ratification by the United States in 2003. Where damages of more than 100,000 SDR are sought, the airline may avoid liability by proving that the accident which caused the injury or death was not due to its negligence. The Convention also amended the jurisdictional provisions of Warsaw and now allows victims or their families to sue foreign carriers where they maintain their principal residence and requires all air carriers to carry liability insurance.

The Montreal Convention also generally increases the maximum liability of airlines for lost baggage. Whereas liability in the Warsaw Convention is based on the weight of the baggage, the Montreal Convention changes liability to a fixed amount of 1000 SDR.

III SPACE LAW

Outer space lies beyond the upper limit of a state's sovereign airspace. In a 1963 resolution, the U.N. General Assembly declared outer space to be free for exploration and use by all states. The resolution outlined rules assigning individual responsibility for dealing with transgressions of international law declared space to be incapable of national appropriation.

The basic legal framework of international space law was established with the Treaty on Principles Governing the Activities of States in the Exploration and Use of Outer Space, Including the Moon and Other Celestial Bodies, colloquially known as the "Outer Space Treaty of 1967." Recognizing the "common interest of all mankind in the progress of the exploration and use of outer space for peaceful purposes" (Preamble OST), the Treaty reiterates the principle that the "exploration and use of outer space, including the moon and other celestial bodies, shall be carried out for the benefit and in the interests of all countries" (Article I OST). The Outer Space Treaty bars states parties from placing in orbit around the earth "any objects carrying nuclear weapons or any other kinds of weapons of mass destruction, [installing] such weapons on celestial bodies, or [stationing] such weapons in outer space in any other manner" and reserves the moon and other celestial bodies for exclusively peaceful purposes (Article IV OST). The treaty also sets out a framework of mutual assistance for the rescue of astronauts in crisis situations (Article V OST) and cooperation in the exploration of outer space (Article IX OST).

The Agreement Governing the Activities of States on the Moon and Other Celestial Bodies (1979), informally known as the Moon Treaty ("MT"), follows the tradition of reserving the regions of outer space to peaceful purposes. It seeks to promote cooperation "in the exploration and use of the moon and other celestial bodies [and] prevent the moon from becoming an area of international conflict" (Preamble MT). It requires the demilitarization of the moon and other celestial bodies and declares that "the moon and its natural resources are the common heritage of mankind" (Article 11.1 MT). However, the effect of the treaty has been minimal, as none of the states engaged in manned space exploration ratified the treaty.

CHAPTER 12
International Economic and Trade Law

Organizations such as the World Trade Organization that write international laws binding on member states fall within public international law, as they do not deal with states' domestic laws strictly speaking.

I THE WORLD TRADE ORGANIZATION

A Overview

The World Trade Organization ("WTO") is an international economic organization that regulates international trade between nations. Through the WTO, states establish and enforce the rules that govern international trade and seek to promote transparency and non-discrimination in trade relations. The WTO agreements are intended to supervise and liberalize international trade and assist producers of goods and services as well as exporters and importers to conduct their business.

The WTO is a member-driven organization whose agreements have been negotiated, signed and ratified by most of the world's trading states. Currently, there are 164 WTO members, in addition to 24 observer governments of states moving toward full membership. Only 16 states are neither World Trade Organization members nor observer governments.

B Key Instruments Underpinning the WTO Framework

A number of multilateral agreements create the WTO framework. The three key international agreements underpinning the WTO system are as follows:

- the General Agreement on Tariffs and Trade, which covers trade in goods;
- the General Agreement on Trade in Services, which covers trade in services; and

- the Agreement on Trade-Related Aspects of Intellectual Property Rights, which covers the trade-related aspects of intellectual property rights.

1 *General Agreement on Tariffs and Trade*

The General Agreement on Tariffs and Trade ("GATT") was formed in 1949 and lasted until 1993. GATT was negotiated during the 1944 U.N. Conference on Trade and Employment and was the outcome of the failure of negotiating governments to create the International Trade Organization ("ITO"). Because GATT lacked a coherent institutional structure, it was modified in 1994, creating the WTO in 1995. The WTO incorporates the principles of GATT, but is better positioned to carry out the principles of GATT as it incorporates an effective dispute resolution system and holds more power.

The text of the original GATT of 1947 is still in effect under the WTO framework but has been modified by GATT 1994, the Final Act Embodying the Results of the Uruguay Round of Multilateral Trade Negotiations. In addition to the texts of the agreements, the Final Act also contains texts of Ministerial Decisions and Declarations, which further clarify certain provisions of some of the agreements.

2 *General Agreement on Trade in Services*

The General Agreement on Trade in Services ("GATS") is a WTO treaty that entered into force in 1995 with dual objectives of creating a reliable and predictable system of international rules for trade in services and facilitating the progressive liberalization of services markets. All WTO members are states parties to the GATS.

The GATS applies to all service sectors, with the exception of services supplied in the exercise of governmental authority on a non-commercial basis (e.g., the provision of education and public health services) and services related to air transport. GATS members are free to choose which sectors are to be progressively liberalized, which mode of supply would apply to a particular sector and to what extent liberalization will occur over a given period.

While members' commitments are not to be wound back, Article XXI of GATS allows members to withdraw their liberalization commitments. However, at the request of any member whose benefits under GATS may be affected by such withdrawal, the modifying member must enter into negotiations with a view to reaching agreement on any necessary compensatory adjustment. In such negotiations and agreement, the concerned members must endeavor to maintain a general level of mutually advantageous commitments not less favorable to trade than that provided for in Schedules of specific commitments prior to such negotiations and compensatory adjustments must be made on a most-favored-nation basis (Article XXI.2 GATS).

3 *Agreement on Trade-Related Aspects of Intellectual Property Rights*

The Agreement on Trade-Related Aspects of Intellectual Property Rights ("TRIPS Agreement") establishes minimum standards of protection for copyrights, trademarks, patents, industrial designs, geographical indications ("GIs"), integrated circuit layout designs and undisclosed information. The TRIPS Agreement also establishes minimum standards for the enforcement of intellectual property rights ("IPRs") through civil actions for infringement and through criminal actions for copyright piracy and trademark counterfeiting.

The TRIPS Agreement plays a critical role in facilitating trade in knowledge and creativity and in resolving intellectual property trade disputes. Section 1 of Part II of the TRIPS Agreement provides protections in the area of copyright and related rights, including for literary and artistic works, performances, phonograms (or sound recordings) and broadcasts. Section 2 of Part II governs trademark rights and protects any sign capable of distinguishing the goods or services of one undertaking from those of other undertakings and makes such signs, and in particular "words including personal names, letters, numerals, figurative elements and combinations of colours as well as any combination of such signs" eligible for registration as trademarks (Article 15 TRIPS Agreement). Patents are governed by section 5 of Part II, which makes patents available for "any inventions, whether products or processes, in all fields of technology, provided that they are new, involve an inventive step and are capable of industrial application" (Article 27.1 TRIPS Agreement).

C Other Agreements

1 *Plurilateral Agreements*

In most cases, all WTO members subscribe to all WTO agreements. However, following the Uruguay Round, there were four "plurilateral agreements" that were originally negotiated in the Tokyo Round that had a narrower group of signatories. All other Tokyo Round agreements became multilateral obligations for all members when the WTO was established in 1995. The plurilateral agreements, in contrast, establish obligations for a smaller number of parties.

The four plurilateral agreements of the WTO are as follows: the Agreement on Trade in Civil Aircraft, which eliminates import duties on civil aircraft, civil aircraft engines and their parts and components, all components and sub-assemblies of civil aircraft, and flight simulators and their parts and components; the Agreement on Government Procurement, which sought to open up as much of government procure as possible to international competition by making laws, regulations, procedures and practices regarding government procurement more transparent and to ensure they do not discriminate against foreign suppliers; and the International Dairy Agreement and the International Bovine Meat Agreement, which were terminated in 1997.

2 *Agreement on Technical Barriers to Trade*

The Agreement on Technical Barriers to Trade ("TBT Agreement"), while recognizing the right of WTO members to implement measures to achieve legitimate policy objectives, such as the protection of health, safety and the environment, aims to ensure that technical regulations, standards and conformity assessment procedures are non-discriminatory and do not create unnecessary obstacles to trade. Aiming to create a predictable trading environment, the TBT Agreement encourages members to base their measures on international standards as a means to facilitate trade.

Among other obligations, the TBT Agreement requires states parties to undertake the following obligations:

- "ensure that in respect of technical regulations, products imported from the territory of any Member shall be accorded treatment no less favourable than that accorded to like products of national origin and to like products originating in any other country";
- "ensure that technical regulations are not prepared, adopted or applied with a view to or with the effect of creating unnecessary obstacles to international trade";
- refrain from maintaining technical regulations "if the circumstances or objectives giving rise to their adoption no longer exist or if the changed circumstances or objectives can be addressed in a less trade-restrictive manner";
- use technical regulations when required and relevant international standards exist, or their completion is imminent, "except when such international standards or relevant parts would be an ineffective or inappropriate means for the fulfilment of the legitimate objectives pursued";
- upon the request of another member, explain the justification for a technical regulation whenever a member is preparing, adopting or applying such a regulation, which may have a significant effect on trade of other members;
- play a full part, within the limits of their resources, "in the preparation by appropriate international standardizing bodies of international standards for products for which they either have adopted, or expect to adopt, technical regulations" (Article 2 TBT Agreement).

D Dispute Settlement Understanding

The WTO dispute settlement system, commonly known as the Dispute Settlement Understanding ("DSU"), was created as part of the WTO Agreement during the Uruguay Round. The DSU provides an enforcement mechanism in cases where a WTO member fails to comply with its obligations. The DSU is embodied in the Understanding on Rules and Procedures Governing the Settlement of Disputes. Found within Annex 2 of the WTO Agreement, the DSU sets out the procedures and rules that define the dispute settlement system.

The DSU seeks to provide security and predictability to the multilateral trade system (Article 3.2 DSU) through an efficient, dependable and rule-oriented system to resolve disputes relating to the application of the provisions of the WTO Agreement. If the parties to a trade dispute fail to reach a solution, the complainant is guaranteed a procedure in which the merits of its claims will be examined by independent panels and an Appellate Body. Only states can bring cases through the DSU. By enforcing a rule-based system, the dispute settlement system makes the trading system more secure. When a ruling is issued against a WTO member, the member must implement the ruling promptly or face the possibility of trade sanctions.

II INTELLECTUAL AND INDUSTRIAL PROPERTY

A range of international instruments and institutions have been established for the protection of intellectual property. Among these are the TRIPS Agreement, discussed under "The World Trade Organization," *supra*, and the Convention Establishing the World Intellectual Property Organization, discussed below.

A World Intellectual Property Organization

The World Intellectual Property Organization ("WIPO") is a specialized U.N. agency headquartered in Geneva, Switzerland, that was formed by the 1967 Convention Establishing the World Intellectual Property Organization ("WIPO Convention"). WIPO began operations on 26 April 1970 when the WIPO Convention entered into force. WIPO's purpose is to develop a balanced and accessible intellectual property system that protects intellectual property globally. This protection is effected through cooperation among WIPO's 193 member states and international organizations.

WIPO hosts a range of fora to discuss and shape the rules governing the protection of intellectual property and provides services for the registration and protection of intellectual property and the resolution of transboundary disputes. WIPO publishes reports and statistics on the state of intellectual property protection globally and in specific countries and administers 26 international treaties, as follows:

- Sixteen intellectual property protection treaties that define internationally agreed basic standards of intellectual property protection in each country: the Beijing Treaty on Audiovisual Performances, the Berne Convention, the Brussels Convention, the Madrid Agreement (Indications of Source), the Marrakesh VIP Treaty, the Nairobi Treaty, the Paris Convention, the Patent Law Treaty, the Phonograms Convention, the Rome Convention, the Singapore Treaty on the Law of Trademarks, the Trademark Law Treaty, the Washington Treaty, the WIPO Copyright Treaty (WCT), the WIPO Performances and the Phonograms Treaty (WPPT).
- Six global protection treaties that ensure that one international registration or filing will have effect in all signatory states: the Budapest Treaty, the Hague Agreement, the Lisbon Agreement, the Madrid Agreement (Marks), the Madrid Protocol and the Patent Cooperation Treaty (PCT).

- Four classification treaties that create classification systems that organize information concerning inventions, trademarks and industrial designs into indexed structures to facilitate retrieval: the Locarno Agreement, the Nice Agreement, the Strasbourg Agreement and the Vienna Agreement.

B Industrial Property: The Paris Convention (1883)

The Paris Convention for the Protection of Industrial Property, adopted in 1883, protects a wide range of industrial property, including patents, trademarks, industrial designs, utility models, service marks, trade names and geographical indications. The Paris Convention requires each state party to grant to nationals of other states parties the same protection that it grants to its own nationals. Nationals of non-states parties are also entitled to national treatment if they are domiciled or have a real and effective industrial or commercial establishment in a state party.

In addition, the Paris Convention establishes a right of priority that allows for the first applicant for a patent, utility model, mark and industrial design to apply for protection in any of the other states parties within a certain period of time (12 months for patents and utility models; 6 months for industrial designs and marks). These subsequent applications are regarded as if they had been filed on the same day as the first application, thus granting the applicant priority over applications filed after the applicant's first application was filed.

C Copyright: Berne Convention for the Protection of Literary and Artistic Works (1886)

1 Overview

The principal international treaty in the area of copyright law is the Berne Convention for the Protection of Literary and Artistic Works (generally referred to as the "Berne Convention"), which was signed in 1886, went into effect in 1887, was revised at Paris in 1896 and at Berlin in 1908, completed at Berne in 1914, revised at Rome in 1928, at Brussels in 1948, at Stockholm in 1967 and at Paris in 1971, and was amended in 1979.

2 States Parties

The following 174 parties have ratified or acceded to the Berne Convention (in addition to 172 U.N. member states, the Holy See and Niue are contracting parties):

> Albania, Algeria, Andorra, Antigua and Barbuda, Argentina, Armenia, Australia, Austria, Azerbaijan, Bahamas, Bahrain, Bangladesh, Barbados, Belarus, Belgium, Belize, Benin, Bhutan, Bolivia (Plurinational State of), Bosnia and Herzegovina, Botswana, Brazil, Brunei Darussalam, Bulgaria, Burkina Faso, Burundi, Cabo Verde, Cameroon, Canada, Central African Republic, Chad, Chile, China, Colombia, Comoros, Congo, Cook Islands, Costa Rica, Côte d'Ivoire, Croatia,

Cuba, Cyprus, Czech Republic, Democratic People's Republic of Korea, Democratic Republic of the Congo, Denmark, Djibouti, Dominica, Dominican Republic, Ecuador, Egypt, El Salvador, Equatorial Guinea, Estonia, Fiji, Finland, France, Gabon, The Gambia, Georgia, Germany, Ghana, Greece, Grenada, Guatemala, Guinea, Guinea-Bissau, Guyana, Haiti, Holy See, Honduras, Hungary, Iceland, India, Indonesia, Ireland, Israel, Italy, Jamaica, Japan, Jordan, Kazakhstan, Kenya, Kuwait, Kyrgyzstan, Lao People's Democratic Republic, Latvia, Lebanon, Lesotho, Liberia, Libya, Liechtenstein, Lithuania, Luxembourg, Madagascar, Malawi, Malaysia, Mali, Malta, Mauritania, Mauritius, Mexico, Federated States of Micronesia, Monaco, Mongolia, Montenegro, Morocco, Mozambique, Namibia, Nepal, Netherlands, New Zealand, Nicaragua, Niger, Nigeria, Niue, Norway, Oman, Pakistan, Panama, Paraguay, Peru, Philippines, Poland, Portugal, Qatar, Republic of Korea, Republic of Moldova, Romania, Russian Federation, Rwanda, Saint Kitts and Nevis, Saint Lucia, Saint Vincent and the Grenadines, Samoa, Sao Tome and Principe, Saudi Arabia, Senegal, Serbia, Singapore, Slovakia, Slovenia, South Africa, Spain, Sri Lanka, Sudan, Suriname, Eswatini (Swaziland), Sweden, Switzerland, Syrian Arab Republic, Tajikistan, Thailand, North Macedonia, Togo, Tonga, Trinidad and Tobago, Tunisia, Turkey, Turkmenistan, Tuvalu, Ukraine, United Arab Emirates, United Kingdom, United Republic of Tanzania, United States of America, Uruguay, Uzbekistan, Vanuatu, Venezuela (Bolivarian Republic of), Vietnam, Yemen, Zambia, Zimbabwe.

Non-states parties to the Berne Convention include:

Iraq, Iran, Afghanistan, Turkmenistan, Eritrea, Ethiopia, Somalia, Uganda, Angola, Western Sahara and Papua New Guinea.

3 *Berne Union*

The Berne Convention establishes a Union for the protection of the rights of authors in their literary and artistic works. The countries to which the Convention applies are members of the Union (Art 1 Berne Convention).

The Berne Union has an Assembly and an Executive Committee. All members of the Union who have adhered to at least the administrative and final provisions of the Stockholm Act are members of the Assembly. The members of the Executive Committee are elected from among the members of the Union, except for Switzerland, which is a member ex officio.

4 *Basic Principles*

The Berne Convention sets forth several basic principles, discussed herein.

a *Principle of National Treatment*

Works originating in one of the contracting states (i.e., works the author of which is a national of such a state or works first published in such a state) must be given the same protection in each of the other contracting states as the latter grants to the works of its own nationals.

For example, if a work is first published in the U.K., then it would receive in all 174 of the contracting parties the same protections that these states offer to their own nationals. Thus, if the work was published in the U.K. but remains under copyright in the U.K., which applies a copyright term of 70 years following the death of the author, it would not enjoy copyright in a country such as Canada, which applies a shorter term of 50 years following the death of the author.

b *Principle of Automatic Protection*

Protection must not be conditional upon compliance with any formality; rather, protection must be automatic.

c *Principle of Independence of Protection*

Protection is independent of the existence of protection in the country of origin of the work. However, if a contracting state provides for a longer term of protection than the minimum prescribed by the Convention and the work ceases to be protected in the country of origin, the contracting state may deny protection once protection in the country of origin ceases. For example, if a work is published in Saudi Arabia in 1960 and the author dies in 1963, copyright protection would cease in Saudi Arabia in 2013, 50 years after the death of the author. While the U.S. offers a term of protection of 70 years after the death of the author, it would not be required to continue to afford protection to the work until 2033, once protection in Saudi Arabia ceases in 2013.

5 ***Right of Reproduction and Free Uses***

a *General Rule*

As a general rule, authors of literary and artistic works protected by the Berne Convention have the exclusive right to authorize the reproduction of these works in any manner or form (Article 9(1) BC).

b *Free Uses*

However, the Convention allows certain limitations and exceptions on economic rights, allowing for protected works to be used without the authorization of the owner of the copyright and without payment of compensation. These limitations are commonly referred to as "free uses" of protected works and include:

i Fair Use

Under Article 9(2) BC:

> It shall be a matter for legislation in the countries of the Union to permit the reproduction of such works in certain special cases, provided that such reproduction does not conflict with a normal exploitation of the work and does not unreasonably prejudice the legitimate interests of the author.

ii Quotations

Under Article 10(1) BC:

> It shall be permissible to make quotations from a work which has already been lawfully made available to the public, provided that their making is compatible with fair practice, and their extent does not exceed that justified by the purpose, including quotations from newspaper articles and periodicals in the form of press summaries.

iii Newspaper Articles

Article 10bis BC similarly provides for the reproduction of newspaper or similar articles and the use of works for the purpose of reporting current events.

iv Ephemeral Recordings

Article 11bis(3) BC allows for ephemeral recordings for broadcasting purposes.

6 Minimum Protections Afforded

a Overview

Under the Berne Convention, states parties agree to protect works originating in other states parties in the same way that they protect works of their own citizens. A work protected under the copyright laws of one state party is generally protected in other states parties to the Convention. It is, however, possible that a state party lodge a reservation with respect to the protection afforded in the Convention.

b Copyright Term Based on Author's Death

i Default Rule: Life + 50

The term of protection granted by the Berne Convention is the life of the author plus 50 years after his death (Article 7(1) BC). Terms for cinematographic, anonymous and photographic works vary per the terms of the Convention and national legislation, as discussed under "Copyright Term Based on Publication and Creation Dates," *infra*.

ii Extended Protection Terms

The countries of the Union may grant a term of protection in excess of those provided by the Convention (Article 7(6) BC). For example, the U.S. affords protection throughout the life of the author plus 70 years for works published since 1978 or for unpublished works. The U.K. similarly affords protection throughout the life of the author plus 70 years and, if there are multiple authors, the life of the last surviving author plus 70 years.

c Copyright Term Based on Publication and Creation Dates

The Berne Convention provides the following copyright terms based on publication and creation dates:

- For cinematographic works, 50 years from the publication date or, if not shown, 50 years from creation (Article 7(2) BC).
- For anonymous or pseudonymous works, 50 years from publication (Article 7(3) BC).
- For photographic works, 25 years from creation (Article 7(4) BC).
- Longer terms may be granted by contracting parties (Article 7(6) BC).

7 Registration

Although most countries do not require copyright registration in order to enjoy copyright protection, registration can offer several benefits, such as proof of ownership. Many countries have bilateral copyright relations with one another, such that each country agrees to honor other countries' citizens' copyrights.

D Patents and Trademarks

A patent or trademark registered in one country does not afford protection in other countries; patents and trademarks must be filed in each country where protection is sought.

1 Madrid System for Trademarks (1891)

a The Madrid Agreement

The Madrid system for the international registration of marks (Madrid System), established in 1891, functions under the Madrid Agreement Concerning the International Registration of Marks (1891) ("Madrid Agreement") and the Madrid Protocol (1989). The Madrid System is administered by the International Bureau of WIPO located in Geneva, Switzerland.

The Madrid Agreement, revised at Brussels in 1900, at Washington in 1911, at The Hague in 1925, at London in 1934, at Nice in 1957 and at Stockholm in 1967 and amended in 1979, has been in operation for more than 110 years with 56 members. The Madrid Protocol, which entered into force in 2004 and currently has 112 members, introduced changes to the Madrid system that enhanced its usefulness to trademark owners. It makes it easier to file for trademark registration in multiple countries. By filing one trademark application, applicants may simultaneously seek trademark protection in up to 66 countries.

b *The Trademark Law Treaty*

The Trademark Law Treaty (1994) ("TLT") aims to standardize and streamline trademark registration procedures through both the simplification and harmonization of certain features of those procedures, thus making trademark applications and the administration of trademark registrations easier across jurisdictions.

2 *Patent Cooperation Treaty (1970)*

The Patent Cooperation Treaty ("PCT") (1970), done in Washington, DC, has made the process of applying for patents and trademarks in various countries much easier. For example, by filing one patent application with the U.S. Patent and Trademark Office ("USPTO"), U.S. applicants can simultaneously seek protection in up to 156 countries (as of 2022).

3 *Patent Law Treaty (2000)*

The Patent Law Treaty ("PLT") was signed in 2000 in Geneva, Switzerland, by 53 States and the European Patent Organisation and entered into force in 2005. It aims at harmonizing and streamlining the requirements to obtain filing dates for patent applications, the content of patent applications and the procedures for obtaining patent protection. Other than filing date requirements, the Treaty sets forth the maximum requirements that states parties may apply for patent applications.

III INTERNATIONAL SANCTIONS

A Overview

Economic and trade sanctions are geopolitical tools used by governments to influence the behavior of other governments and individuals. Governments as well as corporations, when engaged in international trade, must take into account the effect of sanctions on their operations and how to choose courses of action that mitigate and eliminate risk.

Economic and trade sanctions are restrictions that governments impose on certain types of transactions as a tool to achieve foreign policy or national security goals. Sanctions often are imposed in an effort to bring about a change with regard to armed conflict, terrorism, trafficking in arms and narcotics and violations of international human rights law. They are a means of achieving political objectives without resorting to the use of force. Governments as well as corporations, when engaged in international trade, must take into account the effect of sanctions on their operations and how to choose courses of action that mitigate and eliminate risk.

Sanctions can take a variety of different forms, including, without limitation:

- arms embargoes;
- blocking sanctions, consisting of (i) the freezing the funds and resources of targeted persons; and (ii) prohibitions on making funds or economic resources available for the benefit of such targeted persons;
- prohibitions on engaging in specific transactions with targeted persons;
- financial sanctions, including restrictions on the raising of capital by targeted companies and bans on the provision of specific services, such as brokerage services;
- trade sanctions, including export and import bans, prohibitions on investment in sanctioned states and bans on payments to sanctioned individuals;
- flight bans of sanctioned individuals;
- "Smart sanctions" that are intended to target only specific areas of a country's economy or to target specific individuals or groups;
- visa bans on targeted individuals.

Companies face a series of risks from sanctions. These risks include:

- business disruption in cases where governments suddenly impose sanctions on a state, requiring businesses to divest from the sanctioned state;
- loss of assets and other investments in states that become sanctioned;
- Criminal penalties that may be imposed for breaches of sanctions regimes. Such penalties can include company fines and imprisonment of company executives;
- Reputational damage.

Both the normative purpose of imposing sanctions as well as the efficaciousness of sanctions are subject to extensive debate. Some argue that imposing a trade embargo on a state has an undue negative impact on that state's civilian population while failing to have any influence on the behavior of the state's leaders. The Democratic People's Republic of Korea (North Korea) is a case in point. Despite extensive international and unilateral sanctions designed to prevent North Korea from obtaining nuclear weapons, today, North Korea is a nuclear power estimated to have 50 warheads in its nuclear arsenal.[430] Yet despite the controversy surrounding the use of sanctions, states continue to use them as a way of conducting "war by other means."

Sanctions can take the form of multilateral action, where international or regional organizations coordinate a sanctions response, or unilateral action, where states, operating through their domestic lawmaking authority, impose sanctions. With respect to multilateral sanctions, the U.N. Charter provides for the U.N. Security Council to take measures not involving the use of armed force in order to address threats to peace and acts of aggression. These measures "may include complete or partial interruption of economic relations" (Article 41 Charter). Since 1966, the U.N. Security Council has established 31 sanctions regimes, including in Southern Rhodesia, South Africa, the Former Yugoslavia, Haiti, Angola, Liberia, Eritrea/Ethiopia, Rwanda, Sierra Leone, Côte d'Ivoire, Iran, Somalia/Eritrea, ISIL (Da'esh) and Al-Qaida, Iraq, the Democratic Republic of the Congo, Sudan, Lebanon, Democratic People's Republic of Korea, Libya, the Taliban, Guinea-Bissau, Central African Republic, Yemen, South Sudan and Mali. Other international organizations that have established sanctions programs, including the E.U., as discussed below. Most sanctions programs, however, are unilateral national programs. Several examples of such programs are discussed below.

B U.S. Sanctions Law

1 Overview of U.S. Sanctions

a Application and Authority

U.S. sanctions law can apply to any of the following:

- U.S. persons, including U.S. citizens (regardless of where they reside or are located);
- permanent residents;
- entities formed under U.S. law;
- companies whose majority stake is owned by U.S. persons;
- persons physically located in the U.S.; and
- under certain sanctions programs (e.g., Iran, Cuba), any other persons who have sufficient U.S. nexus.

In the U.S., sanctions are generally issued under federal rather than state law. U.S. sanctions may be imposed by the U.S. President, who may issue Executive Orders under statutory authority or by the U.S. Congress through the enactment of sanctions legislation.

430. "Arms Control and Proliferation Profile: North Korea," Arms Control Association (January 2024), available at <https://www.armscontrol.org/factsheets/arms-control-and-proliferation-profile-north-korea#:~:text=North%20Korea%20currently%20is%20estimated,kilograms%20of%20highly%20enriched%20uranium.>.

Under the International Emergency Economic Powers Act of 1977,[431] the U.S. President has the power to declare a "national emergency" based on an "unusual and extraordinary threat to U.S. national security and U.S. foreign policy" and has the power to prohibit commercial practices and block (freeze) transactions. Presidential Executive Orders may take the form of Directives (Sectoral Sanctions) or Determinations (listing sectors that are the target of blocking sanctions). Congress's power to issue sanctions legislation is derived by the U.S. Constitution, which grants Congress power "to regulate trade with foreign nations."[432]

Executive Orders and sanctions statutes are generally implemented by the U.S. Treasury, the U.S. State Department or the U.S. Commerce Department through the issuance of regulations. These executive branch departments have broad authority to investigate and impose civil penalties on persons found to have violated sanctions. The U.S. Department of Justice, U.S. Attorneys' offices and certain state and local prosecutors have the authority to seek criminal penalties through the U.S. courts.

Sanctions that were imposed in the U.S. by the President can be lifted by the President under the same authority through which they were imposed. However, sanctions imposed by the U.S. Congress under its statutory authority generally require Congress to pass new legislation lifting such sanctions.

b *Penalties*

Penalties for sanctions violations under U.S. law may include any of the following:

- Civil penalties
  - The maximum civil monetary penalty for U.S. sanctions violations depends on the statute being enforced. The maximum under the Trading with the Enemy Act ("TWEA") is USD 108,489 in 2024, up from USD 105,083 in 2023. The maximum under the International Emergency Economic Powers Act ("IEEPA") is USD 368,136 in 2024, up from USD 356,579 in 2023.[433]
  - Forfeiture of goods involved or of profits from the transaction.
  - Addition to the Specially Designated Nationals and Blocked Persons List ("SDN List").
- Criminal penalties (for willful violations)
  - Up to 20 years imprisonment.
  - Fines of up to the greater of USD 1,000,000 and twice the pecuniary gain.
- Secondary sanctions penalties
  - Exclusion from U.S. markets.
  - Denial of U.S. loan facilities.

431. 50 U.S.C. §§ 1701 et seq.
432. U.S. Constitution, Art. I, s. 8, Clause 3.
433. *See* OFAC, Inflation Adjustment of Civil Monetary Penalties (89 Fed. Reg. 2,139). *See also*: Appendix A to Part 501—Economic Sanctions Enforcement Guidelines, section V.B.a.

- Prohibition on the opening or imposing conditions on the maintenance of U.S. correspondent banking accounts;
- Addition to the SDN List.
- Prohibition on transactions in foreign exchange that are subject to the jurisdiction of the United States.
- Prohibition on investments.
- Restrictions on imports of goods, technology, or services, directly or indirectly by the sanctioned person.
- Imposition of the above sanctions on principal executive officer or officers, or persons performing similar functions and with similar authorities, of a sanctioned person.

2 **Mens Rea** ***Requirements***

The U.S. Department of the Treasury's Office of Foreign Assets Control ("OFAC") administers and enforces most economic and trade sanction programs. OFAC administers civil enforcement of U.S. sanctions laws based on strict liability. Therefore, OFAC is not required to prove any level of *mens rea* or culpability, including intent (purpose), knowledge, recklessness or negligence, in order to enter an enforcement action or issue civil penalties against an offending party. OFAC may impose civil penalties on a strict liability basis of up to the higher of either twice the value of the underlying transaction or over USD 350,000 per violation.

The U.S. Department of Justice, in contrast, may pursue criminal investigations and criminal enforcement actions for willful sanctions violations, as can state criminal investigatory and enforcement bodies. In many cases, criminal charges have been brought against financial institutions that have both violated sanctions laws and intentionally attempted to deceive U.S. regulatory authorities by covering their sanctions violations. In such cases, the enforcement agency must prove the *mens rea* standard applicable to the underlying crime, which is generally intent or, in some cases, knowledge.

3 ***Primary and Secondary Sanctions***

a Types of U.S. Sanctions

U.S. sanctions may take any of the following forms:

- territorial embargoes that ban the export and import of goods from sanctioned countries;
- secondary sanctions that prohibit non-U.S. persons from engaging in certain specified activities (e.g., selling armaments to Iran);
- prohibitions on the evasion of sanctions and the facilitation of other persons' violations of sanctions;

- restrictions on transacting with entities from certain sectors of the economy of the sanctioned country;
- electronic payments denominated in U.S. dollars are generally prohibited if targeted countries or persons are involved. This prohibition generally applies even if the payments are initiated outside the U.S. since most U.S. dollar payments anywhere in the world will indirectly clear through the U.S.; and
- blocking or freezing the funds or other assets of sanctioned individuals or entities. Blocking sanctions apply to various categories of sanctioned persons and to the individuals and entities on the primary U.S. sanctions list—the SDN List.

b *Primary Sanctions and Derivative Designations for "Material Assistance"*

i Overview

Primary sanctions are asset freezes and trade embargoes that prohibit citizens and companies having nexus with the U.S. from engaging in certain transactions with sanctioned persons or sanctioned countries and that prohibit transactions with sanctioned persons or sanctioned countries when such transactions have nexus to the U.S. Sanctioned persons are generally named on the SDN List, a list published by OFAC of specially designated nationals and blocked persons that have been determined to have engaged in activities of concern covered by sanctions programs or who are designated pursuant to some other regulation. Some persons may, however, be sanctioned without appearing on the SDN List. An example would be where an entity is owned 50 percent or more in the aggregate by one or more individuals, entities and vessels listed on the SDN List, as discussed further below.

ii Specially Designated Nationals

Specially designated nationals ("SDNs") (generally referred to as "blocked persons") are individuals, entities and vessels listed on the SDN List and all entities owned 50 percent or more in the aggregate by one or more individuals, entities and vessels listed on the SDN List (the "50 Percent Rule"). OFAC has stated that:[434]

> any entity owned in the aggregate, directly or indirectly, 50 percent or more by one or more blocked persons is itself considered to be a blocked person. The property and interests in property of such an entity are blocked regardless of whether the entity itself is listed in the annex to an Executive order or otherwise placed on OFAC's list of Specially Designated Nationals ("SDNs").

An SDN can be an individual, including a person designated as a terrorist, or a company, parastatal entity or entity determined to be owned or controlled by, or acting

434. "Entities Owned by Blocked Persons (50% Rule)," OFAC (13 August 2014).

for or on behalf of, targeted countries or groups. The SDN's assets are blocked and U.S. persons are generally prohibited from dealing with them.

iii Difference Between Specially Designated Nationals and Blocked Persons

(1) Overview

As mentioned above, SDNs are generally referred to as "blocked persons." However, there is a key difference between the two concepts under the Iran sanctions program. All Iranian SDNs appear on the SDN List and are blocked persons. However, not all blocked persons are designated persons that appear on the SDN List. This is because under E.O. 13599 ("Blocking Property of the Government of Iran and Iranian Financial Institutions"), all entities meeting the definition of "Government of Iran" and Iranian financial institutions are blocked. However, not all such entities appear on the SDN List.

(2) "Material Assistance" to and "Significant Transactions" with Blocked Persons that Are Not Designated Do Not Trigger Derivative Designation or Secondary Sanctions

Regardless of whether blocked persons appear on the SDN List, U.S. persons are prohibited from transacting with them. However, if blocked Government of Iran entities or Iranian financial institutions appear on the SDN List, then risks of derivative designation for "material assistance" and secondary sanctions for knowingly engaging in "significant transactions" arise for non-U.S. persons without such blocked entities needing to appear on any list other than the SDN List. However, if a blocked Government of Iran person does not appear on the SDN List, then "material assistance" to and "significant transactions" with the blocked person do not trigger derivative designation or secondary sanctions for non-U.S. persons.

Non-U.S. persons transacting with Iranian SDNs should automatically assume that there is a risk of secondary sanctions applying without having to consult any separate list or database of entities subject to secondary sanctions. These risks of secondary sanctions do not apply to non-U.S. persons engaging with blocked persons who are not designated as SDNs.

iv Nexus and Jurisdictional Requirement

(1) Nexus of Persons and Entities to the U.S.

In the U.S., primary sanctions are "prohibitions" that apply only to persons and entities subject to the jurisdiction of the U.S. Such persons and entities must have nexus with the U.S. In general, persons subject to U.S. jurisdiction include:

(i) any person wheresoever located, who is a *citizen or resident* of the U.S.;
(ii) any person *actually within* the U.S.;

(iii) any *corporation organized under the laws of the U.S.* or of any state, territory, possession or district of the U.S.; and
(iv) any partnership, association, corporation, or other organization wheresoever organized or doing business which is *owned* by persons specified under points (i), (ii) and (iii) above.

The Iran and Cuba programs expand the definition of persons subject to U.S. jurisdiction for purposes of nexus, treating foreign organizations owned or controlled by a U.S. person as though they were U.S. persons. Under 31 CFR § 535.329, which defines nexus for the Iranian Assets Control Regulations, the notion of "persons subject to U.S. jurisdiction" includes business organizations that are *controlled* by U.S. citizens, residents, persons in the U.S. and corporations organized in the U.S. The full list of U.S. persons thus includes:

(i) any person wheresoever located, who is a *citizen or resident* of the U.S.;
(ii) any person *actually within* the U.S.;
(iii) any *corporation organized under the laws of the U.S.* or of any state, territory, possession or district of the U.S.; and
(iv) any partnership, association, corporation, or other organization wheresoever organized or doing business which is *owned or controlled* by persons specified under points (i), (ii) and (iii) above.

The Cuban Assets Control Regulations, in CFR § 515.329, defines persons subject to U.S. jurisdiction as follows:

(a) any individual, wherever located, who is a citizen or resident of the United States;
(b) any person within the United States as defined in § 515.330;
(c) any corporation, partnership, association, or other organization organized under the laws of the United States or of any State, territory, possession, or district of the United States; and
(d) any corporation, partnership, association, or other organization, wherever organized or doing business, that is owned or controlled by persons specified in paragraphs (a) or (c) of this section.

(2) Transactional Nexus

In addition, some commentators argue that primary sanctions could also apply to persons who do not fall under any of the foregoing categories if they otherwise have nexus to the U.S. (e.g., by engaging in transactions in or with the U.S., such as by using U.S.-based servers or banks). It may thus be helpful to think of primary sanctions as applying to "transactions" involving a nexus to U.S. jurisdiction. U.S.-nexus transactions include:

- transactions involving a U.S. person,[435] defined as:
  - any person wherever located, who is a citizen or resident of the U.S.;
  - any person within the U.S.;
  - any corporation organized under the laws of the U.S. or of any state, territory, possession, or district of the U.S., as well as their foreign branches;[436]
  - foreign subsidiaries owned or controlled by U.S. companies.
- transactions involving U.S.-origin products, software, or technology;
- transactions causing or involving activity in U.S. territory.
- transaction in U.S. dollars, which generally involve U.S. persons, including U.S. banks, and may also involve clearing and settlement by U.S. financial institutions (U.S. persons).[437] However, a U.S. dollar transaction where no U.S. persons are involved (e.g., where a non-U.S. person purchases a product using U.S. dollars in cash from another non-U.S. person) will not trigger U.S. nexus.

v Application of Primary Sanctions to Non-U.S. Persons

Primary sanctions may apply to non-U.S. persons in the following cases:

- where there is U.S. nexus (e.g., in U.S. dollar transactions);
- in cases of evading, causing, attempting to cause or conspiring to cause a sanctions violation (including aiding and abetting); and
- in cases of derivative designations.

Although these sanctions are similar to secondary sanctions in that they apply to non-U.S. persons, they remain under primary sanctions programs.

(1) U.S. Nexus Transactions

(a) Overview

As discussed above, some commentators argue that primary sanctions could apply to non-U.S. persons if they have nexus to the U.S. (e.g., by engaging in transactions in or with the U.S., such as by using U.S.-based servers or banks). "Transactions" involving a nexus to U.S. jurisdiction include transactions involving U.S.-origin products, software, or technology and transactions causing or involving activity in U.S. territory (including transactions in U.S. dollars).

435. 31 C.F.R. § 535.329.
436. OFAC *Frequently Asked Questions ("FAQ") No. 11*, available at <https://ofac.treasury.gov/faqs/11>.
437. *See* Christine Abely, "Causing a Sanctions Violation with U.S. Dollars: Differences in Regulatory Language Across OFAC Sanctions Programs," 48 *Georgia Journal of International and Comparative Law* 29 (2019).

(b) Consequences

Transactions that involve U.S. nexus and that violate U.S. sanctions laws may be charged by the U.S. Department of Justice and may carry criminal penalties.

(2) Evading, Causing, Attempting to Cause or Conspiring to Cause a Violation

(a) Overview

The term "primary sanctions" can be used to describe "prohibitions" that operate in an extraterritorial fashion when a person not otherwise subject to U.S. jurisdiction "evades or avoids" sanctions or "causes," "attempts to cause" or "conspires to cause" a violation of a primary sanctions prohibition.[438]

(b) Consequences

Evading, causing, attempting to cause or conspiring to cause a violation can result in enforcement action, which consists of criminal prosecution and penalties. In all cases, an activity by a non-U.S. person resulting in an enforcement action against the non-U.S. person *will involve at least one person that is actually a U.S. person or otherwise subject to U.S. jurisdiction*, even if the foreign person penalized is not a U.S. person or otherwise subject to U.S. jurisdiction. The conduct therefore is connected with some underlying activity that would violate substantive prohibitions administered by OFAC.

It may be possible that designation has been imposed on non-U.S. persons for evading, causing, attempting to cause or conspiring to cause a violation, but it is impossible to confirm this because OFAC may designate persons without giving a reason.

(3) Derivative Designations for "Material Assistance"

(a) Overview

Derivative designation criteria are found in many executive orders issued under the authority of the International Emergency and Economic Powers Act ("IEEPA") that involve the blocking of property. Derivative designations pose risks for U.S. and non-U.S. persons of being designated for:

(i) material support or assistance. The language used in E.O. refers to having "materially assisted, sponsored, or provided financial, material, or technological support for, or goods or services to or in support of any person whose property and interests in property are blocked pursuant to this section" (i.e., any person who is designated pursuant to a particular executive order);

(ii) being owned or controlled by, or having acted or purported to act for or on behalf of, directly or indirectly, any designated person (i.e., any person whose property and interests in property are blocked pursuant to a particular

438. *See, e.g.*, 31 CFR § 560.203. *See also* 31 CFR § 561.220.

executive order). This would include a corporation that is indirectly owned by an SDN through an intermediary agency; or

(iii) egregious conduct while operating in sectors that are also targeted by secondary sanctions.

These activities by non-U.S. persons do not trigger a sanctions violation but involve the risk of being designated as an SDN. Under the various Iranian sanctions programs, non-U.S. persons face a risk of derivative designation. In principle, OFAC also has the authority to designate U.S. persons as well for material assistance.

Because OFAC primary sanctions target only individuals and entities subject to U.S. jurisdiction, non-U.S. persons cannot "violate" U.S. primary sanctions. However, non-U.S. persons can be subject to sanctions risks when they transact with SDNs targeted under U.S. primary sanctions. Specifically, some of the E.O.s prohibiting U.S. persons from transacting with SDNs allow for designations of "any person" determined "to have materially assisted, sponsored, or provided financial, material, or technological support for, or goods or services to or in support of, any person whose property and interests in property are blocked."[439] The designation of non-U.S. persons on the basis of "material assistance" is relatively rare and limited to egregious conduct in sectors that are also targeted by secondary sanctions (e.g., the provision of material and technology for weapons[440] or transactions in the Iranian oil sector).[441]

Similarly, OFAC can designate non-U.S. individuals when they act "for or on behalf, directly or indirectly, any person whose property and interest in property are blocked."[442] Although there is some scholarly debate concerning whether designations under sanctions for "material support" or "acting on behalf of an SDN" amount to secondary sanctions since they target non-U.S. persons, they have *not* been traditionally classified as "secondary sanctions," which establish an outright prohibition on non-U.S. persons from engaging in certain transactions.

(b) Executive Orders Designating Persons

There are five Iran-related E.O.s that block property:

439. *See, e.g.*, section 1(a)(iii) of E.O. 13902 of 10 January 2020.

440. *See, e.g.*, Press Release, "Treasury Sanctions Procurement Network Supporting Iran's UAV and Military Programs," U.S. Department of Treasury (19 Apr. 2023). OFAC's action targets the Iran's Pardazan System Namad Arman (PASNA) suppliers procuring electronic components used in unmanned aerial vehicles (UAVs). The front-companies were established in Iran, Malaysia, Hong Kong and PRC.

441. *See, e.g.*, Press Release, "Treasury Targets Network Supporting Iranian Petrochemical and Petroleum Sales," U.S. Department of Treasury (17 November 2022). OFAC sanctioned 13 companies in multiple jurisdictions facilitating the sale of hundreds of millions of dollars' worth of Iranian petrochemicals and petroleum products to buyers in East Asia on behalf of sanctioned Iranian petrochemical brokers Persian Gulf Petrochemical Industry Commercial Co. (PGPICC) and Triliance Petrochemical Co. Ltd. (Triliance), as well as the National Iranian Oil Company (NIOC) and its marketing arm, Naftiran Intertrade Company Ltd. (NICO).

See, e.g., section 1(a)(iv) of Executive Order 13902 of 10 January 2020.

442. *See, e.g.*, section 1(a)(iv) of Executive Order 13902 of 10 January 2020.

(1) E.O. 13606—Blocking the Property and Suspending Entry into the United States of Certain Persons With Respect to Grave Human Rights Abuses by the Governments of Iran and Syria Via Information Technology:
   - This E.O. blocks persons, all of whom have been put on the SDN List, and includes material assistance language.

(2) E.O. 13553—Blocking Property of Certain Persons With Respect to Serious Human Rights Abuses by the Government of Iran and Taking Certain Other Actions:
   - This E.O. blocks persons, all of whom have been put on the SDN List, and includes material assistance language.

(3) E.O.13876—Imposing Sanctions With Respect to Iran:
   - This E.O. blocks "the Supreme Leader of the Islamic Republic of Iran and the Iranian Supreme Leader's Office" and includes standard derivative designation language.
   - Material assistance to the Supreme Leader's Office is an example in which material assistance to a "blocked person" that is not an SDN can trigger derivative designation. This is designed to ensure that the successor to the current Supreme Leader, Ali Khamenei, is blocked even if there is a delay in OFAC's designating his successor.

(4) E.O. 13599—Blocking Property of the Government of Iran and Iranian Financial Institutions:
   - This E.O. blocks all entities meeting the definition of "Government of Iran" and "Iranian Financial Institutions," but it does not enumerate them, and, in any case, not all "Government of Iran" entities are SDNs. However, E.O. 13599 does not include a material assistance provision.

(5) E.O. 13949—Blocking Property of Certain Persons With Respect to the Conventional Arms Activities of Iran:
   - This E.O. blocks property of persons with respect to the conventional arms activities of Iran, but it does not name persons specifically. It grants OFAC the authority to make future designations. When OFAC designates an entity as an SDN, it will do so by identifying the authority pursuant to which the entity is being designated.
   - If an entity is designated pursuant to E.O. 13949, derivative designations will apply, as the E.O. includes a material assistance provision.

(c) Consequences

Once the designations are made pursuant to the designation criteria, primary sanctions prohibitions attach to transactions involving persons subject to derivative designation and to their property. Such persons are added to the SDN List and are treated like SDNs without any distinction.

vi Penalties

Since primary sanctions apply only to persons with U.S. nexus, they can be enforced by OFAC through criminal prosecution or by civil fines, sometimes in conjunction with the Department of Justice and state-level law enforcement. In some cases, designation could also result. Any U.S. person who engages in an unlawful act consisting of violating, conspiring to violate or causing a violation of a license, order or prohibition under primary sanctions can be subject to civil and criminal penalties.[443] U.S. persons can be subject to violations of primary sanctions in the same way they can be subject to violations of any other U.S. criminal provisions.

The applicable maximum civil penalty per violation is the greater of USD 356,579.00 or an amount that is twice the amount of the transaction that is the basis of the violation with respect to which the penalty is imposed. The applicable maximum criminal penalty can be more severe. A person who willfully commits, attempts to commit, conspires to commit, or aids or abets in the commission of an unlawful action can be fined upon conviction with a limit of USD 1,000,000.00, or if a natural person may be imprisoned for not more than 20 years, or both.

The civil and criminal penalties are subject to adjustments depending on the nature of the infringement, the gain and loss resulting from the infringement and other factors. OFAC has published Economic Sanctions Enforcement Guidelines providing a general framework for enforcement of all economic sanctions programs administered by OFAC ("OFAC Enforcement Guidelines" or the "Guidelines"). The Guidelines provide general factors that OFAC considers in determining appropriate administrative actions and appropriate amount of penalty. These factors include, among others, willful or reckless violation of the law, awareness of the conduct at issue, harm to the sanctions program objectives, characteristics of the infringement, having compliance programs in place, remedial responses, cooperation with OFAC, timing of apparent violations, the deterrence effect of sanctions and other factors that are reviewed on a case-by-case basis.[444] In some cases, during the administrative penalty process, OFAC and the respondent will reach a settlement agreement that may be less than the civil penalty that might be imposed in the event of a formal determination of a violation.[445]

c *Secondary Sanctions for "Significant Transactions"*

i Overview

Secondary sanctions are extraterritorial sanctions that apply to non-U.S. persons in transactions having no connection to the U.S. They penalize persons having no U.S. nexus. The U.S. government has imposed secondary sanctions targeting non-U.S.

443. 31 C.F.R. § 501.701.
444. Appendix A to Part 501—Economic Sanctions Enforcement Guidelines, available at <https://www.ecfr.gov/current/title-31/subtitle-B/chapter-V/part-501/appendix-Appendix%20A%20to%20Part%20501>.
445. 31 C.F.R. § 501.710.

persons engaging in certain conduct involving Iran and with persons designated under U.S. sanctions targeting Russia. Though secondary sanctions vary across jurisdictions, most secondary sanctions are triggered upon a determination that a non-U.S. person has "*knowingly*" engaged in a "*significant transaction*" with an SDN.

In determining whether a transaction or financial service is "significant," OFAC considers the totality of the circumstances. As a general matter, OFAC may consider some or all of the following broad factors:

(a) the size, number and frequency of transactions performed;
(b) the nature of the transaction(s) or the goods or services for sale, supply, or transfer, including the type, complexity, and commercial purpose of the transaction(s), or the goods or services for sale, supply or transfer;
(c) the level of awareness of personnel involved in the transaction and pattern of conduct;
(d) the proximity between the person engaged in the transaction and the sanctioned activity;
(e) the impact of the transaction on sanctions policy goals;
(f) the involvement of deceptive practices; and
(g) other factors that OFAC deems relevant on a case-by-case basis.[446]

Under certain sanctions programs, the factors may be more specific. For example, under the Iran program, the nexus between the foreign financial institution involved in the transaction(s) and a blocked Islamic Revolutionary Guard Corps ("IRGC") individual or entity or blocked Iran-linked financial institution will be considered.[447] This is particularly relevant to transactions with the Central Bank of Iran because it has been designated as an agent or affiliate of the IRGC.[448] Therefore, SDR transactions involving the Central Bank of Iran pose a higher risk of secondary sanctions.

Furthermore, § 561.203(f) of the Iranian Financial Sanctions Regulations, 31 C.F.R. part 561 ("IFSR"), authorizes OFAC to sanction a foreign country's central bank, but only if it engages in financial transactions related to purchase or sale of petroleum or petroleum products to or from Iran. Therefore, SDR exchanges with the Central Bank of Iran involving petroleum transactions may expose the Saudi Central Bank to U.S. sanctions risks.

ii Conduct Prohibited by Secondary Sanctions

Secondary sanctions impose penalties on persons and organizations not having U.S. nexus that are engaged in the same dealings prohibited under U.S. primary sanctions. For example, because the Islamic Revolutionary Guard Corps ("IRGC") is subject to

446. *See, e.g.*, 31 C.F.R. § 562.407.
447. FAQ No. 154, available at <https://ofac.treasury.gov/faqs/154>.
448. Press Release, "Treasury Sanctions Iran's Central Bank and National Development Fund," U.S. Department of Treasury (20 September 2019), available at <https://home.treasury.gov/news/press-releases/sm780>.

secondary sanctions, a person who is not a U.S. person and has no U.S. nexus who deals in assets linked to the IRGC may be subject to OFAC penalties. This is true even when there is nothing in the transactions that triggers U.S. nexus, such as the use of U.S. dollars.

iii Application to Persons with No U.S. Nexus

Unlike primary sanctions, which apply only to citizens and companies having U.S. nexus, secondary sanctions apply to persons having no U.S. nexus. Despite their lack of U.S. nexus, such persons may be penalized as described below.

Although secondary sanctions apply to non-U.S. persons, secondary sanctions legislation is often drafted in a manner that includes "any person" within its scope, which could include U.S. persons. However, OFAC targets U.S. persons under U.S. primary sanctions rather than under secondary sanctions. To date, secondary sanctions have only been enforced against non-U.S. persons.

iv Penalties

Because secondary sanctions, unlike primary sanctions, apply to persons with no U.S. nexus, they cannot be enforced by fines or criminal prosecution in the U.S. However, secondary sanctions may be enforced by, *inter alia*, designation as an SDN. Such designation results in a prohibition of dealing with U.S. persons and companies, including banks. Moreover, persons subject to secondary sanctions can be subject to exclusion (immigration bans), banking restrictions (including prohibitions on using the U.S. financial system) and bans on investment and equity ownership in U.S. companies.

d Exemptions and Authorizations

i Overview

OFAC regulations allow for exemptions (general licenses) authorizing the performance of certain categories of transactions. In addition, OFAC issues authorizations (specific licenses) on a case-by-case basis under certain limited situations and conditions to engage in transactions that otherwise would be prohibited.[449]

OFAC authorizations (including general licenses) or exemptions under U.S. sanctions regulations allow U.S. persons to engage in activities otherwise prohibited by U.S. sanctions. OFAC has published a number of general licenses in connection with various sanctions programs administered with respect to Iran. These general licenses are, in effect, written authorizations allowing U.S. persons to engage in specified types

449. For guidance, *see* 31 C.F.R. 501.801.

of activities or transactions that would otherwise be prohibited by the sanctions. Certain general licenses are also codified within the relevant sanctions regulations.

While these authorizations or exemptions are for U.S. persons, they are important for non-U.S. persons both from the standpoint of primary sanctions compliance and secondary sanctions risks. With respect to primary sanctions, non-U.S. persons can rely on an exemption or general license to engage in U.S.-nexus transactions covered by the general license or exemption. Provided the transaction is authorized for U.S. persons under a general license, a non-U.S. person can engage in the same activity and would generally not risk "causing" a U.S. person to violate U.S. primary sanctions (since they are already authorized to participate in the transaction).

With respect to the risk of facing secondary sanctions, OFAC has stated repeatedly in published guidance that non-U.S. persons generally do not risk exposure to sanctions for engaging in activities or facilitating transactions for activities that would be authorized for U.S. persons.[450] In other words, a non-U.S. person may generally engage in activities authorized for U.S. persons under a general license and not risk being designated under secondary sanctions.

ii General Licenses (Exemptions)

The Iran sanctions program provides for certain exemptions, or "General Licenses," from the prohibitions. These General Licenses apply to the public at large. Below, we list some of the available General Licenses.

(1) Personal Communications, Remittances, Publishing and Information Technology

Iranian persons may engage in personal communications (phone calls, emails, text messages) with U.S. persons. In addition, U.S. persons may send personal remittances to Iran and engage in publishing activities in Iran.[451]

OFAC also issued General License D-2 with respect to certain services, on a fee basis, incident to the exchange of communications over the Internet, such as instant messaging, chat, social networking, sharing photos and movies, web browsing, blogging, social media platforms, web maps, user authentication services, as well as cloud-based services.[452]

(2) Exportation of Agricultural Commodities

The exportation or reexportation of agricultural commodities to the Government of Iran, or to any individual or entity in Iran is authorized, with the exception of certain

450. *See, e.g.*, OFAC, FAQ No. 1120, available at <https://ofac.treasury.gov/faqs/1120>; *see, e.g.*, OFAC, FAQ No. 823, available at <https://ofac.treasury.gov/faqs/823>; OFAC, FAQ No. 844, available at <https://ofac.treasury.gov/faqs/844>.
451. 31 C.F.R. § 560.550. *See also* 31 C.F.R. § 560.508.
452. OFAC General License D-2, available at <https://ofac.treasury.gov/media/928096/download?inline>.

excluded agricultural commodities (e.g., fertilizers).[453] The regulations also provide for a General License for payment and financing of exports and reexports of agricultural commodities under certain conditions.[454]

(3) Exportation of Medicines and Medical Equipment

The exportation or reexportation of medicine, medical devices and certain related software and services to the Government of Iran, or to any individual or entity in Iran, with the exception of certain excluded medicines and medical devices, is authorized. The exportation or reexportation of replacement parts for certain medical devices, as well as services and software necessary for the operation, maintenance and repair of medical devices, is also authorized.[455] The regulations also provide for a General License for payment and financing of exports and reexports of medicine, medical devices and certain related software and services.[456]

(4) Household Goods and Personal Effects

The exportation from the U.S. to Iran of household and personal effects, including baggage and articles for family use, of persons departing the U.S. to relocate to Iran is authorized, provided the articles included in such effects have been actually used by such persons or by family members accompanying them, are not intended for any other person or for sale, and are not otherwise prohibited from exportation.[457]

(5) Official Business of Certain International Organizations and Entities

The conduct of official business by entities, employees, grantees and contractors of international organizations such as the UN, the International Centre for Settlement of Investment Disputes ("ICSID"), the European Bank for Reconstruction and Development and the Global Fund to Fight AIDS, Tuberculosis and Malaria is authorized. The General License does not extend to transactions or activities involving the Iranian Red Crescent Society.[458]

(6) Official Business of the U.S. Government

The conduct of official business of the U.S. government by employees, grantees, or contractors is authorized.[459] In addition to the above, the regulations provide that OFAC can issue specific licenses for transactions in connection with awards, decisions or orders of the Iran-U.S. Claims Tribunal in The Hague, the International Court of Justice or other international tribunals, or agreements settling claims brought before tribunals;[460] exportation or reexportation of goods, services, and technology to ensure the safety of civil aviation and safe operation of U.S.-origin commercial passenger

453. 31 C.F.R. § 560.530.
454. 31 C.F.R. § 560.532.
455. 31 C.F.R. § 560.530.
456. 31 C.F.R. § 560.532.
457. 31 C.F.R. § 560.524.
458. 31 C.F.R. § 560.539.
459. 31 C.F.R. § 560.557.
460. 31 C.F.R. § 560.510.

aircraft;[461] exportation of equipment and services relating to information and informational materials;[462] and activities of non-governmental organizations and other entities organized in the U.S. which engage in projects, including conferences and training to support human rights, democratic freedoms, democratic institutions and the establishment or support of independent civic organizations.[463]

(7) Exemptions for Humanitarian Purposes

Most OFAC sanctions programs allow for exemptions for certain donated goods, such as articles donated to relieve human suffering. With respect to Iran, transactions "incident" to "humanitarian donations" are not exempt if they involve a person blocked pursuant to 31 C.F.R. 560.211 (including the Government of Iran and all Iranian Financial institutions). This is because E.O. 13599, which blocks the Government of Iran and all Iranian Financial Institutions, contains no carveout for donations.[464]

iii Specific Licenses

Specific licenses are issued at the request of persons and entities that wish to be allowed to engage in specific transactions that would otherwise be prohibited and which are not permitted under any general license. Entities and individuals can request OFAC to issue a specific license authorizing any other transaction prohibited under the Iranian sanctions regime that is not contemplated in the regulations. To obtain a specific license, the applicant must submit a comprehensive application that includes all relevant documents and a persuasive presentation grounded in U.S. policy considerations as to why OFAC should make an exception and allow the proposed transactions. If a license is granted, it is strictly construed to permit only the conduct specified in the license.

4 *Specific Sanctions Legislation*

a Countering America's Adversaries Through Sanctions Act

The Countering America's Adversaries Through Sanctions Act ("CAATSA")[465] was signed into law on 2 August 2017. Section 231 of CAATSA requires the imposition of sanctions on any person (U.S. or otherwise) that "knowingly … engages in a significant

461. 31 C.F.R. § 560.528.
462. 31 C.F.R. § 560.523.
463. 31 C.F.R. § 560.545.
464. OFAC FAQ 828, available at <https://ofac.treasury.gov/faqs/828#:~:text=The%20making%20of%20humanitarian%20donations,Regulations%2C%2031%20CFR%20Part%20560%20(/>.
465. Public Law 115-44, H.R. 3364, 2 August 2017.

transaction with a person that is part of, or operates for or on behalf of, the [Russian] defense or intelligence sectors."[466]

CAATSA establishes a sanctions regime that includes secondary sanctions as well as an expansion of some of the prohibitions applicable to U.S. persons. It is divided into the following three Acts, which impose sanctions on the Democratic People's Republic of Korea (North Korea), Iran and Russia, respectively:[467]

i Countering Iran's Destabilizing Activities Act of 2017

The Countering Iran's Destabilizing Activities Act of 2017 requires the President of the U.S. to impose sanctions against: (1) Iran's ballistic missile or weapons of mass destruction programs; (2) the sale or transfer to Iran of military equipment or the provision of related technical or financial assistance; and (3) Iran's Islamic Revolutionary Guard Corps and affiliated foreign persons. The law also grants the President authority to impose sanctions against persons responsible for violations of internationally recognized human rights committed against individuals in Iran and to temporarily waive the imposition or continuation of sanctions under specified circumstances.

ii Korean Interdiction and Modernization of Sanctions Act

The Korean Interdiction and Modernization of Sanctions Act increases the President's authority to impose sanctions on persons in violation of certain U.N. Security Council resolutions regarding North Korea and prohibits U.S. financial institutions from establishing or maintaining correspondent accounts used by foreign financial institutions to provide indirect financial services to North Korea. It also imposes sanctions on North Korean cargo and shipping, certain North Korean-produced goods and foreign persons that employ North Korean forced laborers.

iii Countering Russian Influence in Europe and Eurasia Act of 2017 ("CRIEEA")

The Countering Russian Influence in Europe and Eurasia Act of 2017 ("CRIEEA") was enacted in response to Russia's efforts to exert influence throughout Europe and Eurasia, including in the former states of the Soviet Union. It seeks to hinder Russia's efforts to "exert influence throughout Europe and Eurasia, including in the former states of the Soviet Union, by providing resources to political parties, think tanks, and civil society groups that sow distrust in democratic institutions and actors, promote xenophobic and illiberal views and otherwise undermine European unity."[468] CRIEEA

466. Sanctions are to be applied to persons engaging in such activity on or after the date that is 180 days after the enactment of CAATSA. The Countering America's Adversaries Through Sanctions Act, Section 231(e), codified at 22 U.S.C.§ 9525.
467. H.R. 3364—Countering America's Adversaries Through Sanctions Act, 115th Congress (2017-2018).
468. CAATSA, section 2(1).

expands restrictions on U.S. persons and grants the President authority to impose sanctions under the Sergei Magnitsky Rule of Law Accountability Act of 2012 and the Global Magnitsky Human Rights Accountability Act of 2016.[469] In addition, CRIEEA adds secondary sanctions targeting the activity of non-U.S. persons involving Russia and certain operations outside Russia.

Under CRIEEA, U.S. persons are prohibited from providing goods, services (except for financial services), or technology in support of exploration or production for "new" deepwater, Arctic offshore, or shale oil projects involving a sanctioned Russian oil firm or individual with a controlling interest or a 33% or more non-controlling ownership interest. This expanded the geographic scope of the prohibitions under OFAC's "Directive 4" that apply only to deepwater, Arctic offshore, or shale projects "that have the potential to produce oil in the Russian Federation, or in maritime area claimed by the Russian Federation and extending from its territory."

b *Protecting Europe's Energy Security Act of 2019, as Amended*

The Protecting Europe's Energy Security Act of 2019, as amended ("PEESA"),[470] directs the President to impose sanctions on any foreign person that knowingly provides pipe-laying vessels for constructing a Russian-origin energy export pipeline that makes landfall in Germany or Turkey. The sanctions may consist of asset-blocking or inadmissibility to the U.S. (blocking or revocation of visas). An exception is granted for the admission of an alien to the U.S. when required by the U.N. Headquarters Agreement.

c *Iran Sanctions Programs*

The Iran Sanctions Program is one of the most comprehensive and complex programs administered by OFAC. The U.S. has imposed restrictions on activities with Iran under various legal authorities since 1979, including legislation, four sanctions regulations and over 20 executive orders. OFAC has listed thousands of individuals, entities, vessels and aircraft as SDNs under specific authorities targeting Iran. Additional sanctions are imposed under non-country-specific programs (e.g., Global Magnitsky, Foreign Terrorist Organization, Non-Proliferation):

- Under OFAC's 50 Percent Rule, entities directly or indirectly owned 50 percent or more in the aggregate by one or more SDNs are automatically considered SDNs (i.e., they are deemed to be SDNs and are treated as SDNs). Therefore, the true number of sanctioned entities is far greater than what is reported under specific U.S. sanctions programs.
- SDN designations cover most of the sectors of the Iranian economy, ranging from petrochemicals to mining and metals, textiles, construction, media,

469. CAATSA, section 3(10).
470. P.L. 116-92, Title LXXV; 22 U.S.C. 9526 note.

defense, finance and nuclear proliferation. In addition, some of the designations target Iranian ministries, agencies, research centers, foundations and officials.

C E.U. Sanctions Law

1 *Overview*

E.U. sanctions apply to E.U. citizens, business organizations incorporated or constituted under the law of an E.U. Member State and business organizations doing business on E.U. territory, in the E.U.'s airspace and on aircraft or vessels under an E.U. Member State's jurisdiction.

2 *Authority*

In the E.U., sanctions are either imposed by the Council of the E.U. through the implementation of U.N. Security Council Resolutions issued under Chapter VII of the U.N. Charter or they are imposed within the framework of the E.U.'s Common Foreign and Security Policy ("CFSP"). E.U. sanctions are governed by the Guidelines on implementation and evaluation of restrictive measures (sanctions) in the framework of the CSFP. Sanctions imposed under the CFSP may be implemented at either the E.U. level or by national jurisdictions within the E.U.

In some cases, E.U. sanctions are issued with an expiration date. If the legal instruments issuing such sanctions are not amended or renewed, the sanctions are lifted. In addition, the European Council can choose to repeal sanctions if the aim of the sanctions has been fulfilled.

3 *Penalties*

E.U. sanctions regulations assign responsibility for violations to the E.U. member states, providing member states authority to issue rules for effective penalties for infringements of sanctions regulations and to enforce such regulations. Penalties vary from Member State to Member State but generally include criminal liability.

D U.K. Sanctions Law

U.K. financial sanctions are administered by the Office of Financial Sanctions Implementation ("OFSI"), pursuant to the provisions of Part 1 of the Sanctions and Anti-Money Laundering Act 2018 ("SAMLA") and the Russia (Sanctions) (E.U. Exit) Regulations 2019. SAMLA is the primary legislation that allows the government to impose a wide range of sanctions, including financial sanctions (section 3), immigration sanctions (section 4), trade sanctions (section 5), aircraft sanctions (section 6) and shipping sanctions (section 7).

The Russia (Sanctions) (E.U. Exit) Regulations 2019, which have been issued pursuant to SAMLA, make full use of SAMLA's sanctions arsenal. The 2019 Regulations introduce, *inter alia*, extensive financial sanctions, including an asset freeze that prohibits making funds available to or for the benefit of a designated person and forbids making economic resources available to or for the benefit of such a designated person (Regulations 10-15). The Regulations also impose restrictions on dealing with transferable securities or money-market instruments (Regulation 16) and contain provisions restricting loans and credit arrangements (Regulation 17), correspondent banking relationships (Regulation 17A), investments in relation to non-government controlled Ukrainian territory (Regulation 18), the provision of financial services relating to foreign exchange reserve and asset management (Regulation 18A), investments in relation to Russia (Regulation 18B) and trust services (Regulation 18C).

U.K. sanctions law, unlike U.S. sanctions law, does not distinguish between primary and secondary sanctions. In general, U.K. sanctions do not have extraterritorial effects. However, U.K. persons must comply with the provisions of the SAMLA even if their conduct takes place abroad. The Russia (Sanctions) (E.U. Exit) Regulations 2019 have the same territorial scope as the primary legislation they rely on and require persons with nexus to the U.K. to comply with the Regulations when they operate outside of the U.K.

CHAPTER 13
Alternative Dispute Resolution

States may choose from a wide range of mechanisms for resolving international disputes peacefully. We have already examined legal adjudication in international tribunals such as the ICJ or the ECJ. Now, we turn to alternative dispute resolution. Non-binding measures include negotiation, mediation and conciliation. When these fail, states may take recourse to binding arbitration.

I NEGOTIATION

A state may engage in ad hoc negotiation when its leadership believes that the decision or action of another state threatens its well-being or security. These may either be direct negotiations between the parties or indirect negotiations involving third parties, such as the U.N. secretary-general, through good offices. Negotiations are usually pursued through the diplomatic channels of foreign ministries and diplomats, through more formal commissions, or through international summits. The UN, through the General Assembly or the Security Council, may recommend solutions or dispute resolution methods.

II MEDIATION

Mediation, a more formal means of conflict resolution than negotiation, usually involves a neutral third party who hears both sides of the controversy and assists the parties in reaching a resolution by encouraging negotiations, providing additional channels of communication, or proposing solutions.

III CONCILIATION

An even more formal tool is conciliation, whereby a permanent or ad hoc commission is set up to conduct an investigation and search for a set of settlement terms that would likely be accepted by both parties. The parties to conciliation are not, however, bound by the proposed settlement terms.

IV ARBITRATION

A Introduction

Still more formal in the toolkit of dispute resolution is arbitration, where the parties in a conflict submit to an arbitral tribunal that hears all sides and comes to a binding decision. The parties decide the scope of the arbitral tribunal powers.

Arbitration can be used as a means of resolving disputes of both public international law (disputes between two states or between a state and citizens of another state) and private international law (disputes between private litigants from different countries). Although the decisions rendered in international arbitration are binding, the parties have a great deal of discretion in deciding whether to submit to arbitration, the forum in which the arbitration will take place, the body of law to be applied and who will serve as the arbitrator or arbitrators.

B Doctrine of Separability

Under the doctrine of separability, arbitration clauses are considered to be separate from the contracts in which they are embedded. Arbitrators retain their jurisdiction notwithstanding certain challenges to the validity of a contract containing an arbitration clause. Many jurisdictions, including New York, recognize this doctrine.[471]

C Enforcement of International Arbitral Awards

Although the results of arbitration are generally binding, states may challenge arbitral awards. The losing party may commence proceedings in the national courts of the arbitral *situs* to set aside, vacate, or annul the arbitral award, while the prevailing party may commence proceedings in the same national courts to "confirm" the award. The prevailing party may also seek to "enforce" the award in the national courts of the arbitral *situs* or in a foreign court. The 1958 Convention on the Recognition and Enforcement of Foreign Arbitral Awards ("New York Convention"), which entered into force on 7 June 1959 and has been adopted by 142 of the 193 U.N. member states,[472] is

471. New York State Bar Association, Dispute Resolution Section, International Section, "Choosing New York for International Arbitration," p. 6.
472. The following states are party to the New York Convention as of March 2008: Afghanistan, Albania, Algeria, Antigua and Barbuda, Argentina, Armenia, Australia, Austria, Azerbaijan, Bahamas, Bahrain, Bangladesh, Barbados, Belarus, Belgium, Benin, Bolivia, Bosnia and Herzegovina, Botswana, Brazil, Brunei Darussalam, Bulgaria, Burkina Faso, Cambodia, Cameroon, Canada, Central African Republic, Chile, China, Colombia, Costa Rica, Cote d'Ivore, Croatia, Cuba, Cyprus, Czech Republic, Denmark, Djibouti, Dominica, Dominican Republic, Ecuador, Egypt, El Salvador, Estonia, Finland, France, Gabon, Georgia, Germany, Ghana, Greece, Guatemala, Guinea, Haiti, Holy See, Honduras, Hungary, Iceland, India, Indonesia,

particularly key in this area in that it requires courts of contracting states to give effect to private agreements to arbitrate and to recognize and enforce arbitral awards made in other contracting states.

Iran, Ireland, Israel, Italy, Jamaica, Japan, Jordan, Kazakhstan, Kenya, Kuwait, Kyrgyzstan, Lao People's Democratic Republic, Latvia, Lebanon, Lesotho, Liberia, Lithuania, Luxembourg, Madagascar, Malaysia, Mali, Malta, Marshall Islands, Mauritania, Mauritius, Mexico, Moldova, Monaco, Mongolia, Montenegro, Morocco, Mozambique, Nepal, Netherlands, New Zealand, Nicaragua, Niger, Nigeria, Norway, Oman, Pakistan, Panama, Paraguay, Peru, Philippines, Poland, Portugal, Qatar, Republic of Korea, Romania, Russian Federation, Saint Vincent and the Grenadines, San Marino, Saudi Arabia, Senegal, Serbia, Singapore, Slovakia, Slovenia, South Africa, Spain, Sri Lanka, Sweden, Switzerland, Syrian Arab Republic, Thailand, North Macedonia, Trinidad and Tobago, Tunisia, Turkey, Uganda, Ukraine, United Arab Emirates, United Kingdom of Great Britain and Northern Ireland, United Republic of Tanzania, United States of America, Uruguay, Uzbekistan, Venezuela, Vietnam, Zambia, Zimbabwe.

Appendices

GLOSSARY

A

Abrogation Complete revocation of a treaty or other law; the abolition of a law. *Compare* DEROGATION.

Academic Council on the United Nations System ("ACUNS") International institution with a membership of approximately 1,000 scholars, teachers, practitioners and others active in the work and study of the United Nations System and other international organizations. It was founded in 1987 and has been based at Dartmouth College, Brown University, Yale University, and Wilfrid Laurier University (Ontario) before its 2018 transition to Coventry University in England in 2018.

African Court of Justice and Human Rights At an African Union Summit held in Sharm El Sheikh, Egypt, in 2008, heads of state and government signed the Protocol on the Statute of the African Court of Justice and Human Rights. The purpose of this Protocol was to establish the African Court of Justice and Human Rights, a merger of the African Court on Human and Peoples' Rights with the still non-existent African Court of Justice. As of 18 June 2020, eight countries ratified the Protocol on the Statute of the African Court of Justice and Human Rights, out of 15 needed for its entry into force. Therefore, the African Court of Justice and Human Rights has not yet become operational.

Aggression Also known as a CRIME AGAINST PEACE, it is a crime generally defined under customary international law and the Nuremberg Principles as the planning, preparation, initiation, or waging of any war in violation of international law, treaties, or agreements, including participation, conspiracy or complicity in the same (*see* Nuremberg Principles VI and VII).

Air law The body of laws concerning civil aviation. In its broadest sense, it may also refer to all laws involving any use of the air, including but not limited to civil aviation. *Also known as* AVIATION LAW.

Alien Tort Claims Act Section of the USC that grants U.S. federal district courts original jurisdiction "of any civil action by an alien for a tort only, committed in violation of the law of nations or a treaty of the United States" (28 USC 1350). By "law of nations," the statute is referring to public international law that is comprised not only of international treaties, but also customary international law and general principles of law. The statute allows suit to be brought in U.S. federal court by aliens for torts committed outside of the U.S. in violation of international law.

Amiable composition Dispute resolution based on equity and considerations of what is reasonable and just for the parties, rather than on strict adherence to the laws of a particular jurisdiction. Often used in international arbitration between companies governed under distinct bodies of law and commercial customs.

Antarctic Treaty System A system of treaties comprised of the Antarctic Treaty and related agreements, including the Convention for the Conservation of Antarctic Marine Living Resources (1980) and the Protocol on Environmental Protection to the Antarctic Treaty (1991). The Antarctic Treaty, signed by 47 countries and entering into force in 1961, sets aside Antarctica as a scientific preserve free from weapons testing and other military activity and establishes freedom of scientific investigation on the continent.

Armed reprisal Use of military force that follows an armed incident prior to the onset of hostilities. It is normally used as punishment, retaliation or revenge for an armed attack, and it does not fit into the exception that allows the use of force for self-defense. Armed reprisals fall within the *jus ad bellum*. *Compare* BELLIGERENT REPRISAL.

Aviation law *See* AIR LAW.

B

Barrel bomb Type of cluster munition consisting of an improvised unguided bomb typically made from a large barrel-shaped metal container that has been filled with high explosives and, sometimes, shrapnel, oil, or chemicals and dropped from an aircraft. Use of barrel bombs is typically described as inconsistent with the requirements of international humanitarian law because of their tendency to cause superfluous injury or unnecessary suffering.

Baseline Line from which the seaward limits of a state's territorial sea and other maritime zones of jurisdiction (contiguous zone, exclusive economic zone, etc.) are measured. Normally, a sea baseline follows the LOW-WATER LINE of a state's coast (Article 5 UNCLOS), but it may also be drawn from the low-water line of reefs in the case of islands situated on atolls or of islands having fringing reefs (Article 6 UNCLOS) or, in the case of coastlines that are deeply indented and cut into or having fringing islands, straight baselines joining appropriate points may be used (Article 7.1 UNCLOS).

Belligerent reprisal Defined by the ICRC as "an action that would otherwise be unlawful but that in exceptional cases is considered lawful under international law when used as an enforcement measure in reaction to unlawful acts of an adversary. In international humanitarian law there is a trend to outlaw belligerent reprisals altogether. Those that may still be lawful are subject [to] stringent conditions."[473]

Bilateral donor Government or private donor that provides assistance directly to a recipient country or entity or to non-governmental institutions operating in the recipient country. *Compare* MULTILATERAL DONOR.

C

Cabotage The exclusive right of a country to control the air traffic within its borders.

Civilian (international humanitarian law) Negatively defined in Article 50 of Additional Protocol I to the 1949 Geneva Conventions as "any person who does not belong to one of the categories of persons referred to in Article 4A(1), (2), (3) and (6) of the Third Convention and in Article 43 of this Protocol. In case of doubt whether a person is a civilian, that person shall be considered to be a civilian." Article 43 includes in its definition of armed forces "all organized armed forces, groups and units which are under a command responsible to that Party for the conduct of its subordinates" and states that "Members of the armed forces of a Party to a conflict (other than medical personnel and chaplains covered by Article 33 of the Third Convention) are combatants" with the right to participate directly in hostilities.

Cluster munition Explosive weapon that releases or ejects many small explosive bomblets designed to kill enemy personnel, disperse chemical or biological weapons or destroy vehicles, runways or power transmission lines. Because the bomblets are scattered over a wide area and pose risks to civilians both during attacks and afterward, cluster munitions have been prohibited by the Convention on Cluster Munitions.

Commission on Human Rights *See* UNITED NATIONS COMMISSION ON HUMAN RIGHTS.

Conciliation Means of conflict resolution where a permanent or ad hoc commission is set up to conduct an investigation and search for a set of settlement terms that would likely be accepted by both parties. The parties to conciliation are not bound by the proposed settlement terms. *Compare* MEDIATION.

Continental shelf (*Geography*) Extended perimeter of each continent that is underwater by relatively shallow seas (known as shelf seas) and gulfs. (*Law*) Under UNCLOS, the continental shelf was legally defined as the stretch of the sea extending from the coast to the continental shelf.

Continental margin A steep continental slope followed by the flatter CONTINENTAL RISE.

473. Jean-Marie Henckaerts and Louise Doswald-Beck, *Customary International Humanitarian Law*, Vol. I, ICRC, Cambridge University Press (Cambridge, New York, 2009), Rule 145, p. 513.

Continental rise Pile of sediment that cascades down the slope and accumulates at the base of the continental slope. It is found between the continental slope and the abyssal plain.

Continuous combat function Civilian persons belonging to hostile, non-state organized armed groups. They cease to be civilians, can be attacked, are not considered to be prisoners of war if captured, and can be criminally charged. Unlike civilians who directly participate in hostilities and who can only be targeted for such time as they directly participate in hostilities, civilians with a continuous combat function can always be targeted by virtue of their status. *Compare* REVOLVING DOOR FIGHTER.

Convention on the International Sale of Goods *See* UNITED NATIONS CONVENTION ON CONTRACTS FOR THE INTERNATIONAL SALE OF GOODS.

Convention for the Protection of Human Rights and Fundamental Freedoms An international treaty to protect human rights and fundamental freedoms in Europe. It was drafted in 1950 by the then-newly formed Council of Europe and entered into force in 1953. *Informally known as* the EUROPEAN CONVENTION ON HUMAN RIGHTS.

Court An assembly, normally of a permanent nature, of one or more judges with the authority to judge on and adjudicate legal claims or disputes. Normally created by state law. *Compare* TRIBUNAL.

Court of Bosnia and Herzegovina (**Court of BiH**) Domestic court of the State of Bosnia and Herzegovina, which includes international judges and prosecutors. Based in Sarajevo, the Court of BiH was established on 3 July 2002 by the Parliament of Bosnia and Herzegovina, with the Law on the Court of Bosnia and Herzegovina promulgated on 12 November 2000.

Crime against peace *See* AGGRESSION.

Crime of aggression *See* AGGRESSION.

Crimes against humanity Certain enumerated inhuman and odious acts committed as part of a systematic attack against any civilian population that constitute grave humiliation or degradation or a serious attack on human dignity. The SICC enumerates a series of crimes, including murder, extermination and enslavement, that constitute crimes against humanity when "committed as part of a widespread or systematic attack directed against any civilian population, with knowledge of the attack" (Article 7.1 SICC). "Attack directed against any civilian population" is, in turn, defined as "a course of conduct involving the multiple commission of acts … against any civilian population, pursuant to or in furtherance of a State or organizational policy to commit such attack" (Article 7.2 SICC).

Customary international law A source of international law consisting of: (i) a consistent and recurrent state practice, (ii) developed over time, that is (iii) undertaken out of a sense of legal obligation. It thus results from a general and consistent practice of states followed by them from a sense of legal obligation.

D

Derogation Exemption from or relaxation of a treaty or other law; a partial repeal or abolition of a law (e.g., from a human rights treaty in situations of emergency). *Compare* ABROGATION.

Domestic law *See* MUNICIPAL LAW.

Draft Articles on the Responsibility of States for Internationally Wrongful Acts Non-binding declaration drafted by the ILC in 2001 that attempts to codify the rules under customary law for state responsibility. It serves as evidence of customary international law.

Dublin Regulation European law that regulates which European country is responsible for asylum seekers' claims for protection and that permits families separated across various European jurisdictions to be reunited during their asylum claims. Children under 18 years old have a wide range of possibilities to join their family members in other European jurisdictions. Depending on a variety of conditions, spouses and dependent and vulnerable adults may also be eligible for family reunification.

Dual-use objects Defined as "facilities or objects that serve both a military and civilian purpose and may be legitimate military targets."[474] They typically include roads, bridges, power plants and satellites. They may be attacked, subject to taking feasible precautions to avoid collateral damage. Also referred to as a "dual-use facility."

Durable solutions Any of the three solutions that end the problems associated with displacement for the refugee and allow her to resume a normal life in a safe environment. There are three traditional durable solutions available for consideration: voluntary repatriation, local integration and resettlement.

E

Economic object Objects that become legitimate military targets when they "effectively support military operations ... provided their attack offers a definite military advantage."[475] In U.S. practice, economic objects "are typically factories, workshops and plants that make an effective (though not necessarily direct) contribution to an adversary's military capability."[476] Attacking economic objects seeks to break up an enemy's economic potential, which has "a direct influence on the armed forces'

474. "Law of War Targeting Restrictions," *Annex 3-60 Targeting*, U.S. Air Force Doctrine (15 March 2019) 93. *See also* Henckaerts, *Customary IHL* 29-32.
475. Jean-Marie Henckaerts and Louise Doswald-Beck, *Customary International Humanitarian Law*," Vol. I: Rules, ICRC, Cambridge University Press (Cambridge, New York, 2009), Rule 8, p. 32.
476. "Law of War Targeting Restrictions," *Annex 3-60 Targeting*, U.S. Air Force Doctrine (15 March 2019), p. 93.

capacity to resist so that this economic potential also becomes a war objective."[477] The U.S. Law of War Manual classifies "economic objects associated with military operations or with war-supporting or war-sustaining industries" as military objectives.[478]

***Erga omnes* obligation** A wrongful act is deemed to be *erga omnes* ("toward all") if it harms everyone and not merely the injured party. In its judgment of 5 February 1970 in *Barcelona Traction, Light and Power Company, Limited (Belgium v. Spain)* (1962-1970), the ICJ commented on a category of international *erga omnes* obligations, which are owed by states to the international community as a whole and are intended to protect and promote the basic values and common interests of all. The ICJ referenced the "obligations of the state towards the international community as a whole," in whose protection all states have a "legal interest" and which are thus "the concern of all states." Specifically, the ICJ enumerated four *erga omnes* obligations: the outlawing of acts of aggression, the outlawing of genocide, protection from slavery, and protection from racial discrimination. *Compare Jus cogens* NORM.

Ethnic cleansing A war crime that has not been recognized as an independent crime under international law or granted a precise definition. A United Nations Commission of Experts mandated to look into violations of international humanitarian law committed in the territory of the former Yugoslavia defined ethnic cleansing in its interim report S/25274 as "rendering an area ethnically homogeneous by using force or intimidation to remove persons of given groups from the area." In its final report, S/1994/674, the Commission described ethnic cleansing as "a purposeful policy designed by one ethnic or religious group to remove by violent and terror-inspiring means the civilian population of another ethnic or religious group from certain geographic areas." The ICJ reaffirmed this definition of ethnic cleansing in the Case Concerning Application of the Convention on the Prevention and Punishment of the Crime of Genocide, Judgment, 26 February 2007, paragraph 190. Unlike the definition of genocide established by the Genocide Convention and Rome Statute, ethnic cleansing does not require as one of its elements the intent to destroy a national, ethnical, religious or racial group.

European Convention on Human Rights *See* CONVENTION FOR THE PROTECTION OF HUMAN RIGHTS AND FUNDAMENTAL FREEDOMS.

Explosive Ordnance Munition containing explosive or nuclear materials or biological or chemical agents, including bombs, missiles, rockets, torpedoes, mines, artillery, clusters and dispensers, improvised explosive devices and similar munitions of an explosive nature.

---

477. Jean-Marie Henckaerts and Louise Doswald-Beck, *Customary International Humanitarian Law*, Vol. II: Practice—Part 1, ICRC, Cambridge University Press (Cambridge, New York, 2009), § 569, p. 218.
478. Office of General Counsel, U.S. Department of Defense, *Law of War Manual*, Department of Defense, promulgated pursuant to Department of Defense Directive 2311.01E (June 2015, updated December 2016), p. 217.

F

Food and Agriculture Organization of the United Nations ("FAO") U.N. agency that leads international efforts to fight hunger. FAO acts as a neutral forum where nations meet to negotiate agreements and debate policy and serves as a source of knowledge and information to assist developing countries to modernize and improve agriculture, forestry and fisheries practices.

G

GATT *See* GENERAL AGREEMENT ON TARIFFS AND TRADE 1949 *and* GENERAL AGREEMENT ON TARIFFS AND TRADE 1994.

General Agreement on Tariffs and Trade (1949) An agreement negotiated during the U.N. Conference on Trade and Employment that was the outcome of the failure of negotiating governments to create the International Trade Organization ("ITO"). It was formed in 1949 and lasted until 1994, when it was modified by the General Agreement on Tariffs and Trade of 1994, prior to the formation of the WTO in 1995. *Known by its acronym* GATT. *See also* GENERAL AGREEMENT ON TARIFFS AND TRADE (1994).

General Agreement on Tariffs and Trade (1994) The Final Act Embodying the Results of the Uruguay Round of Multilateral Trade Negotiations, signed by ministers in Marrakesh in 1994. In addition to the texts of the agreements, the Final Act also contains texts of Ministerial Decisions and Declarations, which further clarify certain provisions of some of the agreements. The text of the original GATT of 1947 is still in effect under the WTO system, subject to modifications under the 1994 GATT text. *See also* GENERAL AGREEMENT ON TARIFFS AND TRADE (1949).

General Order No. 100 of 1863 *See* LIEBER CODE.

General principle of law A source of international law that serves as a gap filler by international courts when there is no applicable treaty provision or rule of customary international law. The court will try to ascertain general principles of law by finding commonalities among well-development legal systems in the world. These general principles may include both principles of law and principles of equity.

Genocide Defined under the Genocide Convention and the Rome Statute as any of the following acts committed on members of any national, ethnical, religious or racial group with the intent to destroy it in whole or in part: killing, causing of serious bodily or mental harm, prevention of birth, transferring of children to another group, or infliction of conditions of life calculated to bring about its physical destruction (Article II CPPG; Article 6 SICC). The Genocide Convention and the Rome Statute use identical definitions for the crime of genocide.

Global Fund to Fight AIDS, Tuberculosis and Malaria ("GFATM") Public-private partnership international financing organization based in Geneva and incorporated as a foundation under Swiss law to attract and disburse additional funding and resources to prevent and treat HIV and AIDS, tuberculosis and malaria. It began operations in

2002 and until 1 January 2009, Global Fund staff were officially WHO staff members and the WHO provided administrative services to the Global Fund secretariat.

Grotius, Hugo Dutch jurist whose writings established the basis of modern international law. In his treatise *De jure belli ac pacis libri tres* (*On the Law of War and Peace: Three books*), he advances a system of principles of natural law that he holds to be binding on all people and nations regardless of local custom and then goes on to outline the circumstances under which war may be justly executed.

H

The Hague Conference on Private International Law Preeminent organization in private international law formed in 1893 to work for the progressive unification of the rules of private international law by assisting in the implementation of multilateral conventions promoting the harmonization of conflict of laws principles. Sixty-eight nations, including China, Russia, the United States and all of the E.U. countries, are currently members.

Hors de combat Out of combat or "outside the fight." Under Rule 47 of the ICRC's *Customary International Humanitarian Law*, a person *hors de combat* is: "(a) anyone who is in the power of an adverse party; (b) anyone who is defenceless because of unconsciousness, shipwreck, wounds or sickness; or (c) anyone who clearly expresses an intention to surrender; provided he or she abstains from any hostile act and does not attempt to escape."

House of Lords The final appeals court of the United Kingdom.

Human Rights Commission *See* UNITED NATIONS COMMISSION ON HUMAN RIGHTS.

Human Rights Committee HUMAN RIGHTS TREATY BODY of the ICCPR. It has the power to: (i) elaborate on the norms in the ICCPR; and (ii) hear complaints from individuals against states.

Human rights treaty body Committee of independent experts charged with monitoring the implementation of an international human rights treaty and considering individual complaints or communications. Human rights treaty bodies are created by the human rights treaties that they implement.

Human Rights Council *See* UNITED NATIONS HUMAN RIGHTS COUNCIL.

Human shield Civilians used against their will to deter attacks on military targets during armed conflict or civilians who voluntarily protect either military or civilian targets from attack. The use of human shields is forbidden by Additional Protocol I of the Geneva Conventions. Some have argued that an attack that would be disproportionate should be considered proportionate if the presence of civilians is due to the wrongful actions of the enemy.

Humanitarian assistance Under international humanitarian law, any form of aid that seeks to save lives and alleviate suffering of a crisis-affected population provided in accordance with the basic humanitarian principles of:

(i) humanity: the treatment of humankind humanely in all circumstances by saving lives and preventing and alleviating suffering while ensuring respect for the individual;
(ii) impartiality: the provision of assistance based on need without discrimination as to race, nationality, religion, or creed;
(iii) neutrality: not taking sides in conflicts and controversies; and
(iv) independence: the formulation and implementation of policies with autonomy and independently from government policies or actions.

I

Impartiality Within the context of international humanitarian law, IMPARTIALITY refers to the provision of assistance on the basis of need and without distinction based on ethnicity, religion, race, political affiliation, etc. *See* HUMANITARIAN ASSISTANCE.

Incoterms Series of pre-defined commercial terms published by the International Chamber of Commerce that are widely used in international commercial transactions. The Incoterms rules are intended primarily to clearly communicate the tasks, costs, and risks associated with the transportation and delivery of goods. *Also known as* INTERNATIONAL COMMERCIAL TERMS.

Inland waters Lakes, rivers and ports located within the boundaries of a state. States are fully sovereign over their inland waters and may enforce their laws in full against foreign marine ships.

Instructions for the Government of Armies of the United States in the Field. *See* LIEBER CODE.

Inter-Agency Standing Committee ("IASC") Inter-agency forum of U.N. and non-U.N. humanitarian partners founded in 1992 by the U.N. General Assembly to strengthen humanitarian assistance and improve the delivery of humanitarian assistance to affected populations.

International Bill of Human Rights International human rights framework comprised of the UDHR, ICCPR, and ICESCR.

International Commercial Terms *See* INCOTERMS.

International Commission of Jurists ("ICJ") International human rights non-governmental organization headquartered in Geneva and comprised of 60 eminent jurists (including senior judges, attorneys and academics) dedicated to ensuring respect for international human rights through the law. The composition of the Commission aims to reflect the geographical diversity of the world and its legal systems. *Compare* INTERNATIONAL LAW COMMISSION.

International Committee of the Red Cross ("ICRC") Impartial private humanitarian organization based in Geneva, Switzerland that works to protect the victims of international and domestic armed conflicts. Its mandate stems from the four Geneva Conventions of 1949 and states parties to the Conventions and their Additional Protocols of 1977 and 2005 have given the ICRC a mandate to protect the victims of war and armed violence.

The ICRC holds special status under international law as the custodian of the Geneva Conventions and is granted unique privileges and immunities under international law. For example, under Rule 73.4 of the Rules of Procedure and Evidence of the ICC, the ICC "shall regard as privileged, and consequently not subject to disclosure, including by way of testimony of any present or past official or employee of the International Committee of the Red Cross (ICRC), any information, documents or other evidence which it came into the possession of in the course, or as a consequence, of the performance by ICRC of its functions under the Statutes of the International Red Cross and Red Crescent Movement, unless: (a) After consultations undertaken pursuant to sub-rule 6, ICRC does not object in writing to such disclosure, or otherwise has waived this privilege; or (b) Such information, documents or other evidence is contained in public statements and documents of ICRC."

International Conference on Population and Development ("ICPD") Conference coordinated by the U.N. in Cairo, Egypt, on 5-13 September 1994 that resulted in a Programme of Action, which is the steering document for the United Nations Population Fund ("UNFPA"). Conference delegates achieved consensus on the following goals: universal education; reduction of infant and child mortality; reduction of maternal mortality; and access to reproductive and sexual health services, including family planning.

International Court of Arbitration International institution within the International Chamber of Commerce that is committed to the resolution of international commercial disputes by arbitration. It is headquartered in Paris, France.

International crime Internationally wrongful act resulting from the breach by a state, state agent, or non-state actor of a peremptory norm (*jus cogens*) so essential for the protection of the international community's fundamental interests that its breach is classified by the community as a crime (e.g., aggression, torture, genocide).

International Development Association ("IDA") International financial institution headquartered in Washington, DC that is a member of the World Bank Group. It offers loans and grants to the poorest developing countries having the lowest gross national income, troubled creditworthiness or the lowest per capita income.

International Development Law Organization ("IDLO") Intergovernmental organization with a mandate to promote the rule of law and development. It supports emerging economies and middle-income countries to strengthen their legal capacity and rule of law framework for sustainable development and economic opportunity.

IDLO is headquartered in Rome, Italy and has a branch office in The Hague and is one of a number of entities that are United Nations General Assembly observers.

International Federation of Red Cross and Red Crescent Societies ("IFRC") Founded in 1919 and based in Geneva, the IFRC coordinates activities between the 191 National Red Cross and Red Crescent Societies within the International Red Cross and Red Crescent Movement. On an international level, the Federation leads and organizes relief assistance missions responding to *large-scale emergencies*. The IFRC was awarded the Nobel Peace Prize in 1963.

International Finance Corporation ("IFC") International financial institution and member of the World Bank Group headquartered in Washington, DC, with a mandate to offer investment, advisory, and asset-management services to encourage private-sector development in developing countries.

International Forum of Sovereign Wealth Funds ("IFSWF") Non-profit international group of sovereign wealth funds managers established in 2009 in London by the IFSWF's predecessor, the International Working Group of Sovereign Wealth Funds, following discussions with the G20, IMF and the U.S. Department of Treasury. The Working Group created the "Santiago Principles," a set of 24 principles and practices generally accepted and endorsed voluntarily by members of the IFSWF. Following the 2009 Kuwait Declaration, the Working Group became the IFSWF with the mandate of helping members implement the Principles.

As of the date of this writing, the following 36 sovereign wealth funds are full members of the IFSWF: Abu Dhabi Investment Authority (United Arab Emirates); Agaciro Development Fund (Rwanda); Alaska Permanent Fund (United States); BpiFrance (France); Budgetary Income Stabilization Fund (Mexico); CDP Equity SpA (Italy); China Investment Corporation (China); Compañía Española de Financiación del Desarrollo (Spain); Fondo de Ahorro de Panamá (Panama); Fonds Gabonais d'Investissements Stratégiques (Gabon); Fonds Souverain d'Investissements Stratégiques S.A. (Senegal); Fundo Soberano de Angola (Angola); Future Fund (Australia); Ghana Petroleum Funds (Ghana); GIC Private Limited (Singapore); Growthfund (Greece); Indonesia Investment Authority (Indonesia); Intergenerational Trust Fund for the People of the Republic of Nauru (Nauru); Investment Corporation of Dubai (United Arab Emirates); Ireland Strategic Investment Fund (Ireland); Ithmar Capital (Morocco); JSC National Investment Corporation of the National Bank of Kazakhstan (Kazakhstan); JSC Samruk-Kazyna (Kazakhstan); Khazanah Nasional Berhad (Malaysia); Korea Investment Corporation (South Korea); Kuwait Investment Authority (Kuwait); Libyan Investment Authority (Libya); Mubadala Investment Company (United Arab Emirates); New Zealand Superannuation Fund (New Zealand); Nigeria Sovereign Investment Authority (Nigeria); Oman Investment Authority (Oman); Palestine Investment Fund (Palestinian Territories); Qatar Investment Authority (Qatar); State Oil Fund of the Republic of Azerbaijan (Azerbaijan); Heritage Fund Trinidad and Tobago (Trinidad & Tobago); The Pula Fund (Botswana); Sovereign Fund of Egypt (Egypt); Timor-Leste Petroleum Fund (Timor-Leste); Türkiye Wealth Fund (Türkiye). In addition, the following seven sovereign wealth funds are associate members of the IFSWF: Ethiopian Investment Holdings (Ethiopia); Fonds Souverain de Djibouti (Djibouti); Fórum de Fundos Soberanos Brasileiros (Brazil); Maharlika Investment Corporation (Philippines); Mauritius Investment Corporation (Mauritius); National Infrastructure Investment Fund (India); Natural Resource Fund (Guyana).

International humanitarian law ("IHL") Set of rules regulating the conduct of war and armed hostilities. These rules restrict the means and methods of warfare and seek to limit the effects of armed conflict for humanitarian reasons by protecting civilians who are not or are no longer participating in hostilities. *Also known as* LAW OF WAR, LAW OF ARMED CONFLICT and *JUS IN BELLO*. *Compare JUS AD BELLUM*.

International Institute for the Unification of Private Law ("Unidroit") Independent intergovernmental organization with 59 member states whose purpose is to examine ways of harmonizing, modernizing and coordinating the domestic private law of States and, in particular, commercial law. The organization, seated in Rome, is neither a U.N. body nor a U.N. agency.

International Law Commission ("ILC") A commission established by the U.N. General Assembly in 1948 for the "promotion of the progressive development of international law and its codification" (Article 1 of the ILC Statute). It has held sessions in Geneva every year since 1949 that have led to the creation of the Vienna Convention on the Law of Treaties, the Vienna Convention on Diplomatic Relations, and the Draft Articles on the Responsibility of States for Internationally Wrongful Acts, among others. The Commission receives instructions from the UNGA's Sixth (Legal) Committee. *Compare* INTERNATIONAL COMMISSION OF JURISTS.

International Law Institute A private, non-for-profit organization chartered by Georgetown University that conducts scholarly research, publishing and practical legal training and technical assistance in order to promote economic development and rule of law and address the challenges faced by the international community.

International organization A body created by a treaty with a permanent institutional structure whose membership consists either exclusively or in large part of states. The treaty is the constituent instrument of the organization.

International Organization for Migration ("IOM") Principal intergovernmental organization in the field of migration. The IOM promotes humane and orderly policies in the movement of persons across borders, migrant health protections, assisted returns, and counter-trafficking. The IOM also provides humanitarian assistance to refugees, internally displaced persons, and other migrants in need. In September 2016, it became a related organization of the U.N. As of 2019, the IOM had 173 member states and eight observer states.

International Red Cross and Red Crescent Movement International humanitarian movement with approximately 97 million global volunteers, members and staff. It was founded to protect human life and health, to ensure respect for all human beings, and to prevent and alleviate human suffering. The movement consists of several legally distinct organizations that share common basic principles, objectives, symbols, statutes and governing organizations.

International Residual Mechanism for Criminal Tribunals *See* MECHANISM FOR INTERNATIONAL CRIMINAL TRIBUNALS.

International seabed area Portion of the sea that lies beyond the limits of national jurisdiction, underlying most of the world's oceans.

International Trade Centre ("ITC") Joint agency of the WTO and UNCTAD that provides trade-related technical assistance.

International uniform law Refers to the situation whereby the domestic laws of nations have been made uniform by agreement.

International Criminal Police Organization ("INTERPOL") International police organization that facilitates worldwide police cooperation and crime control. It is headquartered in Lyon, France and holds seven regional bureaus worldwide and a National Central Bureau in each of its 195 member states.

Islamic International Court of Justice Principal judicial organ of the OIC established in Article 14 of the OIC Charter. Created in the Fifth Islamic Summit of 1987, it has jurisdiction to resolve contentious disputes between OIC members and to issue advisory opinions.

J

Jus ad bellum (*Lat.*, "Justice in the resort to war") Laws that regulate recourse to the use of armed force. *Compare* *JUS IN BELLO*.

***Jus cogens* norm** (*Lat.*) Fundamental, overriding principle of international law from which no derogation is permitted. *Also known as* a PEREMPTORY NORM OF GENERAL INTERNATIONAL LAW, it is defined by the VCLT as "a norm accepted and recognized by the international community of States as a whole as a norm from which no derogation is permitted and which can be modified only by a subsequent norm of general international law having the same character" (Article 53 VCLT). Under the VCLT, "[a] treaty is void if, at the time of its conclusion, it conflicts with a peremptory norm of general international law" (Article 53 VCLT). Examples of *jus cogens* norms include prohibitions on genocide, crimes against humanity, torture, slavery, human trafficking, and aggression. *Jus cogens* refers to the legal status that certain international crimes reach, while *ERGA OMNES* OBLIGATIONS (*obligatio erga omnes*) refer to the legal implications arising out of a crime's reaching *jus cogens* status. According to some commentators, *jus cogens* norms produce *ERGA OMNES* OBLIGATIONS. *Also known as* PEREMPTORY NORM OF GENERAL INTERNATIONAL LAW. *Compare* *ERGA OMNES* OBLIGATION.

Jus in bello (*Lat.*, "Justice in the conduct of war") *See* International humanitarian law. *Compare* *JUS AD BELLUM*.

K

Kellogg-Briand Pact International agreement concluded in 1928 in which signatory states promised not to use war to resolve "disputes or conflicts of whatever nature or of whatever origin they may be." The Pact was signed in 1928 by representatives from Australia, Belgium, Canada, Czechoslovakia, France, Germany, Great Britain, India, the Irish Free State, Italy, Japan, New Zealand, Poland, South Africa, and the United States. Following subsequent ratifications and accessions, the Pact currently has more than 60 states parties. *Also known as* the General Treaty for Renunciation of War as an Instrument of National Policy (official name) and Pact of Paris.

Kosovo Specialist Chambers and Specialist Prosecutor's Office Temporary institutions seated in The Hague and established pursuant to an international agreement adopted between the Republic of Kosovo and the European Union and ratified by the Kosovo Assembly, a Constitutional Amendment and the Law on Kosovo Specialist Chambers and Specialist Prosecutor's Office with a mandate and jurisdiction over crimes against humanity, war crimes and other crimes under Kosovo law, which were commenced or committed in Kosovo between 1 January 1998 and 31 December 2000 by or against citizens of Kosovo or the Federal Republic of Yugoslavia.

Law of armed conflict *See* INTERNATIONAL HUMANITARIAN LAW.

Law of Nations Name given in the past to refer to international law.

Law of neutrality describes the decision of a state to refrain from participating in hostilities and to undertake: the *duty of abstention* (i.e., the duty not to participate in the hostilities); the *duty of impartiality* (i.e., granting the same rights to and refraining from showing partiality toward belligerents on both sides of the conflict); and the *duty of prevention* (i.e., to resist violations of neutrality). Neutrality also gives rise to the right of the neutral state to the inviolability of the neutral's territory. However, if a neutral state breaches its duties, it forfeits the right of inviolability of its territory and belligerents may retaliate by attacking any of the state's armed forces or military objects. However, violating the law of neutrality does not necessarily make a State a co-belligerent. Merely providing weapons violates neutrality but does not suffice for co-belligerency.

Law of war *See* INTERNATIONAL HUMANITARIAN LAW.

Lex specialis (*Lat.*) A legal principle derived from the Latin *lex specialis derogat legi generali* ("the more specific law has precedence over the more general law"). Under this doctrine, where two laws govern the same factual situation, the law governing a specific subject matter (*lex specialis*) overrides the law governing general matters (*lex generalis*).

Lieber Code One of the first written codes governing the conduct of soldiers and limiting the effects of war. The Instructions were signed by U.S. President Abraham Lincoln and issued in 1863 to the Union Forces of the United States during the

American Civil War to prescribe a code of conduct for soldiers in war. The code was authored by Francis Lieber, a Prussian immigrant, legal scholar, political scientist, and law school professor. Much of the language from the Lieber Code is contained in the modern Geneva Conventions and their Additional Protocols. *Also known as* GENERAL ORDER № 100 OF 1863 *and* THE INSTRUCTIONS FOR THE GOVERNMENT OF ARMIES OF THE UNITED STATES IN THE FIELD.

Low-water line The location of the coastline at low tide. *Also known as* LOW-WATER MARK.

Low-water mark *See* LOW-WATER LINE.

M

Mainland China Geographical area under the jurisdiction of the PRC. According to the Taipei-based Mainland Affairs Council, the term excludes the PRC special administrative regions of Hong Kong and Macau.

Magnitsky legislation Laws that impose governmental sanctions against foreign individuals who have committed human rights abuses or corrupt acts. Named after the Russian tax advisor Sergei Magnitsky, who died in police custody in Russia in 2009 amid allegations of human rights violations, the first Magnitsky legislation was passed in the U.S. in 2012 through the Sergei Magnitsky Rule of Law Accountability Act of 2012, which barred Russian officials believed to be involved in Magnitsky's death from entering the U.S. or using U.S. banks. The U.S. law was expanded with the passage of the Global Magnitsky Human Rights Accountability Act by the U.S. Congress in December 2016, through which the U.S. Treasury has sanctioned human rights violators around the world without the need for a country-specific Executive Order. Similar human rights sanctions programs were later established by the E.U., the U.K. and Canada.

Martens Clause introduced into the preamble to Hague Convention (II) of 1899 with Respect to the Laws and Customs of War on Land and expressed in modified versions in Hague Convention (IV) of 1907 respecting the Laws and Customs of War on Land and Additional Protocols I and II to the Geneva Conventions of 1949. The formulation found in Additional Protocol II states that "[i]n cases *not covered by the law in force*, the human person remains under the *protection of the principles of humanity* and the dictates of the public conscience." The Clause was further restated with slight variations in the Preamble to the Convention on Conventional Weapons and it was paraphrased in Resolution XXIII of the Tehran Conference on Human Rights of 1968 and is cited in various national military manuals, including those of the United States.[479]

479. U.S. Department of the Army, *The Law of Land Warfare* (Field Manual No. 27-10 (1956), para. 6; U.S. Department of the Air Force, *International Law-The Conduct of Armed Conflict and Air Operations*, 1-7(b), AFP No. 110-31 (1976).

Mechanism for International Criminal Tribunals ("MICT") International mechanism established by Security Council to carry out a number of functions of the ICTY and ICTR, namely, continuing the "jurisdiction, rights and obligations and essential functions" of the Tribunals, including securing the arrest, transfer and prosecution of remaining fugitives still wanted for trial by the ICTR. The ICTR branch of the MICT began operations in 2012 and the ICTY branch in 2013. *Also known as* INTERNATIONAL RESIDUAL MECHANISM FOR CRIMINAL TRIBUNALS.

Mediation Means of conflict resolution that usually involves a neutral third party who hears both sides of a controversy and assists the parties in reaching a resolution by encouraging negotiations, providing the parties with additional channels of communication, or proposing solutions. The parties to conciliation are not bound by proposed settlement terms. *Compare* CONCILIATION.

Multilateral donor Government or private donor that provides assistance to a multilateral organization such as the U.N. or U.N. specialized agencies such as the World Bank, which in turn administer aid to several recipient countries. *Compare* BILATERAL DONOR.

Municipal law For the purposes of international law, municipal law is the internal law that applies within a country. *Also known as* DOMESTIC LAW *or* NATIONAL LAW.

N

National law *See* MUNICIPAL LAW.

Non-derogable right Under international law, certain rights have been considered so important that they are non-derogable, i.e., they may not be revoked or in any way compromised. These rights are also known as peremptory norms of international law or *jus cogens* norms. The provisions of international humanitarian law, for example, are non-derogable.

Non-refoulement Principle that establishes a refugee's non-derogable right to be protected against forcible return to territories where his or her life or freedom would be in danger. This principle places an absolute obligation on states parties to the CRSR not to return refugees to countries in which such danger to their lives or freedom would arise.

North Atlantic Treaty that created the NORTH ATLANTIC TREATY ORGANIZATION.

North Atlantic Treaty Organization Alliance of 26 countries from North America and Europe committed to fulfilling the goals of the NORTH ATLANTIC TREATY.

Norwegian Refugee Council ("NRC") Non-governmental organization that promotes and protects the rights of refugees and IDPs who have fled their homes as a result of conflict, human rights violations, acute violence and natural disasters, among other causes.

Nuremberg Principles Text drafted by the ILC in response to the U.N. General Assembly's 1950 request to formulate the principles of international law recognized in the Charter of the International Military Tribunal and in the judgment of the Tribunal with respect to what constitutes a war crime. The text consists of seven principles. *Formally known as* PRINCIPLES OF INTERNATIONAL LAW RECOGNIZED IN THE CHARTER OF THE NUREMBERG TRIBUNAL AND IN THE JUDGMENT OF THE TRIBUNAL.

O

Office of the United Nations High Commissioner for Human Rights ("OHCHR") Geneva-based U.N. agency established by the U.N. General Assembly in 1993 to promote and protect the human rights that are guaranteed under international law and stipulated in the UDHR. The OHCHR is headed by the High Commissioner for Human Rights, who coordinates human rights activities throughout the U.N. and supervises the UNITED NATIONS HUMAN RIGHTS COUNCIL. Formerly known as the Centre for Human Rights.

Opinio juris (*Lat.*, "opinion of law" or "opinion of necessity") An opinion on behalf of a state that it is bound to apply a particular state practice. Along with state practice, *opinio juris* is an element necessary to establish a legally binding custom.

Organisation of Islamic Cooperation ("OIC") An intergovernmental organization established in September 1969 consisting of 57 member states spread over four continents. Founded to safeguard and protect the interests of the Muslim world, it is the world's second-largest intergovernmental organization after the U.N. *Formerly* the Organisation of the Islamic Conference).

Organization of African Unity ("OAU") Established in 1963 to promote the unity and solidarity of the African states, to act as a collective voice for Africa and to eradicate all forms of colonialism. Dissolved in 2002 and replaced by the AU.

Organization for the Prohibition of Chemical Weapons (U.N.) ("OPCW") Implementing body for the Chemical Weapons Convention (1997). The OPCW, with its 193 member states, oversees the global endeavor to permanently and verifiably eliminate chemical weapons.

P

Pacta sunt servanda (*Lat.*) "Agreements must be kept."

Parlementaire Combatant representative of a warring force sent to negotiate terms or ceasefires with the opposing side or to collect casualties. Parlementaires receive special protection under Hague Regulation IV. Fighting must cease to the extent necessary to ensure the safety of parlementaires. To receive this special protection, parlementaires must carry a white flag and, at the conclusion of their mission, they must be allowed to rejoin their own forces.

Peace of Westphalia Series of peace treaties signed in 1648 in Osnabrück and Münster, Germany, that ended the Thirty Years' War (1618-1648) in the Holy Roman Empire and the Eighty Years' War (1568-1648) between Spain and the Dutch Republic.

Peremptory norm of general international law *See* JUS COGENS.

Perfidy Prohibited method of warfare. Additional Protocol I states that it is prohibited to:[480]

> kill, injure or capture an adversary by resort to perfidy. Acts inviting the confidence of an adversary to lead him to believe that he is entitled to, or is obliged to accord, protection under the rules of international law applicable in armed conflict, with intent to betray that confidence, shall constitute perfidy. The following acts are examples of perfidy:
>
> a) the feigning of an intent to negotiate under a flag of truce or of a surrender;
> b) the feigning of an incapacitation by wounds or sickness;
> c) the feigning of civilian, non-combatant status; and
> d) the feigning of protected status by the use of signs, emblems or uniforms of the United Nations or of neutral or other States not Parties to the conflict.

Additional Protocol I contrasts PERFIDY with RUSES OF WAR, which are "not prohibited." *Compare* RUSES OF WAR.

Permanent Court of Arbitration ("PCA") International organization created by the Hague Convention (I) of 1899 for the Pacific Settlement of International Disputes. The Court, in order to facilitate "an immediate recourse to arbitration for international differences" (Article 20 Hague Convention I), provides for the resolution of disputes involving states, state entities, intergovernmental organizations, and private parties. Along with the International Court of Justice, the PCA is housed at the Peace Palace in The Hague.

Permanent Court of International Justice ("PCIJ") Predecessor of the International Court of Justice.

Presumption Acceptance of a proposition as true in the absence of sufficient evidence to the contrary. Within the context of international humanitarian awl, several presumptions are made during armed conflicts to grant individuals favorable status and treatment until and unless sufficient evidence proves otherwise. These presumptions include the following: (i) in international armed conflicts, persons having committed a belligerent act and having fallen into the power of an adverse party are presumed to be prisoners of war until their status has been determined by a competent tribunal; (ii) in all armed conflicts, persons must be presumed to be civilians and objects normally dedicated to civilian purposes (such as places of worship, houses or schools) must be presumed to be civilian objects; and (iii) anyone accused of a criminal offence related

480. Article 37(1) Additional Protocol I.

to the armed conflict must be presumed innocent until proven guilty according to the law.[481]

Principle of equal application All parties to an armed conflict are bound by international humanitarian law, regardless of which party initiated the conflict, whether the onset of hostilities was legally justified, and which party prevails.

Principles of International Law Recognized in the Charter of the Nuremberg Tribunal and in the Judgment of the Tribunal *See* NUREMBERG PRINCIPLES.

Propio motu (*Lat.*) By one's own volition.

Protocol Subsidiary agreement built from a primary treaty, often implementing or applying the primary treaty, incorporating recent political or scientific developments. They often permit countries to enter into an agreement by signing a general framework and to later work out details as to implementation via protocols.

R

Refoulement Forcible return of a refugee to territories where his or her life or freedom would be in danger. *See NON-REFOULEMENT*.

Revolving Door Fighters Individuals who constantly shift between civilians and individuals directly participating in hostilities. The ICRC position is that directly participating in hostilities does not transform civilians into combatants; while combatants may always be targeted, civilians may only be targeted while directly participating in hostilities. However, some critics raise issues with the prohibition on targeting so-called revolving door fighters when they are not directly participating in hostilities. On the one hand, "a civilian who took a direct part in hostilities once, or sporadically, but detached himself from them (entirely, or for a long period) is not to be harmed. On the other hand, the 'revolving door' phenomenon, by which each terrorist has 'horns of the alter' (1 Kings 1:50) to grasp or a 'city of refuge' (Numbers 35:11) to flee to, to which he turns in order to rest and prepare while they grant him immunity from attack, is to be avoided .... In the wide area between those two possibilities, one finds the 'gray' cases, about which customary international law has not yet crystallized."[482] *Compare* CONTINUOUS COMBAT FUNCTION.

Right to innocent passage The right to sail in territorial seas as long as the sailing is not prejudicial to the peace of the coastal state.

Ruses of war Additional Protocol I defines RUSES OF WAR as:[483]

481. "Presumptions," *How Does Law Protect in War?*, ICRC, available at <https://casebook.icrc.org/a_to_z/glossary/presumptions>.
482. "Israel: Practice Relating to Rule 6. Civilians' Loss of Protection from Attack," IHL Database: Customary IHL available at <https://ihl-databases.icrc.org/customary-ihl/eng/docs/v2_cou_il_rule6>.
483. Article 37(2) Additional Protocol I.

> acts which are intended to mislead an adversary or to induce him to act recklessly but which infringe no rule of international law applicable in armed conflict and which are not perfidious because they do not invite the confidence of an adversary with respect to protection under that law. The following are examples of such ruses: the use of camouflage, decoys, mock operations and misinformation.

Unlike PERFIDY, which is prohibited in the law of armed conflict, RUSES OF WAR are permitted. *Compare* PERFIDY.

S

Santiago Principles Set of 24 principles and practices generally accepted and endorsed voluntarily by members of the INTERNATIONAL FORUM OF SOVEREIGN WEALTH FUNDS ("IFSWF"). The Principles seek to promote transparency, good governance, accountability and prudent investment practices and promote open dialogue and deeper understanding of SWF activities, with the following objectives: maintaining a stable global financial system and free flow of capital and investment; complying with all applicable regulatory and disclosure requirements in the countries in which SWFs invest; ensuring that SWFs invest on the basis of economic and financial risk and return-related considerations; and ensuring that SWFs have in place a transparent and sound governance structure that provides adequate operational controls, risk management, and accountability.

Sic utere (*Lat.*) General principle of good neighborliness in environmental law derived from the Latin expression *sic utere tuo ut alienum non laedas* ("so use your own as not to injure another's property").

Special drawing right International reserve asset created by the IMF to supplement member countries' official reserves. Its value is based on four key international currencies and it can be exchanged for freely usable currencies. There are at present 204 billion SDRs (approx. USD 308 billion) at the time of writing.

Special protections Heightened protection status that is granted to certain classes of persons and objects in addition to general protection from attack based on their vulnerability or special role they play during armed conflict. Under most circumstances, special protections are lost when a specially protected person directly participates in hostilities or a specially protected object is misused. Special protections are distinguishable from general protections because they require additional elements beyond status that must be met for the special protections to be triggered.

Specialized agency Autonomous organization working within the U.N. and one another through the ECOSOC coordinating mechanism at the intergovernmental level and through the Chief Executives Board for coordination at the inter-secretariat level. There are at present 15 specialized agencies: FAO, ICAO, IFAD, ILO, IMF, IMO, ITU, UNESCO, UNIDO, UNWTO, UPU, WHO, WIPO, WMO and the World Bank Group.

Specially designated national ("SDN") An individual, entity and vessel listed on the SDN List and all entities owned 50% or more in the aggregate by one or more individuals, entities and vessels listed on the SDN List (the "50 Percent Rule"). An SDN can be an individual, including a person designated as a terrorist, or a company, parastatal entity or individual determined to be owned or controlled by, or acting for or on behalf of, targeted countries or groups. The SDN's assets are blocked and U.S. persons are generally prohibited from dealing with them. *Also known as a* "blocked person."

State actor An actor for whose conduct a nexus to state action may be established.

Strafe Attack with machine guns or cannon fire from a low-flying plane.

T

Terra nullius (*Lat.*, "the land of no one") Land that is not under the sovereignty or control of any state. States may obtain title to *terra nullius* through the occupation thereof.

Transformative occupation where an occupying power makes changes to the legal or political infrastructure of an occupied territory, including where such changes accord with the rebuilding of a post-conflict state along democratic lines. There is a presumption *against* the legitimacy of transformative occupations that change the laws in place of an occupying territory.

Tribunal An assembly, usually of an ad hoc nature, of one or more judges with the authority to judge on and adjudicate legal claims or disputes. *Compare* COURT.

Tripartite Agreement Agreement entered into by the United States, France and Great Britain in September of 1936 to stabilize their national currencies.

U

UNCITRAL *See* UNITED NATIONS COMMISSION ON INTERNATIONAL TRADE LAW ("UNCITRAL").

UNIDROIT *See* INTERNATIONAL INSTITUTE FOR THE UNIFICATION OF PRIVATE LAW.

United Nations Administrative Tribunal ("UNAT") Court established by the U.N. General Assembly as the final arbiter over claims alleging breach of the terms of appointment (including all pertinent regulations and rules) of staff members working in the U.N. Secretariat. 30 June 2009 marked the end of the mandate of the United Nations Administrative Tribunal, which was replaced by the UNITED NATIONS APPEALS TRIBUNAL ("UNAT") from 1 July 2009 onward.

United Nations Appeals Tribunal ("UNAT") Court of second instance within the U.N. internal justice system, hearing cases in which a Court of First Instance allegedly exceeded its jurisdiction, failed to exercise its jurisdiction or erred on questions of fact, procedure or law. It became operational on 1 July 2009, replacing the UNITED NATIONS ADMINISTRATIVE TRIBUNAL. *See* UNITED NATIONS DISPUTE TRIBUNAL ("UNDT").

United Nations Commission on Human Rights U.N. Commission in 2006 was replaced by the UNITED NATIONS HUMAN RIGHTS COUNCIL. It was a subsidiary body of ECOSOC concerned with drafting human rights treaties for adoption by the U.N. General Assembly and was also assisted in its work by the OHCHR as the UN's principal mechanism and international forum concerned with the promotion and protection of human rights.

United Nations Commission on International Trade Law ("UNCITRAL") U.N. body charged with promoting the harmonization of international trade law and regulating international trade in cooperation with the WORLD TRADE ORGANIZATION.

United Nations Commission on the Status of Women ("UNCSW") Functional commission of ECOSOC promoting gender equality and the empowerment of women.

United Nations Convention on Contracts for the International Sale of Goods ("CISG") (Vienna Convention) International sales treaty and uniform law that was developed by the United Nations Commission on International Trade Law ("UNCITRAL") and was signed in Vienna in 1980. The CISG has been ratified by 89 states that account for a significant proportion of world trade. *Also known as the* CONVENTION ON THE INTERNATIONAL SALE OF GOODS.

United Nations Development Fund for Women ("UNIFEM") Fund was established in 1976 as a part of U.N. Women that serves as a partner to women in conflict-affected areas. It brings women together to agree on common positions in peace negotiations, supports women's engagement with security and justice institutions to stop impunity for violence against women, supports women's empowerment and gender equality, facilitates their inclusion in post-conflict planning processes to ensure their needs are addressed, and encourages their engagement with peacekeeping forces to foster creative responses to security threats that women face. The acronym "UNIFEM" is taken from the French "Fonds de développement des Nations unies pour la femme."

United Nations Dispute Tribunal ("UNDT") Court of First Instance within the U.N. internal justice system that became operational on 1 July 2009 with the power to hear cases appealing administrative decisions alleged to be non-compliant with terms of appointment or employment contracts filed by staff members of the U.N. Secretariat; Peacekeeping and Political Missions; International Criminal Tribunals; ECOSOC Regional Commissions; and General Assembly Programs, Organs, Funds and Other Entities. The Tribunal conducts hearings, issues orders, and renders binding judgments. Staff members and the U.N. Administration may appeal the judgments of the United Nations Dispute Tribunal to the UNITED NATIONS APPEALS TRIBUNAL. *Compare* UNRWA DISPUTE TRIBUNAL.

United Nations Foundation Foundation endowed by Ted Turner in 1998 in order to support the U.N. in executing its worldwide programs, including child health, climate change, energy, sustainable development, technology, women and population.

United Nations Human Rights Council ("UNHRC") Successor to the UNITED NATIONS COMMISSION ON HUMAN RIGHTS. As a subsidiary body of the U.N. General Assembly, it is responsible for strengthening the promotion and protection of human rights around the globe. The Council was created by the U.N. General Assembly on 15 March 2006 with the main purpose of addressing situations of human rights violations and making recommendations on them.

United Nations Investigative Team for Accountability of Da'esh/ISIL ("UNITAD") Agency established by the U.N. Secretary-General pursuant to Security Council resolution 2379 (2017), according to which it was mandated to support domestic efforts to hold ISIL (Da'esh) accountable by collecting, preserving and storing evidence in Iraq of acts that may amount to war crimes, crimes against humanity and genocide committed by the terrorist group ISIL (Da'esh) in Iraq.

United Nations Relief and Works Agency for Palestine Refugees in the Near East ("UNRWA") Agency established by the General Assembly in 1949 to provide assistance and protection through relief and jobs to 652,000 Arabs who fled or were expelled from Israel during the Arab-Israeli War. Today, UNRWA provides assistance to some five million Palestinian refugees living in the West Bank, the Gaza Strip, Jordan, Lebanon and Syria to achieve their full potential in human development, pending a just and durable solution to their plight.

United Nations Special Fund Fund established by the UNGA on 14 October 1958 in order to enlarge the scope of the U.N. program of technical assistance with a focus on large projects "in the fields of resources, including the assessment and development of manpower, industry, including handicrafts and cottage industries, agriculture, transport and communications, building and housing, health, education, statistics and public administration."

United Nations special rapporteur Independent expert working on behalf of the United Nations within the scope of "special procedure" mechanisms who holds a mandate from the United Nations Human Rights Council. The mandates can refer to a specific country or theme. Subject matter themes include the Environment; Extrajudicial, Summary or Arbitrary executions; Freedom of Religion or Belief; Hazardous Substances and Wastes; Human Rights Defenders; Internally Displaced Persons; Promotion of Truth, Justice, Reparation and Guarantees of Non-Recurrence; Privacy; Protecting Human Rights while Countering Terrorism; Torture and Other Cruel, Inhuman or Degrading Treatment or Punishment; Transnational Corporations and other Business Enterprises; and Violence against Women. Country themes include Belarus, the Democratic People's Republic of Korea (North Korea), Iran, Myanmar, Palestine, Somalia and Sudan. The special rapporteur is a pro bono role.

Universal jurisdiction Principle under international law that allows national courts to try cases involving the most egregious crimes, such as genocide, that are considered "crimes against all." The principle allows the courts of any nation to try nationals of any other nation without the consent of the accused or of his nation. This is an exception to the general rule that holds that sovereign nations must consent to have their nationals tried by international courts.

UNRWA Dispute Tribunal Court of First Instance that hears and decides cases filed by or on behalf of UNRWA staff members appealing administrative decisions alleged to be non-compliant with their terms of appointment or employment contracts. Staff members and the UNRWA Administration may appeal the judgments of the UNRWA Dispute Tribunal to the UNITED NATIONS APPEALS TRIBUNAL. *Compare* UNITED NATIONS DISPUTE TRIBUNAL.

Uti possidetis (*Lat.*, "as you possess") International legal principle that holds that territory and other property possessed at the end of a conflict remains with the possessor, unless otherwise provided for by treaty. This principle enables a belligerent party to legitimately claim territory that it has acquired by war.

V

Vatican City Independent state enclaved within Rome, Italy, that was established by the Lateran Treaty of 1929. It is under "full ownership, exclusive dominion, and sovereign authority and jurisdiction" of the Holy See. *Officially known as* Vatican City State.

W

War crimes "Serious violations of international humanitarian law."[484] The Rome Statute defines war crimes as: "[g]rave breaches of the Geneva Conventions of 12 August 1949";[485] "[o]ther serious violations of the laws and customs applicable in international armed conflict, within the established framework of international law";[486] and "[i]n the case of an armed conflict not of an international character, serious violations of article 3 common to the four Geneva Conventions of 12 August 1949."[487] The Rome Statute further provides an extensive list of war crimes falling within each of these three categories. For example, the following constitute war crimes under Article 8.2(b) of the Rome Statute: willful killing; torture or inhuman treatment; willfully causing great suffering, or serious injury to body or health; extensive, unlawful, wanton and militarily unjustified destruction and appropriation of property; compelling service in the forces of a hostile power; willful deprivation of the rights of fair and regular trial; unlawful deportation, transfer or confinement; and taking of hostages. The London Charter gave the following examples of war crimes under the jurisdiction of the IMT: "murder, ill-treatment or deportation to slave labor or for any other purpose of civilian population of or in occupied territory, murder or ill-treatment of prisoners of war or persons on the seas, killing of hostages, plunder of public or

484. Jean-Marie Henckaerts and Louise Doswald-Beck, *Customary International Humanitarian Law*, Vol. I, ICRC, Cambridge University Press (Cambridge, New York, 2009), Rule 156, Chapter 44, p. 568.
485. Article 8.2(a) SICC.
486. Article 8.2(b) SICC.
487. Article 8.2(c) SICC.

private property, wanton destruction of cities, towns or villages, or devastation not justified by military necessity."[488]

Women's International War Crimes Tribunal on Japan's Military Sexual Slavery A people's tribunal organized in 2000 by various women's and human rights non-governmental organizations from across Asia to remedy the failure of the International Military Tribunal for the Far East to prosecute groups and individuals for rape or sexual slavery during World War II. The Tribunal met in December of 2000 and issued a judgment convicting the late Emperor Hirohito Showa who, as leader of the country, was deemed ultimately responsible for the sexual slavery policy and World War II "comfort stations" for Japanese soldiers. The Tribunal, organized more than half a century after the trials of the International Military Tribunal for the Far East, was called on to apply the law at the time of World War II as it existed with respect to crimes against humanity. Also known as the TOKYO WOMEN'S TRIBUNAL.

World Food Council ("WFC") Former U.N. organization headquartered in Rome and established in 1974 by the U.N. General Assembly by recommendation of the World Food Conference to serve as coordinating body for national ministries of agriculture to help reduce malnutrition and hunger. WFC was suspended in 1993 and its functions were absorbed by the Food and Agriculture Organization of the United Nations and the World Food Programme.

World Food Programme ("WFP") A U.N. General Assembly subsidiary organ headquartered in Rome that provides food assistance to address hunger and promote food security. The WFP provides food to an average of 90 million people per year, the majority of whom are children.

World Wide Fund for Nature ("WWF") International NGO founded in 1961 working in the field of biodiversity conservation and the reduction of humanity's footprint on the environment. It was formerly named the WORLD WILDLIFE FUND, which remains its official name in Canada and the United States.

World Wildlife Fund *See* WORLD WIDE FUND FOR NATURE.

World Intellectual Property Organization ("WIPO") U.N. specialized agency established in 1967 to promote the protection of intellectual property internationally.

World Trade Organization ("WTO") The only global international organization dealing with the rules of trade between nations. The WTO agreements, negotiated and signed by most of the world's trading nations, are intended to supervise and liberalize international trade and assist producers of goods and services, exporters and importers conduct their business.

488. Article 6(b) IMT.

CHARTS AND SCHEMATICS

Affirmative Duties under International Law

Category	*Legal Basis*
Preventing genocide	The Convention on the Prevention and Punishment of the Crime of Genocide requires that its 140 states parties "undertake to prevent and to punish" genocide (Article I CPPG).
Ensuring the respect of international humanitarian law	States parties to the four Geneva Conventions are required to "*respect* and *ensure respect* for the present Convention[s] *in all circumstances*" (common Article 1).
Agreeing to consignments in occupied territories	An occupying power has an affirmative duty to consent to the relief schemes directed at the civilian population of an inadequately supplied occupied territory (Article 59 GC IV).
Respect for human rights	The ICCPR requires that states agree not only to refrain from violating basic rights, but also that they ensure the protection of these rights from other member states' violations (Article 2(3) ICCPR).

Dispute Settlement Mechanisms of the Arab League and OIC

Arab Investment Court of the Arab League ("AIC")	Established in 1986 by the Unified Agreement for the Investment of Arab Capital in the Arab States (the "Arab Investment Agreement") (1980), which was concluded under the umbrella of the Arab League to provide protections to Arab investors when investing in other Arab signatory states. The AIC was established to adjudicate claims between Arab governments and corporates and individuals from Arab states. Seated in Cairo, Egypt, the AIC is composed of at least five serving judges each with a different Arab nationality which must not be the same nationality as either of the parties to the conflict. The Court was inactive until 2003, when the Arab League renewed its operations. In 2004, the Court heard a dispute in which the Saudi Arabian company Tanmiah for Consultancy Management & Marketing sued the Tunisian government for damages surrounding the execution of sponsorship for the 2001 Mediterranean Games. The court ruled in favor of the Tunisian government. Judgments rendered by the AIC are final and are enforceable in each of the contracting states in the same way a judgment delivered by their national courts.

Arab Court for Commercial Control and Dispute Settlement	The Arab Court for Commercial Control and Dispute Settlement is the legal institution of the *Arab Union for Commercial Arbitration and Dispute Settlement ("AUCADS")*. The AUCADS is an independent Arab international body, a member of the Arab Federations Forum and a member of the Permanent Executive Office of the Arab League. The AUCADS seeks to resolve long-standing disputes outside the courts to support trade and investment in the Arab world. The Arab Court for Commercial Control and Dispute Settlement is a mechanism for achieving AUCADS' objective of dispute resolution. The Arab Court for Commercial Control and Dispute Settlement is derived from the Arab Federation of Commercial Arbitration, Settlement and Disputes. It is an independent judicial authority that rules and adjudicates commercial disputes in the Arab world.
Agreement on Promotion, Protection and Guarantee of Investments among the Member States of the Organisation of the Islamic Conference	The OIC's Agreement on Promotion, Protection and Guarantee of Investments among the Member States of the Organisation of the Islamic Conference (the "OIC Investment Agreement") was opened for signature by Resolution 7/12-E of the Twelfth Islamic Conference of Foreign Ministers held in Baghdad, Iraq, in June 1981 and entered into force in September 1986. Investors may file claims before national courts or arbitral tribunals, but once having chosen a forum, they lose the right of recourse to the other forum. Article 17 of the OIC Agreement provides for the mechanisms of conciliation and arbitration for the peaceful settlement of disputes.

Conditions of a Just War

The conditions of a just war depend on the basis of the school of thought that one follows. Under Thomas Aquinas' theory, which is among the most cited, the following elements are required:

- a legitimate authority;
- a just cause; and
- the right intention.

Other elements have been incorporated into this theory over time. The most frequently cited are as follows:

- exhaustion of all non-violent options; and
- reasonable prospect of success.

Geneva Conventions

Overview

Convention	*Revising*	*Function*
Geneva Convention I for the Amelioration of the Condition of the Wounded and Sick in Armed Forces in the Field, 1949 Original: 1864	The Geneva Convention for the Relief of the Wounded and Sick in Armies in the Field of 27 July 1929 First Geneva Convention (1864)	- Protects wounded and sick soldiers on land during war. - Protects medical and religious personnel, medical units and medical transports. - Contains a draft agreement relating to hospital zones and a model identity card for medical and religious personnel.
Geneva Convention II for the Amelioration of the Condition of Wounded, Sick and Shipwrecked Members of Armed Forces at Sea, 1949 Original 1906	Xth Hague Convention of 18 October 1907 for the Adaptation to Maritime Warfare of the Principles of the Geneva Convention of 1906	- Protects wounded, sick and shipwrecked military personnel at sea during war at sea.
Geneva Convention III relative to the Treatment of Prisoners of War, 1949 Original: 1929	Convention concluded at Geneva on 27 July 1929, relative to the Treatment of Prisoners of War	- Applies to prisoners of war. - Established the principle of repatriating prisoners of war immediately upon the cessation of hostilities.
Geneva Convention IV relative to the Protection of Civilian Persons in Time of War, 1949 Original: 1949	NA	- Protects civilians, including those in occupied territories. - Outlines the rights of those captured during military conflicts. - Protects the wounded and civilians in war zones.

Common Articles 2 and 3 of the 1949 Geneva Conventions

Common Article 2 (international armed conflicts)

In addition to the provisions which shall be implemented in peace-time, the present Convention shall apply to all cases of declared war or of any other armed conflict which may arise between two or more of the High Contracting Parties, even if the state of war is not recognized by one of them.

The Convention shall also apply to all cases of partial or total occupation of the territory of a High Contracting Party, even if the said occupation meets with no armed resistance.

Although one of the Powers in conflict may not be a party to the present Convention, the Powers who are parties thereto shall remain bound by it in their mutual relations. They shall furthermore be bound by the Convention in relation to the said Power, if the latter accepts and applies the provisions thereof.

Common Article 3 (non-international armed conflicts)

In the case of armed conflict not of an international character occurring in the territory of one of the High Contracting Parties, each Party to the conflict shall be bound to apply, as a minimum, the following provisions:

(1) Persons taking no active part in the hostilities, including members of armed forces who have laid down their arms and those placed hors de combat by sickness, wounds, detention, or any other cause, shall in all circumstances be treated humanely, without any adverse distinction founded on race, colour, religion or faith, sex, birth or wealth, or any other similar criteria.

To this end, the following acts are and shall remain prohibited at any time and in any place whatsoever with respect to the above-mentioned persons:

- (a) violence to life and person, in particular murder of all kinds, mutilation, cruel treatment and torture;
- (b) taking of hostages;
- (c) outrages upon personal dignity, in particular humiliating and degrading treatment;
- (d) the passing of sentences and the carrying out of executions without previous judgment pronounced by a regularly constituted court, affording all the judicial guarantees which are recognized as indispensable by civilized peoples.

(2) The wounded and sick shall be collected and cared for.

An impartial humanitarian body, such as the International Committee of the Red Cross, may offer its services to the Parties to the conflict.

The Parties to the conflict should further endeavour to bring into force, by means of special agreements, all or part of the other provisions of the present Convention.

The application of the preceding provisions shall not affect the legal status of the Parties to the conflict.

States Parties to the 1949 Geneva Conventions (195 States)

(1) Afghanistan
(2) Albania
(3) Algeria
(4) Andorra
(5) Angola
(6) Antigua and Barbuda
(7) Argentina
(8) Armenia
(9) Australia
(10) Austria
(11) Azerbaijan
(12) Bahamas
(13) Bahrain
(14) Bangladesh
(15) Barbados
(16) Belarus
(17) Belgium
(18) Belize
(19) Benin
(20) Bhutan
(21) Bolivia
(22) Bosnia and Herzegovina
(23) Botswana
(24) Brazil
(25) Brunei
(26) Bulgaria
(27) Burkina Faso
(28) Burundi
(29) Cambodia
(30) Cameroon
(31) Canada
(32) Cape Verde
(33) Central African Republic
(34) Chad
(35) Chile
(36) China
(37) Colombia
(38) Comoros
(39) Cook Islands
(40) Costa Rica
(41) Côte d'Ivoire
(42) Croatia
(43) Cuba

(44) Cyprus
(45) Czech Republic
(46) Democratic People's Republic of Korea (North Korea)
(47) Democratic Republic of the Congo
(48) Denmark
(49) Djibouti
(50) Dominica
(51) Dominican Republic
(52) East Timor
(53) Ecuador
(54) Egypt
(55) El Salvador
(56) Equatorial Guinea
(57) Eritrea
(58) Estonia
(59) Ethiopia
(60) Fiji
(61) Finland
(62) France
(63) Gabon
(64) The Gambia
(65) Georgia
(66) Germany
(67) Ghana
(68) Greece
(69) Grenada
(70) Guatemala
(71) Guinea
(72) Guinea-Bissau
(73) Guyana
(74) Haiti
(75) Vatican City (Holy See)
(76) Honduras
(77) Hungary
(78) Iceland
(79) India
(80) Indonesia
(81) Iran
(82) Iraq
(83) Ireland
(84) Israel
(85) Italy
(86) Jamaica
(87) Japan
(88) Jordan

(89) Kazakhstan
(90) Kenya
(91) Kiribati
(92) Kuwait
(93) Kyrgyzstan
(94) Laos
(95) Latvia
(96) Lebanon
(97) Lesotho
(98) Liberia
(99) Libya
(100) Liechtenstein
(101) Lithuania
(102) Luxembourg
(103) North Macedonia
(104) Madagascar
(105) Malawi
(106) Malaysia
(107) Maldives
(108) Mali
(109) Malta
(110) Marshall Islands
(111) Mauritania
(112) Mauritius
(113) Mexico
(114) Federated States of Micronesia
(115) Moldova
(116) Monaco
(117) Mongolia
(118) Montenegro
(119) Morocco
(120) Mozambique
(121) Myanmar
(122) Namibia
(123) Nauru
(124) Nepal
(125) Netherlands
(126) New Zealand
(127) Nicaragua
(128) Niger
(129) Nigeria
(130) Norway
(131) Oman
(132) Pakistan
(133) Palau

(134) Panama
(135) Papua New Guinea
(136) Paraguay
(137) Peru
(138) Philippines
(139) Poland
(140) Portugal
(141) Qatar
(142) Republic of the Congo
(143) Republic of Korea (South Korea)
(144) Romania
(145) Russia
(146) Rwanda
(147) Saint Kitts and Nevis
(148) Saint Lucia
(149) Saint Vincent and the Grenadines
(150) Samoa
(151) San Marino
(152) Sao Tome and Principe
(153) Saudi Arabia
(154) Senegal
(155) Serbia
(156) Seychelles
(157) Sierra Leone
(158) Singapore
(159) Slovakia
(160) Slovenia
(161) Solomon Islands
(162) Somalia
(163) South Africa
(164) Republic of South Sudan
(165) Spain
(166) Sri Lanka
(167) Sudan
(168) Suriname
(169) Eswatini (Swaziland)
(170) Sweden
(171) Switzerland
(172) Syria
(173) Tajikistan
(174) Tanzania
(175) Thailand
(176) Togo
(177) Tonga
(178) Trinidad and Tobago

(179) Tunisia
(180) Turkey
(181) Turkmenistan
(182) Tuvalu
(183) Uganda
(184) Ukraine
(185) United Arab Emirates
(186) United Kingdom
(187) United States
(188) Uruguay
(189) Uzbekistan
(190) Vanuatu
(191) Venezuela
(192) Vietnam
(193) Yemen
(194) Zambia
(195) Zimbabwe

Human Rights Bodies at the International Level

U.N. Institutions

Office of the U.N. High Commissioner for Human Rights (OHCHR) (Geneva)	The UN's principal mechanism and international forum concerned with the promotion and protection of human rights. It was established by the U.N. General Assembly in 1993 to promote and protect the human rights that are guaranteed under international law and stipulated in the UDHR.
U.N. Human Rights Council ("UNHRC") (Geneva)	Successor to the United Nations Commission on Human Rights. As a subsidiary body of the U.N. General Assembly, it is responsible for strengthening the promotion and protection of human rights. The Council was created by the U.N. General Assembly in 2006.
U.N. Human Rights Committee (HRC) (New York spring session; Geneva summer and fall sessions)	Human rights treaty body of the ICCPR. It holds the power to review compliance reports submitted by states parties to the ICCPR; issue "General Comments" on the implementation of the ICCPR; and, under the (First) Optional Protocol to the ICCPR, consider petitions from individuals claiming violations of the ICCPR by a state party.

U.N. Commission on Human Rights (Geneva)	U.N. commission that in 2006 was replaced by the United Nations Human Rights Council. It was a subsidiary body of ECOSOC concerned with drafting human rights treaties for adoption by the U.N. General Assembly and was also assisted in its work by the OHCHR.

Human Rights Treaty Bodies

There are nine principal international human rights treaties. Each of these has created a treaty body (committee) of experts to monitor implementation of the treaty provisions by its states parties.

- The U.N. Human Rights Committee ("HRC") monitors implementation of the ICCPR (1966) and its optional protocols.
- The Committee on Economic, Social and Cultural Rights ("CESCR") monitors implementation of the ICESCR (1966).
- The Committee on the Elimination of Racial Discrimination ("CERD") monitors implementation of the International Convention on the Elimination of All Forms of Racial Discrimination (1965).
- The Committee on the Elimination of Discrimination against Women ("CEDAW") monitors implementation of the Convention on the Elimination of All Forms of Discrimination against Women (1979) and its optional protocol (1999).
- The Committee Against Torture ("CAT") monitors implementation of the Convention against Torture and Other Cruel, Inhuman or Degrading Treatment (1984).
- The Committee on the Rights of the Child ("CRC") monitors implementation of the Convention on the Rights of the Child (1989) and its optional protocols (2000).
- The Committee on Migrant Workers ("CMW") monitors implementation of the International Convention on the Protection of the Rights of All Migrant Workers and Members of Their Families (1990).
- The Committee on the Right of Persons with Disabilities ("CRPD") monitors implementation of the International Convention on the Rights of Persons with Disabilities (2006).
- The Committee on Enforced Disappearance ("CED") monitors implementation of the International Convention for the Protection of All Persons from Enforced Disappearance (2006).

International Declarations, Treaties, and Conventions

- United Nations Charter (1945)
- Universal Declaration of Human Rights (1948)
- Convention on the Prevention and Punishment of the Crime of Genocide (1948)

- Convention Relating to the Status of Refugees (1951)
- International Covenant on Civil and Political Rights (1966)
- International Covenant on Economic, Social and Cultural Rights (1966)
- International Convention on the Elimination of All Forms of Racial Discrimination (1966)
- Convention on the Elimination of All Forms of Discrimination against Women (1979)
- Indigenous and Tribal Peoples Convention (1989)
- Convention on the Rights of the Child (1989)

Regional Human Rights Systems

- Council of Europe human rights system
  - European Court of Human Rights
  - European Convention on Human Rights (1950)
- European Union human rights system
  - European Court of Justice
  - Charter of Fundamental Rights of the European Union (2000)
- American human rights system
  - Inter-American Commission on Human Rights
  - Inter-American Court of Human Rights
  - American Declaration of the Rights and Duties of Man (1948)
  - American Convention on Human Rights (1969)
- African human rights system
  - African Court on Human and Peoples' Rights
  - African Charter on Human and Peoples' Rights (1981)
  - Protocol to the African Charter on Human and Peoples' Rights on the Rights of Women in Africa (2005)
- Arab human rights system
  - Cairo Declaration on Human Rights in Islam (1990)
  - Arab Charter on Human Rights (2004)
  - Arab Court of Human Rights

Human Rights Due Diligences

Corporate human rights due diligences are a step that companies can proactively take toward strengthening international human rights. Through human rights due diligences, companies can effectively manage the potential and actual adverse human rights impacts of their business operations and those of their partners. When examining the human rights impact of their own business operations, company due diligences should incorporate the following core components:

- identifying and assessing actual or potential adverse human rights impacts that the company may cause or contribute to directly or which may be linked to its business relationships;
- integrating findings from impact assessments across company operations and taking action according to its involvement in any relevant impact;
- evaluating the effectiveness of measures and processes to mitigate adverse human rights impacts; and
- communicating how impacts are being addressed and showing investors and impacted stakeholders that there are adequate policies and processes in place.

When examining the human rights impact of the operations of potential acquisition targets, JV partners and other business partners, human rights due diligences should incorporate the following core components:

- details of claims brought against the target, with a focus on labor, corruption and bribery, including actual or threatened litigation, disputes, investigations and claims by or against the target with a focus on labor, human trafficking, money laundering, terrorism or other abuses of international human rights law or violations of humanitarian law;
- review of compliance with international human rights standards, including a review of human rights policies and environmental protection charters, if applicable, and the implementation of policies to combat human trafficking, modern slavery, forced labor, child labor, environmental contamination, injury to natural resources, money laundering and terrorism;
- determining if the company is a sanctions target found on the U.N. sanctions list, the E.U. Sanctions Map, OFAC lists or Her Majesty's Treasury list;
- undertaking AML and terrorist links searches through financial crime and sanctions screening tools;
- review of any violations by the target or its employees of any applicable foreign or domestic sanctions or trade restrictions;
- conducting negative news searches in English and the prevailing language(s) in the territories in which the company is incorporated and has its place(s) of business;
- review of the target's governance, compliance and anti-corruption policies;
- review of insurance policies and claims filed and awarded or denied in any areas relevant to human rights, mass torts and environmental protection.

Human Rights Policies: Sample Language

Overview

This section includes language that companies may wish to incorporate into their supply agreements, license agreements, joint venture agreements and other contracts. While boilerplate language exists that can be incorporated into contracts across various sectors, companies should consider tailoring contracts to their specific industry. For example, a supply contract in the energy industry would likely incorporate language relating to pollution that would not be found in a supply contract in the financial services company, whereas a supply contract in the defense industry would likely incorporate language relating to the manufacture of weapons or use of child soldiers that would not be found in a hospitality industry supply contract. While this section provides general examples of language that can be used by companies, the language should be tailored to specific sectors before being finalized and promulgated.

Contracts with Third Parties

One way that companies can ensure the respect of international human rights is to incorporate into their agreements language guaranteeing human rights. This ensures that companies will only do business with like-minded companies that share their commitment to human rights. It will also exclude from company supply chains businesses that breach international human rights law by, for example, subjecting their employees to hazardous work conditions contrary to occupational safety laws; using forced labor; employing children in a manner that is harmful to their health or physical, mental, spiritual, moral or social development; or engaging in human trafficking, sexual exploitation of minors or forced prostitution. Companies that are serious about ensuring respect for human rights may go a step further by reserving a right to audit their counterparties' premises with minimal notice to ensure compliance with their human rights policies.

Companies may incorporate the following sample language into their agreements:

> COMPLIANCE WITH HUMAN RIGHTS AND LABOR STANDARDS
>
> Counterparty [Supplier, Licensee, Lessor, Lessee, Seller, Partner, Investor, etc.] warrants that it does not, and agrees that it will not, conduct business with any vendors, subcontractors or any other third parties that (a) employ children, (b) use forced labor, prison labor, indentured labor or bonded labor, or (c) use corporal punishment or other forms of mental and physical coercion as a form of discipline. Company and Counterparty agree to define "child" as less than sixteen (16) years of age. However, if local minimum age law sets the definition of "child" below sixteen (16) years of age and is in accordance with the standards set forth in International Labor Organization Convention No. 138, then the lower age shall apply.
>
> Counterparty warrants that in the event that it employs persons aged eighteen (18) years old or younger, such employment shall comply with local law and international standards and shall not be inconsistent with Article 32 of the rights in the Convention on the Rights of the Child, which requires that a child shall be protected from performing any work that is likely to be hazardous or to interfere with the child's education, or to be harmful to the child's health or physical, mental, spiritual, moral or social development;
>
> Counterparty warrants that its directors, officers and employees and any other persons controlled by Counterparty to perform any services under this Agreement are not engaged in sexual exploitation, trafficking of persons or other abuses of international human rights law. Should instances of any such abuse come to Counterparty's attention, Counterparty undertakes to investigate any such allegations and take appropriate disciplinary action and, should such abuse rise to the level of a criminal offense under local law, to refer such violations to local law enforcement for prosecution.

Counterparty warrants that modern slavery and forced labor in all of their forms have no place in its operations or supply chains. Counterparty recognizes that no person should be indebted or coerced to work and pledges to combat all forms of modern slavery, forced labor and child labor. Counterparty requires its employees, officers and directors and all third parties acting on its behalf to comply with applicable labor laws and regulations prohibiting forced labor and modern forms of slavery.

Counterparty undertakes to both respect the labor and human rights standards enumerated in this Clause and to ensure that third parties under its control, including Counterparty's agents, subcontractors and assigns, respect the labor and human rights standards enumerated herein.

Company has the right to audit Counterparty's premises to ensure compliance with the provisions of this Clause.

In the energy sector, companies may wish to include a clause that states:

> Counterparty shall refrain from any acts that result in the pollution of the environment, cause injury to natural resources or create hazardous conditions to public waters, soils, the air or other receptors. Counterparty shall take prompt remedial action when it learns of contamination caused by its business operations, whether such contamination is caused directly by its employees or indirectly by its agents or assigns.

In the defense industry, companies may include a clause that states:

> Counterparty shall not engage in the acquisition, manufacture, sale or possession of weapons in violation of international humanitarian law, including chemical, biological or toxin weapons, and shall refrain from recruiting, supplying or working with child soldiers.

Human rights policies of companies in the financial services sector, such as banks and investment institutions, should include language relating to upstream sources and downstream uses of funding to finance operations that breach international human rights law. For example:

> Counterparty shall ensure that its funds are not used to finance, fund or support human trafficking, forced child labor, the use of human carriers to traffic drugs, sexual exploitation, forced prostitution, terrorism, the purchase or use of weapons against civilians or other persons protected from direct attack under international law or other violations of international humanitarian law, international human rights law and local law.

In the legal sector, companies may include a clause that states:

> Counterparty shall support the rule of law and the institutions, processes and frameworks that ensure accountability, predictability and justice in governing economic transactions and social relations and resolving disputes.

International Jurisprudence

Eritrea-Ethiopia Claims Commission

2003 *Partial Award: Prisoners of War—Eritrea's Claim 17* (Eritrea-Ethiopia Claims Commission). Eritrea sought a finding from the Commission that Ethiopia was liable "for loss, damage and injury suffered by the Claimant as a result of the Respondent's alleged unlawful treatment of its Prisoners of War ("POWs") who were nationals of the Claimant [and requesting] monetary compensation, costs, and such other relief as is just and proper."[489] The Commission held that Ethiopia was liable to Eritrea for the following violations of international law: (1) failing to take effective measures to prevent incidents of beating or other unlawful abuse of Eritrean PoWs at capture or its immediate aftermath; (2) frequently depriving Eritrean PoWs of footwear during long walks; (3) failing to protect the personal property of Eritrean PoWs; (4) subjecting Eritrean PoWs to enforced indoctrination; (5) permitting health conditions to be such as to seriously and adversely affect or endanger the health of the Eritrean PoWs; (6) providing all Eritrean PoWs prior to December 2000 a diet that was seriously deficient in nutrition; (7) failing to provide the standard of medical care required for Eritrean PoWs and failing to provide required preventive care by segregating from the outset prisoners with infectious diseases and by conducting regular physical examinations; and (8) delaying the repatriation of 1,287 Eritrean PoWs for 77 days longer than was reasonably required.

2003 *Partial Award on Prisoners of War—Ethiopia's Claim 4* (Eritrea-Ethiopia Claims Commission). Ethiopia sought a finding from the Commission that Eritrea was liable "for loss, damage and injury suffered" by PoWs who were nationals of Ethiopia as well as monetary compensation to be "determined by a mass claims process."[490] The Commission held that Eritrea was liable to Ethiopia for the following violations of international law: (1) refusing permission for the ICRC to send delegates to visit all places where Ethiopian PoWs were detained, to register those PoWs, to interview them without witnesses, and to provide them with relief and services customarily provided; (2) failing to

489. *Partial Award: Prisoners of War—Eritrea's Claim 17*, Eritrea-Ethiopia Claims Commission, Volume XXVI, Eritrea's Claim 17 (1 July 2003), p. 30.
490. *Ibid.*, p. 80.

protect Ethiopian PoWs from being killed at capture or its immediate aftermath; (3) permitting beatings or other physical abuse of Ethiopian PoWs; (4) depriving all Ethiopian PoWs of footwear during long walks from the place of capture to the first place of detention; (5) permitting its personnel to threaten and beat Ethiopian PoWs during interrogations; (6) the general confiscation of the personal property of Ethiopian PoWs; (7) permitting pervasive and continuous physical and mental abuse of Ethiopian PoWs in its camps; (8) seriously endangering the health of Ethiopian PoWs by failing to provide adequate housing, sanitation, drinking water, bathing opportunities and food; (9) failing to provide the standard of medical care required for Ethiopian PoWs and failing to provide required preventive care by segregating prisoners with infectious diseases and conducting regular physical examinations; (10) subjecting Ethiopian PoWs to unlawful conditions of labor; (11) permitting unnecessary suffering of PoWs during transfer between camps; and (12) failing to allow the Ethiopian PoWs in its camps to complain about their conditions and to seek redress, and frequently punishing PoWs who attempted to complain.

ICJ Cases

1949	*Albania v. Great Britain* (*Corfu Channel* case) (1949). Albania was ordered to compensate Britain for damage caused by Albania's mining of the channel.
1974	*New Zealand v. France* (*Nuclear Tests* case).
1982	*United States v. Iran* (*U.S. Diplomatic and Consular Staff in Tehran* case). States are responsible for the conduct of non-state actors if they subsequently ratify the conduct and adopt it as their own.
1984	*Canada v. United States* (Delimitation of the Maritime Boundary in the Gulf of Maine Area).
1985	*Libyan Arab Jamahiriya v. Malta* (*Continental Shelf* case). State practice, together with the *opinio juris* of states, forms the substance of customary law.
1986	*Case Concerning the Military and Paramilitary Activities in and Against Nicaragua (Nicaragua v. United States of America)*[491] (*Nicaragua Contras* case).[492] In a dispute brought before the ICJ by an application filed by Nicaragua on 9 April 1984, the ICJ

491. *Case Concerning the Military and Paramilitary Activities in and Against Nicaragua (Nicaragua v. United States of America)*, 1986 ICJ 14 (27 June 1986), p. 14.

492. The Iran-Contra affair (also referred to as the "Iran-Contra scandal" or simply "Iran-Contra"), was a related political scandal in the U.S. that occurred during President Ronald Reagan's

held that by supporting Contra guerrillas in their rebellion against the Nicaraguan government and by mining Nicaragua's harbors, the U.S. had violated "its obligations under customary international law not to use force against another State," "not to intervene in its affairs," "not to violate its sovereignty," "not to interrupt peaceful maritime commerce," and "its obligations under Article XIX of the Treaty of Friendship, Commerce and Navigation between the Parties signed at Managua on 21 January 1956."[493]

The ICJ held that the duty to respect and ensure respect derived from the Geneva Conventions and from "general principles of humanitarian law to which the Conventions merely give specific expression." The U.S. was "under an obligation not to encourage persons or groups engaged in the conflict in Nicaragua to act in violation of the provisions of Article 3 common to the four 1949 Geneva Conventions."[494]

The ICJ awarded reparations to Nicaragua. The U.S. refused to participate in the proceedings after the ICJ rejected the argument that it lacked jurisdiction. Following issuance of the judgment, the U.S. blocked enforcement through a 1986 Security Council veto of a resolution calling for full and immediate compliance with the judgment, thereby preventing Nicaragua from obtaining compensation.

The ICJ also held that there is a customary international law prohibition on the use of force. However, the ICJ did not discuss in detail the practice of when states use force against each other.

1996 *Advisory Opinion on the Legality of the Threat or Use of Nuclear Weapons*. The principle of distinction in international humanitarian law "is aimed at the protection of the civilian population and civilian objects and establishes the distinction between combatants and non-combatants; states must never make civilians the object of attack and must consequently never use weapons that are incapable of distinguishing between civilian and military targets."[495]

second term of office. Administration officials secretly facilitated the sale of arms to Iran, which was the subject of an arms embargo, to use the proceeds to fund the Contras in Nicaragua.

493. The ICJ also held that "for a new customary rule to be formed, not only must the acts concerned 'amount to a settled practice,' but they must be accompanied by the *opinio juris sive necessitas* [an opinion of law or necessity]."

494. *Case Concerning the Military and Paramilitary Activities in and Against Nicaragua* (*Nicaragua v. United States of America*), 1986 ICJ 14 (27 June 1986), p. 114, para. 220.

495. *Legality of the Threat or Use of Nuclear Weapons*, Advisory Opinion, ICJ Reports (8 July 1996), p. 257, available at <https://www.icj-cij.org/docket/files/95/7495.pdf>.

The ICJ recognized the destructive character of nuclear weapons. The Court observed as follows:[496]

> The Court ... notes that nuclear weapons are explosive devices whose energy results from the fusion or fission of the atom. By its very nature, that process, in nuclear weapons as they exist today, releases not only immense quantities of heat and energy, but also powerful and prolonged radiation. According to the material before the Court, the first two causes of damage are vastly more powerful than the damage caused by other weapons, while the phenomenon of radiation is said to be peculiar to nuclear weapons. These characteristics render the nuclear weapon *potentially catastrophic*. The destructive power of nuclear weapons *cannot be contained in either space or time*. They have the potential to *destroy all civilization and the entire ecosystem of the planet*.

In light of this potential for widespread destruction, many treaties have been adopted that restrict the proliferation and deployment of nuclear weapons. However, "they have not resulted in a treaty of general prohibition of the same kind as for bacteriological and chemical weapons" (pp. 248-249, paragraph 58). Rather, they restrict the acquisition, manufacture and possession of nuclear weapons, the deployment of nuclear weapons in Antarctica, outer space, and the seabed and ocean floor and the testing of nuclear weapons. On this basis, the ICJ held by 11 votes to three that (p. 266, paragraph 105):

> There is in neither customary nor conventional international law any comprehensive and universal prohibition of the threat or use of nuclear weapons as such.

In a split vote of seven votes to seven, by the President's casting vote, the ICJ held that the threat or use of nuclear weapons would:[497]

> generally be contrary to the rules of international law applicable in armed conflict, and in particular the principles and rules of humanitarian law. However, in view of the current state of international law, and of the elements of fact at its disposal, the Court cannot conclude definitively whether the threat or use of nuclear weapons would be lawful or unlawful in an extreme circumstance of self-defence, in which the very survival of a state would be at stake.

496. *Ibid.*, pp. 243-44, para. 35.
497. *Ibid.*, p. 266, para. 105, available at <https://www.icj-cij.org/docket/files/95/7495.pdf>.

The ICJ thus could not definitively conclude whether the threat or use of nuclear weapons would be lawful in such extreme circumstances, thereby leaving the question to individual state interpretation.[498]

In addition, the ICJ observed that international humanitarian law reflects non-derogable customary international law and *jus cogens* (*see* "International Humanitarian Law as Customary International Law and Non-Derogable *Jus Cogens*" above).

1998 *Libyan Arab Jamahiriya v. United States of America* (*Lockerbie* case).

1999 *Botswana v. Namibia*. Territorial dispute in which the ICJ ruled in favor of Botswana's claim over Sedudu Island.

1999 *Yugoslavia v. Belgium* (Legality of the Use of Force Application of the Federal Republic of Yugoslavia). For the ICJ to have jurisdiction over the case, Yugoslavia would have had to have accepted compulsory jurisdiction under Article 36(2) SICJ prior to the occurrence of the events.

2002 *Arrest Warrant of 11 April 2000 (Democratic Republic of the Congo v. Belgium)* (14 February 2002). The Court held that it did not have jurisdiction to consider whether Belgium had a right to invoke universal jurisdiction in issuing an arrest warrant for a Congolese state official and instead decided the question on the basis of immunity of high-ranking state officials, concluding that state officials have immunity under international law while serving in office in order to ensure the effective performance of their functions on behalf of their respective states and when abroad, state officials may enjoy immunity from arrest in another state on criminal charges.

However, the question of universal jurisdiction was addressed in separate and dissenting opinions that recognized the principle as legitimate. The joint separate opinion of Judges Higgins, Kooijmans and Buergenthal concluded with respect to universal jurisdiction that "the international consensus that the perpetrators of international crimes should not go unpunished is being advanced by a flexible strategy, in which newly established international criminal tribunals, treaty obligations and national courts all have their part to play. We reject the suggestion that the battle against impunity is 'made over' to international treaties and tribunals, with national courts having no competence in such matters."

498. The United States does not deem the threat or use of nuclear weapons to be a per se violation of international humanitarian law.

2004 *Mexico v. United States* (Case Concerning Avena and other Mexican Nationals). The U.S. was found to be in breach of the VCDR for failing to inform certain Mexican nationals imprisoned in the U.S. of their right to contact their embassy and was required to review all sentences of the nationals.

2004 *ICJ advisory opinion on Legal Consequences of the Construction of a Wall in the Occupied Palestinian Territory* (the *Wall* case). International humanitarian law (the Regulations annexed to the Fourth Hague Convention of 1907 and Geneva Convention IV) apply to the Palestinian territories that, before 1967, lay to the east of the 1949 "Green Line" and international human rights law (ICCPR, ICESCR, U.N. Convention on the Rights of the Child) apply in the Occupied Palestinian Territory. The ICJ was not required to conclude that Palestine was a state or a "High Contracting Party" in order to trigger the application of Geneva Convention IV; rather, the fact that Israel occupied Jordanian territory was a sufficient basis for the application of the Convention. The Court held that "the Fourth Geneva Convention is applicable in any occupied territory in the event of an armed conflict arising between two or more High Contracting Parties. Israel and Jordan were parties to that Convention when the 1967 armed conflict broke out. The Court accordingly finds that that Convention is applicable in the Palestinian territories which before the conflict lay to the east of the Green Line and which, during that conflict, were occupied by Israel, there being no need for any enquiry into the precise prior status of those territories."[499]

The ICJ concluded that "the Israeli settlements in the Occupied Palestinian Territories (including East Jerusalem) have been established in breach of international law" (*Ibid.*, p. 184, paragraph 120).

While the ICJ noted "the assurance given by Israel that the construction of the wall does not amount to annexation and that the wall is of a temporary nature (see paragraph 116 above), it nevertheless cannot remain indifferent to certain fears expressed to it that the route of the wall will prejudge the future frontier between Israel and Palestine, and the fear that Israel may integrate the settlements and their means of access. The Court considers that the construction of the wall and its associated régime create a '*fait accompli*' on the ground that could well become permanent, in which case, and notwithstanding the formal characterization of the wall by Israel, it would be tantamount to *de facto* annexation" (*Ibid.*, p. 184, paragraph 121).

499. *Legal Consequences of the Construction of a Wall in the Occupied Palestinian Territory* (the Wall Case), Advisory Opinion, ICJ Reports (9 July 2004), p. 177, para. 101.

	The route of the Wall entailed "a risk of further alterations to the demographic composition of the Occupied Palestinian Territory resulting from the construction of the wall inasmuch as it is contributing ... to the departure of Palestinian populations from certain areas." Furthermore, the Wall "severely impedes the exercise by the Palestinian people of its right to self-determination, and is therefore a breach of Israel's obligation to respect that right" (*Ibid.*, p. 184, paragraph 122).
2007	*Bosnia and Herzegovina v. Serbia and Montenegro* (Application of the Convention on the Prevention and Punishment of the Crime of Genocide). Belgrade (Serbia) breached international law by failing to prevent the 1995 genocide in the town of Srebrenica and for failing to try or transfer to the ICTY those accused of genocide.
2010	*ICJ advisory opinion on Kosovo's declaration of independence.* Kosovo's unilateral declaration of independence did not violate international law.

ICTR Cases

2001	*Prosecutor v. Jean-Paul Akayesu* (Appeals Chamber, 1 June 2001). The ICTY Appeals Chamber has developed the test that "[t]here must be a nexus between the violations and the armed conflict" (paragraph 438, n. 807).
2003	*Prosecutor v. Elizaphan Ntakirutimana and Gérard Ntakirutimana* (Trial Chamber, 21 February 2003). "The provision [Article 4(a)] seeks to protect persons not taking an active part in the hostilities in armed conflicts not of an international character" (paragraph 859).
1999	*Prosecutor v. Clément Kayishema and Obed Ruzindana* (Trial Chamber, 21 May 1999). "[T]here must be a nexus between the crime and the armed conflict" (paragraph 169).

ICTY Cases

1995	*Prosecutor v. Dusko Tadić.* The ICTY found that "an armed conflict exists whenever there is a resort to armed force between states or protracted armed violence between governmental authorities and organized armed groups or between such groups within a State."[500] The ICTY acknowledged that the following

500. *Prosecutor v. Dusko Tadić*, IT-94-1AR72, ICTY Appeals Chamber, Decision (2 October 1995), para. 70.

factors are relevant for determining whether violence rises to the level of a *non-international armed conflict*, thus triggering common Article 3: (i) the intensity of the violence (duration, types of weapons, civilians affected, number of casualties, etc.); and (ii) organization of the parties to the conflict (to distinguish from lesser forms of violence, such as banditry, rioting, or individual terrorist activities).

1997 *Prosecutor v. Dusko Tadić*. The test applied to confirm the *existence of a non-international armed conflict* "focuses on two aspects of a conflict; the intensity of the conflict and the organization of the parties to the conflict. In an armed conflict of an internal or mixed character, these closely related criteria are used solely for the purpose, as a minimum, of distinguishing an armed conflict from banditry, unorganized and short-lived insurrections, or terrorist activities, which are not subject to international humanitarian law."[501]

1999 *Prosecutor v. Dusko Tadić*. An *international armed conflict* may exist if a foreign state exercises "*overall control*" (i.e., "overall political and military authority")[502] over an organized armed group or an armed non-state actor's military activity by equipping, financing, or training and providing operational support, and coordinating or helping the general planning of the organized armed group or armed non-state actor's military activity (*see generally* paragraphs 88-162). "Effective control" (including activities that are "specifically imposed, requested or directed by the State" (paragraph 122)) is not necessary, though that test is relevant to "State responsibility rather than individual criminal responsibility" (paragraph 70). The Appeals Chamber held that "the armed forces of the Republika Srpska were to be regarded as acting under the overall control of and on behalf of the FRY" and, therefore, "the armed conflict in Bosnia and Herzegovina between the Bosnian Serbs and the central authorities of Bosnia and Herzegovina must be classified as an international armed conflict" (paragraph 162).

1999 *Prosecutor v. Dusko Tadić*. The "requirement that the conflict be international for the grave breaches regime to operate pursuant to Article 2 of the Statute has not been contested by the parties."[503] The Appeals Chamber therefore did not consider that question. However, the Appeals Chamber did hold that grave breaches did not necessarily require violations by state actors; non-state armed groups could be held liable for such violations. Therefore, even non-state armed groups that have not formally accepted the terms of the Geneva Conventions may be prosecuted for war crimes that constitute "grave breaches" of the Geneva Conventions.

501. *Prosecutor v. Dusko Tadić*, IT-94-1-T, ICTY Trial Chamber (7 May 1997), para. 562.
502. *Prosecutor v. Dusko Tadić*, IT-94-1-A, ICTY Appeals Chamber (15 July 1999), para. 160.

2008 *Prosecutor v. Ramush Haradinaj et al.* (3 April 2008). Factors used to determine whether a disturbance rises to the level of an armed conflict for the purpose of Additional Protocol II of the Geneva Conventions include "the number, duration and intensity of individual confrontations; the type of weapons and other military equipment used; the number and calibre of munitions fired; the number of persons and type of forces partaking in the fighting; the number of casualties; the extent of material destruction; and the number of civilians fleeing combat zones. The involvement of the U.N. Security Council may also be a reflection of the intensity of a conflict."[504]

Israel Cases

1969 *Prosecutor v. Kassem*, the Israeli Military Court in Ramallah. The second condition for prisoner of war status requires "a fixed distinctive sign recognizable at a distance." The rule applies while combatants are engaged in an attack or in a military operation preparatory to an attack. Wearing "mottled caps and green clothes" fulfilled this condition because such attire was unconventional for civilians at the place of capture. However, they failed to meet the third condition for prisoner of war status, that of carrying arms openly.

2006 *Public Committee against Torture in Israel v. Government of Israel*, Supreme Court, HCJ 769/02, 14 December 2006. Petitioners argued that Israel's targeted killing policy violates the domestic criminal law of Israel, which governs the armed conflict between Israel and terrorist groups. In the alternative, the targeted killing policy violates the rules of international law "even if we apply the laws of war to the armed conflict between Israel and the Palestinians. These laws recognize only two statuses of persons—combatants and civilians. Combatants are legitimate targets for attack, but they also enjoy the rights that are granted in international law to combatants, including immunity against indictment and the right to a status of prisoners of war. Citizens enjoy protections and rights that are granted in international law to civilians in times of war … The petitioners therefore reject the state's position that the terrorist organizations' operatives should be regarded as unlawful combatants. The petitioners discuss how the state itself refuses to give these

503. *Prosecutor v. Dusko Tadić*, IT-94-1-A, ICTY Appeals Chamber (15 July 1999), para. 4.
504. *Prosecutor v. Ramush Haradinaj, Idriz Balaj and Lahi Brahimaj*, IT-04-84-T, ICTY Trial Chamber, Judgment (3 April 2008), para. 49.

operatives the rights and the defences given in international law to combatants, such as the right to a status of a prisoner of war. The result is that the state wishes to treat them according to the worse of both worlds: as combatants, to justify killing them, and as civilians, for the purpose of arresting them and bringing them to trial. This result is unacceptable. The operatives of the terrorist organizations, even if they take part in combat activities, are not thereby excluded from the application of the rules of international law. The petitioners' position is therefore that the operatives of the terrorist organizations should be regarded as having the status of civilians."[505] The petitioners further argue that "a civilian who takes part in combat may lose some of the protections given to civilians in times of war. But this is only when he takes a direct part in the combat activities, and only as long as this direct participation lasts. These two conditions are provided in article 51(3) of the First Additional Protocol to the 1977 Geneva Conventions (hereafter—the First Protocol). This article, with all of its conditions, reflects, according to the petitioners, a customary rule of international law. These conditions were adopted in international case law, and they are mentioned in additional international documents, as well as in the army manuals of most Western countries. In order to preserve the clear distinction between combatants and civilians, these conditions are given a narrow and precise interpretation. According to this interpretation, a civilian will lose his immunity against attack only when he actually takes a direct part in hostilities, and only during the time when this direct participation is continuing."[506]

With respect to the legality of targeted killing, the Court held that it should be "done within the law. The maxim 'When the cannons speak, the Muses are silent' is well known. A similar idea was expressed by Cicero, who said: *silent enim leges inter arma* (laws are silent in times of war). These statements are regrettable. They do not reflect the law either as it is or as it should be ... It is precisely when the cannons speak that we need laws ... Every struggle of the state—whether against terrorism or against any other enemy—is carried out in accordance with rules and laws. There always exists a law that the state is liable to follow. Black holes do not exist (see J. Steyn, *Democracy through Law: Selected Speeches and Judgments*

505. *Public Committee against Torture in Israel v. Government of Israel*, Supreme Court, HCJ 769/02 (14 December 2006), p. 466-467.
506. *Ibid.*, p. 467.

(2004), at p. 195). In our case, the law is determined by customary international law relating to armed conflicts of an international character. Indeed, the struggle of the state against terrorism is not waged 'outside' the law. It is waged 'within' the law and with tools that the law makes available to a democracy."[507]

On the basis of the law, "it cannot be determined ab initio that every targeted killing is prohibited under customary international law, just as it cannot be determined ab initio that every targeted killing is permitted under customary international law. The laws relating to targeted killings are determined in customary international law, and the legality of each individual attack needs to be decided in accordance with them."[508]

PCIJ Cases

1928 *Island of Palmas* case. Island dispute between the U.S. and the Netherlands. The Court held that cession between states is one means by which territory may be transferred, and moreover, if a state exercises continuous, open, actual sovereignty over a territory with good title and a discoverer of the territory does not contest this claim, the claim by the sovereign that exercises authority is greater than a title based on mere discovery.

U.S. Supreme Court Cases

2006 *Hamdan v. Rumsfeld*, 548 U.S. 557 (2006). The defendant, Hamdan, a Yemeni national and detainee at Guantanamo Bay, was captured by militia forces, turned over to the U.S. government, and tried by a military commission for terrorism conspiracy and providing material support for terrorism. The defendant challenged the trial by a military commission. The Court held that the military commission lacked the power to try the defendant because its structure violated the Uniform Code of Military Justice, and no statute provided that a military commission may try such a defendant or offense. Furthermore, the lower court erred in its holding that because Al Qaeda was not a "High Contracting Party" to the Geneva Conventions, the Geneva Conventions did not apply. In fact, common Article 3 to

507. *Ibid.*, p. 516.
508. *Ibid.*, p. 519.

the Geneva Conventions applies to all individuals in non-international armed conflicts between a high contracting party and a non-state armed group, as was the case of the conflict between the U.S. and Al Qaeda. The Court held:[509]

> [T]here is at least one provision of the Geneva Conventions that applies here even if the relevant conflict is not one between signatories. Article 3, often referred to as Common Article 3 because, like Article 2, it appears in all four Geneva Conventions, provides that in a "conflict not of an international character occurring in the territory of one of the High Contracting Parties, each Party to the conflict shall be bound to apply, as a minimum," certain provisions protecting "[p]ersons taking no active part in the hostilities, including members of armed forces who have laid down their arms and those placed hors de combat by ... detention." ... One such provision prohibits "the passing of sentences and the carrying out of executions without previous judgment pronounced by a regularly constituted court affording all the judicial guarantees which are recognized as indispensable by civilized peoples."

Common Article 3 requires trial by a regularly constituted court:[510]

> While Common Article 3 does not define its "regularly constituted court" phrase, other sources define the words to mean an "ordinary military cour[t]" that is "established and organized in accordance with the laws and procedures already in force in a country." The regular military courts in our system are the courts martial established by congressional statute. At a minimum, a military commission can be "regularly constituted" only if some practical need explains deviations from court-martial practice. No such need has been demonstrated here.

Common Article 3 guarantees fair and humane treatment for all detainees, prohibits indefinite detention and binds the U.S. The Court further held:[511]

> Common Article 3 obviously tolerates a great degree of flexibility in trying individuals captured during armed conflict; its requirements are general ones, crafted to accommodate a wide variety of legal systems. But requirements they are nonetheless. The commission that the President has convened to try Hamdan does not meet those requirements.

509. *Hamdan v. Rumsfeld*, 548 U.S. 557, 629 (2006).
510. *Ibid.*, p. 736.
511. *Ibid.*, p. 635.

2011 *United States v. Hamdan*, 801 F. Supp. 2d 1247 (2011). In *dicta* contained in a footnote, the U.S. Court for Military Commissions Review, in an overturned decision, provided the following member instruction for the purpose of determining the existence of armed conflict:[512]

> With respect to each of the ten specifications [of providing material support for terrorism] before you, the government must prove beyond a reasonable doubt that the actions of the accused took place in the context of and that they were associated with armed conflict. In determining whether an armed conflict existed between the United States and al Qaeda and when it began, you should consider the length, duration, and intensity of hostilities between the parties, whether there was protracted armed violence between governmental authorities and organized armed groups, whether and when the United States decided to employ the combat capabilities of its armed forces to meet the al Qaeda threat, the number of persons killed or wounded on each side, the amount of property damage on each side, statements of the leaders of both sides indicating their perceptions regarding the existence of an armed conflict, including the presence or absence of a declaration to that effect, and any other facts or circumstances you consider relevant to determining the existence of armed conflict. The parties may argue the existence of other facts and circumstances from which you might reach your determination regarding this issue. In determining whether the acts of the accused took place in the context of and were associated with an armed conflict, you should consider whether the acts of the accused occurred during the period of an armed conflict as defined above, whether they were performed while the accused acted on behalf of or under the authority of a party to the armed conflict, and whether they constituted or were closely and substantially related to hostilities occurring during the armed conflict and other facts and circumstances you consider relevant to this issue. Counsel may address this matter during their closing arguments, and may suggest other factors for your consideration. Conduct of the accused that occurs at a distance from the area of conflict can still be in the context of and associated with armed conflict, as long as it was closely and substantially related to the hostilities that comprised the conflict.

512. *United States v. Hamdan*, 801 F.Supp.2d 1247, 1278 n.54 (U.S.C.M.C.R. 2011), *rev'd with orders to vacate*, 696 F.3d 1238 (D.C. Cir. 2012).

International Red Cross and Red Crescent Movement

Overview

The International Red Cross and Red Crescent Movement is an international humanitarian movement with approximately 97 million global volunteers, members and staff. It was founded to protect human life and health, to ensure respect for all human beings, and to prevent and alleviate human suffering.

The ICRC, IFRC and National Societies form the American Red Cross and Red Crescent Movement. All of the organizations are legally distinct and independent bodies, none working for the other but bound together by a common set of unifying humanitarian principles, objectives, and symbols.

International Committee of the Red Cross (ICRC)

Impartial private humanitarian institution founded in 1863 in Geneva. Its 25-member committee has a unique authority under international humanitarian law to:

- protect the life and dignity of the victims of international and internal armed conflicts; and
- provide assistance in armed conflicts.

The ICRC was awarded three Nobel Peace Prizes.

International Federation of Red Cross and Red Crescent Societies

Founded in 1919 and based in Geneva, the International Federation of Red Cross and Red Crescent Societies ("IFRC"):

- serves as a clearing house to coordinate the efforts and activities between the 191 National Red Cross and Red Crescent Societies within the Movement; and
- focuses on disaster response, disaster preparedness, and community health and leads and organizes relief assistance missions responding to large-scale emergencies.

The IFRC was awarded the Nobel Peace Prize in 1963.

National Red Cross and Red Crescent Societies

National entities that work in their home countries according to the principles of international humanitarian law and the statutes of the International Red Cross and Red Crescent Movement. National Societies may take on additional humanitarian tasks that are not directly defined by international humanitarian law or the mandates of the International Movement. In many countries, these tasks are tightly linked to the respective national healthcare system by providing emergency medical services. The ICRC recognizes and the IFRC has admitted as members 191 National Societies.

Just War Theory under the *Catechism of the Catholic Church* and the ICISS Guidelines Combined

Catechism of the Catholic Church	*ICISS Guidelines*
1. *Just cause.* The cause must be just (i.e., defense of the innocent against an armed attack, redressing an injury, punishing evil, restoring territory unjustly seized).	(1) *Just Cause Threshold.* "To be warranted, there must be serious and irreparable harm occurring to human beings, or imminently likely to occur."
2. *Right intention.* The central intention of the war must be reestablishing a just peace (as opposed to conquest, expanding territory, spreading the seeds of revolt or acquiring power or material possessions).	(2) Precautionary Principles. *Right intention*: "The primary purpose of the intervention, whatever other motives intervening states may have, must be to halt or avert human suffering."
3. *Last resort.* All non-violent options must be exhausted before the use of force is justified.	(2) Precautionary Principles. *Last resort*: "Military intervention can only be justified when every non-military option for the prevention or peaceful resolution of the crisis has been explored, with reasonable grounds for believing lesser measures would not have succeeded"
4. *Proportionality.* The use of arms must not produce evils graver than the evil to be eliminated; the peace established by the war must be preferable to the peace that would have prevailed had the war not been fought.	(2) Precautionary Principles. *Proportional means*: "The scale, duration and intensity of the planned military intervention should be the minimum necessary to secure the defined human protection objective."
5. *Reasonable prospect of success.* Deaths and injuries incurred in a war not having a reasonable chance of success are not morally justifiable.	(2) Precautionary Principles. *Reasonable prospects*: "There must be a reasonable chance of success in halting or averting the suffering which has justified the intervention, with the consequences of action not likely to be worse than the consequences of inaction."
6. *Legitimate authority.* War must be waged by a legitimate civil authority (i.e., a state, in accordance with Romans 13), not individuals or groups who do not constitute an authority sanctioned by whatever the society deems legitimate.	(3) *Right Authority.* "There is no better or more appropriate body than the United Nations Security Council to authorize military intervention for human protection purposes ..."

Catechism of the Catholic Church	*ICISS Guidelines*
7. *Grave damage from the aggressor.* The damage inflicted on the people under the control of the legitimate authority must be lasting, grave and certain.	(4) Operational Principles A. Clear objectives B. Common military approach among involved partners C. Acceptance of limitations, incrementalism and gradualism
	D. Rules of engagement which fit the operational concept E. Acceptance that force protection cannot become the principal objective F. Maximum coordination with humanitarian organizations

Landmark Decisions of *Prosecutor v. Dusko Tadić*

Date	*Subject*	*Holding*
2 October 1995	Criteria for determining when armed conflict exists	An "armed conflict exists whenever there is a resort to armed force between states or protracted armed violence between governmental authorities and organized armed groups or between such groups within a State."[513]
7 May 1997		The test applied to confirm the *existence of a non-international armed conflict* "focuses on two aspects of a conflict; the intensity of the conflict and the organization of the parties to the conflict."[514]
15 July 1999	Overall control of an organized armed group as sufficient for triggering international armed conflict	An *international armed conflict* may exist if a foreign state exercises "*overall control*" (i.e., "overall political and military authority")[515] over an organized armed group or an armed non-state actor's military activity by equipping, financing, or training and providing operational support, and coordinating or helping the general planning of the organized armed group or armed non-state actor's military activity.[516]

513. *Prosecutor v. Dusko Tadić*, IT-94-1AR72, ICTY Appeals Chamber, Decision (2 October 1995), para. 70.
514. *Prosecutor v. Dusko Tadić*, IT-94-1-T, ICTY Trial Chamber (7 May 1997), para. 562.
515. *Prosecutor v. Dusko Tadić*, IT-94-1-A, ICTY Appeals Chamber (15 July 1999), para. 160. *Ibid* (*see generally* paras. 88-162).
516. *Ibid.* (*see generally* paras. 88-162).

Date	*Subject*	*Holding*
	Application of the grave breaches regime to non-state armed groups	The "requirement that the conflict be international for the grave breaches regime to operate pursuant to Article 2 of the Statute has not been contested by the parties,"[517] but the Appeals Chamber held that non-state armed groups that have not accepted the terms of the Geneva Conventions may be prosecuted for war crimes under the "grave breaches" regime.

Maritime Zones of Jurisdiction

Category	*Geography*	*Rights of Coastal State*
High Seas	Beyond the continental shelf, in the deep seabed.	- Ships are subject to international law and the law of the state. - The right of hot pursuit for violations of its laws if the pursuit began in its internal or archipelagic waters, territorial sea, or contiguous zones and is uninterrupted.
Continental Shelf	Based on geology survey, but no more than 350 miles from baselines or 100 miles from 2,500-meter isobath	- Sovereign exclusive rights for exploring it and exploiting its natural resources (mineral and other non-living resources and living *sedentary* organisms)
Exclusive Economic Zone	Up to 200 miles from baselines	- Exclusive rights to fish, exploit biological resources, mine minerals from and exploit the seabed, produce energy from the currents and wind, etc.
Contiguous Zone	Up to 24 miles from baselines	- Jurisdiction for enforcing customs, fiscal, sanitary and immigration laws and punishing infringements thereof. - Exclusive rights to fish, exploit biological resources, mine minerals from and exploit the seabed, produce energy from the currents and wind, etc.

517. *Ibid.*, para. 83.

Category	*Geography*	*Rights of Coastal State*
Territorial Sea	Up to 12 miles from baselines	- Coastal state may enforce its criminal jurisdiction. - Jurisdiction for enforcing customs, fiscal, sanitary and immigration laws and punishing infringements thereof. - Exclusive rights to regulate airspace above. - Exclusive rights to fish, exploit biological resources, mine minerals from and exploit the seabed, produce energy from the currents and wind, etc.
Internal waters	Inland lakes, rivers and ports	- Territorial sovereignty. - Coastal state may enforce its civil and criminal jurisdiction. - Jurisdiction for enforcing customs, fiscal, sanitary and immigration laws and punishing infringements thereof. - Exclusive rights to regulate airspace above - Exclusive rights to fish, exploit biological resources, mine minerals from and exploit the seabed, produce energy from the currents and wind, etc.

Nuremberg Principles

Principle I

Any person who commits an act which constitutes a crime under international law is responsible therefor and liable to punishment.

Principle II

The fact that internal law does not impose a penalty for an act which constitutes a crime under international law does not relieve the person who committed the act from responsibility under international law.

Principle III

The fact that a person who committed an act which constitutes a crime under international law acted as Head of State or responsible Government official does not relieve him from responsibility under international law.

Principle IV

The fact that a person acted pursuant to order of his Government or of a superior does not relieve him from responsibility under international law, provided a moral choice was in fact possible to him.

Principle V

Any person charged with a crime under international law has the right to a fair trial on the facts and law.

Principle VI

The crimes hereinafter set out are punishable as crimes under international law:

(a) Crimes against peace:
  (i) planning, preparation, initiation or waging of a war of aggression or a war in violation of international treaties, agreements or assurances;
  (ii) participation in a common plan or conspiracy for the accomplishment of any of the acts mentioned under (i).

(b) War crimes:
Violations of the laws or customs of war, which include, but are not limited to, murder, ill-treatment or deportation to slave labour or for any other purpose of civilian population of or in occupied territory, murder or ill-treatment of prisoners of war, of persons on the seas, killing of hostages, plunder of public or private property, wanton destruction of cities, towns, or villages, or devastation not justified by military necessity.

(c) Crimes against humanity:
Murder, extermination, enslavement, deportation and other inhuman acts done against any civilian population, or persecutions on political, racial or religious grounds, when such acts are done, or such persecutions are carried on in execution of or in connection with any crime against peace or any war crime.

Principle VII

Complicity in the commission of a crime against peace, a war crime, or a crime against humanity, as set forth in Principle VI, is a crime under international law.

People's Tribunals

Tribunal	*Description*
Russell Tribunal on Vietnam (1966-1967) (International War Crimes Tribunal/Russell-Sartre Tribunal/Stockholm Tribunal)	Private body constituted in 1966 by Bertrand Russell and Jean-Paul Sartre and conducted in 1967 to investigate and evaluate the American military intervention in Vietnam following the 1954 defeat of French forces at Diên Biên Phu and the establishment of North and South Vietnam. The tribunal did not investigate alleged war crimes by the Viet Cong.
Russell Tribunal II on Latin America (1973-1976)	Continuation of the Russell Tribunal on Vietnam to deal predominantly with Latin America. It held a meeting in Rome in 1974 focusing on the dictatorships of Argentina and Brazil and from 1974 to 1976 focusing on Chile's military *coup d'état*.
Permanent Peoples' Tribunal	Established in Bologna, Italy, in 1979 as a continuation of the Russell Tribunals in Vietnam and Latin America with a view to transforming the Russell Tribunals into a permanent institution that could become an institution to give recognition, visibility, and a voice to the peoples suffering violations of their fundamental rights. According to the Universal Declaration of the Rights of Peoples, adopted in Algiers in 1976, these peoples were marginalized in international law, which had become the guarantor of the interests of the powerful.
Women's International War Crimes Tribunal on Japan's Military Sexual Slavery (Tokyo Women's Tribunal)	Organized in 2000 by various women's and human rights non-governmental organizations from across Asia to remedy the failure of the International Military Tribunal for the Far East to prosecute groups and individuals for rape or sexual slavery during World War II. The Tribunal issued a judgment convicting the late Emperor Hirohito Showa who was deemed ultimately responsible for the sexual slavery policy.
Subsequent Russell Tribunals	The Russell Tribunal was subsequently convened to investigate: - Human Rights in Psychiatry (Berlin, 2001) - Iraq (Brussels, 2004) - Palestine (Barcelona, 2009-2012)

Persons Holding Combatant Immunity

Geneva Conventions I to III apply and issue protections to the following categories of persons who also enjoy combatant immunity (Article 4A GC III; Article 13 GC I; Article 13 GC II):

(1) Members of the armed forces of a party to the conflict, as well as members of militias or volunteer corps forming part of such armed forces;
(2) Members of other militias and members of other volunteer corps belonging to a party to the conflict and operating in or outside their own territory, provided that such militias or volunteer corps:
  (a) are *commanded by a person responsible* for his subordinates;
  (b) have a *fixed distinctive sign* recognizable at a distance [normally worn on a uniform, though a uniform alone could also count];
  (c) *carry arms openly*;
  (d) conduct their operations in *accordance with the laws and customs of war* (*combatant prisoners of war*).
(3) Members of regular armed forces who profess allegiance to a government or an authority not recognized by the detaining power.
(4) Inhabitants of a non-occupied territory, who on the approach of the enemy, spontaneously take up arms to resist the invading forces without having had time to form themselves into regular armed units (i.e., in the sense provided under sub-clauses 4A(1) and 4A(2)), provided they carry arms openly and respect the laws and customs of war ("*levée en masse*").

Promissory Notes and Bills of Exchange Compared

The following chart compares the elements of bills of exchange and promissory notes under the Convention providing a Uniform Law for Bills of Exchange and Promissory Notes (1930):

Bill of Exchange	*Promissory Note*
(1) The term "bill of exchange" inserted in the body of the instrument and expressed in the language employed in drawing up the instrument	(1) The term "promissory note" inserted in the body of the instrument and expressed in the language employed in drawing up the instrument
(2) An unconditional order to pay a determinate sum of money	(2) An unconditional promise to pay a determinate sum of money
(3) A statement of the time of payment	(3) A statement of the time of payment
(4) A statement of the place where payment is to be made	(4) A statement of the place where payment is to be made
(5) The name of the person to whom or to whose order payment is to be made	(5) The name of the person to whom or to whose order payment is to be made
(6) A statement of the date and the place where the bill is issued	(6) A statement of the date and the place where the promissory note is issued
(7) The signature of the person who issues the bill (drawer)	(7) The signature of the person who issues the instrument (maker)
(8) The name of the person who is to pay (drawee)	

Public versus Private International Law

Question or Scenario	*Public*	*Private*
Rights between several nations	✓	
Human rights abuse by a state of an individual person	✓	
Expropriation by a state of the property of an alien corporation	✓[518]	
Activities of and relations between natural and juridical persons when they cross national borders when governed by domestic conflict of laws provisions.		✓

Public International Law versus Conflict of Laws

Organization	*What it Does*	*Category*
HCPIL	Harmonizes domestic rules for conflict of laws. Concluded 36 multilateral treaties.	Private international law
UNIDROIT	Harmonize states' substantive domestic laws, especially commercial laws.	Private international law
UNCITRAL	Harmonizes international trade law.	Private international law
WTO	Supervises and liberalizes international trade through agreements negotiated and signed by trading nations.	Public international law

Recognized Sovereign States

Internationally Recognized Sovereign States

Following is a list of the 194 recognized sovereign states, consisting of the 193 U.N. member states and Vatican City (the Holy See), a U.N. permanent observer.

(1) Afghanistan
(2) Albania
(3) Algeria
(4) Andorra
(5) Angola
(6) Antigua and Barbuda
(7) Argentina

518. Assuming that the alien sues the expropriating state under an international legal provision, such as a treaty, the case would fall under public international law. However, if he sues under the state's domestic alien tort statutes, the case would fall under private international law.

(8) Armenia
(9) Australia
(10) Austria
(11) Azerbaijan
(12) Bahamas
(13) Bahrain
(14) Bangladesh
(15) Barbados
(16) Belarus
(17) Belgium
(18) Belize
(19) Benin
(20) Bhutan
(21) Bolivia
(22) Bosnia and Herzegovina
(23) Botswana
(24) Brazil
(25) Brunei Darussalam
(26) Bulgaria
(27) Burkina Faso
(28) Burundi
(29) Cambodia
(30) Cameroon
(31) Canada
(32) Cape Verde
(33) Central African Republic
(34) Chad
(35) Chile
(36) China
(37) Colombia
(38) Comoros
(39) Costa Rica
(40) Côte d'Ivoire
(41) Croatia
(42) Cuba
(43) Cyprus[519]
(44) Czech Republic
(45) Dem. People's Rep. of Korea
(46) Democratic Rep. of the Congo
(47) Denmark[520]
(48) Djibouti

519. Northern Cyprus is recognized as a sovereign state only by Turkey.
520. Greenland is an autonomous constituent territory within the Kingdom of Denmark.

(49) Dominica
(50) Dominican Republic
(51) Ecuador
(52) Egypt
(53) El Salvador
(54) Equatorial Guinea
(55) Eritrea
(56) Estonia
(57) Ethiopia
(58) Federated States of Micronesia
(59) Fiji
(60) Finland
(61) France
(62) Gabon
(63) The Gambia
(64) Georgia
(65) Germany
(66) Ghana
(67) Greece
(68) Grenada
(69) Guatemala
(70) Guinea
(71) Guinea-Bissau
(72) Guyana
(73) Haiti
(74) Honduras
(75) Hungary
(76) Iceland
(77) India
(78) Indonesia
(79) Iran
(80) Iraq
(81) Ireland
(82) Israel
(83) Italy
(84) Jamaica
(85) Japan
(86) Jordan
(87) Kazakhstan
(88) Kenya
(89) Kiribati
(90) Kuwait
(91) Kyrgyzstan
(92) Laos

(93) Latvia
(94) Lebanon
(95) Lesotho
(96) Liberia
(97) Libya
(98) Liechtenstein
(99) Lithuania
(100) Luxembourg
(101) Madagascar
(102) Malawi
(103) Malaysia
(104) Maldives
(105) Mali
(106) Malta
(107) Marshall Islands
(108) Mauritania
(109) Mauritius
(110) Mexico
(111) Monaco
(112) Mongolia
(113) Montenegro
(114) Morocco
(115) Mozambique
(116) Myanmar
(117) Namibia
(118) Nauru
(119) Nepal
(120) Netherlands
(121) New Zealand
(122) Nicaragua
(123) Niger
(124) Nigeria
(125) Norway
(126) Oman
(127) Pakistan
(128) Palau
(129) Panama
(130) Papua New Guinea
(131) Paraguay
(132) Peru
(133) Philippines
(134) Poland
(135) Portugal

(136) Qatar
(137) Republic of the Congo
(138) Republic of Korea
(139) North Macedonia
(140) Republic of Moldova
(141) Republic of South Sudan
(142) Romania
(143) Russian Federation
(144) Rwanda
(145) Saint Kitts and Nevis
(146) Saint Lucia
(147) Saint Vincent and the Grenadines
(148) Samoa
(149) San Marino
(150) Sao Tome and Principe
(151) Saudi Arabia
(152) Senegal
(153) Serbia
(154) Seychelles
(155) Sierra Leone
(156) Singapore
(157) Slovakia
(158) Slovenia
(159) Solomon Islands
(160) Somalia[521]
(161) South Africa
(162) Spain
(163) Sri Lanka
(164) Sudan
(165) Suriname
(166) Eswatini (Swaziland)
(167) Switzerland
(168) Sweden
(169) Syria
(170) Tajikistan
(171) Thailand
(172) Timor-Leste
(173) Togo
(174) Tonga
(175) Trinidad and Tobago

521. Somaliland is an autonomous region of Somalia. Although Somaliland declared independence in 1991, it has not received recognition as a sovereign State from any foreign government.

(176) Tunisia
(177) Turkey
(178) Turkmenistan
(179) Tuvalu
(180) Uganda
(181) Ukraine
(182) United Arab Emirates
(183) United Kingdom
(184) United Republic of Tanzania
(185) United States
(186) Uruguay
(187) Uzbekistan
(188) Vanuatu
(189) Vatican City (Holy See)[522]
(190) Venezuela
(191) Vietnam
(192) Yemen
(193) Zambia
(194) Zimbabwe

Disputed or Partially Recognized States

See "Disputed States" in Chapter 4 (States and Governments in the International Order), page 82, *supra*, for details.

Quasi-Independent Countries

Country	*Characteristics*
Cook Islands	Quasi-sovereign country in the South Pacific in free association with New Zealand
Hong Kong	Special administrative region of the PRC (the other being Macau). Common law judiciary is independent of China's civil law. However, issues of foreign affairs are deferred to China.
Macau	Special administrative region of the PRC (the other being Hong Kong)
Niue	Quasi-sovereign country in the South Pacific in free association with New Zealand

522. The Holy See is headquartered in, operates from, and exercises exclusive dominion over the independent Vatican City State in Rome, Italy.

United Nations Internal Justice System

	Tribunal	*Jurisdiction*	*Notes*
Courts of First Instance	United Nations Dispute Tribunal ("UNDT")	Claims by staff members of the U.N. Secretariat; Peacekeeping and Political Missions; International Criminal Tribunals; ECOSOC Regional Commissions; and General Assembly Programs, Organs, Funds and Other Entities	Court of First Instance within the U.N. internal justice system that became operational on 1 July 2009 with the power to hear cases appealing administrative decisions alleged to be non-compliant with terms of appointment or employment contracts.
	UNRWA Dispute Tribunal	Claims filed by UNRWA staff members	Court of First Instance that hears and decides cases filed by or on behalf of UNRWA staff members appealing administrative decisions alleged to be non-compliant with their terms of appointment or employment contracts.
Appeals Court	United Nations Appeals Tribunal ("UNAT")	Appeals to judgments issued by the United Nations Dispute Tribunal and other courts of first instance, such as the UNRWA Dispute Tribunal	Court of second instance within the U.N. internal justice system, hearing cases in which a Court of First Instance allegedly exceeded its jurisdiction, failed to exercise its jurisdiction or erred on questions of fact, procedure or law. It became operational on 1 July 2009, replacing the United Nations Administrative Tribunal.

United Nations Peacekeeping Missions

- MINUJUSTH U.N. Mission for Justice Support in Haiti
- MINURSO U.N. Mission for the Referendum in Western Sahara
- *MINUSCA* U.N. Multidimensional Integrated Stabilization Mission in the Central African Republic
- *MINUSMA* U.N. Multidimensional Integrated Stabilization Mission in Mali
- *MONUSCO* U.N. Organization Stabilization Mission in the Democratic Republic of the Congo
- UNAMID UN-African Union Mission in Darfur
- UNIFIL U.N. Interim Force in Lebanon
- UNISFA Interim Security Force for Abyei (Sudan and South Sudan)
- UNMIL U.N. Mission in Liberia

- *UNMISS* U.N. Mission in South Sudan
- UNDOF U.N. Disengagement Observer Force (between Israeli and Syria forces)
- UNFICYP U.N. Peacekeeping Force in Cyprus
- UNMIK U.N. Interim Administration Mission in Kosovo
- UNSOS U.N. Support Office in Somalia

United Nations Principal and Subsidiary Organs and Agencies

SECURITY COUNCIL	GENERAL ASSEMBLY	INTERNATIONAL COURT OF JUSTICE

Security Council

- Peacekeeping Operations and Missions
- International Tribunals
  - ICTY
  - ICTR
- Military Staff Committees
- Standing Committees & ad hoc Bodies
- U.N. Compensation Commission

General Assembly

Committees
- Main committees
- Other sessional committees
- Standing committees and ad hoc bodies

Other subsidiary organs
Expert Bodies

Programs, Organs, Funds
- UN-INSTRAW
- UNCHS
- UNCTAD
  - ITC (UNCTAD/WTO)
- UNDCP
- UNDP
  - UNIFEM
  - UNV
- UNEP
- UNFPA
- UNHCR
- UNHSP (UN-Habitat)
- UNICEF
- UNITAR
- UNRWA
- WFP

Research and Training Institutions
- INSTRAW
- UNICRI
- UNITAR
- UNRISD
- UNIDIR

Other UN Entities
- OHCHR
- UNOPS
- UNU
- UNSSC
- UNAIDS

SECRETARIAT	ECOSOC	TRUSTEESHIP COUNCIL

SECRETARIAT

OSG
OIOS
OLA
DPA
DDA
DPKO
OCHA
DESA
DGAACS
DPI
DM
OIP
UNSECOORD
ODC
UNOG
UNOV
UNON

ECOSOC

Functional Commissions

Commission for Social Development
Commission on Human Rights (replaced by the Human Rights Council, a subsidiary body of the UN General Assembly)
Commission on Narcotic Drugs
Commission on Crime Prevention and Criminal Justice
Commission on Science and Technology for Development
Commission on Sustainable Development
Commission on the Status of Women
Commission on Population and Development
Statistical Commission

Specialized Agencies*

FAO
ICAO
IFAD
ILO
IMF
IMO
ITU
UNESCO
UNIDO
UNWTO
UPU
WHO
WIPO
WMO
World Bank Group
- CGIAR
- IBRD
- ICSID
- IDA
- IFC
- MIGA

Regional Commissions

ECA
ECE
ECLAC
ESCAP
ESCWA
UNFF
Sessional and standing committees
Expert, ad hoc and related bodies

Related Organizations

IAEA
WTO (trade)
WTO (tourism)
CTBTO
OPCW

* Autonomous organizations working within the U.N. and one another through the ECOSOC coordinating mechanism.

U.S. Statutes that May Be Invoked in Prosecuting International Crimes

Criminal Statutes

U.S. War Crimes Act ("WCA") 18 U.S.C. § 2441 (1996)

Key Provisions	*Notes*
Act that punishes "war crimes," defined as grave breaches of the Geneva Conventions of 1949, certain breaches of the Hague Conventions, grave breaches of Common Article 3 and violations of the provisions of the Protocol on Prohibitions or Restrictions on the Use of Mines, Booby-Traps and Other Devices as amended at Geneva in 1996 (Protocol II), when the U.S. is a party to the Protocol and leads to the willful killing or causes serious injury to civilians.	The WCA applies if either the victim or the perpetrator is a national of the U.S. or is a member of the U.S. armed forces. The penalty may be life imprisonment or, if the conduct resulted in the death of one or more victims, the death penalty.

Justice for Victims of War Crimes Act ("JVWCA") Amendment to 18 U.S.C. § 2441 (2023)

Introduced in 2022; became Public Law No. 117-351 in 2023

Key Provisions	*Notes*
Broadens the scope of individuals who are subject to federal prosecution for war crime offenses under the WCA, which provides federal jurisdiction over war crime offenses committed anywhere if the victim or offender is a member of the Armed Forces or a U.S. national.	Extends federal jurisdiction over war crime offenses committed anywhere to offenses where: (1) the victim or offender is an alien lawfully admitted for permanent residence; or (2) the offender is present in the U.S., regardless of the nationality of the victim or the offender. Also expands federal jurisdiction to war crime offenses that occur in whole or in part within the U.S., regardless of whether the victim or offender is a member of the Armed Forces, a U.S. national, or an alien lawfully admitted for permanent residence.

Civil Statutes

The Federal Tort Claims Act ("FTCA") 28 U.S.C. § 1346 (1946)

Key Provisions	*Notes*
Federal statute that permits private parties to sue the U.S. in a federal court for most torts committed by persons acting on behalf of the U.S.	The FTCA constitutes a limited waiver of sovereign immunity by the U.S., permitting citizens to pursue some tort claims against the federal government.

The Alien Tort Claims Act ("ATCA") 28 USC § 1350 (1948)

Also called the Alien Tort Statute ("ATS")

Key Provisions	*Notes*
Grants the U.S. federal district courts original jurisdiction "of any civil action *by an alien* for a tort only, committed in violation of the law of nations or a treaty of the United States" (28 USC 1350). The Supreme Court has ruled that the ATCA allows claims *against natural and legal persons, not sovereign governments*. By "law of nations," the statute refers to public international law comprised of not only international treaties but also customary international law and general principles of law. The statute allows suit to be brought in U.S. federal court by aliens for torts committed outside of the U.S. in violation of international law. Courts have generally interpreted the ATCA to allow foreign nationals to seek remedies in U.S. courts for human rights violations committed outside the U.S., provided there is a sufficient nexus to the U.S. Case law has differed on what characterizes sufficient nexus in the U.S. The controversy is particularly pronounced with respect to corporate entities.	The personal jurisdiction of U.S. federal district courts over defendants in ATCA claims has been debated, but it has been "almost uniformly that the same [personal jurisdiction] standards [in other federal cases also] apply" in ATCA cases.[523] In 2021, the U.S. Supreme Court held in the case *Nestlé USA Inc. v. Doe et al.*, Docket No. 19-416, that a "plaintiff does not plead facts sufficient to support the domestic application of the ATCA simply by alleging 'mere corporate presence' of a defendant" in the U.S.,[524] thereby narrowing the extraterritorial scope of the ATCA.

523. Richard Buxbaum and David Caron, "The Alien Tort Statute: An Overview of the Current Issues," 28(2) *Berkely Journal of International Law* (2010), p. 513.
524. *Nestle USA Inc. v. Doe et al.*, Docket No. 19-416 (decided 17 June 2021), p. 5.

Foreign Sovereign Immunities Act ("FSIA") 18 USC § 1602 et seq. (1976)

Key Provisions	*Notes*
"A foreign state shall not be immune from the jurisdiction of the courts of the United states or of the States in any case not otherwise covered by this chapter in which money damages are sought against a foreign state for personal injury or death that was caused by an act of *torture, extrajudicial killing, aircraft sabotage, hostage taking, or the provisions of material support or resources for such an act* if such act or provision of material support resources is engaged in by an official, employee, or agent of such foreign state while acting within the scope of his or her office, employment, or agency."	The FSIA allows victims to sue only designated state-sponsors of terrorism, which at the time of writing are Cuba, Iran, Democratic People's Republic of Korea (North Korea) and Syria. Key cases include: - *Thuneibat v. Syrian Arab Republic*, 167 F. Supp. 3d 22 (D.D.C. 2016) (holding Syria was liable for terrorist attack that killed U.S. citizens in Jordan) - *Colvin et al. v. Syrian Arab Republic*, Order, Case 16-cv-01423 (ABJ) (D.D.C. 12 December 2018) (awarding Plaintiffs USD 302,511,836 in compensatory and punitive damages for the extrajudicial killing of a journalist, which was characterized as a war crime attributable to Syria)

Torture Victim Protection Act ("TVPA") 28 USC § 1350 (1992)

Passed in 1991 and signed into law in 1992

Key Provisions	*Notes*
Gives rights to *U.S. citizens and non-citizens (aliens)* to bring claims for torture and extrajudicial killing committed in foreign countries.	Both plaintiffs and defendants can be U.S. citizens or foreigners. Creates a cause of action for torture and extrajudicial killing (including attempt).

Anti-Terrorism Act ("ATA") 28 USC § 2333 (1992)

Key Provisions	*Notes*
"Any national of the United States injured in his or her person, property, or business by reason of an act of international terrorism, or his or her estate, survivors, or heirs, may sue therefor in any appropriate district court of the United States and shall recover threefold the damages he or she sustains and the cost of the suit, including attorney's fees."	The victim must be a U.S. national; the plaintiff, who can be an heir, can be a U.S. citizen or a foreigner.

Trafficking Victims Protection Reauthorization Act ("TVPRA") 18 USC § 1595 (2005)

Key Provisions	*Notes*
"An individual who is a victim of a violation of this chapter may bring a civil action against the perpetrator (or whoever knowingly benefits, financially or by receiving anything of value from participation in a venture which that person knew or should have known has engaged in an act in violation of this chapter) in an appropriate district court of the United States and may recover damages and reasonable attorneys fees."	Plaintiffs can be foreign nationals.

Justice Against Sponsors of Terrorism Act ("JASTA") Public Law 114-222 (2016)

Key Provisions	*Notes*
Enacted by the U.S. Congress to narrow the scope of state sovereign immunity. It amends the FSIA and the Anti-Terrorism and Effective Death Penalty Act in regards to civil claims against a foreign state for injuries, death or damages from an act of international terrorism on U.S. soil.	Key cases include: - *Thuneibat v. Syrian Arab Republic*, 167 F. Supp. 3d 22 (D.D.C. 2016) (holding Syria was liable for the terrorist attack that killed U.S. citizens in Jordan) - *Colvin et al. v. Syrian Arab Republic*, Order, Case 16-cv-01423 (ABJ) (D.D.C. 12 December 2018)

War Crimes and Grave Breaches Compared

States are prohibited from violating any of the provisions of the Geneva Conventions and other conventions to which they are parties. However, certain violations carry elevated gravity. These violations are known as war crimes and grave breaches, each of which is discussed below.

Grave Breaches

Geneva Conventions I and II define grave breaches as any of the following acts if committed against persons or property protected by the Convention (Article 50 GC I; Article 51 GC II):

- wilful killing;
- torture or inhuman treatment, including biological experiments;
- wilfully causing great suffering or serious injury to body or health;
- and extensive destruction and appropriation of property, *not justified by military necessity and carried out unlawfully and wantonly.*

Geneva Convention III includes the following crimes (Article 130 GC III):

- compelling a prisoner of war to serve in the forces of the hostile Power;
- wilfully depriving a prisoner of war of the rights of *fair and regular trial* prescribed in Geneva Convention III.

Geneva Convention IV includes any of the following acts if committed against persons or property protected by Geneva Convention IV:

- *unlawful deportation or transfer or unlawful confinement of a protected person;*
- *wilfully depriving a protected person of the rights of fair and regular trial prescribed in Geneva Convention IV;*
- *taking of hostages.*

These scenarios are restated in Article 8.2(a) of the Rome Statute.

War Crimes

War crimes are "[s]erious violations of international humanitarian law"[525] that include grave breaches of the 1949 Geneva Conventions, other serious violations of the laws and customs applicable in international armed conflict, and, in the case of non-international armed conflict, serious violations of common Article 3 of the Geneva Conventions. By way of example, the Rome Statute provides the following acts as examples of serious violations of the laws and customs applicable in international armed conflict that do not fall within the definition of grave breaches (Article 8.2(b) SICC):

525. Jean-Marie Henckaerts and Louise Doswald-Beck, *Customary International Humanitarian Law*, Vol. I, ICRC, Cambridge University Press (Cambridge, New York, 2009), Rule 156, Chapter 44, p. 568.

(i) intentionally directing attacks against the civilian population as such or against individual civilians not taking direct part in hostilities;
(ii) intentionally directing attacks against civilian objects, that is, objects which are not military objectives;
(iii) intentionally directing attacks against personnel, installations, material, units or vehicles involved in a humanitarian assistance or peacekeeping mission in accordance with the Charter of the United Nations;
(iv) intentionally launching an attack in the knowledge that such attack will cause incidental loss of life or injury to civilians or damage to civilian objects or widespread, long-term and severe damage to the natural environment, which would be clearly excessive in relation to the concrete and direct overall military advantage anticipated;
(v) conscripting or enlisting children under the age of 15 years into the national armed forces or using them to participate actively in hostilities.

The Rome Statute further provides the following acts as examples of war crimes in the case of non-international armed conflicts when committed against persons taking no active part in the hostilities, including members of armed forces who have laid down their arms and those placed *hors de combat* by sickness, wounds, detention, or any other cause (Article 8.2(c) SICC):

(i) violence to life and person, in particular, murder of all kinds, mutilation, cruel treatment and torture;
(ii) committing outrages upon personal dignity, in particular humiliating and degrading treatment;
(iii) taking of hostages;
(iv) the *passing of sentences and the carrying out of executions without previous judgment pronounced by a regularly constituted court*, affording all judicial guarantees which are generally recognized as indispensable.

Bibliography

Articles

Christine Abely, "Causing a Sanctions Violation with U.S. Dollars: Differences in Regulatory Language Across OFAC Sanctions Programs," 48 *Georgia Journal of International and Comparative Law* 29 (2019)

Fareda Banda, "Blazing a Trail: The African Protocol on Women's Rights Comes into Force," *Journal of African Law*, Vol. 50, Issue 1 (2006)

John B. Bellinger III, "Obama's Announcements on International Law," Lawfare (8 March 2011), available at < https://www.lawfareblog.com/obamas-announcements-international-law >

Jochen von Bernstorff, "The Changing Fortunes of the Universal Declaration of Human Rights: Genesis and Symbolic Dimensions of the Turn to Rights in International Law," *European Journal of International Law*, Vol. 19, No. 5 (2008)

Michael Bothe, "The Status of Captured Fighters in Non-International Armed Conflict," in Christian Tomuschat, et al. (eds.) *The Right to Life*, Brill (2010)

Ayana Bowman, "Reframing Sexual and Gender-based Violence: Proposed Practices for an International Tribunal in Syria," *Temple International & Comparative Law Journal*, Vol. 34, No. 1 (2019)

Richard Buxbaum and David Caron, "The Alien Tort Statute: An Overview of the Current Issues," *Berkely Journal of International Law*, Vol. 28, Issue 2 (2010)

Lee M. Caplan, "State Immunity, Human Rights and *Jus Cogens*," *The American Journal of International Law*, Vol. 97 (2003)

Antonio Cassese, "Affirmation of the Principles of International Law recognized by the Charter of the Nürnberg Tribunal," Audiovisual Library of International Law, United Nations (June 2009)

Elena Chachko and Ashley Deeks, "Who is on Board with 'Unwilling or Unable'?" International Law, *Lawfare* (10 October 2016)

Christian M. de Vos, *From Rights to Remedies: Structures and Strategies for Implementing International Human Rights Decisions*, Open Society Foundations (New York, 2013)

Jack Donnelly, "The Relative Universality of Human Rights," *Human Rights Quarterly*, Vol. 29, No. 2 (2007)

Jörn Oliver Eiermann, "Investigating Nationals of States Not Party to the Rome Statute," *UCLA Journal of International Law and Foreign Affairs*, Vol. 24, No. 2 (2020)

Major Ryan M. Fisher, "Defending Taiwan: Collective Self-Defense of a Contested State," *Florida Journal of International Law*, Vol. 32, Iss. 1, Article 3 (2020)

David Forsythe, "The UN Security Council and Human Rights: Promising Developments, Persistent Problems," *Journal of Human Rights*, 13(2) (2014)

Felice D. Gaer, "A Voice Not an Echo: Universal Periodic Review and the U.N. Treaty Body System," *Human Rights Law Review*, Vol. 7, Issue 1 (2007)

Nicolas Goeglin, "UN General Assembly Adopts a Resolution Establishing an International Investigation Mechanism in Syria on Grave Violations of Humanitarian Law and Human Rights," *Derecho Internacional* (2016)

Ryan Goodman and Eric Messinger, "U.N. Committee Criticizes U.S. Record on Torture, Praises U.S. on Extraterritorial Reach of Treaty" *Just Security* (28 November 2014), available at <https://www.justsecurity.org/17837/un-committee-torture-concluding-observations-united-states>

Priya Gopalan, "Rejecting Notions of 'Honour' to Mitigate Stigma," *LSE Women, Peace and Security Working Paper Series*, 27/2021 (2021)

Oona A. Hathaway, "Do Human Rights Treaties Make a Difference?" 111.8 *Yale Law Journal*, Vol. 111 (2002)

Oona A. Hathaway et al., "Human Rights Abroad: When Do Human Rights Treaty Obligations Apply Extraterritorially?" 43 *Arizona State Law Journal* (2011)

Kevin Jon Heller, "The Civil War and the Blockade of Gaza (a Response to Posner)," *OpinioJuris* (4 June 2010), available at <http://opiniojuris.org/2010/06/04/eric-posners-incomplete-editorial-on-the-blockade-of-gaza>

Anna Hood and Monique Cormier, "Prosecuting international crimes in Australia: the case of the Sri Lankan president," *Melbourne Journal of International Law*, Vol. 13, Issue 1 (June 2022)

Eric Talbot Jensen, "Presidential Pronouncements of Customary International Law as an Alternative to the Senate's Advice and Consent," *Brigham Young University Law Review*, Vol. 2015, Issue 6 (December 2015)

Hersch Lauterpacht, "Recognition of States in International Law," 53 *Yale Law Journal* (June 1944)

Miguel Lemos, "The ICC as a 'Tool' of the United Nations Security Council and the 'Absurdity' of Head of State Immunity with Regard to International Crimes," *Indiana International and Comparative Law Review*, Vol. 32 (2022)

Konstantinos Magliveras and Gino Naldi, "The Arab Court of Human Rights," *Revue québécoise de droit international*, Vol. 29, Issue 2 (2016)

Eve Massingham, "Military intervention for humanitarian purposes: does the Responsibility to Protect doctrine advance the legality of the use of force for humanitarian ends?," *International Review of the Red Cross*, Vol. 91, No. 876 (December 2009)

Theodor Meron, "The Martens Clause, Principles of Humanity, and Dictates of Public Conscience," *American Journal of International Law*, Vol. 94, No. 1 (2000)

Simon O'Connor, "Corporations, international crimes and national courts: a Norwegian view," *International Review of the Red Cross*, No. 887 (September 2012)

Mehrdad Payandeh, "With Great Power Comes Great Responsibility? The Concept of the Responsibility to Protect Within the Process of International Lawmaking" *Yale Journal of International Law*, Vol. 35 (2009)

"Proposed Arab Court of Human Rights: An Empty Vessel Without Substantial Changes to the Draft Statute," *Human Rights Watch* (6 June 2014)

Deanna Rafla-Yuan, "The IIIM on Syrian War Crimes: What It Does and Doesn't Do," *Journal of Global Rights and Organizations* (2018-2019)

Steven R. Ratner, "Belgium's War Crimes Statute: A Postmortem," *American Journal of International Law*, Vol. 97, No. 4 (2003)

Voker Röben, *Le Precedent dans la jurisprudence de la Cour Internationale*, German Yearbook of International Law *32* (1989)

Hernando Salazar, "Colombia: beligerancia polémica," BBCMundo.com (18 January 2008), available at <http://news.bbc.co.uk/hi/spanish/latin_america/newsid_7196000/7196558.stm>

Andrew Shacknove, "Who Is a Refugee?" *Ethics*, Vol. 95, No. 2, *The University of Chicago Press Journals* (January 1985)

Jane E. Stromseth, "Justice on the Ground: Can International Criminal Courts Strengthen Domestic Rule of Law in Post-Conflict Societies?" *1 Hague Journal on the Rule of Law* (2009)

Rüdiger Wolfrum and Christianne E. Philipp, "The Status of the Taliban: Their Obligations and Rights under International Law," *Max Planck Yearbook of United Nations Law*, UNYB 6 (2002)

Books and Monographs

Georges Abi-Saab, Marcelo G. Kohen (ed.) and Magnus Jesko Langer (ed.), *Le développement du droit international—réflexions d'un demi-siècle*, The Graduate Institute of Geneva: Théorie générale du droit international public (Volume 1) (Geneva, 2013)

Shahram Akbarzadeh and Benjamin MacQueen (eds.), *Islam and Human Rights in Practice*, Routledge (London, 2008)

Anthony Aust, *Handbook of International Law*, Cambridge University Press, 2d Ed. (Cambridge, 2010)

M. Cherif Bassiouni, *Al-Qānūn Al-Dawlī al-Insānī* [International Humanitarian Law], Dar al-Nahḍa al-'Arabiyya (Cairo, 2007)

Peter Baehr, *The Role of the Nation-State in the 21st Century: Human Rights, International Organizations and Foreign Policy*, Kluwer Law International (Cambridge, 1998)Andrea Bianchi and Alexis Keller (eds.), *Counterterrorism: Democracy's Challenge*, Hart Publishing (Oxford, 2008)

Andrea Bianchi and Yasmin Naqvi (eds.), *International Humanitarian Law and Terrorism*, Hart Publishing (Oxford, 2011)

Alan Boyle and Christine Chinkin, *The Making of International Law*, Oxford University Press (Oxford, 2007)

Serge Brammertz and Michelle Jarvis (eds.), *Prosecuting Conflict-Related Sexual Violence at the ICTY*, Oxford University Press (Oxford, 2016)

James Leslie Brierly, *The Law of Nations: An Introduction to the International Law of Peace*, Clarendon Press, 5th Ed. (Oxford, 1955)

Herbert W. Briggs, *The Law of Nations: Cases, Documents, and Notes*, Appleton-Century-Crofts, 2nd Ed. (1952)

Antonio Cassesse, *International Law*, Oxford University Press, 2nd Ed. (Oxford, 2005)

Hilary Charlesworth and Christine Chinkin, *The Boundaries of International Law: A Feminist Analysis*, Manchester University Press (Manchester, 2000)

Marcus Tullius Cicero and Walter Miller (tr), *De officiis (On Moral Duties)*, Harvard University Press (Cambridge, 1913)

Andrew Clapham, *Human Rights: A Very Short Introduction*, Oxford University Press (Oxford, 2015)

Andrew Clapham and Paola Gaeta (eds.), *The Oxford Handbook of International Law in Armed Conflicts*, Oxford University Press (Oxford, 2014)

Andrew Clapham, Paola Gaeta and Marco Sassòli (eds.), *The 1949 Geneva Conventions: A Commentary*, Oxford Commentaries on International Law, Oxford University Press (Oxford, 2015)

Jean Combacau, Serge Sur, *Droit international public*, Éditions Montchrestien (Paris, 2001)

James Crawford, *The Creation of States in International Law*, Oxford University Press, 2nd Ed. (Oxford, 2007)

Customary International Humanitarian Law, Vol. I, ICRC, Cambridge University Press (Cambridge, New York, 2009)

Marie-Bénédicte Dembour, "Critiques," in Daniel Moeckli, Sangeet Shah and Sandesh Sivakumaran (eds), *International Human Rights Law*, Oxford University Press (Oxford, 2018)

Yoram Dinstein, *War, Aggression and Self-Defence*, Cambridge University Press, 5th Ed. (New York, 2011)

Martin Dixon, Robert McCorquodale and Sarah Williams, *Cases and Materials on International Law*, Oxford University Press (Oxford, 2011)

Jeffrey Dunoff, Monica Hakimi, Steven R. Ratner, David Wippman, *International Law: Norms, Actors, Process*, Aspen Publishing, 5th Ed. (2020)

Paola Gaeta (ed.), *The UN Genocide Convention: A Commentary*, Oxford Commentaries on International Law, Oxford University Press (Oxford, 2009)

Judith Gardam and Michelle Jarvis, *Women, Armed Conflict, and International Law*, Kluwer Law International (2001)

Geneva Academy, *Rules of Engagement: Protecting Civilians through Dialogue with Armed Non-State Actors* (Geneva, October 2011)

Terry D. Gill, *Yearbook of International Humanitarian Law* (various volumes), Springer (Berlin, 2016)

Priya Gopalan, Daniela Kravetz and Aditya Menon, "Proving Crimes of Sexual Violence," in Serge Brammertz & Michelle Jarvis (eds.), Prosecuting Conflict-Related Sexual Violence at the ICTY, Oxford University Press (2016)

Leslie C. Green, *The contemporary law of armed conflict*, Juris Publishing, Manchester University Press (2000)

Sohail H. Hashmi (ed.), *Islamic Political Ethics: Civil Society, Pluralism and Conflict*, Princeton University Press (Princeton, 2002)

Jean-Marie Henckaerts and Louise Doswald-Beck, *Customary International Humanitarian Law*, Vols. I-II, Cambridge University Press (Cambridge, 2005)

Louis Henkin, *How Nations Behave*, Columbia University Press (New York, 1979)

Louis Henkin (ed), *The International Bill of Rights*, Columbia University Press (New York, 1981)

Tamás Hoffman, *The Crime of Genocide: Then and Now*, Brill (Leiden, 2022)

Mark Janis, John Noyes, Leila Sadat, *International Law: Cases and Commentary*, West Academic Publishing (American Casebook Series), 6th Ed. (2020)

Hersch Lauterpacht, *Recognition in International Law*, Cambridge University Press (Cambridge, 1947)

C.S. Lewis, *The Abolition of Man*, HarperOne (2015)

Peter Malanczuk, *Akehurst's Modern Introduction to International Law*, Routledge (1997)

Karl Marx, *On the Jewish Question*, Grapevine (1843, republished in 2023)

Nils Melzer, *Interpretive Guidance on the Notion of Direct Participation in Hostilities under International Humanitarian Law*, ICRC (Geneva, 2009)

Guénaël Mettraux, *International Crimes: Law and Practice*, Volume I: Genocide, Oxford University Press (Oxford, 2019)

Guénaël Mettraux, *International Crimes: Law and Practice*, Volume II: Crimes against Humanity, Oxford University Press (Oxford, 2020)

Daniel Moeckli, Sangeet Shah and Sandesh Sivakumaran (eds), *International Human Rights Law*, Oxford University Press (Oxford, 2018)

Usha Natarajan, John Reynolds, Amar Bhatia and Sujith Xavier (eds.), *Third World Approaches to International Law: On Praxis and the Intellectual*, Routledge (London, 2017)

Atalia Omer, R. Scott Appleby, David Little (eds.), *The Oxford Handbook of Religion, Conflict, and Peacebuilding*, Oxford University Press (Oxford, 2015)

Anne Orford and Florian Hoffmann (eds.), *The Oxford Handbook of the Theory of International Law*, Oxford University Press (Oxford, 2016)

Jean Pictet (ed.), *Commentary to Geneva Convention (IV) relative to the Protection of Civilian Persons in Time of War*, ICRC (Geneva, 1960)

Anthea Roberts, *Is International Law International?* Oxford University Press, reprint ed. (Oxford, 2019)

Tilman Rodenhäuser, *Organizing Rebellion: Non-State Armed Groups under International Humanitarian Law, Human Rights Law, and International Criminal Law*, Oxford University Press (Oxford, 2018)

Cecily Rose, *An Introduction to Public International Law*, Cambridge University Press (Cambridge, 2022)

Yves Sandoz et al. eds., *Commentary on the Additional Protocols of June 1977 to the Geneva Conventions of 12 August 1949*, ICRC (Geneva, 1987)

Ben Saul (ed.), *Research Handbook on International Law and Terrorism*, Edward Elgar Publishing (Cheltenham/Northampton, 2014)

William Schabas, *Genocide in International Law*, Cambridge University Press (Cambridge, 2000)

Michael N. Schmitt (ed.), *Tallinn Manual 2.0 on the International Law Applicable to Cyber Operations*, Cambridge University Press (Cambridge, 2017)

Malcolm Shaw, *International Law*, Cambridge University Press, 9th ed. (Cambridge, 2021)

Moines de Solesmes, *La Paix Internationale*, Desclée (Paris, 1956), Vol. I

Hugh Thirlway, *British Yearbook of International Law 116* (2005)

Hugh Thirlway, *The Law and Procedure of the International Court of Justice: Fifty Years of Jurisprudence, Volume II*, Oxford University Press (Oxford, 2013)

Hugh Thirlway, *The Sources of International Law*, Oxford University Press, 2nd Ed. (Oxford, 2019)

Christian Tomuschat et al. (eds.), *The Right to Life*, Brill (2010)

Arthur Travers Harris and Sebastian Cox, *Despatch on War Operations: 23 February 1942, to 8 May 1945*, Routledge (1995)

Table of Cases and Advisory Opinions

Other Sources

Index

W

www.ingramcontent.com/pod-product-compliance
Lightning Source LLC
LaVergne TN
LVHW020647300926
849161LV00004B/855